RUSSIA

UNDER WESTERN EYES

RUSSIA

UNDER WESTERN EYES

FROM THE BRONZE HORSEMAN TO THE LENIN MAUSOLEUM

MARTIN MALIA

THE BELKNAP PRESS OF
HARVARD UNIVERSITY PRESS
Cambridge, Massachusetts
London, England
1999

Library of Congress
Cataloging-in-Publication Data

Malia, Martin E. (Martin Edward)
Russia under western eyes : from the
Bronze Horseman to the Lenin Mausoleum /
Martin Malia.
p. cm.
Includes bibliographical references and index.
ISBN 0-674-78120-1 (alk. paper)
1. Russia—Civilization.
2. Soviet Union—Civilization.
3. Russia—Foreign public opinion.
4. Soviet Union—Foreign public opinion.
I. Title.
DK32.M18   1999
947—dc21   98-39769

FOR BILL, PAUL, RICK, TOM, AND DEBORAH,
my nephews and niece, to whom this book was promised at that now remote time when Russia seemed eternally set on a course of divergence from the West. Fortunately, I tarried long enough for all concerned to discover that the Spectre would dwindle down into something like a kitten after all.

CONTENTS

PROLOGUE: IN SCYTHIA   IX

INTRODUCTION:
THE RUSSIAN RIDDLE   1

**1 RUSSIA AS ENLIGHTENED
DESPOTISM: 1700–1815   15**

The Birth of the Concert of Europe   21
Russia as Old Regime   27
The Ottoman Control   39
Russia as Philosophic Fable   42
Exegi Monumentum Aereum Perennum I   50
The Legend Redux   51
Enlightenment and the Police State   59
The Twilight of the Old Regime   73

**2 RUSSIA AS ORIENTAL DESPOTISM:
1815–1855   85**

Europe as the Two and the Three   89
Culture and the German *Sonderweg*   103
The Romantic Chiaroscuro   111
The New Historical Canon   124
A Fractured Image   130
The Russian *Sonderweg*   139
Russia Outcast   146

**3 RUSSIA AS EUROPE REGAINED:
1855–1914   161**

Obverse: The Curve of Convergence   166
Russia Reformed   167
Mitteleuropa   175
Russia for Liberals   179
Russia for Socialists   182
Russia for Nationalists   187
Reverse: Fin de Siècle and Russian Soul   192
Art for Art's Sake   193
From Symbolism to Modernism   198
The Russian Prophets   205
Soul for Export   207
The Roots of Aesthetic Nihilism   217

**4 WAR AND REVOLUTION:
1914–1917   233**

The Hinge of Darkness   236
A Dawn amidst the Night?   245
The Socialist Riddle   247
Socialism as an Ideal Type, or,
the DNA of a Unicorn   252
Marxist Theory   256
Leninist Practice   271

**5 THROUGH THE SOVIET-RUSSIAN
LOOKING-GLASS, AND WHAT
THE WEST FOUND THERE:
1917–1991   287**

Prologue: In the Eye of the Beholder   289
Heads, the Experiment: 1917–1945   295
The Ride of the Troika   298
Exegi Monumentum II   313
The Fascist Counterpoint   314
Where the Twain Meet   335
The Ride of Rozinante   339
International Class Struggle   352
Tails, the Empire: 1945–1991   357
The Cold War   359
Kaleidoscopic Vision   361
Khrushchev's Thaw   373
The Road to Détente   383
The Waltz of the Models   388
Voices Off   391
Over and Out: Gorbachev   401

CONCLUSION   409

Whither the Troika Now?   411
And Whither the Spectre?   420

NOTES   437

ACKNOWLEDGMENTS   483

INDEX   485

PROLOGUE: IN SCYTHIA

These are the researches of Herodotus of
Halicarnassus, which he publishes in the hope
of preserving from decay the remembrance . . . of
the great and wonderful actions of the Greeks
and Barbarians.

Fourth Book, "Melpomene, Muse of Tragedy"

According to the account which the Scythians themselves give, they are
the youngest of all nations . . .

The Greeks tell a different story . . . Heracles came into the region
now called Scythia and rewarded a strange being, half-maiden
half-serpent, who saved him, with three sons . . . From Scythes, the
youngest, descended the kings of Scythia.

There is a different story, however, in which I am inclined to put
more faith . . . that the wandering Scyths once simply dwelt in Asia, and
after losing a war migrated to Europe . . . The Euxine sea has nations
around it more unpolished than those of any other region that we know
of . . . there is not within this region a single nation which can put
forward any claim to wisdom, or which has produced a single person of
high repute.

Yet the Scythians have indeed in one respect . . . shown themselves
wiser than any nation: . . . accustomed one and all to shoot from horseback, they make it impossible for the enemy who invades them to escape destruction, while they themselves are entirely out of his reach . . .
having neither cities nor forts, and carrying their dwellings with them
wherever they go . . .

The Scythian soldier drinks the blood of the first man he overthrows
in battle. Whatever number he slays he cuts off all their heads and

carries them to the king. . . . The Scyths blind all their slaves, to use them in preparing their milk . . .

Scythia has an abundance of soothsayers, who foretell the future by means of willow wands . . . Whenever the Scythian king falls sick, he sends for the three soothsayers of most renown at the time . . . They say that he is ill because such and such a person . . . has falsely sworn by the royal hearth . . . The man accused is arrested and brought before the king . . . If [the soothsayers] find the man guilty . . . straightaway he is beheaded.

When the king dies . . . they take the corpse . . . and cleaning out the inside, fill it with chopped cypress and frankincense . . . enclose the body in wax and carry it through all the different tribes.

The Scythians have an extreme hatred of all foreign customs, particularly those in use among the Greeks, as in the instance of Anacharsis . . . There is no doubt that Anacharsis suffered death on account of his attachment to foreign customs after his sojourn among the Hellenes.

The country has no marvels except its rivers, which are larger and more numerous than those of any other land. These, and the vastness of the plain, are worthy of note . . .

Thus far the land is known, but beyond . . . lies a region of which no man can give any exact account. Lofty and precipitous mountains bar further progress . . . Some say (though it does not seem credible) that the people who live there . . . sleep during half the year. Above them dwell men with one eye . . . and beyond these the Hyperboreans, who extend to the sea . . . The whole region has winters of exceeding rigor . . . eight months of frost . . . unlike that of the same season in any other country.

I have now related all that is said of the most distant part of the continent whereof any account is given . . . of the Hyperboreans . . . the men beyond the northern winds.

But the ultimate boundaries of Europe are quite unknown, and there is not a man who can say whether any sea girds it round either on the north or on the east . . . For my part, I cannot conceive why these names [Europe and Asia] should ever have been given to a tract of land which is in reality one . . . Libya after an African woman, and Asia after the wife of Prometheus. As for Europe, no one can say whence the name is derived, unless we say that Europe was so called after the Tyrian maiden Europa. But it is certain that Europa was an Asiatic and never even set foot on the land which the Greeks now call Europe, only sailing from Phoenicia to Crete.

The same steppes twenty-five hundred years later:

The researches of N. V. Gogol from Poltava Province in Ukraine have uncovered the epic of one Pavel Ivanovich Chichikov, "Collegiate Assessor and landowner, traveling on personal business." The hero, after having purchased his last Dead Soul, climbs on his troika and heads for the horizon . . .

Chichikov smiled slightly as he bounced on his leather cushion, for he loved fast driving. And what Russian doesn't like fast driving? . . .

The milestones, the merchants' carts are coming toward you; and the forest on either side is flying too, with its rows of dark pines, its thumping axes, and the cawing of its crows; the whole road is flying, God knows where, into the hazy distance, and there's something sinister about flashing past objects that disappear even before they've come into focus; and only the sky overhead, with its clouds split by the moon appears to be standing still. O troika, O birdlike troika! Who invented you? Only a people full of life could have done so, a people that refuses to be daunted by anything, a people whose land spreads out evenly across half the world, so that you may race ahead full-speed and count the milestones until they flash like spots before your eyes and you grow dizzy.

And to think there's nothing complicated about a troika—no screws, no metal; all it took to build it was an ax, a chisel, and a smart Russian peasant. And your driver doesn't wear fancy foreign gaiters, he's all beard and mittens and he sits on God knows what . . . And there she goes, goes, goes! And already there's nothing to see but the dust rising in the distance.

And you, Russia—aren't you racing headlong like the fastest troika imaginable? The road smokes under you, bridges rattle, and everything falls behind . . . O horses, horses! Are there cyclones concealed in your manes? . . . a flow of air, and the whole troika flies along inspired by God!

And where are you flying to, Russia? Answer me! But she gives no answer. The carriage bells burst forth with a marvelous peal. The air roars, is torn to shreds and turns into wind; everything on earth flashes past, and all other peoples and nations casting worried sidelong glances, step out of her path and make way for her course.

RUSSIA

UNDER WESTERN EYES

INTRODUCTION:
THE RUSSIAN RIDDLE

Yes, we are Scythians! Yes, we are Asiatics,
With slanted, greedy eyes! . . .

Oh old world! so long as you have not yet
   perished . . .
Halt, perplexed, like Oedipus,
Before the Sphinx with its ancient riddle!

—Aleksandr Blok, "The Scythians" (1918)

After a thousand years of marching in the laggard Eastern train of Europe, forever hobbled by the double burden of poverty and despotism, Russia in 1917 had thrust upon her an improbable vanguard destiny. In the wake of Lenin's Red October, the "Spectre of Communism" proclaimed by Marx in 1848 to be haunting Europe at last received a local habitation and a name: Soviet Socialist Russia. For the next three-quarters of a century, the Soviet-Russian hybrid stood as the prime catalyst of both the hopes and the fears of the West, indeed of mankind.

Henceforth the Soviet "experiment" loomed as the great Other in terms of which the world was obliged to define itself. To the hopeful, it represented the socialist antithesis to capitalism, and the future as against the past. To the fearful, it became the totalitarian menace to the free world of the West, and the enemy of civilization. And for everyone, it figured as the pivotal second world setting off the first world of advanced nations from the third world of colonized peoples. Yet the very multiplicity of these perceptions meant that the newfound land of the Soviets would always remain in large measure an enigma.

The riddle the Red Sphinx posed to Western wayfarers, therefore, was often facilely resolved by declaring the spectre of Communism to be little more than the new face of eternal Russia. For those hostile to the experiment, Communism was simply a mutation of tsarist autocracy and thus an enduring menace to Western freedom. For those friendly to the brave new Soviet world, its difficulties, its shortcomings, and at times its crimes were to be explained away by the same tsarist heritage;[1]

4

and if the Socialist state appeared menacing, this was only because it was unfairly treated by a hostile world. Yet both evaluations presupposed, in some measure, an inherent difference of civilizations between "Russia" and the "West."

Although the modern sense of this difference was created by the shock of Lenin's October and Stalin's "construction of socialism" in the 1930s, this did not as yet make Red Russia a global force; for the prewar Soviet Union remained only one of six or seven major powers, and hardly in the first rank among them at that. The full measure of Soviet Russia's otherness did not strike the world until a second shock, her victory in the Second World War, made it seem that one day she might well overwhelm the West. And that victory, in truth, marked one of the most profound changes of the world equilibrium in modern history.[2]

During the three hundred fifty years since the failure of the Habsburgs' aspirations to universal empire in the sixteenth century, Europe had lived under a multistate system of international relations, eventually designated as the concert of Europe and held to be founded on a balance of power. This order, though challenged successively by Louis XIV, Napoleon, and Wilhelmian Germany, nonetheless invariably reemerged. Then, suddenly the Second World War, consummating a development begun during its predecessor of 1914–1918, precipitated what has been called the "political collapse of Europe."[3] The European masters of the international arena, the victors no less than the vanquished, not only forfeited their continent's hegemony in world affairs, but even lost full control over their own national destinies. Global power shifted to the peripheries of the former system—the United States and the Soviet Union—while Europe itself was partitioned by the newcomers into two zones of allied or dependent states, which in the East were transformed into outright satellites. Although the passage of time blurred this sharp division of the world, notably with the Chinese secession of 1959–1962 in the East, the polarization of international politics inaugurated in 1945 was institutionalized for half a century in the Cold War.

This polarization was reinforced by the institutional and cultural gulf that the experiment had opened between East and West. For the two superpowers, together with their respective associates in the "free world" and the "bloc," represented radically contrasting systems—the one democratic and open, the other autocratic and totalitarian. Nor was this circumstance changed by the Sino-Soviet break, for until 1980 China's internal order remained resolutely socialist, while Russia retained her role as the archetype of Communist societies everywhere, even in dissident form. Although world Communism as a unitary movement came to an end in the early 1960s, Communism as a world force was still very much alive as the antithesis to Western civilization. Its enduring ascendancy from the Elbe to the China Seas gave the West apparently good reason throughout the Cold War to view Red Russia as irredeemably "Oriental."

Not content to derive this category from Communism alone, some commentators pursued the roots of the Soviet Union's otherness back to distinctively Russian institutions and national traits of character. Accordingly, the herdlike collectivism of the Communist kolkhoz was attributed to the servile tradition of the old Russian peasant commune; or the Soviet police state was held to descend from the Third Section of spies and gendarmes maintained by Nicholas I; or Stalinism was traced to the autocracy of Peter the Great and Ivan the Terrible, indeed to the khans of the Golden Horde. And some writers, in their quest for the key to the Soviet Kremlin, eventually wound up in the Sacred Palace of Byzantium. For was this not the source of the Eastern autocratic tradition descending from Constantine the Great to Stalin? Surely, the argument went, the Byzantine ideal of Caesaro-papism was the prototype of that fusion of absolute state power, ideological orthodoxy, and messianic zeal which, in secular guise, was the essence of Soviet totalitarianism.[4]

The application of such reasoning to Russia's international behavior yielded an equally static explanation. Supposedly, absolute power in internal affairs fuels a drive for absolute power in relations with other nations. Thus conquest has always been Russia's goal, beginning in the fifteenth century, when the monk Philotheus of Pskov, speaking for the first Russian prince to call himself tsar, or Caesar, boasted that Moscow was the Third Rome predestined to be the final seat of world empire—an ambition continued into the twentieth century by the conspiracy of the Third International intended to give Moscow universal dominion through world revolution. In short, the inevitable concomitant of autocracy, whether white or red, is aggression and imperialism.[5]

Not even Communism's great crash in the years 1989–1991 effaced this sense of otherness. True, for some, that event was enough to proclaim the "end of history," as socialist Russia rallied to market democracy. Yet for others, Communism's fall meant not so much Russia redeemed as eternal Russia's return in native garb. This suspicion was aggravated when it became apparent that the Soviet mode of modernization had hardly ended Russia's economic backwardness, and still less had it readied her for democracy.

The world's troubles with Russia thus were clearly not over with the eclipse of the Spectre. At the least, the new situation foreboded the prospect of anarchy and ethnic strife over much of Eurasia; at the worst, it presaged revived Muscovite aggression throughout the same area, indeed into Central Europe. These apprehensions were magnified by the fear that nationalism had superseded Communism worldwide as the menace to liberal civilization: for did not twentieth-century history teach that nationalism is the antechamber to fascism? Many in the West therefore responded to the reborn Russia with a Pavlovian reaction of yesteryear: the "Russian tradition," whether white, red, or now white-blue-and-red, was despotism and chauvinism at home leading to expansionism and imperialism abroad.

Such persistent recourse to the dichotomy of Russia versus Europe points up its derivation from a still broader antithesis: the Occident versus the Orient, understood as civilization versus barbarism. In this venerable perspective the West is the home of freedom, reason, and dynamism; and its obverse is the realm of despotism, obscurantism, and stagnation known as Asia—a barren society in which an omnipotent state is the proprietor of the land and all its inhabitants. "Eternal Russia" thus is a subspecies of "Oriental despotism," a trope as old as Herodotus's epic account of the struggle of free Greece against Persia's King of Kings.

In the modern age, Montesquieu made Oriental despotism a sociological category designating the most primitive type of polity; Hegel made it a metaphysical category defining the most servile stage of

World History; and Marx recast it as "the Asiatic mode of production," the lowest form of economic life. Leaving aside the relevance of such thinking for understanding the vastness and variety of "Asias" since the time of the Great King of Persia, suffice it to note that this heavy conceptual baggage inevitably accompanies the dichotomy of Russia versus the West.[6]

Yet how valid is this "essentialist" perception of Russian history? And how real is the cultural determinism underlying it? In other words, is the antithesis of Russia and the West a given of history? Or is it itself relative to historical circumstances? The purpose of this study is to answer these questions by exploring the three centuries since Peter the Great—in Pushkin's famous phrase from *The Bronze Horseman*—first "cut a window through to Europe."[7]

For a start, the elementary historical facts of the last three centuries are distinctly more complex than the vulgate of eternal Russia would have it—as indeed should be obvious to anyone who has perused a survey of Russian history beyond the prophecies of Philotheus of Pskov to, say, Voltaire's cult of Catherine the Great. In reality, the West's sense of difference from Russia has rarely attained the acute pitch of the Cold War years. Instead, from the time Russia entered the modern European world under Peter, this sense of difference has registered dramatic fluctuations in intensity. And during considerable periods, and for important segments of Western opinion, it has faded away entirely, to be replaced by a sentiment of kinship, even of adulation.

Much less obvious is the fact that these fluctuations do not coincide, in any simple or commonsense pattern, with the real trends of divergence or convergence between the practical interests of Russia and Western nations. A heightened sense of hostility toward Russia is not inevitably caused by aggressiveness on her part; nor are periods of Russian reasonableness invariably rewarded by more kindly sentiments on the part of the West. A case in point is, again, Voltaire's apologias for Catherine's voracious expansionism in contrast to the panicked reaction of a later Left to the great status quo sovereign of his day, Nicholas I. It is thus an illusion to suppose either that the West's attitude toward Russia has always represented a rational response to real conflicts of interest, or that Europe's periodic bouts of Russophobia can be accounted for by the objective threat of Russian power. Quite to the contrary, the West is not necessarily most alarmed when Russia is in reality most alarming, nor most reassured when Russia is in fact most reassuring.

Because Russia's behavior offers only a partial explanation for the uneven response to her presence in Europe since Peter, the full explanation must be sought in forces acting within the body politic of the West. Russia has at different times been demonized or divinized by Western opinion less because of her real role in Europe than because of the fears and frustrations, or the hopes and aspirations, generated within European society by its own domestic problems. The prime example of Russia refracted through the prism of Western crises and contradictions is, of course, the combined attraction-repulsion of the Red Spectre in the twentieth century.

Yet is it even possible to speak of the "West" in the singular? Or are the fluctuating European images of Russia the reflection of a number of contending "Wests"? Indeed, we find that the Left and the Right, the rationalists and the romantics, or in another sphere, the English, the French, the Germans and the Poles, have simultaneously perceived the same Russia in different ways. In the eyes of one Western nation or ideological camp, Russia's international actions have seemed menacing; yet in a different period, or in the eyes of another Western social or political constellation, essentially similar actions have inspired indifference or even admiration. Thus, during the Cold War the Western Left and Right had very different perceptions of the Soviet system and its international intentions; nor was the relative weight of the two ideological camps the same in vulnerable Europe and imperial America.

The present study, therefore, is concerned only secondarily with questions of *Realpolitik*, that is, with the "rational" responses of the various European powers to concrete conflicts of interest between them and Russia. The primary concern here, rather, is the cultural and social context, the affective and intellectual climate, in which Europe's political relations with Russia have been conducted, an ambiance which more often than not produced "irrational" international results. Our subject thus is the West's judgments about Russia as a power, to be sure, but even more as a civilization.

Indeed, perception of Russia as a civilization has often influenced her status as a power—as in the irrationality of the West's underreaction to Catherine II and its overreaction to Nicholas I. A central task of this discussion is to contrast the fluctuations of these less rational Western reactions to Russia with the quite different pattern of conflict or concordance in the real interests of both parties. In fact, so great is the discrepancy between Russian reality and Western reaction that at times the European climate of opinion, as distinct from relations of force, has itself become a force that weighs in the balance of power between Russia and her neighbors—as, again, the global swath cut by the late great Soviet Spectre amply illustrates.

In sum, any judgment of Russia's position in Europe must begin with recognition of the great weight of subjectivity that has always governed it. The necessary emphasis given here to this fact, however, entails nothing so recondite as claiming Russia to be a "construct" of the Western mind. In the present context, "subjectivity" has only the ordinary meaning of an inner predisposition to view the world through the feelings and temperament of the subject rather than the attributes of the object observed. It is by such all-too-human subjectivity that we have, to a significant degree, produced our images of Russia out of ourselves.

It is the chronicle of the West's varying assessments of Russia, therefore—taken in conjunction with their origins in internal Western conditions—that furnishes the narrative structure of the chapters which follow.[8] This narrative commences with Russia's dramatic impact on Europe following Peter's victory over Sweden at the Battle of Poltava in 1709, and it unfolds in four phases.

The first extends from Poltava to the Congress of Vienna in 1814–15, a period when Russia presents, in the guise of the "enlightened despotism" of Peter I, Catherine II, and the young Alexander I, the most benign visage she has ever displayed to the West. The second, begun in 1815 by Alexander's Holy Alliance and brought to its climax by the most unbending autocrat of the century, Nicholas I, offers the antithesis of the first, with Russia plunging to the nadir of her fortunes under Western eyes in her role as the "gendarme of Europe." During the third phase, opened by the Great Reforms of Alexander II following the Crimean debacle of 1854–1856 and closed by the fall of the imperial regime in 1917, the West's negative opinion of Russia is progressively nuanced and attenuated to the point where, by the early twentieth century, most observers again viewed her as an integral, though no longer idealized, part of Europe. The last chapter of the story, begun with the October Revolution, defies all clear characterization, for it offers the starkest antitheses of white and black, reproducing simultaneously the idealization of the eighteenth century and the denigration of the early nineteenth, yet, despite a constantly shifting balance, never fusing these extremes into a coherent image, capable of dominating Western opinion.

The method to be followed here can only be as eclectic as the subject matter itself is varied. This method is, in the first instance, comparative. For tracing the West's evolving perceptions of Russia inevitably entails assessing the West's own evolution. And, since the West is no monolith, defining it means contrasting the national evolutions of its components, for example distinguishing Germany from France as sharply as Russia is usually distinguished from the two together. It is only by such comparisons that one can determine what is lacking—or present—in Russia to qualify her for European status. And this exercise, in turn, means posing the question of the nature, or the essence, of European civilization as such, as well as of the modern world it produced. For modernity, if no longer Eurocentric, was indubitably born in Europe before going on to revolutionize the rest of the planet.

A second point of method relates to the already mentioned fact that in Western-Russian relations the cultural climate has often translated into political power. "Climate" here, however, does not mean public opinion at any given moment; nor does "culture" designate the *mentalités* of the population at large, which before the twentieth century played little role in Europe's assessment of Russia. What is significant in the present context, rather, is high or elite culture—those long-term constellations of ideas that have been conventionally treated under the rubric "intellectual history," which privileges such luminaries as Voltaire and Hegel, or Marx and Nietzsche. For it is this level of discourse that has governed the West's representations of Russia.

The relevant constellations of ideas are such classical cultural currents as the Enlightenment and Romanticism and, later, positivism, Marxism, and symbolism. These movements—as well as the key concepts they invoke, from "reason," to "people," to "nation," to "art"—must be treated in two stages. They are discussed first in their own right, as an exercise in *Begriffsgeschichte*, or the history of concepts, to clarify which of the meanings they have accumulated over time is relevant here. Yet, since ideas assume full significance for this study only when they become forms of power, in the second stage they are explored at their intersection with politics, where they are transformed into ideologies capable of acting on the world. Culture, then, is ultimately examined here in the form of those great sociopolitical ideologies of modernity: liberalism, nationalism, socialism, and fascism.

Moreover, since ideas and ideologies in modern Europe clearly vary from one institutional or national situation to another (J. S. Mill could hardly have been Russian or Fedor Dostoevsky English), they must be treated in concrete historical context. This approach, however, is not meant to privilege social environment, of which ideas would in some sense be the "superstructure"; nor is the looser, but still reductionist, framework of a hypothetical "sociology of knowledge" appropriate. The relevant historical context, rather, is a multifaceted one: political, social, economic, and indeed geographic, all at once. In this nexus each element functions as an independent variable; and connections among them are seen not as causes but as correlations—an unsatisfyingly imprecise model no doubt, but still the most expedient way to square the circle of defining history's motive forces.

Given so extensive an agenda, and so varied a methodology, a selective sampling of European opinion regarding Russia is unavoidable; yet if the catalog offered can hardly pretend to be comprehensive, it may at least hope to be representative. Thus what follows is an "essay" in the basic meaning of that term—an attempt, a testing or a trying out of

concepts—in an effort to stake out the overall pattern of Russia's relation to the West.

Subjective and diverse though Western images of Russia have been,
their mutations are not arbitrary nor is their sequence accidental, since
all may be grounded in one basic perspective—which gives us a third
point of method. That perspective is furnished by the degree to which
institutions and culture evolve in similar, or in different, ways at the
western and eastern ends of Europe. During times when internal developments at these two poles converge, the West's evaluation of Russia
tends toward the positive; when these evolutionary paths diverge,
Europe's judgment veers to the negative.

Now the term "convergence," when applied to Soviet Russia and the
West, requires circumspect definition. In the post-Stalin years, when
the Cold War was mellowing while the Soviet economy still appeared
imposing, the illusion was born in many quarters that Western political
liberty could be fused with Soviet socialism to produce a society both
affluent and just—an illusion which returned briefly during Gorbachev's *perestroika*. This "convergence theory," as it was called, was of
course resoundingly refuted by events, and nothing like it is intended
here.[9]

The failure of *Soviet-Western* convergence, however, does not mean
that *Russian-Western* convergence was not underway before 1917, or
that it is impossible in the post-Soviet present. Indeed, the thesis advanced here is that Russian Russia since Peter the Great has generally
moved toward convergence, however halting, with the West, and that it
is Marxist-Leninist, Soviet Russia that represents both maximal divergence from European norms and the great aberration in Russia's own
development. Seen in this perspective, therefore, Russia threatened the
West most when she was least distinctively Russian—under Communism.

So the possibility of a new convergence with Russia returns us to the
problem of Europe's own essence. The comparative method, however,
permits us to transcend habitual essentialist thinking, since, if comparison is systematically pursued, it presents geographic Europe not as two
cultural zones—a West and an East—but as a spectrum of zones graded

in level of development from the former to the latter. Recent German historiography, reflecting a most uncomfortable national position between modern Europe's two extremities, expresses this perception as *das West-östliches Kulturgefälle*, the West-East cultural gradient or declivity.[10] It is this perspective that is followed here—with Russia at the bottom of the slope to be sure, but part of Europe nevertheless.

Viewing Europe in terms of such a differential, however, parallels what is generally known as the transition from traditional to modern society. To frame matters, then, in these familiar (and at bottom economic) categories, the fluctuations in Western-Russian relations are due to the fact that Russia embarked on her modernization later than the rest of Europe and, because of the persistent drag of "backwardness," pursued her development either out of phase with, or less smoothly than, her neighbors. There is surely much value in this mode of explanation, and it will be partially employed here. Still, it should not be forgotten that the kindred category of "industrial society" gave us the illusion of Western democracy's convergence with Communism. Our standard social-science categories—which apply as readily to Turkey or China as to Europe—clearly omit something from the conceptual framework necessary for the purposes of this study. And the variable they lack is those specifically European cultural and institutional coordinates which have governed Russia's relation to the West.

The discussion here, therefore, will be conducted less in terms of general social-science concepts than with respect to historical categories specific to European institutions and culture. Such a distinctively European mold is most succinctly designated by the name it received when, in 1789, it at last gave way to what is now called modernity: *Ancien Régime*. And this Old Regime is by no means a designation for an age when Europe itself was backward, or underdeveloped, or unenlightened. It designates rather a millennial order—sacred, hierarchical, and monarchical—that became the matrix of our dynamic modernity. It is this distinctive Old-Regime world, and its revolutionary transition to a secular, liberal, and democratic order, that furnishes the conceptual axis of this study. This general transition, though of course related to

14

economic development, is not reducible to it. In fact, the economic dimension of the process is the one least relevant to deciding modern Russia's fate; ideology has been much more crucial.

So, from one question to another, this study arrives at its ultimate purpose. And that is to transcend the presumed polarity *between* Russia and Europe by proposing a definition of Russia's place *within* Europe. In the narrative that follows, charting Russia's appearances under Western eyes is not an end in itself; it is a means for situating her in pan-European context. Indeed, the title of this book might well have been, precisely, "Russia in European Perspective." Yet since Russia viewed in this manner changes the customary contours of Europe itself, another alternative title could easily be "Europe: The View from the East" or, better yet, "Europe in the Russian Mirror."[11]

And perhaps the reflection that this inverted approach sends back can yield an answer to the riddle of the Russian Sphinx—and thus provoke the demise of that fabulous creature.

RUSSIA AS ENLIGHTENED DESPOTISM: 1700–1815

Beside the desolate waves stood *He,*
And charged with mighty thoughts, stared out . . .

Here shall a city be laid down
In defiance to a haughty neighbor
Here nature has predestined us
To break a window through to Europe . . .

I love thee, work of Peter's hand,
I love thy harmonies severe:
The Neva's imperial flow,
Her embankments of granite sheer.

—Aleksandr Pushkin, *The Bronze Horseman* (1836)

The equestrian statue of Peter I stands on the edge of the Neva. . . . His severe countenance gazed on the river. . . . On these desolate shores Peter founded his capital and created subjects. His terrible arm is still extended over their posterity, which huddles around the august effigy: one looks and does not know if that hand of bronze is raised to protect or to threaten.

—Joseph de Maistre, *Les soirées de Saint-Pétersbourg* (1809–1821)

Muscovite Russia inaugurated her career as a European power with one of the sharpest reversals of national fortune in modern history. Although in the eleventh century it was in no way surprising that a king of France should marry a princess of Kievan Rus to secure an alliance against the German emperor, by the mid-thirteenth century this first European "Russia" had been destroyed and fragmented by the onslaught of the Mongols. Even after Muscovy's liberation from this Tatar Yoke around 1480 (and though Florentine architects had already arrived to rebuild the Kremlin), the Russia of onion-domed churches and boyars in flowing robes kowtowing to their tsar seemed to Renaissance Westerners scarcely less exotic and remote than it had before. Throughout the sixteenth and seventeenth centuries, Europeans continued to relegate Muscovy almost to the same alien and Asiatic category as the Ottoman Turks. With Poltava, all this changed drastically.

Politically, Peter's eruption into Europe promoted the Muscovite backwater to full membership in the European state system. Culturally, it propelled its inhabitants from the religious Middle Ages to what contemporaries were then beginning to call the modern era. For it was Russia's fate that, at the moment Peter cut his famous window through to Europe, Europe cut a window through to secular enlightenment. In this new climate, Russia was able to gain acceptance for an international aggrandizement that a quarter of a century earlier would have produced a clash of worlds.

The cultural gulf existing before Peter, however, was not one that can meaningfully be described as an antithesis between "Russia" and the "West," since neither term then carried the connotation of distinctiveness as a civilization. Before the eighteenth century, "Europe" was largely a geographical expression, and its inhabitants customarily thought of their world as "Christendom"—*Christianitas*, or the *Respublica Christiana*. These terms, going back to the Carolingians, denoted the Latin West's sentiment of difference from and superiority to all heathens and infidels, especially those of Islam, with whom they had been continuously at war since Charles Martel halted the Saracens at Poitiers in 732. Nor did the Protestant Reformation alter the sentiment of the Christian West's unity vis-à-vis outsiders: the Spanish naval victory over the Turks at Lepanto in 1571 was acclaimed as a deliverance in Reformed no less than in Catholic countries. Indeed, as late as 1683 Vienna was besieged by the Turks, who were driven off only in extremis by King Jan Sobieski of Poland. It was thus toward the turn of the century that the term "Europe," increasingly used since the fifteenth century as a synonym for Christendom, finally displaced the latter: the Treaty of Utrecht in 1713 was the last international agreement to make reference to the *Respublica Christiana*. The reason for this change was momentous: "Europe" now designated not a place but a civilization; and this civilization was defined by the fact that the balance within its high culture had tipped decisively toward secularization.[1]

Although the Muscovites, too, were Christian, before Peter they had not belonged to the Christendom just described. True, they were counted by the Latins to be part of a single community of apostolic faith; but they had never been included in the Christendom of the West, with its central papal jurisdiction and international religious orders, or still less in any of the subsequent Protestant confessions. Instead the Muscovites identified their world as "Orthodoxy." (There is in fact no word in Russian or Greek for Christendom as a society.) Orthodoxy, of course, means "right opinion," or the one correct doctrine: and, after being utilized in eighth-century Byzantium to combat the Iconoclasts, it was employed to set the Greek East apart from the Latin West and the "heresies" that had led it to the schism of 1054. Indeed, after that event, and especially after the Fourth Crusade captured Constantinople in 1204, "Orthodoxy" acquired an increasingly defensive connotation, as the Greek East steadily declined in area and strength while the once "barbarian" West grew in power and prosperity. The Latin West, therefore, came to consider it legitimate to use persuasion, even force, to return the Orthodox schismatics to the one, universal fold. Then, as the Turks closed in on Constantinople, and as the desperate Greeks sought protection by reuniting with Rome at the Council of Florence in 1439, the relationship between Catholics and Orthodox became one of proselytizer to supplicant and subordinate. And so the remnants of the once proud Byzantine Commonwealth acquired the consciousness of a humiliated and offended community, a stunted second Christendom.[2]

This aggrieved consciousness was passed on to the Russian Church after the Turkish conquest of the Balkans and, in 1453, the fall of Constantinople, events that made Muscovy the only independent Orthodox community in the world. It was for this reason that the overly quoted Philotheus of Pskov came to speak of Moscow as the third and final Rome, by which he meant, however, not the power of the Muscovite state, but the purity, the "right teaching," of Muscovite Christianity, the only church free of both the Latin and the Greek heresies; for the See of Constantinople, too, had fallen into error by uniting with Rome.[3]

As for Muscovy's polity, it called itself the "Grand Prinicipality of Moscow," or later the "Muscovite state" *(Moskovskoe gosudarstvo)*, or sometimes the "Tsardom" *(tsarstvie)* of Moscow. The more general term, "Russia," adopted from the Latin through Poland, began to be used as an alternative designation only in the seventeenth century. Still, this political identity was secondary to the religious one, and the inhabitants of Muscovy thought of themselves in the first instance not as the "Russian people," but as "Christians" (the Russian word for peasant, or everyman, is *krestianin*) or the "Orthodox people."

Thus, until the late seventeenth century, in both the western and eastern portions of geographic Europe, people thought of their civilization primarily in religious terms. In such a culture, the relationship of Orthodox Muscovy to Latin Christendom, especially in its original Catholic form but also in its dissident Protestant versions, was largely one of hostility. And tension continued unabated almost until the end of the seventeenth century; after Moscow had repudiated the Union of Florence, the Papacy and the Jesuits still sought to bring Russia into the fold of a unitary Christendom, a process that reached its apogee when a Western fringe of the Orthodox community went over to Rome at the Union of Brest in 1596.[4]

This effort at conversion appeared all the more threatening since it was paralleled by military pressure along Muscovy's western frontier from the *Rzeczpospolita*, the *res publica* or Republic, of Poland-Lithuania, a term also translated as "commonwealth." Indeed, the pressure of this enormous realm led in 1610 to the temporary occupation of Moscow itself. At the same time, another Western power, Sweden, cut Muscovy off from the Baltic Sea, which became virtually a Swedish lake; and in the south, Russia too had her infidels, with the Turks controlling the entire coastline of the Black Sea, thereby making Russia landlocked except for the Arctic route through Arkhangelsk. Thus Muscovy's three neighbors, for a combination of geopolitical and religious reasons, sought to isolate her from the developed parts of Europe and so keep her weak. And this quarantine in backwardness served to aggravate the sentiment of mixed pride and humiliation deriving from her religious isolation.

It was in this situation of high tension between Russia and the outside world that the negative Western image of Muscovy was formed. Stubbornly schismatic in the crucial matter of religious faith, old Russia was deemed to have inherited from her erstwhile Tatar overlords the most slavish political despotism, to which was adjoined the savagery and poverty of the ancient Scythians—a combination of qualities that for Western Christendom denoted Asia. This, indeed, was the message conveyed by the memoirs of such early travelers as Sigismund von Herberstein, Jacques Margeret, and Giles Fletcher, whose accounts proved useful to later historians but aroused little interest at the time. Until Peter, Russia appeared to the West as no more than a barbarous backwater which, if inspiring any reaction at all, incited only revulsion, yet on the whole left Europe indifferent, since her actions hardly affected the interests of the truly significant portions of mankind.

All this changed dramatically as a result of Peter's triumph in the Great Northern War with Sweden between 1700 and 1721. The change in the relationship between Russia and Europe was, of course, in the first instance military and diplomatic: Russia had suddenly become a Great Power, self-promoted moreover to the rank of empire in the lineage of Rome.[5] But soon the change came to be institutional and social, as this power acquired the forms of a European Old Regime. Finally, with the century's advance the change became cultural, as this newest Old Regime opened itself to the Enlightenment and indeed became an object of admiration for the intellectual vanguard in the West.

The Birth of the Concert of Europe

In the military and diplomatic domain, then, Russia under Peter not only broke out of landlocked quarantine to the Baltic and established direct maritime contact with the major Western nations; her armies by the end of his reign had secured a virtual protectorate over the vast but declining monarchical republic of Poland-Lithuania and had even appeared as far west as the mouth of the Elbe. In the brief interval of twenty years, from 1700 to 1721, Russia had thrust herself into power politics on a European scale. Henceforth, little could take place in continental affairs in which she could not claim a voice, nor was there much that she initiated which would not affect in some measure the other powers of Europe. Overnight she had become an international actor almost equal to France, England, or Austria, and ahead of declining Spain, Holland, or rising Prussia. Never again until her victory in the Second World War would Russia experience a larger or more sudden increase of power vis-à-vis her most formidable contemporaries.

Indeed, Petrine Russia must be considered a founding member of the modern concert of Europe.[6] That precise term dates from the Congress of Vienna in 1815, when it was used to indicate the intention of the powers to ensure henceforth the equilibrium of Europe. A rough anticipation of such a system, however, in the form of a "conflictual balance of power," appeared at the same time that Russia emerged on the European scene.[7] Throughout the sixteenth and early seventeenth centuries international affairs had been dominated by the rivalry between the House of Habsburg in Austria and Spain, on the one hand, and France under the Valois and Bourbons, on the other. Most weaker states participated in international affairs largely as allies of the two principal rivals, as when Charles II mortgaged the foreign policy of England to France in exchange for a subsidy and, later, when Holland had to accept a Habsburg alliance to escape French domination. The concert of Europe emerged only after the two chief rivals had been successively defeated in their bid for hegemony.

The Spanish Habsburgs had lost out by the death of Philip II in 1598, and the lesser threat from their Austrian cousins had been beaten back by 1648 and the Treaty of Westphalia, an agreement which also established the diplomatic framework of the European state system. But it was only with the War of the Spanish Succession between 1701 and 1713, which finally thwarted Louis XIV's bid for hegemony, that Europe possessed a number of approximately coequal powers. By the time of the Treaty of Utrecht (in 1713), Spain, Sweden, and Holland had been reduced to secondary rank. England, a marginal state before this, became a major European power as Great Britain, as between 1689 and 1713 for the first time since Agincourt she was able to put an army on the continent. Austria, after the defeat of her German ambitions in the Thirty Years' War, had been recently refounded on a larger scale through the reconquest of Hungary from the Turks by Eugene of Savoy. Frederick William I, after 1713, gave emerging Prussia its mature form as a military autocracy.

All these transformations were contemporary with Peter's Great Northern War.[8] Although Russia had made a modest debut in European affairs in 1684 as a junior partner in the Holy League of the Papacy, Venice, and Austria against the Turks, it was only with the Northern War that she challenged a Western power and campaigned in Europe itself. Thus, in the opening years of the new century, what John Churchill, duke of Marlborough, and Prince Eugene of Savoy did for British and Austrian power in Western and Central Europe, Tsar Peter did for Russian power in the East.

After the wars of Marlborough, Eugene, and Peter, moreover, the European states ceased to function in separate western and eastern compartments. By the time of the War of the Polish Succession in

1733–1736 (or at the latest by the opening of the War of the Austrian Succession in 1740), they had been fused into a single international system of five dominant states from the Atlantic to the Urals. And all members of this now unitary concert of Europe viewed the others as juridically equal partners in a European family of states. Furthermore, all subscribed to the principle that the balance of power among them, though highly competitive, should not be upset unduly in favor of any one state, and that when such a danger threatened, other states could legitimately seek territorial "compensation" to achieve a new balance of forces. This European concert would pursue its conflictual course until it was destroyed in the Second World War.[9]

Given Russia's spectacular promotion under Peter, one might expect that the arrival of Muscovy's Asiatic hordes at the Elbe, together with the appearance of a Russian fleet in the Baltic, would have produced panic in Europe, for the Russians, their sovereign included, hardly displayed a refinement commensurate with their military strength. And indeed, there was a flurry of anxiety during the first years following Poltava over the raw nature of this force and its sudden emergence. Yet at no time did apprehension stiffen into panic; and within a few years after the Treaty of Nystadt, in 1721, had consecrated Peter's victory, thereby bringing his troops home, the initial sense of menace waned, and Russia was accepted into the European concert with remarkable ease considering the gains she had made. After Peter's death in 1725, when the succession fell to weaker rulers, the powers quickly fixed their attitude toward Russia for the rest of the century according to their various geopolitical interests, quite without regard for her once reputedly Asiatic civilization.

The Prussians in particular, who had gained significantly from collaboration with Peter, faced the new situation with equanimity from the beginning. At midcentury, the closeness was such that Frederick II arranged the marriage of his protégée, Princess Sophie of Anhalt-Zerbst (later Catherine II) to the heir of the Russian throne. Soon, however, Frederick's overweening ambition brought Russia into the coalition of the Seven Years' War of 1756–1763 against him; but the trauma of the Russian occupation of Königsberg and Berlin in 1761 convinced him that Prussia's future security depended on strict adherence to the policy of cooperation she had pursued toward Russia under Peter. Prussia therefore inaugurated an era of ever closer collaboration between Potsdam and St. Petersburg which lasted until Bismarck's fall in 1890 and which was to exercise the most profound influence on the destinies of Europe.

The Austrians, for their part, though at first alarmed by Peter's advance into Germany, moved toward friendship with his new Russia once they realized the damage he had dealt to France's traditional friends, Sweden and Poland. Throughout most of the century, furthermore, Austria shared a common cause with Russia in seeking to push the Ottomans southward into the Balkans. And between 1740 and 1763 Vienna found a more urgent mutual interest with St. Petersburg in resisting the extension of Frederick the Great's power in the north. Even after Frederick had learned his lesson from his near destruction during the Seven Years' War, the proximity of Russian power to East Prussia remained the Habsburgs' surest guarantee that the Hohenzollerns would continue to respect the existing equilibrium in the Germanies. Thus Austria not only accepted Russia's influence in Europe, but with a few lapses positively welcomed it—an alignment that would endure until the 1850s.

The French, by contrast, became the focus of antagonism toward the new Russia. All Peter's gains had been made at the expense of the Bourbons' heavily subsidized *barrière de l'est* against the Habsburgs—Sweden and Poland—an alliance system now called on also to wall off Russia. To manifest this new intent, the court of Versailles refused until the 1740s to recognize the Russian sovereign's "usurpation" of the title of emperor. Indeed, in the 1760s French diplomats, working with a variety of Ukrainian, Hungarian, and Polish political figures, produced a forged "Testament of Peter I," purporting to reveal Russia's "grand design" to conquer most of Europe. This document was still taken seriously by governments during the Napoleonic Wars; and as late as the Cold War President Harry Truman found it helpful in explaining Stalin.[10] Thus, even as Russia acquired full membership in the concert of Europe, the argument was staked out that she could never be trusted to play by the rules of civilized nations.

England, unlike France, became almost as constant a Russian partner as Austria. Although at first fearful that Russia's new power threatened the importation from the Baltic of cordage, timber, and tar for her fleet, she soon realized that Russia counterbalanced Sweden's strength in the area, thereby making it an open sea, more accessible to British shipping than when it had been Stockholm's private preserve. The cabinet of Westminster concluded that, so long as Russia did not intend to annihilate Sweden, her power in the Baltic should be encouraged. The English discovered further that Russia had as vital a need for Western manufactured goods—from armaments for the state to colonial and luxury products for the aristocracy—as England had for northern raw materials, and that she desired nothing better than to purchase these from their most abundant supplier, Great Britain.

With the commercial treaty of 1734 England became Russia's chief trading partner, and Russia a significant factor in England's own economy. Indeed, so indispensable was this commerce for both parties that during the Seven Years' War, when England was Frederick's only ally and Russia his most dangerous foe, each refrained from hostilities against the other in order not to imperil their Baltic exchanges. Most Englishmen of sense now held that a mutual economic interest and a shared antagonism toward their traditional enemy, France, made Russia their "natural ally." They fully agreed with the almost constant policy of their government that everything should be done to supply Russia's armies; to construct, to fit out, even to officer her ships of war; and to urge her increased participation in European affairs—an orientation that endured until the 1830s.[11]

Over and above these specific instances of concordance or conflict between the practical interests of Russia and those of other powers, certain general factors help to explain her easy integration into Europe. From the moment Peter broke the vise of Swedish power until Catherine's great wars of expansion against Turkey in the last third of the century, Russia was favored in her international enterprises by her location on the periphery of the European system and her consequent freedom from the vigilance, and the vengeance, of powerful neighbors. In the poor and scarcely populated eastern reaches of the continent, from Finland to Bessarabia, a shift in the balance of power disturbed fewer entrenched interests than it did at the system's nerve center, from the Low Countries to northern Italy, where the coveting of a canton could occasion a greater perturbation throughout Europe than the wresting of whole provinces from Sweden, Poland, or Turkey. Louis XIV and Frederick the Great, for every notable acquisition they made, were compelled to fight a return engagement against a coalition of most of Europe, whereas each conquest of Peter or Catherine, once accomplished, was accepted by Europe as definitive almost without challenge. Only England at the other periphery of the European system enjoyed similarly favorable conditions as a "flank power."[12] The isolation of her principal theater of action, the high seas, facilitated her colonial conquests from France and Holland—despite the notable exception of the French revanche in the War of American Independence.

On the European concert's other flank, Russia continued to profit from an underreaction to her advance until Catherine II and Alexander I completed their conquests in Poland, Finland, and along the Black Sea littoral. Only after these annexations was Russia brought cheek by jowl with other major powers, at a time moreover when the European system as a whole had grown more taut than a century earlier. She was thereby confronted for the first time with geopolitical conditions which made further acquisitions difficult, short of an explosive challenge to the entire European order. Yet, throughout the eighteenth century, during which Russia launched her career as a Great Power, she enjoyed a luxury of impunity unique in modern European history—a free gift of geography that does much to explain both her phenomenal westward expansion and the relative equanimity with which Europe viewed it.

In all international encounters, then, from the time of Peter to Catherine's early years, Russia's friends and foes alike responded to her promotion quite "rationally": that is, they reacted in terms of relationships of interest and power, without concern for the nature of her civilization. The first secret of her eighteenth-century success, therefore, was that her advance was readily accommodated to the emerging European state system of five predominant powers. For when Russia gained, Austria, Prussia, and England usually did so too; and only France (whom her neighbors thought too mighty anyway) habitually lost. Still, accommodation to the balance of power does not fully account for Russia's easy entry into Europe. The underlying premise of such acceptance, the factor making possible the primacy of *raison d'état* among the powers regarding her, lies outside the sphere of international politics as such.

Russia as Old Regime

The crucial factor in her acceptance is that Russia's rise did not do violence to the higher values of contemporary European society. In no way did she appear impervious, still less inimical, to what thinkers by the late 1760s began to call civilization.[13] This neologism lacked one of its two modern meanings: it did not signify a particular civilization in the sense of a unique set of qualities inherent in a given society; nor did it denote an organic historical community. Instead, in the eighteenth century, "civilization" possessed only its second modern meaning: an advanced level of material, intellectual, and moral development. It was the culmination of mankind's ascent from the "savage" state, such as could still be observed among America's natives, through the "barbarous" condition of most Asiatic realms as well as of Europe's own past. This advanced state, moreover, was viewed either as the attainment of high social rank or as a universal value capable, eventually, of extension to all mankind by diffusion from its European homeland.

In both senses the term was applicable in some degree to Peter's empire, where borrowed Western ways had been introduced by autocratic fiat. This method, however, was considered only normal; for almost until the eve of 1789 Europeans saw civilization proceeding from the top down, from the enlightened few to the ignorant many. This elitist perspective explains why, until the 1760s, Europeans designated the highest state of human development not by the abstract concept of civilization, but by the more concrete, institutional notion of "police"—*la police* in France and *Polizeiwissenschaft*, or "police science," in Germany.

This term designated the agent of law enforcement empowered by the prince to apply physical coercion for the maintenance of order, that is, a "police force" in the most concrete sense, the only one the word retained into the nineteenth and twentieth centuries. But in the seventeenth and eighteenth centuries *la police* signified enlightened govern-

28

ance, that is, the promotion of civil order in the state, the rational regulation of law and the economy, and the fostering of refined social norms. In this sense the word reveals its illustrious lineage, for it stems from the Greek *politeia* (itself derived from *polis*) signifying both the civil polity and citizenship in that polity. Although the modern term "police" appears to degrade the concept of a civilized society, in its eighteenth-century meaning it was still close to its original and nobler sense.

This use of "police" in roughly the later sense of "civilization" was no semantic accident. In both French and English, the verb "to civilize" and the participle "civilized" had existed at least since the seventeenth century. But it took a hundred more years for their obvious substantive, "civilization," to make its appearance. In the meantime, the term "police," which indicated both the agent and the effect of the civilizing act, stubbornly remained the designation for the coercive and judicial apparatus of princely authority. The consistency of this usage signifies that until almost the eve of 1789 Europeans viewed the development of civilized conditions as the result of action by the state rather than of the spontaneous operation of society. Improvement came from above, from the prince and the upper orders, not from below, from the people. Progress meant the development of social order and law far more than of individual freedom. Throughout most of the eighteenth century, therefore, an *état policé* and an *état civilisé* meant roughly the same thing; or rather, as time went on, the former came increasingly to be regarded as an immature form of the latter.[14]

It was through the cultural norms of *la police* that the Petrine empire was integrated into the emerging concert of Europe. And it must be emphasized that it was the Russian state, not the Russian nation, that was involved. For in the eighteenth century the state was not conceived of as the expression of a nation; rather it was a dynastic polity, whose peoples were subjects, not citizens. To be sure, the subjects of the more advanced polities of Europe—England and France—had long thought of themselves in significant measure as nations. Yet in international affairs even they often behaved as dynastic polities. Thus, so well-formed a nation as the France of Louis XIV after 1700 made acquisition of the Spanish inheritance for the House of Bourbon the cornerstone of its international policy; and eighteenth-century Britain's involvement in continental affairs was in part governed by the concerns of the House of Hanover, a connection necessary to ensure the Protestant dynastic succession at home. Such states as Austria and Prussia were entirely the creation of their ruling dynasties, not an emanation of society. It is no accident that half of eighteenth-century wars were wars of one or another succession.

As regards the dynastic polity's social structure, it is best considered as a political regimen; it was organized as a legally prescribed hierarchy of "orders" or "estates," each defined by its relationship to the sovereign. In the dynastic polity's absolutist ideology, the state was not considered the creation of society; rather, it was the prince that gave order and form to the body social of the realm by the power of *la police*. Legitimate authority was thus superordinate authority, viewed as coming from above, from God or nature, not from below, from the population. Although these traditional assertions had already been challenged by theories of contract, such as Locke's, or of intermediate bodies, such as Montesquieu's, the European norm remained patriarchal and absolutist. Similarly, society was seen as a divinely or naturally ordained hierarchy of ranks, founded on unequal hereditary status. (Natural inequality was characteristic also of such premodern "republics" as the Netherlands, the Swiss Confederation, and Venice.) And the principles of superordinate authority and legitimate social inequality together defined the internal structure of the dynastic polity—that sacred sociopolitical order baptized "Old Regime" after its paradigmatic example was overthrown in 1789.

Yet this Old Regime was not a "despotism," a concept that implies lawlessness; rather, it was, in Montesquieu's term, an *état de droit*. It operated according to a kind of social contract under which service was rendered to the monarch by his subjects in their various capacities, while the monarch maintained internal order and external security, and assured the "liberties"—that is, corporate privileges—of the various categories of his servants.[15] Thus Western European absolutism, as epitomized by the rule of Henry IV, Richelieu, and Louis XIV, in effect rested on an implicit, nonwritten constitutionalism—an administrative pluralism that drew on feudal rights, municipal franchises, and ecclesiastical immunities that went back to the Middle Ages. The task of seventeenth-century absolutism was to pacify and unify the variegated world it had inherited from this past—in other words, to "police" it—in order to supply the military and fiscal means for interdynastic rivalry. Since the Bourbons undertook this effort in the richest zone of Europe, their mobilization of society never became so onerous as to transform the *état de droit* into a despotism (although farther east monarchical power became increasingly more stringent).

The rise of royal absolutism, therefore, had as its counterpart the creation of what classical political theory called civil society as distinct from the now "sovereign" monarchy. And this occurred as a protracted process of interaction between the monarchy and its corporate subjects.[16] Beginning in the thirteenth century the Capetian kings organized the medieval groups of "those who pray, those who fight, and those who labor" into the three juridically defined corporate estates of the realm. Even when the Bourbons ceased, after 1624, to consult with these orders on the national level, provincial elected assemblies continued to function. The fact of a division of powers under absolutism was expressed even more clearly in the monarchy's "sovereign courts," in its judicial *parlements*, and in the mentality of the elite.

Peter's Russia entered the policed world of the Old-Regime dynastic state from a rather different point of departure from her more Western neighbors. The medieval Rus of Kiev, of course, had originated like the rest of Europe of the year 1000: it was a barbarian kingdom which had received Christianity, clerical literacy, and a modest classical heritage from East Rome, comparable to what Western barbarians, from the Franks of Clovis to the Magyars of St. Stephen, had received from West Rome. This changed radically, however, after the Mongol conquest in the mid-thirteenth century. The old heartland of Rus, from the merchant republic of Novgorod in the north to Kiev in the south, gravitated westward, the latter eventually being absorbed by Poland-Lithuania. The northeastern Rus of Muscovy became a backwater largely cut off from the rest of Christian Europe until the end of the fifteenth century, that is, for some two hundred years.

Muscovy was not alone in such a fate. Her lot was analogous to

Spain's for some five hundred years after the Arab conquest of 712, and to Hungary's for almost two hundred years after the Turkish conquest of 1526. Yet, unlike Spain or Hungary, Muscovy was not occupied or colonized; and contrary to widespread opinion, no Mongol institutions were implanted in Russia. Muscovy's basic institutions remained the prince and his comitatus, or *druzhina*, of boyars, which until the late fifteenth century functioned under a contractual regime of what may fairly be called incipient feudalism.

During this long isolation, Muscovy's extreme poverty in combination with the military pressure from the nomads of the southern steppes and then later from Poland-Lithuania led to maximum mobilization for survival. Thus by the sixteenth century Muscovy had become a military autocracy founded on a universal service society. The hereditary, or boyar, nobility was amalgamated with the new non-noble service gentry, or *dvorianstvo*, and both were obligated to military duty to the tsar; at the base of the system the peasantry was bound into serfdom to the gentry and tax or infantry tribute to the state. The church and the towns suffered similar subordination to the service principle. Finally, the city-state of Novgorod had been destroyed by Moscow, and in the seventeenth century half of Cossack-cum-gentry Ukraine had been conquered from Poland.

The essence of Peter's reforms was to bring Muscovy's universal service system to its culmination by recasting it in the contemporary European mold. The impetus to this change was quite simply military necessity. From the fifteenth century until the seventeenth the principal threat to Muscovy's security had come from the southern steppe frontier;[17] and this could be met by a militia of horsemen using bows and arrows. By the late fifteenth century, however, the Turks had acquired gunpowder weaponry from the West; and in the sixteenth century Russia came into increasing military conflict with advanced Western states themselves. These circumstances made it imperative for Russia to adapt to what has been called the early-modern military revolution.

Between the early sixteenth century and the mid-seventeenth, the contest between the Spanish Habsburgs and France in Italy and the Low Countries transformed European warfare. First, gunpowder magnified offensive power; then, dense fortification multiplied defensive strength—only to be answered by sophisticated artillery and massed infantry, organized into standing armies. Soon this revolution had spread west to the British Isles, north to Sweden, and east into Germany; and after the Thirty Years' War, numerous of its veterans took up service in Russia. Peter, from his boyhood infatuation with boats and "toy regiments" to his adult passion for artillery and fortification, adapted the new European methods to produce a standing army of some 200,000 men.

The transformation of warfare also transformed statecraft. Warfare, after all, was the first business of European Old Regimes, consuming up to 80–90 percent of the tax revenues of most states. All of them were therefore obliged to strengthen their fiscal and administrative systems; and these "reforms" meant the rationalization of the bureaucratic and economic support systems of war through policies of mercantilism and cameralism—and this, too, was part of "police." All these changes, finally, had important consequences for the social structure of the dynastic polities. It was through militarization and rationalization in this mode that, under Peter, Muscovy's primitive universal service system first converged with Old-Regime Europe.[18]

This initial step toward convergence, of course, did not mean that Peter's Russia had become just another European Old Regime. Serfdom had disappeared in most of Western Europe by the thirteenth century; Peter strengthened it in Russia. Even his nobles were bound to lifetime service to the state, thus precluding the formation of a civil society. Nevertheless, Russia had taken a genuinely European first step toward the emergence of such a civil order. For Europeanization would not stop with improved military technology and a rationalized organization of administration and finance. These practical innovations, promoted as they were by the philosophy of state building through princely "police," required the assimilation of European higher culture to produce their full effect. And this step would inevitably open the country to grander values and more intoxicating ideals.

Still, Russia had no choice but to step on the European cultural escalator. So great was the military pressure in Old-Regime Europe for a more coherent ordering of the state that every society had to respond to it in some manner or go under. Even in relatively secure and insular England, it was only at the cost of two revolutions, a civil war, and fifty years of withdrawal from European affairs that civil society was able to thwart the efforts of the Stuart kings to develop Tudor absolutism into a militarized polity on the French model. Nevertheless, British civil society after 1640 was obliged to appropriate the task of military modernization and state building for itself. Indeed, it was Cromwell's New Model Army that for the first time brought the whole of the British Isles under London's control. By contrast, east of France, and in response to her challenge, from the mid-seventeenth century onward the backward polities of Prussia and Austria developed more onerous military monarchies than that of the Bourbons.

One cause of this stringency was the greater natural poverty of Central Europe; another was the fact that its lands possessed a more rudimentary heritage of estates and intermediate bodies than postfeudal France,[19] thereby facilitating monarchical centralization. Thus the Central European dynasties were able, with varying degrees of ruthlessness, to impose elements of a general service order on the nobility, the towns, and the church—and of course the peasants. Conversely, the price of failure to militarize in this manner was paid by municipal and ecclesiastical Italy, which largely succumbed to foreign occupation, and gentry-republican Poland, which was simply expunged from the map of Europe.

Muscovy was only the last European society to respond to this universal pressure; and, given the paucity of her resources, she did so in an even more ruthless manner than the Central European monarchies. Still, in one crucial respect Russia's similarity to these neighbors was greater than theirs was to the maritime West of Europe: beginning in the sixteenth century "second serfdom" was established in all of Europe east of the Elbe, at the same time that first serfdom took hold in Russia. Although in Central Europe the impetus to this development was largely economic mobilization for the export of grain to the West, and in Russia it was military mobilization for national survival, the overall result was to divide Europe into two social zones—thereby creating a frontier which would endure into the nineteenth century (and which the Iron Curtain would follow in the twentieth). It was under these

34

onerous conditions that the domains of the House of Romanov were accepted into Europe as the last-born dynastic polity of the European Old Regime.

At the same time that Russia reentered the European cultural universe at its eastern end, those British outposts which would one day become the United States first entered history on its western fringe. Yet, whereas Russia was obliged to take the military, statist route, the remote North American colonies, because of the English monarchy's relative weakness, had the freedom to take the obverse route of a civil society emancipated from most Old-Regime forms; and in this sense, America was "born modern."[20]

Yet despite the differences between eighteenth-century British North America and Russia, the two may plausibly be seen as contrasting faces of a single expansion of Europe. For Europe—or, as it would now be better to say, the West—cannot be conceived of as a fixed entity.[21] Although all cultures obviously change, the historical particularity of Europe was its exceptionally rapid and creative development; and its motto since the late fifteenth century had been to increase and multiply. After 1492 Atlantic, Columbian Europe had been consciously seeking out new worlds in the West from New Spain to New England and New France; and after 1640 this same dynamic Europe, simply by its creative pressure, inadvertently and without progress aforethought, was generating new European worlds in its own Baltic backyard, along the dunes and marshes from Stettin and Königsberg to Petersburg. Indeed, the emergence of both Vienna and Berlin as significant cities and dynastic capitals preceded St. Petersburg by only some twenty years. All this was not without its price, to be sure. The development of both the Western and Eastern extensions of the European heartland was paid for by the creation of new forms of servitude: African slavery in the West and second serfdom in the East. At the same time, however, in each of these extensions of the West, European culture also brought the seeds of the Enlightenment; and over the long haul these would mature to challenge both slavery and serfdom.

The result of these transformations was that by Peter's death, Europe presented a series of gradations of severity in Old-Regime structures, from the mild militarization of France, to the intermediate rigors of Austria and, especially, Prussia, to the brutal simplicity of Russia. Yet at the ultimate point of contact of this middle zone with Russia—East Prussia—society was not notably different from what it was in the Romanovs' provinces across the Nieman River. Indeed, Peter's reforms are best understood as the application to a vaster, poorer territory of the methods of military and bureaucratic state building from above employed by the Great Elector of Brandenburg some fifty years earlier, or by his own half-contemporary, Frederick William I.

After Peter's death, the gap between Russia and her nearest neighbor was narrowed further still. The gentry exploited its control of the guards' regiments of the capital to determine the succession, obtaining as a reward the gradual reduction of its service obligations. By 1762, it had achieved complete "emancipation," while retaining lands and serfs as private property. Catherine solidified the gentry's rights with the Charter of the Nobility of 1785, which gave it the status of an estate. Thereby the Russian *dvorianstvo* at last became a nobility approximately on the Western model, and Russia acquired the first basis for a civil society.[22] The most fundamental lacunae of Peter's rough-hewn Old Regime had been filled in. Of course, the peasants remained serfs—but this was true in republican Poland and the German Old Regimes as well.

The parallelism between the two most militarized dynastic polities of Europe, Prussia and Russia, would continue to operate, with the same lag of fifty years, into the twentieth century. And indeed, this parallel offers the prime illustration of that West-East cultural gradient, the downward slope of cultural maturity from West to East, already mentioned as the overall framework of this book. This *West-östliches Kulturgefälle* took form only shortly before Russia reentered Europe.

From the fifteenth century to the late sixteenth, the course of civilization's development in modern Europe had been from south to north, from municipal Italy to the transalpine monarchies—in the arts and letters, in economic organization, in diplomacy and military technology, indeed in everything but state building. With the beginning of the seventeenth century, the course of civilization began to run from west to east, from the dynamic Atlantic polities to their Central and Eastern European emulators.

Nor is this merely a perception of later historiography. The Italian Renaissance was obviously perceived at the time to be the European center of innovation. Frederick the Great held that mid-eighteenth-century Prussia had barely attained the level of civilization of Richelieu's France a century earlier, while he saw Russia as still half-barbaric and no more than marginally European.[23] As for Peter himself, he saw only a difference of level of development between his empire and its immediate Western neighbors, yet at the same time he never doubted Russia's ability to close the gap. And so, for most eighteenth-century observers, Russia was the farthest march of Europe, the outer band in an international spectrum of Old Regimes.

Yet in the dynastic polity, while the prince was served in one way or another by all categories of his subjects, he was served more directly by some than by others. The most noble of these servants were the warriors and higher magistrates who permitted him to fulfill his prime function as monarch—the safeguarding of external security and internal order—on which the welfare of all humbler categories of the population depended. In such a world, the primary distinction among people was not so much national as social. What counted most in the lives of individuals, and in the social intercourse between them, was not whether they were Frenchmen or Germans or Russians, but whether they were noble or non-noble servants of their respective monarchs. Thus, service to the Russian emperor automatically conferred patents of nobility, not only according to the Table of Ranks established by Peter, but also in the eyes of the European aristocratic establishment.

But acceptance as a noble was fully confirmed only if the emperor's officers also displayed the bearing of gentlemen. The eighteenth-century nobility did not consider their status to be derived solely from service to the prince; they also held it to be founded on the inherent worth of certain cultural norms deriving from birth and breeding, and representing the *summum* of the virtues of civilized society. These values were generically designated as *civilité*, or civil comportment, *politesse*, or a polished demeanor, and *courtoisie*, or courtly manners. As the century wore on, *moeurs douces*, in the sense of restrained and humane norms of conduct as much as of gentlemanly manners, were increasingly regarded as an essential component of the older ideal of civility. The refined manners and ethos designated as *moeurs douces*, however, although perhaps first expressed by the nobility, could also become the property of society as a whole, whereas civility remained more closely associated with the "polished" influence of the princely court. And all this added up to the moral dimension of what by 1770 was called civilization.[24]

Cultivation of these qualities, of course, presupposed not only literacy—still a rare commodity at the time—but also a significant degree of material well-being and, in most cases, the security of legal class privilege. Those who might qualify as civilized, then, came, in Eastern Europe, almost invariably from the nobility, and in lands west of the Rhine, only from the nobility and the higher echelons of the Third Estate. And these strata were separated by an immense gulf from the masses, in the West no less than in Russia. In the eighteenth century, therefore, civilization was primarily an attribute of the upper orders, and barbarism was a quality not just of non-European societies but also of the common brutes at the base of all societies. A Chinese mandarin, a Persian sage, or even that noble gentleman Saladin the Turk was more civilized than a Norman or Brandenburg peasant. So, too, was a Muscovite boyar if, as Peter commanded him, he shaved off his beard, put on a powdered wig, and acquired civil manners.

The upper-class West throughout the eighteenth century saw in Russia largely this powdered, polished elite; it paid little attention to the near absence of a Third Estate beneath it. As for the Russian serf, Western nobles were hardly aware of his exceptionally wretched condition, the most degraded of any peasantry in Europe, since they displayed a similar indifference to the state of their own rustics at home: for Frederick the Great peasants were simply the "beasts of burden of society." According to the standards of the age, however, acceptance of the Russian elite meant acceptance of Russia as a whole. In the eyes of the dynastic and aristocratic establishment of the day, a *gentilhomme russe, officier de Sa Majesté Impériale*, providing he possessed reasonably refined manners (and standards were no longer exacting by the time one reached Pomerania or Galicia) and spoke passable French so that one could communicate with him, was as European as anyone. The fact that his Muscovite name ended with "off" or "sky," was secondary.

A command of French was necessary not only as a means of communication, but also as an international warrant of both civility and nobility. In eighteenth-century Europe, until the emergence of literary German after 1750, there were only two languages capable of expressing fully modern secular culture: French and English. English, however, was confined to its native island and overseas colonies, while French was the vehicle for the higher values among the upper orders throughout Europe. Classical French, moreover, beginning with the founding of the Académie Française in 1635 had been quite deliberately molded by the royal court; it was thus especially suited to be the class language of international aristocratic culture, since it had first articulated the ethos of nobility and the norms of civility that were the ideal of the dynastic polity everywhere.[25] Russia's cultural accommodation to these values was accomplished to the satisfaction of most of aristocratic Europe as a result of the passable gallicization of its elite under Peter's daughter, Elizabeth, in the middle of the century.[26] And after the emancipation of the gentry from compulsory state service in 1762, imperial Russia's social and cultural assimilation into the European establishment was largely complete.

Evidence for this assimilation is found not only in the adoption of Western ways by the Russian nobility but also in the political connections of the Western nobility with the Russian state. The eighteenth century provides many examples of aristocratic internationalism, or more properly "interdynasticism." A son of the king of Saxony could become the French Maréchal de Saxe. The "ethnically" (or culturally) French Eugene of Savoy could become the chief servant of the Austrian emperor and the leader of his forces against his former patron Louis XIV. And Marlborough, too, had learned his trade in Louis's army before becoming his most dangerous foe. Finally, Frederick William I could make the widest view of French Huguenots at all echelons of his service; and in 1700 nearly half the population of Berlin was French. In Russia such phenomena were perhaps even more frequent.

The tradition began under Peter with such humble adventurers as the Swiss Francis Lefort, and the Scot Peter Gordon. It continued with the virtual rule of the Germans—Court Chamberlain Ernst-Johann Biron, Field Marshal Burkhard Münnich, and Foreign Minister Andrew Ostermann—under Empress Anna between 1730 and 1740. Although under Elizabeth and Catherine II the already gallicized local stock—the Shuvalovs, Vorontsovs, Rumiantsevs, and Panins—tended to crowd the foreigners from the front of the stage, they by no means eliminated them, especially the omnipresent Germans from Russia's Baltic provinces. This tradition extended well into the nineteenth century, and indeed culminated then, for the revolutionary and Napoleonic upheavals in the West made Russia the principal refuge and bastion of international aristocratic society. Outstanding examples of foreigners in the Russian service include the prominence of the Corsican Pozzo di Borgo in the immediate entourage of Alexander I; the role of the duke of Richelieu, a future prime minister of France, as governor-general of New Russia and founder of Odessa; and the importance of Freiherr Heinrich vom Stein, a former first minister of Prussia, in the Russian emperor's inner councils on the eve of the Napoleonic invasion of 1812. Finally, under Nicholas I such Baltic or ethnic Germans as Foreign Minister Count Karl Nesselrode, Finance Minister Egor Kankrin, and Chief of Gendarmes Count Alexander Benkendorff for decades occupied some of the most exalted offices in the state. Not only had Peter introduced Russia into the political concert of dynastic Europe; he had introduced her into the social concert of international aristocracy as well.

The Ottoman Control

That the two initiations were substantive may be illustrated by a glance at Europe's relations with that "scourge of Christendom," Turkey, with which Russia before Peter had been so frequently equated by Westerners. Beginning as early as the mid-fifteenth century—a full two hundred and fifty years before Russia's introduction to Europe—the Ottoman Empire had borrowed Western military technology and imported Western technicians quite as much as did Russia beginning with Peter.

Yet despite these contacts, Turkey never came to function as part of the European concert. Its only notable alliance with a Western power, France, amounted to little more than a haphazard coincidence of Turkish aggressiveness with French need for a counterweight to the Habsburgs during the sixteenth and seventeenth centuries.

The Turks' alien and resolutely unsecularized religion was, of course, the chief cause of their failure to become a member of the European concert. For the Ottoman fusion of political sultanate and religious caliphate gave the Turkish polity a sacred character, transforming its foreign policy into a religious messianism. In Ottoman eyes, the world was divided into the "abode of Islam" for the faithful and the "abode of war" for the infidel; and every war in which they engaged became a holy undertaking—not just a conflict between states, but a confrontation of civilizations. Accordingly, until the seventeenth century the Sublime Porte refused to accord its foes more than a temporary "truce" after each war; nor, after it had accepted formal peace treaties, as at Carlowitz in 1699, did it maintain regular diplomatic relations with most of the powers until the late eighteenth century.

Just as important in keeping the Ottomans out of Europe was the fact that they never developed the institutional and cultural forms of an Old-Regime polity, or even approached the "refinement" of its mores. The differences in this domain between the two successor empires of East Rome are glaring.[27] The central Ottoman institution was that of the janissaries, a landless class of praetorian slaves conscripted as children from the subjugated Christian population of the Balkans, converted to Islam, and bound wholly to the service of the sultan. By its very nature it could hardly have been transformed in any conceivable span of time into a European type of aristocracy; and when the sultan's control began to loosen, the janissaries turned into predatory local satraps, thereby helping to provoke the early nineteenth-century Greek, Serbian, and Albanian revolts and transforming the once mighty Porte into the "sick man of Europe." In contrast, the Russian service gentry, despite its origins as a creature of the autocracy, possessed the institutional leverage to win its freedom in the course of the eighteenth century and become a noble estate. Still less did the Porte attempt to make its despotism enlightened. Although the Ottomans eagerly accepted military technology from the West, they were resolutely hostile to its infidel ideas, even refusing to have a printing press in Constantinople until 1729 (only to close it again in 1742). The Muscovites, by contrast, had founded their first press in 1553—in order to print religious books, it is true, but this had been the priority of Gutenberg himself. Under such circumstances there was never any question of the Ottomans establishing, like Peter, such a medium of secular civilization as an Academy of Sciences. In every aspect of its internal order Turkey adamantly remained what the age called barbaric.

Muscovy, furthermore, had never been a monolithic sacred polity, despite a Byzantine legacy of church subservience to the state (though not of Caesaro-papism, as is often alleged). Although the division between the secular and sacerdotal powers in both Muscovy and Byzantium was much weaker than in the Latin West, the tsar or emperor was not also the patriarch, in a pattern of separation general to Christian societies. By virtue of this distinction, as well as of the customary weakness of the Orthodox Church vis-à-vis monarchical authority, it was easy for Peter to make his empire essentially secular. In an Erastian spirit common to much of contemporary Europe, especially in Protestant countries, he subordinated the church to state control by replacing the patriarch with a governing board of bishops, the Holy Synod, presided over by a layman, thereby largely separating religion from politics. Thus, whereas the Porte continued to conduct its international affairs in a medieval atmosphere of jihad, the Russian monarchy successfully disentangled the sacred from the political, "de-ideologizing" its foreign relations at a time when both Protestant and Catholic powers had recently done the same.

Before Peter, therefore, Russia had the advantage over Turkey of being Christian and hence, to a degree, akin to Latin Europe; after him, she had the further advantage of being able to develop secularized political and cultural forms that were congenial to the one ethos no less than to the single idiom of Versailles, Schönbrunn, and Potsdam. Indeed, it is a striking commentary on the central theme of this inquiry that Turkey, during five centuries of occupation of the oldest civilized

portion of the continent—the land of the Parthenon and Santa So-
phia—became far less a part of "historic Europe" than did the back-
woods of Muscovy in twenty-five years under Peter.

More interesting still than the acceptance of Russia by the established
courts of Europe, as well as by the strata of society which thought in
estate terms, was her idealization by a circle of men who viewed the
world in universal terms, those for whom *moeurs douces* and civilization
were grounded not in hereditary status, but in that "natural reason"
common to all mankind. Such individuals were Western Europeans
who were fortunate enough to possess civility, but not so fortunate as to
enjoy nobility, men of letters who attacked the aristocratic establishment in the name of Humanity—in short, the enlightened, the *philosophes*. For it was this "republic of letters" which produced the first
major work that presented Europe with an articulated image of the new
colossus of the north: Voltaire's *History of Charles XII*, published in
1731, a date which symbolically marks Russia's full welcome into the
European cultural concert. It is indeed a date well worthy of note, for
Voltaire's tribute, together with the long series of eulogies it inaugurated, was not the least of the laurels that Peter had won for Russia with
his victory over Charles at Poltava.

Russia as Philosophic Fable

The roseate image of Russia held by Voltaire and his successors may be
understood only if one bears in mind that the *philosophes'* attack on the
existing order was not a frontal assault but rather an undermining action conducted from within the framework of the dynastic polity's institutions and values. The universal norms of philosophy emerged only by
degrees from the elitist norms of nobility, while the prince and the state
spanned both sets of values at once. The particularized civility of court
and aristocracy in the seventeenth century became, by the early eighteenth century, the refined mores of a broader but as yet ill-defined
society; and only later still, around 1770, did it develop into the generalized notion of civilization as the potential endowment of all men.

It was by virtue of this escalation of the concept of princely police that Voltaire was able to annex Russia to the cause of philosophy in his *History of Charles XII.* The work was undertaken for its own sake by an author of thirty-seven who was not yet internationally famous and who could thus expect no reward from a mighty and perhaps munificent power in St. Petersburg—a motive too often alleged as the inspiration of the *philosophes'* encomia of Eastern autocracy. Already in his youth Voltaire had been drawn to his subject by witnessing the revolution in Europe's affairs wrought through Russia's rise, and especially by the contrast this presented between Peter's uninterrupted success and the relative failure of Louis XIV in his last, bigoted, and despotic years. Since Voltaire, moreover, understood history as "philosophy teaching by example," he also saw in the contest between Charles and Peter a means of dramatizing the difference between traditional, predatory monarchy and creative, "enlightened" statecraft. In Voltaire's account, Charles, for all his dash and brilliance, was essentially a purposeless figure, who succeeded only in wasting his kingdom's wealth and in depopulating her provinces. Though Peter too was a conqueror and shared the uncouth customs of his nation, he at least conquered with a constructive aim: he brought civility to his benighted subjects, carved a noble capital out of the wilderness, and encouraged the material improvement of his realm in every way.[28]

Soon this became the accepted Western opinion of Russia. In 1748 the high Enlightenment was launched with Montesquieu's *Spirit of the Laws.* In it the author declared that Peter had indeed "given the manners of Europe to a European nation"; at the same time—since Montesquieu firmly equated Europe with freedom, as contrasted with Oriental despotism—he was at some pains not to rank autocratic Russia among the despotic powers.[29] The mature Voltaire, however, had no such problem. In 1748 he resumed his praise of Russian autocracy with *Anecdotes of Peter the Great.* A decade later, the now celebrated author extracted an invitation from his hero's daughter, the Empress Elizabeth, to compose a full history of the reformer's reign and for that purpose was furnished with official papers. The result was the appearance, in 1759 and 1763, of the two volumes of his *History of the Russian Empire under Peter the Great.* In this new work the emphasis was shifted from

Peter's external contest with Sweden to his internal struggle for reform, thereby for the first time presenting the European public with an account of Peter's achievements as a "legislator."[30]

To begin with, Peter had established administrative regularity and public order; that is, he had made Russia *policée*. Although he had also devoted much energy to waging war and for that purpose had even given Russia its first modern army and a navy, his ultimate object in stooping to such relatively unenlightened activities had been to ensure peaceful conditions for his empire's development. Voltaire, antimilitarist though he was, recognized too well the crude character of European society not to appreciate the necessity for a firm martial hand at the helm of state if the higher values of civility and refined mores were to develop at all. Besides, war for Peter was a means, not an end. He conquered only to win access to the more civilized regions of Europe, and thereby to speed the flow of commerce and the importation of useful mechanical inventions, to encourage the implantation of manufactures, and to advance the material development of his domains in every sphere. Peter's method in these enterprises was as admirable as his goal. He was forever curious to learn new things and to introduce all known improvements, whether in the arts of warfare, of industry, or of state administration. Among the sovereigns of his age, he was uniquely free from slavery to the irrational prejudices of the past: experimentation and practicality were his guides in any undertaking.

Peter struck equally vigorous blows for progress in his efforts to forge an improved social and political order. He repressed the factious gentry, though at times by deplorable expedients, as in the case of the mass beheading of his rebellious palace guards, the *streltsy*. He curtailed clerical "superstition" and "fanaticism" by instituting lay control over the church through the Holy Synod, by limiting the number of "dronish" monks through appropriation of their landed wealth, and by practicing toleration toward religious dissenters, indeed Muhammadans. When certain disgruntled nobles and monks fought back by pitting his heir, Alexis, against him, the emperor defended his reforms even at the cost of his son's life. Although Peter's severities might appear offensive to delicate natures, they were justified by his nation's immaturity and redeemed by their results. "Who would have said in 1700," exclaimed

Voltaire, "that a magnificent and polished court would [now] be established on the gulf of Finland . . . that an empire of two thousand leagues . . . would be policed in fifty years?" The creation of Peter's empire "represented perhaps the greatest revolution [*époque*] in European life since the discovery of the New World."[31]

On his last page, Voltaire drew the moral from this extraordinary story: "Sovereigns of states that have long been policed can only say to themselves: if in the frozen climes of ancient Scythia a man aided by his genius alone has accomplished such great things, what could we not achieve in kingdoms where the accumulated labors of centuries have made all things easy?"[32] In other words, Voltaire challenged Louis XV to turn the infinitely more favorable climate of France to even greater advantage for promoting the cause of progress and reason. Indeed, this was the point that Voltaire had already urged on him by eulogizing the example of his predecessor in the *Century of Louis XIV* in 1751 and by his still more provocative, and unpublishable, panegyric of 1723 to the tolerant Henry IV, *The Henriad*.

Peter's Russia thus was in a sense a slogan and a symbol in Voltaire's campaign for reform at home, a battering ram against the "irrational" institutions and "prejudices" of the supposedly civilized states of old Europe. As such, the Russian reformer was akin to that semimythical pantheon of humane, reasonable, and tolerant Chinese, Persians, and even red-skinned Hurons whose civilized example the *philosophes* often employed to point up the vices of Old-Regime society. Yet there was one crucial difference between Peter and his fellows in the *philosophes'* Areopagus of "lawgivers": whereas most of these exotic figures were largely mythical, Peter was real, and a number of his accomplishments in fact represented crude approximations of policies dear to his admirers. Thus despite significant exaggerations on Voltaire's part, stemming from his polemical intent, his eulogies of Peter constituted a serious commitment to imperial Russia as the embodiment of one of the greatest values of the age—an enlightened monarchy, or a well-policed state, a notion which nineteenth-century historiography would rebaptize enlightened despotism to characterize the three governments in Eastern Europe so venerated by the Western republic of letters.[33]

Such a high assessment of Peter's rule was not just the retrospective

judgment of a polemically minded *philosophe* who had had no direct
contact with his hero. Although Voltaire was unaware of the fact, his
opinion had been anticipated by a far more important philosopher,
Leibniz, who, moreover, actually made a contribution to Peter's reforms. Leibniz was deeply impressed by Russia's incursion into Europe
and Germany in the later years of his own life. At first, the philosopher
thought that hitherto barbaric Russia might serve as a bridge between
civilized Europe and an equally civilized China, whose high accomplishments he had come to appreciate through the Jesuits' accounts of
their efforts to convert Beijing to Christianity. Later the philosopher,
disturbed by the still recent division of Christendom at home, and less
of a secularist than Voltaire, hoped that Orthodox Russia, now under an
enlightened tsar, might reunite all branches of Christianity into one
church. And still later Leibniz came to consider that Russia's recently
"barbarous" state made her a *tabula rasa* unencumbered by the historical clutter of Europe and, therefore, an ideal terrain for constructing a
polity that would fuse the "*civitas dei* of religion with the philosophy of
la république des lettres."[34]

Moved by these various messianic concerns, the philosopher paid
assiduous court to Peter, eventually obtaining two personal meetings
with him, in 1711 and 1713, which were followed by a regular correspondence with the tsar and his entourage. In the course of these contacts, Peter seriously sought advice on how to improve his country's
administration; and Leibniz saw in Peter's interest a major opportunity
to mold a truly rational society, an undertaking for which he would be,
appropriately, the "Solon." To implement this grand design Leibniz, in
1711, devised a plan for a Russian Academy of Sciences, just as in 1700
he had drawn up the plan for the Prussian Academy of Sciences. The
new academy was intended by philosopher and tsar alike to be unique in
Europe, taking as its purpose the application of man's knowledge to the
practical problems of terrestrial existence, thereby transforming from
above the whole of society—a mission which prefigured the program
enunciated at midcentury by the *Encyclopédie.* The academy was actually
founded in 1725, though with more modest ambitions, after the death
of both Leibniz and the tsar; and it was staffed essentially by Germans,
just as the Berlin Academy in 1750 was refounded by Frederick the

Great and staffed with Frenchmen. Thus did enlightenment descend the European cultural gradient, with apprentices becoming masters as they sought out opportunity in the East.

The degree and durability of the commitment of European reformers to Russia should not be underestimated, for the image of Russia established by Voltaire (and adumbrated by Leibniz) dominated enlightened opinion until roughly the last quarter of the century as his tradition was taken up by other, almost equally influential, men of letters. In return the Russian monarchy itself, during almost every reign of the century, seemed to conspire to give its admirers new pledges of a developing enlightenment. Even Peter's unimpressive daughter Elizabeth could be counted in the tradition, as was emphasized not only by Voltaire but also by the more judicious legal reformer Sir William Blackstone. She was the first European sovereign to abolish capital punishment, whereas Louis XV had offered Paris the barbaric spectacle of the public dismemberment of his would-be assassin, Damiens. But the most glorious of all the lineage, for Voltaire and the whole republic of letters, was Catherine, the great "Semiramis of the North," whose *lumières* dazzled them far more than the bolder but ephemeral reforms of Joseph of Austria, and whose only rival for their favor was the great, though less constant, Frederick of Prussia.

The *philosophes'* cult of Catherine, inaugurated shortly after her accession in 1762, began with Voltaire himself; and the epistolary dialogue between them continued, to the great advantage of both parties, until the philosopher's death in 1778.[35] Catherine, on her side, was vulnerable since all of Europe knew she had attained power by deposing her husband and excluding her son from the succession; and it was widely suspected that her husband's subsequent death was in fact murder. She therefore sought legitimacy by posing as Peter the Great's moral heir, which entailed both a policy of imperial glory and an opening to enlightened Europe. Voltaire, for his part, was once again in search of a crowned head to patronize his cause: in the 1740s his impudent wit had ended his career at the court of a suspicious Louis XV, and in the 1750s it did the same at the court of his admirer Frederick II. Hence, at age seventy, the acknowledged patriarch of the European republic of letters was still banned in Paris and confined to gilded exile on his estate of Ferney near Geneva. Catherine seized the occasion to publicly proclaim herself the "pupil" of the Sage of Ferney, while Voltaire boasted his intimacy with power by referring to her as "la belle Cateau" in correspondence with philosophic friends. And so, these two cosmopolitan adventurers sought the maximum of publicity for their respective causes in the luster that the fame of each could lend to the other.

Just as important an acquisition for Russia's cause was Denis Diderot, editor of the century's central monument of enlightenment, the *Encyclopédie*. Like Voltaire, he corresponded assiduously with Catherine in the 1760s and 1770s, but unlike Voltaire, Diderot actually made the arduous voyage to St. Petersburg in 1773, just as a younger Voltaire had gone to Berlin in 1750 to be Frederick's court *philosophe*. And Diderot took his role as "Solon" so seriously that in the egalitarian animation of conversation he allegedly pinched Catherine's thigh with such vigor that she was obliged to put a table between them—an endearing story that also soon made the rounds of the republic of letters. But the favorable image of Semiramis created by such anecdotes might have been blurred by certain less encouraging impressions that Diderot brought back from his visit, for the philosopher, taking his benefactress's protestations of enlightenment somewhat too literally, had given her such liberal advice on how to rule Russia that he eventually provoked a rebuff. Desiring to preserve the practical advantages that accrued from public friendship with the empress, however, he took care not to give undue notoriety to this disappointment.

Another advocate of Catherine's cause was Diderot's colleague in the *Encyclopédie*, Jean D'Alembert. On the empress's assumption of power he had been invited, in a striking gesture, to become the tutor of her heir, an offer he reluctantly declined because he did not wish to leave his editorial work and move to remote St. Petersburg. By the 1780s, however, D'Alembert too became disturbed by some of his benefactress's policies, in particular her designs on Turkey and Poland; and, unlike Diderot earlier, he took no pains to conceal his disillusion. By contrast, her most assiduous if not her most illustrious correspondent, Frédéric-Melchior Grimm, the press agent, as it were, of the republic of letters, not only served for years as her confidential agent in Paris, but until the end of her reign faithfully flooded Europe with her praises and justifications of all her policies.

Simultaneously in England, where philosophy, though less militant and dogmatic than in France, was nonetheless well entrenched, the liberal jurist Blackstone extolled the English translation of Catherine's projected code of laws. His radical critic Jeremy Bentham, who had traveled to Russia and whose brother had even entered Russian service, was long an ardent enthusiast of the empress, publicly defending her every action until the eve of the final partitions of Poland.[36]

The enlightened of the West had quite solid reasons for pouring forth such praise. Catherine's largesse supported one of the major battles for civil liberties fought by the *philosophes*, defense of the Calas family, who in supposedly civilized France were being persecuted for their Protestant faith. She gave Diderot what was in effect a life pension by purchasing his library for a handsome sum while allowing him use of his books for the rest of his days. When the publication of the *Encyclopédie* was for a time forbidden in Paris, she offered to transfer the entire operation to St. Petersburg at her expense, thereby attempting to outbid Frederick in Berlin.

Not only did she subsidize the propagation of enlightenment abroad; she observed its precepts at home. Early in her reign, she demonstrated her concern for the physical welfare of her superstitious subjects by publicly submitting herself and her son to the new and ill-understood practice of vaccination against smallpox. Late in her reign, she provided for their moral welfare by entrusting the education of her grandsons to the Swiss *philosophe* and republican Frédéric-César de LaHarpe, thereby providing for the future enlightened governance of her empire. And she proceeded to hem in the "superstition" of the clergy through the definitive secularization of ecclesiastical lands, thereby completing Peter's work of subordinating the church to the state.

But it was as a "lawgiver" that Catherine made her principal bid to appear as the most progressive monarch of Europe. Beginning in the seventeenth century, the combined pressure of the new rationalistic philosophy stemming from Descartes and of the revival of a universalistic natural law by Hugo Grotius made the reform and codification of law a primary concern of progressive governance. Every ruler was thus summoned to be a Lycurgus or a Solon, while Montesquieu and Black-stone undertook to produce theories for a renovated science of juris-prudence. The aim of this movement was to bring order to the clutter and inconsistencies of customary law by submitting it to the norms of reason. In fact, by the end of the century most of the states of Europe had received their first modern legal codes, a process of which the Code Napoleon, completed in 1810, was the belated culmination.

Catherine joined this movement almost at its inception, and did so with fanfare by convening, in 1767, an *elected* Legislative Commission to reform Russia's laws. For its guidance, she personally wrote a *Nakaz*, or *Instruction*, which drew liberally on the ideas of Montesquieu. The document began grandly by proclaiming that "Russia is a European state," since Peter had finally given her customs truly suitable to her "climate." In the next paragraph, however, the empress asserted that "the Sovereign is absolute," for no other authority "can act with a vigour proportionate to the extent of such a vast dominion."[37] With these two affirmations the *Nakaz* encapsulated the enduring dilemma of imperial Russia: the ultimate incompatibility of dynamic Europeaniza-tion and irresponsible autocracy. Indeed, this contradiction was mani-fested in the document itself, where Montesquieu's separation of pow-ers became a mere division of bureaucratic functions; and no modern Russian code of law would see the light of day until the 1830s. Cather-ine triumphed before Europe, nonetheless: the *Nakaz* was translated at her order into French and English, and its boldness made such a stir that the king of France, through fear of its subversive effect on his own subjects, forbade its publication in his realm.

Exegi Monumentum Aereum Perennum |

The romance of the Western children of light with eighteenth-century Russian absolutism left a monument of bronze and stone more durable, and symbolically more potent, than any of the *philosophes'* written hom-ages to Russia. From the time of its foundation by Peter in 1703, Rus-sia's new capital had been laid out in a geometric grid that reflected the rationalistic and classical spirit of the century. Now Catherine, under the influence of her philosophic friends, gave the city a dramatic new focus. In 1766 Diderot, before his voyage to Russia, recommended to

Catherine his protégé, the sculptor Etienne-Maurice Falconet, to create a monument to Peter. Placed in a commanding position on the embankment of the Neva River, the monument bore the inscription, in Latin and Russian, "To Peter I from Catherine II." Modeled on a renowned equestrian statue of Louis XIV by Bernini, it was inaugurated in 1782, the centennial of Peter's accession to the throne.[38]

Its base is a rough block of natural stone curving upward and symbolizing the raw, unformed nature of the Russia that Peter had inherited. The horseman and his mount are cast in bronze, with the horse's forelegs rearing high above the rock; Peter is clad in a Roman toga, his outstretched arm wielding an emperor's baton. As Joseph de Maistre later observed, "one looks and does not know if that hand of bronze is raised to protect or to threaten." Ever after, this Bronze Horseman would be the symbol of imperial Russia in its dynamic and Westernizing guise. Pushkin in 1836, in his masterpiece, *The Bronze Horseman*, celebrated the grandeur of the Petrine empire; yet at the same time, drawing consciously on the ambiguous judgment of de Maistre,[39] he recognized, in the person of the counterhero, the poor clerk Eugene, the human cost of bringing civilization to Russia by despotic power.

The Legend Redux

That cost, and the shortcomings of the new Russia, were well recognized by a number of eighteenth century observers. In particular, in the second half of the century, as travelers to St. Petersburg became more frequent, Europeans who actually saw Russia received a much less rosy impression of Catherine's achievements as a lawgiver than did those who only read about them in the *Nakaz*.[40] In fact, much of the travel literature on Russia in the second half of the century painted a grim picture of primitiveness barely lacquered over by a semblance of civilized manners. Some of these travel books, notably one by Chappe d'Auteroche in 1768, were sufficiently telling in their criticisms and caused enough stir in the West for Catherine and her philosophic allies to take alarm and publish counterattacks, whose excessive protestations constituted an indirect admission that Semiramis in reality had some dark secrets to hide.[41] Yet despite the basic veracity of this black literature on Russia it was not the informed and obscure Chappe d'Autero-che but the uninformed though illustrious Voltaire and Diderot who carried the day before cultivated European opinion.

Such a perception was called increasingly into doubt, however, during the last quarter of the century, a movement of dissent inaugurated by that maverick in the party of humanity, Jean-Jacques Rousseau. A poor boy from the Republic of Geneva, he began his Parisian career in the 1750s in the company of Diderot and the Encyclopedists, but soon turned against these rationalists to celebrate the powers of sentiment and spontaneity. In so doing he developed a particular detestation for Voltaire, and through him for Catherine's Russia—an animus which naturally drew him to Russia's quintessential antithesis, the Republic of Poland-Lithuania.

Yet by the mid-eighteenth century the *Rzeczpospolita's* extraordinary constitution had become a menace to the nation's very survival. For this nominal kingdom was in fact a loose federation of provinces; its central Diet, where decisions could be blocked by a single vote, the *liberum veto*, was more a diplomatic congress than a national parliament; and its elective monarchy was a prize available to the highest foreign bidder. Although more must be said later about Catherine's relations with Poland, suffice it to mention here that after 1764 she intervened regularly in the republic's affairs to keep it weak, an action that produced a movement of defense and reform. To this end, the Polish resistance sought the advice, and the moral support, of the now famous "citizen of Geneva" and author of the *Social Contract*, Rousseau. He replied in 1771 with the essay *On the Government of Poland*,[42] which countered Voltaire's idealized Russia with his own idealized Poland, and which rejected all despotism, enlightened or otherwise, in the name of popular self-government.[43]

Yet, like Voltaire, Rousseau only half understood his chosen East European nation. He of course recognized, as did all Europe, that Poland's extreme decentralization was dangerous to the freedom it was supposed to preserve, since it rendered the republic defenseless against its autocratic neighbors. All the same, he believed that the existing constitution could be preserved in its main outlines, including even the infamous *liberum veto*. In his optimistic view, therefore, reform rather than wholesale reconstruction would suffice to make the system work. In a more realistic vein, he advised the Poles to proceed most cautiously with reform, since the innate viciousness of Russian despotism was always ready to devour them.

Despite appearances, Rousseau's defense of aristocratic Poland was basically consonant with the democratic principles he had advocated since becoming famous, in 1754, with his *Discourse on the Origins of Inequality*. In his scheme of things, the corruption of existing society was founded on the scandal of human inequality; and inequality arose from the very accomplishments, both intellectual and material, that contemporaries vaunted as civilized. Hence Rousseau condemned the sophistication of rationalistic civilization as both artificial and elitist, and advocated returning to a simpler, more egalitarian condition. Yet since mankind had already fallen from the natural state, he also recognized that improvement could come about only through a long process, not a revolutionary break: Poland's existing though imperfect liberties were therefore a good place to begin. This view of reform, of course, his erstwhile philosophic colleagues condemned as retrograde; and it was clearly incompatible with admiration for Catherine's rationalistic and statist concept of progress. Thus his idealization of republican Poland and his condemnation of mainstream Western enlightenment were two aspects of the same crusade.

Detestation of Russia was still another aspect of it. Indeed, already in the *Social Contract* of 1762, Rousseau had explicitly attacked Voltaire's eastern utopia:

> the Russians will never be really *policés*, because the task was attempted too soon. Peter had [only] the talent of an imitator. . . . He saw that his people were barbarous, but he failed to see that they were not yet ready for *la police*; he wanted to civilize them when what they needed was to be tamed. . . . He tried to turn them into Germans or Englishmen instead of making them Russians. He urged his subjects to be what they were not and so prevented them from becoming what they might have been.

Then came a warning that anticipated the dominant view of the next century: "The Russian empire would like to subjugate Europe and will

54

find itself subjugated. The Tartars, its subjects or neighbors, will become its masters—and ours."[44] And this negative reaction was amplified by Rousseau's radical epigones, the abbés Guillaume Raynal and Gabriel Mably.

In other words, criticism of Russia took hold with the second generation of *philosophes*, who were more impatient for progress, and more democratically inclined than Voltaire or the Encyclopedists had been before about 1775. As the century drew to a close, these skeptics came to believe more readily the reports of such detractors of the Russian monarchy as Chappe d'Auteroche. Until 1789, however, their skepticism divided rather than dominated enlightened Western opinion about Russia. Even as disenchantment with Catherine grew in more radical European circles, her unabated zeal for education, toleration, and material progress continued in the eyes of the majority to lend credibility to that body of eulogistic literature about her empire which the first generation of *philosophes* had put into circulation. The new skepticism merely adumbrated Russia's destiny in the next century; it was not itself the real beginning of her fall from Western grace.

In view of this undercurrent of doubt, and its basis in fact, ought one not conclude that Voltaire and the Encyclopedists had sold the Western public a fraudulent bill of goods, and that their glittering image of Russia was only a mirage? Certainly there was much self-interested politics and disingenuous propaganda on both sides in Catherine's idyll with the children of light. After all, the empress had first sought out the *philosophes* and exploited their prestige to bolster her shaky legitimacy at home. And later she would employ the republic of letters to win friends for Russia's voracious ambitions abroad. In return, the *philosophes* obtained an ally during the "battle of the *Encyclopédie*," at a time when they were politically vulnerable, impecunious, and harassed by censorship. So the support of the Russian empress, as well as of the Prussian king, against the proscriptions of their own monarch and of the Sorbonne's theologians was of real practical importance. For this mutual aid, each side was willing to pay the price of a measure of duplicity, even self-delusion: Catherine played the coquette about her *âme républicaine*, while Voltaire waxed ironical about the unpleasantness caused her by that rogue, the "marquis de Pugatschef."[45]

The frivolity of this reference in particular reveals the shallowness of philosophy's comprehension of Russian realities. No marquis at all but a fugitive Don Cossack, Emelian Pugachev claimed to be Catherine's dead husband and thus the true tsar. In 1773–74 he led a mighty serf revolt that was in effect a response to the gentry's emancipation a decade earlier, the movement's logic being that since the landowners had been freed from compulsory service to the state the peasants should be freed from service to the landowners. Indeed, so flagrant was the injustice of the existing system that the spectre of a new *Pugachevshchina* would hang over Russia's Old Regime until the end, the dark counterpoint to the enlightenment with which the autocracy sought to transform the nation. But this, of course, was something Western philosophy chose not to ponder.

Nevertheless, beneath the hyperbole of the protestations on both sides there was a substratum of truth. According to the lights of philosophy, as well as of the empress herself, rough Russia was not to be judged by the same exacting standards as polished Europe, for Russia was still being raised by the firm hand of princely police from barbarism to the initial stages of civilization. In the context of her nation's development, therefore, Catherine, by supporting the *Encyclopédie*, appeared to the enlightened to be forcing the pace of progress with astonishing energy and rapidity, while Louis XV, by harassing the Encyclopedists, in the context of civilized France was downright guilty of obstructing progress.

And Catherine's policy was in fact to promote as vigorously as possible those values of public order, material progress, and education represented by the ideal of *police*.[46] Within the limits imposed by an extremely brutal social system that made her beliefs relevant only to a tiny elite, she even believed in progress toward human betterment and its pursuit unfettered by superstition—an ensemble of values denoted by the neologism "civilization," which had emerged during her reign. What she did not believe, however, was that *police* and civilization could ever be dissociated. But then only a few in the West, such as the close-

56

mouthed Diderot or the atrabilious Rousseau, as yet placed popular government higher than princely governance. The *philosophes*, of course, in their desire to shame the king of France into action, greatly overstated the case for Catherine's zeal on behalf of *les lumières;* and in their ignorance of her empire, they thoroughly underestimated the difficulties in illuminating the darkness of Russian life. Yet there remains a half-truth in the half-legend of Semiramis: no more than Peter, was Catherine some mythical Chinese sage born of the exhalations of the *philosophes'* imagination, or some fabulous symbol of their wishful thoughts.

The golden legend of Russian monarchy did end with 1789 and Catherine's turn to reaction. True, a somber decade intervened between 1790 and the end of the century. When the empress learned of the democratic horrors being perpetrated in Paris, she ordered that Houdon's bust of Voltaire be removed to the attic, and she condemned two of her most enlightened subjects, Aleksandr Radishchev and Nikolai Novikov, the one to Siberian exile and the other to prison, for presuming to draw in print some obvious conclusions from the liberal principles she herself had formerly championed. In turn, Jacobin Paris, deeming that her enjoyment of a legion of lovers had definitively eclipsed her *lumières,* now called Semiramis the Messalina of the North. In fact, the change of epithets indicated less a change in Catherine than in the Atlantic West. The reforming eighteenth century had now crossed the threshold into the revolutionary nineteenth century—but more on this great divide of modernity shortly.[47]

Then, at the end of the decade, the demented despotism of Catherine's son, Paul, further dimmed Russia's aura under Western eyes. In 1801, however, with the accession of her grandson, Alexander I, the northern phoenix rose again from the ashes. Indeed, it soared aloft on a bolder wing than ever before, for the Russian monarch now declared that his enlightenment would no longer be confined within the bounds of princely police but would reach out instead into the freer spaces of constitutional government.

Again the West responded to the old lure. In England, Russia's cause was taken up once more by that apostle of the rational recodification of

ancient, barbaric laws and advocate of renovated representative government, Jeremy Bentham. An old admirer of Catherine, he was so encouraged by recent reports from his brother in the Russian service as to
pour forth suggestions to Alexander about how best to implement his
manifest intentions of reform.[48] Moved by similar hopes, the president
of the new North American republic, Thomas Jefferson, who even kept
a bust of the emperor in his study, wrote to another paragon of contemporary enlightenment, Joseph Priestly:

> The apparition of such a man on a throne is one of the phenom-
> ena which will distinguish the present epoch so remarkable in the
> history of man. But he must have an herculean task to devise and
> establish the means of securing freedom and happiness to those
> who are not capable of taking care of themselves. Some prepara-
> tion seems necessary to qualify the body of a nation for self-
> government. Who could have thought the French nation incapa-
> ble of it? Alexander will doubtless begin at the right end, by taking
> means for diffusing instruction and a sense of their natural rights
> through the mass of his people, and for relieving them in the
> meantime from actual oppression.[49]

A few years later, in 1806, Jefferson addressed Alexander himself:

> It will be among the latest and most soothing comforts of my life
> to have seen advanced to the government of so extensive a portion
> of the earth, and at so early a period of his life, a sovereign whose
> ruling passion is the advancement of the happiness and prosperity
> of his people; and not of his own people only but who can extend
> his eye and good will to a distant and infant nation, unoffending in
> its course, unambitious in its views.[50]

Even more significant than the testimonials of Bentham and Jefferson,
who were far removed and safe from Russian power, was the faith of the
dispossessed Pole Prince Adam Czartoryski. Though taken as a hostage
to Russia by Catherine in 1795, he yet believed for twenty years in her
grandson's enlightened intentions toward mankind in general and Poland in particular, and was long willing to serve in the inner councils of
Alexander's government, even as his foreign minister.

Alexander's deeds, like those of Peter and Catherine before him, appeared to Europe to be as good as his intentions. He fought the wars of 1812–1814 under the slogan of the liberation of the nations of Europe from the tyrant Bonaparte, and he was accepted by them as the Agamemnon of the coalition against the perturber of the peace of mankind. After Alexander's entry into Paris it was he, more than any other statesman, who was instrumental in persuading the Bourbon whom the allies had restored to the throne to grant a constitution. In 1815 he became the first European sovereign to bestow voluntarily on any of his subjects a parliamentary form of government—a privilege moreover which he vouchsafed to the Poles, who had invaded his lands by the side of the "lawless" Bonaparte. Even more remarkable, Alexander let it be understood that this Polish Diet was to be a model for constitutionalism in Russia proper. As former President Jefferson then wrote, without the slightest hint of alarm, "To the wonders of Bonaparte's rise and fall, we may add that of a Czar of Muscovy, dictating, *in Paris*, laws and limits to all the successors of the Caesars, and holding even the balance in which the fortunes of this new world are suspended."[51]

The tradition launched by Voltaire in 1731 had enjoyed a stunning success. Russia in the eighteenth century was not only an enlightened despotism but the most enduring and successful of them all. No other monarchy in Europe could boast a tradition of nearly a century and a quarter of enlightened rule, nor had any other monarchy adapted better to the constantly rising level of expectation evoked by the notion of *les lumières*. Peter had made Russia *policée* at the beginning of the century, when lawful order was all that the enlightened had asked. Catherine had made Russia *civilisée* at a time when the growth of legality and of *moeurs douces* had led the enlightened to make their prime concern the cultivation of the more fragile quality of reason. Now the young Alexander seemed about to crown the edifice of civilization with the gift of liberty, which would entrust the safeguard of law and reason both to the responsibility of the citizenry. By the dawn of the new century the enlightened despotism of imperial Russia seemed to be on the point of transcending its original nature and of attempting to raise that nation to heights of civilization which the French had fallen short of achieving in their abortive revolution, which even the English were far from attaining, and which had until then been approximated only in the raw American republic. As of 1815, in the eyes of some of the most enlightened spirits of the West, such as the Sage of Monticello, Russia could quite plausibly be placed in the vanguard of the world's progressive forces.

Enlightenment and the Police State

Yet all that has been adduced so far does not explain the seeming *trahison des clercs* on the part of the Old-Regime republic of letters. Although it was natural for the European aristocracy of the day to find the Russian dynastic state acceptable, it is less comprehensible that radical European reformers should have been so blind to the defects of their idol, which was in fact the most brutal government in Europe and one under which they would have found it quite intolerable to live. The answer to this apparent enigma lies in the deep cultural and institutional roots of the eighteenth century's commitment to enlightened absolutism. For we should not fall into the frequent error of dismissing that commitment as superficial, because it eventually proved ephemeral.

To dig down to these roots, however, it is necessary to ask once again the question Kant famously posed on the eve of 1789: what is enlightenment? And this means examining the philosophy of the *philosophes* per se. For if we are to understand any aspect of the eighteenth century, it is necessary to take seriously the ideology that earned for it the title Age of Reason.

It is no accident that the men of letters of the time viewed themselves first of all not as writers, but as philosophers. Indeed, one of the particularities of eighteenth-century culture is that its republic of letters demoted imaginative literature to the second rank and exalted instead the rigors of rational philosophy. Lyricism and poetry gave way to logic and prose; and the aesthetic mode of the day, from Nicolas Boileau and Alexander Pope to Voltaire the verse dramatist (his first métier), was a classicism founded on universal rules, an aesthetic which resonated in belles lettres to the universal categories of philosophy.

We have already seen one aspect of the new rationalism's impact on Russia's relation to the West: because the Age belonged to Reason,

secularized Europe could easily accommodate a Russia whose Orthodox identity Peter and Catherine had subordinated to universal enlightenment. Russia was therefore able to become European in the space of
a generation, because Europe itself was undergoing the most profound
cultural revolution since the end of the ancient world.[52]

Briefly, the essence of the revolution was this: Western European
high culture from Christianity's triumph in the fourth century until the
emergence of modern science in the seventeenth century had been an
amalgam of the revealed religion of Scripture and the deductive reason
of Greek philosophy, a compound manifested most notably in medieval
scholasticism. In this fusion, the natural truths of reason had always
been subordinated to the revealed truths of religion, because eternal
salvation depended on the latter, whereas the former gave merely terrestrial knowledge. Granted, the hegemonic position of religion had
been progressively challenged from the late Middle Ages onward. Thus
Marsilio of Padua in his *Defensor Pacis* in 1324 had staked out a sphere
of autonomy vis-à-vis the papacy, which he called "civil society"—that
is, lay society. And this term, of course, was later used to denote self-
constituted society in opposition to royal absolutism.[53] Renaissance humanism then pushed the process of secularization further still. But the
cultural hegemony of religion was really broken only by the scientific
revolution of the seventeenth century. For the new science offered a
certitude far greater than did either faith or deductive logic, since it was
able (at least at its best in physics) to formulate its results in universal,
mathematical laws that were at the same time empirically verifiable.
These results, moreover, applied to the natural world, the here and now
in which men lived.[54]

The new knowledge thus was qualitatively different from any that
mankind had hitherto possessed. To put the matter in the simplest
terms, one could believe, or refuse to believe (though at the risk of
pursuit for heresy), in divine revelation and still be regarded as a sane
person; and one could agree or disagree with the syllogisms of Plato
and Aristotle and still be considered a rational being; but, after a certain
lapse of time, one could not disagree with the laws of Galileo and
Newton and still claim full possession of one's faculties, because these
laws could be demonstrated empirically. For the first time in history,

mankind had a form of knowledge that was, if not infallible, at least incontrovertible as far as the human mind could range. Man thus appeared to have acquired absolute knowledge, of the sort that had previously been attributed only to God. Although most of the creators of the new empirico-mathematical method—from Galileo to Kepler to Descartes to Newton—were, in one or another degree, devout, the result of their labors was to furnish an intellectual instrument that eventually meant the end of revealed religion's hegemony in European culture.

This came about because of the metaphysical conclusions soon drawn from the miracle of the new science. Since the laws of nature were clearly derived from observation of the real world, both a priori logical deduction and ideas innately planted in our minds by God or nature were ruled out, or at least marginalized, as sources of truth. Instead, all knowledge was deemed to come to us by induction through our five material senses. From John Locke onward one or another variant of this empiricism was the regnant philosophy in both England and France. Voltaire and the Encyclopedists in particular held that Locke's empirical philosophy was the logical counterpart of, and just as scientific as, Newton's laws of universal gravitation. Moreover, if all knowledge came from the sensory, or material, world, of which man was a part, then improvement of man's lot in that world constituted the only "sound" (saine) philosophy. As Alexander Pope famously summed things up in the new classical mode: "God said 'Let Newton be' and all was light," to which the inescapable corollary was, "The proper study of mankind is Man." Or as D'Alembert put the new creed in the idiom of the more radical French Enlightenment: "philosophy is the experimental physics of the soul."[55] Thus science was expected to produce, in Condorcet's phrase, "the indefinite perfectability of the human species," a view that led him to ask: "Would it be absurd then to suppose . . . that the day will come when death will be due only to extraordinary accidents or to the decay of the vital forces, and that ultimately the average span between birth and decay will have no assignable value?"[56]

It was the task of the eighteenth-century Enlightenment to apply the scientific method developed by the previous century not just to the natural world, but to law, government, society, economics, ethics, and indeed to the inner workings of the human soul. Execution of this "systematic" program of total, positive knowledge was the mission of the *Encyclopédie*, and in carrying it out the philosophers of the republic of letters were by implication challenging the entire existing order of Europe.

The entering wedge of this revolution was the circumstance that in the Old-Regime world, there was no such thing as the separation of church and state; everywhere, not only was the church established, but it was coextensive with the existing political and social order, for it was religion that gave moral sanction and legitimacy to all human institutions. Attacking superstition in the name of reason, therefore, was not simply a matter of personal conviction; it automatically called into question all the terrestrial political and social institutions justified by divine authority.

Yet the new rationalism was not just negative; it also pointed the way to what the succeeding order might be. First, philosophical empiricism and "sensationism" signified that the material and social worlds were entirely natural phenomena, and that natural reason gave mastery equally over both. Social engineering was thus as feasible an enterprise as mechanical or hydraulic engineering. Concretely, the goal of the new philosophy was the rationalization, the "uniformization," of the clutter of inherited institutions, going back to the Dark Ages (as the formative centuries of Christendom were now called), that composed the Old Regime. And the method of this reform was to subject all traditional institutions to the tests of human rationality and social utility.

The new rationalism, moreover, though most decidedly an elite movement, was paradoxically egalitarian in its implications. Descartes had inaugurated the intellectual revolution born of the new science by asserting that henceforth proper philosophical method rested on recognizing that "common sense is the thing most evenly distributed in the world," for "reason is naturally equal in all men." Kant had brought the spirit of the new rationalism to its most refined culmination by proclaiming that the categorical ethical imperative of the modern age was, "Act so as to treat man, in your own person, as well as in that of anyone else, always as an end, never merely as a means." He justified this claim, not on the traditional grounds that all God's children possess immortal souls, but on the secular principle that all men are endowed with reason, and "rational nature exists as an end in itself." Again only on the theoretical level, he concluded that all men ought to become equal citizens of a future rational polity.

The philosophers of Europe, of course, were not aware at the time of the full practical implications of their devotion to reason. Only gradually were the abstractions of philosophy transformed into concrete politics, as the *philosophes* proceeded to attack one or another irrationality of the existing order. Nor did they discover until the eve of 1789 that their various reformist causes amounted, cumulatively, to the demand for an entirely *new* order. And so by stages, the campaign of the *philosophes* against the "fanaticism" and intolerance of the church escalated into an attack on irrational and nonfunctional social inequalities, or the "society of orders" as such; and only at the end of the process did it lead to an attack on royal absolutism. This transmutation of abstract reason into revolutionary politics, in sum, was what the Enlightenment was all about.

A few decades after this process had culminated in the Revolution of 1789, Hegel characterized the "world-historical" uniqueness of the eighteenth century with an image of inversion that would recur down to the twentieth century: "Ever since the sun has stood in the heavens, and the planets revolved around it, never have we known man to walk on his head, that is, to base himself on the Idea and to build the world in accordance with it."[57] Marx would later claim this honor for his own generation and for the advocates of socialism, famously turning Hegel on *his* head and asserting that the time had come for philosophy to progress "from understanding the world to changing it."[58] In fact, philosophy had already made this transition with the *philosophes*, as Hegel correctly saw: the Enlightenment had indeed stood the millennial civilization of Christendom on its head, making it an Old Regime in thought before it became one in historical fact.

The progress of this cultural revolution was furthered by other contemporary developments. First, it was only at the end of the seventeenth

64

century, after Louis XIV's ambitions had been checked by Protestant England and Holland, that it at last became clear that the religious wars begun by the Reformation had ended in a draw, and that the unity of Christendom, whether under Catholicism or Protestantism, could never be restored. This outcome inevitably relativized both contenders, indeed diminished revealed religion per se. Toleration and often down-right skepticism, therefore, increasingly gained legitimacy in both religious camps. In such a Europe the intrusion of a still schismatic but now rather archaic Orthodoxy was hardly upsetting.

Second, it was only in the second half of the seventeenth century, after the defeat of the Fronde in France in 1653 and the end of the English revolutionary interregnum of 1640–1660, that the major states of Western Europe came to enjoy durable domestic order, and that the king's writ ran unchallenged throughout the realm. This internal peace also facilitated economic development, or what the age referred to as *le doux commerce* and "public opulence." As a result, eighteenth-century Europe first came to know what the modern world calls sustained growth and, for the upper classes at least, an unprecedented level of material comfort, which Voltaire celebrated in verse with a provocative hedonism in *The Worldling (Le mondain).*[59]

In these newly pacified and "policed" national areas, moreover, by the mid-seventeenth century there had emerged standardized and "pol-ished" vernaculars capable of expressing the gamut of cultural concerns from high philosophy and science to popular journalism and entertain-ment. Latin was thereby dethroned as the chief medium of serious learning: Newton's *Principia Mathematica* of 1687 (two years before Peter's active reign began) was among the last pivotal works to appear in that language. With this "vernacular revolution" the range of influence of advanced ideas was extended far beyond the learned world itself, even to the hitherto untutored women of aristocratic and bour-geois society, as is made clear by Molière's fun at the expense of Paris's "learned ladies" *(les femmes savantes).*

It is out of the conjunction of this vernacular breakthrough and the religious stalemate with the sunburst of the new science that the broad movement of the Enlightenment was born. Yet of these three forces it is science, with its attendant imperial rationalism, that is the sine qua non of the whole movement. And this circumstance, finally, determined a new attitude toward history.

Until the late seventeenth century Europeans had as their highest cultural ambition to return either to the timeless aesthetic norms of Greece and Rome (the Renaissance) or to the purity of original Christianity (the Reformation). Both movements, although they in fact mightily changed European culture, were perceived by contemporaries as restorations not as revolutions. With the scientific revolution of the seventeenth century, however, Europeans at last knew that they had gone well beyond the ancients, and that the civilization they had created was new and unique in human history. This awareness was dramatized in the 1690s in the ranks of the French Academy of Sciences by the "Quarrel of the Ancients and the Moderns," in which the latter won hands down. The result was the birth of the idea of progress, with Europe of course leading the cortege. By the midcentury, our present periodization of history was beginning to emerge as the triad—antiquity, the Middle Ages, and the modern era—in which the last term was viewed as an open-ended triumphal march.[60]

The Enlightenment exerted pressure for the reform of inherited, traditional structures all over Europe, but pressure for reform was greatest in the most developed, northwestern portion of the continent, and pressure was greatest of all in France. There the Old-Regime structures common to all Europe were still capped by a royal absolutism that was essentially unchanged since the middle years of Louis XIV, yet a prosperous and educated civil society was already robust and mature. In England, pressure for reform, though mounting, was less acute because a comparable civil society had by 1688 already achieved partnership with the monarchy, and religious dissenters enjoyed a modest toleration. And so the classical, radical Enlightenment came to have France as its focus.

For what forces or interests did this radical French Enlightenment speak? Or, as some would ask, what was its "social base"? There was a time, not so long ago, when the answer to this question in many quarters would have been, following Marx, the "rising bourgeoisie."[61] The bourgeoisie was indeed rising in the eighteenth century, and the

Physiocrats' antimercantilist, laissez-faire doctrines, arguably expressions of its interests, were part of the arsenal of philosophy. Still, the new commercial class was even more prominent in England and in Holland, while philosophy assumed its most militant form in France. The reason for this disparity, therefore, was political, not social, for in France the entrepreneurial classes were enveloped in a far vaster entity, the Third Estate. So it is necessary to ask once again Sieyès's famous question of 1788: what is the Third Estate?[62]

Sieyès's answer to his own question, of course, was that in law the Third Estate was "nothing" but that by rights it should be "everything," for it was indeed the "nation." In fact, the Third Estate had only a negative unity, since it included everyone, from great bankers to lowly peasants, who was not a member of the privileged orders of the clergy and the nobility. In other words, this philosophical abbé was calling for the suppression of the "society of orders" and its replacement by a modern polity of "citizens," a call that paralleled on a practical, political level Kant's theoretical assertion of mankind's rationality. Thus the "base" of "sound" philosophy was not social, but ideological, and it was furnished by any group that supported the program of "rationalizing," or leveling, the Old-Regime hierarchy.

It is now clear that the clientele of philosophy was drawn from the most diverse groups in society.[63] Contributors as well as subscribers to the *Encyclopédie* were more often abbés or marquis, clerics and royal officials, than *roturiers*, or non-nobles, such as Voltaire, Diderot, D'Alembert, and Rousseau—crucial though these great commoners were in articulating the first principles of the movement. Indeed, the spokesmen of philosophy ranged from the establishment of the Old Regime to what have been called "Rousseaus of the gutter."[64]

In fact, the partisans of philosophy constituted what nineteenth-century Russians first identified as an "intelligentsia," that is, a group defined not by social status, but by its superior education, the content of its ideas, and its oppositional stance. But why should this first European intelligentsia have emerged when and where it did? The answer that best fits the obvious multiclass facts of the case is that of Tocqueville: it was the very success of the Old Regime in creating a "well-policed" society that bred the iconoclastic aspirations of its privileged elements.

The centralizing monarchy, by introducing civil order into the realm, had deprived the first two estates, especially the nobles, of their autonomy and social function, while leaving them their now too conspicuous privileges.[65] In short, the monarchy had leveled the Old Regime spiritually, while preserving intact all its inequalities institutionally; and this outcome could only nurture a thirst for libertarian and egalitarian change (not without an element of resentment and envy) among the unprivileged of that great negative unity which was the Third Estate. The philosophic intelligentsia of the republic of letters thus spoke for all those subjects of the eighteenth-century dynast, from whatever social category, who as a result of the long development of secular refinement and civility founded on the free exercise of individual talent had become impatient with a traditional hierarchy based on hereditary privilege and supernatural sanction. The mission of philosophy, therefore, was to promote leveling reform in the name of that universal, natural reason, as first manifested in science, which made all men free and equal brothers. Thereby the philosophic camp of natural reason became, in Hume's words, the political "party of humanity."[66]

Its leadership was naturally furnished by what the age called *les hommes à talents*, those professional intellectuals, whose real roles in society, and hence whose abilities and accomplishments, were no longer defined by military or bureaucratic service to the prince. From the inevitable conflict between the awareness of their own worth and the limited scope allowed them by the existing religious and political order, these "men of parts" derived a sense of oppression that permitted them to articulate a still more general pattern of disaffection generated by a society whose real structures were changing rapidly while its legal forms remained fixed. The *philosophes*, in sum, were the spokesmen of a mature civil society pressing against an ossified absolutism which had long since completed the task of welding its feudal subordinates into a nation. Since the *philosophes'* central objection to the Old Regime was that hereditary privilege and function in relation to the monarch took precedence over intrinsic human merit, their aim was to reorganize society so that precedence would accrue to individual accomplishment and not to traditional status. Such an order they termed "natural" or "rational."

The ultimate goal of the *philosophes*, therefore, was to transform the Old Regime into what would now be called a liberal—and to a degree an egalitarian—society.[67] This future order would not necessarily be democratic, however, since liberty meant only freedom enough to rise in the world, given the requisite talent; and equality meant only equality of legal status and of opportunity, not of real condition. The "rationalizers" thus envisaged that the new society, like the old, would be organized in a hierarchy in which the "populace," *le bas peuple*, would remain inferior to the enlightened and fully civilized at the top.

Since this type of "free and equal" order was the *philosophes'* goal, it might appear surprising that they found imperial Russia so admirable when its society was much more rigid and offered far less scope to their kind than did the crumbling structure wanly presided over by Louis XV, which so mightily provoked their ire. The reason was that the enlightened of the West saw in Russia not its society but only its monarchy, and half felt they wanted a similar institution at home. Historically the first model for rationalizing society envisaged by European reformers was not the complex system of representative government that they came to demand by 1789, but a strong monarchy that would limit from above both the hereditary privilege of the aristocracy and the supernatural claims of the clergy, so as to open a free career to native, human ability.

Reasons were not lacking for such an assessment of monarchy's role. As Voltaire argued at length in his *Essai sur les moeurs* of 1756, all over Europe monarchy had developed at the expense of aristocratic independence by turning the turbulent nobles into disciplined servants of its will.[68] Only strong monarchy had created the policed world of law and peace, which had made possible the professional and economic activities of the intellectual and commercial classes. Moreover, monarchy had everywhere developed at the expense of the autonomy of the church, an institution that irked the men of parts even more than did the nobility. Not only did these men hold its privilege, influence, and wealth to be inordinate for so "useless" an organization; they also chafed at the "irrationality" of its values, at its lack of concern for earthly betterment, at the "idleness" of its clergy, and at the innumerable restraints its moral code imposed on the preferred cultural and economic pursuits of the fruitfully occupied portions of mankind. Finally, strong monarchy was necessary to control and, if need be, repress the ignorant, superstitious, and unruly people, who otherwise could prove a menace to civilization.

With so many enemies in the world, both above and below, it is small wonder that the Third Estate, while it was still weak, should have looked to monarchy to protect both itself and all the civilized values it revered. To aspire to take the state over on its own, by establishing representative government, would have been pure folly. Only under the unusually favorable conditions of insular England, where the military force of the state rested more in a mobile navy than a standing army, had elements similar to the upper echelons of the continental Third Estate obtained a measure of participation in government. There the Commons of the realm—country gentry, urban burgesses, and some London men of parts—were thoroughly integrated into a liberal if narrowly oligarchic representative polity. Yet even in England this result had entailed a complex compromise with the interests of great aristocracy, established church, and monarchy, achieved moreover at the cost of a half-century of civil strife. As much as continental reformers might admire the constitutional results of this process, they hardly desired to see a repetition of the fanatical and "enthusiastic" zeal of the Puritans who had produced it. They thus had no choice but to cooperate with their own monarchies at home.

Once again, Voltaire's example provides the best illustration of this point. He began his career, in the *Philosophical Letters* of 1734, as a eulogist of tolerant and constitutionalist Britain. He then moved on, in 1750, to become court *philosophe* to Frederick of Prussia (and to laud retrospectively the century of Louis XIV that same year). Finally, in the 1760s, he took up the cause of Peter and Catherine. Yet at each stop on this eastward way his politics remained the same, namely, to use whatever institutional means the Old Regime afforded to promote the rationalization of its structures—and thereby, ultimately, their subversion.[69]

But after 1700 in the West the heroic nation-building monarchy of the century of Henry IV, Richelieu, and the young Louis XIV was a

thing of the past. In the new century, only east of the Elbe was monarchy in advance of society. It was precisely out of this disparity between
the two ends of Old-Regime Europe that the cult of enlightened despotism grew. The cult flourished largely in the West; the reality to
which it referred existed principally in the East. To be sure, the Mediterranean south, by now something of a backward zone, had its lesser
enlightened despots: in Spain under the new Bourbon dynasty and
especially in parts of Italy. But it was only east of the Elbe that enlightened absolutism had been enthroned by leading members of the European concert. And it was this marriage of power with enlightenment,
which seemed to hold out the promise of instant progress, that above all
allured the philosophic dissidents of the West.[70]

In the Atlantic West itself they lacked comparable access to the
summit of the state; there they could act on power only indirectly,
through public opinion. Since revolutionary action was unthinkable,
moreover, their chief political recourse was to celebrate their monarchy
as it had existed in its creative prime, a century before, and in this spirit
slowly to infiltrate its modern institutions. Thus, D'Alembert and Condorcet became, respectively, "perpetual secretaries" of the Académie
Française and the Royal Academy of Sciences. Only late in the century,
in 1774, did the party of philosophy see one of their own, the physiocrat
Turgot, temporarily become Louis XVI's first minister. But such efforts to capture the monarchy from below invariably ended in failure
and frustration, for king and court correctly sensed that conceding too
much to civil society might end by abdicating to it wholly.

In Central and Eastern Europe, however, philosophy rested on very
different foundations, for there civil society was weak to nonexistent.[71]
It not only posed no threat to the absolutist state, but indeed its stunted
growth obliged the state to create a surrogate for it in the form of
bureaucracy. Only by such authoritarian action from above could the
backward dynastic polities of the East become competitive internationally. Enlightened despots therefore seized upon the *philosophes'* radical
critique of tradition, their down-to-earth approach to wealth, and their
cult of science and technology to promote the rational organization of
the state. For in the late-starting Old Regimes beyond the Elbe only

autocratic initiative could foster the creative forces which civil society had generated on its own in the West. And since of all European states, Russia possessed the weakest civil society, the initiative there remained longest with the state, and the ideal of enlightened absolutism was longest held in honor by its sovereigns.

Obversely, on the other flank of the European cultural orbit, in England or her American dependencies, enlightened despotism could not be a force at all—even though such radicals as Bentham and Jefferson fully appreciated its necessity in less mature lands. And enlightened despotism was despised in societies which were either threatened or dominated by foreign autocratic power, as in Switzerland, in Italy's surviving republics, and in Poland. In all these countries the reformist energies common to the age found expression in moderate constitutionalism, as in England, or in overt republicanism, as in her colonial commonwealths, parts of Italy, Geneva, and Poland.

But over the rest of Europe, the ideal of civilizing "police" functioned as a mutually enriching duality. Radical Western ideologues had need of real Eastern accomplishments to whet their critical appetite for reform at home; and much of what the enlightened despots stood for did, in fact, adumbrate the transforming work of 1789. At the same time, the state-building absolutisms beyond the Elbe had need of imported critical ideology to propel their revolutions from above; and this Eastern market did, in fact, stimulate Western social theorizing. The result was the strange eighteenth-century symbiosis of Western radicalism and Eastern autocracy, in a common devotion to liquidating the legacy of a dark past on behalf of a luminous future—which the twentieth century would call modernity.

Throughout most of the eighteenth century, then, while the civil society of the Third Estate was still gathering strength, the favorite utopia of its philosophic avant-garde remained a strong, reforming monarchy. Even on the threshold of 1789, the cry of reformers was almost as much for a new Henry IV as for a return of the Estates General. But the monarchy could no longer give the nation such an ideal king. The agitation of the *philosophes* was in effect summoning royal power to choose the interests of the Third Estate over those of the two privileged orders, a preference that could only destroy all existing institutional arrangements and, along with them, the monarchy's position itself.

Confronted with mounting pressure for this drastic option, the king became increasingly the prisoner of those guardians of the threatened establishment, the aristocracy. Louis XIV had suppressed the nobility and elevated the Third Estate because this course had served the power of the state as a whole, which was also the power of the king. Louis XV could pursue this policy no further because the same Third Estate now threatened to become both state and king in his place. Hence, while the intellectual spokesmen of this growing and aggrieved order awaited the day when they could dispense with any Louis at all, they sought their ideal in "the frozen climes of Scythia." Frustrated in their hope for an ideal prince, and baffled at his failure to appear, the disgruntled of the West cast longing eyes, first on the Prussian, then on the Russian, monarchy. Since that monarchy was still introducing elementary "police" into its rude domains, it could safely exercise a despotic yet enlightened vigor for the apparent welfare, not of any privileged groups, but of the nation as a whole.

The cult of enlightened despotism cannot be dismissed either as the quaint fantasy of a few men of letters seeking flattery and patronage from the mighty of this world, or as the exploitation of their vanity by ambitious and cynical crowned heads, such as Frederick and Catherine. On the contrary, enlightened despotism was one of the most serious political myths of the day, with deep but different roots in the conditions of the West and of Russia. It faded in the West only on the eve of 1789, when men began to demand, along with a new Henry IV, new Estates General. And it disappeared entirely only in the course of the Revolution, when civil society discovered that the very nature of its demands precluded the existence of such an ideal king and concluded that parliamentary, even democratic, government alone was worthy of free citizens.

Indeed, before 1789, the transitional nature of the ideal of enlightened despotism had been made explicit. As the crisis of the French Old Regime deepened after the accession of Louis XVI in 1774, advanced thinkers came increasingly to hold that the most important—in fact, the sole—purpose of monarchy was to prepare its uncouth charges for liberty and participation in the affairs of government by promoting the downward penetration of civilization through the development of education. The enlightened monarchs themselves, by assuming the role of "first servant of the state" (in Frederick's well-known formula) transformed their relationship to the people into a kind of social contract, thereby undermining traditional divine right well before the coup de grace of 1789.[72]

This evolution explains the differing reactions of the various generations of the Enlightenment toward Catherine: for Voltaire, her policies were sufficient in themselves; for Diderot, they were sufficient as transitional means; for Rousseau, they were already an anachronism. It was precisely because Alexander seemed to understand his grandmother's failure to keep pace that at the demise of the original ideal of enlightened despotism in 1789 imperial Russia's reputation survived—as it did in the opinion of such a sterling democrat as Jefferson. Nor had the good president been crassly taken in. Alexander himself believed just as deeply in the "withering away" of monarchy, a view which he had first imbibed from the Swiss republican LaHarpe. This conviction had been reinforced by the spectacle of the extravagant tyranny of his father, Paul I; and once in power, he had begun to act on it by charging his chief minister, Mikhail Speranskii, with the task of constitutional reform.

This belief was to remain a cardinal premise of Alexander's policies until after 1815, when he, like Western monarchs before him, encountered the intractable resistance to reform of his own aristocracy and so at last became its prisoner. In the last analysis, by the very nature of his princely office, he was also the existing order's first guardian.

The Twilight of the Old Regime

Eighteenth-century Russia, then, was accepted into the European concert as it was understood at the time by all segments of society. The men of the dynastic, the aristocratic, and the enlightened systems of value, no matter how ambivalent toward one another, were in essential agreement with respect to Russia: she was Europe's new and raw eastern extension, but a part of Europe nonetheless. No one spoke in antithetical fashion of "Russia and the West," since no one had as yet formulated the cultural categories for such a sheep-and-goats distinction.

An episode from the Seven Years' War may serve to illustrate the favorable convergence of opinion among the three value systems of the age. Toward the close of the conflict, victorious Russian armies were occupying Berlin and East Prussia—an area where the presence of their Soviet successors after 1945 caused both scandal and foreboding throughout the West. In 1761, however, the Russian authorities in East Prussia were at pains to make their then three-year occupation a model one, and thus win over the province's population for annexation after the war. As a result, throughout the countryside the Junker nobility, deeming the Hohenzollerns' cause to be lost, actively prepared to transfer allegiance to the Romanovs—a quite reasonable attitude in light of the way their cousins, the barons of the Baltic provinces, had prospered in changing from Swedish to Russian service under Peter. For these intimations of treason to the Prussian crown, Frederick the Great never forgave them, refusing thereafter even to set foot in the perfidious province. In his "Testament" of 1768 he pressed out the sour grapes still more by declaring that civilized nations would come to rue the day they allowed huge, "barbarian" Russia—"Huns," no less—into the European fold. Nevertheless, as a practical matter he felt no rancor toward the Romanovs, for he would have proffered the same temptations in their place. Indeed, a few years later he proposed to Russia that together they undertake the partition of Poland.

The same year, in the East Prussian capital of Königsberg—after 1945 annexed by the Soviets, demolished, resettled, and rebaptized Kaliningrad to honor their late "president"—the Russian military command encouraged its officers to follow courses at the university. The Russian authorities approved a petition of the university's professors for collective promotion that had previously been rejected by the Prussian government, and this just as a budding scholar, Immanuel Kant, came under consideration for advancement to the rank of magister. In the meantime, moreover, Kant advertised in the local gazette to give private lessons in natural and moral philosophy for officers of the Russian garrison, as he had previously done for Frederick's officers. Whatever benefits resulted for the intellectual improvement of the Russian nation are not known, but Kant himself clearly did not feel that his action was incongruent with the lights of philosophy, or that his clients were closed a priori to the universal and necessary categories of the one Pure Reason that shines for all mankind.[73]

What, then, is the moral we may draw from the story of Europe's generally favorable reaction to Russia in the eighteenth century? In particular, how does this reaction relate to her constant westward expansion?

To recall the first phase of that aggrandizement: from Peter's victory at Poltava in 1709 to the beginning of Catherine's career of conquest in 1768, Europe's response to Russia's ambitions took the rational form of ignoring her character as a society and judging her only as a power. Whether this response was favorable, as during most of the period, or unfavorable, as at the end of Peter's Northern War, it was governed on both sides by relationships of military strength and political interest. Since Russia's interests complemented those of a majority of the powers—England, Austria and, for much of the century, Prussia—and conflicted with those of only one, France, she was able to expand with the consent of the European concert. In a situation where most of the important courts of the West gained when Russia gained, few had an incentive to raise any notable outcry over her advance.

Yet, when all due allowance is made for the play of *Realpolitik*, the decisive factor governing Russia's first century as a power remains this: her integration into the political concert of European states was contingent on her assimilation into the cultural concert of dynastic-aristocratic Old Regimes. It was only by virtue of this deeper convergence that other powers applied to her the same norms of international law that they observed among themselves, thereby legitimizing the gains that her arms and her alliances had so abundantly afforded her. Thus the security of Russia's territories, no matter how newly acquired, was guaranteed both by her power and by her legitimacy as a civilized state. By contrast, it was for want of any similar cultural convergence that "barbaric" Turkey's centuries-long dominion in the Balkans was accepted by the powers only as a cruel necessity, and hence was forever precarious.

More interesting than this play of power politics, however, was the impact on Russia's fortunes of less "rational" cultural and ideological considerations. For if Russia was correctly received into Europe by the Old-Regime establishment, her promotion was positively welcomed by the enlightened opposition. And this occurred during the reign of Catherine, a period of unmatched Russian aggrandizement. It was thus under the sign of Semeramis that for the first time the European climate of opinion became a force weighing in the balance of power between Russia and the West.

It was the sum of Catherine's conquests, even more than her *lumières*, that earned her the title "Great." The annexations resulting from her two Turkish wars and her three partitions of Poland brought Russia a larger increment of power relative to other states than at any time since Peter, or, for that matter, until Stalin's victory in the Second World War. And she achieved these gains in the record time of twenty-eight years. Yet all this occurred without provoking notable hostility in Europe, much less fear of a Russian menace to civilization. True, there were diplomatic protests, particularly regarding Poland, from France;[74] yet no Western government ever even contemplated a military riposte. Quite to the contrary, at every stage of her aggrandizement Russia was assisted by one or another European power—and not least by the power of enlightened opinion. Neither before nor since has the West reacted with such insouciance to so flagrant a display of Russian imperial enterprise.

Catherine promoted Russia's fortunes in two bouts of conquest, the first between 1768 and 1774 and the second between 1787 and 1795. During both campaigns she juggled a Turkish war and a Polish partition concurrently, in the century's most stunning game of imperialist poker.

Catherine's opening move was to secure the election in 1763 of a former lover, Stanislas Poniatowski, to the Polish throne, thereby strengthening Russia's role as guarantor of the *Rzeczpospolita's* constitution, a "protection" ensured by the presence of Russian troops on its soil. Yet Catherine carefully combined this assertion of power with the purist enlightenment; for she also imposed on Poland religious toleration for the republic's Orthodox and Lutheran minorities (who in fact had greater rights than did dissenters in either England or Holland), a policy for which she received Frederick's support. The anti-Russian party in Poland then rose in revolt, and in answer the French prevailed on Turkey to launch a war against Catherine. The empress thus received a golden opportunity to march into the Balkans, and indeed to sail into the Mediterranean, with no less an aim than provoking the Ottoman's Christian subjects to rise and destroy the infidel empire. Even though no uprising resulted, Catherine's success against Turkey so alarmed Vienna that, in 1772, Frederick mediated a tripartite amputation of Poland to "compensate" both himself and Maria Theresa of Austria for Russia's major gains against the Porte.

There were several reasons for this success, over and above the freedom of maneuver and impunity from retaliation afforded Russia as a flank power.[75] Politically the moment was exceptionally favorable to Russian ambition. The Polish-Lithuanian Republic, which in 1610 had been far stronger than Muscovy, and as late as 1683 was still a major European force, by the mid-eighteenth century had become a constitutional invalid seeking the philosophic ministrations of the "citizen of Geneva": the erstwhile "Golden Freedom" of the noble republic had now become the "Polish anarchy." Moreover, Poland's geopolitical position on the open northern European plain, always a perilous one, had been rendered untenable by the military revolution in Prussia and Russia. At the same time, to Russia's south even the once terrible Turk could no longer muster the means to defend his holdings in the steppes north of the Black Sea. Both Poland and Turkey, in sum, needed allies to maintain their positions.

Among the powers only France and England had a practical interest in offering such support—France because Catherine's victims were its traditional clients, England because Catherine's victory over the Porte would bring a rival sea-power into the Mediterranean. Yet neither state was then able to act. France had emerged militarily and financially exhausted from the Seven Years' War shortly before. England was distracted by the onset of crisis with her North American colonies. Of course Austria, too, had an interest in setting bounds to Russia's expansion at Turkey's expense; but she could be effectively appeased by compensation in Poland for Russia's gains against Turkey.[76]

Still, neither the geopolitical circumstances of the day nor Catherine's personal daring can account fully for Russian expansion during her reign: the ultimate factor easing her way was the cultural climate of the age. In the eyes of most Europeans the Ottomans remained a thoroughly barbarous lot, despite the philosophic fable making Saladin a champion of enlightenment against Christian bigotry. Catherine's victories over the Turks were thus widely greeted as victories for the progress of mankind; and Voltaire in particular trumpeted her successes as a triumph not only of Russia, but of civilization itself. All of enlightened Europe applauded the brilliance of her audacity, no less than of her *lumières*, when in 1770 the Russian fleet sailed from the Baltic around the whole of Europe to smite the Turk at Chesmé in his home waters of the Aegean. Not even the English, who normally took a dim view of such resounding maritime exploits, were significantly alarmed. Indeed, not only had they granted Catherine's fleet free passage through the Channel, but they had built her ships and even commanded them at Chesmé.[77]

Progressive European opinion was similarly indulgent regarding the first partition of Poland, for that nation's freedom then was hardly the sacred cause it became in the next century. On the contrary, the republic's mainstay, the *szlachta* or gentry, who made up almost ten percent of the population, presented an egregious example of everything the enlightened liked least. The most fractious nobility of Europe, these petty squires had degraded their "aristocratic republic" into the exact antithesis of an *état policé*. Even worse, they had made it the most priest-ridden and superstitious nation of Europe. It was merely fitting, therefore, that Catherine should intervene to protect religious "dissidents" from popish persecution, a laudable action which had then raised the Turks against her. In the face of this unholy alliance of fanaticisms, it was only legitimate that enlightened Russia should conquer, and annex, until the evil was eradicated. At the same time, however, progressive Western opinion failed to notice that Catherine's advance into the Ukrainian steppes also brought the advance of serfdom. Indeed, that institution reached its apogee during her reign.

Of course, Catherine did not enjoy philosophy's support for her second Turkish war, between 1787 and 1792, or for her last two partitions of Poland, in 1793 and 1795. Yet she could now do without the enlightened, since the international situation alone offered opportunity enough for expansion. When Catherine went to war, England was still recovering from her recent American losses and was distracted by demands for reform at home and in Ireland; and France was absorbed in a crisis of reform so grave that it would soon lead to revolution. By the time Catherine gathered in her final gains, in 1795, the foreign victories of revolutionary France had so disrupted the concert of the powers that her hands were completely freed in the East.

In fact, even before this international collapse, Catherine's earlier triumphs in Turkey and Poland had made her bolder than in her first foreign adventures. Thus in 1780 during the American Revolution she had bated Albion on the high seas by organizing Europe's lesser powers into a League of Armed Neutrality to protect their commerce with Britain's American allies, France and Spain.[78] Still more revealing of Catherine's ambition, however, was her famous "Greek project."

The treaty of Kuchuk-Kainardji in 1774, which had consecrated Russia's first victory over Turkey, gave her certain rights of protection over the Porte's Balkan Christian subjects. Soon Catherine's viceroy in the south, Prince Grigorii Potemkin, proposed exploiting these rights to drive the Turks from Europe altogether and reestablish a Greek Orthodox empire at Constantinople.[79] In 1779 her second grandson was christened Constantine, and given Greek nurses, to prepare him to become the first emperor. Remembering Austria's hostility in 1772, however, Catherine in 1781 persuaded Joseph II to join in an alliance for partitioning Turkey's European provinces. Protected by this complicity, in 1783 she annexed the Crimea; and in 1787 she and her impresario, Potemkin, shepherded the hapless Joseph and a host of international celebrities on a triumphal inspection of the new territories (hence the expression "Potemkin villages" to designate Russian progress as a fraudulent facade). In response, the Turks, fearing they were about to suffer Poland's fate, declared war, thereby activating Catherine's Austrian alliance and giving her a chance at Constantinople. And she truly intended to get there; for her Greek project, unlike the imperial ambitions set forth in the purported "Testament" of Peter the Great, was all too real. If she in fact failed to launch a campaign toward the Turkish capital, it was only because she was unexpectedly compelled to fight on other fronts.

Catherine's final imperial gamble hence turned out to be the riskiest of her career. England, by now concerned about her ambitions, refused to let the Russian fleet sail out of the Baltic to the Mediterranean; and an equally anxious Sweden attacked from the north while the empress's armies were engaged in the south. In 1790 Joseph II's death took Austria out of the war. And the unanticipated strength of Turkish resistance guaranteed a long conflict.

The most ominous development of all, however, was the emergence of a Polish reform movement.[80] In gestation since the terrible lesson of the first partition, this movement saw Catherine's involvement with Turkey as a golden opportunity to challenge Russia's "guarantee" of the republic's incapacitating constitution. The Polish reformers drew on the arsenal of the Enlightenment far more unambiguously than Catherine ever could have done, since her protégé, Stanislas Augustus, had during the preceding twenty-five years become one of philosophy's most active patrons.[81]

Although the monarch wished to reform cautiously, Russia's preoccupation with Turkey inevitably fanned the ardor of the Polish Patriot party. Meanwhile, the new king of Prussia, seeking to profit from the involvement of *both* Russia and Austria in the south, actively encouraged the Polish reformers—in the hope, of course, of taking Russia's place in the republic. Therefore, when the Diet convened in 1788, Stanislas was overrun on his Left: in what amounted to a revolutionary coup d'état, the deputies gave themselves a four-year term and constituent powers. The next year Catherine, herself overrun by two wars and Anglo-Prussian hostility, withdrew her troops from Poland in a feigned gesture of conciliation.

In the midst of all this, in 1789, the French Estates General, in a revolutionary coup far bolder than that of the Four-Year Diet, transformed themselves into a National Assembly. The cult of enlightened absolutism was now interred under the Rights of Man and the Citizen. Philosophy, at last unadulterated by despotism, had come to power in both Paris and Warsaw.

The outcome in Poland was the Constitution of May 3, 1791, which provided for a genuine central government: a hereditary monarchy; a veto-free, bicameral Diet; and a standing army. Although conflated by many with the French constitution of the same year, the charter of May 3 in fact was a moderate document, closer in spirit to the relatively conservative American Constitution of 1788 than to the radical, unicameral new order of France. No wonder that Edmund Burke approved of the Polish action.

Catherine, of course, could accept no part of the Polish revolution, for it meant both the end of Russia's overlordship in Poland and the presence on her doorstep of a version of the Enlightenment quite incompatible with autocracy. Soon her hands were freed: by 1792 both the Swedes and the Turks had been obliged to make peace on Russia's terms. The same year France became a democratic republic, and in 1793 Louis XVI was executed. Catherine now branded the Polish reformers the eastern wing of Jacobinism and mobilized her army. Prussia, duly impressed, reneged on her Polish alliance. So In 1793 the two autocracies invaded Poland to preserve the "liberties" of her old constitution, at the same time reducing her territory to a rump. (Austria this time did not participate, for she had no great geopolitical stake in Poland, preferring to preserve the republic as a buffer.) This second partition provoked an armed revolt, led by a hero in the War of American Independence, Thaddeus Kościuszko. The revolt was of course crushed; and Austria joined in the final invasion to keep pace with her neighbors' expansion. In 1795, therefore, Poland was expunged from the map of Europe—the first time the powers had ever done such a thing to a civilized European state.

Liberal opinion in England and France now waxed indignant at such vast and shameless despoliations. Yet this belated attack of conscience scarcely absolved the enlightened of the West from complicity in Poland's demise. Philosophy had prepared the way for just such an outcome by lending moral justification to Poland's first amputation: not only did that act set an obvious precedent for future dismemberments, it made them well-nigh inevitable.

Partition, of course, was an accepted practice of eighteenth-century diplomacy, but it usually occurred as a result of defeat in war. The first partition of Poland, however, came about when she was at peace with her neighbors; and it resulted from a war against Turkey in which she was not a party, thereby demonstrating the republic's unique vulnerability among European states. The three eastern powers thus concluded that anytime they needed "compensation" for a rival's gain (and sooner or later another international crisis would require such a solution), Poland was the easiest place to find it. To the Poles, however, the precedent of the first partition demonstrated that they could survive only by recovering national power through reform. Yet Poland's republican tradition mandated that any reform would yield a liberal polity, which would appear as a danger to her autocratic neighbors. In the context of Eastern Europe, therefore, Polish reform inevitably constituted a provocation to everyone else—and hence also an invitation to further partition.

Yet all this took decades to work itself out. And in the meantime, philosophy's benediction of the first partition obscured the real issue between Catherine and Poland until Europe awoke to discover that Poland had disappeared, with Russia receiving the lion's share. But even by the time of Poland's extinction, Europe was still not scandalized in a manner commensurate with the scandal that had actually occurred: six million new subjects, or almost the population of Prussia, had been absorbed into Catherine's empire.[82] By the time of Catherine's death, a year later, Russia had a population of some forty million: she was now not only the largest, but also the most populous state in Europe. Thus the power base for Russia's continental hegemony after the Napoleonic wars had already been created by Catherine.[83]

Here, at last, we must conclude that a disproportionate shift in the balance of power toward Russia had indubitably occurred. But how are we to explain it? And how are we to account for Europe's supine reaction? An accumulation of causes has already been advanced: geography, the political conjuncture, philosophic fatuity, and Catherine's infinite audacity. But—it will be objected—was there not an even more basic cause: Russia's inveterate aggressiveness, as manifested by the Orthodox messianism of Catherine's infamous Greek project? Indeed, Catherine returned to dreaming of Constantinople in her last year, once she had finished off Poland. A whiff of comparative method, however, reveals a number of competing messianisms.

Philip II and Louis XIV, after all, had campaigned with notable zeal for Catholicism; and Gustavus Aldolfus of Sweden had quite equaled their ardor on behalf of Lutheranism, as had Cromwell for Calvinism. The religious motivation of all these leaders was far more sincere than Catherine's. Moreover, the Russian empress acted not so much in the name of Orthodoxy as in that of protecting religious minorities—that is, in the name of the Enlightenment ideal of toleration. True, this justification (or pretext) was inextricably linked with promoting Russian power. Yet in mixing her motives Catherine was again not alone, nor was she being particularly Russian: all her predecessors in ideologically justified conquest had done the same. The real secret of the masters of the European Old Regime, therefore, whether religious or secular, lies elsewhere, namely, in the logic of the European state system itself and its competitive balance of power. Their common creed was perhaps best expressed by the *chef de file* of Old-Regime monarchs, Louis XIV, when he confessed of his glorious conquests that "to aggrandize oneself was the worthiest and most agreeable occupation of a sovereign."[84]

In sum, Catherine got away with her imperialism in part because the enlightened of the West had smoothed over the moral obstacles in her path. But she succeeded in even greater part because the dynastic and aristocratic polities of Central Europe actively conspired with her; and they did so because the dynamic of the European state system, founded on a conflictual balance of power maintained by compensation, made them Russia's natural accomplices. Clearly, neither of the Central European monarchies felt the slightest divergence in interests, methods, or values from the Russians. And the common sharing of the Polish booty, by imposing on all three powers the necessity of defending their spoils together to avoid losing them separately, cemented their union for decades to come. The spectre of Poland—like Banquo's ghost—

would haunt the partitioning powers until their simultaneous demise in 1917–18.[85]

Even without this partnership in crime, however, by the turn of the century a new community of values was emerging among the three "Cours du Nord"—as the Eastern absolutisms were now collectively designated—which henceforth would give them a special kinship within the concert of Europe. In the aftermath of the French Revolution, Russia's internal order could no longer be considered a kindred one by the whole continent; it appeared cognate only in the eyes of her two nearest neighbors, Prussia and Austria.

At the beginning of the century, when Louis XIV was still on the throne of France and Peter was on his way to becoming a sovereign in the Sun King's image and likeness, the dissimilarities between the senior policed polity of Europe and the most junior had not seemed to be fundamental in nature: they appeared as a difference of degree of civilization, not a difference of kind as between civilizations. But by the end of the century the possibility of so simple an appraisal was a thing of the past. Russia no longer measured up to the ideals of that nascent liberal Europe west of the Rhine, which, since the Revolution, had been attempting in clumsy though determined fashion to run society on its own, free of the tutelage of any despot except one of its own creation, such as Bonaparte, and for the most liberal spirits, free also of him. Russia now resembled merely the rump Old Regime of trans-Elbean Europe.

For the first time since her intrusion into Europe, the transformation of the more advanced nations of the "West" began to make of Russia something truly alien or, more exactly, something anachronistic. Then in one short decade after 1815, her new destiny overtook her: the golden legend of Russian Enlightenment came abruptly to an end; the black legend of inveterate Russian autocracy was about to begin.

RUSSIA AS ORIENTAL DESPOTISM: 1815–1855

We are not related to any of the great human families. . . . We have not been affected by the universal education of mankind. . . .

In our houses we are all like campers . . . in our cities like nomads, more nomadic than the herdsmen who let their animals graze on our steppes, for they are more bound to their deserts than we to our cities. This is a natural consequence of a culture based wholly upon importation and imitation. . . .

Peoples are moral beings just as individuals are. It takes centuries to educate them . . . Europeans have a . . . family resemblance. Despite the general division of these people into Latin and Teutonic branches . . . there is a common bond which unites them . . . not very long ago all Europe was [Roman] Christendom. . . .

What have we to substitute for that in our country? . . . Suspended between the East and the West, with one elbow on China and the other on Germany . . . we have given nothing to the world . . . contributed not a single thought to the human fund of ideas. . . . If the barbarian hordes . . . had not passed through the country we inhabit before throwing themselves upon the West, we would scarcely have furnished a chapter in world history.

Forced by a fatal destiny, we sought the moral code which was to constitute our education in miserable Byzantium.

—Necropolis, December 1, 1829, Petr Chaadaev, *Lettres philosophiques* (for publishing this essay, he was declared mad by Nicholas I)

Russia, the unwashed, farewell!
Land of masters, land of slaves,
Farewell, all ice-blue uniforms,
And you, their fawning people.

Perhaps behind Caucasus' wall
I may hide from all your pashas,
From their all-seeing eyes,
From their all-hearing ears.

—Mikhail Lermontov, on going into administrative exile in 1841

There are at present two great nations in the world, which started from different points, but seem to tend towards the same end: the Russians and the Americans. Both have grown up unnoticed . . . and the world learned their existence and their greatness at almost the same time. . . .

The American struggles against the obstacles which nature opposes to him; the adversaries of the Russian are men. The former combats the wilderness and savage life; the latter civilization with all its arms. The conquests of the American are therefore gained by the ploughshare; those of the Russian by the sword.

The Anglo-American relies upon personal interest to accomplish his ends, and gives free scope to the unguided strength and common sense of the people; The Russian centers all the authority of society in a single arm. The principal instrument of the former is freedom; of the latter, servitude.

Their starting-point is different, and their courses are not the same; yet each seems marked out by the will of Heaven to sway the destinies of half the globe.

Alexis de Tocqueville, *Democracy in America* (1835)

Russia's fall from grace in Western eyes began at the very moment when, at the Congress of Vienna, she seemed to have arrived at the pinnacle of her glory. As that conclave opened in 1814, the armies of Alexander I had just completed a triumphant march across the whole of the continent from Moscow to Paris—a feat of arms unmatched by either Peter or Catherine, even at their greatest, and which conferred on Russia the novel position of first arbiter of Europe's destinies. She appeared, moreover, as a generous arbiter, who came not in the furtherance of a selfish national ambition, but as the liberator of oppressed Europe from the "despotism" of Bonaparte and as the champion of international law, peace, and stability. In the Germanies her advance was positively welcomed as the only means of driving out the French. Even in France herself, the behavior of the Russian troops was so exemplary, and the charm and European cultivation of their officers so compelling, that they soon could claim an undeniable popularity in the capital of their former foes.

What is even more significant, by 1814 Russia emerged as one of the two great victors, along with Great Britain, of the Revolutionary and Napoleonic Wars. For twenty years the French revolutionary impetus had rolled across Europe, absorbing the Low Countries, Germany, and Italy, and partially reconstituting Poland. This flood was in part a "modernizing" force, for everywhere within the occupied zone it dismantled, or at least greatly simplified, Old-Regime structures by introducing the Code Napoleon. At the same time, however, it brought liberation from the past at the cost of servitude in the present, as the old

European state system was supplanted by a monolithic French imperium. Yet the Revolution's man on horseback did not know when to stop riding; and so in 1812–1814, with his ambition stretched from Madrid to Moscow, his empire crashed to the ground.

Although the important European states were restored to their former positions, it is the two flank powers of the European system that gained the most: England now had unchallenged mastery of the high seas and clear colonial supremacy, and Russia was just as clearly the first power on the continent. For the first time, therefore, the empire of the tsars became a status quo power in Europe. With Alexander I's acquisitions in Finland, Congress Poland, and Bessarabia, its western frontiers were fixed for the remainder of the imperial regime. Its European policy henceforth was simply to defend them.

In a kindred conservative spirit the five principal powers formed what was called, in so many words, the concert of Europe. With this formula they proclaimed that they had learned their lesson from the previous century's conflictual balance of power and the Napoleonic Wars: such costly practices had to give way to concerted diplomatic action to maintain the international equilibrium. (Ottoman Turkey, of course, was not included in this concert; despite her presence in the Balkans, she remained an Asiatic outsider until the end of the century.) And indeed, although periodic congresses met for only a decade after Vienna, the tradition of concerted action it established continued until the Congress of Berlin in 1878. To be sure, the most explosive problems of the century—Italian and German unification—were resolved by force of arms between 1859 and 1870. Nonetheless, the residual idea of European collective security helped make the nineteenth century, overall, the most peaceful ever in European history.

As symbolic acknowledgment of Russia's full membership in this European family, the Congress of Vienna formally placed the continent's eastern frontier at the Urals. The reason was that the territorial exchanges decided by the Congress required calculating the relative value of the areas transferred; and these were assessed on the principle that territory in the rich and populous west was worth more than in the poor and thinly settled east. Thus, since Prussia was to receive the valuable Rhineland, she could not have the whole of equally valuable

Saxony, which she also wanted. And if Russia desired all of Poland, which she at first claimed, this meant knowing how much stronger this would make her overall, which entailed assessing how large she was to begin with. The problem was solved by counting only "Russia in Europe"—thus cutting Europe off at the Urals.[1] Indeed, eighteenth-century Russian geographers had long advocated fixing the frontier at these unimposing mountains so as to make good the boast of Catherine's *Nakaz* that "Russia is a European state." Her claim was now written into international law.

Europe as the Two and the Three

Despite this legitimation, at the conclusion of the congress in 1815 Russia had become the object of growing suspicion throughout Europe. At first, this changed attitude resulted from a wholly rational and political cause. As a consequence of Napoleon's defeat, Russian military strength on the continent was not only of major magnitude, as it had been since Peter, but for the first time emerged disproportionate to that of every other power. Alexander's acquisitions in Finland, Bessarabia, and especially Poland, together with his penetration as far west as Paris, made the cup of Russia's power, already so amply filled by Peter and Catherine, seem at last dangerously near to spilling over. Russia had assumed France's traditional position as the preponderant and hence potentially most aggressive power on the European continent. All Europe was acutely aware that Russia maintained the largest military establishment of the age, a standing army of some one million men, and the quality of this force had been demonstrated when it defeated the foremost captain of modern history. Only Prussia, which was indebted to Russian strength for her very survival under the Napoleonic occupation as well as for her territorial aggrandizement following the French defeat, and in fact by 1815 was almost a Russian satellite, remained unperturbed by this altered state of affairs. In all other quarters, the fear was abroad that Europe had thrown off the hegemony of France only to risk falling under that of Russia. Alexander's might at Vienna for the first time gave the West the sense of a "Russian menace."[2]

At Vienna this sentiment focused with special acuity on the problem of Poland. Alexander, alleging his desire to atone for Catherine's injustices toward that nation and proclaiming his devotion to liberal principles for its internal governance, sought the powers' consent to a restored, constitutional Polish kingdom. At the same time, however, he insisted that the crown of the revived state be held in perpetual union with the Russian crown, an arrangement buttressed by a permanent military alliance, so as to safeguard the legitimate interests of his principal dominions. Yet, because the balance of power had now tipped so drastically in Russia's favor, Alexander's relatively sincere declarations were discounted in the West, whereas when Russia had been less mighty and more remote, Catherine's crass propaganda regarding Poland had been taken at face value. Hence most of Europe took Alexander's protestations of solicitude for the Poles as a subterfuge for advancing Russian power permanently into the heart of Europe. And his policies provoked the inevitable response in such situations: formation of the Triple Alliance of Vienna, an embryonic coalition grouping England, France, and Austria. Although only transitory, this was the first combination of Great Powers against her that Russia had faced. Alexander was consequently obliged to retreat, receiving only two-thirds rather than the whole of the Polish territories previously beyond his frontiers, in a settlement soon referred to as the fourth partition of Poland.

Russia's good reputation in liberal circles was immediately called into question. As Alexander's old admirer, Thomas Jefferson, commented in 1816:

> I sincerely wish that the history of the secret proceedings at Vienna may become known, and may reconcile to our good opinion of him his participation in the demolition of ancient and independent States, transferring them and their inhabitants as farms and stocks of cattle at a market to other owners, and even taking a part of the spoils himself. It is possible to suppose a case excusing this, and my partiality for his character encourages me to expect it, and to impute to others, known to have no moral scruples, the crimes of that conclave, who under pretense of punishing the atrocities of Bonaparte, reached them themselves, and proved that with equal power they were equally flagitious.[3]

As such tempered disillusionment makes clear, the growing negative reaction to Russia was as yet no more than the opinion that she had succumbed to the classic corruptions of power. The fear she inspired was of the same sort that the France of Louis XIV or of Napoleon had aroused: alarm because one of the Great Powers had grown significantly greater than all the others. It was not, at least initially, experienced as the fear of an encroaching alien civilization.

Europe's view of Russia as an alien civilization emerged only in the decade following Vienna, when the spectre of her might was conjoined with the antiliberal ends that might was increasingly made to serve.[4] This new orientation of Russian policy first became manifest in connection with the Holy Alliance, a covenant foisted by Alexander on all the powers but England in 1815. Originally no more than a nebulous league of Christian sovereigns pledged to moral governance and the preservation of international order, the Holy Alliance was soon transformed under the leadership of Prince Metternich of Austria into the ideological adjunct of the status quo created by the Congress of Vienna. Despite Alexander's moralizing liberalism, that status quo represented nothing less than an attempt to restore the international Old Regime of the previous century. Thus, Alexander, hemmed in by his position as one of the chief architects and guarantors of the Vienna system, and increasingly frustrated by his failures to effect reform at home, became ever more preoccupied with preserving "legitimacy" and the established order throughout Europe. Although this transformation reassured the chief status quo powers, notably Austria, as to Russia's moderate intentions and made them forget the alarm they had experienced at Vienna, it also brought Russia into her first conflict with European liberalism.

In part influenced by Metternich and in part moved by growing legitimist conviction, Alexander energetically urged intervention by the powers against the constitutionalist revolutions of 1820–21 in Spain, Portugal, Piedmont, and Naples. For the first time it became apparent that Alexander would accept liberty only insofar as it was granted from above, on the sovereign's terms, not when it was wrested from below, in accordance with its beneficiaries' own aspirations. Even more scandalous was the tsar's attitude toward the national and liberal revolt the Greeks raised against Turkey in 1821. As this desperate and heroic struggle continued through the rest of his reign, Alexander was besieged by philhellene and liberal elements at his court and in his army urging him to intervene on behalf of his Orthodox brothers; for Christian legitimacy clearly did not extend to the sovereignty of the lawless and infidel Ottomans. Yet so fearful had Alexander become of the contagion of sedition that he adopted the position that revolution was revolution, even against the Turk, and all aid to the rebels was forbidden. Outrage against him spread across Europe and penetrated deep into his own army. It seemed that the Russian autocracy by its very nature could never be a liberal force, and that only direct action might change it.

The irreformable nature of tsarism was confirmed on Alexander's death in 1825, when liberal sedition finally reached Russia herself. The Russian autocracy was for the first time challenged, arms in hand, by a movement for constitutionalism; its members, moreover, were heroes of Alexander's "wars of liberation" of 1812–1814. These Decembrists, as they came to be called, failed, but the shock of their action stripped the Russian monarchy of its last pretenses of enlightenment. For the new sovereign, Nicholas I, made it clear from the outset that he was a strict dynastic legitimist with no other creed than to rule in the tradition of Peter the Great, and that Peter's heritage meant integral autocracy, military order, and bureaucratic government. As Nicholas inaugurated his reign with a cannonade that left seventy dead on Senate Square, followed by five executions and Siberian exile for two hundred of his most enlightened subjects, Russia began her career as "gendarme of Europe."

The metamorphosis of Russia's image was completed five years later with the repression of the Polish insurrection of 1830; for this veritable war, far more than the poorly understood Decembrist affair, occasioned the most profound shock throughout Europe. Not only had the Polish patriots been ruthlessly put down, but they were summarily stripped of their constitution and their separate army, thus abolishing the autonomous status guaranteed them by the Vienna settlement. Their universities were suppressed, their Catholic religion penalized, and many thousands of them sent to Siberia or forced into Western exile. For the first time the system of Russian autocracy—not simply the sovereignty of the Romanovs—had been imposed on an indubitably European land. The West's new image of Russia as the continental bastion of inveterate, militant reaction was now in full focus.

This perspective was further darkened by recollection of Russia's imperialistic past, for which she was at last held to account. The reconquest of Warsaw called up resentful memories of Alexander's gains at Vienna and even more of the infamous partitions. Westerners began to recall, and for the first time appreciate, the gallant participation of the exiled General Thaddeus Kościuszko in the American Revolution and, more poignant still, his valiant yet futile struggle against Catherine in 1795 in Poland itself on behalf of both national independence and the Constitution of 1791. They remembered with even greater emotion the Poles' association with the cause of liberty during the Revolutionary and Napoleonic Wars, when the legions of Prince Józef Poniatowski had fought beside the French on all the battlefields of Europe, in the elusive hope that their sacrifices would be rewarded by the integral restoration of their country's freedom. Suddenly it became clear to all men of good will in the West that, after France herself, Poland possessed the most heroic revolutionary and libertarian tradition of any nation in Europe.

With the rise of liberal nationalism in the wake of the revolutions of 1830, Poland became a cardinal symbol of the most progressive values of the age. With the concurrent rise of the Napoleonic legend, she received an added aura of glory as the most faithful of the great emperor's allies. The mounting Polish claims on Europe's attention were enhanced by the appeal which this chivalric yet doomed nation exercised upon the new Romantic sensibilities of the day. The Polish legend was proclaimed to an avid public in the mystical rhetoric of the poet Adam Mickiewicz, from the new chair of Slavonic literature at the Collège de France, and in the sentimental harmonies of Frederic Chopin, from all the keyboards of Europe.

As Poland's fortunes waxed in Western eyes, those of Russia correspondingly waned. The more Poland appeared a virtuous martyr, the more Russia seemed an ignoble executioner. By 1830, enlightened opinion saw the two nations as exactly the reverse of what they had been in 1772. Personifying this change was Prince Adam Czartoryski, the friend of Alexander's progressive youth and his one-time foreign minister, who now stood against Nicholas on the "Western" side of the barricades as head of the provisional government in Warsaw.

The impact of Russia's actions in Poland was all the more powerful because it coincided with the first triumphs of Western liberalism since its forward movement had been deflected by Napoleon and then halted by the Restoration. Slowly overcoming the fears inspired by the Revolution's excesses, a more circumspect generation of liberals began to attack the Old Regime that Vienna had partially restored. This renewed impetus culminated in the July Revolution of 1830 in France and the Reform Bill of 1832 in England, which marked the full emergence of that liberal, individualistic civilization that had been in gestation since the time of the *philosophes.* Though still tremulous before absolutist spectres from the recent past, as well as fearful of the unruly "people" below, this liberal civilization would henceforth dominate the society of westernmost Europe, whether through a parliament or a new plebiscitary Bonaparte. For, though parliamentary government was the new society's preferred politics, in a crisis Bonapartism could also embody its social, economic, and national programs, and thus was regarded as a progressive force by much of Europe until late in the century. Granted, in France, and especially in England, traditional aristocratic and clerical forces were hardly swept away by the liberal turn of 1830–1832; indeed, in the latter country they acquired the name "establishment." Still, the tide of the times was irrevocably running against them.

In the two decades following 1830, the classical liberals were challenged by competition on the Left. The modest results of the July overturn—a constitutional monarchy founded on a property suffrage yielding only some two-hundred thousand voters—simply whetted society's appetite for more drastic change. The demand was therefore voiced by the heirs of Rousseau and the Convention of 1792 to go beyond a property suffrage to the universal (manhood) suffrage of full "democracy" (an ancient term now revived in a broader meaning), and from "bourgeois" monarchy to a "radical" republic. Soon an even bolder cry was raised: for the first time the Left proclaimed that the democratic ideal required going beyond the political to the social republic. Disappointment with the outcomes of 1789 and 1830 thus pushed the premises of the *philosophes* to their most ruthlessly logical conclusion: the result was the new ideal of Socialism, together with its most radically egalitarian variant, Communism.[5]

But more than the precise political circumstances of 1830 was involved in this escalation of democratic expectations. The fundamental cause was that the abolition of the society of orders had only laid bare another form of human oppression: the division of humanity into unequal social classes—rich and poor, masters and laborers, and hence also exploiters and exploited. This oppression was all the more invidious in that it was camouflaged by formal, legal equality. The "citizen" of 1789, therefore, with his abstract Rights of Man, now appeared to many as a sham behind whom stood in fact the "bourgeois," a term which thus acquired its present negative meaning. In this perspective the mass of society became propertyless "proletarians," another ancient word revived with a specifically modern meaning, the degradation of whose condition was an intolerable affront to the dignity of Man.

In this way were the basic premises of the *philosophes* brought up to date. Advanced thinkers insisted that a truly rational order did not signify the substitution of a hierarchy of merit or wealth for one of birth. Rather, it meant that hierarchy must be swept away utterly; that no man could be free unless all were free; and that the social and economic inequalities subordinating the many to the few must be overcome. The means for achieving such a just society was the abolition, or at least the limitation, of the right of private property on which the bourgeoisie's domination rested. So liberalism at the moment of its first great triumph, and in response to the very inadequacies it revealed in practice, inadvertently opened the way to maximalist projections of its own ideal. Alexis de Tocqueville in 1835 summarized this irresistible movement of modern times:

The gradual development of the equality of conditions is thus a providential fact, it has the principal characteristics of such a phenomenon: it is universal, it is enduring, and it constantly eludes the power of the human will. All events, just as all men, serve to promote its development. Would it be sensible to believe that a social movement whose impetus comes from such depths can be suspended by the efforts of one generation? Can one really think that, after having destroyed aristocracy and the kings, democracy will stop short before the bourgeoisie and the rich?[6]

Accordingly, as Europe after 1830 again moved leftward, in England Chartism became a significant movement, seeming to threaten British society with the continental revolutionary virus; and in France socialism, emerging from the barricades of Paris and Lyons in 1832–1834, presaged further democratic storms. At the same time, the previously silent *Bürgertum* of Prussia and Austria, as well as of their various dependencies in the "third Germany" and Italy, first raised its voice against autocracy and aristocratic privilege. Heinrich Heine sang and Giuseppe Mazzini conspired to bring the modern world beyond the Rhine and the Alps, thereby continuing the interrupted work of Napoleon; and in the wings, by 1848 Karl Marx sought to make men believe that the spectre of Communism was already haunting Europe. The progeny of the *philosophes*, though now differentiated into liberals, radicals, and socialists of various sorts and divided among a dozen newly self-conscious nationalities, had multiplied prodigiously. Never before had there been such a European-wide assault on the remnants of the Old Regime or such a universal outcry for reason, humanity, liberty, and equality. In all Europe, only Russia was mute and unshaken. Yet there she remained, the monolithic Eastern flank of the still tenacious establishment of the previous century—huge, sullen, and terrifying in her might.

In international relations, therefore, after 1830, the unitary Old Regime restored at Vienna gave way to a Europe of "the Two and the Three," in the phrase of British Foreign Minister Lord Palmerston. On one side stood the liberal "maritime powers," England and France, on the other, the autocratic "northern monarchies," Prussia, Austria, and Russia. The ideological divide between the Old Regime and the New had become embodied in a geographical dichotomy between East and West, in a pattern that would persist throughout much of the century. And neither camp approached the other in a spirit of peaceful coexistence. While statesmen and public opinion in the West placed their trust for victory in the logic of historical progress, and in the East rulers invoked the favors of divine Providence, in reality both sides felt quite uncertain as to the outcome of the struggle. The autocratic monarchies, ever mindful of the lessons of 1789, feared a universal return of the revolutionary scourge, whereas the maritime powers, haunted by the memory of the Holy Alliance, dreaded a Second Coming of the Cossacks. In the Atlantic West, apprehension was especially acute, both because liberalism's gains were recent and precarious and because the possibility of further revolution and hence renewed reaction still appeared very real. The Victorian age began its grand century of success, which only in retrospect seems serene and inevitable, in anything but a mood of self-confident complacency.

Hence the first half of the nineteenth century was an age when politics was exalted and ideological, and when international affairs were cast in a Manichaean perspective. States fought not merely for power, but for the triumph of good over evil. Neither camp could view any change in the domestic status quo of the other camp as a purely internal affair. Repression of liberty in Warsaw or Budapest automatically posed a threat to liberty in Paris or Milan. Revolution in Brussels or Rome seemed to forebode the outbreak of anarchy in Vienna or Berlin. So each side magnified every initiative in the camp of the other quite out of proportion to its real import.

Russia, more than any one power, became the focus of the fears and hopes of the two Europes. More stable politically than Prussia or Austria and more powerful militarily than any other continental state, she supplied the muscle for the reduced Holy Alliance of the three Eastern absolutist states after 1830 and, by the same token, appeared as the most dangerous single enemy of Western liberty and progress. In the years following the July Revolution, the regime of Nicholas I loomed ever more ominously, like some impregnable granite cliff raised up for no other purpose than to dash the best hopes of enlightened mankind.

The second quarter of the nineteenth century was thus the age par excellence of black literature about Russia. Indeed, it was then that the repertory of negative stereotypes regarding Russia first emerged, judgments that persist in our day. Perhaps the greatest single source of these clichés was the travel account of the marquis de Custine, *La Russie en 1839*, which immediately upon publication became an international success.[7] This sensational volume was all the more convincing since its author was an avowed legitimist and opponent of the liberal overturn of 1830. As Custine explained, he had gone to Russia expressly to observe, and to praise, a society uncontaminated by the revolutionary virus gnawing at Europe. Given these intentions, moreover, his entrée into all corners of the empire had been facilitated by a government anxious to counterbalance the bad publicity resulting from its suppression of the recent Polish revolt. (The government later tried to recruit Balzac, then courting Mme. de Hanska of Ukraine, to counterbalance Custine, but the novelist declined.)[8]

Yet even this marquis, nostalgic for the Old Regime, was appalled by the repressive measures Nicholas employed to promote order. The tsarist empire appeared to him as a gigantic prison whose inmates, hounded by police spies, were afraid to speak frankly to one another, even to think for themselves. The sterility of Russian life was compounded by its self-imposed isolation from the West, which made the population suspicious of all strangers, distrustful of alien ways, and envious of superior foreign achievements. So oppressive was the atmosphere that the traveler rushed to the Nieman River frontier. And, upon crossing it into the West, he felt an almost physical sense of release, an intoxication of free air.

Reversing the dominant judgment of the previous century, Custine's book declared Peter's work a failure. The reformer's task had turned out to be intrinsically impossible, since his nation was by nature too "barbaric" and "Asiatic" to absorb European civilization. The result was a simulacrum of Western society: "un Empire de façades. . . . La Russie est policée non civilisée."[9] Accordingly, Custine warned Europe to beware:

> An ambition, inordinate and immense, one of those ambitions which could only possibly spring in the bosoms of the oppressed, and would only find nourishment in the miseries of a whole nation, ferments in the heart of the Russian people. That nation, essentially aggressive, greedy under the influence of privation, expiates beforehand, by a debasing submission, the design of exercising a tyranny over other nations: the glory, the riches which it hopes for, consoles it for the disgrace to which it submits. To purify himself from the foul and impious sacrifice of all public and personal liberty, the slave, upon his knees, dreams of the conquest of the world.[10]

Thus was formulated in all its plenitude the axiom that the despotism and servitude of Russia's internal order inevitably spawned aggression and expansion in her relations with the external world.

A few years later in England David Urquhart, Scottish member of Parliament and romantic Turkophile, launched a campaign to alert the West to that expansionist danger. In the wake of the Revolution of 1848 his Free Press poured forth pamphlets warning Europe against Russia's sinister designs on Turkey and the Near East. For a time he was aided in this enterprise by an émigré German socialist, Karl Marx, who had sought refuge in London after the collapse of the recent revolution. Marx was drawn to Urquhart's Russophobia since his emigration had initially been caused by Russian power: in 1843 his Cologne newspaper, the *Reinische Zeitung*, had been closed on Nicholas's personal intervention with the Prussian authorities for attacking the imperial "gendarme." Confirmed thereby in his belief that St. Petersburg's influence in Berlin and Vienna was the prime obstacle to progress everywhere east of the Rhine, Marx undertook to arouse the West against the Russian menace with virulent contributions to Urquhart's Free Press.

The essence of his argument was that Russia's "Oriental" autocracy bred such a lust for conquest that it could be sated only by destroying Western civilization. Thus in his *Revelations of the Diplomatic History of the Eighteenth Century* he sought to give historical "depth" to Custine's by now established stereotype of Russia:

> The bloody mire of Mongolian slavery, not the rude glory of the Norman epoch, forms the cradle of Muscovy, and modern Russia is but a metamorphosis of Muscovy. . . . Peter the Great, the creator of modern Russia, divested the old Muscovite system for conquest of its purely local character and generalized its purpose by exalting its object, which is unlimited power. Modern Russia's drive for Constantinople is but the continuation of the policy of the Rurik dynasty which transferred its capital from Novgorod to Kiev, in order to be nearer to Byzantium. Byzantium became the model of Russian religion and civilization, as well as the goal of Russia's everlasting aspirations.[11]

Marx, of course, buttressed this assessment with the apocryphal "Testament of Peter I" and an exegesis of Catherine's Greek project. Indeed, this economic materialist grew so overwrought that he failed to notice the incongruity of explaining Russia's "messianic" drive for world domination by the metaphysical and essentialist notion of eternal Eastern despotism.

In a similar vein, for a time he shared the radical suspicion that Russian émigrés such as Mikhail Bakunin, who preposterously claimed to represent Russian socialism, must be "provocateurs" sent by the Third Section to confuse Western revolutionaries. To cap it all off, he and Urquhart were able to explain the British government's "criminal" apathy toward Russia only by assuming that so nationalistic a foreign minister as Lord Palmerston was a secret agent of the tsar.[12] The pattern of the previous century was thus stood on its head: the European Left, only lately open to suspicion of being Russia's agent in the West, had now become the chorophaeus of Western Russophobia.

More telling, however, than this shrill condemnation were the consequences for Russia's position in Europe of a new historical consciousness emerging in more moderate quarters of the Western Left, a consciousness that redefined both "Europe" and "civilization." To the philosophic historians of the eighteenth century, civilization began only with modern science and the Enlightenment; they dismissed the Middle Ages as a time of darkness and barbarism. If Voltaire and Gibbon wrote so extensively on that period it was to denounce its superstition and, by contrast, to extoll the intellectual emancipation of their own age. Otherwise, their view of history was a fairly static one, offering an abrupt passage from darkness to light with only an occasional golden age in ancient Athens, the early Roman Empire, or Renaissance Florence to prefigure modern *lumières*.

The shock of the French Revolution demolished this simple view. For the startling vicissitudes of the years 1789–1815 demonstrated that history is a development in many stages, and that the path to civilization and liberty is not a straight line but a zigzag replete with paradox. History, in short, was process; and exploring its record was a search less for reason than for roots.

Of course, among the first to draw this conclusion was Edmund Burke. As early as 1789 he argued that the Revolution would surely go awry because its abstract principles had disrupted that incremental constitutional growth which alone can produce true liberty in a viable society. To make his point, he offered the example of British representative institutions, as consolidated in the Glorious Revolution of 1688; for these had their origins not in timeless reason, but in contractual relations going back to the Middle Ages, a system moreover grounded in revealed religion. Thereby he staked out one national pattern of historical particularity.

This approach was generalized from a single case to the historical particularity of Europe as a whole in Restoration France, again with the enigma of the Great Revolution as the stimulus. Thus François Guizot—moderate liberal, constitutional monarchist, and Anglophile, for whom 1830 was to be the French equivalent of 1688—in 1829 published his *History of Civilization in Europe*.[13] For Guizot, European "civilization" meant the interdependent development of social cohesion and individual liberty, and it began with the conversion of barbarian Europe to Roman Christianity in the fifth century. Europe launched its grand career, however, in twelfth-century France with the revolt of the merchant bourgeoisie against its feudal and ecclesiastical overlords to obtain corporate status as self-governing "communes." This "class struggle" continued over the centuries, even as the monarchy turned to absolutism; and it culminated with the Third Estate's victory in 1789 and the bourgeoisie's return to power in 1830. (Incidentally, it was from this work that Marx picked up not only the principle of class struggle, but also much of what he knew about the Middle Ages.) In the present context, the relevance of this first notable general history of Europe is that it simply ignored Russia. Indeed, it offered a definition of civilization as middle-class progress toward constitutional liberty quite incapable of accommodating her.

This exclusion was amplified and made explicit on Guizot's left by Jules Michelet—radical democrat, Romantic, and Germanophile—for whom 1789 was the culmination of French, indeed of human, history. In this spirit, during the 1830s and 1840s, his monumental *History of France* traced the process by which the nation had been created by the "people." This epic moved from the religious patriotism manifested in the simple shepherdess Joan of Arc to the fulfillment of the national destiny in the democratic explosion of the Revolution.[14] Once again, seeking liberty's roots in Europe's multilayered past implicitly excluded Russia from "real" history. Michelet made this verdict explicit by bringing Adam Mickiewicz to the Collège de France as the first professor of Slavonic literature in the West and by himself writing *Democratic Legends of the North*, which employed his populist vision of humanity's development to depict free Poland's struggle against despotic Russia.[15]

Thus the historiography of the years 1830–1848, by rehabilitating the feudal and religious Middle Ages in a liberal-to-democratic version, redefined Europe as coterminous with the Latin Christendom that the *philosophes* had earlier cast out from civilization. As regards Russia, the only conclusion one could draw from this change was that she was not part of Europe at all. For Peter had brought her into the West's venerable civilization only in its most recent phase, the Enlightenment; yet that brief, borrowed candle had been snuffed out by the obscurantism of Nicholas. With the new century, therefore, Russia was once again thrust out into the cold of her Asiatic steppes.

This, indeed, was the conclusion that in Russia herself Petr Chaadaev in 1836 famously drew by applying the canons of the new French historiography to Nicholas's realm. Barren and despotic Russia, he affirmed, was a "gap in the intellectual order of things" which existed only "to serve as a terrible lesson to mankind." And her history was such a cultural void because she had derived her civilization from the wrong spiritual fount, "miserable Byzantium."[16]

His fellow countrymen, of course, could not let this condemnation stand, and so a group soon to be known as the Slavophiles turned it on its head.[17] Adapting, in their turn, the cultural and religious perspective of the new historiography, they declared that Peter, the Enlightenment, and the West were alien to Russia's essence, which derived precisely from the pure Christianity of Orthodox Byzantium.

Culture and the German *Sonderweg*

The rebirth of liberalism and radicalism in the maritime West was not the only force redefining the West. Even more potent were the cultural innovations emerging in Germany at the turn of the century. Indeed, it can plausibly be claimed that the nineteenth century is divided from the eighteenth not only by the year 1800 but by the Rhine. What France had done for secular rationalism and political radicalism in the previous century, Germany now did for aesthetic Romanticism and philosophical Idealism.

So novel was this culture that German intellectuals of the nineteenth and twentieth centuries periodically debated whether their nation was, or ought to become, a part of the West, somewhat the way Russian Westernizers and Slavophiles debated their national destiny. After the Second World War the term *Sonderweg* was introduced to describe this "special" or "separate" German path, which left-leaning historians then saw as leading from the failed Revolution of 1848 to Hitler.[18] That convenient term has been appropriated here, though with a different analytical intention. It designates, first, the undeniable cultural and political distinctiveness of nineteenth-century Germany. By extension, it denotes the "special path" of *each* nation along the West-East cultural gradient, in a series of *Sonderwege* from the Atlantic to the Urals.

The notion of "civilization" had emerged in eighteenth-century France and England as secular Europe's definition of itself, and at the same time as a universal value capable of acclimatization anywhere in the world. When this concept crossed the Rhine, however, its ecumenical pretensions were unexpectedly challenged by the counterconcept "culture." This word, whose Latin root is as old as the tilling of fields and the rearing of children, was now written *Kultur;* and it meant something both less universal and more exalted than the Western idea of civilization.

As the value *Kultur* was elaborated from the late eighteenth century onward it acquired ever new layers of meaning.[19] It meant, in the first instance, something close to the Latin original, that is, the nurturing of the inner man, the molding of his soul or spirit, for which the term *Bildung* (formation or education) was also used. By extension, *Kultur* also signified the nobler religious, artistic, and intellectual fruits of this nurturing—the arts and sciences, the poems and paintings, the symphonies and philosophies, that the community of cultivated men produce. Still, such exaltation of *Kultur* was not intended to deny the merits of *Zivilisation.* The latter continued to mean the material, scientific, technological, and even moral or behavioral improvement of society; and civilization in this sense remained the basis of the European community as a whole. In the new German perspective, however, this basic civilization was only a preliminary to the higher human attainments, the fostering of inner *Bildung* and national "cultural" creativity. Thus *Kultur* had escalated from meaning a quality of the individual's inner life to signifying the collective qualities of a given people or nation, above all the German nation. Such was emerging Germany's answer to the pretension of France and England that their civilizational norms had delimited humanity's horizons once and for all. *Kultur*, in sum, was the definition that Romantic and Idealistic Germany gave of *her*self.

There are many causes of this challenge to the West after 1800, but they are all related to Germany's position as the first eastward plateau along the West-East gradient of modern Europe's development.[20] Or, in other language, Germany at the time was "backward." Yet this had not always been the case. As Germans were acutely aware, in the era of Luther and the Fuggers they had been in the forefront of European innovation. After 1555, however, the religious wars occasioned by the Reformation, especially the Thirty Years' War, had devastated the country so thoroughly that by the mid-seventeenth century it had become a backwater—just when the policing of the Western monarchies was culminating in the creation of a scientific and secular culture. By the mid-eighteenth century, when Germany began to recover, she had decades of lost development to make up, a task given added urgency by her memories of past greatness recalled through present humiliation. But given also Germany's now meager resources, regeneration could only be promoted by an even stronger hand of princely police than had been the case farther West.

The "well-ordered police state" in post-1648 Germany took the form of a simplified Old Regime in which the territorial princes employed the aristocracy to officer their armies and administrations and "civilized" them through the court, a society where the simple people worked as "beasts of burden" or were impressed as soldiers, and where there was hardly any equivalent of a Third Estate, or civil society, in between. There did exist, to be sure, a *Bürgertum*, especially in such "free imperial cities" as Hamburg and Frankfurt; but on a national scale, it did not count for much socially and amounted to even less politically. The principal intermediate group in the German Old Regimes, therefore, was constituted by non-noble petty officials, the Lutheran clergy (who also served as school teachers), and their lay counterparts, university professors. In the age of the scientific revolution, when in the Western monarchies the forces of innovation were concentrated in royal academies, Germany preserved its medieval universities as its principal cultural institutions.

Hence, in Germany, the chief intermediate "social" group was an intelligentsia (to use again the later Russian term). At the same time, the fragmentation of the country into a number of sovereignties, and the political separation of the territorial states from the more dynamic free cities, stunted this intelligentsia's sense of national cohesion. By the same token, these divisions diminished civil society's leverage vis-à-vis the princes and impeded development of a unified ideological "market" (as Frederick the Great pointed out to Voltaire), such as served to magnify the power of the brokers of the Enlightenment in centralized France and England. Shakespeare had been an occasional court impresario for James I and Molière for Louis XIV, whereas Goethe's patron was only the petty duke of Weimar. Unlike the men of parts of Paris who moved with ease between "la cour et la ville," frequenting both the high nobility and the grand bourgeoisie, German intellectuals in provincial courts and cloistered universities largely had themselves as a public.[21] This modest, yet comfortable, intelligentsia thus hardly had an incentive to become radical or activist; its natural bent was contemplative, aesthetic, and philosophical. Germany's pride therefore was to be the land of "poets and thinkers," of *Dichter und Denker.*

Yet in its pursuit of this high vocation the German intelligentsia had to forge its personality in the shadow of the accomplishments accumulated by the West during the previous century and a half. This task was made doubly difficult since Germany's princes had already taken the shortcut to a policed society by importing its Gallic neighbor's civilization ready-made—the language, the manners, the art, and the philosophy. Frederick's highest ambition was to be a French poet, and it was to learn this métier that he first paid court to Voltaire. But the gallicization of the Old-Regime elite, though it brought the country intellectually up-to-date, did nothing to develop a German culture accessible to ordinary citizens. Rather, it threatened to replace what German burghers saw as the robust, moral, and pious native tradition with the shallow and impious ways of France.

In consequence, the German middling strata reacted with ambivalence to the absolutist princes and their imported civilization. This vulnerable group of course understood that the raw state of German society made princely police necessary to force the nation toward *Aufklärung*, as well as to protect their own "liberties" as *Aufklärer* from religious orthodoxy.[22] At the same time, even though the German intelligentsia resented the new civilization in so far as it was foreign, it recognized that civilization as such was indispensable to promote enlightenment in Germany. Hence, unlike the Western republic of letters, the emerging German men of parts never aspired to challenge the established order. As Kant imagined Frederick addressing the tiny educated elite among his subjects, "Argue all you want, but obey"; for German civil society was not yet "mature" enough even to think of self-government.[23]

As if to compensate for this civic immaturity, the German intelligentsia sublimated its resentment at the princes and foreign civilization by forging a culture that would equal, indeed surpass, the highest Western standards and still be distinctively native. Drawn from the manses of its Lutheran pastors and the halls of its universities, Germany's exceptionally studious and learned yet non-noble elite was awakened to secular civilization only in the 1760s. But in the space of a generation this group became the most critically acute and creative intellectual community in Europe. By adapting the literary forms of Shakespeare, it quickly made its "vernacular revolution" with the self-consciously national, didactic, and bourgeois dramas of Gotthold Lessing. It then proceeded, in the person of Kant, to devise a philosophy that would subsume—but critically—all Western thought from Descartes to Hume and reconcile reason with the ethical concerns of German and Christian inwardness.[24]

Thus *Kultur*, as contrasted with *Zivilisation*, acquired a class connotation in Germany.[25] The latter quality was the province of alien and superficial court society; the former was the domain of the humble but profound world of native burgers, pastors, and professors. By the turn of the century, as literature with Goethe and Schiller and philosophy with Kant reached a stunning maturity, the efforts of this intelligentsia added up to what later historiography called *die deutsche Bewegung:* the self-conscious elaboration of a national identity founded on cultural creativity.

The impact on Germany of the French Revolution and Napoleonic occupation then gave *Kultur* its ultimate meaning: from a class concept within the Germanies it was transformed into a national concept setting Germany off from France, and indeed from all Europe.[26] *Zivilisation* now meant the material, instrumental, indeed soulless civilization of France and England, whereas *Kultur* signified the deeper, moral and spiritual culture of Germany. Thus was the Enlightenment's notion of Europe as a single civilization of universal import fragmented into Romanticism's concept of civilization as a multiplicity of particular national cultures.

Yet the German cultural nation, divided between the Prussian and Austrian monarchies and a host of lesser sovereignties, did not exist as a state and still less was it a polity of citizens. Thus, Germany's "poets and thinkers," though proclaiming themselves the "self-consciousness" of the World Spirit (in Hegel's words) in the realm of pure reason, were nevertheless aware that they counted for precious little in the realm of practical affairs. On the one hand, they were tantalized by the revolution across the Rhine, and this impelled them to absorb its aspirations into the realm of thought. On the other hand, they were frustrated by the irrelevance of Western politics to German conditions, and this drove them to circumvent the Western challenge by construing German art and philosophy as the consciousness of the European body social, of which France and England were the unthinking, material limbs. It was these terms that Schiller used in 1795 in his "fragment" *die deutsche Grösse;*[27] or, as Jean-Paul Richter satirically framed the same thought: "the English have the empire of the sea, and the French have the empire of the land, but the Germans have the empire of the air."[28]

In this situation of practical impotence and intellectual superachievement, the German concept of culture came to focus with particular acuity on the then emerging idea of nationality.[29] To be sure, before 1789 both England and France—for centuries structured under a single sovereignty and since the sixteenth century possessed of well-developed vernacular languages and literatures—had gone a long way toward the creation of a genuine national consciousness. Still, in both countries all men, no matter how proud the rights they enjoyed, remained after all subjects. The modern concept of the nation was born when the French Revolution, by leveling the Old-Regime hierarchy of estates, for the first time made all men citizens.

Indeed, the Revolution had been made explicitly in the name of the "nation."[30] In 1789 this old Roman term for tribe or people was equated with the Third Estate, or the commonalty, as opposed to the two privileged orders. Thus the first modern meaning of nation was "the people," and they were invested with the majestic "sovereignty" of the erstwhile absolute monarchy. But soon the French Republic's struggle against the "despotism" of its unregenerated Old-Regime neighbors necessitated the *levée en masse* of all citizens to defend *la patrie*. And so Europe's first attempt at democracy revealed that the egalitarianism of universal suffrage had its logical counterpart in the fraternity of universal military service. "Nation" thereby acquired a second meaning, and the only one it has today, namely, one popular sovereignty as opposed to other such sovereignties. Clearly, from the moment it came into the world, modern democracy has invariably entailed nationalism.

It should be emphasized, however, that the French concept of the nation as fatherland was political, not cultural or ethnic. All citizens of the republic, whether German-speaking Alsatians or Italian-speaking Corsicans, were as French as any Parisian simply by virtue of legal citizenship, as Generals Johann Kleber and Napoleone Buonaparte well knew. When France then challenged Europe with this formula of popular-cum-national mobilization, no major state but England had the institutions and the heritage to respond with comparable collective cohesion.

The problem for Germany, therefore, was to adapt the double meaning of nation to the intact German Old Regimes. Yet even under the French occupation of Prussia after 1807, when patriotic intellectuals like Fichte urged the Hohenzollern king to place himself at the head of the whole "German nation," and to liberate it both from the foreigner and the servitudes of its own past, the most the dynasty would accept was a bureaucratically controlled "revolution from above." The result was the Stein-Hardenberg Reform Movement of 1808–1812.

Basically, this movement sought to implement that part of the French revolutionary agenda which was compatible with the preservation of autocracy and aristocratic estate privilege. In attempting this marriage of opposites, moreover, the Prussian Reform Movement set the pattern for the reaction of the backward Center and East of Europe to the challenge of the West for the rest of the century. Concretely, the program of this limited preventive revolution was the abolition of serfdom, the extension of education, a measure of local self-government, and—as the crowning measure—universal military service. This was a far-reaching program indeed, but it was clearly designed less to elevate society than to strengthen the state for international competition.[31]

To be sure, the patriotic sentiments of the "cultivated" public were mobilized to effect this reform; and the intellectuals were given the magnificent new University of Berlin to spread *Aufklärung*, though chiefly for purposes of improving the bureaucracy. Indeed, when the moment of liberation from Napoleon came, in 1813, the Prussian king went so far as to promise the nation a constitution. But once the French had been driven from Germany the monarch abandoned this momentary alliance with cultural nationalism and its disturbing liberal overtones. For the essence of the Prussian formula of progressive revolution from above was precisely to avoid what was the essence of the French Revolution: the nation as a sovereign people giving *itself* a constitution. In fact, the Prussian Reform Movement was much more in the spirit of enlightened despotism than in that of 1789.

When the dust of the revolutionary era settled in 1815, therefore, the German nation could be defined only as an ethnic-linguistic *Kultur* in contradistinction to its Old Regimes. Anyone who spoke German and was nurtured in German folk ways belonged to the true nation, whatever political obedience he might owe to one or another dynastic house. Participation in the *Volksgeist* conferred spiritual citizenship in Germany in place of the political citizenship practiced in France. Ambivalence nevertheless remained. For the cultural nation was regarded as the matrix out of which the political nation would one day be born—in the reverse of the French and English process of nation building.

In the wake of the French, Belgian, and Polish revolutions of 1830, the issue of crowning the Stein-Hardenberg Reforms with a national assembly was once again placed on the agenda of the German intelligentsia. And there the matter would fester for two frustrating decades until it burst forth in revolution during the euphoric "Springtime of the Peoples" in 1848.

By then, however, Germany was no longer the only people aspiring to become a political nation. As 1848 approached, her cultural definition of nationality had acted on her neighbors as potently as the original French political definition had acted on Germany. For if early-nineteenth-century Germany was backward with respect to France, she was advanced with respect to the rest of Europe; and so her influence spread eastward to the ends of the European cultural gradient.

In those lands on which Germany's new cultural dynamism exerted pressure, or where German dynasties reigned, there emerged in the 1820s and 1830s a similarly frustrated cultural-linguistic nationalism: in Italy, Hungary, Czech Bohemia, Poland, and—on the last ricochet—Russia. In most of these lands, as in Germany, there was an ancient people but no modern state; and in Russia there was an ancient state which had not yet developed a higher culture to justify its international power. Throughout this backward Europe, each emerging people employed the concepts worked out by Germany's quest for *Kultur*, each time adapting them to local conditions and traditions—with relative sobriety in classical Italy but with increased headiness in the immature East.

Yet none of these new culturally defined nationalisms could simply translate the German ideal of *Kultur* into the local language, for culture is by definition specific to a particular people. The new concept, therefore, became multiform, and its varied manifestations were historicized. World culture was now seen as developing from lower to higher stages of achievement, and from one people to another. In this perspective, each nation had its appointed "moment" of destiny, as Athens, Rome, and France had enjoyed in their day, a view which obviously conferred future advantages on latecomers to the creative cultural process. More often than not, in these lands of the "unhappy consciousness" of nationalism, the new democratic-patriotic identity was forged through a love-hate relationship with the Teutonic mentor akin to that which Germany had experienced toward France.

And so, Romantic nationalism moved on in lyrical waves across Europe, presaging the storms of 1848, and indeed the hecatombs of 1914. As the twentieth century would come to recognize, a terrible beauty had in truth been born.

The Romantic Chiaroscuro

Nationalism and historicism inevitably bring us to the intellectual heart of the cultural revolution that began with the new century: literary Romanticism and philosophical Idealism. Early-nineteenth-century culture in fact offers a compound of the new history, the new aesthetics, and the new philosophy. Let us, therefore, call the whole of this amalgam Romanticism—in part for the convenience of discussion, but even more for the substantive reason that all the components of the mix arose through a common opposition to the Enlightenment and the French Revolution.

Yet the Romantic reaction to the Enlightenment, though it had its first and clearest focus in the first quarter of the nineteenth century, especially in Germany, is not a phenomenon limited to that period. In fact, both Enlightenment and Romanticism, if given a broad construction, may be considered ideal types furnishing the contrapuntal forms of modern culture in general. Thus the pair, in a variety of mutations, and whether acting in alternation or in one and another combination, would recur throughout the nineteenth century, indeed on into the twentieth. The forms of this double eternal return would change—the rationalistic impulse evolving into positivism and utilitarianism, and the mythopoeic into symbolism and modernism—but generic Enlightenment and generic Romanticism would always continue to be recognizable.

Europe's oscillation between these two currents is quite relevant to Russia's position in the modern world (even though Russia did not participate in launching them, and though she will thus be absent in the present discussion of Romanticism's genesis). The oscillation is relevant here, first, because it governed the West's perception of Russia down to the twentieth century. Second, and just as important, the compound of Enlightened and Romantic currents during the 1820s and 1830s, once it penetrated Russia, produced the great period of her cultural creativity and thus her fullest convergence with the West. Finally, the years 1830–1848 produced the ideological foundations of Russia's later false grandeur—and her greatest divergence from the West—in her Soviet Socialist guise.

For there is no understanding modern Russia without socialism and Marxism; and there is no understanding Marx without Hegel, and thus also Romanticism. The origins of generic socialism in France have been looked at briefly, and more will be said in Chapter 4. Hegel and his background are examined in the present section. His relation to Marx will be analyzed at the moment Marxism produced its worldwide impact, after October 1917. The present excursus into high culture, therefore, is in no way a detour, but a case of *reculer pour mieux sauter*.

What, then, is Romanticism? Unlike Kant's bold interrogation of *Aufklärung*, this question is often dismissed as unanswerable. For, if the Enlightenment possesses an intrinsic clarity, or at least lends itself to a manageable summary of its chief tenets, Romanticism eludes definition, since the various currents that have been termed Romantic are not only diverse but often mutually contradictory. For this reason some specialists would use the term "Romanticism" only in the plural.[32] Let us begin, then, with what these Romanticisms declared they were *not*.

They all began with the premise that, as of 1800, the Enlightenment project had failed in its objective of remaking mankind through the accumulation of knowledge and the fostering of reason. The French Revolution, which had begun so hopefully, by the end of the decade had fallen far short of creating the new world dreamt of by such diverse visionaries as Condorcet, the young Wordsworth, and the aged Kant. This is not to say that it is plausible to claim that the Revolution had simply "failed." For it had obviously succeeded in leveling the Old Regime in the name of a society of citizens, and it had irreversibly rationalized life by improvements ranging from the metric system to the Code Napoleon. But it had palpably failed to create a *new man* (after all, its highest ambition); and it had destroyed many beautiful, venerable things.

Even more important, the Enlightenment's relative defeat lay in its inherent insufficiencies as a worldview, as a moral and cultural code for living. Well before the troubling surprises of the Revolution, from the Terror to Bonaparte's dictatorship, it left men hungry for the psychological, even spiritual, nurture that the rational faculties alone could not provide. Even before the Enlightenment began, indeed at the dawn of the new science, its fatal flaw had been divined by Pascal: "le coeur a ses raisons que la raison ne connait pas." It was out of this moral and emotional lack that Romanticism would be born.

Arising from this general preoccupation, generic Romanticism may be given either a broad or a narrow construction, a minimal or a maximal meaning. And the problem of the multiplicity of Romanticisms may be met by regarding them as a series of concentric circles, building from the narrow to the broad meaning, and widening both over time, from about 1800 to the threshold of the Revolution of 1848, and across the areas of culture embraced, from art and religion to history and philosophy.[33]

There exists, then, an *Ur-Kreis*, a primal circle of meaning, going back well before 1800 and often designated as pre-Romanticism. This movement originated at the high point of the Enlightenment itself, in Rousseau's critique of Anglo-French empiricism. This critique began with refusal of the belief that the derivation of all knowledge, especially of man's inner life, from sensory experience could not yield an adequate theory of ethics. This mechanistic view transformed morality into a calculus of mere physical pleasure and pain, a cold utilitarian response to useful or harmful external stimuli, whereas our heart instinctively tells us that "virtue" is all about something deeper. Only the inner "voice of conscience" can teach us how to "love" ourselves and our fellow man. So with Rousseau, the "sensation" of Locke and the Encyclopedists was transformed into "sentiment," and reason was subordinated to "feeling."

Rousseau's celebration of sentiment and inwardness was taken up most fervently in Germany, where it was elaborated to produce the national literary and philosophical culture already discussed. After 1770 it helped foster the cult of the "genius rebel" in the *Sturm und Drang*, or storm-and-stress movement, of the young Goethe and Schiller. This literary movement, furthermore, was given a theory by the "father of historicism," Johann-Gottlieb Herder.[34] A Lutheran pastor from the eastern fringes of *Deutschtum* (about whom more will be said shortly), Herder fused the Christian idea of Providence with the Enlightenment idea of progress, and then adapted this amalgam to the feebly developed societies of Central and Eastern Europe. In his view, human history offered a single, ascending line of development, as willed by God, but into which the various peoples entered only successively, each new nation bringing its contribution to the common treasure of humanity. And in this view of world history he was a "cosmopolitan."

In his definition of what constitutes a people, however, he laid the basis of what later would become nationalism. Each people was defined by its language, which articulated its unique spirit or essence; and this spirit was at its purest, not in prose or rational philosophy, but in the folk art of its "youth," for "poetry is the mother tongue of peoples," as Herder's mentor, Johann Hamman, was the first to declare. The quest of then provincial Germany for a distinctive cultural identity involved looking to the past and to the *Volk* for sources of inspiration in the present. These sources Herder found in Germany's medieval and gothic art forms (as well as in the kindred "medieval," multifaceted, and "folk" art of Shakespeare), models the *Sturm und Drang* sought to employ to create a distinctively German literature superior to that of France. This movement, therefore, shows us the nativist, anti-Enlightenment face of nascent German *Kultur*.

But its emphasis on national identity by no means meant nationalism in an exclusive or militant sense. Rather, it situated national particularity in a thoroughly *weltbürgerlische*, or cosmopolitan, perspective, and in the context of a mutually enriching brotherhood of peoples. Thus Goethe's *Faust*, initially medieval in form, ultimately acquired a heavily Hellenic and secular second part, and so wound up with a thoroughly melioristic content quite compatible with the humanistic and progressive traditions of the Enlightenment. Indeed, the Weimar humanists, as Goethe and Schiller were later called, increasingly sought their inspiration, not in gothic shadows and penumbras, but in the luminous classicism of Greece and Italy. Nonetheless, with the *Sturm und Drang* for the first time art, history, and national particularity had been associated to yield a novel cultural syndrome: in truth, an alluring cultural beauty had been born.

A second circle of meaning opened in the midst of the French Revolution and yielded the term "Romantic" itself, in its strict and narrow construction. In the critical studies of the brothers Friedrich and August Schlegel this new movement received an explicit programmatic statement.[35] In their usage, Romanticism signified the principled rejection of both Greco-Roman and French classicism with all their constraining and rationalistic "rules" in favor of a turn to the "universal-poetic," free-flowing modern *roman*, or novel, as practiced by Goethe in *Wilhelm Meister*, or a return to the lyrical and "many-sided" *romans*, or romances, of the medieval troubadours. This anticlassicism automatically entailed rejection of its ideological counterpart, the "soulless" and "desiccating" reason of the *philosophes*, and a return to the inner light of revealed religion. All these values, moreover, had found their perfect historical expression in the chivalry of feudalism, the spirituality of gothic art, and the unitary society of papal Christendom. These allegiances meant, finally, adherence to the "medieval" and "feudal" Old

Regime then being leveled by the Revolution. This creed was given perhaps its most intransigent formulation by the Schlegels' colleague, the poet Friedrich Hardenberg, better known as Novalis, who declared that his crisis-racked age must choose either "Christendom *or* Europe," and who summoned a still spiritual Germany to lead the continent back to its primal religious origins.[36]

Such was, roughly, the nexus of ideas expressed between 1798 and 1810 by the first generation of Romantics *strictu senso*, not only the Schlegels and Novalis, but also Samuel Taylor Coleridge and René de Chateaubriand in the "West." Slightly earlier Edmund Burke (whose *Reflections on the Revolution in France* enjoyed immense success in Germany) had expressed similar traditionalist views in more directly political form. Since all of these thinkers were consciously protesting against either the rationalism of the Enlightenment or the radicalism of the Revolution, or both, the whole movement has sometimes been characterized as conservative in its fundamental inspiration, the ideological counterpart of the Restoration in politics, or the "Romantic reaction." And this is roughly true for the first two decades of the century.

But a third, and quite different, circle of meaning emerges with a younger generation of Romantic artists who appeared on the scene between 1820 and 1830. These new rebels against the old rules of classicism reconstrued Romanticism antithetically to their mentors: it became "liberalism in art," in Victor Hugo's programmatic definition on the eve of the Revolution of 1830, an event which indeed had as one of its triggering causes the staging of his Romantic play *Hernani*.[37] His redefinition of Romanticism, moreover, characterizes equally well the art and politics of Lord Byron, Percy Shelley, and Heinrich Heine. And so, from one bard to another, the powers of the new lyricism were enrolled all across Europe in the cause of revolt and liberation.

In yet another domain—music—Ludwig van Beethoven, the supreme composer for all Romantics, from his Eroica Symphony in 1804 to his Choral Ninth in 1822, had consistently celebrated freedom and the brotherhood of man. As the text of the latter work, Schiller's "Ode to Joy," put it: "Seid umschlungen Millionen . . . alle Menschen werden Brüder."

From such a fraternal apotheosis, under the yoke of the dynastic

Holy Alliance, it was only a step to viewing Romanticism as nationalism in art, a permutation that occurred with the Pole Adam Mickiewicz, the Italian Giacomo Leopardi, and the Hungarian Eötvös Petöfi (and, though largely unbeknownst to Europe, the Russian Aleksandr Pushkin). All of them drew inspiration from the founder of the tradition of ethnic and historical local color, Sir Walter Scott, who for all intents and purposes had "invented" Scotland. But the nation also means the simple people, who in their very lack of cosmopolitan and rationalistic sophistication, express the "soul" or "spirit" of the community in its deepest authenticity. Thus in the early nineteenth century the words *peuple* and *Volk*, in the sense of the lower classes, shed their earlier derogatory connotations and acquired the nobler meaning of the "nation" as defined by 1789. (At the same time, the Russians created the term *narod* with the same double meaning.) Thereby Romanticism also became populism in art, as with the fairy tales of the brothers Grimm, the rhapsodic democratic history of Jules Michelet, and the revolutionary lyrics of George Herwegh and Ferdinand Freiligrath.

A fourth and outer circle of meaning emerges, finally, if one turns from "romanticism for the heart to idealism for the head," in Aleksandr Herzen's phrase. In German "classical" philosophy it turns out that reason itself, originally the *bête noire* of all the heirs of Rousseau, could be given a construction that may plausibly be termed Romantic. As Heine was among the first to point out to the West, while the French were making their revolution in the external world of society, the Germans were quietly making an equally momentous revolution in the inner world of thought.[38]

The Anglo-French Enlightenment, it will be recalled, had founded all knowledge on man's sensory experience of the material world. Moreover, it either merely tolerated religion, as did Locke, or was downright hostile to it, as were Voltaire and the Encyclopedists, as well as Hume and Gibbon. The German *Aufklärung*, however, took a diametrically opposed position on these two great issues. In epistemology it was idealistic, deriving man's knowledge from the internal structure of the mind, not from the external world of nature. And in its attitude toward religion, if it was no longer pietistic, it remained filially reverent, seeking to strip away Christianity's historical integument of "superstition" and recasting its ethical core in rational terms. Thus the supreme *Aufklärer* who initiated this transmutation of the Enlightenment, Immanuel Kant, appropriately viewed his enterprise as the "Copernican revolution" of European philosophy.

His revolution was triggered by the fact that the Anglo-French Enlightenment, which had made reason contingent on external nature, had ended in a crisis of skepticism. This crisis was due to Hume's strict reformulation of empiricism, which demolished as mere metaphysics the concept of "cause" on the grounds that sense data could yield only "constant conjunction," not universal laws. But the validity of science, the cornerstone of the Enlightenment, rested precisely on universal laws. To save science from skepticism, Kant, on the eve of 1789, made modern reason "pure," that is, independent of and unconditioned by any external sensory experience; and he made it "transcendental," that is, freed from contingency upon and placed above all "phenomenal," or empirical, appearances as their "universal and necessary" organizing principle.

In other words, he held that we can have ironclad laws of science because the a priori "categories of the understanding" of our minds give flawless order to our sense perceptions. As for the "things-in-themselves," or the world lying behind our phenomenal perceptions, they cannot be known scientifically, even though we must "postulate" that they do exist. Kant thereby removed the seat of Reason from the external world of nature, where the *philosophes* had placed it, and lodged it transcendentally in the knowing subject, or the human mind. From this single center of "apperception" philosophy then derived the lawful pattern of external nature and the rational moral will of the inner man.

Kant had, in truth, realized his ambition to effect that Copernican revolution of modern thought after which the age's coordinates of understanding would be reversed. In making this reversal, however, he intended his "critique" of previous metaphysics to be the capstone rather than the repudiation of the Enlightenment. His intent was firmly in the mainstream enlightened tradition, for his new epistemology was designed to account for the perfection of modern science, just as the reverse epistemology of the Encyclopedists had been; and he had the same "never-ending awe" for the infallible laws governing the "starry heavens above him" as any Diderot or D'Alembert.

Yet he had an equal awe for "the moral law within him," a sentiment the crudely utilitarian Encyclopedists did not share.[39] And this concern, which sprang from the pietistic strain of German Lutheranism, brought Kant to Rousseau's critique of empiricist ethics. Accordingly, he sought to give the latter's "voice of conscience" the same absolutely binding character as Newton's laws of physics. He achieved this end by construing conscience to mean the Categorical Imperative, or the rational "duty" of following only those norms of conduct that we would will to be "universal and necessary" laws. He buttressed this argumentation with a lay piety of "religion within the bounds of reason alone," a pallid faith that, for want of scientific proof, simply "postulated" God's existence and the immortality of the soul as necessary for moral action. In short, God was no longer divine; he was merely an adjunct of our ethical needs.

The master's exposition of this summa of Idealistic reason was indeed awesome intellectually, and by 1789 it had conquered the German cultural world. Yet at the same time it was unsatisfying psychologically, since in the last analysis we do not really *know* anything outside ourselves. Moreover, even though Kant sought to furnish an ethics capable of inspiring virtue, the Categorical Imperative was hardly an emotionally uplifting code for living. Thus, Kant's impact was in the last analysis a paradoxical one: in order to defend the scientific values of the Enlightenment he had enthroned subjectivity at the heart of his system; yet since this system retained all the Enlightenment's rationalistic dryness, its radical subjectivity ultimately fueled the Romantic revolt against reason.

Politically, Kant was to the left of the Enlightenment, for—again drawing on Rousseau—he was committed to "reverence for the common man." He thus not only welcomed the French Revolution, as did many intellectuals in Germany, but steadfastly supported it throughout its most radical phases, as most of them did not. Hence Kant, despite his subliminal pietistic inclinations, must be counted with the mature Goethe among the Westernizers and cosmopolitans of the German tradition. Indeed, he was very disturbed by the *Sturm und Drang* and Herder, both for their vatic irrationalism and their parochial nativism.

Nevertheless, Kant's transcendental categories of understanding, and especially his celebration of the will, readily lent themselves to the intuitionism he himself deplored. This transformation of Idealism was promoted by a new generation of thinkers who had been reared, not on the austerities of Newtonian science, but on art, Greek philology and above all Lutheran theology.[40] Their Idealism indeed often harkened back to prescientific modes of thought, whether the unorthodox mysticism of Jacob Boehme in the sixteenth century or that of the heterodox medieval monk Joachim of Floris, with his vision of history divided into the ages of the Father (Old Testament law), the Son (New Testament grace), and the Holy Spirit (the beatific future of mankind).

These post-Kantians, moreover, were the exact contemporaries of the literary Romantics and like them had first welcomed the Revolution, only to turn against it toward various forms of conservatism, corporatism, and nationalism. They therefore are the prime representatives of the nativist tradition in German thought, hostile in varying degrees to the "cosmopolitanism" of Frederick, Goethe, and Kant. As Goethe himself saw so well, in his own person and in his greatest creation, Faust, two warring yet inseparable souls dwelt within the breast of the emerging German intellectual class.

Thus in the 1790s Johann-Gottlieb Fichte, in his initial Jacobin response to the Revolution, construed Kant's moral reason as a manifestation of the striving will; later, in his anti-Napoleonic phase, he associated this will with emerging German nationalism. In the 1810s the former seminarian Friedrich Schelling, in close communion with Novalis and the brothers Schlegel, transformed the transcendental faculty still further into a predominantly aesthetic impulse. He then associated this, first, with a world of nature now "de-Newtonized" and interpreted as animate and poetic and, subsequently, with the folk art of cultural nationalism. In the same decade, finally, the greatest former seminarian of them all, Georg Wilhelm Friedrich Hegel, fused the speculations of his predecessors from Kant onward into a single cosmic unity called the Absolute Idea.[41]

Hegel's starting point was the problem created when Kant made reason "universal and necessary" yet denied that its reach extended to the things-in-themselves and to God. Hegel resolved this dilemma by positing that we could understand the world around us because Reason resided equally in our minds and in everything outside ourselves, be it material or divine. The link between the subjective and the objective aspects of reason, moreover, was given by the interchange of the dialectic. This neo-Platonic principle meant that internal and external Being were joined by a perpetual process of Becoming, in which one form of existence was "negated," and thereby "sublated" or transcended (*aufgehoben*), so as to yield a higher form of existence. Similarly, progress through negation governed the dialogic evolution of "concepts" that give consciousness to the successive forms of existence.

The process of Becoming-through-negation was a conflictual one, unfolding in a recurring rhythm of loss and renewal, of destruction and re-creation, of objectification or "alienation" (*Entfremdung*) and return into one's self at a higher level. Alienation was in fact self-enriching, as the great chain of Being-as-Becoming spiraled upward to attain full "self-consciousness" of the cosmic life in the Absolute Idea. Self-consciousness moreover was also freedom, since the seat of this Idea was the human mind; thereby humanity, through understanding the necessary laws of the universe, was itself liberated from external necessity. In this way Hegel sublated and transcended Kant's cautious critical Idealism into an intoxicating absolute Idealism in which man could know everything, both inside and outside himself.

In Hegel's cosmic process of self-enriching alienation, the life of the Absolute began with the pure logic of Reason; it then exteriorized itself in the living yet unconscious world of Nature; and finally it turned back into itself in the self-conscious social, aesthetic, religious, and philosophic development of Man. With this odyssey of the World Spirit through time, reason became something it had never before been in human thought: historical. By the same token history became rational, indeed the living embodiment of Reason, the Logos of pure consciousness made temporal flesh. History was now the vehicle for the self-revelation over time of the Idea, which was also God; and this Reason-God-Idea manifested itself immanently and completely through the mundane workings of human society and culture. The vulgar, utilitarian notion of progress of the *philosophes* had been transmuted into a grandiose secular pantheism. Conjoined with this pantheism was a rationalistic theodicy of the bloody and destructive, yet eternally creative, ascent of the World Spirit through all the stages of the dialectical unfolding of human destiny.

The paltry lights of the previous century were thus sublated into a kind of philosophic theology, indeed a latter-day secular gnosticism, offering certain understanding of the designs of divine Providence amidst the disorder of human affairs. This knowledge was retrospective, not predictive, coming to the philosopher, like the owl of Minerva, only after historical events had run their course. Nonetheless, the rational pattern of history's seemingly random events was indubitably real. Hegel called this principle the Cunning of Reason; and we shall have occasion to observe its operation as our investigation moves from Hegel himself to Marx, to Lenin, to Stalin.

For the moment suffice it to say that by this paratheological principle Hegel meant that historical actors, whether individuals or nations, are unwittingly yet purposefully led by a "logic" of events of which they themselves are unaware. Thus, Hegel, on seeing Napoleon enter Jena in 1806, declared him to be the "World Spirit on horseback," yet added that the emperor was only an unconscious agent of Reason in history, whereas he himself, as philosopher, was its conscious agent.

Of course, Hegel did not believe these positions made him a Romantic; he indeed scorned the Romantics in the narrow sense, whom he considered wooly obscurantists. And he clearly considered himself a rationalist in the tradition of the Greeks and the modern Enlightenment. He even maintained that he was the ultimate rationalist, who had synthesized the one-sided reason of the previous century with the older verities of religion and art. Moreover, outside his commitment to the spiritual superiority of Lutheranism over Catholicism, he was not notably nationalistic but cosmopolitan in his views and range of interests. Nor did he revere the simple people and their folk ways as the source of cultural creativity, in the new spirit of *Volkstum* expounded by Hamman and Herder. Rather, in politics Hegel was a believer in progress through the dynastic state and its corporate social hierarchy as updated by the Prussian Reform Movement, a renewed polity he also viewed as consonant with the economic civil society of Adam Smith. Overall, then, through his service to the reformed Prussian monarchy during the Restoration, Hegel was still in large measure in the eighteenth-century tradition of enlightened absolutism.

Nevertheless, a rationalist for whom mind is also Spirit, and for whom this mind-spirit, or *Geist*, is not so much an intellectual faculty of man as a veritable being, a cosmic *daemon*, moving as a demiurge upon the waters of history, is a new sort of rationalist. Or, rather, he is an old, prescientific sort of theologian, who has rearticulated in post-Enlightenment terminology the basic structure of a neo-Platonic, Joachimite, and Boehmian tradition still alive in Germany under the surface of recently imported, positive *lumières*. Many of the things that Hegel's Absolute carried throughout history—the values of art, religion, and a corporate social organization—but above all the priority accorded to a dialectical History itself, were quite foreign to the trans-Rhenan and Kantian Enlightenment and very close to the positions held by those of his contemporaries who unabashedly called themselves Romantics.

Thus the rational-dialectical historicism of post-Kantian Idealism constitutes the outer circle of meaning and delimits the broad construction of Romanticism. It is in this broad construction—Romanticism as a compound of reason and art with historical becoming—that the term is understood here.

If a single label is to be assigned to this amalgam, perhaps the best is "natural supernaturalism."[42] This concept was proposed to account for the genesis of Romanticism proper at the end of the 1790s. It signified that in a culture imbued with the Christian apocalyptic tradition yet already half-secular, the Revolution in France was widely greeted among foreign intellectuals as the advent of the final age, the social redemption of mankind. When the Revolution turned to tragedy in 1793–94, its disappointed literary votaries sought an alternative but still secular redemption in beauty and art. Thus Wordsworth and Coleridge in England and the brothers Schlegel and Novalis in Germany in 1798 were the first to treat art as a form of religion and the poet as a kind of priest. Their aim was not to displace the old religion and clergy but to supplement them with a vatic lyricism and an aesthetic clerisy. If the French did not get around to this new cult until 1802, when René de Chateaubriand won fame by celebrating religion for its beauty in *The Genius of Christianity*, it was because until then their millenarian energies had been absorbed by the Revolution itself.

The final step in this process was taken by German classical philosophy. Kant's Categorical Imperative can easily be read as a secular surrogate for the Golden Rule. And Hegel's historicized pantheism is most plausibly interpreted as a philosophical religion and a form of secularized Christian providentialism. When read into the human record this lay soteriology yields the triad: in the Orient one was free, in Greece and Rome some were free, and in the Germano-Christian West all are free—a progression that echoes the mysticism of Joachim of Floris. The philosophers, just like the poets, viewed these emendations of theism, which to Orthodox believers were quite scandalous, not as refutations of religion but as its culmination.

Early-nineteenth-century Romanticism consequently represents an effort to save what could be salvaged of the consolations of a prescientific, prepolitical ethos and to adapt them to a world where an "enlightened," protopositivistic culture had become predominant. Thus, Romanticism met needs that had traditionally been provided for by religion, yet did so with purely this-worldly and aesthetic means. In sum, it may be understood as an attempt to resolve the cultural crisis unleashed by the French Revolution by seeking to have both Christendom *and* Europe together.

The New Historical Canon

The fact that Romanticism thus conceived combined eighteenth-century reasons with early-nineteenth-century sentiments is precisely the relevant point for the purposes of this study. By 1830 the time had passed when Romanticism signified an antirationalistic and conservative reaction against the Enlightenment and the Revolution, of the heart against the head, or of poetry against prose. It had become at one and the same time an overcoming and an adaptation of the *philosophes*, both a repudiation and an appropriation of *les lumières*. Hegel's philosophy, completed by 1830, marks the culmination of the syncretistic process of gathering all culture into one totality. And the same date marks the beginning of this Romantic amalgam's fusion with political activism.

This second Romantic age, which extended until 1848, produced a politics that eschewed clear cultural polarities and fused values that were incompatible in the sharply focused lights of the *philosophes*, who had pitted bright reason against dark superstition and divided history into distinct phases of barbarism and civilization—a transition so clear-cut it could be promoted in a short span by the single agency of the prince. The social Romanticisms of the midcentury, rather, perceived history in evolutionary terms, in which the nations advanced by stages from "lower" to "higher" forms in a great chain of historical Becoming—a process so complex and protracted it could be driven only by the "genius" of the people rather than by the initiative of the state.

In the postrevolutionary age, therefore, political argumentation grew more eclectic. Those who wished to defend Old-Regime values and institutions were obliged to resort in some measure to the weapons of their adversaries. Even such a foe of the Enlightenment as Burke argued that religion was socially more useful than rational self-interest, and that a traditional inegalitarian order was more natural than the philosophical abstractions of universal rights. Chateaubriand preached religion with the argument that the beauty created by religion instilled faith in men's "natural conscience" as understood by Rousseau. Conservatives of all stripes, in order to deny the legitimacy of revolution, argued that human progress was secured only by the organic evolution of social forms, as was done, in various modes, by Justus Möser or by the "historical school of law" of Karl Friedrich von Savigny. Yet all of these arguments partially accepted the categories, if not the goals, of the opposition.

Conversely, once the new tenets of Romanticism had been put into circulation, the political descendants of the *philosophes* could no longer proceed as before. Thus, to the left of the medievalizing liberalism and democracy of Guizot and Michelet we find Henri de Saint-Simon, who advocated a socialism founded on technological progress by framing it as a New Christianity (his disciple, Pierre Leroux, in 1831 was the first to use the term "socialism" to describe this doctrine). At the same time

126

the former Dominican priest Félicité de Lamennais carried natural supernaturalism into the political realm by preaching democracy as the highest form of charity. In the more backward parts of Europe we find the messianic nationalisms of Adam Mickiewicz and Guiseppe Mazzini, in which martyred Poland and Italy were both seen as the "Christ among nations." And we will later see how Marx amalgamated the cause of a materialist proletarian revolution with the paratheological agency of Hegel's dialectic, reinterpreted as Guizot's class struggle.

This ever more frequent syncretism of Enlightenment and Romanticism was furthered by Europe's awareness of the acceleration of history after 1789.[43] Europeans had, of course, been conscious of change earlier, from the Renaissance and Reformation to the scientific revolution. But none of these changes had given contemporaries the impression of transiting from one historical age to another in a single lifetime. The French Revolution for the first time did just that: in a decade a millennial civilization had become an "Old Regime," and Europe was now embarked on an adventure of open-ended change. Another way of putting this awareness after 1789, and especially after 1830, was to speak of politics, and eventually culture, as a permanent struggle of "Left" against "Right," of the "party of movement" against the "party of resistance." Hence contemporaries concluded that historical process is of the essence of the human condition, that change per se is the very warp and woof of reality. And this new consciousness is what distinguishes early-nineteenth-century historicism from the eighteenth-century idea of progress.

Though initially owing more to conservative than to progressive thinkers, the Romantic sense of history as organic continuity between the past, the present, and the future, was a sword that in politics could cut both ways: it could strike to the left as easily as to the right. Insofar as historicism extolled continuity and insisted that the slow labor of the ages alone could produce the good society, it represented a critique of the Revolution and so lent itself to the defense of the old order—as with Burke. Yet insofar as Becoming also emphasized the inevitability of change, it could fuse with the Enlightenment idea of progress and so promote the gradual liberalization of inherited values and institutions—as with Hegel. Or it could serve to anticipate the apocalyptic transcendence of the past—as with Marx. The Romantic sense of historical Becoming, Janus-like, looked backward and forward, to the right and to the left, at one and the same time.

Yet whichever way it looked, by the eve of 1848, it had produced a single historical canon, one which is largely with us still. This canon offered a thousand-year-old European civilization, and the leitmotif of its history was humanity's ascent to freedom. Depicting the European epic, moreover, was no longer the work of such amateurs as Voltaire and Gibbon; it was a professionalized, archive-based endeavor of professors, such as Guizot and Michelet, who could plausibly claim that their craft was a science. But even their work was surpassed in rigor and scope in the German cultural renaissance by Leopold von Ranke.[44] Not surprisingly, he was able to arrive at his magisterial perspective by looking westward from the relative backwardness of Prussia.

In answering the question of what unites Europe, he did not take generic Christianity as the standard because it included the laggard East of Greek Orthodoxy, and he eliminated Latin Christendom as a whole because it included Slavs and Magyars; he even refused to define Europe as the Great Powers of his own day because this would mean taking in Turks and Russians.[45] The position he set forth in his first work, in 1824, was that Europe emerged from the fusion of the Romance and Germanic peoples through the reception by northern barbarians of Roman and Christian culture. The axis of European institutional and spiritual development thus began with the Holy Roman Empire of the German Nation, and led from the contest of Papacy and empire to the Renaissance and Reformation, and on to the modern state system dominated by France, England, and Prussia. Over the decades of the midcentury Ranke devoted massively researched volumes to Europe's formative centuries and her three major modern states, thereby creating a more comprehensively European historiography than that of any of his contemporaries farther west.

Unlike those contemporaries, however, Ranke was no democrat, or even a liberal. A devoted Prussian civil servant, he was deeply upset by the revolutions of 1830 and 1848, and even by the radical way Bismarck achieved unification in 1871—although he did approve of the result.

Nonetheless, like his Western colleagues, he too believed that history offered a pattern of progress, consisting in the stage-by-stage manifestation of God in the European state system, as papal Christendom developed into the purer Reformation and then into the great national monarchies. He strongly approved of Europe's mission to expand through crusades, whether against Muslims in Spain and the Near East or Slavs and Balts in the north. For Ranke European history represented human-cum-divine self-realization, and as such the culmination of world history. Although he greatly disliked Hegel for the latter's abstract approach to the past, behind Ranke's own densely empirical narratives (once mistakenly considered positivist) lurked a kindred secular theology. Thus, the Germanic version of the new historicism privileged the Romano-Germanic world as the homeland of freedom, just as surely as did Guizot and Michelet, though freedom was now interpreted in a spiritual more than a political sense.

By the eve of 1848, therefore, the maritime West and Germany together, the European Left and Right in tandem, had produced an Enlightened-Romantic redefinition of European civilization. Despite differing conceptions of freedom within this consensus, the actual genealogy of liberty unearthed by both parties was roughly the same: the fraternal comitatus of the German barbarians, medieval Christianity, the chivalry of feudalism, the humanism of the Renaissance, the "Christian liberty" of the Reformation, the science of the seventeenth century, and the rationalism of the Enlightenment. Whether construed in a radical, French sense or in a statist, Prussian one, this was the high lineage of freedom for all authentically Western peoples.[46]

This lineage, moreover, did more than describe where contemporary Europe came from; it also defined Europe as an essence, a cultural being endowed with a unique soul. The European essence was present from the birth of the Romano-Germanic world, and all its subsequent stages of development emerged from this genetic code. Hence Europe was an entity that nations belonged to from the beginning; it could not be joined en route to its culmination in freedom. Such a view, obviously, stood in stark contrast to the Enlightenment definition of Europe as a civilization emancipated from its primitive roots and universal in import. The early-nineteenth-century pedigree of freedom, therefore, in conjunction with its essentialist concept of civilization, left to raw Russia—which could at best claim a dubious share in the European heritage through the stagnant Christianity of Byzantium or the medieval communes of Kiev and Novgorod—only the most tenuous toehold among the "historically significant" nations of the world.

Certainly the nineteenth-century historical canon is a great improvement over the eighteenth century's simple darkness-to-light emplotment of European history, which had written off the Middle Ages as a kind of cultural black hole, ignoring what was in fact the *Grundzeit* of Europe itself. Indeed, the new canon may be considered "true" as a broad outline of Western development from around the year 1000 to 1789. Nevertheless, we should not forget that history's meaning is in large measure defined by its denouement at any given moment; and the "end" of the European story now is hardly that of the nineteenth century. In particular, beginning in the sixteenth century Europe constantly expanded both West and East, yet the diminution of Europe itself that this expansion produced did not become apparent until the twentieth century. As regards Europe's internal development, furthermore, the somber events of the last century make the early-nineteenth-century canon appear much less adequate than it did on the eve of the Springtime of the Peoples. Time has added many layers to the story told by Guizot, Michelet, and Ranke. And it is self-evident that Russia has bulked ever larger in these new strata, beginning with the moment the canon was set. Cultural "essences" are not fixed; they evolve over time, if indeed they exist at all.[47]

Nonetheless, from 1848 to the present day the historical canon of Romano-Germanic development has invariably lurked in the back of people's minds whenever the question of Russia and the West is raised. As a result, the question is invariably answered with a check list of negatives: Medieval Church and Empire? No. Feudalism and chivalry? No. Renaissance and Reformation? No.[48] If one adds to this a national history that certainly did not culminate in freedom, the verdict is clear: Russia is of non-European essence, and all that is non-European is Asian and barbaric. It is as simple as that. As the nineteenth century was pleased to sum up this wisdom: "grattez un Russe et vous trouverez un Tartare."

A Fractured Image

Yet since the Romantic worldview could also be adapted to the most diverse political positions, from Left to Right, Russia's fate under the early-nineteenth-century constellation of values was by no means automatically assigned. Her fortunes plummeted in Western eyes only when the stars of historicism and nationalism aligned with those of liberalism and democracy. When conservatism was in the ascendant, however, her very backwardness could bring her luck.

Still, this differentiation took some time to emerge. In the meantime the notion of civilization as a plurality of national cultures kept Europe's door open to Russia, a view best revealed by a closer look at the "father of historicism," Herder. Although he knew no Slavic language, he had been born on the cultural divide between Teuton and Slav in East Prussia, and from age fourteen to eighteen he lived under benevolent Russian occupation. His first assessment of Russia was an ode to Peter III (Catherine's unfortunate spouse), who on acceding to the throne in 1762 had saved Frederick the Great, and probably also the existence of Prussia, by withdrawing unilaterally from the Seven Years' War. After crossing paths with Kant at Königsberg, for five years Herder taught at Riga in the Russian empire, indeed becoming a Russian subject. There he drafted an ode to Peter I, whom he praised after the manner of Leibniz and Voltaire as the genius who had imprinted European civilization on the *tabula rasa* of Russia. In 1769, during his first visit to the great world of the West, he traveled to France, where he concluded that enlightened Europe had perhaps passed its prime; so when he learned of Catherine's victories over Turkey, he opined that the Ukrainian steppes might well blossom into a new Greece. By this point, moreover, he had discovered Rousseau's critique of Peter as a baleful imitator who made the Russians into pseudo-Europeans instead of permitting them to become their authentic selves. As he migrated onward to Weimar, where the *deutsche Bewegung* was accomplishing just that for the Germans, he declared that someday the Slavs (by which he meant primarily the Russians), would develop their unique national personality.[49]

Thus, in his mature philosophy of history, Herder became the first

major thinker to view Europe as a spectrum of cultures, arranged moreover in a gradient (although, of course, he did not use that image) in
which civilization moved first from Greece and Rome to the Barbarians, and then across northern Europe from the Atlantic eastward. In
this perspective, the future obviously belonged to the "younger" nations—in his day Germany in relation to France, and later the Slavs in
relation to Germany. For to Herder, unlike to the *philosophes*, each
people was a nascent cultural entity in its own right, not simply an
empty vessel to be filled by a ready-made civilization; and the sum of its
cultural achievements manifested the will of God in human history.[50]
And what might the Slavs' future contribution be? Herder's answer was
to contrast them with the warlike Franks and Saxons: the Slavs were a
pacific, even passive, people, whom destiny had unfortunately placed
between the Germans on the one side and the Tatars on the other,
while their love of peace and domestic labor had prevented them from
building a permanent military organization. Yet if their lands were ever
cultivated and opened to European progress, then "at last they would
be awakened from their long inert slumber and delivered from their
chains." From the Don to the Elbe they "would celebrate their ancient
rites of labor and peaceful commerce," and "mankind" *(Menschheit)*
thus would attain a higher "humanity" *(Humanität)*. Small matter that
this famous passage confuses Slavs and stateless Balts, and even more
that it fails to mention the imperial Russian state; for decades to come it
would warm populist hearts from the Vistula to the Volga.[51]

A similar attitude characterized the Weimar humanists generally, for
whom the new idea of cultural distinctiveness was still compatible with
"cosmopolitanism" and the universalist concept of civilization they
shared with the *philosophes*. Thus, Schiller, whose principal artistic interest had long been verse dramas portraying characteristic episodes in
the history of the various European peoples—as in *Don Carlos*, *The
Maid of Orleans*, and *Maria Stuart*—became in his unfinished play *The
False Dmitrii* the first writer of international stature to attempt a theme
purporting to depict the specific quality of Russian life. To him, as to
Goethe and Herder, civilization was the sum of national cultures, each
offering its distinct contribution to the common treasure of humanity.
This view was still held by the brothers Schlegel in the 1810s, who were

favorably disposed to Russia's cultural potential, in the same manner as they were interested in the Hindu Vedas or the religious dramas of Spain. Their disciple Mme. de Staël, who first revealed German Romanticism to France, after visiting Goethe in Weimar pushed on to Moscow in 1810 in the conviction that culture existed there, too.[52]

But this cosmopolitan mood was a thing of the past after 1806 for Fichte, with his embattled nationalism, and for Hegel, with his cultural statism and elitism. Both had hard-headedly concluded from the vicissitudes of the Revolution that civilization was a progression through struggle from one society to another, in which latecomers subsumed the creations of their predecessors and in which weak competitors were eliminated altogether. Humanity was therefore divided by Hegel into creative, world-historical societies and nonhistorical ones. He held further that in the present the only significant nations were in Romano-Germanic, Christian-Enlightened Europe.

Indeed, one of the most striking characteristics of liberal and rationalistic thought after 1815 was its deafening silence regarding Russia. Whereas the author of the formula "philosophy of history," Voltaire, had written whole books on her, and the father of historicism proper, Herder, had produced lyrical and empathetic chapters, the grand metaphysician of historicism, Hegel, who had seen with his own eyes Russian armies drive the "*Weltgeist* on horseback," Napoleon, out of Germany, and who lived in the city whose central square was called Alexanderplatz after Russia's emperor, could muster only one paragraph for all the Slavs:

> We find, moreover, a great Slavic nation in the East of Europe.
> . . . These people did indeed found kingdoms and sustain spirited
> conflicts with the various nations that came across their path.
> Sometimes, as an advanced guard, as an intermediate nationality,
> they took part in the struggle between Christian Europe and un-
> christian Asia. The Poles even liberated beleaguered Vienna from
> the Turks; and a part of the Slavs were conquered by Western
> Reason. Yet this entire body of peoples remains excluded from
> our consideration, because hitherto it has not appeared as an inde-
> pendent phase in the series of configurations of Reason in the

world. Whether it will happen hereafter does not concern us here; for in history we have to do with the past.[53]

Thus was the new historical canon of Romanticism cast in "rational" terminology. Even though it was offensively dismissive of everyone east of Berlin, what Hegel had in mind was nonetheless quite real. Turning Herder on his head, in speaking of the "configurations of Reason in the world" he meant not peoples but states; and none of the Slavs other than the non-European Russians any longer possessed an independent polity. The Poles, the Czechs, the Balkan Slavs, and also the Hungarians had all lost out to the more rational dynastic empires. Thus was staked out a widespread German view that the lesser breeds in the East were inherently incapable of state building, and hence fit only to be ruled by others. As for the Russians, who clearly possessed a state, it was by now a common German opinion that they had not created it themselves: it had been imposed on them by Scandinavian Varangians and perfected in modern times only by imported Teutonic talent.

Yet soon the spirit of Herder would have its revenge. As Germany's concept of cultural particularity was adapted by her eastern neighbors, they reacted against the historical canon of a Romano-Germanic Europe by producing a transnational cultural-linguistic configuration: Slavdom. The eighteenth-century definition of Europe as civilization had made it possible to ignore the ethnic and historical particularities of Central and Eastern Europe. The early-nineteenth-century sensitivity to historical roots made it impossible to avoid coming to terms with them.

To be sure, Europeans had always been aware of ethnic and linguistic differences beneath the overarching unity of Christendom or civilization: German speakers had long scornfully called Romance speakers the *welsche*, and the Teutonic *Drang nach Osten* against barbarian Slavs and Balts had been a bloodily bitter affair. Even so, until the nineteenth century the nations of East Central Europe had usually defined themselves vis-à-vis Germany in political terms, that is, by speaking of the "aristocratic republic" of the *Rzeczpospolita* and of the "liberties" of the lands of the Crown of Bohemia or of the Crown of St. Stephen. Yet since these polities and their liberties had long since disappeared, and since their oppressors in Berlin and Vienna regarded their own culture as Romano-Germanic, in answer intelligentsia spokesmen for the submerged peoples of East Central Europe began to define their common culture as Slavic.

During the Springtime of the Peoples in 1848, this collective awareness produced in Prague an assembly known as the first pan-Slav congress. Convened to agitate for the emancipation of Slavs everywhere, this body was directed in the first instance against the two Germanic monarchies. But the legacy of the Polish partitions also turned the congress against Russia, or at least against the Russian empire. Indeed, the lone Russian present, Mikhail Bakunin, had come with the message that pan-Slav nationalism could destroy the three Eastern monarchies together, thereby launching a socialist revolution across Europe. For in his anarchist eyes the bureaucratic empire of St. Petersburg was more Mongol-Germanic than Slavic—*un empire knuto-germanique*, as he later put it.[54]

As a practical matter, however, little came of the democratic pan-Slav movement. True, there was a "second" pan-Slav congress in Moscow in 1867, but this was essentially a gathering of scholars and clerics, not activists, and internationally it was concerned primarily with the Orthodox Slavs of the Balkans.[55] Yet democratic pan-Slavism failed above all because the Slavic peoples had never constituted a political or cultural unit comparable to the Holy Roman Empire of the German Nation and its various modern descendants; nor did the modern Slavs really think of themselves as a unit. They were riven by national antagonisms, especially between Catholic Poles and Orthodox Russians. Moreover, only Russia was an independent state. The unity of Slavdom thus was largely the negative one of common stateless subjection to Germans or Turks; and, except for the Poles, this meant a measure of attraction to the possible protective power of Russia. On this score, however, Bakunin's intuition had been basically correct: until almost the end of the century St. Petersburg felt itself politically akin to Berlin and Vienna, not to its putative little Slavic brothers in Mitteleuropa, a feeling reciprocated by the two Germanic emperors.

Behind the facile musings about the unity of Slavdom, however, lies a different and harsher historical reality. The zone between Germany and Russia does indeed have a distinctive character, but it is not defined by the ethnic-linguistic Romantic mirage of pan-Slavism. Reference has often been made here to the division of Europe along the Elbe River. The time has now come to divide the lands to the east of that line into two plateaus along the European gradient: an East Central Europe and an Eastern one. The former has at times been called a second Europe, to distinguish it both from the first Europe to its west and a third zone, or non-Europe, of Russia to its east.[56] Whatever name or number it is given, its distinctiveness is unmistakable; and it is determined by a political destiny that cuts across ethnic-linguistic groupings.

In this East Central Europe, there are first the German military marches of Mark Brandenburg in the north and the Ostmark of the Danube, which in the seventeenth century became the foundation stones of modern Prussian and Austrian power. In the poorer regions beyond these marcher states, the Hungarian, Bohemian, and Polish kingdoms had earlier adopted a diluted version of the feudal institutions, and eventually the urban life, of Europe west of the Elbe. On this basis these kingdoms lived their golden ages as independent nations between the fourteenth and sixteenth centuries. Yet in all three, in contrast to the Plantagenet and Capetian realms, the nobility constantly developed its power at the monarchy's expense. So when circumstances at last brought a test of national strength, the East Central European kingdoms were extinguished one after another by Ottoman Turkey, by Habsburg Vienna, and (the last of them, Poland) by Hohenzollern Prussia, the Habsburgs, and Romanov Russia together. By the eighteenth century trans-Elbean Europe had established the configuration it would keep until the First World War: three dynastic empires astride the three defunct East Central European national monarchies.[57]

The early nineteenth-century fragmenting of the European cultural map did not invariably cast Russia into the outer darkness of Asia. The notion of Russia's separateness could also be given a positive valence if one adopted a spiritual-organic as opposed to the rational-dialectical concept of culture. Thus after 1815, as a general rule traditionalist conservatives, especially in Germany, were Russophile, as were the heirs of Romanticism in the narrow meaning of the term. So too were most ultramontane Catholics, who totally rejected the postrevolutionary world and blamed 1789 on the "atheism" of the Enlightenment, and the Enlightenment on the religious "individualism" of the Reformation. Thus in the early years of the Restoration, the Catholic philosopher Franz von Baader was so moved by Alexander I's Holy Alliance as to visit Russia and press on the emperor still grander spiritual schemes. Baader's aim was to restore a Europe ravaged by revolution through a return to the ecumenical Christianity that had existed not just before the schism of Protestantism, but indeed before the schism of the Western and Eastern churches in 1054. This was essentially Novalis's vision of "Christendom *or* Europe" but with Orthodoxy now counted in. (It was also similar to Leibniz's approach to Peter's Russia.) Even though later rebuffed by Nicholas, Baader continued to praise Russia's Orthodox heritage, untainted by any spirit of modernity, such as had touched even the Papacy.

In a similar spirit the older Schelling, now quite overshadowed by Hegelianism, as he moved toward Catholicism and his final "philosophy of Revelation," was gratified by the unexpected audience he had gained among such Russians as the religious Westernizer Chaadaev and the young Slavophile Ivan Kireevskii, both of whom came to seek his wisdom in Munich. To one of his visitors, Prince Vladimir Odoevskii, he confided that "Russia is destined to great things." Finally, the aged Friedrich Schlegel expressed his satisfaction that thanks to the very "artificiality" of Peter's reforms "many good things already lost in Western Europe had in consequence been preserved in Russia."[58]

Farther to the West, in Burkean England, a similar conservative symbiosis occurred. The Slavophile Alexei Khomiakov, though generally hostile to the West, made an exception in the case of England. He saw her Anglicanism as untainted by the "legalistic and formal" Christianity of Rome, the "individualistic and rationalistic" Protestantism of Germany and the "crypto-atheism" of Hegel, and the revolutionary impiety of France; thus her reformed, Episcopal Church alone could be compared to the apostolic and conciliar purity of Orthodoxy. Similarly, only England in the West preserved the organic social and political institutions celebrated by Burke. Khomiakov visited Oxford at the height of the Tractarian, or High Church, Movement in the 1830s. He there developed a lifelong friendship with the theologian and fellow of Magdalen College William Palmer, who in turn visited Russia three times. Indeed, Palmer soon came to conclusions regarding Orthodoxy analogous to those of John Henry Newman regarding Rome: it represented the one holy and apostolic church while the Anglican communion did not. Although Palmer finally chose Rome, he retained his private views that Orthodoxy was not in schism with the see of Peter. To the end of his life he remained concerned with Russia, publishing an account of his travels there with a preface by (now) Cardinal Newman and composing a lengthy scholarly monograph on the greatest patriarch of Moscow, Nikon.[59]

Admiration for Russia was expressed in a more tough-minded conservative vein by Joseph de Maistre. De Maistre, a radical pessimist, held that man's innate sinfulness made necessary strong moral and social authority, indeed a significant measure of servitude, to ensure the survival of civilization. He therefore viewed the French Revolution as an apocalyptic judgment on the presumptuous belief, engendered by the *philosophes*, that society could sweep away the institutional restraints of the ages and start history anew in a state of natural innocence. He held, further, that once the catastrophe had occurred only armed force could undo it. Thus de Maistre, who had lived out the Napoleonic years in emigration in St. Petersburg, always considered Russia to be a crude but indispensable rampart of antirevolutionary and Christian Europe. To keep Russian force free of Protestant and Enlightened contagion, he sought as early as 1810 to moderate Alexander's zeal for founding universities. He therefore argued to the emperor's minister of education that Russia could not have things both ways—the way of autocracy and serfdom on the one hand and of perfectionistic Enlightenment on the other, of the Old Regime and the New—but that she must choose. And he drove home his argument with one of the more prescient observations ever made by a foreigner about the empire of the tsars: that in a country as raw as Russia, excessive openness to Europe might well end with a *Pougatcheff d'université*.[60]

In a softer conservative mode than de Maistre spoke Freiherr von

Haxthausen, who had been encouraged by St. Petersburg to visit Russia in the hope he would produce an antidote to Custine's defamatory broadside. Both a Catholic and an *alt-Preussisch* conservative, in the early 1840s he traveled the length and breadth of Russia observing her folk life through the prism of Romantic corporatism. In two abundantly documented volumes, he praised the "organic" nature of her peasant communes as a bulwark of Russian stability, and hence also of European order, in the face of new revolutionary threats. He even suggested that Russia could consider herself more blessed than the West, since her communes, like the medieval corporate institutions that Germany was rapidly losing, protected the people from the scourges of atomistic individualism and "pauperism" now afflicting the liberal, industrial nations. While Europe was paying the wages of revolutionary sin with the endemic social convulsions, Russia remained unshaken, since her communes already provided the fraternal virtues that the latest Western utopia, socialism, promised in vain.[61]

Nor were such friendly sentiments toward the Russian people expressed only by conservative Catholics. In the special case of Poland, where Romantic Catholicism was associated with nationalism and revolt, a positive attitude toward Russia emerged on progressive lines. Thus Mickiewicz, an old friend of Pushkin and long a resident of Russia, thought that Russia had two souls, one authentically "Slavonic" and libertarian, the other "Asiatic-German," as expressed in an autocratic-bureaucratic order common to Berlin and St. Petersburg and imposed by both on fractured and martyred Poland. Even the protosocialist Joachim Lelewel and the Polish Democratic Society in emigration after 1830 did not think of Russia as an Oriental despotism but stressed her "slavonic soul" as expressed by the free commune of old Novgorod and the constitutionalism of the Decembrists.[62] Indeed, Lelewel was perhaps the first European thinker to note that the folk commune once common to all Germans and Slavs had survived only in the Russian *mir* or *obshchina*, thereby offering a promise of future democratic development for the tsarist empire. In 1848 the first Russian socialist, Herzen, took up this hint, reinforced it with borrowings from the Slavophiles, and documented it with Haxthausen. Brandishing his anticipatory theory of Russian peasant socialism, he succeeded in convincing such Russophobic democrats as Michelet and Mazzini that the empire of the tsars, after all, might one day become democratically European.[63]

Despite the ideological and polemical cast of these various Russophile views, they often offered an informed grasp of important aspects of Russian life. In particular, it is clear in retrospect that the writings of de Maistre, Palmer, and Haxthausen displayed more real insight than did the shrill pronouncements of Custine, Urquhart, or Marx. Yet it was the latter camp that carried the day before majority opinion in the West, for most Europeans were too terrified by the tsarist state, standing athwart the path of human progress, to sympathize with the values or institutions of the tsar's mute subjects. For Westerners who saw themselves locked in mortal combat with reaction, it was far simpler to believe that since Oriental despotism was enthroned at the top of Russian society, its power must rest on a base of a Tatar barbarism below.

The Russian *Sonderweg*

One cause of the disparity between civilizations now generally called, almost without reflection, Russia and the West was the quickening tempo of European development between 1789 and 1848. Another cause was the penetration of Western civilization itself into Russia, a process proceeding ever faster during the same years when Russia appeared most Asiatic to Europe. By the accession of Nicholas, Russia had at last produced a cultivated and creative elite, which had made as bold as to demand, in the persons of the Decembrists, that tsarism liberalize with the times. Voltaire, it turned out, had been more prescient than Rousseau in wagering on the civilizing outcome of the enlightened despotism of Peter and Catherine.

The cruel paradox of Nicholas's reign was that it was precisely the emergence of this creative European culture in Russia that produced her divorce from Europe. The deepening Westernization of the elite, and especially its liberal political corollary, forced the autocracy onto the defensive at home, thereby making tsarism the natural champion of reaction abroad. This did not mean, however, that Nicholas no longer saw Russia as a European state; it meant, rather, that the Europe to which she belonged was the Europe of his grandmother, the Europe of paternalistic absolutism and the international concert of the previous century. For Nicholas, it was not Russia that had betrayed a once common heritage; it was the West that had done so.

The divorce between the two set the mold for Russia's *Sonderweg* until the fall of tsarism. The problem for imperial Russia was that it had become a full-fledged European Old Regime—in the latter half of Catherine's reign—just as that regime collapsed in its Atlantic heartland. Henceforth Russia's lot was to be permanently out of phase with a West she yet could not cease taking as a model.

The reversal of the autocracy's relation both to Europe and to the educated elite it had called into being occurred around 1815. From Peter to Alexander the autocracy had been the vanguard of civilization in Russia, goading a reluctant population along the ways of modernity, more or less as the *philosophes* had believed. After the Napoleonic Wars the initiative passed from the monarchy to cultivated society, for the process of Europeanization had become too complex to be controlled any longer by the heavy-handed paternalism of the state. Contrary to the opinion of Voltaire, Russia had only been *policée* in the eighteenth century, despite all the glitter of Catherine; but contrary also to the opinion of Custine, Russia was fast becoming *civilisée* in the early nineteenth century, despite the dark shadow of Nicholas.[64]

This transformation was manifested first in the domain of letters. Until Peter, Russian had not really been a written medium, and still less was it a literary one. The country made do with the ancient liturgical language, Church Slavonic. During the eighteenth century contemporary Russian was elaborated into a usable vehicle for the range of European literary forms; and in the three decades after 1820 Russia made her "vernacular revolution" in the domain of high culture. Though this development went unnoticed by Europe during the reign of the frightful imperial gendarme, the poetry of Aleksandr Pushkin and the prose of Nikolai Gogol attained a level of humanism and aesthetic refinement quite comparable to anything in the contemporary West.

Yet these authors did not simply reproduce European values. Just as *die deutsche Bewegung* had earlier effected the cultural construction of Germany, so too the writings of Pushkin and Gogol inaugurated the literary construction of Russia.[65] Both writers were consciously creating an art that "smelled of Russia," as Pushkin said in versifying a folk tale.

He also put this thought in the grand tradition of European letters. And just as Horace had asserted the eternal glory of his work in the ode *Exegi monumentum aere perennius* (I have built a monument more durable than bronze), so Pushkin adapted these lines to proclaim the immortality of his own name throughout the Russian land.[66] Although he did not say so directly, any reader with a smattering of Latin would understand that he now claimed to do for Russian culture what the Bronze Horseman, Peter, had done for Russia's international stature. And this was indeed true: with Pushkin, Russian literature was launched on its golden age, that great half-century of creativity extending to the early 1880s, which would make her a first-class cultural power.

In these same decades Russia for the first time attempted to rise to the challenge of the modern Western political tradition. It has already been noted that Catherine's Enlightenment had, by the 1790s, produced the first critics of autocracy and serfdom, Novikov and Radishchev. Under Alexander I such criticism became a movement, first in the entourage of the emperor himself, notably with the constitutional project of his chief minister Mikhail Speranskii, and then in his army, after its return from Paris, with the more radical projects of the Decembrists. The aspiration of both emperor and rebels was to apply Enlightenment principles to society with the aim of emancipating the peasants and replacing autocracy with responsible government. Though both parties failed, the political goals to which the Enlightenment logically led had at last been put on the national agenda.

The evidence since 1789 indicated, however, that implementing such an agenda is no simple matter. As Jefferson noted apropos of Alexander I's reformist intentions, and in the light of 1789's outcome, it is a "Herculean task" for a government to diffuse enlightenment downward into a "dark" population while at the same time preserving order and stability. Belying the optimism of the *philosophes*, Alexander's failure showed that the engineered humanization of the Old Regime could only give rise to problems of staggering difficulty; and the Decembrists' revolt proved that the penetration of liberal expectations through Old-Regime structures was fraught with unpredictable and perilous consequences. By Nicholas's accession, the autocracy's efforts in the previous century had brought Russia roughly to the point of France at the death of Louis XIV a century earlier: the tsarist empire was beginning its *crise de l'ancien régime*.[67]

Yet the onset of this familiar crisis did not mean that Russia could retrace, in the same manner and at a comparable pace, the development of maritime Europe, any more than Germany, after her mid-eighteenth-century awakening, had been able simply to repeat the previous evolution of France. Still less did the lateness of the stirrings of liberalization in Russia mean that her way would be illumined and made easier by the West's prior experience. On the contrary, as the last and rawest plateau on the West-East cultural gradient, her task could only be more difficult than that of all her predecessors.

After 1815–1825, therefore, Russia was caught in a permanent dilemma. Confronted in every domain, from economic organization to philosophy, by models of achievement too complex to be readily imitated, given the poor resources bequeathed by her antecedent development, she nonetheless could not escape the challenge of adaptation if she were to maintain her position in the conflictual European concert. Yet when she chose to adapt, she was compelled to telescope into decades developments that elsewhere had taken a century, thereby only aggravating the dislocations within her existing skewed and laggard order. Her backwardness served at one and the same time as a psychological stimulus to progress and as a practical impediment to its achievement.

Russia's road to Europe was further complicated by the forced and precipitate manner in which her Old Regime had been launched under Peter. Politically, all power resided in the autocracy and its bureaucracy; socially, all power belonged to the gentry, who officered the armed forces and owned their peasant serfs outright. Until well into the nineteenth century, the nation was almost without a developed civil society and "intermediate" public bodies between the state and service gentry, on the one hand, and the sullen peasant mass, on the other. In particular, serfdom, which in the conditions of pre-1789 Europe had been a national asset furnishing cheap military manpower, after the emancipation of the gentry in 1762, became a liability because of the contrast it offered both with the free elite at home and with postrevolutionary societies abroad. Indeed, the exceptional misery of this 90 percent of the population—half enserfed to private landowners and half to the state—made the "dark" masses a source of instability such as existed in no other European state.

It was in these conditions that the Russian intelligentsia, the last class of men of parts to appear in Europe, emerged as a surrogate civil society.[68] Although the word "intelligentsia" itself would not appear until the next reign, and would not become current until the end of the century,[69] the phenomenon nevertheless was present in the 1830s and 1840s. And this intelligentsia, given the lack of intermediate corporate bodies and of modern economic middle strata, was a more purely ideological substitute for civil society than any of its predecessors in the West. Harassed by the suspicious autocracy above and unheeded by the distrustful peasant mass below, it was perilously suspended in midair.

This intelligentsia first appeared with the competing intellectual camps of the Westernizers and the Slavophiles. The Paris Revolution and the Polish rising of 1830 made clear that Europe was on the march again, and that this time Russia too would be affected (as the Decembrist revolt had already demonstrated). The Slavophiles wanted Russia by all means to avoid this turbulent Western path. They therefore argued that she should develop her native traditions as manifested in the fraternal village *mir*, or commune, and the "conciliar," or consensual, tradition of the Orthodox Church (*sobornost*). These country gentlemen wished to soften, though not dilute, the autocracy by fostering the loyal corrective of a rurally based, spiritual civil society. To make this point in the new historicist mode, they condemned Peter's Westernizing revolution and venerated the devout and patriarchal society of seventeenth-century Muscovy as the icon of the true Russia—in the same way Western Romantic conservatives slightly earlier had idealized the pious and organic Middle Ages.[70] Thus did the Slavophiles offer the vision of a moderate conservative *Sonderweg* for Russia, not so much within Europe as parallel to it.

The mainstream Westernizers, by contrast, sought to make Russia a liberal society by abolishing serfdom and limiting the autocracy. They consequently argued that Peter's work marked the beginning of civilization in Russia, and that his mission should now be brought to its logical conclusion along the lines of the contemporary West, of which Russia was simply an immature part. Accordingly, the majority of the Westernizers took the July Monarchy as a model of what reformed Russia might someday become. For these professors of history, philosophy, and law, there existed no Russian *Sonderweg* at all, but only different degrees of being European.[71]

However, a minority of Westernizers—those best known to history—took as their model the radical opposition to the July Monarchy. The peasant socialism of Herzen and Bakunin has already been mentioned in passing. But how did they arrive at such an aberrant idea? As young men in the early 1840s both proclaimed their commitment to an amorphous revolutionary socialism at the same time as the young Marx.[72] Initially they expected that socialism, as the most advanced stage of history, would triumph first in the West. But the failure of the Revolution of 1848 led them to conclude that Europe's "moment" in history had perhaps passed, and that the socialist future would dawn in "young" Russia. Thus did they hold forth the hope of a radical Russian *Sonderweg*, unfolding within Europe yet leading beyond it—a perspective that indeed would have a future when combined with the more potent theories of Marx. Marx's own itinerary is examined in the next chapter; yet it must be emphasized here that Herzen and Bakunin arrived at socialism in a manner parallel to his.

The pair belonged to the generation of Russian intellectuals who, following the collapse of Russia's Gallic Enlightenment with the Decembrist adventure, sought solace in the inner illumination of German Idealism. Yet they served only a telescoped apprenticeship in philosophy by skipping over Kant's sober *Aufklärung* and plunging directly into the heady pantheisms of Schelling and Hegel. At first this led to political quietism, as it had in Germany. But soon the dynamic of the dialectic had its way; again like the German Left, Herzen and Bakunin liberated themselves from metaphysics by appropriating Ludwig Feuerbach's critique of Hegel's parareligious Absolute as an alienated projection of human aspirations.

Herzen and Bakunin drew the same practical conclusion from this emancipation as did the Left Hegelians, namely, that if the rational powers of German philosophy were combined with the revolutionary activism of France, then Europe would have the formula for a universal socialist upheaval. Indeed, this belief was common to all Europe east of the Rhine; Polish radicals, after their defeat in 1830, sought a similar fusion of German thought with French politics to fuel their inevitable next rising. Thus Herzen and Bakunin reinterpreted the Hegelian dialectic as a radical instrument: to Herzen it was the "algebra of revolution," and to Bakunin it meant that "the desire to destroy is also a creative desire."

At this point, however, the two Russians diverged from the Germans. Borrowing from the Slavophiles, they proclaimed that Russia's peasant commune was already protosocialist, and that on this basis the Russian serf-Prometheus could propel the tsarist empire directly from autocracy to socialism. Young Russia, they believed, could leap over the "bourgeois" West that had betrayed democracy in 1848, thereby showing "advanced" Europe the way to a truly free society. Although the metaphysical underpinnings of this peasant socialism were primitive compared with that of Marx's "proletarian" system, and although Marx abominated both Herzen and Bakunin for their cult of backward peasants, the impulse governing the Russians' vision was akin to that of their German rival. In the two cases, revolutionary intellectuals, by looking westward through the prism of dialectical Idealism, discovered the progressive promise of their respective nations' backwardness.

The consequences of this discovery were momentous. By Nicholas's death in 1855, Russia, though still an immense distance from constitutional liberalism, had been summoned by her radical intelligentsia to aim immediately for socialism. The foreshortening of history is the habitual lot of backward countries; with the emergence of peasant socialism, in the empire of the tsars this foreshortening became the inversion of the hitherto "normal" order of European history. At a time when Russia's real problem was autocracy and serfdom, converting a part of her elite to the West's most radical politics so distorted the national agenda as to make the perfect egalitarian society an immediate goal.

For the rest of the century the precocious primacy of socialism over liberalism would embolden the Russian opposition quite out of proportion to its numbers. Correspondingly, the autocracy was made more unbending, an attitude reinforced by another aspect of Russia's backwardness: the spectre of a new peasant *Pugachevshchina*. This syndrome of fears first took form under Nicholas, who beginning in the period 1825–1830 saw his empire threatened with disintegration from combined foreign contagion and internal subversion. Each time Europe entered into revolutionary ferment, therefore, he felt Russia had no choice but to attempt whatever international intervention was feasible. At the same time he cordoned off his subjects from baleful alien influences, restricting their right to travel abroad, controlling their import of foreign books, and censoring all that they found to read at home—as Custine had endlessly stressed.

Nicholas justified these policies by agreeing with his Western detractors that Russia was indeed not a part of their seditious new Europe. She was part of the true Europe to which she had been introduced by Peter and which had been reestablished by Alexander's Holy Alliance. Mixing Petrine tradition with revealed religion and a dash of the age's new sense of national uniqueness, Nicholas proclaimed that Russia's eternal way was "Orthodoxy, Autocracy, Nationality."[73] Taking its stand on this ultraconservative *Sonderweg*, the autocracy adamantly refused to go beyond cultural to political Europeanization for the rest of its existence.

The pressure generated by Europe's advance, combined with the drag of native backwardness, would continue until 1917 to complicate Russia's way to modernity. It is the action of these two forces, not the hoary memory of the Sacred Palace of Byzantium or of the Mongols' Golden Horde, that constitutes the true anomaly of Russia's modern history. The quantitative burden of her backwardness has been so much greater than her neighbors' as to produce, by the twentieth century, a qualitative difference in her destiny.

Russia Outcast

The predominant European judgment of Russia as Oriental soon received final and apparently irrefutable confirmation. Disappointed after the Revolution of 1830 by the modest achievements of classical liberalism in power and appalled by the dislocations resulting from early industrialism, progressives dreamed ever bolder dreams of an ultimate liberating upheaval, a universal 1789, in the name of humanity, progress, and democracy. In Central Europe they dreamed of national liberation as well. Europe—a term now understood usually to exclude Russia—stood on the eve of its first general revolution. With a euphoric anticipation, during the Springtime of the Peoples all of Europe's discontented looked forward to the imminent arrival of a Romantic-Enlightened millennium. Though divided by a variety of concrete goals, ranging from extension of the suffrage to establishment of a socialist republic, the European Left was nonetheless united, and its common faith was warmed, by recognition of a single enemy: the surviving Old Regime, as defined by the Vienna treaties, blessed by the Holy Alliance, and defended by the tsarist barbarians. The forthcoming revolution, clearly, would have to be a revolution against Russia.

When the long-awaited upheaval at last arrived in 1848, it produced a paroxysm of Russophobic rage as universal as the revolution itself. Indeed, during 1848 and its aftermath the spectre haunting Europe was not Marx's variety of Communism, a movement almost unnoticed at the time, but Nicholas and his Cossacks. On May 15 revolutionary socialism made its first appearance on the European stage, and precisely in response to this Russian spectre. Auguste Blanqui and Armand Barbès, at the head of a band of workers, invaded the Chamber of Deputies in an effort to overthrow the political republic for a social one; their rallying cry was war to drive Russia out of Poland and all Europe. After the insurrection of the June Days, the Russian spectre appeared all the more terrible to the Left, since European conservatives now did not hesitate to call for a second coming of the Cossacks in answer to this second coming of 1789; only this could save a "decadent" West from the furies of democracy, just as the Cossacks had delivered Europe from the tyranny of Bonaparte in 1813–14. Indeed, Napoleon himself had declared: "l'Europe sera républicaine ou elle sera cosaque!"[74]

When the revolution failed almost everywhere to achieve even its minimal goals of political democracy and national unification (let alone socialism), in much of Europe this outcome could, with varying degrees of plausibility, be blamed on Russia. And even in ultraconservative quarters, which had welcomed Nicholas's armed intervention in Hungary in 1849, the fear was expressed that Russia's strength could threaten as well as save. Thus the marquis de Valdegamas, Donoso Cortés, in 1850 caused an international sensation by warning in the Spanish parliament that revolutionary anarchy and socialism had so weakened Europe as to make her vulnerable, like ancient Rome, to conquest by the barbarians of Slavdom under Russia.[75]

Although Nicholas's threat, on the outbreak of revolution, of marching to the Rhine turned out to be rhetorical, German liberals in fact had reason to revile him for the political support he gave his indecisive brother-in-law, Frederick William IV of Prussia, in resisting the democratic aspirations of both the Diet in Berlin and the National Assembly in Frankfurt. When the assembly declared that German unification would bring with it Polish liberation, Nicholas redoubled his pressure on Berlin. Thus when Frederick William finally spurned the constitutional "crown of shame" offered by the assembly, thereby wrecking the chances for a liberal-national triumph in Germany, the Russian tsar deserved his share of the obloquy that enveloped the two brothers-in-law. German nationalists received further reason to hate Russia when Nicholas, through a show of naval force in the Baltic, thwarted the efforts of both the Frankfurt Assembly and the Prussian king to wrest the duchies of Schleswig-Holstein from Denmark. Nationalist rage was compounded in 1850, when Russia vetoed a Prussian and princely scheme of German unification in the name of the Vienna treaties, almost completely restoring the prerevolutionary status quo in Germany.

More nefarious still in Western eyes was Russia's role in the Habsburg domains. Russia contributed both diplomatic support and money to Austria's struggle against the revolution in her north Italian provinces. He exulted publicly when Marshall Joseph Radetzky retook Milan from Piedmont and later when Prince Alfred Windischgrätz recaptured Prague and Vienna from democracy. The most heinous Russian deed during the entire revolution, however, was the 1849 intervention against the democratic nationalism of Hungary, where Nicholas went beyond political pressure to overt military action. On the appeal of the Austrian emperor, Franz-Joseph, the tsar dispatched 200,000 men under the viceroy of Poland, Prince Ivan Paskevich, to crush the Hungarian Republic led by Louis Kossuth and inspired by the poet Petöfi. The Russians were all the more ruthless in this action because the Hungarians were aided by numerous Polish volunteers, driven from their homeland when the same Paskevich had repressed the constitutional regime in Warsaw in 1831. The Cossacks had at last come; and without them it is doubtful that Franz-Joseph could have won alone in Budapest. For the second time in less than twenty years the primitive force of Russian peasant soldiers had deprived an ancient European people of its renascent liberty. As a codicil to this testament of crime Nicholas even found time to thwart, again by military occupation, the timid national and constitutional aspirations of the Romanians.

By the end of these campaigns, Nicholas, together with his Hohenzollern and Habsburg "brothers," had reaffirmed the Vienna treaties, reconsecrated the Holy Alliance, and restored the Restoration everywhere east of the Rhine. Before the revolution, Russia had stood guilty of extinguishing Poland's liberties; after it, the liberties of Hungary, Germany, and Italy as well could be counted the victims of either her might or her machinations. The devastation staggered the liberal imagination. Even when the failure of the Central European revolutions was the result of internal weakness more than of Russian intervention—as was clearly the case in Germany and Italy—this very fact made it more bearable psychologically to seek an external scapegoat in the Third Section and the Cossacks of Nicholas. As the party of humanity, in exile in London or Geneva brooded over its defeat, Russia became the *diabolus ex machina* of the revolutionary tragedy. By 1850, Russia stood without a friend in Europe save the masters of Berlin and Vienna and such of their servants as Ambassador Otto von Bismarck or Chancellor Prince Felix Schwarzenberg. Even to the Prussian and Austrian sovereigns, their Russian brother at times appeared too big.

The hatred of Russia now felt by men of civilized values was intensified by the fact that she had become a monstrous anachronism socially. Prussia had abolished serfdom after her defeat by Napoleon in 1806, and Austria had liquidated it under the impact of the Revolution of 1848. Only in Russia did this barbarous institution remain intact and continue to find apologists. Politically, even the Junker king, his hand forced by the revolution, had finally granted the semblance of a constitution in 1849, whereas Nicholas celebrated a cult of autocracy more retrograde than that of Peter. The years following 1848 thus marked Russia's farthest remove from Europe since the two had first made significant contact a century and a half before. Although politically and militarily triumphant over half the continent, morally Russia had been cast into the outer darkness of Asia, from which, it was now clear, she should never have been allowed to emerge.

In response, after 1848 Nicholas withdrew his outcast nation to winter quarters and retrenchment in cultural isolation. Amidst this withdrawal Russia completed her sesquicentennial as a European power.

What, then, was the balance sheet of her gains for his hyperborean reign? And what moral may be drawn from the story of Russia's alienation from Europe for understanding the fortunes of war and diplomacy? In part, the pattern of Western reactions is familiar, representing a continuation of the rational response to Russian policy exhibited by the dynastic establishment of the eighteenth century. In larger part, however, the pattern is new, reflecting the *volte-face* of enlightened opinion regarding Russia.

To begin with the familiar, after 1815 Russia's civilization continued to be felt as kindred, and so was regarded as a neutral factor in international affairs, by Europe's other two Old Regimes, Prussia and Austria. It does not follow that they invariably viewed Russia's international undertakings with a benign eye; but it does follow that their conflicts with her stemmed from considerations of political interest. Such had been the case when Austria at the Congress of Vienna temporarily aligned herself with England and France to limit Russia's gains in Poland, and when Prussia in 1850 incurred the combined opposition of Russia and Austria by attempting to unify Germany under her hegemony.

Only power, however, was at issue in such conflicts. There was never a question of good versus evil, civilization versus barbarism. And even such conflicts were exceptions in the age of the Holy Alliance, for the ideological and social pressures that pitted the Eastern Three against the Western Two tended to submerge political differences within the Eastern camp. In that part of Europe where a rational view of Russian policy prevailed, potential conflicts were subordinated—as in the great crises of 1830 and 1848—to a more visceral instinct of cohesion among the menaced societies of the Old Regime. This subordination in turn meant submission, with whatever qualms, to the leadership of Russia, alone impregnable among the Eastern Three. To play rational power politics at all, it was necessary to survive, and for the Central European regimes in the early nineteenth century an alliance with Russia was the first condition of survival.

More interesting than this calculated concord was the strident hostility toward Russia displayed by maritime Europe. Most Westerners had come to hold, in the words of one London editorialist, that the Muscovites were not "accessible to the ordinary motives of the human family." Russia's foreign policies were regarded by the liberal West as what would later be designated imperialism and aggression but which were then called the "dark ambitions of despotism."[76] Yet what justification existed for such allegations?

True, in 1801 Russia had annexed Georgia. She did so, however, on the invitation of Georgia's last prince, no longer able to defend his Orthodox lands against the predatory Turks. True, too, Russia had proceeded from this new base during the next half-century to absorb the rest of Transcaucasia, while at the same time scoring gains over Persia and beginning to advance into Central Asia. Yet these were turbulent and lawless regions that presented a danger to Russia's exposed southern frontier—territories, in short, of the sort that the British in India and the French in Algeria thought it legitimate to "pacify" during the same period. Nor did Russia's Asian advance touch the interests of any civilized power, since it still left her armies a phenomenal distance from India and was conducted, contrary to London's suspicions, quite without designs on the subcontinent.

It is true also that Russian forces had been conspicuously active in Poland and Hungary, that the weight of her diplomacy was felt heavily throughout Central Europe, and that she had twice threatened to march to the Rhine. Yet the talk about the Rhine was mere rodomontade, not the expression of a serious intent to launch a crusade against Western liberalism. In Central Europe, though Russia clearly did what she could diplomatically to shore up her natural allies, she was careful not to become involved militarily. Sincerely though Nicholas detested all revolution, he was no Don Quixote of international reaction, and as a practical matter, he wished to reserve his forces for defense of the immediate interests of his empire. This aim, in 1848 as in 1830, meant above all keeping control of Poland, both because it served as the advance bastion of Russian power in Europe and because a liberated and liberal Polish state could only have a disruptive effect on the rest of his empire. Even Nicholas's intervention in Hungary was dictated largely by this concern: if the Hungarians, aided as they were by Polish volunteers, had succeeded in breaking away from Vienna, Poland itself would surely have attempted to imitate their example. It was to this set of limited imperatives that Nicholas's seemingly megalomaniac European policy boiled down.

Actually, Russia's numerous European enterprises under Nicholas failed to net her a verst of new territory; nor had she sought to acquire any. On the contrary, instead of profiting from the disarray of Prussia and Austria in 1848 to make gains at their expense, after the manner of Catherine during the French Revolution, Russia bent all her efforts to restoring her allies to their full territorial as well as social integrity. Indeed, after 1815 Russia's whole policy toward Europe, like her Polish policy, was one long holding operation against liberal nationalism, a conservative rather than an aggressive stance. It is striking that during the thirty years of Nicholas's reign—when Russia appeared more threatening to the West than ever before in her history or than she ever would again until Stalin—she failed for the first time since Peter to register any westward advance.

Whence, then, did Europe's obsession with Russia's "dark ambitions" derive? The most obvious rational cause of this foreboding was the "Eastern Question," that is, the anticipated dissolution of the Ottoman Empire, a matter which after all brought or threatened to bring Nicholas's armies to Constantinople and the Straits on four occasions in twenty-five years.[77] On this issue Westerners could most plausibly evoke the idea of Russian megalomania.

As tension mounted over the Straits, learned specialists like the historian of Byzantium Jakob Fallmerayer, in his *Fragmente aus dem Orient*, could elaborate this fear in the spirit of the new historicism. He brought all the weight of his scholarship to show that "Tsargrad," or Constantinople, was the cradle of Russia's culture and the source of the imperial heritage of East Rome whose double-headed eagles, and ambitions, she still flaunted. It was only to be expected, the argument ran, that Russia should be drawn by an atavistic urge to the home of the despotic and Caesaro-papist messianism she continued to embody. Nor did Fallmerayer, and such of his journalistic popularizers as Marx, fail to draw the political conclusion that if Russia triumphed in the Balkans her ultimate hegemony over all Europe would be assured.[78] The Eastern Question clearly seemed to provide a case of Russian imperialism sufficiently blatant to justify Europe's worst apprehensions.

Now it is true that Nicholas would not have been averse to acquiring Constantinople under appropriate conditions, or at least to obtaining paramount influence there; it is also true that such a breakthrough to the Mediterranean would have represented a shift in the European balance of power. Even so, access to the Aegean would not have made Russia a major naval power; and occupation of any significant portion of Turkey would have been as troublesome as occupation of Poland or the North Caucasus. Moreover, Russia's actual involvement in Turkey's affairs under Nicholas came about in more prosaic fashion and was pursued much less from metaphysical, pan-Orthodox motives than Europe supposed. Yet it brought the apogee of Western-Russian estrangement in the nineteenth century.[79]

Nicholas first intervened in Turkey in 1828–29 as a result of the crisis provoked by the Greek revolt and the arrival of the forces of the Porte's powerful Egyptian vassal, Mehemet Ali, to crush the insurgents. Acting at first in concert with Great Britain and France, then, as they grew hesitant, acting alone, the tsar sought to impose by force of arms an orderly settlement of Turkey's internal affairs which would at the same time guarantee his own interests in the area. Advancing eventually as far as Adrianople, he exacted as the price of such a settlement the cession of southern Bessarabia, thereby bringing his frontiers to the mouth of the Danube. This was Russia's one European acquisition under Nicholas, though not from a Western power. The war had as a second result Greek independence. Yet this victory gave more influence in the Balkans to the West than to Russia, for constitutional Greece soon gravitated into the orbit of the maritime powers.

Nicholas's second intervention came in 1833, when Mehemet Ali again moved north, this time nearly destroying his nominal Ottoman master: Russia came to the sultan's "rescue" by landing troops in the Bosphorus. As the price for this aid, Nicholas extorted the Porte's agreement to the Treaty of Unkiar Skelessi, which gave St. Petersburg a virtual protectorate over Turkey, theoretically with broad rights to intervene in her internal affairs. Never before had Russian power loomed so large in the East, and all of Europe took serious alarm. Thus, when in 1839–40 Mehemet Ali erupted a third time, Russia was prevented from repeating the unilateral triumph of Unkiar Skelessi by the concerted action of the powers, who intervened to jointly guarantee Turkey's territorial integrity.

This collective assurance of stability along Russia's southern border and the closing of the Straits to foreign warships were acceptable to Nicholas as temporary measures. At the same time, he sensibly feared that the Ottoman state would eventually disintegrate under the impact of further crises. He began to make overtures, particularly to the British, to convince the powers that they should consider an orderly and equable partition of Turkey among themselves in order to forestall chaos in the Near East. But as word of these advances spread abroad, Europe was reminded of the scandalous fate of Poland under Catherine the Great, which had also enjoyed Russia's "protection," and the tsar's diplomatic frankness was interpreted as a cloak for sinister ambitions.

In this mood of mounting distrust, a trivial dispute in 1853–54 between France and Russia over the respective rights of Catholics and Orthodox in the Holy Places of Palestine led to a crisis which diplomacy could not resolve. In this impasse, Nicholas clumsily attempted to impose his solution on the Porte by reoccupying its Romanian, or Danubian, Principalities, evacuated after the Revolution of 1848. The maritime powers, suspecting him of annexationist designs, sprang to Turkey's defense with a surprise attack on his home territory in the Crimea. And hitherto friendly Austria applied diplomatic pressure and bellicose threats to oblige Nicholas to withdraw from the Danubian Principalities and to divert much-needed Russian forces from his sagging Crimean front.

In this "most unnecessary of wars," Nicholas's aim was not to achieve unilateral territorial aggrandizement. Rather, his conduct in the Eastern Question was of a piece with that commitment to a conventional balance of power which characterized his policies toward Central Europe. He sought above all to secure agreement about Turkey's future with the responsible governments of Europe. His main miscalculation involved the citizenry of the maritime powers, who turned out to be too overwrought ideologically to respond with similar Old-Regime calculations. And it was from this ideological incompatibility that the conflict derived.

From the vantage of the Winter Palace the Crimean imbroglio appeared as an excessive, almost incomprehensible reaction to a reasonable international stance. Nicholas, as a conservative sovereign whose numerous difficulties at home made him fearful of disorder everywhere, was interested primarily in maintaining quiet throughout Europe as much as in his own domains. Yet in addition to his Polish troubles, he had a worrisome problem on his southern border in the form of what he called the "sick man of Europe," Turkey, whose impending demise threatened to precipitate a whole zone of the continent into chaos, with what frightful consequences for neighboring states no one could foretell. Then, too, he had legitimate strategic interests to safeguard, which centered on the question of who would control the Straits leading to his Black Sea coast, and under what conditions passage through them would be open. Since at the same time he believed in an evenly adjusted balance of power within the European concert, in the best Old-Regime tradition, he understood that his own rights at the Straits could be secured only if other interested sovereigns participated in whatever settlement was made of Turkey's affairs.

As one Mehemet Ali crisis after another convulsed the "sick man," Nicholas tried to interest the responsible powers in arriving at a common settlement before anarchy engulfed the Balkans. But on each occasion when he was obliged to show his armies in the south in order to prevent the worst, a clamor was raised against him in the West. The turbulent French, from whom little better was to be expected in view of their record since 1789 and their recent election of a new Bonaparte, cried revenge for the humiliations of the Congress of Vienna and for martyred Poland. Thus it was hardly surprising that they should covertly encourage Mehemet Ali and incite the Latin monks of Palestine to usurp the rights of other faiths. But the conservative British were a different matter; for this was the great antirevolutionary land of Burke and the duke of Wellington, Russia's old ally against Napoleonic France, a nation which Nicholas had visited as a young man and admired only second to Prussia. Yet the English were now in alliance with Bonaparte, and their press waxed hysterical about Nicholas's supposed ambition and the "menace" he constituted for the "order" of Europe— he who stood only for order. Even the Austrians, "ungrateful" for Nicholas's aid in 1849, refused to believe that his power would always be used for the benefit of the concert of reasonable states.[80] Viewed from the last redoubt of the integral Old Regime that the Winter Palace had become by 1854, Europe appeared strange and contradictory indeed.

The alarm of the Austrians was largely rational, since the conflict of interests between them and their huge protector was real and immediate. If Russia advanced farther into the Balkans, all avenues of expansion would be closed to the Habsburgs, and their international security would become much too dependent on Russian good will. The French and the British, however, on their road to war gave one of the least rational performances in modern international politics. Indeed, in the Crimean conflict metaphysical messianism was preponderantly on the side of the liberal heirs of *les lumières*. To be sure, messianic impulses were displayed on the Russian side as well, most notably by the Slavophiles and the Russian envoy to Constantinople, Aleksandr Menshikov; but such figures had far less influence on policy than did the ideologically inflamed British and French press.

The French had a long-standing involvement in Levantine trade and an even more venerable role as protector of Latin Christians in the

Near East, both interests dating back to their Old-Regime connection with the Porte, indeed to the Crusades. In the Crimean affair, however, the French were moved far less by these interests, which were hardly menaced by Russian policy, than by the desire to undo the Vienna settlement, guaranteed by Russia, and the quarantine it imposed on their international ambitions. In pursuing this aim, the French sought also to promote the forces of heroic progressivism embodied by the Napoleonic legend. For this mission, whether exercised for the liberation of Italy, Poland, or the Holy Places, always redounded to the greater glory both of France and of "civilization."

Even more interesting and less rational was the case of the British. Industrial Britain had a growing, if recently acquired, interest in commerce with Turkey. She had an even greater strategic stake in keeping Russian naval power bottled up in the Black Sea and out of the Mediterranean. Substantial though these points of conflict were, they were not the whole story, for England had encountered Russian naval power in the Mediterranean before and had displayed a far milder reaction. And she had been Nicholas's naval ally as recently as the campaign of 1829. But the great case in point for understanding Britain's role in the Crimea is the reign of Catherine.

Catherine had been motivated by the most genuine imperialism. To recall: in two Turkish wars she had brought Russian power across the southern steppes to the shore of the Black Sea; and between 1787 and 1792 she had escalated her hitherto nominal right of protectorate over Turkey's Balkan Christian subjects into a Greek project aiming at the dismemberment of the Ottoman state and the reestablishment of a revived Orthodox empire at Constantinople. Only the actual destruction of Poland—but by three powers, not one—was a more brutal assault on the European balance of power. Despite her messianic designs on Turkey, however, Catherine had marched her armies into the Balkans, and even sailed her fleet past Dover into the Mediterranean, without provoking Albion's ire. Not even the direct challenge of Armed Neutrality during the War of American Independence elicited more than the routine protest that eighteenth-century states expressed in such concrete conflicts of interest. Yet throughout most of the nine-

158   teenth century, the British were constantly agitated by the Russian menace around the rim of Asia, concerned not only with the real problem of the Straits but also with such chimeras as Russia marching over the Himalayas to India.

Changing patterns of trade and sea power alone did not account for this dramatic reversal of British attitudes. The full answer lay in the new mood of England after the reform of 1832. No longer the conservative land of Burke and Wellington, she had assumed her proud Victorian role as standard-bearer of Whig progress for the lesser breeds of Europe—the St. George of constitutional liberalism and champion of such causes as Greek and Italian independence. It was this Whig progressivism that stimulated the public's hostility to all "continental despotism," of which Russia was the quintessential representative, and fed the Russophobic fury of Urquhart and Marx. The most striking instance of such ideologically driven foreign policy came in the reign of Nicholas, of all Russian sovereigns since Peter the least imperialistic and most devoted to accommodation with the status quo powers, especially Britain.

Yet to the maritime powers of the West Nicholas indeed appeared sinister. The real issue between him and his antagonists, however, was not his imperialism but the contest between the Old Regime and the New. The Straits were largely the symbol and the focus of liberal Europe's moral indignation at the presence at their side of this monstrous relic of despotism. Although they could not reach him in Poland or in Hungary, they could at least strike at him through the Straits.

But when they struck in the Crimea, in 1854, they discovered that the spectre that had been haunting them since 1830 was no more than an insubstantial ghost out of the past, a monstrous force in their imagination only. For during the forty years since the Russian army's triumphant march across the continent to Paris, behind the facade of imperial power the "tsarist hordes," like everything else over which Nicholas presided, had become a sorry remnant of an earlier age. Russia had found it easy enough to defeat the isolated Poles and Hungarians or the Asiatic Turks. But when she confronted the industrially based power of England and France, the largest army in Europe was routed on its own soil. Overcome by shame, the hyperborean gendarme himself melted away (or perhaps took his life) in his redoubt of the Winter Palace, amidst the ruin of his policies.

The liberals of the West thus feared tsarism most when it had passed its prime, in the early nineteenth century, whereas they had trusted it most when it was at the height of its powers, in the late eighteenth century. After the Crimean War, tsarism would never seriously disquiet the West again, although a residual fear of it persisted into the twentieth century. Henceforth imperial Russia would lose every major struggle in which she engaged. In a new war with Turkey in 1877–78, although she painfully got as far as the suburbs of Constantinople, she was deprived diplomatically of full victory by the powers at the Congress of Berlin; in the conflict of 1904–5 with Japan she was squarely defeated on land at Mukden and at sea at Tsushima by an Asiatic upstart. And in 1917 the inability of the Russian Old Regime to wage successful modern war spelled its doom.

RUSSIA AS EUROPE REGAINED: 1855–1914

Two souls, alas! reside within my breast
And each withdraws from, and repels, its brother:
One clings to the world with ardent desire,
The other soars impassioned from the dust,
To the higher spirits and Elysian fields.

—Goethe, *Faust*

n the early nineteenth century, Westerners had viewed Russia as a "civilization" apart and by and large decided that her lack of "culture" excluded her from authentic Europe. In the second half of the nineteenth century they still saw Russia as sui generis but progressively softened this perception until, by the early twentieth century, she appeared not as an alien entity but as one national culture within a common European civilization. The older, negative image hardly disappeared, but it receded ever farther into the background.

This change of perspective resulted from major changes in both Russia and the West after 1856. In the 1860s Russia experienced her second revolution from above since becoming a European power. Her first revolution from above, that of Peter, had transformed Muscovy's universal service state into a crude version of a contemporary European military absolutism. Catherine had liberalized this Petrine structure enough to create a rudimentary but genuine European Old Regime; and under Alexander I and Nicholas I further Europeanization bore fruit in an intelligentsia and a secular national culture. On this basis, Russia's second revolution from above, that of Alexander II, was able to narrow the gap between Russia and the West more dramatically than at any time since Peter. The Great Reforms of the 1860s emancipated the peasants and established independent courts and local elective assemblies, thereby giving Russia the basis of a modern civil society.

Equally important changes occurred in the West around 1870. With the Second English Reform Bill of 1867 and the foundation of the

Third French Republic in 1870, liberalism was at last securely in control in maritime Europe. This liberalism, however, was much bolder than that of the first half of the century: in France the July Monarchy's property suffrage was discarded completely for universal (manhood) suffrage, and in England the limited franchise of the Whigs was greatly extended. The two countries were now closer politically to the United States than they were to Europe east of the Rhine.

Similarly profound changes occurred in Central Europe between 1862 and 1870, though with a different valence. In 1848 national-constitutional forces had failed to wrest the Germanies from the Old Regime, obtaining only a modest constitution granted from above. After 1862 Bismarck definitively routed these forces by appropriating a part of their program and distorting the rest. He realized the national ideal of unification in 1870 by the bayonets of the Prussian aristocratic caste, and he undercut liberal constitutionalism by conceding a Reichstag with universal suffrage but subordinated to a semiautocratic monarchy and limited by the class suffrage of the dominant federal state, Prussia. In Germany's wake the Austrian monarchy at long last reformed itself, creating through the Compromise *(Ausgleich)* of 1867 with Hungary a second hybrid traditional-modern order in Central Europe.

As a result of these transformations a new alignment of European states, foreshadowed in the failed Revolution of 1848, came fully into the open. After 1870 the division of the continent between the maritime powers and the courts of the North was no longer pertinent. Europe was now separated into three rather than two zones: the mature liberal society of the maritime West; the mixed world of what was later called Mitteleuropa; and the reformed yet still Old Regime of Russia. Russia, in other words, was confronted by two Wests, a farther and a hither Europe.

In both of these Wests, however, two cultural souls contended for the body European, as ever new varieties of generic enlightenment were challenged by ever more resistant mutations of generic Romanticism. Yet in each West a different soul tended to predominate. During the midcentury in the farther West the majority, extrapolating from the empiricism of the Encyclopedists and the utilitarianism of the Benthamites, and blending these traditions with the positivism of Auguste Comte, believed that unilinear progress toward constitutional democracy and a rational economic order was the norm of history. Although Romanticism and conservatism, of course, still prospered in this farther West, until late in the century they did so in the shadow of progressive positivism. By contrast, in Mitteleuropa, in high tension with its more modern maritime neighbors, the midcentury turn to positivism proved less potent and the hold of Romanticism more tenacious. Then, at the fin de siècle in both West and Center the Romantic heritage was transformed into a new antirationalism, with the mission of combating the "sickness" of modern civilization through the creation of a more aesthetic, spiritual culture. Yet given Central Europe's stronger Romantic tradition, the new antirationalism there was more precocious, and went deeper, than in the Atlantic West.

Thus, Russia's Great Reforms appeared to part of European opinion as a harbinger of her "convergence" with universal civilization, whereas to those disillusioned with that civilization, her archaic rural society seemed an oasis of primal "Slavic soul," a spiritual quality rapidly disappearing in the industrial, urban world of the West. In view of the differences within that world, farther Europe tended to privilege Russia's potential for convergence with progressive norms, while hither Europe was given to fantasizing about the spirituality of her Eastern neighbor. So Russia, even as she was regained for Europe, continued, Janus-like, to be emblazoned with her two-headed eagle: observed from the Left, she signified convergence, and from the Right she betokened soul.

OBVERSE: THE CURVE OF CONVERGENCE

For I dipt into the future, far as human eye could
  see,

. . .

Saw the heavens full with commerce, argosies
  of magic sails,
Pilots of the purple twilight, dropping down with
  costly bales;

. . .

Till the war-drum throbb'd no longer, and the
  battle-flags were furl'd
In the Parliament of man, the Federation of the
  world.

. . .

Let the great world spin for ever down the
  ringing grooves of change.

. . .

Better fifty years of Europe than a cycle of
  Cathay.

—Tennyson, "Locksley Hall" (1842)

You may be a poet if you wish,
But a citizen you have to be
And what is meant by citizen?
A worthy son of the fatherland.
Let us produce merchants, officers,
Bourgeois, officials, improving landlords,
We've had quite enough of poets,
What we need is citizens, more citizens!

—Nikolai Nekrasov,
"The Poet and the Citizen" (1860)

Of the several causes for this transformation the most obvious, though not necessarily the most important, was the fact that following the Crimean debacle Russia was no longer the foremost military power of the continent. After 1870, Russian strength appeared still further diminished when, as a result of the Franco-Prussian War, European military supremacy passed to Bismarckian Germany. To be sure, the British still showed signs of hysteria every time the Muscovite bear advanced in the Balkans, as in 1877–78, or in Central Asia, as in the 1880s; and even as late as 1904, Nicholas II's designs on the Far East provoked an anachronistic panic over the accidental clash of Russian warships with British fishing trawlers in the Dogger Bank incident off Dover. It was not until minuscule Japan in 1905 defeated mammoth Russia on both land and sea, demonstrating the latter's gross ineptitude as an imperialist, that England at last gave up the ancient ghost of Urquhart and began to worry instead about the growing threat of German naval armament.

But no one else in Europe was fooled for so long. After 1870, the French had much more cause to fear Germany than Russia. Indeed, hostility to Germany in republican France helped kindle a romantic sympathy for Russia, tsarist though she remained, thus preparing the way for a military alliance with the enemy of the two Napoleons. Most discerning about St. Petersburg's real power and intentions, however, was official Germany, as opposed to certain demagogic pan-German elements. Bismarckian Prussia and later the German empire long enjoyed cordial relations with official Russia. Even after Bismarck's fall in 1890 brought about less friendly relations, imperial Germany still felt that her security was amply guaranteed by the contrast between her military and economic superiority and Russia's invariably inadequate attempts to rejuvenate her war machine. And indeed, despite the efforts of Army Minister Dmitrii Miliutin following the lesson of 1870 and those of his successor, Vladimir Sukhomlinov, after the lesson of 1905, that machine always turned out to be one war behind the times. Germany therefore feared neither a Russia in isolation nor one in alliance with France alone, for until the Anglo-Russian Convention of 1907 she cherished the belief that England could be used as a counterweight to such a coalition, and thereafter she expected that in a crisis England would remain neutral. By degrees, between 1856 and 1905 the spectre of the Russian menace to civilization faded throughout Europe. No longer an alien force of monstrous dimensions, Russia became once again, as in the eighteenth century, simply another of the Great Powers and, at that, hardly one of the most formidable among them. Since Westerners feared her less, they had the serenity of spirit to understand her more.

Russia Reformed

Just as important in producing a change of perspective was the convergence of social and political forms between Russia and the West marked by the Great Reforms.[1] The autocracy was driven to enact them by the Crimean debacle, just as Prussia had been forced to reform after her defeat by Napoleon in 1806. Since Russia, like Prussia, was essentially a military absolutism, failure in war was the severest possible condemnation of her internal structures; and in 1856 the verdict of arms was that Nicholas's attempt to maintain the iron autocracy of Peter was no longer tenable. Russia had no choice but to adapt to the ever higher level of achievement offered by industrial and liberal Europe, or else go under as a power.

Russia's Great Reforms of 1860–1874 were similar in all major particulars to the Prussian reforms of 1807–1812. Like the latter, they aimed to implement that part of the French revolutionary agenda which was compatible with preserving the two pillars of the Old Regime: absolutism in politics and aristocratic supremacy in society. And so, as the terminus of the West-East cultural gradient, Russia once again followed, with a fifty-year lag, the Prussian model of adapting to westernmost Europe's challenge, just as she had done since the Great Elector and Peter I.

The cornerstone of the reforms was the abolition, in 1861, of the great social anomaly that set Russia apart from civilized Europe, serfdom. In 1864 a modicum of local self-government was introduced by establishing elected zemstvos in most provinces, followed in 1870 by the creation of (more modest) municipal dumas in the major cities. In 1864 also, a judicial system was introduced providing for trial by jury and an independent judiciary and founded on the standard Western principles of due process of law, irremovable judges, and respect for individual rights. Education at all levels was expanded, and the universities were granted autonomy. And in 1874 Russia's transformation was capped with the most nearly "democratic" of all the reforms, universal military service.

Even more boldly, in 1861 broad autonomy and parliamentary government were accorded the Grand Duchy of Finland. And efforts were made to achieve a similar solution to the eternal problem of Poland by, in effect, restoring the constitution of 1815–1830. But what Alexander adamantly refused to consider was the "crowning of the edifice" hoped for by liberals: a national legislative assembly. As he constantly repeated: "surtout, pas d'Assemblée de notables!"—the aristocratic body which had been the prelude to the revolutionary Estates General of 1789. However timid Russia's reforms might appear to Westerners after 1848, when even Prussia had a parliament, they at least indicated that civilized men with comprehensible human aspirations existed behind the hitherto opaque mask of autocracy. Thus, in the wake of the Great Reforms, Russia acquired features which in the Western view she had lacked under Nicholas: a political personality, a civil society independent of the state, and a capacity for change.

But, as Tocqueville had noted of Louis XVI's enlightened minister, Turgot, "the most dangerous moment for a bad government is when it starts to reform itself." For reform unleashes expectations in society that a genuinely bad government can neither readily satisfy nor effectively repress. Less fortunate than Prussia after 1806, Russia in the wake of 1861 was therefore confronted with a runaway movement from below for more radical change than existing structures could accommodate. No sooner had the Emancipation edict been published than its terms—inevitably a compromise between peasant and gentry interests—led to cries of "swindle" and "betrayal" from the Left intelligentsia. This circumstance transformed Russian peasant socialism, hitherto a merely cerebral affair in the minds of a handful of émigrés, into an embryonic revolutionary movement within Russia herself. Herzen, now writing freely abroad, launched the slogan: "To the people!"[2]

This appeal fell on fertile ground among the "nihilists" of the 1860s. With their appearance, emerging Russian civil society reached the great caesura in its development: the displacement, in Ivan Turgenev's famous dichotomy, of the aristocratic, idealist, and liberal "fathers" of the 1840s by the plebeian, materialistic, and socialist "sons" of the 1860s. The great figure in this new generation was Nikolai Chernyshevskii. He began his annihilation of the heritage of the 1840s by rejecting "art for art's sake" in favor of a "civic art" useful for instructing and uplifting the people, as exemplified by the poet Nikolai Nekrasov. In veiled terminology (he was writing under censorship), he preached to the intelligentsia an ideology combining Feuerbach's atheism with French utopian socialism, Comte's positivism, and British utilitarian ethics. In his novel *What Is to Be Done?* he summoned the "critically thinking" youth to take as their sacred duty devotion to the cause of the masses. He held out to these "new people" the vision of the future as a "Crystal Palace," a metaphor taken from the London Exposition of 1851 and symbolizing both material progress and the just society.[3]

A year after the Emancipation there appeared the first underground political organization in Russia. Called Land and Freedom, it marked the beginning of the revolutionary tradition later known as Populism (*narodnichestvo*). The next year, in 1863, Alexander's efforts to liberalize Poland led to a new insurrection for independence and, this time, for democracy as well. Even though it was again put down by force of arms, it had been supported by Russia's apprentice revolutionaries in St. Petersburg as well as by Herzen and Bakunin abroad. The government, seeing in this conjunction of seditions a mortal danger to the empire, answered with repression; the leading radical journals were closed and Chernyshevskii was exiled to Siberia.

Although reform did not stop in 1863, from that date onward the government was quick to repress any presumption by society to participate in power. The first victims of this attitude were the heirs of the moderate Westernizers, those gentry liberals so instrumental in promoting the Great Reforms. In 1862 these loyal squires made so bold as to petition for a constitution; in answer their press was curtailed and some of the leaders sent into administrative exile. With Russia's incipient civil society silenced, the way was cleared for the domination of Russia's shadow politics by the revolutionary opposition, which, though minuscule, yet had the power to drive the government into reaction by its calls for a socialist *Pugachevshchina*.[4]

In consequence, the Russian tendency to telescope Western developments to the point of inverting their "normal" historical order was pushed a great step further. Indeed, the crisis of 1862–63 made this inversion the permanent structure of modern Russian politics: henceforth Russian liberalism would labor in the shadow of socialism, in constant danger of being wildly overrun on its Left. (Constitutionalist Britain as yet did not even have a separate Socialist Party.) Thus a society barely emerging from serfdom, and with no legal political activity, after 1861 lived under the threat of a permanent revolutionary movement. Although there are parallels to this situation in the carbonari and other secret societies of pre-1848 Europe, nowhere before the twentieth century would there be revolutionary underground as enduring and institutionalized as that of the final sixty years of Russia's Old Regime.

This institutionalization was completed in the 1870s, when the radical intelligentsia "went to the people" with a call to rise up against the autocracy and the gentry. The effort, of course, failed. A fragment of this movement, the People's Will, then launched a campaign of terror to force the autocracy to convene a constituent assembly whose peasant majority would vote agrarian socialism into being. In 1881, they at last succeeded in assassinating Alexander II (in their view an "execution"), a deed of political boldness the like of which no major state had witnessed since 1793.

Indeed, the whole extraordinary Populist episode from 1862 to 1881 may be considered a fantasy reenactment of the French Revolution, though with the "higher" aim of socialism. In this respect, it resembled the anticipatory revolutionary fantasies of the 1840s West (of which more is said in the next chapter) in the sense that belief in revolution as the driving force of history was not the automatic outcome of Russia's social processes. It came to her as a reflection of Western experience, not only the Aeschylean tragedy of 1789, but the more immediate "farce" of 1848 (in Marx's epigram) and the grim Commune of 1871. Yet the Russian Populists' fantasy was far more unreal than any earlier Blanquist attempts at engineering revolution. With no serious practical program, and without any base in society, the People's Will ended in pure disaster: the only result of its "triumph" of 1881 was to halt reform for a quarter-century, thus retarding the maturation of zemstvo-based civil society as the autocracy's prime opposition.

Another outcome of the Populist episode was, of course, that it introduced Marxism to Russia, and revolutionary Russia to Marx himself—but, again, this subject will be treated more fully in the following chapter. The point here is that the Russian revolutionary intelligentsia, from its inception in Left Hegelianism in the 1840s to the 1880s, was in constant symbiosis with German and French radicalism. In fact, in Russia no less than in Germany or France, the Socialism of the intellectuals was a variant of modern Europe's common quest for a perfect, egalitarian democracy founded on the people. Russian Populism was not a radical species apart, as is usually assumed; it was an adaptation to backward Russian conditions of a common European aspiration.

At the time, however, the Populist episode was judged by most in the West as negatively as the nearly contemporary Paris Commune had been. In particular, the shocking events of March 1881, led moderate elements abroad to fear that Russia risked veering from the extreme of reaction to that of anarchistic revolution. In many quarters during the late nineteenth century the term "nihilism" carried almost as foreign and ominous a connotation as "tsarism." Still, in all quarters of the West the stirrings of society under Alexander II led to the conclusion that Russia could no longer be subsumed under the simple category of Oriental despotism. Instead, the presence of a movement for liberal reform and of agitation on behalf of socialist revolution bore witness to the workings of a familiar European process: the unbinding of the authoritarian and hierarchical ties of the Old Regime, which had been the dominant theme of the West's own history since the late eighteenth century. Thus, the life of Russia, too, was characterized by development and not, as had appeared to be the case under Nicholas, by the timeless stagnation of the East. And this development tended in the same direction and was governed by the same laws as in the West. Like all other modern nations, Russia was moving from absolutism to some form of liberalism or democracy, and her evolution revealed the familiar oscillation between radical pressure and conservative resistance.

Even during the quarter-century of reaction following 1881, Russia's Europeanization did not cease. Whereas the imperial government was politically retrograde in the person of the ober-procurator of the Holy Synod, the state governing board of the church, Konstantin Pobedonostsev, it was economically progressive in the person of Finance Minister Sergei Witte. During the 1890s this bureaucratic tycoon promoted an industrial boom that was perhaps more rapid and revolutionary than any previously experienced by a Western nation. Its most spectacular symbol was the construction of the Trans-Siberian Railroad, the longest in the world, an exploit not without comparison with the dynamic winning of the American West. Of greater substantive significance was the dramatic industrial growth of the European portions of the empire, which forged a new kind of link between Russia and the West, drawing her for the first time into a modern system of interlocking economic relationships.

Although Russia had traded extensively with Europe, especially England, since the time of Peter, she had done so largely as an exporter of raw materials and an importer of manufactured goods; her role was that of a rudimentary commercial accessory for the industrial nations. Now, however, though still a junior partner in the consortium, she was integrated into the international market economy of capitalism. Because of Witte's exertions, notably his introduction of the gold standard in 1897, she became an attractive field for Western investment, much as the United States had been at the start of industrialization: Russia began to absorb masses of capital and equipment from Germany, Great Britain, and especially France. By 1900, her market was almost as necessary to European economic prosperity as was Europe's financial and technological assistance to her own economic development. Russia was tied to an international capitalist system by bonds yielding the most concrete sort of mutual interest, in a manner that to many observers seemed to herald the definitive end of her old isolation and backwardness.

Drawn by this dynamism, in 1904 Henry Adams visited the new Russia of Witte. Indeed, he came on something of a pilgrimage, for he remembered that, when his grandfather, John Quincy Adams, had been American minister to Alexander I, the "personal friendliness" of the tsar had "saved his fortunes" and a career leading "to the White House." He had an even deeper "gratitude" of his own for the "firm neutrality" of Alexander II and his dispatch of a naval squadron to New York during the Civil War. This was the only gesture of support for Lincoln forthcoming from Europe, and it had been made while liberal England was aiding the slave-holding South and conniving to destroy the Union, and when neo-Bonapartist France was trying to conquer Mexico. On seeing Russia, Adams, though moved to awe by the enormous "force of inertia" of her traditional ways, and bemused by his parting vision of a Russian peasant "lighting his candle and kissing his icon before the railway Virgin in the station at St. Petersburg," nonetheless felt his final image of Russia was that of "a retreating ice-cap." He had seen enough of Russia, he concluded, "to sympathize warmly with the railways and . . . de Witte's industries. The last and highest triumph of history would . . . be the bringing of Russia into the Atlantic combine. . . . At the rate of unification since 1840, this end should be possible within another sixty years."[5]

Soon, however, the imperial regime reaped unforeseen political dividends from Witte's economic portfolio. In 1905 the social transformations wrought by industrialization helped trigger an unmistakably modern revolution. Its goals and leadership were supplied by the liberal and radical intelligentsia, for the first and last time pulling more or less in tandem; its shock troops were furnished by the proletariat, in its historical debut, and the restive peasantry, on the move for the first time since Pugachev. Forty years after Alexander II's revolution from above, Russia produced an answering revolution from below.[6]

This event clearly resembled the Central European Revolution of 1848, where, forty years after the Stein-Hardenberg revolution from above, Germany experienced an echoing revolution from below. The outcome in Russia was similar, too. For Russian civil society, in gestation only since the Great Reforms, was defeated on its first bid for power. The monarchy's back was not broken, and Witte, now prime minister, resolved the crisis with a semiconstitution granted from above, which established a modest parliament, the Duma, based on a class suffrage. This was almost exactly the Prussian formula of 1849, or the Austro-Hungarian formula of two decades later. Once again, a half-century after Germany, Russia had taken another half-step toward the farther West. Yet she did so with a much less solid social structure and a weaker civil society, and with none of Bismarck's genius to make the half-modern formula work. After Witte's fall in 1906, therefore, it was only to be expected that the imperial regime would try to revert to the national conservatism descended from Nicholas I's doctrine of Official Nationality.

Even so, in 1905 an irrevocable step had been taken. Russia's integration into the European capitalist nexus, achieved through Witte's gold standard, had been complemented by her integration into the full aspirations, if not the full accomplishments, of European liberalism through Witte's October Manifesto and the Duma. Russia's integration into the movement of European radicalism was even more advanced, as demonstrated by the general strike that had extorted the October Manifesto from the tsar—the first successful use of the new syndicalist weapon in Europe. Although not a genuine constitutional order, Russia had still ceased to be an integral Old Regime.

After 1905, the great question for men of progressive temper in the farther West was how long matters could remain teetering between two worlds—the same question posed to European liberals after 1848 by the precarious equilibrium of Prussia-Germany. This question was put with greater anguish regarding tsarism, however. In the wake of the assassination of Alexander II in 1881, Russia had produced Europe's first anti-Semitic pogroms (a new word in the European vocabulary); and such popular violence was even more conspicuous in the revolutionary events of 1905. Well publicized in the Western press, this development made many liberals doubt that Russia was as yet enlightened enough to aspire to self-government.

Beginning, then, with the Great Reforms, but especially after 1905, Russia for the first time since the eighteenth century made sense in the light of categories familiar to all segments of European society rather than merely, as in the early nineteenth century, to diehard conservatives or nostalgic Romantics. She was now equally comprehensible to conservatives, liberals, and socialists, no matter how differently each might evaluate her evolution, since all three could view her internal struggles though the same political prism that refracted their own domestic battles.

To the majority of Westerners, therefore, Russia appeared no longer as an alien world but rather as an extension of their own civilization, though still in a immature stage of development. Consequently, just as the decline of Russia's military power after the Crimean War permitted increased understanding, so too the liberalization of her internal order further diminished fear.

Mitteleuropa

This new Western attitude was due not only to changes within Russia; it derived equally from the internal transformation of the West. The liberal West's fear of Nicholas had been produced not just by the shadow of his power over Central Europe; it arose also from the apprehensions generated by liberalism's weakness in its heartland, England and France. In neither country after 1830–1832 did the liberal middle classes have undivided control of the state or domination in society. In both countries, they were troubled by the hold of a Tory or "Ultra" aristocracy above, and by the turbulence of "les classes laborieuses et dangereuses" below.[7] Indeed, in France the revolutionary action of the people produced the eclipse of the political, if not the economic and social, manifestations of liberalism under Napoleon III. In such conditions of insecurity, French and English liberals were hardly capable of a rational, detached view of benighted and militant Russia. Even more fearful of her were the weaker liberals of Central Europe, whom Nicholas had actively thwarted in 1848–1850.

This situation had changed drastically, however, by 1870. France at last became a democratic republic for good. In 1871 the bloody defeat of the Paris Commune marked the end of popular insurrection not only in France but throughout the West; after 1871 Western workers in fact would never revolt again, although fear of another such explosion lingered on. In England the evolution toward modern constitutionalism occurred in less dramatic fashion: as early as Chartism's failure in 1848 it was clear that English workers were not revolutionary at all; with the repeal of the protectionist Corn Laws in 1846 and the franchise reforms of 1867 and 1884 it was equally apparent that the nation could legislate Tory reaction from one retreat to another. By the century's end in France and England there thus remained no significant barriers to full democracy.

Equally profound changes occurred in Central Europe between 1862 and 1870. The imposed or "granted" *(octroierte)* Prussian constitution of 1849 soon proved to be a precarious accommodation, and it was by no means certain that the liberal-national forces of 1848 had been definitively defeated. Indeed by 1862, the Prussian king was confronted with a rebellious majority of liberals in his granted Diet. On the verge of despair, he summoned home his then ambassador to Paris, and his former ambassador to St. Petersburg, Otto von Bismarck. During three years in the latter post Bismarck had become a Russophile and had learned Russian; he had grown to appreciate the common Prussian-Russian interest in keeping Poland down and in opposing Austrian power; above all, he had seen first hand how his good friend, Alexander II, had been able to apply the old Prussian formula of engineered change from above.

In only a few months in Paris, however, Bismarck had learned even more from his future enemy, Napoleon III. For this imperial parvenu explained that universal suffrage, nationalism, and even social welfare for workers need not constitute a menace to authority. They could just as easily be turned to conservative uses to build a national consensus behind the established order. Bismarck, combining his Russian and French lessons, in 1862 embarked on a policy of what may be called legitimist Bonapartism. And this revolutionary conservative, after the most stunning game of political poker of the century, had by 1870 transformed the second-rank Prussian kingdom into the German empire and the first power of continental Europe.[8]

Bismarck's game rested on two interdependent gambles, a foreign and a domestic one; and success abroad governed success at home. Three powers stood in the way of a Prussian conquest of Germany—Russia, Austria, and France—and Bismarck's tactic was to neutralize them one by one. In 1863 he assured Alexander's benevolence by dispatching half the Prussian army to his eastern frontier, thereby sealing off the Polish insurrection for mopping up by the Cossacks. In 1866 he expelled unreformed Austria from Germany in a war so swift that France lacked the time to react. Then in 1870 he drove an isolated France from the German Rhine and detached her provinces of Alsace and Lorraine. And this dazzling succession of international successes made possible the unfolding of the domestic half of his gamble.

Here Bismarck proceeded by appropriating, and denaturing, the ideals of 1848 so as to give the Prussian Old Regime the foundation of a hitherto lacking national consensus. In 1871 he brought all German states except Austria together in a new Reich, an empire formed under the Prussian crown on the invitation of the princes, not of the people. The empire's lower house, the Reichstag, was elected by universal suffrage—a concession to modernity carefully circumscribed by an upper house dominated by Prussia, which retained its class-based constitution of 1849. Social welfare was disbursed more precociously and generously than anywhere else in Europe, but after 1878 the Socialist Party was outlawed. And Bismarck retained the linchpin of the Prussian formula for revolution from above: there would be no sovereign national assembly. The chancellor was responsible to the king-emperor alone, and the Reichstag thus was less a vehicle for expressing the nation's will than a means for mobilizing it behind the monarchy and affording the chancellor a permanent plebiscite—a set of arrangements that unreconciled liberals and Social Democrats called *Scheinkonstitutialismus,* or sham constitutionalism. The result of these measures was a paradoxical structure in which the most modern economy and the most dynamic society in Europe remained under the political control of the trans-Elbian Prussian Old Regime.[9] In a manner roughly analogous to that in which old Muscovy had once slowly absorbed more advanced Novgorod, Ukraine, and Poland to build the Russian empire, so too did old Brandenburg-Prussia rapidly absorb advanced western Germany to build a nineteenth-century Reich.

So irrefutable was Bismarck's success that after 1870 most German liberals made their peace with military Junkerdom and irresponsible monarchy and on the whole felt they had made it not too badly with respect to their perceived immediate interests. With varying degrees of reluctance the middle classes either diluted their constitutional ideas or deferred indefinitely the hope of seeing them realized. In the meantime, they enjoyed the economic and social advantages of liberalism, so effectively guaranteed by Prussia's *Rechtsstaat* bureaucracy and the regime's adamant stand against the mounting pressure of socialism. They found further satisfaction in the glory of national unity at last achieved, and in the power and prestige bestowed on them by Bismarck, whose ruthless genius even his enemies were compelled to admire.

At roughly the same time, the Austrian monarchy, under the impact of Bismarck's "conservative radicalism" and of its own expulsion from Germany, was forced at long last to reform itself. Through the granted constitution and the Compromise of 1867 with the Hungarian aristocracy, the Habsburgs conceded half of what they had refused to both liberalism and nationalism in 1848–49. In essence, a second traditional-modern order emerged in Central Europe. At this acceptable price to the masters of the Old Regime, democracy was contained for decades to come everywhere east of the Rhine. Thus was born the bicephalous West of fin-de-siècle Europe.

Yet these two Wests had one thing in common: both were far more successful than Russia, and after Nicholas's Crimean defeat, for the first time since 1815 both felt secure in the face of Russian power. Nor was it clear as of 1870 that the internal division of Western Europe along the Rhine would be as deep and enduring as it eventually proved to be. Rather, the economic dynamism of Mitteleuropa made it seem to most men of good will that further change along liberal-democratic lines was inescapable. And so, as regards Russia, the uniformly dynamic, if politically dual, world to the west of Königsberg and Budapest basked in a feeling of common modernity. From the heights of its superior civilization it could afford to be rational, comprehending, and even sympathetic in observing crisis-racked Russia's struggle to climb to its level. And although this bourgeois Europe was often patronizing in its view of Russia's problems, it could also perceive them with a new clarity in the reflected light of its own once turbulent but now orderly process of self-civilization.

And so, for the first time since Russia's introduction into Europe under Peter the Great, opinion makers in the West began to view Russia in roughly realistic terms. Only after the Crimean War, and especially after 1870, were internal conditions in the West conducive to a diversified understanding of internal conditions in Russia—in contrast to the semimythologies of the *philosophes* or of Custine and the early Marx.

Russia for Liberals

The dramatic telegraphic dispatches describing the Crimean campaign—the first war to be reported by the daily press—awakened among Westerners a new interest in the land and people behind the facade of tsarism. The volume of literature on Russia suddenly increased and thereafter maintained a steady growth until 1914, stimulated by each major new event in the empire of the Romanovs. Much of this output consisted of travel accounts, retailing elementary information and exotica, as is often the case for "newly discovered" countries, and it bore such titles as *Russia, Land of the Nihilists* or *The Country of the Cossacks*. The information was often superficial or erroneous, in the spirit of what the Russians took to calling a *kliukva*, or "cranberry bush," after a scene in Alexander Dumas's travel memoirs depicting country squires drinking tea "in the shade of a majestic *kliukva*."[10] Some Western visitors found Russia intriguing but baffling. Such was the Reverend Charles Dodgson, alias Lewis Carroll, who, in 1867, saw in

Moscow a "city . . . of conical towers that rise one out of another like a fore-shortened telescope; of bulging gilded domes, in which you see as in a looking glass distorted pictures of the city." The impression of Russia's strangeness was increased by the "bewildering jabber of the natives" and their inverted alphabet.[11] Could it be that his *Through the Looking Glass*, published four years later, owed something to the feeling of exotic inversion received from this, his only trip abroad?

Some of the new writing on Russia, however, was very informed, produced by men who knew its inverted language, who often had spent several years in the country, and who felt some empathy for its real problems. Among the first works of this sort were the academic histories of Alfred Rambaud and Alexander Brückner, which began to appear in the late 1870s.[12] By the 1890s, studies of high quality, from scholarly research to eyewitness surveys of the contemporary scene, provided a significant body of literature in the major Western languages. And their studious approach began to filter down to magazines and newspapers, dispelling the legends and *kliukvas* of earlier decades.

The largest part of this literature was produced by men of varying degrees of liberalism, who viewed constitutional democracy, tempered by a touch of tradition, as the norm of civilization, and who wrote in the vein of the Europeanization of Russia. This liberal interpretation received its first notable, though at times tentative, expression in 1877 in Mackenzie Wallace's *Russia*. Still, it was a novelty that a compatriot of Urquhart and Palmerston could write in calm tones about Russia, particularly in a year when she once again seemed to be grasping with greedy hands at the Straits: "Now the reader must endeavor to realize that Russian peasants, even when clad in sheepskins, are human beings like ourselves." Having thus challenged the doubts of the British public, he advanced the populist claim that "no class of men in the world are more good-natured and pacific than the Russian peasantry" and that their village communes, despite the supposed horrors of Russian administration, "are capital specimens of representative constitutional government of the extreme democratic type." Given these virtues of the peasantry at the base of society and the "humane despotism" of Alexander II above, Wallace was hopeful about the chances for civilization in Russia—despite the lice, dirt, and inefficiency of her present state. Wallace was not only sympathetic but sufficiently accurate in his picture of postreform Russia so that his book can serve as a good introduction to that period even today.[13]

A decade later a similarly sympathetic view was set forth in more learned fashion by Anatole Leroy-Beaulieu in his three-volume *L'empire des tsars et les Russes*, still the most satisfactory survey of late-nineteenth-century Russia. True, the author was disturbed by many features of the Russian government and its bureaucracy, by certain traits of the nihilist intellectuals, and even by some characteristics of the peasants, who were nonetheless described as upholding "the beautiful and simple habits of another age." Yet despite his many nuances of judgment, his general conclusion was unambitious: "Under Alexander II the gates were thrown open and the reform came at last that was to reconcile Russia with herself as well as with Europe. . . . Until the emancipation of the serfs, the work of Peter the Great, having left out the bulk of the nation, lacked a basis; the emancipation gave it one." While Russia was clearly moving along the one prescribed path of European civilization, this did not mean that she would cease to be national. The Western values of liberty and humanity would inevitably be molded, as they should be, by the native historical, religious, and folk traditions, thereby enriching both Europe and Russia. More admiring than Wallace in his approach to Russia, Leroy-Beaulieu also placed her more firmly within the European family of nations.[14] Just as significant as this learned labor was the novelistic Europeanization of Russia achieved by the most popular writer of the fin de siècle, Jules Verne, who, after delving *Twenty-Thousand Leagues under the Sea* and going *Around the World in Eighty Days*, in 1876 made Russia a familiar country to the youth of middle-class Europe through the adventures of *Michael Strogoff, Courier of the Tsar*.[15]

During the three decades after the completion of Leroy-Beaulieu's work in 1889, as its substantial volumes went through successive editions in the major Western languages (and as *Michel Strogoff* was reprinted almost annually in every European language), it looked as if the liberals' hope might be realized. Although in the reactionary interlude under Alexander III an American student of Russia, George Kennan, registered shock at the rigors of tsarist repression and the Siberian exile system, unmasking them in two abundantly documented volumes published in 1891, his judgment of Russia herself was by no means negative. He at the same time expressed admiration for the fortitude of the simple people and especially for the valor of the radical opposition, and in these qualities saw the real hope for her future.[16]

With the new century, as Russia offered Europe its first democratic revolution since 1848, the liberal West was reminded of its own heroic past; and in countries where 1848 had been a failure, Russia's exploit appeared as a reproach, and even an example for the future. In Germany, Max Weber suspected that Russia, because she had not yet been subdued by the "bureaucratic rationalism" of mature capitalism, might be on the verge of a fuller freedom than the German Reich. At the age of fifty he taught himself Russian to follow the revolution daily and soon produced two books on that event. Although he concluded that his hope for Russian reform—or his fear of Russian strength—was unfounded and that Russia would go the way of a bureaucratic rationalism even less satisfactory than the West's, it was nonetheless a novelty that a German liberal nationalist should look to the empire of the tsars for a model of freedom and rationality.[17]

Farther west, although there was no expectation that Russia might serve as a model, there was sympathetic interest in her progress. In 1903, as agitation against the imperial regime mounted, the dignified liberal gentleman and historical scholar Paul Miliukov could win sympathy from a receptive public in Chicago by arguing that Russia's crisis, no matter how painful, was certainly not the desperate, semi-Asiatic affair that Kennan's recent exposé might be taken to imply.[18] And in 1917, the presence of this same Miliukov as foreign minister of the Provisional Government made it easier for President Woodrow Wilson to bring America into the war, for it signified that Russia, like all the other Allies, had at least become a democracy.

Russia for Socialists

Although Western liberals understood much about postreform Russia, Western socialists perceived part of what the liberals missed. Among the first to gain insight was Marx himself. Like the liberals, Marx was awakened by the Emancipation of 1861 to the existence of Russian society, hitherto obscured by the pall of Mongol-Byzantine tsarism. In contrast to the liberals, however, he interpreted the Great Reforms and the ensuing Polish ferment as harbingers of a social revolution that might shake not only the Russian monarchy but the Prussian and Austrian ones as well. The crushing of the Polish revolt for a time revived Marx's belief that Muscovy was hopelessly uncivilized; but then in 1868 he received a request for permission to translate his *Capital*, which had appeared only the year before, from a "socialist" in St. Petersburg! This request astounded Marx, since according to the logic of his system, interest in his work should have been greatest in the advanced West, not in backward Russia, where the very existence of socialists appeared to be a contradiction in terms. Yet the proposed translation (which in fact appeared in 1872) would be the first in any language; the alacrity of the Russian response even constituted a compliment he had not yet received in Germany, where Engels had to write reviews under pseudonyms to get the book talked about at all.[19]

Marx was so impressed by interest from this unexpected quarter that at the age of fifty (like Weber later) he learned Russian in order to read such Populists as Chernyshevskii and Petr Lavrov and to investigate for himself the economic and social changes which were clearly creating a new Russia. In 1870, a group of Russian revolutionaries abroad asked him to become their representative on the council of the First International. A prophet still largely without honor in his own country, for the remainder of his life Marx was reverently consulted by Russian radicals about their forthcoming revolution. By 1881, the vigor of Russian radicalism had won from him the acknowledgment that in the event of a general European upheaval, the peasant commune, if it survived the eastward spread of capitalism, could indeed become the basis for socialism in Russia. In his public statement of this position the following year, however, the more Russophobic Engels persuaded him to make this prognosis strictly contingent on the success of a prior Western revolution.[20]

The transformation in Marx's views from the days of his collaboration with Urquhart was amazing. Yet his new position was no more exceptional in the changed context of the age than had been his Russophobia before 1861. In both periods the evolution of his thinking paralleled that of the liberals, progressing from the theory of Oriental despotism to the acceptance of Russia as part of Europe and to the view that she was developing according to the same universal historical laws, though later and more slowly. Like the liberals also, Marx became assimilationist because Russia was in fact becoming assimilated into modern Europe. Again like the liberals, he let his desires for Western society largely determine his insights with respect to Russia. But this propensity led him to a different evaluation of Russia's march. As a socialist, he was sensitive to the revolutionary rather than the evolutionary potential of the Great Reforms. And in contrast to the liberals, he could no more believe in the progressive intentions of the Russian monarchy than he could in those of its Prussian cousin. He continued to denounce tsarism as virulently as in his youth, a tradition maintained in the socialist press by Engels for a decade after his associate's death in 1883. Marx's attitude toward Russia was thus more ambivalent than that of the liberals: on the one hand, he accorded her a grudging admiration for her unexpected revolutionary potential, but on the other hand, he hated her as the worst enemy of progress in Europe because of her still barbaric autocracy, supported by her benighted peasant masses.

In general, this remained the view of most European socialists until 1905. At successive congresses of the Second International, European Marxists found the learned Georgii Plekhanov quite as congenial a comrade as contemporary Western liberals found Professor Miliukov; and only the most radical socialist leaders, such as Rosa Luxemburg, were sufficiently versed in the obscure differences between Bolsheviks and Mensheviks to suspect that comrade Lenin, with his Blanquist conception of revolutionary strategy and his idea of a vanguard party, might not be as good a democrat as Plekhanov. Then the upheaval of 1905 suddenly thrust Russia into the front rank of European socialist attention. The October general strike and the St. Petersburg workers' "soviet," or council, of that year were the first expression of proletarian combativeness since the Paris Commune of 1871.

Western socialists and syndicalists, who for decades had accomplished nothing more heroic than mouthing revolutionary slogans from the past, were made aware of their own passivity and of the subtle pervasion of liberal, parliamentary moderation. At the same time, the example of Russian action indicated a way out of this dilemma. For 1905 had been not a revolution of barricades in the classic nineteenth-century manner, but a movement adapted to mature industrial conditions: a nationwide general strike, founded on a concentrated working class's ability to paralyze all components of an interdependent society.

In Germany, the idea of the mass strike was seized upon by such representatives of the Social Democratic left as Rosa Luxemburg and Karl Liebknecht in an effort to infuse the largest but most complacent working-class party in Europe with a revolutionary spirit, an effort that met with little immediate success but that prepared the way for the wartime radicalization of a large part of the German movement, in the Independent Socialist Party and the Communistic Spartacus League.[21] In France, the Russian example was a contributory cause of the syndicalist agitation which raged between 1906 and 1910, while in England the strike waves of 1911–12 and 1914, connected with the constitutional and Irish crises of those years, owed something to the French example and hence indirectly to Russia.[22] Even in the remote United States, the Industrial Workers of the World found an audience for the idea of the revolutionary strike, especially among unskilled workers who were often of East European origin.

In countries where constitutionalism was still weakly developed, 1905 had a different kind of impact. Just across Russia's borders in the Dual Monarchy of the Habsburgs, it lent impetus to socialist agitation for universal suffrage, which was at last conceded by Vienna in 1907. In more aristocratic Budapest, however, the reaction was one of fear, thereby contributing to the refusal of a democratic suffrage in 1906. More novel still, the impact of 1905 extended beyond the borders of historic Europe into the now far decayed Ottoman Empire, where it helped inspire the constitutionalist revolt of the Young Turks in 1908; and a similar shock was felt in Persia, which by 1906 had a constitution and a parliament. Finally, the events of 1905 impinged on the domestic affairs of the Far East by ricochet, for the defeat of European and autocratic Russia by Asiatic but constitutionalist Japan offered some inspiration to the Chinese Revolution of 1911.

For the first time in her history a tremor in Russia's internal life touched off reverberations that were felt in the farthest corners of the West, indeed outside the West. St. Petersburg was beginning to lay claim to the role that radical Paris had played throughout the nineteenth century. In fact, though no one suspected this at the time, the capital of the tsars had already produced most of the theories, and the leadership, that would soon propel it far beyond any radicalism that had ever emanated from Paris.

Although the agitation in Russia soon subsided, it left a legacy. After 1905, the symbiosis of the German, Polish, Bundist (Jewish), and Russian Marxist movements grew to be increasingly accepted as a fact of international socialist life, as demonstrated by the careers of Rosa Luxemburg, Karl Radek, and Aleksandr Helphand-Parvus. All three were born in Poland (two as Russian subjects), all were Jewish, and after working in the Polish Marxist party all moved on to the German Social Democratic Party, while maintaining close links with the Russian Social Democrats. From this base the first became a Communist foe of Lenin, the second became one of his chief lieutenants, and the third was the godfather of Trotsky's theory of "permanent revolution" and the man with the connections in Berlin to get Lenin back to Russia in the famous sealed train in 1917. Thus as 1914 approached, Russian Social Democracy, though the least flourishing branch of the European Socialist family, was nonetheless a prominent member of the International, while even those holdovers from peasant Populism, the Socialist Revolutionaries, were allowed to camp on its fringes.

Yet Russia was accepted into Europe by prewar socialists much less completely than by liberals, a reflection of the changing fortunes of the two groups in the fin-de-siècle West. The very fact that the Second International had been founded in Paris on the centenary of the French Revolution in 1889 was a declaration that the era of "bourgeois" liberalism was over and that the proletariat's day was at hand. And indeed, in the twenty-five years of the International's existence the European working class grew steadily in strength. Correspondingly, classical liberals and republicans, most of whose enemies had hitherto been on the Right, now discovered an increasing number on the Left as well. Inevitably, liberalism became more cautious and conservative.

As Western liberalism added water to the wine of its once heady principles, the principles underlying tsarism became increasingly a matter of indifference to much of the West, and relations with Russia hence were approached in terms of national rather than ideological considerations. Conversely, as socialism became the main force of movement throughout Europe, it inherited the heroic mentality and internationalist fervor that had formerly characterized liberalism. In the eyes of this new Left, even though tsarism was no longer the threat it had been under Nicholas, democratic morality mandated that Russia's regime could not be a matter of indifference: it remained on principle offensive to all progressive citizens.

Russia for Nationalists

As the century wore on, the changing fortunes of nationalism further nuanced Russia's reintegration into Europe. To recapitulate nationalism's course hitherto: The protoliberalism of the *philosophes* had been innocent of the idea of nationality; and Herder, when he came to place it on the agenda of intellectual debate, inserted it squarely in the prevailing cosmopolitan context. Early-nineteenth-century liberalism continued this cosmopolitan view, in the thought of Mazzini and Mickiewicz and in the sympathy displayed among liberals in England and France for Greek, Polish, and Italian independence. Civic and national emancipation, moreover, were widely regarded as two facets of a single process, and the national cultures of Europe were seen as complementary rather than competing. The various nationalities thus admired one another's folklore and history, as when Walter Scott or the dramatists of the *Sturm und Drang* furnished models for the articulation of national identity everywhere.

Emerging nationalities, therefore, felt they were destined to work together to overthrow the supranational dynastic states which denied to each of them the possibility of self-fulfillment. Although lacking formal organization other than such ephemeral conspiracies as the multinational carbonarism of Mazzini's Young Europe, what may be called a Liberal International clearly existed during the first half of the nineteenth century. Aided and abetted by the more fortunate liberal nationalisms of England and France, this movement was everywhere pitted against the Old-Regime "International" of the Holy Alliance. Only the

Russians were denied admission to this brotherhood of peoples, because their patriotic ambitions appeared unredeemed by any aspiration to liberty (the Decembrist movement was unknown except to the Poles).

Then, in 1848–49, the Liberal International had its first—and fleeting—experience of power; and the clash of Teuton and Magyar with Slav revealed that the aspirations of one nationality could usually be realized only at the expense of another.[23] Nationalism clearly meant conflict more often than cooperation. The dismal outcome of the Springtime of the Peoples also demonstrated that ethnic conflicts could not be resolved, nor national unification achieved, by good will alone: these goals required the use of state power. This awareness prepared the way for realizing the national idea in much of Central Europe between 1859 and 1870 by the *Realpolitik* of Napoleon III, Cavour, and Bismarck.[24]

But this route was available only of the largest frustrated nationalisms, those of Italy and Germany, which already possessed the nucleus of a nation-state in Piedmont and Prussia. There thus remained all the stateless nationalisms of East Central Europe, the West and South Slavs together with the Magyars and the Romanians. And in this area, despite its great heterogeneity, the spectre of pan-Slavism, unsuccessfully launched in 1848, did at last come to play a role in European politics through its association with the only Slavic state, Russia. This attraction of course could not operate for the two major peoples of the area, the Poles and the Magyars, but it did have appeal among the South Slavs and even the Czechs. Hence it was only in the Balkans that Russia, in the 1870s, came to partially support the pan-Slav and Orthodox cause, for there it conveniently ran parallel to her strategic interest in the Straits.

Yet, despite the autocracy's circumspect attitude toward the pan-Slav idea, it evoked vociferous support among Russian conservatives. This agitation inevitably appeared to Germanic Europe as the pretext and prelude of a Russian drive for continental hegemony. And just as inevitably pan-Slavism provoked the answer of pan-Germanism in Mitteleuropa. Thus by the early twentieth century Bakunin's assessment, in 1848, of the revolutionary potential of emergent Slavdom would be proved correct, though not in the way he had anticipated. The effort to transform the peoples of East Central Europe into states would indeed spell the end of the three Eastern empires (and of the Turkish one as well). The result, however, would not be Socialism but general conflict; for the two world wars, though they of course had more general causes, were actually ignited on the fault line between Teuton and Slav.

Indeed, ever since the Springtime of the Peoples of 1848 the great European dilemma had been to adapt the formula of the nation-state—as worked out before 1789 in the Atlantic world of England, the Low Countries, France, Spain, and Portugal—to the world of dynastic states east of the Rhine and the Alps. It is surely no accident that all European wars after the midcentury were wars of national liberation or national unification: the Italian War of 1859, the Prusso-Austrian Seven Weeks' War of 1866, the Franco-Prussian War of 1870, the Russo-Turkish War over Bulgaria of 1877–78, and the Balkan Wars of 1911 and 1912. Yet each time, the still surviving concert of the powers prevented the conflagration from becoming general. In 1914, however, the concert could no longer contain the pressure and the European state system collapsed.

Nationalism has been appropriately defined as the demand that states should be made to coincide with peoples, conceived of as ethnic-linguistic units. The problem, then, is to explain why this demand became general and insistent only in the nineteenth century. Perhaps the most frequently heard answer is that it was required by "capitalism," whether to create a large market or to transform peasants into an educated, modern labor force.[25] Another form of this answer is that national identities are "imagined communities" of culture created by "print capitalism."[26] The trouble with such explanations is that the development of nationalism does not correspond at all well with the map of capitalism, which spread at an uneven pace in the early nineteenth century while nationalism was well-nigh ubiquitous.

What the proliferation of nationalisms does correspond with, however, is the political and cultural map of Europe. As we have seen, democracy introduced nationalism into the old, established states of the Atlantic West; and culture, from Germany's *deutsche Bewegung* to its various imitations in East Central Europe, brought it to the dynastic

Old Regimes beyond the Rhine and the Alps. The literary construction of nationalism is thus a prime case in which culture has weighed as a force in the European balance of power, indeed by 1914 helping to destroy the two-century-old European concert.

As Europe approached 1914, moreover, classical liberalism was increasingly caught up in the escalation of nationalism. The abandoned banner of cosmopolitan progressivism was therefore reclaimed after 1864 by the International Workingmen's Organization of Marx and Bakunin, a tradition continued and reinforced after 1889 by the Second International. The proletariat was now held to constitute the true European brotherhood of peoples, expressed in the mutual aid of workers across state boundaries against the "holy alliance" of the national bourgeoisies. Still, until 1905 this cosmopolitan socialism, like liberalism earlier, acted by and large to exclude Russia from progressive Europe, since, despite the anarchists Bakunin and Petr Kropotkin, the land of the tsars seemed to lack proletarian brothers.

In retrospect, liberalism's drift toward nationalism after 1848, and socialism's inheritance of the cosmopolitan ideal, were the first chapter in the by now familiar life cycle of movements for radical social change: they are internationalist when out of power but nationalist when in power, or even only near to power. The Second International socialists encountered this dilemma in August 1914, when they voted war credits for national defense. The Soviet leaders discovered it in turn after the Second World War, with the secession first of Tito's Yugoslavia and then of Mao's China from the Third International of Communism.

In sum, the diminishing cosmopolitanism of Western liberalism after 1848 proved to be a force for Russia's reassimilation into Europe. Although the upsurge of hard-headed nationalism led to a new kind of Russophobia, ethnic rather than ideological, as with pan-Germanist hostility to pan-Slavism, this nationalism also made Russian culture appear less alien within Europe taken as a whole. For opinion now emphasized the distinctive qualities of each nation rather than the unity of the Romano-Germanic world, thus making Russia one of many nations in a divided continent. Russia's internal regime also dwindled in importance as Western liberals were increasingly pitted against their counterparts across the nearest border, or against their "unpatriotic" working classes at home. By the early twentieth century, therefore, liberalism's fragmentation had created still another opening through which half-reformed Russia could creep back into Europe, if not exactly as a brother, then at least as one of the pack.

So it came about that as early as the 1890s, tsarism with reforms, but without a Duma, appeared to be a tolerable if not an admirable ally to French Radicals. These heirs of the Jacobin Mountain had been thoroughly sobered by the events of 1870–71, which revealed to them both the national threat from Germany and the social danger from the Commune at home. Thus Alexander III, the most reactionary tsar after Nicholas I, was honored in 1895 in the heart of republican Paris by a sumptuously gilded bridge dedicated to his memory, after having a few years before bared his head to the strains of the "Marseillaise" on the occasion of the good-will visit of a French naval squadron to Kronstadt—a pair of gestures that would have been unthinkable on both sides fifty years earlier.

But tsarism, even after the October general strike and with a Duma, remained abhorrent to socialists. The German Social Democrats in 1914 deemed its pogroms and knout-wielding Cossacks sufficient cause for approving war credits to defend, however reluctantly, their imperfect but nevertheless superior culture against Russian "barbarism." And to justify the Marxist orthodoxy of their stand, they mobilized quotations from the Russophobic declarations of Engels at the time of the Franco-Russian alliance of 1894.

REVERSE: FIN DE SIÈCLE AND RUSSIAN SOUL

Are you from heaven or hell, oh Beauty!
Your gaze is both infernal and divine,
Pouring forth good and evil blended;
So men have likened you to wine.

By "modernity" I mean the ephemeral, the fugitive,
the contingent, the half of art whose other half is
the eternal and the immutable.

—Charles Baudelaire,
"Hymn to Beauty" (1857) and "Modernity" (1863)

Art, rather than ethics, constitutes the essential
metaphysical activity of man.

—Friedrich Nietzsche,
The Birth of Tragedy (1870–71)

These villages so poor,
This meager, barren nature:
My native land of long suffering,
Land of the Russian people!

Proud eyes of foreigners
Will never grasp nor note
The inner light beneath
Your humble nakedness.

Crushed by the cross's burden,
The Heavenly Tsar has traveled
In servile guise across you,
My native land, with blessing.

Not by the mind is Russia understood,
Nor is she measured by a standard rule:
She has a special measure of her own;
In Russia it is possible only to believe.

—Fedor Tiutchev (1855)

At the same time as Russia's slow political convergence with the worlds of liberalism and socialism claimed Europe's principal attention, a more exciting and disturbing image of Russian culture was taking form in the background, reflecting a new and unexpected artistic creativity. Although the political foundations of the threefold division of Europe along the Rhine and the Niemen had been laid between 1848 and 1870, the cultural consequences of this realignment did not become fully apparent until the turn of the century. Western awareness of this change developed in two phases. Initially, a sober image of Russia's aesthetic achievements emerged in the wake of the Crimean War and became predominant in liberal and rationalistic circles of the maritime West. Toward the end of the century, however, the West's representation of Russia's creativity acquired an intoxicating neo-Romantic cast that made it the special appanage of fin-de-siècle antirationalists, above all in Mitteleuropa.

Art for Art's Sake

In the early nineteenth century the West's rejection of Russia as alien had been easy to maintain because to the outsider she evinced no discernible sign of creativity in the arts and sciences, a quality regarded as indispensable to a genuinely European nation. In fact, before 1855 Russia had less to offer in this domain than did her neighbors— although her accomplishments were greater than Westerners suspected. As we have seen, during the 1830s and 1840s Pushkin and Gogol had already inaugurated what would rapidly become the golden age of Russian literature.

And the West soon found this out. In the midst of the Crimean campaign, Prosper Mérimée offered an antidote to prevailing Russophobia by launching Ivan Turgenev before the French public with a translation of *A Sportsman's Sketches*. The moment was propitious: the hegemony of Romanticism and poetry had ended, and the novel of contemporary life was the dominant literary form, yet despite this "realism" art for its own sake continued to be viewed as the highest spiritual accomplishment of man. For the next two decades the West's impression of Russian culture was formed largely by translations of each new work of Turgenev and by elementary critical and historical essays elucidating Pushkin and Gogol, with Mérimée still serving as chief exegete. To Mérimée, Russia, like the Spain he had depicted earlier in *Carmen*, was of interest largely as a source of exotica, which for a time was the main quality Europe sought in its literary imports from the East.[27]

Turgenev soon took over the movement in his own right, in part because the nihilist proponents of "civic art" in Russia drove him to spend most of his time in the West, where he formed well-publicized friendships with such figures as Gustave Flaubert, Gustav Freitag, and Henry James. But his impact was due above all to the thoroughly modern quality of his fiction, which presented the West with the image of an unmistakably civilized, creative, and European culture. His sensitive yet sober psychological portrayals of character transformed Custine's monsters and phantoms into comprehensible human beings. His classi-

cal yet lyrical style, in conjunction with his realistic treatment of subjects, convinced readers that his characteristically Russian themes also
reflected an innately reasonable and universally applicable view of man.
Both as an international intellectual figure and as an artist, Turgenev
came to symbolize Russia's participation in a single tradition of European humanism, an impression that paralleled in impact the emerging
liberal image of Russia as a society aspiring to a common European
civic ethos.

Around 1880, the West began to discover those still more colossal
figures of Russian literature, Tolstoy and Dostoevsky. The French edition of *War and Peace* appeared in 1879, just ten years after its publication in Russia. Turgenev immediately prevailed on such literary opinion makers as Flaubert, Hippolyte Taine, and Henry James to read, and
to praise, this extraordinary prose epic. By the 1880s most of Tolstoy's
work up to that point was available in some form in the West; and by
the time of the publication of *Resurrection* in 1899, reverence for the
sage of Yasnaya Polyana was so widespread that the new novel appeared
in German, French, and English almost simultaneously with the original. Similarly, by the 1880s the basic works of Dostoevsky had begun to
filter through to the West. By 1886 they were widely enough circulated
for Nietzsche to chance upon a copy of *Notes from the Underground* in a
bookstore in Nice, and he immediately proclaimed its author "the only
psychologist from whom I learned something," whose discovery was
"the greatest stroke of good luck in [his] life."[28] By the early twentieth
century, as a result of the impact of these two giants, the European
public had become acquainted with the astounding succession of Russian prose writers from Gogol and Aleksandr Goncharov to Nikolai
Leskov, Anton Chekhov, and Ivan Bunin. By 1914 this corpus of works,
in both size and quality, appeared to equal if not surpass that of any
other national literature, and an increasing number of Western critics
were prepared to acclaim the Russian novelists as the masters of the
foremost school of fiction in Europe.

It was widely agreed that this school's chief merit lay in its advanced
realism, the usual, if not entirely appropriate, term employed both in
Russia and abroad.[29] Russian fiction explored, with a verisimilitude un-
attained in any other literature, both the diversified sweep of a whole

society, as in the novels of Tolstoy, and the arcane depths of the inner man, as in the writings of Dostoevsky. It mirrored the human condition, whether individually or in the aggregate, as it "really" is, and did so more minutely and penetratingly than any previous aesthetic movement in European culture. This impression of mastery was amplified around the turn of the century when a comparable preeminence was accorded to the Russian drama, in recognition of the seminal impact on all the stages of Europe of the Moscow Art Theater and the Stanislavsky method of psychological and scenic realism.[30]

Of Russia's nineteenth-century literary glories, only her poetic tradition remained unappreciated abroad, because of the linguistic barrier that usually confines poets to an exclusively national fame. Since Russian literature was unsustained by any comparable impact in other areas such as business and politics, it lacked the support of a knowledge of the Russian language. Thus, despite Russia's acknowledged literary preeminence, she remained in a category separate from England, France, or Germany: she continued to be viewed as through a glass darkly, in translation only. Her literature, though familiar, remained remote. This circumstance doubtless facilitated the eventual deduction from Russian "realism" of extravagant conclusions about Russian national character.

Still, exceptional as Russian realism appeared to the European public, it was not in an aesthetic sense revolutionary, for it came to the West as a re-export of forms and techniques that had originated there. Although these models returned greatly enriched, they remained easily recognizable. Thus while they aroused admiration and excited imitation, they hardly inspired radical formal innovation. That role first fell to Russia in another domain, music, where her cultural fruition produced some of the most potent seeds of the twentieth-century "modernist" reaction against realism.

Russia's international debut in music was reminiscent of her introduction into world literature. In the third quarter of the nineteenth century the magnificently sentimental, mellifluous, and Italianate scores of Tchaikovsky and Anton Rubinstein revealed that Russia had creatively assimilated the tradition of European harmony. By the turn of the century, the Western public was beginning to discover Aleksandr Borodin and Nikolai Rimsky-Korsakov, who, though they innovated little in matters of musical form, developed a titillating (if artificial) strain of Slavonic, even Oriental, local color. As early as the 1870s their populist concern with native themes began to give Russian composition a radically original cast, which eventually made of the Russian school a prime source, second only to Wagner, of musical modernism throughout Europe.

With the discovery of the exuberant and exhilarating genius of Modest Mussorgsky, untamed by the Italianate tradition of the conservatories, Russia moved into the avant-garde of music. Mussorgsky was at once a revolutionary composer in a technical sense and an inspired transposer of Russian folk melody and speech rhythms. Roughly contemporary with Tchaikovsky, he had long been neglected in his native land, where his *Boris Godunov* was a failure on its premier in 1879. He was first appreciated only toward the close of the nineteenth century, and then only in the West. Through his influence on a few Western figures such as the young Debussy, he helped inaugurate the modernist movement in Europe, as a prelude to achieving triumphant acclaim, in both Russia and the West, at the beginning of the twentieth century. Modernist music reached its culmination between 1910 and 1913 in Igor Stravinsky's ballets *The Firebird, Petrushka*, and especially *Le sacre du printemps*, whose premieres were as much Parisian and even European as Russian events.[31]

Russian music brought with it the Russian ballet, as the new composers reached the West primarily on the stage rather than in the concert hall, and more often through dance than opera. The stunning originality of this music lay in its sonic transposition of drama and movement rather than of mood or contemplation. It reflected animate intensity and vital exuberance, qualities the ballet epitomized. In this art form Russia soon achieved a hegemony so durable that the norms it established have endured without fundamental challenge to the present day.

In the last decade of the old century, Tchaikovsky and Marius Petipa, the French choreographer of the Imperial Ballet, brought classical dance to its acme, and also its final flowering, with *Sleeping Beauty* and *Swan Lake*. At the beginning of the new century, the revolutionary

choreography of Mikhail Fokine, aided by the surpassing prowess of
Vaslav Nijinsky and Anna Pavlova, created the modern ballet. In 1909,
Sergei Diaghilev took his company, Les Ballets Russes, to Le Châtelet
Theater in Paris for the first in a series of seasons extending until the
war. In the course of these performances, as the music of Borodin gave
way to that of Stravinsky against a backdrop of resplendent decors by
Nicholas Roerich, after the manner of Benois, the Western public for
the first time received the almost sensual impression, whose legend has
not yet faded, of a veritable cultural revolution stemming from that
ancient citadel of barbarism, tsarist St. Petersburg.[32]

Just as Russian music had brought with it the ballet, the ballet now
introduced Russian painting to Europe, thus completing the revelation
of Russian creativity in every domain of artistic endeavor. Aleksandr
Benois was not only a designer of stage sets and costumes but also a
painter of some accomplishment and, above all, a theorist of the unity
of the arts for the purpose of achieving the full transcendence of reality.
Since 1898 he had edited the review of nascent Russian symbolism, *The
World of Art*, which drew its inspiration from Baudelaire, Nietzsche,
and Wagner and in the name of pure beauty set out to overthrow the
literal-minded, civic realism preached by Nikolai Nekrasov and
Chernyshevskii. The success of the Ballets Russes, therefore, was much
more than a theatrical event; it was a statement in the most vivid terms
of an even more militant philosophy of "art for art's sake" than any
hitherto preached in the West. Yet the fireworks at Le Châtelet should
not be allowed to outshine those other domains in which, on the eve of
1914, Russia for the first time moved into the avant-garde. In Munich
Wassily Kandinsky, and slightly later Marc Chagall in Paris, though
not prime innovators like Stravinsky, contributed prominently to that
disintegration of representational forms which expressed the modernist
revolt in painting.[33] Indeed, Kandinsky took the rare step for a painter
of translating his revolutionary practice into an equally radical theory of
the deeper meaning of modern art. Called *On the Spiritual in Art*, it was
published in 1910 and was quickly translated into the major European
languages; its message was that the dissolution of natural forms into an
"abstract" art was the prelude, indeed the prophecy, of a new spiritual
era for mankind.[34] And so Russia went beyond the export of nineteenth-

century realism to assume a leading role in the elaboration of fin-de-siècle symbolism and of twentieth-century modernism.

From Symbolism to Modernism

Indeed, this silver age of Russian culture, projected abroad by the Ballets Russes, made Russia a major catalyst of the revolt of modernity then reaching its culmination in every domain of European art, an aesthetic dissidence that in the wake of the First World War would level the "philistine" realism of nineteenth-century "bourgeois" culture. Diaghilev's Ballets Russes, combining as they did three art forms, reflected and amplified an existing Western perspective, which went back to the 1840s—the same seminal decade that had produced the worldview of Marx and the first counter-Enlightenment intuitions of Dostoevsky.

In the late 1840s the old natural supernaturalism of Romanticism, and the more recent creed of art for art's sake, were transmuted into a radically new sensibility, one appropriate to what Baudelaire was the first to call "modernity." In his *Salon of 1846*, he redefined the ideal of his elders:

> Romanticism is precisely neither in the choice of subjects nor in exact [historical] truth, but in the manner of feeling. Men have sought for it outside of us, and it is only *inside* that it was possible to find it. For me, Romanticism is the most recent, the most up-to-date form of the beautiful. . . . Whoever says Romanticism, says modern art—that is, intimacy, spirituality, color, aspiration toward the infinite, expressed by all the means that all the arts contain.[35]

But in this world of Romanticism redefined as modernity, even the vestigial remnants of God as represented by the pantheism of original Romanticism (or indeed by Enlightenment deism) were absent. Instead, for Baudelaire, the only supernatural presence was Satan, not of course as a real being, but as a symbol of man's own capacity for self-destruction.

In this fallen world there remained only the lonely individual and his suffering. Hence man's sole means of salvation lay in the creed enunciated through the programmatic sonnet "Correspondances": "Nature is a temple of living pillars" where man "passes as through a forest of symbols . . ." and where "the perfumes, the colors, and the sounds answer each other." In other words, all the arts were one, in a single system of magic *correspondances*. Art thus became all there is, a kind of aesthetic sacrament, a form of grace without redemption, that permitted man the only salvation he could know. And in this earthly vale of tears, the damned yet divine poet had a special sacerdotal mission; for only art could transubstantiate the "evil" of life into the "flowers" of poetry, the "mud" of experience into the "gold" of art, the incurable "spleen" of the modern condition into an "ideal" of aesthetic perfection.[36] Through this sacro-satanic alchemy the artist ascended to a world of pure beauty, in an eternity of art beyond and above time.

Thus was supernatural religion replaced by a secular sacramentalism of art. But so, too, were all the Enlightenment idols of reason and progress cast down at the very moment, in the wake of 1848, when science, positivism, and materialism began a half-century of hegemony. Similarly, original Romanticism was repudiated. Its indulgence of emotion was now viewed as sick sentimentality, a part of the modern malaise, for which the new art of transcendence through the glory of symbols was the antidote. Moreover, whereas the pantheistic God of Romanticism had its being in history, and in the particularities of immemorial rootedness, the anti-God of modernity denied the contingencies of history and spurned the past for the present and the eternal. With symbolism, as with emerging modernism (there is no sharp line between the two), pure and timeless art replaced historical Becoming, the cosmic demiurge for Hegel (and through him of Marx), as the organizing principle of human existence.

In the same decade (the 1840s), Richard Wagner in Germany effected a kindred transvaluation of Romanticism by appropriating certain of its historic themes and giving them a new meaning.[37] Until the Revolution of 1848 he had expected that art, in particular opera, would assume the revolutionary task of offering myths that both expressed and fueled the revolt of the people. After the Revolution's failure he deemed the cause of social regeneration to be lost, and so, under the influence of Arthur Schopenhauer, he construed art to be an end and a value in itself, a refuge from the vileness of the present. His new view of art nonetheless remained revolutionary, for it summoned society to transcend the vulgarity and the fragmentation of "progressive" modernity by recreating timeless and heroic myths, which indeed might one day revivify society. Although these myths were ostensibly taken from the medieval Christian past or the primeval paganism of Germany, they were in fact lodged in an eternal Valhalla of beauty and symbolic truth. Thus Wagner, too, preached a doctrine of *salus sola arte*, of salvation by art alone, and of the regeneration of the fallen modern world by the splendor of ideal myth.

He also held that all the arts were one, in a *Gesamtkunst* of poetry, painting, and symbolic drama, whose combined power might restore a sense of wholeness to modern society, just as artistic communion in the Olympic Pantheon had once given wholeness to the Greek polis. To convey this message, he dissolved the structured musical phrase and abandoned the clear divisions within compositional forms practiced by Beethoven and the Italians; his *Gesamtkunstwerk* was carried endlessly onward in a continuous flow and ebb, a crossing and a mingling of symbolic leitmotivs. In the late 1870s, this doctrine was incarnated in the neopaganism of his Teutonic temple at Bayreuth. Baudelaire, from the very overture of *Tannhäuser*, in 1861, had understood that Wagner's revolutionary opera expressed his own creed of mystical, symbolic correspondences.[38] And so, between the pair of enchanters, there opened the first circle of post-Enlightenment *and* post-Romantic modernity.

A second circle appeared around 1870 with the arrival of a new generation and a new genre on the scene. Painting had followed literature's evolution from the Old-Regime neoclassicism of Jacques-Louis David to the Romanticism of Eugène Delacroix to the midcentury realism of Gustave Courbet. Beginning with the *salon des refusés* in 1866, however, a new avant-garde, in the persons of Édouard Manet and later Claude Monet, abandoned the academic tradition entirely to depict ordinary scenes from contemporary life and to do so in a fluid style that, after a private exhibition in 1874, was called Impressionism. Indeed, these Impressionists, emerging as they did in the wake of the Commune, were

also called "Communists" by a hostile public, since they had demolished the world of visual reality as thoroughly as the Communards had
worked to destroy traditional social reality.[39] For their art in truth
marked more than a change of manner; it brought to an end the grand
tradition of European painting that had begun with the Renaissance
and the discovery of perspective. Painting, even though inevitably styl-
ized, no longer attempted to reflect the external world; it offered only
our subjective perception of its forms and shadings.

The "color" of painting was thus made to answer the "sound and the
perfume" of poetry and music through the appropriation of the visual
world as (in Baudelaire's definition of "modernity") "the transitory, the
fugitive, the contingent." By the same token, Impressionism began the
destruction of the classical canons of representational form, which
would culminate in the first decade of the new century in Cubism and
abstract art. Simultaneously, in poetry, Stéphane Mallarmé developed
Baudelaire's vision of the "ideal" into a crystalline Nirvana of "pure"
symbol and inward aesthetic self-contemplation; he and Arthur Rimbaud together inaugurated the disintegration of traditional verse forms
into a structureless verbal "throw of the dice" and into fragmentary
"illuminations" of poetic prose. And in England, Algernon Swinburne,
and later Oscar Wilde, imported the new French tastes and developed
Baudelaire's perception of "spleen" into an outright delectation in sickness and perversity called "decadence."[40]

But above all, during the 1870s in Germany Friedrich Nietzsche
transposed these aesthetic tendencies into philosophy.[41] In this enterprise he had, of course, a precursor, Schopenhauer, who in *The World as
Will and Representation* of 1818 had rejected the systematic rationalism
of the mainstream post-Kantians, especially Hegel, and taken instead
Kant's doctrine of the moral will as the keystone of philosophy. He
transformed this will into something radically different, however: from
being a transcendental faculty of "practical reason" it became a restless
striving, a Will to life, through which the philosopher, like some secular
Buddha, was able to find surcease from the pain of mortal existence in a
timeless Nirvana of art. For the first time, art became the head and the
corner of philosophy. Long ignored by the public, Schopenhauer's
message was suddenly made relevant by the collapse of Europe's En-

lightened-Romantic illusions in 1848. Wagner, as we have seen, found inspiration in it for his mature work; what is less well known is that Europe's first two Russian discoveries, Turgenev and Tolstoy, did so too.

Nietzsche transformed Schopenhauer's quietistic Will to life into a kinetic faculty of heroic self-creation through art. The universal void of modern existence could be filled only by the beauty of myth, for "art, rather than ethics, constitutes the essential metaphysical activity of man."[42] Inspired by Wagner's revolution in music, Nietzsche set out, first of all, to demolish both the Apollonian classicism of Weimar humanism and the Socratic reason of German classical philosophy from Kant to Hegel (he seems never to have heard of Marx). On their ruins he created a new pantheon, not of Gods, but of moral-cultural symbols, by developing Wagner's mythopoeic antiprogressivism into a philosophy of Dionysian vitality, heroic Will, and neopagan amoralism.

In a later phase he undertook a similar demolition—and transcendence—of Christianity. The Enlightenment and Romanticism between them had for all practical purposes killed off the Devil; and Goethe had pointed up the moral by saving Faust and damning Mephistopheles. God Himself, however, survived in immanent form in the natural supernaturalism of early-nineteenth-century Romanticism, whether in the nature pantheism of Wordsworth, the philosophic Absolute of Hegel, or the aesthetic religion of Chateaubriand. It was only in the 1840s with the Left Hegelian critique of religion by such figures as Ludwig Feuerbach (of whom more later) that modern atheism assumed its most sophisticated form: it was no longer the simple assertion of the *philosophes* that rational proof of God's existence is impossible; it became instead the affirmation that He is merely an idealized projection of Ourselves, not the Creator but a mere by-product of earthly, human needs. Thus by the 1880s Nietzsche could declare that the news that "God is dead" is the "greatest event of recent times."[43] This left Man alone in a valueless universe—but at the same time limitlessly free to make himself truly human.

The trouble was that the "slave morality" or "herd mentality" of Christianity lived on in secular guise in modern democracy and, worse still, in socialism. Similarly, on an intellectual level, modern science and the utilitarian ethics of empiricism promoted another leveling of humanity in mediocrity. The result was the perpetuation in secular political form of the culture of *Ressentiment* created by the ancient Jews, universalized by the crucified God of Christianity, and presently democratized among the underlings of mass society—an ethic of envy by which the losers of history transformed their failings as human beings into virtues, thereby putting down the noble and the strong. This culture of *Ressentiment* now thwarted the emergence of heroes and geniuses, daring spirits able to recreate themselves as works of art by the power of Will. Post-Christian European culture, for Nietzsche, was thus in deep, indeed mortal, crisis.

The only recourse was a critique of existing values as radical as the crisis itself. A "philosophy with a hammer" was needed, an "ecstatic nihilism"[44] that would produce a "transvaluation of all values," the displacement of dead religious and philosophic values by vivifying, noble ones—such as had existed, Nietzsche believed, in primitive, pre-Socratic Greece or among the aristocrats of the French *ancien régime*. (The new German empire of Bismarck was a vulgar travesty of the true Old Regime, and Wagner, in triumph at Bayreuth, had sold his Dionysian birthright by celebrating this pompous, nationalistic Reich.) "Nihilism," therefore, was a creative negation out of which would emerge a "caste" of new aristocrats, supermen (or "overmen"), a type that, for Nietzsche, combined the qualities of Goethe and Napoleon, "Roman Caesar with Christ's soul."[45] In Nietzsche's anti-evangel, therefore, an aestheticized Will to power would permit a portion of mankind, at least, to say "Yea" to the "eternal return" of the miseries of existence, to "joyously" affirm the burden of life.[46]

Thus did Nietzsche transform philosophy from a rational, logical endeavor into an aesthetic, psychological quest, largely expressed through fragmentary aphorisms. The modernist-aesthetic worldview thereby found its vatic Zarathustra, articulating overtly what Baudelaire, Wagner, and the Impressionists had expressed through symbols and the play of sounds, colors, and forms. Indeed, he went a good ways beyond them to give the world the *ne plus ultra* of negation of modern civilization, the most extreme point on the continuum of Romanticisms inaugurated by the shock of the French Revolution.

The Enlightenment, it will be recalled, had "failed" as a comprehensive belief system because the scientific method could not found a compelling ethics, as both Rousseau and Kant argued; and this failure opened the way to the natural supernaturalism of Romanticism. This surrogate supernaturalism, however, turned out to be in fact an earthly aestheticism, as both Baudelaire and Nietzsche eventually made so bold as to proclaim. But can art offer a valid ethics any more than can science? The two questions together have never ceased to haunt modernity.

Once the aesthetic revolution of the midcentury had been assimilated by the avant-garde of Europe, in the 1880s and 1890s there appeared in the West Tolstoy, Dostoevsky, and Mussorgsky, and soon the Firebird on the magic stage of Le Châtelet. They arrived with the primal vitality of a soul both Dionysian and Ideal: it seemed that the gods might in fact be reborn, that the void of spleen and ennui could be filled, and that supermen might again walk the earth.

Thus opened a third circle of modernity, in which symbolism's aesthetic negation of the modern world became an effort to subvert it, a categorical refusal of existing reality for which the term "nihilism" had occasionally been used since early in the century, and which Nietzsche now revived with a vengeance (it seems his attention had been focused on the term by Turgenev's *Fathers and Sons*). This aesthetic nihilism reached its culmination with the generation of the 1890s and gave to that decade the meaning of overripeness, decadence, and the closure of civilization. But it was not just one century that was thus foreclosed. What fin-de-siècle aestheticism negated was the whole past of modern Europe—the civilization and the culture alike—all that Europe had produced since the scientific revolution, indeed since the Renaissance and the Reformation, and all that the Enlightenment had drawn together into the long-term perspective of "progress."

Nor did the revolutionary negation of aesthetic modernism end with the fin de siècle that produced it. In the new century, this force moved onward with constantly widening reverberations, and through an ever greater variety of modernisms, beyond the First World War to the outbreak of the Second.[47] To each new surge of this modernist assault on classical European culture, Russian experimental art—from Vladimir Maiakovskii's futurism to Kazimir Malevich's suprematism, to Sergei Eisenstein's cinematographic montage—contributed as a matter of routine, in constant communion with the avant-garde of the West.

The Russian Prophets

Indeed, the Russians had been in this movement from the very opening of the first circle in the late 1840s. Dostoevsky was of the same generation as Baudelaire and Wagner, while Tolstoy was only slightly younger. And both stood in a similar transitional relationship to Romanticism and the question of God. Dostoevsky on the eve of 1848 first began to discover his aesthetic vocation by transforming the fantastic Romanticism of Gogol and E. T. A. Hoffmann into a means for exploring the psychology of the morbid, the sick, and the perverse. After his Siberian exile and return to Russia in the midst of the Great Reforms of Alexander II, he fused this psychological probing with a critique of what, in his eyes, was the demonic rationalism of the Russian "nihilists" of the 1860s, who epitomized for him the invasion that the modern, Western world had mounted against Holy Russia.[48]

In the case of Tolstoy, behind his apparent realism lay a cognate aesthetic-spiritual reaction against modernity and the West. He, too, could not accept the Great Reforms and the liquidation of traditional, rural and gentry Russia, even though he did his best to act the enlightened squire during the Emancipation. Filled with foreboding by Tocqueville's recently published analysis of the fall of Old-Regime France, and under the influence of the current vogue of Schopenhauer, he concluded that the power of art alone could exorcise the anguish of his revolutionary age. *War and Peace* is thus in large measure an epic idealization of old, prereform Russia, and *Anna Karenina* and *Resurrection* are indictments of the soullessness of a reformed, modern Russia that had already succumbed to the Western invasion launched in the 1860s.[49]

Yet neither he nor Dostoevsky, in searching for a divine solution to the pain of modern existence, ever really recovered the old, personal God. They could only believe in those who still believed in Him—the simple Russian peasants. The "Tolstoyan religion," created after his abandonment of art and his "conversion" in 1881, was clearly in part a transposition of religion into a form of national populism. Even the more supernaturally oriented Dostoevsky would say, through the semi-autobiographical Shatov in *The Possessed*: "I believe in Russia, in her Orthodox Church, I believe in the body of Christ! I believe that the Second Coming will occur in Russia. I believe. . . . But in God? But in God? I . . . I *will* believe in God."[50] The compensation for the Divine absence which Baudelaire found in the grace of poetry and Wagner in the "Good Friday Spell" of music, their Russian *semblables et frères* found in Russia herself.

It was in the context of this modernist refusal of the modern world, then, that beginning in the 1880s or 1890s Russia for the first time became a constant cultural influence on the rest of Europe, a creator and exporter, not just an adapter of artistic forms. By 1914, men everywhere looked to St. Petersburg and Moscow as centers of innovation in the routine way that they looked to London, Paris, Berlin, or Vienna. *Ex Oriente lux* had become as indelible a feature of Russia's image as was the surviving shadow of the Tatar knout. And so, the casual acceptance that Europe had accorded her Eastern hinterland after the discovery of Turgenev, by the ascendancy of Dostoevsky and the Ballets Russes had turned increasingly to admiration, even adulation.

Of course, the light that the West perceived in the East was only a part of the light that actually shone there; and Russian culture by 1900 had become a very complex affair. For nineteenth-century Russia, like the West, had two souls, a neo-Romantic and a rationalistic one.

The same generations that produced the great Russian prophets produced greatness of a different kind. By the early nineteenth century, Peter's investment in Leibniz's Academy of Sciences, and Alexander I's in a university system, started to pay off handsomely. By 1900, in the domain of high culture there was no longer a West-East gradient, but a single European concert of scholarly and scientific professions. Nor were Russian institutions of higher learning any longer staffed by Germans; their luster now came from native sons, such as the inventor of non-Euclidean geometry, Nikolai Lobachevskii, the chemist Dmitrii Mendeleev, and the psychologist of conditioned reflexes, Ivan Pavlov. At the same time in the social sciences the populist historian Vassilii Kliuchevskii, beginning in the 1870s, in effect created modern agrarian social and economic history. One of his pupils, Sir Paul Vinogradoff, an émigré of 1905 and professor at Oxford, inspired the great medievalist Frederick Maitland to introduce that discipline into England with *Domesday Book and Beyond*. And still another pupil, Michael Rostovtseff, an émigré of 1917, did the same for the economic and social history of the ancient world. At the end of the century, the Russian economic school of Mikhail Tugan-Baranovskii and Nikolai Kondratiev had pioneered the analysis of what came to be called development economics, an enterprise that, again in emigration, led to the seminal work of Wassily Leontief and Simon Kuznets. So, eventually, the West did find out about Russia's second, rational soul after all.

Still, it is no accident that her sober seekers after positive knowledge never came to define their country under Western eyes; for Old-Regime Russian culture never defined itself in such rationalistic terms, but rather sought its identity in literary and aesthetic achievement. It did so because the telescoping of the Western itinerary in Russia put inordinate pressure on her small intelligentsia to serve as the mind and guide of the enormous mass of the "dark" and suffering people. Hence the "Russian word" acquired the sacred mission of giving voice to the nation's moral conscience, which was in the first instance an egalitarian, social conscience. Inevitably, Russian writers grappled with the Great Questions of the human condition in a "naive" mode that jaded Westerners no longer dared employ. This distinctively Russian culture of moral concern of course limited what fin-de-siècle Europeans could find in the East. But these Western aesthetes were not looking for Russia's second, rational soul anyway.

Soul for Export

Initially, the emergence of a creative culture in Russia had an effect parallel to that of her postreform political and social development: it made her seem still more a part of Europe. Yet this cultural assimilation, even in its realistic phase, opened vistas onto something more exciting than her likeness to the West, for Russian art also bore the profound imprint of national originality. Although this quality at first appealed to fin-de-siècle Europe merely as exotic and refreshing, it rapidly came to be felt as vital, invigorating, and ultimately intoxicating.

Even the reasonable Westernizer Turgenev, by the very power of his realism, inadvertently revealed to bourgeois Europe an alluringly romantic Russia of fields and peasants and isolated gentry manor-houses; a world imbued with the gentle grace, the timeless calm, the stable roots, and the enduring human values of the land and tradition; a pristine poetry which, in the urban, industrial West, was rapidly disappearing.

Mérimée's successor as the chief European popularizer of Russian culture, Melchior de Vogüé, attributed to Turgenev "the dominant qualities of every true Russian: natural kindness of heart, simplicity and resignation. With a remarkably powerful brain, he had the heart of a child." As a devout Catholic and a nostalgic aristocrat who was ill at ease in the new secular French Republic, de Vogüé consciously used the spiritual realism of the Russians to combat the critical realism of Flaubert and the positivistic naturalism of Émile Zola, which he held responsible for the decline of French vitality vis-à-vis Germany after 1870. The "childlike heart" of Turgenev thus became *l'âme slave, l'âme russe*, and de Vogüé's lyrical pen began to transform Russian realism into the vehicle for a new religiosity.[51]

This transformation became fully apparent only with the discovery of Tolstoy in the 1880s. Tolstoy, according to de Vogüé, gave realism the cosmic sweep of Shakespeare by achieving a "curious union of epic grandeur and infinitesimal analytical detail . . . this author may be said to possess the skill of an English chemist with the soul of a Hindu Buddhist." This Buddhist soul, typified in Platon Karataev, the serenely sage peasant of *War and Peace*, was elemental spirit, authentic primordial humanity: "The spirit of Buddhism in its great effort toward the extension of evangelical charity has penetrated the Russian character, which naturally has such intense sympathy for human nature, for the humblest creatures, for the forsaken and unfortunate. This spirit decries reason and elevates the brute, and inspires the deepest compassion in the heart." Europe's impression of Russia's spirituality was further enhanced when in his later years Tolstoy the novelist became Tolstoy the prophet, a contemner of the state, of the official church, of scientific rationalism, of progress, indeed of all modern civilization, "a true Nihilist—that is, subject to no faith or creed whatsoever."[52]

The transvaluation of European values through the appropriation of Russian culture was completed with the revelation of Dostoevsky to the West in the 1890s. Dostoevsky not only explicitly denounced modern rationalism, as did Tolstoy, but he exemplified this denunciation in every aspect of his art. He eschewed Tolstoy's meticulous description of the external world viewed in the daylight of realism to move instead in the mysterious inner world of the psyche, where the only guide was the nighttime illumination of vital instinct and primal intuition—blood, the will, and the spirit. More powerfully than any writer in any language, Dostoevsky revealed to men of the fin de siècle an "underground" world of demonic yet sublime passions, tenaciously surviving beneath the orderly surface of modern, rational civilization. The conviction was widespread that Dostoevsky's power of insight into the lower depths and the higher yearnings of the human soul was peculiarly Russian, born at once of the Russian people's intimate acquaintance with suffering and of their unusual vitality of character. Dostoevsky could fathom so much because the Russian people, still "young" and uncorrupted by civilization, were more deeply alive, more fully attuned to the pulse of basic humanity and elemental existence, than were the shriveled up, rational bourgeois of the West. This conviction could only be reinforced by the supernatural tones of the plaint of the Holy Fool in Mussorgsky's *Boris Godunov* or by the exuberance of the Ballets Russes. Viewed in this context, Dostoevsky came to be regarded as at once the most authentic oracle of the Russian spirit and the most profound chronicler of the human condition. "There never was," André Gide later wrote, "an author more Russian in the strictest sense of the word and withal so universally European."[53]

In England the indefatigable devotion of Constance Garnett furnished the public with readable, if homogenized, translations of most of the Russian classics. In introducing her rendition of Dostoevsky, so sober a naturalist as Arnold Bennett declared that he wished all British writers would submit to the influence of these "most powerful works of the imagination ever produced."[54] Slightly later the "decadent" yet socialist Oscar Wilde was inspired by Russian events to write a now forgotten play, *Verochka*, whose nihilist, bomb-throwing heroine was portrayed as a Baudelairean manifestation of satanic beauty.[55] Still later, from "the dungeon and chains" of Reading Gaol, in *De Profundis* he placed "the note of pity in Russian novels" in the same category with *Les fleurs du mal*. After declaring that "Christ's place is indeed among the poets" against "the Jews of Jerusalem in Christ's day [who] were the exact counterpart of the British philistines of our own," he asserted: "Two of the most perfect lives . . . are Verlaine and Prince Kropotkin: . . . the first, the one Christian poet since Dante; the other, a man with a soul of that beautiful white Christ which seems to be coming out of Russia."[56]

In prewar France the new idol was taken up by the young Gide, then a little-known rebel against the stifling ethical conventions of bourgeois society, for whom Dostoevsky's impulse-driven heroes were the heralds of his own "immoralistic" quest for self-affirmation in opposition to a philistine, conformist world.[57] At the same time, in other intellectual quarters, Dostoevsky the God seeker lent comfort to those, such as Paul Claudel or François Mauriac, who urged a return to religion purged of bourgeois concern for the respectability of the proper parishioner and informed instead with a spirituality both anguished and transcendent. They thus sought to replace the prevalent "counting-house" religion of morality—balancing merits against demerits, quanta of grace against quanta of sin—by a faith that de Vogüé had called "the religion of suffering": a faith in which redemption could originate in degradation, and in which the humiliation and heroism of psychological crucifixion became the "dark night of the soul" of modern man.

To the votaries of this tradition of Western thought, which extended from Baudelaire's *Fleurs du mal* to at least Georges Bernanos's mournful *Joy* and T. S. Eliot's *The Wasteland*, the satanic-cum-divine message of Dostoevsky soon became one of the four evangels, along with those of Baudelaire, Wagner, and Nietzsche. What T. S. Eliot, mixing Dante with modernist pessimism, wrote of Baudelaire he might just as aptly have written of Dostoevsky: "it is better, in a paradoxical way, to do evil than to do nothing: at least we exist. It is true to say that the glory of man is his capacity for salvation; it is also true that his glory is his capacity for damnation. The worst that can be said of most of our malefactors, from statesmen to thieves, is that they are not men enough to be damned."[58]

But in this aesthetico-Dantesque perspective all Dostoevsky's hero-villains were capable of either salvation or damnation. It must therefore follow that Russians in general were similarly superior spiritual beings, unlike the petty bourgeois of the West, who were neither hot nor cold but only decent. After 1917, Nikolai Berdiaev, preaching the gospel-according-to-Fedor-Mikhailovich, would disseminate this point of view in the West, alleging the titanic demonism of Bolshevism as proof of Russia's instinctive rejection of the Western *via media*, and thus para-doxically the sign of her superior spirituality.[59]

It was in Germany, however, that Holy Russia's impact was most pro-found and pervasive. To the intellectuals of fin-de-siècle Germany, as to those of no other Western nation, the Russians appeared primarily as *Seelenmenschen*, or men of spirit, and Dostoevsky's sacral satanism could evoke in them a properly religious response, as it did from the future Jesuit theologian Romano Guardini. Yet as often as not Russian spiritu-ality was voided of religious content and construed as idealism in the sense of a concern for the "higher," immaterial values of life, or as a heroic voluntarism and self-willed individualism, both being considered antidotes to the conformism of the ordered bourgeois world. From this perspective it was only a step to seeing the Russians as *Naturmenschen*, or men of nature, and the bearers of a childlike simplicity and youthful vitality, and hence also as *Machtmenschen*, or men of might, for the untapped creativity of youth ultimately meant a potential for power that "old" Europe no longer possessed.[60]

Not only the proponent of "God-manhood," Dostoevsky, but also the advocate of a return to the vivifying freshness of nature and the soil, Tolstoy, were revered in the German-speaking lands as veritable prophets, Slavonic Zarathustras. In the 1890s, Rainer Maria Rilke, in aesthetic dissent from Western philistinism, set out to seek the fountain of spiritual youth in a pilgrimage to the sage of Yasnaya Polyana; and he found his mystic-poetic vocation somewhere between the Neva and the Volga. His female companion in this quest, Lou Andreas-Salomé,[61] the friend of Nietzsche, Freud, and Gustav Mahler, mingled the themes of Russian youth and Russian spirituality in a poem, "Old Russia," remi-niscent of Tiutchev:

You seem to dally on your mother's knee,
Not yet to even grasp your woe,
So childlike seems your every deed,
　　While others grow.
You paint your buildings every shade,
As though you played through misery:
Red, green, blue, white on gold brocade,
　　Those are your livery.
And yet: whoever looks long will discover
And refrain respectfully from ridicule:
A child has made this Russia over
　　Into God's footstool.[62]

Similarly Thomas Mann, under the spell of Tolstoy and Dostoevsky—who appeared to him, as to many others, like reincarnations of
the Apostles of primitive Christianity—called Russian literature *die
heilige*, or Holy Writ, in his youthful work of 1903, *Tonio Kröger*. At the
same time Hermann Hesse took a more terrestrial, vitalistic, and
neopagan view of the Eastern utopia when he spoke of the Russian
people as *Urstoff, ungestaltetes Seelenmaterial* (primal human matter, unformed soul material), or when he appropriated a Russian symbol for
the title of his parable of modernist anomie, *Steppenwolf,* the wolf of the
steppes.[63]

Even more portentously, Dostoevsky was extolled by Nietzsche and
by all those who followed, or claimed to follow, in his tradition. Indeed,
after Nietzsche himself, Dostoevsky was one of the most potent cultural influences, especially on the Right, in early-twentieth-century
Germany. Russia returned the compliment Germany had made her in
adopting Dostoevsky by giving Nietzsche the largest audience he enjoyed in any foreign country: thus in Russia, the pair, along with Baudelaire, furnished the intellectual stimulus of the symbolists' revolt against
the civic aesthetics of the Populist tradition.[64] In Germany, a different
synthesis occurred: though it seems that Nietzsche himself never read
the four great novels of Dostoevsky's maturity, later German critics saw
in them the embodiment of his "overmen"—in the Christlike "idiocy"
of Prince Mishkin, the immoral egoism of Raskolnikov, the half-child-

ish, half-barbaric lust for life of Dmitrii Karamazov, the demonic intellectual pride of his brother Ivan, and the self-transcending spirituality of their junior, Alyosha. The conclusion was often drawn that all "true" Russians displayed the larger-than-life vitality and the primal Dionysian force of these fictional archetypes. The true Russian therefore was a superior being of the sort that had long since disappeared in the utilitarian, money-grubbing West, sunk in the mass vulgarity and moral puniness that its middle classes foolishly called "civilization."

Indeed, it was Nietzsche himself who, in his last active years, at the end of the 1880s, first sketched the synthesis between his doctrine and that of Dostoevsky: "This *deep* man, who is ten times correct to think little of the superficial Germans, knew the Siberian prison-camps and the inmates among whom he lived, plain hardened criminals for whom there was no path back into society . . . [for he] was cut from the best, hardest and most valuable wood which grew anywhere in Russia."[65] Dostoevsky was thus a kind of superman; and through him Nietzsche came to see Russia herself as a kind of supercountry, capable perhaps of resolving the crisis of post-Christian culture that so haunted him at the end of the 1880s.

It is in *Beyond Good and Evil* that Nietzsche gives the fullest scenario for the unfolding of Europe's century-long "crisis of nihilism." This most somber of his works gives a critical inventory of the sickness of the modern spirit, in philosophy, in religion, in ethics, in science, and in the life of the various European nations. After finding each branch of culture, and each nation, fatally wanting, he asks what new "aristocracy" can bring Europe the unity that alone can save her?[66] Elsewhere he evokes the parallel with the fall of Rome: "Where are the barbarians of the twentieth century?"[67] Yet he rejoices in the impending catastrophe.

I am a *bearer of glad tidings*. . . . I know lessons of such elevation that we as yet have no concept of them; only beginning with me is there hope again. . . . For when truth enters into struggle with the lies of millennia we will have convulsions . . . the like of which has never been dreamed of. The concept of politics will be entirely dissolved in ideological war [*Geisterkrieg*], all power structures of the old society will be blown into the air . . . there will be wars

214

such as there never have been on earth before. Only beginning with me will the earth know *grand politics*.[68]

And how might this apocalypse work itself out? At times, Nietzsche thought that some "blond beast" might restore life to Europe. For a moment he contemplated racial mingling with the Jews. He also glanced at the classic alternative to Europe, the new world of America. Yet he wound up turning Tocqueville's prophecy about the two masters of the twentieth century on its head: America was resolutely dismissed in favor of Russia. "The mark of the next hundred years: the entry of the Russians into culture. A grandiose goal, the approach of barbarism, the awakening of the arts, the magnanimity of youth, and a fantastic madness and real strength of will."[69] Even so, the regeneration of Europe would require great internal revolutions. One variant might be "the fragmenting of the [Russian] empire into small units, and especially the introduction of imbecilic parliamentarianism." But this would be a disaster.[70] The Russia Nietzsche longed for was a thoroughly premodern one: "Russia is the *only* power which has any endurance left in it, that can wait, that can still promise something—Russia embodies the very opposite concept to the pathetic division of Europe into petty [national] states and that febrility which entered into a critical condition with the founding of the German Empire."[71] Thus "Russia must become the master of Europe and Asia," and in this "new Imperium Romanum" the little nations of Europe will be like the Greek city states under old Rome, cultural centers. Nietzsche concluded that, amidst the wars of the twentieth century, an infusion of Slavic blood and a political alliance with Russia could alone save Germany from the creeping rot of Western democratic and scientific "progress."

In the decade preceding 1914, a self-declared disciple of Nietzsche, Artur Möller van den Bruck, was instructed in the mysteries of Holy Russia by the symbolist novelist and self-appointed exegete of Dostoevsky, Dmitrii Merezhkovskii, who was also a mentor of the future philosopher of National Socialism, Alfred Rosenberg. Under this influence, Möller began to preach the idea that the "Slavs [that is,

Russians] alone can still give birth to a Jesus or a Buddha"[72]—figures whom he viewed not as religious leaders (for in his eyes, as in Nietzsche's, God was dead) but as exemplars of a prerational force of creative idealism.

Thus was the religious and ethical message of the Russian apostles adulterated into a secular cult of antirationalism and amoral instinctualism. The psychological insights of the Russian novelist were forged into political weapons with which to combat the rationalism of dominant liberal society on behalf of a desperate drive to escape the constraints of the bourgeois world and to return to a simpler, more organic past. This neo-Romantic yearning to revert to a society more high-minded than that of the present—a society such as had presumably existed in the West before the triumph of industrialism and which, one might believe, continued to survive in that still unsullied garden of Mother Earth which was rural Russia—yielded a conglomeration of pessimistic and millenarian sentiments which has been variously designated the "conservative revolution" or the "politics of cultural despair."[73]

So strongly did the celebrants of this creed feel the need to combat soulless modernity in the name of the vivifying return of a simpler age that in 1906 Möller van den Bruck, again with the aid of Merezhkovskii, launched a monumental edition of the Slavonic Noble Savage, a series which by 1914 had run to twenty-three volumes. It began with *The Possessed*, which it proclaimed the most probing commentary on the Russian Revolution of 1905. (The novel would, more appropriately, be put to a similar use after 1917.) This choice "allowed Möller from the start to affix to Dostoevsky a predominantly mystical and political interpretation of a radical conservative cast."[74] This enterprise was followed by complete editions of most of the great Russian "primitives," from Gogol to Leskov. As a result, Germany soon could boast the most complete and aesthetically satisfying corpus of translations from the Russian of any Western nation. Gide, for instance, was obliged to have recourse to the German version of *The Brothers Karamazov* for his first acquaintance with the full text. Not only were these series an artistic success; they were a commercial triumph as well. By the First World War, over 100,000 volumes of Dostoevsky were being sold per year and

216

by 1922 annual sales had reached almost twice that figure—a good fortune that did not befall Constance Garnett until after the Second World War.* [75]

Yet it would be much too simple to claim that Dostoevsky's success in Germany was due to the enthusiasm of the antirationalistic Right alone. Enthusiasm could be just as great with men of progressive opinions and a positivistic worldview. The great case in point is Sigmund Freud, who avowed that he had developed the central concept of psychoanalysis, the Oedipus complex, from three literary works: Sophocles' tragedy of course, Shakespeare's *Hamlet,* and Dostoevsky's *The Brothers Karamazov.* Long after his first acquaintance with this work,

---

*At the height of these mystico-metaphysical lucubrations, in 1911, a more sober note was sounded, in Joseph Conrad's *Under Western Eyes,* written in answer to Dostoevsky's *Possessed* and to those European men of letters who knew nothing about Russia beyond their own intoxication with Dostoevsky. Conrad's father had participated in the Polish Rising of 1863 and after its failure was deported with his family to Siberia. This experience, and the drastic Russian repression in Poland itself, led his son to abandon hope for civilization under tsarism and to seek instead the *grand large* of the West and the high seas of the world. Late in life, however, he returned to examine the enigma of his origins in *Under Western Eyes.* Although the novel had little impact when published, it made more sense than most of what passed for wisdom in the West; indeed, after the Revolution it was highly regarded in what remained of liberal and anti-Bolshevik quarters in Russia.

The strength of the novel is its combination of a Polish perception of Russia with a British distrust of high-flown metaphysics. Its message was simple and blunt: the heroic Russian revolutionary movement was a mirror image of the despotism it sought to combat. Radical Russia offered an unrelieved cultural tragedy, for "the moral and emotional reactions of the Russian temperament . . . could be reduced to the formula of senseless desperation provoked by senseless tyranny." This led to "a purely Utopian revolutionism, encompassing destruction by the first means to hand, in the strong conviction that a fundamental change of hearts must follow the downfall of any given human institution. These people were unable to see that all they can effect is merely a change of names" (Anchor Doubleday edition of 1963, p. 11).

All this is perceptive as far as it goes, that is, as applied to the most radical wing of the Russian "social movement," the People's Will, the Combat Organization of the neo-Populist Socialist Revolutionaries, and the Bolsheviks. However, Conrad vastly over generalizes about the Russian "temperament" as a whole, ignoring completely the rational, liberal, and Westernizing elements in Russian culture and politics, represented for example by the Kadets, with whom the moderate Polish Kolo was allied in the Duma. It might be added that Conrad was similarly disabused about the heroic Polish insurrectionary tradition.

Yet for all Conrad's hostility to Russia, and to the myth of her spirituality, he does have something in common with his authorial mirror image, the myth maker and archfoe of Poland and the West, Dostoevsky. For both, in their respective oversimplifications, correctly identified two crucial components of the tragedy of 1917: *Under Western Eyes* points to the inherent brutality of the Russian political situation; *The Possessed* highlights the lethal hubris of mystic rationalism, which is universal.

Freud in 1928 wrote the introduction to one of the supplementary volumes of Möller's series; in it, he produced a retrospective analysis of Dostoevsky's "parricidal neurosis" and claimed it underlay the insights of genius in *The Brothers Karamazov*—"the most magnificent novel ever written."[76]

Thus by 1914 "youthful" and "spiritual" Russia had become in a variety of European circles, but especially in Germany, an object of admiration, even of envy. The result can only inspire a mixed evaluation. On the one hand, the transmigrations of the Russian soul fostered the remarkable aesthetic flowering of modernism; on the other hand, they contributed to the emerging currents of ethical nihilism and integral nationalism that have earned for the age the title "seedtime of totalitarianism." Yet in both cases, Russia's position in European culture had been turned upside down with respect to her status at the time of Peter: just as she had once been a rationalistic utopia for the *philosophes*, she now became a spiritualistic utopia for all dissenters from rational philosophy.

But what transformations in European culture itself produced this inversion of Russia's fortunes? What is the nature of such paradoxical phenomena as a "conservative revolution" or negation as the acme of affirmation? Why had two centuries of Enlightenment culture suddenly been turned on *its* head?

The Roots of Aesthetic Nihilism

In fact, it was the very completeness of the triumph of classical liberalism and positivist values that bred the fin de siècle's ennui with what such a man of science as Alfred North Whitehead once called "one-eyed reason." This backlash unfolded according to a by now established pattern. Just as the protoliberalism and prepositivism of the Enlightenment had engendered the Romantic reaction of the early nineteenth century, so now the radicalized ultra-Romanticism of symbolism challenged liberalism and positivism triumphant. And just as the early Romantics of westernmost Europe, following the lead of Mme. de Staël and Coleridge, had taken "Gothic" and "spiritual" Germany as their model and ideal, so too (now that Germany herself had become bourgeois and philistine) did neo-Romantics throughout fin-de-siècle Europe, following Gide, Wilde, and Rilke, take "young" and "holy" Russia as their guide and inspiration.

Germany and Russia in their respective phases as Romantic utopias in fact offered much of what their foreign admirers sought, for both had developed precocious critiques of the rationalisms of their day—Germany from the time of the *Sturm und Drang* to Romanticism proper, and Russia from the time of Dostoevsky to the symbolism and supernaturalism of the silver age in the early twentieth century. Both nations had developed probing criticisms of rationalism, since each had experienced its impersonal and universalistic categories as in some measure an alien and Western force, a menace to their own cultural identities. So each nation in turn could furnish authentic apostles of *Geist* or "soul," whether the brothers Schlegel or Merezhkovskii and Berdiaev, to bring to Western Gentiles the glad tidings of spiritual rebirth.[77]

Now that the heroic age of liberalism had passed, its heirs and beneficiaries could no longer believe the ancestral creed with their original fervent simplicity. Indeed, as early as 1870, John Stuart Mill, the "saint of rationalism," expressed his own ennui with a lifetime's combat for Enlightenment values:

> In England, I had seen . . . many of the opinions of my youth obtain general recognition, and many of the reforms in institutions, for which I had through life contended, either effected or in course of being so. But these changes had been attended with much less benefit to human well-being than I should formerly have anticipated, because they had produced very little improvement in that which all real amelioration in the lot of mankind depends on, their intellectual and moral state: and it might even be questioned if the various causes of deterioration which had been at work in the meanwhile, had not more than counterbalanced the tendencies to improvement. I had learnt from experience that many false opinions may be exchanged for true ones, without in the least altering the habits of mind of which false opinions are the result.[78]

In other words, a near-century of enlightened reform had failed to overcome the deficiencies of human nature or satisfy human aspiration to some higher than human good.

By the 1890s, it was becoming clear that triumph of a liberal-democratic and industrial order did not necessarily mean a more rational or happier world. Mass literacy produced a debased mass culture as often as it did a mature and informed citizenry; universal suffrage and parliamentary government led to demagogic politics as often as they facilitated the intelligent articulation of social needs; industrial expansion and developing prosperity failed to end either poverty or injustice. Instead, progress in all domains seemed to aggravate rather than assuage class tensions, thereby encouraging the organized pressure of socialists, syndicalists, and other utopian visionaries. Finally, the grouping of the major European peoples into nation-states had produced chauvinism and the threat of general war rather than human fraternity and the prospect of perpetual peace; and the sharpening of national sentiment, together with the entry of the masses into politics, gave rise to jingoistic xenophobia and the new phenomenon of political anti-Semitism.

Altogether, then, the mass society of modernity, by the very irrationalism of its politics, seemed to offer a living refutation of the Enlightenment culture that had fostered it. Accordingly, the attention of fin-de-siècle sociologists and psychologists was increasingly directed toward the irrational in human affairs; intellect, as celebrated by positivism, was now seen as a surface phenomenon barely veiling the depths of the unconscious, whose dark drives were the real motive force of human actions. Some of the new explorations of the unconscious, such as Freud's psychoanalysis, sought to contain its destructive force by understanding it, and so help us live with our burdensome but necessary civilization. Other investigations, such as Gustave Le Bon's study of the "psychology of the crowd," sought to manipulate the mass unconscious so as to transcend what was deemed to be a failed civilization. And the artists of decadence, in their symbolic idiom, exalted the irrational so as to escape from rationalistic civilization, thereby aggravating that civilization's sense of crisis.

Although this mood of crisis obtained in Europe as a whole, there existed important differences between the pattern of liberal disillusion in the Western democracies and in Mitteleuropa, differences that explain the contrast between the fortunes of Constance Garnett and those of Möller van den Bruck as popularizers of Russian culture. In westernmost Europe, the individualistic liberalism born of the Enlightenment had by 1905 entered into crisis because it had fulfilled its program; in Mitteleuropa, it fell into even deeper crisis because it had failed to fulfill that same program.

This common program was parliamentary government, universal suffrage, the rule of law, universal education, and a predominantly secular public sphere, whether under a constitutional monarchy or a political republic. With this achieved, liberalism's role as the principal force for change in Europe was over. In Great Britain, its last heroic age was the period of Lloyd George's People's Budget of 1909, of the resultant constitutional struggle in 1911 against the power of the House of Lords, and of the unsuccessful fight in 1914 to enact Irish Home Rule—a combination of crises that brought normally well-ordered Britain to the brink of civil war but out of which the liberals nonetheless emerged victorious. In France, liberalism's last great hour came at the end of the 1890s with the Dreyfus Affair and the consequent separation of church and state between 1901 and 1905, a traumatic cultural civil war that, all the same, ended in liberal victory. In both countries, therefore, the traditional aristocratic, landed, and clerical foes of liberalism, though hardly annihilated, were eliminated as effective opponents of a democratic order.

And so, by 1914, the British had by and large completed turning Mill's utilitarian agenda of "true opinions" into law; and in France the Radical Republicans had quite completed the Jacobin agenda of 1793. If progress were to go any further, it could only be through a leap into the dark of socialism, or possibly even syndicalism, both of which promised the liquidation of "bourgeois" society. Not only did classical liberalism no longer have anything positive to do, it was threatened with seeing its previous work undone, and so dug in to hold the ancestral fort.

This conservative turn was all the sharper because liberalism's culminating victories had been achieved only through an alliance with the working class against Tories and anti-Dreyfusards, thus stimulating labor agitation. Indeed, socialism, largely dormant in maritime Europe since the failure of Chartism and the Revolution of 1848, had reemerged in the 1890s, leading to mass parties by 1905; and trade unions, largely illegal until the 1870s and 1880s, became a real force with the new century. Both the British Labor Party, with the elections of 1906, and the French SFIO (Socialist Party), formed in 1905 through the merger of smaller groups, emerged as strong political forces, seconded by increasingly belligerent trade-union organizations. English Liberals and French Radicals, at the very moment they freed themselves from the menace of the old Right, found themselves caught in the toils of a new Left. This surprise reawakened fears harking back to the Commune and even to the Chartist movement and the June Days of 1848. Under the shock of these developments, the middle classes of both countries increasingly put patriotism before progress, with the result that by 1909 the former Radical and Dreyfusard Georges Clemenceau, and by 1910 even the former Socialist Aristide Briand, had become nationalistic strikebreakers, while during the war the erstwhile author of the People's Budget, Lloyd George, adopted an equally patriotic stance.[79]

Still, English Liberals and French Republicans, though increasingly conservative, hardly felt defeated. No matter how inadequate their achievements as measured against their original ideals, they had succeeded in one crucial respect: they had attained preponderant political power in their respective societies, and the satisfactions of power can sustain self-confidence in the face of failure to achieve nobler ends. In westernmost Europe, the neo-Romantic revolt against bourgeois civilization was confined largely to the realms of ethics and aesthetics.

Thus, that midcentury precursor of antimodernity John Ruskin forsook the grimy bricks of Britain for the resplendent stones of old Venice, and William Morris abjured industrialism for the handicraft production of art objects and chairs. Somewhat later Joris Huysmans sought a perfected social ideal in the organic world of the medieval cathedral builders, as did Henry Adams later still in the glories of Mont-Saint-Michel and Chartres. Maurice Barrès reviled the republic and celebrated successively the anarchistic *culte du moi* and the tribal cult of *la terre et les morts*. Affluent circles in London and Paris indulged in pre-Raphaelite escapism, or sought spiritual satisfaction in aesthetic decadence, or renounced Ernest Renan and returned to the church, as did Paul Claudel and Charles Péguy. Yet this pessimism about modern culture posed no substantial threat to the stability of existing society.

This remains true even though the rejection of modernity by part of the French middle class produced the neoroyalist Action Française, which has often been considered protofascist.[80] This organization's formal program advocated restoration of the two institutions dear to the traditional French Right, the monarchy and the Catholic Church. It endorsed both, however, essentially as utilitarian means to promote cohesive, authoritarian nationhood for an anticipated revanche against Germany, an ideal known as integral nationalism. Its ideology, moreover, though set forth with vehemence, also sought to convince through what it called Latin clarity and would-be scientific positivism. In consequence, although Action Française embraced the mounting anti-Semitism of the day, it had little gift for the unbridled irrationalism necessary for mass politics of a genuinely fascist sort. It remained, throughout its career, antidemocratic and elitist, and thus hardly a menace to the republic, which, following the Dreyfus Affair and the separation of church and state, was more firmly entrenched than ever before.

Hence, in England and France, the political and cultural terrain was such that Russian spirituality could work the emancipation of individuals, generate powerful aesthetic reactions among the elite, or titillate the *beau monde*. But it could not contribute to the overwhelming of those liberal values by which established society, in spite of all its disenchantments, continued to live so comfortably.

By contrast, in Germany conditions existed which made possible a more devastating impact of the Slavonic genius. Intuitionist and subjectivist modes of thought had, after all, bulked large in the formation of modern German culture at the turn from the eighteenth into the nineteenth century. To be sure, after the failure of the lyrical illusions of 1848, Germany, like the rest of Europe, underwent an anti-Romantic reaction—an era of materialism, positivism, and a scientistic, "Darwin-ian" Marxism. Nonetheless, the strength of the Romantic legacy meant that a predisposition to intuitionist, mythopoeic thinking lay ready and waiting in the national tradition to be exploited by the neo-Romantics of the fin de siècle.

This predisposition acted all the more strongly because of the "special way" by which Germany had become a modern nation-state. France and England had first been defined as polities, and only later did these polities become the bearers of a distinctive national culture. Modern Germany, however, had been defined as a culture before becoming a polity. Political problems, therefore, tended also to be problems of culture, in particular the articulation and defense of a specifically German culture vis-à-vis a universal, modern civilization. It is surely no accident that the refusal of modernity by such figures as Wagner and Nietzsche was primarily a critique of culture, or that this critique simultaneously idealized a supposed harmony between culture and society in the past and projected this idealization into the future. Archaic Greece, or the Middle Ages, or the *Goethezeit* had to be recreated in modern myth to give society heroes to reign in some equally mythic future. Neither Baudelaire nor Ruskin entertained such bold "political" ambitions.

This conflation of politics and culture interacted with Germany's actual institutional *Sonderweg* to give her nineteenth-century liberalism its distinctive and troubled cast. Despite Germany's economic and cultural triumphs, by 1914 more striking than those of England and France, her men of *Besitz und Bildung*, of property and culture, had fallen lamentably short in the all-important political domain where her Western rivals had succeeded: as a result of the liberals' defeats during the Revolution of 1848, and then again under Bismarck in 1862–1871, the middle classes failed to capture power in the state or even a preponderant position in society. And after 1871, under the Kaiserreich, these same liberals, despite sporadic efforts to free themselves from Junker domination, were constantly driven back under the protective tutelage of the monarchy by the growing strength of Social Democracy. For this movement, organized in the 1860s and fully mature by 1891, was far stronger than its French and British counterparts. After its Erfurt Congress of the latter year, it was officially committed to revolutionary

Marxism and supported by the most imposing trade-union apparatus in Europe. In the elections of 1912 these antinational "reds" received a third of the votes, thereby becoming the largest party in the Reichstag.

Confronted with this force, German liberals were far more frightened by socialism than were British Liberals or French Dreyfusards, and hence dared not ally with it against the monarchy and aristocracy. As 1914 approached they largely abandoned the quest for democracy and sought the self-realization denied them at home in vociferous support of the imperial establishment's striving for "a place in the sun" abroad. They were convinced that Germany's economic power, organizational ability, and flourishing culture—all essentially middle-class accomplishments—entitled her to just such an international position. With this submission of middle-class liberalism to the Kaiserreich, in conjunction with the semiautocratic regime's conversion to mass nationalism, the political gap between Germany and the West, which in 1870 had appeared relatively modest and temporary, had by 1914 widened into a gulf. Its extent would become apparent with the outbreak of war. Although the public in all belligerent nations greeted war with enthusiasm, the young generation of Germany did so with particular ardor. To the German generation of 1914, the test of arms appeared both as a heroic release from the prosaic modern world and as the fulfillment of some newfound national vocation.[81]

At the same time as Germany's liberals fell captive to the imperial establishment, they were challenged on still another front. Since these men of "property and culture" had manifestly failed to realize the classic Enlightenment program, after 1870 the ideals of democracy, universal reason, and positive science which had once been theirs were successfully claimed by socialism. By the 1890s, therefore, the German middle classes found themselves simultaneously in bondage to the monarchy above and menaced by socialist leveling from below. In consequence, any political appeal to the ideas of reason and humanity, now appropriated by the socialists, became suspect in numerous liberal quarters.[82]

In this impasse some German liberals, such as Max Weber, chose simply to cling to their values and wait out the situation. Other spokesmen for the world of property and culture, however, made a virtue of necessity by endorsing the existing political system and seeking only corrective improvements in its social and economic policies. Such were the *Katherdersozialisten*—professorial "socialists of the chair"—and the great proponent of the special destiny of Mitteleuropa, Friedrich Naumann.[83] This camp held that the German order represented a unique combination of tradition with modernity, paternalism with social welfare, religious and moral values with industrial and bureaucratic rationalism, a balanced system in which qualified professionals ruled not for their own benefit but for that of the entire nation. Their political ambition was to give the organic German synthesis a heightened social conscience and so safeguard it against the onslaughts of modernity. By the same token, they sought to reaffirm Germany's superiority over the plutocratic democracies of England, France, and the United States, dominated as they were by atomistic liberalism and unbridled profit seeking.[84] In this new political climate, the old distinction between organic German *Kultur* and mechanistic Western *Zivilisation* revived; and during the two decades leading up to the First World War it came to permeate public discourse from high scholarship to mass journalism.[85]

Yet, at the turn of the new century, the defenders of German uniqueness faced a problem that had not existed a hundred years before: Germany's relation to the East. In this regard, one segment of the population, no doubt a majority, held that Germany was both more cultured *and* more civilized than Russia, indeed than all Slavdom. German-speaking Mitteleuropa thus assumed the role of defender of "European civilization" against the Asiatic "barbarism" of tsarism; and pan-Germanism accordingly gathered strength as an antidote to the pan-Slavism presumably promoted by Russia, indeed as civilization's shield against all the lesser breeds of Eastern Europe.

The fin-de-siècle revival of the German idea of *Kultur* did not invariably act to exclude Russia from Europe, however. Since this concept remained first of all an ideological defense against the overcivilized West, one could also conclude that undercivilized Russia, though not as cultured as Mitteleuropa, was nonetheless uncontaminated by Western materialism and hence an ally of authentic Europe. It was by this reasoning that establishment votaries of German uniqueness such as the young Thomas Mann became Romantic Russophiles: in their eyes, it was Russia's uncorrupted primitive nature that enabled her prophets to warn Germany against the West more penetratingly than could German writers themselves.

Still other intellectuals, socially more marginal, pushed these conservative-nationalist positions to extreme, nihilistic conclusions, producing what has been called a "politics of cultural despair." Half-fearing, half-despising the socialist plebs below, and half-idealizing, half-hating the haughty aristocrats above, but most of all detesting the pusillanimous middle classes—that is, in a sense, themselves—this group gave vent to sweeping resentment against the rationalism, liberalism, and socialism of the modern world. Although these nihilists of the Right saw the "rotten West" as the seat of modern decadence, they also held that the constant advance of "red" Social Democracy was bringing that same rot to Wilhelmine Germany. Indeed, they even believed that the imperial establishment at times betrayed its conservative vocation by accepting too much Western progress. The struggle against Western *Zivilisation* was thus essentially a cultural civil war within the Kaiserreich. In consequence, the marginal intelligentsia dreamed of a still more conservative order (which Möller later called a "Third Reich") purged of Western corruption and dedicated to the rejuvenation of native *Kultur*.[86] Of course, intelligentsia voices were raised against such lucubrations: Thomas Mann's brother, Heinrich, pointed out as early as 1910 the danger that the radical conservative mentality presented for society. Yet such liberal, Westernizing dissent was a minority position in Germany's fin-de-siècle aesthetic intelligentsia.[87]

The explanation of this intelligentsia's increasing antimodernism is best sought in the paradoxes of Germany's now markedly skewed *Sonderweg*. The Wilhelmine Kaiserreich was economically dynamic but socially and politically rigid; it encouraged creativity yet simultaneously refused full civic participation; it was open to men of talent yet at the same time denied them a chance at real power. Amid such frustrations resentment abounded; and marginal men of parts experienced most strongly the resulting envy and ire.

Such alienation could not find an outlet in revolutionary commitment on the Left (as was habitual among the Russian intelligentsia). For that would have meant becoming déclassé, falling to the moral level of the proletariat, a degradation which men of *Bildung*, if not always of *Besitz*, could hardly accept. The solution for marginal men of education was to turn conservatism on its head by transforming it into a radicalism of the Right. Thus did activist conservatives direct resentment of their own marginality against the established conservative order, which now stood accused of failing to preserve Germany from alienating modernity. And so the way was opened for Nietzsche's charge that the meek Christian ethic of charity, as well as its liberal and socialist surrogates, were manifestations of a "slave morality." It is surely no accident that the "psychology of *Ressentiment*," first so penetratingly explored by Nietzsche, was a discovery of imperial Germany.

Whatever Nietzsche's motives in enunciating this message (and opinion is divided as to whether his intentions were ethical or political), in the hands of his early twentieth-century epigones, his theories clearly served to stigmatize the religious and humanistic culture of Germany's middle class as a source of national impotence. The ethical values that had formerly been the pride of the educated classes were now castigated as shackles of servitude for superior beings, false gods whose worship blunted the will to struggle against the degradation of modern, mass civilization.

Thus in Germany at the end of the century the self-doubt common to European liberalism as a whole turned increasingly to self-denigration among a part of the middle classes that had once fostered liberalism. Yet in a manner consonant with the contradictory nature of the crisis, cultural masochism did not cease to be compatible with an ardent, even arrogant nationalism. For the destruction of the perverse power of modernity in Germany was held to be only the prelude to her rebirth as a "cultured" nation, a hope which generated a conservative yet revolutionary variant of populism.[88] A part of the aesthetic intelligentsia, in its revulsion against Western progress and the socialist proletariat it had spawned, idealized what it took to be the true *Volk*, nurtured by the land and ancestral tradition, rooted in both blood and soil. This *Volk*, it was held, had furnished Germany's greatness in the past; and once the present invasion of modernity had been halted, it would restore her greatness in the future. With such fantasies the new *völkisch* ideology anointed a mythic "people" as an all-encompassing community that would return society to primal wholeness by abolishing antagonistic classes. In this respect, the *Volk* offers a nationalist replacement for international Marxism's class to end all classes, the proletariat.

In the context of this mythology, any appeal to the universal reason of the liberal tradition could only profit the socialist rabble. Therefore, the argument went, away with reason utterly, history having proved that force and will, not the spineless imitation of universalistic foreign models, were the path to national grandeur. This bizarre and nihilistic logic, which surrendered to resentment of existing German structures in an effort to transcend them, lay at the heart of what the poet Hugo von Hofmansthal later (approvingly) called the "conservative revolution."

In consequence, after the 1890s, when both Nietzsche and Dostoevsky had become major cultural forces in Germany, some nationalist intellectuals belonging to an educated class that since 1848 had been the most stridently Russophobic in Europe discovered a kinship with the antibourgeois writers of Russia. The very vehemence of the outcries of both Russian and German foes of modernity attests that their perceived kinship arose from a sharing of the sentiments of Aesop's fox regarding grapes. In effect, both Germans and Russians often felt excluded from participation in the plenitude of modern civilization, reserved with exasperating injustice for the philistines of England and France. After 1890, as German internal conditions diverged from those of the Western democracies, a part of the defeated German middle classes felt drawn toward an idealized Russia by what they took to be a mutual quest for spirituality but was in fact a common *Ressentiment* of the admired yet despised bourgeois West.

Much of this agitation stemmed from the extravagant, déclassé elements of the German intelligentsia, such as Möller himself. Yet in the last years before the war such sentiments found an ever broader audience in society at large. The poet Stefan George quite equaled Möller as propagator of irrationalism with his lyrical advocacy of returning the nation to an ill-defined aristocracy of the spirit. Even more portentous

was the Free Youth Movement, an organization dedicated to respiritu-
alizing Germany through the cult of nature, many of whose members
would be among the first and most enthusiastic combatants of 1914. In
short, the problem of politics was increasingly transformed into a problem of culture. In consequence, the rhetoric of German *Kultur* versus
Western *Zivilisation*—of spirit versus matter, of a heroic past and future
versus the mediocre present—became the intellectual idiom of the day.

A kindred though less extreme disillusion with liberal values was
expressed by more established and responsible members of the intellectual community. In this instance, the result was more often creative
than nihilistic, for suspicion of a flat rationalism gave to German social
thought of the fin de siècle a deeper sense of complexity than was found
in Auguste Comte's "positive" sociology or Herbert Spencer's evolu-
tionism. The great case in point, of course, is Max Weber's reintroduc-
tion of cultural, in particular religious, forces into the workings of the
socioeconomic process, especially as that process was defined by Marxists. Other figures with doubts about modernity made parallel contributions. Werner Sombart deprecated the modern acquisitive spirit
through a historical investigation of the origins of capitalism that in fact
did much to open the subject up to comparative analysis. The legal
historian Otto von Giercke displayed his reservations regarding egalitarian democracy by investigating medieval corporatism, which in fact
underlay representative institutions that were later deemed "liberal."
The sociologist Ferdinand Tönnies, in his suspicion of unilinear
schemes of progress, staked out a framework of European development
from *Gemeinschaft*, organic traditional community, to *Gesellschaft*, individualistic modern society, that in fact illuminates the transition from
the Old Regime to the New far better than the liberal notion of Progress.

Yet, whatever face of Kaiserreich culture one emphasizes, it remains
true that Germany's exceptional divergence from the liberal tradition
opened the way for an exceptional penetration of her intellectual life by
themes derived from the largely preliberal culture of Russia. For the
Russian prophets, Tolstoy and Dostoevsky, with all the power of their
genius, had anticipated the rest of Europe in denouncing the ills of

230　　rationalistic and liberal civilization, indeed of the modern West per se. At the same time, they celebrated that inwardness which German intellectuals could easily construe as the source of cultural regeneration.

Nonetheless, despite the affinities between these currents of thought and the more visceral emotions that later fed National Socialism, it would be an exaggeration to claim that all the pre-1914 idealizations of Russia were in essence protofascist. More often than not, as in the case of Nietzsche himself, the enthusiasts of Russia in this period were equivocal in their attitude toward politics, interested primarily in an ethical or aesthetic critique of bourgeois civilization. After the war, German intellectuals such as Hermann Hesse and Thomas Mann moved increasingly toward a liberal interpretation of the higher individuality they had first found in the Russian novelists.

Other enthusiasts of the Russian soul, such as Möller, who exulted in the present failure and impending doom of bourgeois Europe, truly belonged to the revolutionary Right, and so later welcomed the beginnings of National Socialism. To these incendiary conservatives the raw youth and spirituality of Russia seemed to mirror Europe's lost past and to offer hope for a future rebirth. Indeed, this ambivalence was first expressed by the founder of the tradition, Nietzsche, in *Beyond Good and Evil*:

> Will is strongest and most astounding [among European nations] in that enormous frontier empire where Europe, as it were, flows back into Asia, in Russia. There the strength to will has long been stored up and accumulated, there the will waits menacingly—uncertain whether it is a will to deny or a will to affirm—to be unleashed. . . . I have in mind an aggravation of the Russian danger such that Europe would have to find the resolve to become dangerous herself, that is, by means of a new European master-caste to *create a single will*, a persistent, dreadful will of its own that can set itself goals thousands of years ahead. Thus would end the comedy that has lasted too long already, the division of Europe into petty states. The time for trivial politics is over; the next century will bring the struggle for world-mastery, the *compulsion* to begin grand politics.[89]

Granted, Nietszche's will to power may be understood as a metaphysical statement about life in general. Even so, projecting it onto historic nations gives it a clear political cast. Thus the Zarathustra of aesthetic nihilism did indeed anticipate Europe's fate in the twentieth century: something like the to-and-fro of wills to power he imagined would in truth mark its middle years.

And so it was that, at roughly the moment the Revolution of 1905 thrust Russia forward as an example for the radical Left, Russian culture made her a utopia for the radical Right. For the first time since the eighteenth century, Russia had advanced beyond assimilation into European life and begun to appear as a leader. Or at least she did so in the eyes of the extremes of Western society—on the Left in the role of a revolutionary guide, and on the Right as a new kind of menace that nonetheless might serve as a model.

WAR AND REVOLUTION:
1914–1917

Snowdrifts covered the Nevskii Prospéct . . .
  And along the [Horesman's] legendary quay,
    There advanced, not the calendar,
      But the real Twentieth Century.

> —Anna Akhmatova, *Poem without a Hero*,
> anent the last prewar winter (1940–1962)

———————————————

Di rider finirai
Pria dell'aurora
(You will finish laughing
Before the dawn).

> —Akhmatova's main epigraph to *Poem* (the voice of
> il commendatore in Mozart's *Don Giovanni*)

———————————————

Surely some revelation is at hand;
Surely the Second Coming is at hand . . .
A shape with lion body and the head of a man . . .
Is moving its slow thighs . . .
The darkness drops again; but now I know
That twenty centuries of stony sleep
Were vexed to nightmare by a rocking cradle,
And what rough beast, its hour come round at
    last,
Slouches towards Bethlehem to be born?

> —W. B. Yeats, "The Second Coming" (1918)

My times—my wild beast,
Who will dare to peer into your eyes
And to stick together with his blood
The severed vertebrae of two centuries?
But your spine has been smashed forever,
My beautiful, pitiful age,
And with an inane, bewildered grimace
You now look back, both cruel and weak,
    Like a beast that once was supple,
At the tracks of your own paws.

> —Osip Mandelshtam, "My Age, My Beast" (1918)

The First World War was the matrix of the contemporary world, the beginning of Akhmatova's "real Twentieth Century"—the century of international and social violence par excellence. It produced the Russian Revolution while the conflict still raged, and in its wake the fascist and Nazi revolutions. These competing revolutions prepared the way for a second world conflict, ending in the victory of the Red Spectre over its Black-Brown fascist adversaries. And this outcome in turn produced the Cold War between the heirs of a now imperial Soviet Union and the Western victors of the first and second hot conflicts.

Nor were these twentieth-century *guerres en chaine*,[1] in Raymond Aron's characterization, traditional wars. The first two were total wars in the material sense, fought by mass citizen armies at the front and entailing the mobilization of civilian society in the rear. The second two were total wars in the moral sense: they were not just political conflicts, but ideological crusades, wars of good against evil, thus making the twentieth century the ideological century par excellence.

The year 1914, moreover, at last brought the end of the European Old Regime. Contrary to the wisdom of the textbooks, 1789 had only begun the dismantling of the world of divinely sanctioned monarchy, aristocracy, and plebeian subordination, and at that only in maritime Europe. It took the whole of the political nineteenth century, from 1815 to 1914, for parliamentary government to spread from west to east, and for suffrage to creep downward to the "people," a process that reached Russia only in 1905. Yet in all European states as of 1914 there

236 was one institution that was uniformly "democratic": the conscript armies with which the coming patriotic war would be fought.

It is this circumstance that produced the end of the Old Regime everywhere east of the Rhine. For the mass armies of Central and Eastern Europe became, in defeat, the breeding ground for the century's rival revolutions. After the war was over, democracy—in the sense of the repudiation of all superordinate authority and hereditary social hierarchy—became the obligatory starting point of politics everywhere in Europe. Yet in nations where democracy was new, it was captured by ideologies that erected, on the mass base it afforded, authoritarianisms more awesome than any the Old Regime had ever known. Thus, the international violence of total war turned into the social violence of total revolution, and the twentieth century received its dominant apocalyptic face.

THE HINGE OF DARKNESS

Dulce et decorum est pro patria mori
(It is sweet and fitting to die for the fatherland).

—Horace, *Odes*

As of 1914 such a chain reaction of disasters was inconceivable to a Europe confident of its power and the planetary superiority of its civilization. Its preferred self-image was that of the *belle époque*, a time of technological progress, democratic advance, and ostentatious *joie de vivre*. Anna Akhmatova, in her great lament for the city of Peter and for Russia, retrospectively saw the time as the last feast of Don Giovanni, an age that refused to believe its libertine ways could ever be ended by war. And consciously echoing the ambivalence about the national fate of Pushkin's *Bronze Horseman*, she evoked the Bolsheviks' iconic cruiser *Aurora* firing its salvos against the Winter Palace only to inaugurate an era of darkness.

However, until these catastrophes cut short the revels of the last prewar years, most Europeans considered Russia as regained to their cause for good. Although not up to the highest Western standards, she was certainly a nation with which civilized societies could do business, whether economic, cultural, or diplomatic. It was under this favorable conjunction of conditions that Russia arrived at her bicentennial as a European power.

In international affairs the predominant belief in Russia's convergence with Europe permitted a reversal of the more extreme patterns of Western behavior toward her. Whereas in the years 1768–1774 French and British opinion had been thoughtlessly complacent about Catherine's policies in Poland and Turkey, and in the period 1830–1855 had been irrationally apprehensive about Nicholas I's activities in the same areas, during the years leading up to 1914 all European states determined their attitude toward Russia in eminently rational fashion—that is, not in terms of her character as a civilization, but with regard to her role as a power and the conflict or correspondence of her interests with theirs, just as they had in the times of Peter the Great and Alexander I.

Until 1890 the early-nineteenth-century alignment of the cabinets of Europe according to social and ideological affinity survived more or less intact in international affairs.[2] To be sure, the intimate Holy Alliance of the age of Metternich, Nicholas I, and Frederick William II had been shattered during the Crimean War by Austria's resistance to Russian designs in the Balkans. As a result, in 1866 Russia stood by complacently while Prussia, her staunchest friend, expelled the Habsburgs from Germany in the Seven Weeks' War. Acute tension again erupted between Austria and Russia as a result of the latter's war with Turkey in 1877–78. At the resulting Congress of Berlin Russia was frustrated in her pursuit of the full fruits of her victory while Austria was gratuitously awarded compensation in Bosnia and England in Cyprus. Russia's frustration also spilled over into a measure of hostility toward imperial Germany for the latter's allegedly pro-Austrian "honest brokerage" in determining Turkey's new frontiers.

Nevertheless, despite the chronic irritant of Balkan affairs time and again between 1872 and 1890 the last and most prodigious statesman of the European Old Regime, Bismarck, patched up the Eastern system of autocratic solidarity with a succession of *Dreikaiserbünde*, or Leagues of the Three Emperors, and a Reinsurance Treaty. In so doing, he acted not only out of considerations of *Realpolitik*, maneuvering to keep revanchist France isolated from possible allies, but also out of a belief, shared with the three emperors concerned, in their community of interests as a matter of conservative principle. Each understood quite well that the surest way to preserve the status quo at home was to avoid conflict among themselves abroad.

At the same time, as the century progressed the liberal Atlantic powers, France and England, ceased to constitute a loose bloc, as they had when they lived in the shadow of the Holy Alliance. Instead, they fell out increasingly over colonial interests, thereby reverting to their traditional pattern of relations as competing maritime powers. Yet, though they no longer allowed their affinity as societies to moderate their international rivalry, they also felt no affinity for the three Eastern empires. Thus they collaborated with them only sporadically and opportunistically, as in the late 1850s, when Louis Napoleon courted Russia, still smarting from Austria's betrayal in the Crimea, in order to isolate Vienna while he promoted the unification of Italy; or as in 1878, when England supported Austria in resisting Russia's encroachment on the Balkan territories of Turkey.

Despite this midcentury exchange of services between East and West, however, the ideological division of the powers into the Two and the Three remained the most important factor in European diplomacy until 1890. And the long shadow cast by this persistence of the Old Regime furnishes a striking illustration of the impact of internal forces on international relations. For in the relative calm of this "century without general war," the interval of restricted conflict between 1854 and 1870 wrought changes in European power relations more profound than those produced by most general wars.

Ever since the Treaty of Westphalia in 1648, the balance of power in Europe had been founded on the division of Germany and to a lesser extent of Italy, and the resultant existence of buffer zones between the major states of the continent. The unification of Italy, and especially of Germany, between 1859 and 1870, together with the consequent relative decline of France and Austria, destroyed these long-standing foundations of international life. The result was the greatest revolution in the alignment of forces in Europe until the Second World War, and equal to that occasioned by Russia's entry into the concert of the powers under Peter. Yet for thirty years after this revolution began, recognition of the new bases of international relations in Europe was so obscured by the lingering consequences of Old-Regime affinities as to remain without practical effect—a result which owed much to Bismarck's political wizardry but even more to Russia's ideological antipathy to republican France and her reciprocated predilection for semi-autocratic Prussia.

But after 1890, the accumulated changes of decades burst through the heritage yielded by the Congress of Vienna and the Revolution of 1830.[3] Immediately following Bismarck's fall, Germany severed her reinsuring but also confining ties with Russia and embarked on a policy of a "free hand," confident that her growing might would permit her to choose allies in specific situations according to her own interests, much as England had always done. This initiative, however, freed other hands as well. Between 1891 and 1894, isolated France seized the occasion to press an alliance on a reluctant but now isolated Russia, in order to create a counterweight to the Triple Alliance of Germany, Austria, and Italy forged between 1878 and 1884. In a world of such tightening diplomatic bonds, England found her traditional "splendid isolation" distinctly less splendid, particularly in view of Germany's growing economic competition and even more ominous determination after 1900 to build a "fleet second to none," as William II declared. Britain therefore composed her colonial differences with France in the Entente Cordiale of 1904; and once Britain's Japanese ally had halted Russian expansion in the Far East, in 1907 she entered into a similar agreement with St. Petersburg to delimit spheres of influence in Persia. Thereby the way was cleared for the transformation of these isolated agreements into the Triple Entente.

In the short span of sixteen years between 1891 and 1907, the old grouping of powers according to political and ideological affinity was effaced, and the major states of Europe were realigned into two ever more rigidly demarcated camps, founded on considerations of international power and security alone. The diplomatic revolution presaged by the Prussian unification of Germany in 1870, and delayed for the next thirty years by Old-Regime allegiances, was at last consummated.

In form, the new division of Europe established two comparable blocs, the Triple Alliance and the Triple Entente. In reality, it represented a confrontation between a league of the more vigorous states of Europe and the single most vigorous nation, Germany. Italy was weak as a power and ambivalent to the point of desertion in her allegiance to her partners. Germany's only staunch ally, Austria, which had never been counted the equal of her protector, after 1900 increasingly burdened the Berlin government because of the centrifugal pull of her national minorities. This factor indeed made it impossible for her to function effectively in a world dominated by homogeneous nation-states, a weakness made more glaringly apparent after 1914 under the impact of war. The progress of the war revealed still further the realities underlying the alliance system, as first Italy and then the major nations of the non-European world, the United States and Japan, joined the Entente against the Central Powers. In short, the pattern revealed by the buildup to the conflict of 1914–1918 was one in which an oversized and dynamic power, by the mere fact of preponderant strength, provoked a coalition of most of Europe against her.

By the eve of 1914, Europe had reverted to the type of alignment that prevailed in the successive coalitions against Louis XIV and his ally Charles XII of Sweden, against Frederick the Great during the Seven Years' War, and against Napoleon—a type of situation in which Russia's assistance could be solicited against the challenger of the existing international equilibrium. In each of these coalition situations, moreover, Russia's associates accepted her aid with the knowledge that in the event of victory her participation would lead to her expansion westward. And on each occasion her partners accepted this eventuality with no more than the usual apprehension entertained by any power in a coalition regarding the potential gains of an ally.

Indeed, it was the defense of Russian interests in the Balkans that eventually drew the Western Allies into war with Germany. Although the heart of the conflict of 1914–1918 was a contest between Germany and the advanced West for European hegemony, the war was actually triggered by a dispute between the two most backward members of the rival alliance systems, Austria and Russia. Without the Austro-Russian conflict in the Balkans, it is highly doubtful that Germany would have challenged England directly and unilaterally, and it is wholly improbable that England or France would have launched a preventive war against Germany.[4]

Both Austria and Russia proved intransigent in their stands toward Serbia because each feared the internal consequences of a Balkan defeat. Austria feared that failure to eliminate the menace of South Slav nationalism centering in Serbia might precipitate the dissolution of the Dual Monarchy, and Russia feared that further humiliation in the Balkans would feed domestic revolutionary agitation, as had the defeats of 1878 and 1905. Germany, too, calculated her international moves partly with an eye to domestic concerns, for she anticipated that a victorious war would definitively shore up the archaic Prussian-German imperial structure against the rising tide of socialism. But France could not let Russia go down alone, and survive; nor could England risk a German victory over France, and feel secure herself.

So it was that the two most backward members of the alliance system drew their more advanced partners into the maelstrom; and the three most conservative states of Europe, because of their growing inability to dominate the forces of modernity stirring among their populations, precipitated a conflict which could only turn out to be the most revolutionary since the Napoleonic era. As Sir Edward Grey, the British foreign minister, declared in August 1914, "the lights are going out all over Europe." But for the three dynastic empires of the East this eclipse in August would turn out to be even more portentous than for the West: it marked the beginning of the collective Götterdämmerung of Europe's surviving Old Regimes.

The device that brought them down was universal military service. We have seen how this institution came into the world as one of the first fruits of the modern democratic idea born of 1789.[5] It was invented by the French Republic in 1793 as a temporary *levée en masse* to defend the new regime of popular virtue against the corrupt Europe of aristocrats and kings. In more institutionalized form it became the basis of Napoleon's stunning victories over his Old-Regime adversaries; then, after his fall, it was in effect abandoned by his less ambitious successors, even his nephew. In the meantime, however, Europe's remaining Old Regimes had adapted the device of their more advanced enemy to their own purposes. Following her defeat at Jena in 1806 Prussia adopted it to survive the Napoleonic challenge; and after 1862 Bismarck perfected it further and wedded it to the new impulses of German patriotism. Only with this perfected instrument could he humiliate France and unite Germany under the Prussian officer caste. In response to this challenge, the French in the 1870s took up their old invention in defense of their new republic and wedded it to the impulses of democratic patriotism. At the same time, in 1874, Russia prematurely gave her peasant masses this last full measure of democracy and wedded it to an archaic patriotism "for mother Russia, for father tsar." Finally, in the course of the conflict of 1914, the British were obliged to follow suit, and in 1917 the Americans also, the better to wage a "war to end war" and to "keep the world safe for democracy." So mass militarization moved on in iron columns across the modern world into the hecatombs of the Marne and the Masurian Lakes, and into four years in the trenches.

This democratic bloodletting is indeed the fundamental cause of the revolutionary impact of the conflict of 1914–1918.[6] Antidemocratic Old Regimes could hardly adopt the democratic and nationalistic device of citizen warfare without implicitly admitting the corollary principles of popular sovereignty and national self-determination. This process of decomposition began with the emergence of the alliance system leading up to the war, in which dynastic empires took to acting as national states. And it accelerated during the conflict as each alliance discarded its previous commitment to the balance of power in pursuit of an ever more total concept of victory.

And so, in the course of the first total war the dichotomy of Russia and the West, which had long been a dichotomy between the Old Regime and the New, was obliterated in favor of pan-European *Machtpolitik*. All the social and affective coordinates of nineteenth-century international politics were unrecognizably reordered; the ideological cards with which the games of war and diplomacy had been played for a hundred years were completely reshuffled.

Hence, when the chips at last were down in 1914, France and Britain, Russia's oldest ill-wishers and the societies most unlike her in

Europe, allowed the defense of tsarist interests in the Balkans to plunge them into a general war because they dared not countenance the destruction of Russian power by Germany under any circumstances. This same concern for their own security led the Entente powers to wage war without regard for the consequences to Western civilization of the claims their Eastern ally could legitimately make once victory had been achieved. In 1915, the British promised by treaty to let Russia annex the long-disputed Straits in order to cement the new union between the two states. In 1916, the French agreed to the incorporation of Austrian Galicia and Prussian Posnania into Russian Poland, thereby delivering over to St. Petersburg's good graces the whole of that martyred nation without even the restrictive guarantees that Alexander I had been obliged to accept at the Congress of Vienna.

At the same time, Germany and Austria, Russia's oldest friends and the two states most like her in Europe, in order to escape the vise of a war on two fronts, so far neglected the bonds of autocratic solidarity as to seek the destruction of the Russian empire, and to do so by means that were as dangerous to themselves as to their adversary. In Germany, during 1915–16, the imperial regime subsidized various fantastic but unsuccessful schemes to subvert the Romanovs; and once the tsarist throne had fallen of itself General Erich von Ludendorff returned Lenin to Petrograd in 1917 in the hope he would foment a socialist revolution that would plunge Russia into chaos, as if unmindful of the fact that 35 percent of the German electorate had voted for socialism on the eve of 1914. But the conservative Ludendorff had been radicalized by the categorical imperative of war, victory. And as of 1917 the Central Powers were desperate not only to throw all their weight to the West before the Americans arrived in strength, but also to obtain from the East the food and raw materials denied them by the Allied blockade. Ludendorff added to his program of social revolution for Russia a program of separatism for her national minorities. And Austria, in even more desperate straits than her ally, so far forgot her own restive national minorities as to join Ludendorff's efforts to "liberate" Russia's Polish, Baltic, and Ukrainian borderlands.

Thus the Central Powers, by subjecting their more backward neighbor to the pummeling of three years of modern war, achieved Russia's

244

dissolution. In February 1917, the Romanovs fell; by the time the Bolsheviks seized power in October Russia's economy had collapsed and her army had disintegrated. With the Treaty of Brest-Litovsk in March 1918, the Central Powers had won their gamble in the East.

After this astonishing victory, even if they had also triumphed in the West, it is doubtful that they could have avoided reaping at home a part of the whirlwind they had helped sow in Russia. As matters turned out, their own defeat the following year made certain the end of the imperial orders of both Austria and Germany, thereby bringing about the very political and national revolutions that the two powers had fought to forestall. At the same time, this defeat guaranteed the survival of the nascent Soviet regime; for there was now no organized force near enough to its borders to unseat it.

And so, in the closing years of a conflict touched off by the schism among the traditional monarchies, the defeat of all three together brought down in ruin that half of the European Old Regime which the exertions of Metternich, Nicholas I, and Bismarck had successfully maintained east of the Rhine for a century. Nor did the catastrophe stop there: out of the rubble left by this "suicide of the empires" came the social and national convulsions, as well as the fanatical ideologies, which in twenty years' time would generate a second, even more deadly cataclysm.[7]

If there is any moral to be derived from the conclusion to this chapter of Western-Russian relations, it might well be that the nineteenth-century propensity for determining international policy by the "irrational" criteria of ideological affinity may not have been so irrational after all. The forces of modernity, which had proved relatively beneficent in the West, turned out to be more intense than the archaic societies of the Center and the East could adapt at a peaceful pace.

A Dawn amidst the Night?

Marxism is the inescapable philosophy of our age.

—Jean-Paul Sartre (1960)

Marxism has been the greatest fantasy of our century.

—Leszek Kolakowski (1978)

It was out of the ruins of the easternmost and weakest redoubt of the European Old Regime that the world's first socialist regime emerged. Marx's Spectre of Communism, which had haunted the West in vain since 1848, at last came to power where its advent was least expected. It did so, however, not through the predicted mechanism of class struggle, but through a chain reaction of destruction triggered by war.

By 1917 the war had mobilized some eight million Russian peasants along a thousand-mile front, a concentration that for the first time gave them real political power, if largely a power of negation.[8] The war also disrupted the still fragile Russian industrial economy, creating severe shortages of food and fuel. And since the war turned out to be a losing one, it reignited the constitutional crisis pending since 1905: the monarchy now used the wartime emergency to govern without the Duma, and the opposition responded by demanding a government of public confidence—in effect a constitution.

Against this background, in February 1917, Petrograd was shaken by large-scale strikes protesting food shortages. When peasant soldiers refused to fire on the crowds, the street action escalated into military mutiny. This mutiny became a revolution when the army high command deserted Nicholas, and the frightened Duma liberals stepped in to form a Provisional Government.

The government was never able to govern, however, since the workers and soldiers, under socialist leadership, simultaneously formed "councils," or "soviets," to monitor the "bourgeois ministry"—bodies that in fact had more authority than the nominal government. The Revolution of 1917, unlike that of 1905, began with the socialists, not the liberals, in the vanguard. Under the pressure of the "dual power" of socialist soviets and the Provisional Government, the administrative and military structures of the state unraveled. With the state withering away, workers asserted their control over industry; the peasants moved to expropriate the gentry without waiting for the promised Constituent Assembly; and the peasant soldiers deserted the front en masse: rural Russia at last had its full measure of "land and freedom." By autumn the government had been thoroughly eclipsed by the soviets; yet these bodies, which were in effect permanent mass meetings, could not themselves govern. Amid this descent into anarchy, there existed no realistic possibility of establishing a constitutionalist order.

Into the political void stepped Lenin and the Bolsheviks. Fired to ideological incandescence by the social implosion of 1917, they mounted a coup d'état to seize state power in the workers' name. Their first act was to appeal to the soldiers of all the belligerent powers "to turn the imperialist war into a international class war." And soon, to expiate the "crime" of the Social Democratic vote for war credits in 1914, they changed their party's name to Communist, the preferred term of Marx and the proclaimed goal of his *Manifesto*. So another terrible beauty was born; and a new light now flamed in the East against the darkness of universal war.

With this brusque turn of fate Russia's relationship to the West was stood on its head. She ceased being Europe's laggard Eastern train; she now embodied, or claimed to embody, Europe's most advanced ideal, Socialism. And this claim, for the first time since her entry into the concert of Europe, made her the continent's premier power ideologically. For the next seven decades she would be judged less as a nation than as humanity's pilot socialist society—that is, when she was not seen as a second coming of the Tatars.

As if in doubt himself, the symbolist bard of October, Aleksandr Blok, in 1918 summoned the West to reflect in awe and trembling on the riddle of the Russian Sphinx. For the rest of the century the world would indeed stand before it in perplexed interrogation: Was Red October truly a socialist dawn amidst the night of war? Or was it a new descent into darkness and despotism?

THE SOCIALIST RIDDLE

By Socialism I mean a form of society in which men and women are not divided into opposing economic classes, but live together under conditions of approximate social and economic equality, using in common the means that lie to their hands of promoting social welfare. Socialism as I understand it, means four closely connected things—a human fellowship which denies and expels distinctions of class, a social system in which no one is so much richer or poorer than his neighbours as to be unable to mix with them on equal terms, the common ownership and use of all the vital instruments of production, and an obligation upon all citizens to serve one another according to their capacities in promoting the common well-being. Nothing is Socialism that does not embrace all these four things; and, given the means of realising these four, nothing further is needed to make a Socialist society. . . . Our Socialism is, then, ardent, passionate, an affair of the heart as well as of the mind. We are in love with Socialism.

—G. D. H. Cole, *The Simple Case for Socialism* (1935)

The riddle put to Western wayfarers by the Russian Sphinx then, is this: by what signs shall we recognize "real" socialism? Both those who are for and those who are against capitalism would agree that the United States, for example, is a "capitalist" society. But "socialist" societies are far more difficult to evaluate, and there is no agreement as to whether Social Democratic Sweden or Communist Russia, Laborite Britain under Clement Atlee or China under Mao Zedong ever achieved "true" socialism. Even though much of humanity in our century has believed that we were ultimately headed for "socialism" (and since the Soviet extinction this belief is perhaps only in hibernation), there was never a consensus as to what we would find when we got there. Thus, despite a century of earnest questing, authentic, indubitable socialism remains an undiscovered country whose bourn no traveler has yet reached. We must therefore ask: what is socialism?[9]

If the empire of the tsars had successfully navigated the passage to constitutional democracy tentatively begun in 1905, the West, while lauding that feat, would hardly have viewed Russia as a beacon, since she would only have followed the West's example. It was Russia's gift to mankind of Communism that first made her appear a world-historical nation in the Hegelian sense, the (putative) home of the *Weltgeist* for the present age. Marx recast this perspective to make socialism the telos of mankind, the end of "prehistory" and the beginning of an authentically human society. Since this prediction was tested first in Russia, throughout the twentieth century the Russian riddle has in fact been the riddle of socialism.

Something has already been said about the origins of the socialist ideal, in the 1830s, as a critique of the political republic aspired to by the French Revolution. The burden of this critique was that formal, political equality cannot ensure real, human equality, and that a social republic, founded on the limitation or suppression of private property, is necessary for human emancipation.[10] The genesis and implications of these propositions must now be explored more fully.

All modern socialist theories originated between the revolutions of 1830 and 1848.[11] To be sure, these theories would be elaborated on greatly in the ensuing decades, but the basic principles (including those of Russian peasant socialism) were staked out in the *entre-deux-révolutions*. The process of elaboration was completed by the turn of the century with the emergence, on the one hand, of the reformism of British Fabianism and Eduard Bernstein's Marxist "revisionism" and, on the other, of Lenin's theory of the vanguard party designed to act in the context of what Trotsky called "permanent revolution." The twentieth century, the century of actual socialist revolution, would live entirely off this ideological heritage.

The years between 1830 and 1848 also produced another legacy that would dominate the modern age, namely, the religion of revolution as the motive force of history. This phenomenon emerged through a long escalation of Europe's conceptualization of historical change. The Renaissance and Reformation, though they obviously transformed Europe, were nonetheless viewed by their initiators not as new departures, but as returns to ancient and noble origins. The seventeenth-century English, although they most definitely made a revolution in the modern sense of an "overturn," never admitted it, and wound up instead viewing its "glorious" outcome, in 1688, as a restoration, thereby largely expunging the radicalism of their deed from the national consciousness. The Americans knew very well that their rebellion was a revolution, at least in outcome if not as a process; but its radicalism was quickly encapsulated in a stable constitutional system and so led to no cult of revolution per se. The French made a revolution so radical with respect to Europe's millennial past that for the first time revolution as an implacable historical force became apparent to all.

And it is this example that furnished the modern world the model of revolution as process, as a veritable force of nature acting independently of human will. Henceforth radicals believed, and conservatives feared, that revolutions are the way history happens—the "locomotives of history" in Marx's metaphor. If not all socialist sects between 1830 and 1848 were committed to violent revolution, all still lived in expectation of an immanent new order, an anticipation that was broadly speaking "revolutionary."

Hence, beginning with the ostensible restoration of the Old Regime in 1815 the European Left was able to anticipate a replay of the scenario of 1789 on a "higher," more progressive level. The uprising of 1830 was thus Europe's first anticipated revolution. But its modest outcome in a mere "bourgeois monarchy" simply raised the level of anticipation for the next, truly democratic round. This new event was envisaged by the far Left as a veritable second coming of 1789, the definitive achievement of human emancipation, since it would be Socialist.

But what is the connection between these expectations and what is usually taken to be socialism's source, industrialization? The common assumption is that the Industrial Revolution was the matrix of socialism, a movement that moreover represented the class consciousness of the new proletariat. But the relationship of industrialization to the rise of socialism is by no means as simple as common assumption has it. To illustrate, in a footnote of Engels to a translation of the *Communist Manifesto*, he explained that he and Marx had taken England as "typical" of the economic development of the "bourgeoisie," and France as "typical" of its political development.[12] Yet he was quite unaware of the non sequitur involved in deriving French politics from English economics, even though the historical division of labor between the two countries is, in fact, obvious.

The focus of nascent socialism was France in the wake of the republicans' failure, in 1830, to hold onto power after the "three glorious days" of the July insurrection by the people of Paris. The new movement was nourished by the theories of such "utopians" as Henri de

Saint-Simon, Charles Fourier, and Pierre-Joseph Proudhon, specula-
tion that elaborated on the legacy of the egalitarian Jacobin Republic of
1792. Indeed, the first adumbration of revolutionary socialism emerged
directly from the Great Revolution itself, in the Conspiracy of the
Equals of Gracchus Babeuf of 1796, which aimed at reversing the Jacobins' defeat in Thermidor 1794 and the consequent failure of Europe's
first attempt at universal-suffrage democracy. The Babouvists' proposed remedy was armed action by an enlightened minority to level all
social inequalities. This desperate enterprise, of course, failed; but it left
behind an insurrectionary tradition transmitted in the 1830s by
Philippe-Michel Buonarroti to Auguste Blanqui and Armand Barbès,
and ultimately Karl Marx. Thus the peaceful utopian socialism of Saint-
Simonians and Fourierists was from the beginning supplemented by
militant utopian Communism.

The first noticeable industrial proletariat, however, emerged in contemporary England, in the wake of the Reform Bill of 1882. Even so,
despite Robert Owen's cooperatives, there was little socialism in Britain
until almost the end of the century, and there was no Communism at
all. What there was in Britain, rather, was an embryonic labor movement, launched in the years preceding 1848 in the form of Chartism.
This movement was essentially the creation of workers themselves; and
its priority was political struggle for universal suffrage to gain parliamentary representation as a prelude to social reform. They failed in this
objective in 1848, thereby blunting the workers' power for thirty years.
When labor revived after the suffrage reform of 1884, it did not found a
class, or socialist, party but pursued its melioristic goals under the wing
of the Liberals until the early twentieth century.

The origins of the socialist ideal, then, lie not in economic and social
circumstances, but in political and cultural ones. To be sure, by the end
of the century most European working-class movements would call
themselves "socialist." All the same, throughout the century socialist
theory and politics—as distinct from the labor movement—remained
the province of what Lenin, quoting Karl Kautsky, later called the
"bourgeois intelligentsia." Thus, although there were occasional working-class socialist leaders, such as Wilhelm Weitling or August Bebel,

the majority of socialist chiefs were nonproletarian intellectuals, beginning with Marx and Engels themselves.

The predominately intelligentsia origins of socialism are related to the word's special status in the modern political vocabulary. "Socialism" in the generic sense (including its higher derivative, "Communism") is unique among terms designating a type of society in that it was created before, not after, the fact of that society's existence. "Feudalism," "Old Regime," "liberalism," "capitalism," and "constitutional democracy," for example, all emerged either after or simultaneously with the fact of their existence and hence designate something real, however imperfectly these societies may have embodied whatever ideals they proclaimed. But the term "socialism" appeared in the 1830s, almost a century before the first attempt was made, in 1917, to achieve a corresponding reality. Socialism thus does not designate in the first instance an actual society; it designates rather an ideal alternative to existing society. The old society is therefore given the antithetical label "capitalism," a term created, not by the owners of capital, but by their socialist adversaries. And the socialists produced this neologism only well after their own emergence on the scene; in fact, the new term did not become current until the 1890s.[13] In sum, "socialism" is first of all a hope, indeed a utopia, in the literal meaning of that word: a "non-place" or a "no-where."

"Socialism" is thus not a descriptive historical term or social-science category; it is a verbal standard raised to mobilize the disaffected and excluded of modern society; and as such it is a messianic, indeed something of a magical, term. "Capitalism," by contrast, carries no such stirring connotations; instead it evokes, at best, a dynamic economic mechanism and, at worst, selfishness and greed. Capitalism and socialism, therefore, are not symmetrical concepts pertaining to empirical society; rather, one designates a present reality, the other a future vision. Yet such is the potency of the socialist aspiration that commentators perennially take it for a social-science category or a putative historical reality, its foes no less than its friends, to the compounded confusion of most discussions of the subject.

This confusion is aggravated by other vagaries of usage. Both before and after 1917 socialists have given to their generic label two basic meanings. One refers to the socialist *movement*, understood as a moral fellowship devoted to the pursuit of a just society, as this pursuit is expressed through political parties, trade unions, cooperatives, or similar undertakings; and this movement is what people who write about "the history of European socialism" mean by their subject. The other designates a form of *society*, as in the Marxist succession of "slave-holding society, feudalism, capitalism, socialism." The confusion arises because the members of the moral fellowship are still waiting to go beyond capitalism to socialism, whereas the Communists claim to have done just that; and so each group accuses the other of betraying true socialism. Despite this mutual disavowal, however, significant programmatic overlap exists between the clean-handed socialist movement in opposition and the "dirty-handed" socialist society of Communism in power. Both have the same enemy, "capitalism," and both propose to replace it with some measure of the socialization, nationalization, or "étatization" of wealth.

Thus socialism in all forms came into the world as a negation. Indeed, the socialist ideal emerged through a series of negations of democratic and industrial society. The result was a composite concept, built up by successive extrapolations from the existing modern world.

Socialism as an Ideal Type, or, the DNA of a Unicorn

Historically, the first phase of this extrapolation was a backward look at a rural "world we have lost."[14] For the socialist aspiration springs in part from a visceral sense of scandal that modern liberalism, after destroying the organic social ties of the Old Regime, had transformed human relationships into market relationships, and replaced all affective social bonds with the soulless mediation of money—the "cash nexus." Such sentiments, for example, were the staple of the English radical William Cobbet in his criticism of early industrialization. They were particularly strong in late eighteenth- and nineteenth-century Germany, where such conservatives as Justus Möser and Adam Müller inveighed against the social rationalism of revolutionary France and extolled the traditional world of fraternal solidarity.[15] This current of thought culminated at the end of the century in Ferdinand Tönnies's sociology of

Gemeinschaft (community) as opposed to *Gesellschaft* (society).[16] And from Fourier's dream of "harmony" to William Morris's advocacy of "guild production" the organic community of the Old Regime has been seen as akin to the socialist future. In this perspective, socialism appears as a revolt against what Max Weber called the "iron cage" of rational-bureaucratic modernity. In other words, the first face of socialism is an aspiration to turn "society" back into a "community."

A second phase in the formation of the socialist ideal is given by extrapolation from the goals of the French Revolution as summarized in the triad Liberty, Equality, Fraternity. By 1830 Liberty had of course been abandoned to the bourgeoisie, and Equality had become the *patrie* of the proletariat; but what of the most mysterious and unprogrammatic member of the republican trinity, Fraternity? Was it evoked simply because a triad was necessary to make a ringing slogan? Or was it present because the slogan itself was a calque on Faith, Hope, and Charity? Since the greatest of Christian virtues was of course Charity, is not Fraternity therefore the highest revolutionary goal, the loving community of all humanity—or Socialism? Of course, nothing can be proved in this matter. But it is reasonable to suppose that in a culture both Christian and incipiently democratic, Charity and Fraternity together equaled a subliminal suggestion of Socialism.[17]

Be this as it may, it is clear that nascent socialism derived its basic programmatic orientations from the Revolution: on the one hand, it rejected the atomization of liberal society, but on the other it found its greatest strength in extrapolations from the liberal ethos itself. Although classical liberalism, politically, practiced a property suffrage in most of Europe until the turn of the century, philosophically it was committed to the sovereignty of natural reason in human affairs; and in this Enlightenment perspective, reason, as the endowment of all men, ultimately meant equality. Classical liberalism's property suffrage hence was foredoomed to give way to universal suffrage.

Nevertheless, even political democracy left intact society's division into unequal classes, a stratification of humanity as invidious to the enlightened as the Old-Regime hierarchy of estates had been in its day. Thus political democracy was in turn predestined to give way to something higher, at least as an ideal; and this was Socialism. For if one is

254

ruthlessly logical about the democratic quest for justice as equality, then differences of wealth become rationally suspect and morally odious. The obvious remedy is the narrowing, or indeed the abolition, of class differences through the social control of wealth.

Hence socialism turns out to be the most uncompromising form of the equation of reason with equality first formulated by the Enlightenment. By the same token, socialism de facto prolongs the mixture of natural religion and rationalistic Enlightenment put forth by Rousseau and Kant: since all men are equally endowed by their Creator, nature, or reason with the same attributes—and therefore with equal rights—artificial divisions among them deny their common humanity, and so profane the sacred person of Man. The core concept of socialism thus is not one or another economic program, but the moral principle of human equality as the supreme good.

Still, this core concept must be translated into concrete social measures to have practical effect. And at this point generic socialism diversifies into a spectrum of instrumental programs. Historically, these have ranged from a progressive income tax and a comprehensive welfare state to full nationalization and centralized planning of the economy. And it is these differing, indeed often conflicting, programs that have made socialism's meaning so elusive. Nevertheless, behind this fractious diversity, we may discern an ideal type of generic socialism.

The first element of such an ideal type is the goal of combatting inequality through some degree of the public control of wealth; and the practical, programmatic question, of course, is always the degree of control. Since we are discussing an ideal type, however, the most extreme programmatic goals best define its contours. Thus, maximal socialism means that ending mankind's division into dominant and dominating classes requires abolishing the bases of all social differentiation: private property and capital wealth. This, in turn, signifies replacing the selfish profit motive as the motor of the economy with the humane organization of production to satisfy "real" human needs; private ownership of the means of production and distribution must therefore give way to their public ownership. And this, finally, requires that the anarchy of the market must be abolished, together with money, in favor of the "rational" ordering of society. The essence of socialism thus emerges as a global negation of existing society. In a word, socialism is noncapitalism, to be achieved by the abolition of private property, profit, and the market. Although most early socialists approached this program only asymptotically, a few, such as Babeuf, Blanqui, and Marx, made the ideal type their actual instrumental program. It is to these few that the term "Communism" best applies.

The second element of the socialist ideal type is faith that its negations are not just destructive, but also creative. Suppressing the "anarchy of the market" is expected to produce the triumph of "rational planning." Ending the quest for individual profit is calculated to refound society on the basis of collective labor, and this fraternal formula is deemed superior, both morally and economically, to private self-interest. Finally, doing away with the class state is supposed to permit the new people's state to manage society's planning and coordinate its collective labor without coercion. Thus, the ideal type of socialism offers a constant oscillation between moral and instrumental concepts, with faith as the chief bond between them.

Another ideal-typical facet of the socialist aspiration is the belief that commitment to the above amalgam of ideals is innate in those who are supposed to benefit from their application—the exploited classes of existing society. These classes are held to be natural socialists, innocent of the crime of exploitation and hence endowed with the moral right and the preternatural grace to expropriate their former exploiters without falling into crime themselves.

Belief in the natural virtue of the exploited and the oppressed, if pushed far enough, transforms the moral aspiration of socialism into a redemptive or religious one. The Saint-Simonians referred to their doctrine as the New Christianity. Philippe-Joseph Buchez and Pierre Ballanche conceived of socialism as a "palingenesis," or rebirth, of humanity. And in this guise the more radical forms of socialism—from Proudhon's to Bakunin's to Marx's—aspired to the anarchist utopia of a classless and stateless society. Such an antinomian world would be a world without human alienation; indeed (though few socialists would put matters so baldly), it would be a society at last without evil. In this rhapsodic culmination socialism shades off into a secularized millenarianism of the final age, the age of the Holy Spirit.

Now the moral aspirations that have aggregated around the socialist banner indeed represent some of the noblest ideals of modern man, and almost no one can be insensitive to their compassionate appeal. The question nevertheless remains: will these moral ends in fact be achieved through the instrumental programs of socialism, whether the abolition of private property and the market or the institution of planning by the state? Or is socialism, arrived at by a process of negative extrapolation from the ills of existing society, simply a fabulous spectre composed of the accumulated negations of the existing world? Is it not, therefore, no more than the composite sum of contradictory policies that can exist separately but not together in a functioning society—a beauteous ideological unicorn that itself exists nowhere in reality?

Marx, to be sure, recognized this danger and claimed that he had put an end to all "utopian" varieties of socialism and replaced them with a "scientific" one. Millions, moreover, have accepted his demonstration as founded in fact, and by 1991 a third of humanity had come to live under regimes that invoked his name. Of all the doctrines of revolutionary modernity launched on the eve of 1848, his has been the world-historical winner. His claims, therefore, must be taken with the utmost seriousness. Yet this justifiable regard for Marx as one of the great social thinkers of modernity should not obscure the fact that in his own view, inscribed as a testament on his monument in London's Highgate Cemetery, "Hitherto philosophers sought only to interpret the world; the point, however, is to change it."[18] The true test of theory, he always held, lies in the praxis of revolution.

Marxist Theory

Marx, for all the scorn he heaped on his French and English "utopian" predecessors, shared one major trait with them: in accordance with the historical norm for socialism's development, he spoke not with a proletarian voice, but in the idiom of high culture, indeed European culture at its highest, drawing as he did on the languages of classical antiquity as well as the major tongues of modern Europe, including, as we have seen, Russian. Moreover, his socialism was the supreme synthesis of the Enlightenment and the Romantic traditions, a combination of ostensible opposites so frequent in early nineteenth-century culture.

As Marx defined the origins of his science, it was a synthesis of German philosophy, French socialism, and British economics.[19] His purpose was to "demystify" British political economy as a bourgeois ideology of exploitation, and so to devise a proletarian economics that would promote the socialist revolution then awaited by the extreme Left in France. As for German philosophy, by which he meant essentially Hegel, it supplied the dialectic of history moving the socioeconomic process to its socialist consummation. As Marx put it, he found Hegel's dialectic "standing on its head" and so he "turned [it] right side up again," that is, he transformed it into the class struggle. In so doing he carried one step further the process which Hegel claimed the Enlightenment had begun: bringing reason down from heaven to walk on earth.[20]

Marx achieved his transformation by taking to a logical extreme the critique of the master launched by the Young, or Left, Hegelians. For Germany in the 1830s and 1840s was at last going through the militantly irreligious Enlightenment that it had missed in the eighteenth century. But the religion now challenged was not the supernatural faith attacked by the *philosophes;* it was the philosophical religion of classical German philosophy from Kant to Hegel. The pivotal figure in this challenge was Ludwig Feuerbach. His central idea was that God was an externalized, or "alienated," projection of idealized human attributes; Man's emancipation therefore consisted in "demystifying" the "inverted" world of heaven, thereby returning humanity's higher essence, its "species-being" *(Gattungswesen),* to earth for fulfillment in the practical world. And by implication, since the monarchical state idealized by Hegel rested on divine sanction, demystifying religion also meant demystifying the state; thus humanity's recovery of its true self necessarily entailed replacing monarchy with universal-suffrage democracy.[21]

Marx took up Feuerbach's "transformative" method to produce his own critique of both Hegel and Feuerbach. For Marx, Feuerbach's undifferentiated Man was no less of an illusion than Hegel's philosophic God. Moreover, Feuerbach had thrown out Hegel's dialectic along with his philosophic God, so Marx had to bring it back again to show that undifferentiated humanity was in fact riven by class exploitation. The democratic state would be no less oppressive than its monarchic predecessor, since it too was the instrument of the propertied, exploiting classes. Hence the only way to end human alienation, whether Old-Regime or liberal, was revolutionary Communism, which would level "bourgeois" civil society *(bürgerliche Gesellschaft)* and make all men equal in their common species-being. Through this double critique, Hegel's idealistic dialectic was transformed into a materialistic one, and class warfare became the demiurge of history. To be sure, Marx later made his terminology more empirical, but this underlying metaphysic of humanity always remained.

In this heady amalgam, Anglo-French social science at first glance seems to dominate, as indeed Marx himself intended. And there was never a more scathing critic than he of the "spooks" of German metaphysics, as in *The Holy Family* or *The German Ideology.* Thus Engels at Marx's grave could assert that his colleague was "the Darwin of social science." Moreover, Marx's properly sociological and economic pronouncements—that is, the bulk of his writing—in fact echo French and English modes of social analysis, whether the productivist cult of technology of Henri de Saint-Simon or the labor theory of value of David Ricardo. Still, no French or English thinker could ever have made the totalizing synthesis that Marx did; and here the decisive element was the German, Hegelian one. Only this grandiose metaphysical form could give to the mundane Anglo-French content its universal sweep and its world-historical dynamic. It is largely for this reason that by the end of the century Marx's theory had won out over all competitors, replacing Proudhon and Ferdinand Lassalle in the West and Bakunin and the Russian Populists in the East. For the genius of Marx's system—and it is indeed a construct of genius—is to present a secular eschatology as a positive social science, and to do so with such verisimilitude that even his liberal enemies argue with him mostly in empirical, sociological terms.

The basic coordinates of Marx's system were first set forth in the *German Ideology* of 1845. However, this fact was not known until that work, together with other of Marx's youthful writings—a corpus often called "original" Marxism—were fully published in the 1930s. Until then "Marxism" consisted of the slogan-like condensation of *Ideology* given by the *Manifesto;* the great "scientific" monument of *Capital;* and such brilliant tracts as *The Eighteenth Brumaire of Louis Bonaparte.* Even more perhaps, Marxism, as perceived at the end of the century, meant Engels's positivistic popularizations of the system in such works as *Anti-Dühring* and *Socialism: Utopian and Scientific.* And these works of "mature" Marxism indeed read like social-science treatises.

The mature face of Marxism offers three interdependent lines of argument which constitute the most familiar part of the system. First, there is a sociology in which the economic mode of production, or "base," determines the cultural, political, and ideological "superstructure" of society. Second, there is a theory of history in which humanity, driven by the class struggle, progresses from slave-holding, to feudal, to bourgeois society, toward the end of its "prehistory" in socialism. Finally, there is a theory of economics setting forth the "internal contradictions of capitalism"—the confiscation of the "surplus value" of labor, leading to the "accumulation of capital," leading to the "law of the falling rate of profit," leading to the terminal crisis that would at last produce the socialist revolution. This revolution, though violent in the manner of 1789, would nonetheless be democratic in the sense that the victorious working class would be the overwhelming majority of society; its "dictatorship," therefore, would be transitional, a simple prelude to "the withering away of the state" in a society now "classless."

The unfolding of these stages in a "lawlike" (*gesetzmässig; zakonomerno* in Russian) pattern of development defines the "logic of history" for Marx; and it is this logic that in the days of the Second International constituted "orthodox" Marxism, an evaluation still shared by most commentators on the subject. This orthodox Marxism, furthermore, obviously designates the advanced industrial nations of the West as the mandatory point of passage from prehistory to socialism. It is these "logical" tenets of classical Marxism that constitute the Enlightenment face of the system; for what they come down to is the eighteenth century's theory of progress, in conjunction with its materialism, recast in more agonistic terms.

What is of greater importance for our purposes, however, is pre-cisely the conflictual force driving historical progress—the dialectic of the class struggle. This Romantic element of Marx's system is the key to understanding why his utopia was first tried out, not in the advanced West, but in the backward East. The material dialectic of Marxism operates according to the same principle of loss and alienation leading to self-realization and freedom as Hegel's spiritual dialectic. Moreover, for Marx as for Hegel, the dialectic of fulfillment-through-alienation operates to produce the self-realization of one supreme entity. For Hegel this entity is the Absolute, which is both rational and divine; for Marx it is Humanity, which contains in itself the perfections that priests and philosophers formerly attributed to God and Reason. Yet when Marx speaks of humanity, he does not mean an aggregation of individu-als, as do classical liberals, for man is by nature a social being. Like Feuerbach, he means man as species-being, a kind of collective person that comes to realize its essence only through the travails of the histori-cal process; and individual self-fulfillment, which does exist as such for Marx, can be achieved only in this collective context.

Marx's logic of history starts when a "division of labor" (a core con-cept of Adam Smith) appears among men to promote the progress of the species. This first step into alienation, or creative "contradiction," is the "division of labor in the sexual act," which produces the basic social unit, the family; yet the nurturing family is also a unit "where wife and children are the slaves of the husband" and thus "the first property" (a core theme of the Saint-Simonians).[22] The latent slavery of the family develops fully as man begins to produce his means of subsistence by creating tools to conquer nature. This leads to a further division of labor between different kinds of economic activity; and in this process, man's essence is again alienated, since he is now dependent on the instruments of production he himself has created, just as he is depend-ent for survival on the social formations spawned by the diversification of production. Yet the supreme dehumanization of the species emerges when economic development leads to private property in the means of production. Thus does man produce his material and social world only by losing himself in servitude to his own creation.

And so history spirals bloodily upward through new forms of the division of labor and alienation, from the "contradiction" between town and country, on to increasingly creative yet exploitative modes of production—from slave-holding society to serf-based feudalism, to the "wage slavery" of the proletariat under capitalism. Yet in each of these stages of progress-through-subjugation the slave does not submit passively to the master; he reacts by struggling to reclaim his confiscated humanity, and this class struggle is the driving force of progress to the next stage of the species's development.

Three forms of alienation are of special importance in Marx's system. The first is the division between physical and mental labor, which produces the false consciousness of priests and philosophers that they are above the contingencies of material existence, and indeed that their Consciousness determines Being. They therefore produce "ideologies" that serve to obfuscate the relationships of exploitation that rule the real, material world. The second form of alienation is the division between society and the state, a repressive institution which ideologues hypostatize as the impartial embodiment of law and justice in order to mask its real class nature. The third and supreme form of alienation is private property, the cruelest social contradiction of all, since it is the basis of the class slavery that characterizes all of prehistory.

Prehistory reaches its culmination when these three forms of alienation interact to produce an eschatological "leap from the realm of necessity to the realm of freedom," in Engels's famous phrase. This occurs when humanity's enslavement to private property, expressed in its highest form by capitalism, at last generates among the exploited consciousness of the dehumanizing reality of all class society. This liberated consciousness then ignites a revolutionary explosion that destroys both class society and its political expression, the state. Humanity thereby recovers its immemorially alienated species-essence; and labor is transformed from servitude into the means for expressing man's creativity in the egalitarian harmony of Communism. Thus Marx's Communism—is it necessary to insist?—is not just a form of society; it is the collective redemption of mankind.

The redeemer in this drama of profane salvation is the most dehumanized class of the old society—the proletariat. Indeed, it is the proletariat's very degradation that makes it the logical agent for ending all degradation, and thus consecrates it as the "universal class," the class to end all classes. Hegel had called the rational bureaucracy of the enlightened state the universal class, the highest expression of Reason in the world. Marx now assigned the role of universal class to the proletariat as the productive and yet suffering class. For the proletariat was the only class whose self-interest coincided with the interests of humanity as a whole and thus with universal rationality itself. As he wrote in a famous passage in 1843,

> A class must be formed which has *radical chains*, a class in civil society which is not a class in civil society, a class which is the dissolution of all classes, a sphere of society which has a universal character because its sufferings are universal, and which does not claim a *particular redress* because the wrong which was done to it is not a *particular wrong* but *wrong in general*. . . . [It must be a class,] finally, which cannot emancipate itself without emancipating all these other spheres, which is in short, a *total loss* of humanity and which can only redeem itself by a *total redemption of humanity*. This dissolution of society, as a particular class, is the *proletariat*. . . . Philosophy is the *head* of this liberation, the proletariat is its *heart*. Philosophy can only be realized by the abolition *(Aufhebung)* of the proletariat and the proletariat can only be abolished by the realization of philosophy.[23]

Thus was Hegel's Absolute Idea, compounded of God and Reason, transmuted into Marx's Absolute Proletariat, still compounded of Reason and of a God now wholly immanent in Man as a collective social being. Since God had always been defined as the perfection of Being—eternal, omniscient, omnipotent—the perfection of humanity under Communism can best be understood as the self-deification of Man. Thus did Marx's historical materialism stand itself on its head by transforming Hegel's theological philosophy into a theological politics.

Marx transformed Hegel in still another way. Hegel had claimed knowledge of totality and the Cunning of Reason solely for the past: "the owl of Minerva takes flight only as the shades of night are falling."[24] But Marx's owl of Minerva took flight at dawn; and he claimed positive knowledge of totality and the Cunning of Class Struggle on into the future, beyond the horizon of the prehistory in which human society, until now, has suffered.[25] This is true even though he ostentatiously foreswore, in favor of science, the utopian trap of proposing blueprints for the future, of that world on the far side of his "dictatorship of the proletariat." Yet this "science" is oriented toward a future which is all the more alluring because it is not described in detail, but only posited as a "negation" of an intolerable present. In one of the grander crescendos of *Capital*,

> The monopoly of capital becomes a fetter upon the mode of production. . . . Centralization of the means of production and socialization of labor at last reach a point where they become incompatible with their capitalist integument. This integument is burst asunder. The knell of capitalist private property sounds. The expropriators are expropriated . . . capitalist production begets, with the inexorability of a law of nature, its own negation.[26]

But, alas, there can be no science of the future, and positive knowledge of that which does not yet exist is an elementary contradiction in terms. It follows, then, that all forms of Socialism are utopian, and that the supreme utopianism is to believe that there is one form that is scientific. Marx had in fact created what he himself termed an "ideology," or an intellectual transmogrification of reality. His system therefore was a kind of "superstructure" in search of a "base"—which he presumed was so real that it lay waiting in the historical conditions of the immediate future, in the next revolutionary round after 1848.

Behind this grand ideological construct there was, of course, much that was real in the present. There was first of all the human suffering caused by the still recent destruction of the Old-Regime guild system in favor of a laissez-faire economy, suffering apparent in the German "hungry forties," the Irish famine of 1847, and the tragic *ateliers nationaux* of 1848. In more general terms, the socioeconomic logic of Marx paralleled Tocqueville's "providential" law of the democratic movement of modern times, advancing from "the destruction of aristocracy and the kings to that of the bourgeoisie and the rich." The difference between the two was that Marx saw this advance governed by a precise scientific scenario culminating in an explosion of social leveling, whereas Tocqueville (who never heard of Marx) saw it as indeterminate in its details and hoped, above all, that it would remain compatible with individual liberty.

Marx cast the advent of democracy in a wrathful and vengeful mode. And there is in him much of what Tocqueville said of those contemporary French socialists, such as Barbès and Blanqui, whose militancy Marx admired: "they seemed to love liberty, but in fact they only hated the master."[27] It is indeed curious that Marx described his Communism not as a roseate dawn, but as an avenging spirit. Of course, the *Manifesto* used the metaphor of a spectre ironically, to mock the bourgeoisie's fear of revolution; the image nonetheless wound up adhering to its author's own doctrine. So Hegel's *Geist* of Reason became Marx's *Gespenst* of Communism, and the panlogic dialectic evolved into a Darwin-like history "red in tooth and claw." The fraternal emancipation of socialism would come into the world through the wrath of the class struggle waged by "those who have nothing to lose but their chains" and with violence as its "midwife." Karl Marx was decidedly not a Social Democrat.

But why, we may wonder, should the inexorable logic of history have need of such vehement emotions to fuel its advance? Indeed, the link between the objective logic of history and the subjective consciousness driving the class struggle is the weak point of Marx's synthesis. For the dialectic of the class struggle contains the germ of what orthodox Marxists called voluntarism—an overdose of subjectivity making political will predominant over historical logic, thus causing revolutionary Consciousness to deflect the lawlike pattern of historical Being. It was this dynamic, Romantic element of the Marxist synthesis that eventually proved to be the entering wedge for creating the world's first socialist society—in the East.

What produced this perverse turn of the Cunning of Reason? The answer is best sought, after the manner of Marx himself, in the historical conditions that produced his system. Just as generic socialism originated in the French political tradition rather than in British economic conditions, so the "scientific" socialism of Marx originated in those uneven German cultural conditions that we have already examined. As he himself emphasized, Restoration Germany remained a society whose politics and economics were still largely Old-Regime. At the same time he believed that Germany's very backwardness conferred on her one great advantage: the poverty of her real life had given her a superior capacity for philosophical understanding. Germany thus constituted the "theoretical consciousness" of what more advanced nations had already "done" in politics.

As a young man he was filled with "shame" at German backwardness, scornfully describing his homeland as "medieval" and even castigating its top-heavy philosophical culture as "inverted." Yet, since he was also both a philosopher and a German patriot, he saw the solution to Germany's retardation in a revolution that would propel her in one leap to the level of France and England. Indeed, he entertained the messianic view that Germany would surpass them both because her philosophic superiority alone could give the all-European revolution the necessary scientific consciousness.

He and the other Left Hegelians were stimulated to such bold hopes by their disappointment with Germany's reaction to the French Revolution. As already noted, the French impact first brought the revolution from above of the progressive Stein-Hardenberg reforms of 1807–1812. The War of Liberation of 1813–14 generated even greater expectations of progress among the German *Bürgertum* and intelligentsia: their goal now was self-government under a constitution, which indeed the king of Prussia promised in 1813. But these hopes were dashed by the reaction of the Restoration and frustrated still further when Prussia refused to follow the liberal lead of France in 1830.[28]

These events for the first time politicized part of the hitherto speculative and contemplative German intelligentsia. Given the "inverted" nature of the German situation, however, this politicization began not with politics, but with the Left Hegelians' critique of religion and idealist philosophy. But this critique quickly radicalized, moving from religion through the gamut of political positions advocated across the Rhine—from constitutional monarchy, to democratic republic, to revolutionary Communism. And Marx was on the far Left of this new German radical intelligentsia.

It is these circumstances that produced the original Marxism of the

1840s. So accustomed are we to viewing Marxism as a theory reflecting the world of mature capitalism that we overlook the fact that it was born in a society where industrialism, even in England, was only at its beginnings. Even more important, we fail to situate it historically as one of the first anticipatory theories of revolution produced in the springtime of such theories, the 1840s. For Marxism was devised, quite precisely, not to analyze capitalism in general, but to forecast the structure of the coming German revolution.

Marx's scenario for this event was that France, which had already made her "bourgeois" revolution in 1789, would now produce a socialist successor; and this explosion would trigger a bourgeois-cum-socialist revolution in still "medieval" Germany. Thus, in the just-quoted article consecrating the proletariat as universal class, he concluded: *"The day of German resurrection will be proclaimed by the crowing of the Gallic cock"* (emphasis in the original). Indeed, he suggested that Germany would be in a sense the universal nation, because *"the emancipation of Germany* will be an *emancipation of Man."*[29] As late as 1850 Marx continued to adhere to this scenario of a telescoped, or "permanent," revolution, as he called it in his "Address to the Communist League" of that year. And such a combined revolution, of course, is the scenario that Lenin and Trotsky would propose for Russia in 1917. Indeed, the Bolsheviks once in power would point to this "Address" to argue the Marxist authenticity of their October.

Of course, none of Marx's anticipatory fantasies was realized in 1848; in France there was only what he called a farcical replay of 1789, and in Germany there was no 1789 at all. Louis Bonaparte stole away the Parisian half of this "permanent revolution," while in Germany the "legitimist Bonapartism" of Bismarck outwitted Marx again, as the Iron Chancellor proved to be a far better practical radical than did the avowed revolutionary. So Marx had no choice but to retire from praxis to the British Museum, with full leisure to produce his "mature" system centering on the logic of history—thereby becoming one of the century's seminal social thinkers.

In sum, Marxism, which in the twentieth century turned out to be an ideology not for revolutionizing the advanced West, but for crash-modernizing the backward East, was appropriately born as the ideology of a leap out of backwardness in the German 1840s. This inverted relationship of Marxism to its supposed base in advanced societies would pertain until 1917: the zone of Marxist influence in Europe always coincided with areas of political or economic backwardness, from highly industrialized but still semiautocratic Germany to increasingly laggard Austria-Hungary, Congress Poland, Russia, and, to a lesser degree, Italy. Moreover, almost all the creative figures of Marxism in the days of the Second International were from this zone: Karl Kautsky, Rosa Luxemburg, Rudolf Hilferding, Victor Adler, Antonio Labriola, and of course the Russians, Lenin, Aleksandr Helphand-Parvus, and Trotsky. By contrast, constitutionalist and industrialized France knew at best a bastard Marxism (Jean Jaurès was closer in spirit to Michelet than to Marx); English Fabianism was not Marxist at all; and in the United States Marxism was the affair of a handful of East European immigrants. Marxism did not really arrive west of the Rhine until after 1917, and as a result of Lenin's exertions on its behalf. In fact, everywhere the potency of Marxism, and of the socialist idea in general, is in inverse proportion to the degree of development of "capitalism"; conversely, the power of both Marxism and generic socialism stands in direct proportion to the persistence of Old-Regime political and social structures.

This inverted manner of Marxism's appeal is no accident. Since advanced Europe shows mankind its future, as Marx stressed, it is hardly surprising that the more backward parts of Europe should be the most curious about his vision. For this vision is an ambiguous affair. On the one hand, Marx's capitalism was alluringly dynamic and creative, the acme of human achievement to date; on the other hand, it was oppressive and dehumanizing, the nadir of human degradation in the present. This ambiguity governed the diverse fortunes of Marxism in pre-1917 Europe.

Since backwardness was not a problem for the English and the French, they largely ignored Marx's vision. Since political, though not economic, backwardness was a major problem for Mitteleuropa, the Left in Germany and in Austria-Hungary welcomed the vision, but more to agitate against their half-surviving political Old Regimes than to dispossess the economic bourgeoisie. Since political and economic backwardness were equal problems for the Russians, they bought into Marxism in three stages. In the 1870s, the Populists willfully misread *Capital* as a warning to avoid capitalism, since it would destroy the existing socialist democracy of the peasant commune. But in the 1890s, after Populism's failure, the Russian Marxists greeted capitalism in more orthodox fashion as the first step toward socialism. Some of them, however, such as the "legal Marxist" Petr Struve, grew so enthusiastic for capitalism that they forgot about its alleged socialist sequel and plumped for industrialization and classical democracy as ends in themselves.[30]

Thus did the Enlightenment face of Marxism backhandedly promote progress in modern Europe. In Central Europe its task was to advance "bourgeois democracy," and in Russia, in its initial phase, it was to foster bourgeois economics.

Even more important than these inverted uses of Marxism's historical determinism, however, is the potential the system offered for the inverted use of its Romantic face. Note has already been made of the latent incompatibility between the objective and subjective aspects of Marxism—the socioeconomic process and the class struggle—and the resulting temptation of accelerating history by an act of political will. Impatience was clearly intrinsic to the Marxist theory of revolutionary anticipation.

This impatience would come to the surface during Marx's own career twice after 1848: in 1871, when he misappropriated the neo-Jacobin radicalism and patriotism of the Paris Commune for his own cause; and in 1878, when he mistakenly anticipated that a European revolution would be launched from Russia (rather than Germany) as a result of tsarism's poor showing in the latest war with Turkey. As late as 1885 Engels was writing that the next European upheaval would begin in the East and was "now soon due (the European revolutions, 1815, 1830, 1848–52, 1870 have occurred at intervals of fifteen to eighteen years in our century)."[31] Anticipatory impatience emerged again in the East in 1905 with Rosa Luxemburg's misperception of the Polish national revolt as proletarian, and in her resulting belief that the general strike was the key to international revolution. Yet each time, the expectations of the Marxist intellectuals were thwarted by the proletariat's deficit of revolutionary consciousness. And so from 1848 onward the fate of the socialist intelligentsia was to be uninterruptedly disappointed by its popular base.

This long disappointment would be broken only when the Bolsheviks escalated impatience into voluntarism. Thus, a theory devised to overcome the backwardness of the first, German plateau of the West-East cultural gradient was finally put into practice on the last and lowest level of the European system, Russia. The receptivity of the empire of the tsars to the new doctrine was due in part to Finance Minister Witte's crash industrialization of the 1890s, which at last gave Russia a noticeable working class. But even more important than this brute social fact was its perception by the revolutionary intelligentsia. And the intelligentsia's tradition prepared it quite well to receive the Marxist message.

The Russian radical intelligentsia had an itinerary close to that of the German Left. Recall that in the 1840s, Herzen and Bakunin, aided by the thought of Feuerbach, fused Hegel with French socialism to produce a dream of revolution in which the peasantry would be the universal class, or at least the all-Russian class. In the 1860s, the generation of Chernyshevskii, drawing on the positivism of Mill and Comte, updated the dream of peasant socialism by grounding it in a militant materialism designated nihilism by its critics. And in the 1870s, the next generation of emancipated youth at last "went to the people" with a message of active revolution, the movement called Populism *(narodnichestvo)*. In all these stages of the intelligentsia's radicalization, though the metaphysical underpinnings of nihilism and Populism were much less elaborate than those of Marx's system, the basic logic was quite parallel to his own premise that the last shall be first, whether as a class or as a nation.[32]

It is therefore hardly surprising that Marx found his first foreign audience not in enlightened England, but in darkest Russia. Despite the formal differences between mentor and pupils, the two shared a common aspiration to social leveling and violent revolution. Indeed, Marx at the end of his career, when all was quiet on the western front, was so impressed by the Populists' *élan* that he allowed that if the coming

Russian revolution coincided with a Western one, then the peasant commune could permit the tsarist empire to leap directly into socialism without an indigenous capitalist phase—a reprise of his own scenario for Germany in 1848 and a preview of Lenin's in 1917.[33]

However, the failure of the revolutionary strategy of the People's Will in 1881 convinced part of the radical intelligentsia that the *muzhik* made a poor revolutionary and that Russia therefore lacked the objective conditions for socialism. Still, the intellectuals themselves remained as revolutionary as before. At this juncture Witte's industrialization offered them a more promising universal class than the peasantry—the proletariat. So the revolutionary movement divided, the more hard-headed abandoning the peasants for the workers, and moralistic Populism for scientific Marxism. One wing of former Populists, led by Georgii Plekhanov, in 1883 came to form the Emancipation of Labor Group to propagate orthodox Marxism in Russia.

Yet this change was less fundamental than either party at the time believed, or than most historians since have assumed. To be sure, the obvious social differences between peasants and workers, and their unequal capacity for participation in modern politics, governed in part the move to Marxism. But the intellectuals were not interested in either class only out of revulsion at its oppressed state. They were equally interested in release from their *own* oppression—they who were the bearers of enlightenment to Russia yet who found themselves beset on every hand by a "barbaric," "lawless," and "Asiatic" despotism. And in this perspective, the "people," of whatever class, were valued above all in terms of their potential as agents of revolution. The most fundamental commitment of the radical intelligentsia was neither to workers nor to peasants; it was to Revolution. Marxism did not come to Russia because industrialization had produced a proletariat; it came to Russia because, after Populism's failure, the radical intelligentsia needed a new theory of revolution.

And so, the longstanding affinities between the half Old Regime of Germany and the full Old Regime of pre-1905 Russia prepared the way for grafting Marx's theory of revolution onto the half-cognate heritage of Bakunin and Chernyshevskii. The outcome of this amalgam was that, in 1917, Marx's logic of history quite skipped over Germany and landed his utopia in a Russia still more "medieval" than its now advanced neighbor. This result is not as improbable as it might appear to the orthodox Marxist eye: for if the proletarian heart of Marx's emancipation had waxed strong in the advanced West, its philosophical head swelled primarily in the backward East. But this unforeseen separation of philosophy from social base raises the vexed question of whether Lenin was a true Marxist and his Red October was the authentic realization of the socialist promise.

Leninist Practice

During the seven decades of Soviet Communism's existence, this question was by no means an academic one, for the regime's legitimacy depended on a positive answer. Lenin's Marxist credentials were challenged by fellow socialists, Western Social Democrats and Russian Mensheviks; and their arguments were then taken up by Western historians unconcerned for socialism but inveterately suspicious of Russia.[34]

The burden of these accusations is that Lenin departed from Marxism by telescoping the bourgeois and proletarian revolutions into one, thereby making his October a Blanquist coup d'état; furthermore, the resulting Jacobin dictatorship, since it was exercised in an immature peasant country, could only lead to "barracks socialism." Beneath Lenin's Marxist veneer, therefore, he was a throwback to the unscientific and conspiratorial People's Will, even to the idea of "preventive revolution" against capitalism advocated by Petr Tkachev in the mid-1870s; and the Bolshevik regime had in consequence turned out to be the mirror image of the backward autocracy it replaced. In this view, Soviet socialism in fact was no more than eternal Russia painted red, whereas true socialism represented both the most advanced economy and the highest form of democracy—in short, it was Western. Thus, the question of Lenin's Marxist orthodoxy fuses with the question of Russia's Europeanness per se. Indeed, the non-Marxist character of Leninism is the clinching argument for Russia's non-Western nature overall.

Lenin, of course, had the highest reverence for Chernyshevskii's intransigence toward all liberals and considerable respect for the People's Will. Nonetheless, the elitist revolutionary tradition of Populism is hardly an exclusively Russian phenomenon. It was recurrent in early nineteenth-century Europe from the Italian carbonari, to the secret societies of the July Monarchy, to the German Communist League for which Marx wrote his *Manifesto*. And it appeared whenever strong ideological goals were thwarted by rigid political circumstances. Moreover, there was a more recent source than Populism for organizational Leninism, namely, the centralized and hierarchical German Social Democratic (SD) Party. This organization, even after its legalization in 1891, remained something of a bunker party—no longer underground but still a beleaguered subsociety in the Kaiserreich and thus structurally mobilized for survival. It was this model that the Russian Marxists adopted for their own party in 1903. And this structure can readily be adapted to top-down bureaucratic authoritarianism, as Robert Michels was the first to demonstrate in his classic study of the German SDs in 1911.[35] As for Lenin's exploitation of rural radicalism, it can be plausibly accommodated to Marxism by classifying the peasants as a "democratic petty-bourgeoisie" and thus a natural ally of the proletariat in the first phase of the revolution. The class categories of Marxism have always been flexible, and Lenin's worker-peasant alliance is analogous to Marx's own view, expressed notably in the *Eighteenth Brumaire*, of the urban petty bourgeoisie as a part-time "democratic" ally of the proletariat.

What is more, in Lenin's day the Populists, now called the Socialist Revolutionaries (SRs) were still very present. Indeed, they had the largest base of support of any Russian party and in addition a conspiratorial arm, the Combat Organization, which in truth replicated the People's Will. Thus the question arises: why was this specifically Russian revolutionary organization so incompetent at the actual business of revolution? If Leninism is simply Populism with a Marxist face, why did it triumph so easily over its giant rival? Moreover, is it possible to imagine a specifically Russian socialist movement, once in power, forcibly collectivizing peasants to finance steel mills, or mesmerizing the planet for decades with its internationalism? A partial answer to these questions is that the neo-Populists lost out because they possessed little talent for disciplined organization, theoretical clarity, or decisiveness in a crisis—deficiencies that some would unkindly call specifically Russian. Thus the real question is not whether Lenin was a throwback to Populism, but why, of all the competing Russian revolutionary parties, his Bolsheviks alone were able to seize power and build a "socialist" regime. So perhaps we would get farther in assessing Lenin's orthodoxy, as well as the Russianness of his regime, by relating his alleged heterodoxy to the ambiguities of Marxism itself.

The first of these is the intrinsic difficulty of adapting orthodox Marxism to Russia. This difficulty was highlighted in a famous phrase of Petr Struve in the first manifesto of the Russian Social Democrats in 1898: "The farther east one goes in Europe, the weaker, meaner, and more cowardly in the political sense becomes the bourgeoisie, and the greater the cultural and political tasks which therefore fall to the lot of the proletariat."[36] This paradox, of course, was not intended as a reprise of the Populist fantasy that Russia could pass directly from autocracy to socialism. The Marxists insisted that Russia would have to follow the orthodox Way of the Cross from its current "feudal" (or "Asiatic") mode of production to capitalism before reaching socialism, and that it would have to do so in two separate revolutions, bourgeois and proletarian. Nonetheless, since Russia already had something of a proletariat, the workers would play a major, even leading, role in the first revolution (as Marx had supposed the proletariat would do in Germany in 1848). Yet at the same time, the Russian workers would have to restrain themselves and assume power only in the second revolutionary round. However faithful this scholastic scenario was to orthodox Marxism, psychologically it was almost an impossible position for a revolutionary party to maintain in practice.

The built-in ambiguity of Marxism as applied to Russia was aggravated by a more general crisis of the doctrine at the fin de siècle. When the essentials of Marxism were created in the 1840s, neither capitalism nor constitutional democracy were well developed in the West; and they were not yet triumphant when "mature" Marxism was worked out in the years 1850–1870. Yet by 1870 the "bourgeois mode of production" (Marx never spoke of "capitalism") had spread to most of Europe west of Russia and across the Atlantic to the United States. And by the founding of the Second International in 1889, there indeed existed worldwide what was coming to be called the "capitalist system," and, though temporarily in depression, it was still raising productivity and living standards. Moreover, universal suffrage, only a first draft in 1792, and again a failure in 1848–1851, after 1870 was an established system in France and, in diluted form, in imperial Germany (it applied only to the lower house of parliament and did not apply at all to the dominant state of Prussia). By 1884 it had practically been achieved in Britain. Hence socialists in most countries could enter parliament and work for piecemeal reform, which, though well short of their full ideal, was still of benefit to workers; and these same conditions at last made possible a solid labor movement in the form of trade unions. By 1900 the conjunction of these economic and political changes revealed, first, that capitalism was not producing increasing "immiseration" but was instead improving the workers' lot and, second, that parliamentary reform might well make revolution unnecessary.[37]

But historical circumstances were not the only factor making for a crisis of Marxism. The deeper cause lay within the system itself, in those underlying tensions which have already been examined. Recall that the system proposes, first, an objective socioeconomic logic of history, leading mankind implacably from feudalism, to capitalism, to socialism; second, it offers a subjective dynamic of the class struggle driving this advance; and, third, it sets forth the goal of socialism as noncapitalism, to be achieved by the abolition of private property, profit, and the market—the whole process culminating in the classless, stateless society. The inherent contradictions of this amalgam began to become apparent at the end of the century as events increasingly indicated that the logic of history, by itself, was leading neither to capitalism's collapse nor to the honing of the workers' revolutionary class consciousness.

The crisis of Marxism during the Second International was at its most acute in the especially contradictory conditions of imperial Germany, now Europe's industrial giant, yet still an Old Regime by half. The German Social Democratic Party, legalized in 1891, in the Erfurt Program of that year began by proclaiming maximalist revolutionary aims (roughly in the terms of Marx's *Manifesto*, minus his endorsement of violence). Yet at the same time this party, until then dominated by intellectuals, increasingly acquired a mass base in the form of trade unions, which were dominated by workers. The marriage of an organized socialist party with a mass labor movement, which at the time appeared to constitute the unique strength of German Social Democracy, became the source of its increasing moderation and "embourgeoisment."

In the course of the decade, the actual policy of the SDs became electoral and reformist, and the revolutionary goal receded indefinitely into the future. It was only a step from such de facto reformism to the conclusion that mature industrial society was refuting Marx's postulate that the economic struggle under capitalism generated a proletarian revolutionary consciousness. Instead, the logic of the system was leading to what would now be called a welfare state. In 1898, Eduard Bernstein said all this clearly by declaring: "the socialist movement meant everything," and the "final goal nothing." But such a view, of course, eviscerated Marx's Marxism, in which the goal of exiting prehistory was the whole point of the theory. Accordingly, Bernstein's position was anathematized as "revisionism" by the "orthodox" leadership of the party under Kautsky.

The underlying contradiction in Second International Marxism, however, remained unresolved, as is apparent from Kautsky's effort to reconcile SD reformist practice with Marx's revolutionary goal. Kautsky did this by adding to the logic of history what was in effect a new stage: universal-suffrage democracy. Surely, Kautsky believed, this instrument would give the socialists an eventual majority; Marx's transitional dictatorship of the proletariat would turn out to be a mild affair, quite compatible with classical liberal rights and freedoms. Nevertheless, Kautsky's ultimate goal remained Marx's noncapitalism: a nationalized economy, centralized planning, and collectivized agriculture—a program that amounts to the revolutionary destruction of civil society. For all its apparent democratic legalism, therefore, Kautsky's orthodoxy in fact offers an agenda that could only provoke massive resistance and civil strife, as nineteenth-century history to his day had rather clearly demonstrated. It is precisely for this reason that no social democratic government, from Sweden of the "middle way" in the 1930s, to Laborite Britain of 1945, to François Mitterrand's France in 1981—all with the authority in an overwhelming majority—has ever proceeded to the wholesale expropriation of society. Instead, they settled for taxing capitalism to fund a welfare state.

Kautsky's orthodoxy therefore amounts to the paradox of an evolutionary revolution—"revolutionary waiting," as he put it. It in fact subverts Marx's Marxism without saying so and puts its own internal contradictions in place of the master's. Hence Second International orthodoxy, in its own way, must be considered as much a fantasy as Marx's insurrectionary big bang. At the same time, since it remained safely in the realm of utopia, it also preserved the moral high ground from which to criticize Lenin's dictatorship, while yet believing that it had not become an accomplice of capitalism.

There is, however, a third way to meet the dilemma of fin-de-siècle Marxism, and that is, precisely, Lenin's own.[38] His starting point was in effect the same as Bernstein's, namely, that the logic of capitalism does not automatically lead to socialist revolution since the working class, by itself, produces only a reformist class consciousness: as Lenin famously put the matter, the "spontaneity" of the workers' movement can produce only a "trade-union consciousness." Lenin's solution, however, was the reverse of Bernstein's: to Lenin, the revolutionary goal of Marxism was everything, and the lawlike historical process, though hardly nothing, had to be mightily bent to make sure it led there. Specifically, this meant that the chosen instrument of the logic of history, the proletariat, could not be left to its own spontaneous devices. "A scientific revolutionary consciousness" had to be brought to it "from without" by a "vanguard" party of Marxist intellectuals who would lead and direct the revolution. Thus, Lenin substituted a party of full-time, "professional revolutionaries" for the real, flesh-and-blood workers. And he was adamant that "without theory there can be no revolutionary movement."

In sum, the Leninist party represents a metaphysical, not an empirical, proletariat—or in plain language, it was the intellectuals, not the workers, who were to lead the revolution. In Lenin's worldview ideological commitment rather than actual social status defined "class" identity. To hammer this point home, he asserted that when actual workers fell into the reformist trap, they ceased being true proletarians and became "petty bourgeois"—the supreme infamy in his, as in Marx's, lexicon.

> Since there can be no question of an independent ideology formulated by the working masses themselves in the process of their movement, the only choice is—either bourgeois or socialist ideology. There is no middle course—for mankind has not created a "third" ideology, and in a society torn by class antagonisms there can never be a non-class or an above-class ideology.[39]

The reasoning here is obviously cruder and more oriented to immediate action than Marx's soaring dialectical "unity of theory and practice." Nonetheless, the general import is the same: there was only one scientific social theory, and it corresponded to the interests of the one revolutionary class. There can be no supraclass neutrality in politics.

But, Lenin's critics would retort, does not this slashing subordination of proletarian Being to party Consciousness stand Marx on his head? And in a formal sense, this is indeed true. However, since history by 1900 had demonstrated that the workers, by themselves, are not revolutionary, there was no other way to reach Marx's goal of noncapitalism, which was the be-all and the end-all of his system. Thus, Lenin's theory of the vanguard party in reality supplied the hitherto missing link in Marx's doctrine. In fact, the germ of Lenin's theory of the necessity of an intelligentsia avant-garde in the proletarian revolution is clearly present in Marx's *Manifesto:*

> The Communists, therefore, are on the one hand, practically, the most advanced and resolute section of the working-class parties of every country, that section which pushes forward all others; on the other hand, theoretically, *they have over the great mass of the proletariat the advantage of clearly understanding the line of march,* the conditions, *and ultimate general results* of the proletarian movement.[40]

Small matter that at the time, in 1848, when Marx attributed this view to "the Communists," he could have meant only himself and Engels, for as yet no one else knew of his "theory." Small matter, too, that there then existed no movement to back it up: the theory was the only correct one all the same. True, there is no direct precedent for a Leninist-type party in Marx. Still, when Marx got his hands on what he hoped would be an appropriate vessel for his theory, the First International, he manipulated in a manner somewhat similar to Lenin's later tactics with the Russian SDs: he used his leadership position to split his own organization, indeed to sink it, rather than let it fall to socialists with the wrong theory, that is, Bakunin's anarchists.

Moreover, Lenin's "inversion" of Marx was more apparent than real. Marx's proletariat-as-the-universal-class had always been essentially a metaphysical construct; and Lenin's substitution of an intelligentsia party for this construct was the only way to bring Marx's metaphysics into the real world. Thereby Lenin transformed into practical politics the premise of the young Marx that "philosophy is the head" of the movement of "human emancipation of which the proletariat is the heart." However, since the actual workers were not conscious that this was their role, philosophy had to become a political party to put some muscle in their heart. With such a "party of a new type" Lenin proposed to "overturn all Russia"—and indeed the world.

Lenin's choice of party over people, moreover, reflects not just the dilemma of Marxism in Russia but the predicament of anticipatory revolution per se. For the masses in the aggregate, workers and peasants combined, *never* generate the scientific consciousness predicated by the intellectuals' theories of anticipation. Thus if the German Revisionists (and Kautsky, unwittingly) made the choice of abandoning the theory for legalistic democracy, this was because there was little prospect of large-scale upheaval in Germany (as the relatively mild nature of the German November Revolution of 1918 confirmed). And if Lenin made the putchist choice of assuming the proletariat's "true" role, it was because he was acting in a genuine revolutionary situation, and so stood a real chance of gaining power for his scientifically motivated intelligentsia.

In this eagerness, he was not alone. All Russian political parties were created in the two or three years before 1905; and they emerged because all Russian political actors (and the autocracy as well) knew that the grand national showdown between the opposition and the Old Regime was imminent. For the first time since the modern Left began anticipating revolution in 1848, a major European state was actually about to make one; and the race was on to shape the coming democratic order, whether in a liberal-constitutionalist sense or a socialist one. Thus, the orthodox Marxism of Germany, blunted by an overly long wait for capitalism to ripen for revolution, when imported into volatile Russia could only re-radicalize. Yet this hardly amounts to a betrayal of Marxism. It simply means that the Marxist theory of a two-stage revolution against an Old Regime is wrong.

In Russia in 1905 the real problem was not "capitalism"; it was autocracy. Russia after 1900 was preparing neither for a bourgeois nor a proletarian revolution; she was gearing up for her variant of the classic European revolution against absolutism and aristocracy. It is thus misleading to talk of this approaching watershed in terms of the transition from capitalism to socialism, as the retrospective shadow of October would make it appear. A more appropriate terminology is the transition from "traditional" to "modern" society—that millennial point of passage from a world that is simply given by God or history to a world where men create their own polity and society. Although the Marxist discourse of the intelligentsia victors of October obscured its real meaning for decades, the transition of 1917 was in fact a deformed version of the passage to modernity common to all European Old Regimes.

Indeed, the categories of Marxist discourse created a dilemma for Russia's new Social Democrats from the very beginning.[41] So long as they were struggling against the revolutionary romanticism of the Populists, the Russian Marxists remained united in applying the master's logic of history to Russia literally: there would have to be two separate Russian revolutions, bourgeois and socialist. As actual revolution approached, however, the Marxists had to devise a policy for worker participation in the lesser of these events. And on this issue they faced an acute dilemma. Since Russia was both a feudal autocracy (or an Asiatic despotism) and a partially capitalist country with something of a proletariat, what should be the role of socialists in a revolution that by definition could not be theirs? The solution that emerged was to claim that, given the Russian bourgeoisie's cowardice, the proletariat would have to play a "hegemonic" role in the revolution of its class enemy.

It is the stumbling block of this political oxymoron that sundered the Russian SDs, after their organization as a party in 1903, into Mensheviks and Bolsheviks. The Mensheviks stuck to the two-stage theory of revolution literally, and hence interpreted hegemony as compatible with a tactical alliance with the liberals and a policy of caution. But the Bolsheviks, emboldened by actual combat, increasingly extended hegemony to mean, in fact, the telescoping of the two revolutions into one. Tactically, this led them to spurn collaboration with the liberals and to seek instead an alliance with the now awakened "democratic" peasantry.

Yet for Lenin's theory of a "party of a new type" to be operative and still lay claim to being Marxist, the orthodox view of the logic of history had to be updated. Lenin accomplished this by the systematic adaptation of Marxist categories to a succession of new, twentieth-century problems. It is indeed strange that commentators should attempt to read out of Marxism a figure who throughout his adult life called himself a Marxist and who argued his every turn of policy with quotations from the Marxist canon.[42] Granted, he had first been a Populist. But what Russian Marxist of his generation had not started there too? After his "conversion," around 1890, he functioned constantly in the intellectual world of the Second International, indeed until 1914 considering himself a faithful disciple of Kautsky.

Thus, as the world approached 1914 the Second International increasingly feared that the scramble of the European powers to partition Africa and Asia would lead to general war. To accommodate this change, Marxists everywhere had to revise the internal contradictions of capitalism. In Austria, Rudolf Hilferding elaborated a theory of "imperialism" as "finance capitalism"; and Rosa Luxemburg in Germany argued that capitalism needed to expand into backward areas to keep afloat. During the war itself, Lenin developed this line of reasoning to add the political corollary that the "chain" of world capitalism would break at its "weakest link," the colonial and semicolonial dependencies of Europe. Thus backward Russia, as a semicolonial country—exploited by Europe but an exploiter of Asia—could logically begin the world revolution. Even though the proletariat was a minority in Russia, its revolution would nonetheless have democratic legitimacy, for it would certainly spread to the advanced West, thereby making it a majoritarian affair overall. Furthermore, if world revolution could begin in backward Russia, it was logical that her most laggard class, the peasantry, could contribute to the Russian revolutionary breakthrough—a corollary Lenin added to his scenario by stages between 1905 and 1917. With the addition of this "revolutionary alliance of workers and peasants" (as he called it after October) to his theory of imperialism and his concept of the vanguard party, Lenin's revision of Second International Marxism was complete.

Yet in making these revisions Lenin believed in all good conscience that his Marxism was the truly orthodox one. To him the essence of Marxism—its real not its formal logic—was the dialectic of class struggle driving history to its appointed goal of noncapitalism. And this dialectic is indeed the core principle of Marxism, the motive force of the process of self-enriching alienation animating the deterministic logic of history. It is, in fact, the element that ties the whole system together. Lenin's emphasis on political will generated by class struggle, therefore, is just as orthodox as anything the Second International orthodox found in Marxism. Or to put the matter another way: Lenin subordinated the Enlightenment, rationalistic element of Marxism to its Romantic, Promethean component; yet his revisions of Marx's own historical scenario still retained the formal framework of the Enlightenment's faith in ineluctable progress.

Hence even Lenin's cascade of revisions cannot suffice to brand him as unorthodox and Soviet Russia as non-Marxist. The real answer to the question of who among Marx's heirs is the true one is that the question itself is a false one. And this is so because Marxism presents to all its practitioners an intrinsically *impossible* task. The lockstep logic of history does not mesh with the system's motive force, the class struggle; nor does either one separately lead to the system's communist goal, which is simply an unattainable utopia. No matter how "mature" capitalism becomes—anywhere, anytime—the schizophrenic Marxist fantasy can never be realized in its entirety.

The question of Marxist orthodoxy is unanswerable for an even deeper reason: the conceptual framework necessary to pose such a question is itself founded on an illusion. In Marxism's grand vision, the course of modern history leads from a bourgeois revolution, which creates capitalism, to a proletarian revolution, which produces socialism. But there is no such thing as a proletarian revolution: never in history has the proletariat seized power. The only possible case is October 1917, but the time has long since passed when one could plausibly claim that this was a worker, rather than a Party, seizure of power. The notion of a proletarian revolution is only an anticipation, an ideological extrapolation from a presumed antecedent "bourgeois revolution."

But there is no such thing as a "bourgeois revolution," either. Of course, there was a great revolution of the Third Estate in France in 1789, followed by an egalitarian Jacobin Republic in the years 1792–1794. The real issue is the meaning of these events. What is indisputable is that for the first time in history they posed the question of "democracy" in its modern sense—that is, a polity founded on the proposition that all men, simply by virtue of being human, are equal before the law and endowed with full rights of participation in government—principles summed up as "the Rights of Man and the Citizen" and "universal suffrage." (The American Revolution, by contrast, despite the ringing "All men are created equal" introducing the Declaration of Independence was not fundamentally about equality; it was about liberty, both national and individual. White male suffrage came only in the 1820s, and full manhood suffrage only with the Fourteenth Amendment in 1868.) The French Revolution did not succeed in institutionalizing universal suffrage democracy; but this is not to say it "failed," as is often averred. It accomplished the epochal feat of mortally wounding Europe's millennial Old Regime, thereby putting egalitarian democracy at the heart of the agenda of modernity.

Marxism purports to offer a deeper perception of the Revolution than this by construing it as a bourgeois seizure of power. In this view, behind all the high-flown rhetoric about the "nation" and the "Rights of Man" the real purpose of 1789, and the hidden hand of the republic, was to create the "objective" conditions for capitalist development by abolishing guilds, internal tariffs, manorial dues, and other aspects of "feudalism" (all projects, incidentally, entertained by enlightened absolutism). Yet this perspective (which, it will be recalled, emerged only under the July Monarchy) hardly corresponds to the real map of industrialism's emergence overall; the economic development of Holland and England, of North America and Prussia-Germany, can be aligned with the politics of France only through an embarrassment of metaphysical legerdemain.[43] Indeed, the case can be made that the Revolution was bad for business in France herself; for it resulted in a society with too many small peasant proprietors and not enough grand entrepreneurs.

In fact, the progression from the bourgeois to the proletarian revolution is not a succession of real historical events but a sociological eschatology. It is hence futile to debate who had, or has, the correct Marxist road map to get from one revolution to the other, since the road itself does not exist. To be sure, all this was not so apparent in 1900 as it came to be at the end of the century. Yet even at the end of the century, decades of historiography treating the Soviet experiment on its own terms still obfuscates what was really involved.

The same unreality of discourse bedevils the discussion of which class is the chosen vessel for a "socialist" revolution. "Bourgeoisie" and "proletariat" are not just social groupings and the "real" actors of politics; they are also moral-ideological categories, mobilizing concepts in the battle of egalitarian politics.[44] Seen in this context, the usual sharp distinction between the "utopian" peasant socialism of Russia and the "realistic" proletarian socialism of the West loses much of its meaning. Achieving socialism on the basis of the peasant commune was, of course, a utopian ambition; but so, too, as it turned out, was building it on the revolutionary community of factory workers.

Clearly, there is a vast practical difference between workers and peasants in any modern revolution. Industrial workers are concentrated in urban nerve centers, and hence can have a disproportionate political impact on events, whereas peasants are scattered across a vast countryside, "like a sack of potatoes" in Marx's contemptuous phrase in the *Eighteenth Brumaire*, and hence are disproportionately difficult to mobilize for politics. It is true also that workers are a modern, technologically literate class, whereas peasants are closer to immemorial and conservative ways. All the same, these political and cultural differences do not indicate any special aptitude of either group for giving birth to the unicorn of Socialism. And so, once again, and in the West no less than in Russia, the "social" common denominator of all socialisms turns out to be the intelligentsia; and its various industrial or agrarian programs are in fact variants of modern Europe's common quest for a perfect, egalitarian democracy founded on the suffering and swindled People.

It is thus artificial to treat the "Russian revolutionary movement" as a phenomenon radically apart in Europe because it looked primarily to peasants not to workers. In clear historical fact there was constant overlap between the Russian and the Western movements. The Russian Populists first became an active force in the early 1870s, at the very moment they discovered Marx's *Capital*; and throughout the decade they used his analysis to steel their resolve to keep capitalism out of Russia.[45] At the same time, Marx himself, after the failure of the Paris Commune in 1871, had no better revolutionary prospect than Russian Populism, and hence edged closer to its program. The Marxist-Populist symbiosis continued until the founding Congress of the Second International in 1889, which the old *narodnik* Petr Lavrov and the neophyte Marxist Georgii Plekhanov attended as Russian delegates. Is it not best, consequently, to speak of a single European movement of anticipatory democracy from 1830 to the end of the century, which, depending on national and temporal circumstances, varied in its level of activism and the priority it accorded to one or another face of "the masses"?

Indeed, by the turn of the century, Russian Populism was obliged to recognize that capitalism had arrived in Russia; henceforth the worker took his place alongside the peasant in their ideology, and this extended universal class was called the "toilers." At the same time, in the West the artisan socialism of Proudhon was transformed into industrial syndicalism. Yet in both East and West Marxism was hegemonic intellectually, imposing on all forms of socialism a base-superstructure sociology and a two-stage, bourgeois-proletarian, vision of revolution.

Sooner or later, all classical Marxists had to choose one or another of Marxism's basic components. Bernstein chose to go where the "logic" of industrial society really led, into welfare-state social democracy; thereby he in effect opted out of Marxism, for it is not necessary to be

Marxist to build a mere welfare state. Kautsky thought he did not have to choose and continued to believe that history's logic would one day produce the goal; he thus prolonged beyond October a phantom orthodox Marxism, eternally in pursuit of the unicorn of a full noncapitalism that would yet be democratic. Lenin, trusting to the creative powers of the class struggle, chose to forge ahead to the Communist goal, adjusting history's logic as he went; and in this he remained as faithful to the master as is possible, for it *is* necessary to be Marxist to strive for the Communist utopia.

And so, after 1914–1917, Marx's feuding heirs went their separate ways. But a strong difference divides their political fates: socialists who remained committed to political democracy in fact never achieved Socialism as the transcendence of capitalism, for even the Swedes could never claim that their "middle way" was as yet the real thing; but Communists who dismissed political liberty as a "formal" bourgeois sham in fact built socialism as noncapitalism, and did so many times over, from China to Cuba. For it *is* possible, if not to arrive at the Communism of the Crystal Palace, then at least to suppress capitalism in the form of private property, profit, and the market—and with them, all the freedoms of civil society.

It is this cruelly ambiguous result that for seven decades fueled a Western debate as to which of Marx's heirs was the legitimate one. The dispute raged on and the ink flowed red between several kinds of Marxist "humanists," revisionists, and reformed Communists proposing Prague Springs and "socialisms with a human face." Still, none of the contending parties ever produced an answer that would bring Soviet Russia into unambiguous focus. For the Sybil of the British Museum was now and forever silent, and not even the posthumously discovered manuscripts of original Marxism could make it speak again with a single, infallible voice.

Yet the answer to the conundrum of Marxism's true meaning may simply be that Marx, like so many of his compatriots, had two warring souls within his system, a Western and an Eastern one, an Enlightenment and a Romantic one, a positivistic and a paratheological one, a Social Democratic and a Communist one. And perhaps Marx had these two souls for more than Middle European reasons. It is most probably true that the composite unicorn of socialism itself has two souls, a libertarian and an egalitarian one, an individualistic and a collectivistic one. Yet—and here is the rub—as Tocqueville argued in Marx's own day, in the real world society cannot have both in full measure and at once, but must choose its order of priorities.[46] Indeed, the modern record indicates that it is quite feasible to expand equality in a liberal polity, but that it requires a revolutionary break to introduce liberty into a would-be egalitarian Communism.

At all events, as an empirical, historical matter, in the domain of revolutionary praxis—for Marx the decisive verdict in questions of theory—it is the Eastern soul of his socialism that won out: Cain slew Abel, and the seed of Ishmael prevailed over that of Isaac. Thus as the Cunning of Reason finally determined, Marx entered into eternity not as emancipator of the First World, but as herald of the servitudes of the Second and patron of the fumblings of the Third.

THROUGH THE SOVIET-RUSSIAN LOOKING-GLASS, AND WHAT THE WEST FOUND THERE: 1917–1991

PROLOGUE: IN THE EYE OF THE BEHOLDER

JABBERWOCKY

'Twas brillig, and the slithy toves
Did gyre and gimble in the wabe
All mimsy were the borogoves,
And the mome raths outgrabe.

JABBERWOCKY

'Twas brillig, and the slithy toves
Did gyre and gimble in the wabe
All mimsy were the borogoves,
And the mome raths outgrabe.

—Lewis Carroll

(An antiphony of Hyperborean and lunary voices is heard from the far side of the mirror:)

THE HERALD, Vladimir Ilich Lenin:

All Power to the Soviets! (1917)

Socialism = soviet power + electrification! (1920)

THE CORYPHAEUS, Iosif Vissarionovich Stalin:

Forward to the Five-Year Plan in four years! (1929)

And to the liquidation of the kulaks as a class! (1930)

The most valuable capital of all is People! (1935)

Life has become better, life has become more joyous! (1936)

(Everyone stands. Thunderous applause, turning into an ovation.)

FIRST DEMICHORUS,
Vladimir Maiakovskii:

About face, march!

No time for wordy palaver.

Quiet, all windbags!

You

Have the floor,

Comrade Mauser.

Enough of life by the law

Handed down from Adam and Eve

We'll ride the nag of history to death.

Left!

Left!

Left!

("Left, March!" 1918)

                    this
                    is Mister European Official
                    taking
        my red-skinned
            piece of passport . . .
                as if it
                    were a bomb;
            . . . my hands hold
                    the hammered-and-sickled
                        Soviet passport . . .
        Read it
            with envy:
                I'm a citizen
                    of the Soviet Union!
("Verses on the Soviet Passport," 1930)

Aleksandr Blok:

The wind whirls, the snow flies.
And twelve men march forth . . .

The bourgeois stands across their way,
His nose in his fur collar . . .
The bourgeois stands like a hungry hound . . .
And the old world, like a mongrel cur,
Tail between legs, slinks down . . .

Forward, forward, forward
You toiling masses!

Hey, comrade, it's going to be rough,
Come out and begin to shoot!

            Trak-tak-tak . . .

The people march on with commanding stride—
Behind them lies the hungry hound,
And at their head—with a bloodied flag,
Behind the screen of whirling snow,
Untouched by any bullet,
Walking weightless over the drifts
In a dust of snowy pearl,

In a white nimbus of roses—
At their head marches Jesus Christ.
(*The Twelve*, 1918)

Yes, we are Scythians; yes, we are Asiatics—

Once and for all: come to your senses, time-worn world!
To the fraternal feast of labor and of peace—
For the last time—to the bright fraternal feast
You are summoned by strains of a barbarian lyre!
("The Scythians," 1918)

SECOND DEMICHORUS

Osip Mandelshtam:

The transparent spring above the black Neva
Has been shattered, the wax of immortality is melting.
Oh, if you my star, are Petropolis, your city,
My brother, Petropolis, is dying. (1918)

In Petersburg we shall meet again,
As though we had buried the sun there . . .
In the black velvet of the Soviet night,
In the night of universal emptiness . . . (1920)

One hears only the Kremlin mountaineer,
Soul-destroyer and peasant-butcher,
A smile on his cockroach mustachios
And a gleam on his great polished boots. (1934)

Anna Akhmatova:

One must not live in the Kremlin—Peter's Guard was right—
There all is crawling still with microbes of ancient hate
Boris's savage fear and all the Ivans' spite
The pride of the self-crowned Impostor—in place of the people's right
("Moon of the Streltsy," 1937)

And the road then opened before me
Along which so many had trod . . .
And long was the funereal path
Through the majestic and crystalline
    Silence of Siberia.

Seized by a deathly terror
Before all that had turned to dust,
And knowing the full measure of vengeance,
Her dry eyes cast downward,
And wringing her hands, Russia
Went before me into the East.
(*Poem without a Hero,* 1940–1962)

(The Coryphaeus reappears atop the Lenin Mausoleum.)

FULL CHORUS IN UNISON:

East March!

. . . Alice, turning fiercely upon the Red Khan whom she considered as the cause of all the mischief—but the Khan was no longer at her side—he had suddenly dwindled down to the size of a rubicund, bald-headed doll, and then of a beatle-browed, bushy one, and then of another bald-headed, birth-marked one, merrily running round and round after its own train.

Catching hold of the little creature . . .

SHAKING . . .

WAKING

—and it really *was* a kitten, after all.

(Reentry to sublunary prose and the near side of the mirror.)

Before 1917 Russia, to most Westerners, was an "East European country which happened to extend into Asia."[1] But can we reverse the proposition and say that after 1917 she appeared as an Asiatic country which extended ominously into Europe? One might well think that so radical a break with the past as October would have replaced hope for Russia's convergence with her neighbors with belief in her radical otherness, as demonstrated by the resemblance of the tsarist and Communist autocracies and the transfer of the capital from European St. Petersburg to Byzantine Moscow with its Oriental Kremlin. A number of commentators did immediately draw such conclusions. But for most of Western opinion perception of such a sharp difference was slow to develop; and when it did emerge, Europe was never unanimous in categorically opposing Russia to the West or in finding a direct filiation from "the white to the red eagle."[2]

On the contrary, after 1917 the West oscillated between a number of different and often incompatible representations of Soviet Russia. Nor did these images fall into any simple pattern. Although various images tended to predominate at different times, they also frequently coexisted within the same period and on occasion merged one into another. Soviet Russia never came into stable focus under Western eyes, as imperial Russia had done earlier, but presented instead a kaleidoscope of conflicting perceptions.

Some order may nonetheless be found in this confusion; for the contradictory evaluations of the Soviet phenomenon in fact offer a recapitulation of all previous images of Russia, taken up again either simultaneously or in rapid succession. Thus the Bolshevik regime after 1917 was seen successively as enlightened despotism and as Oriental despotism; or it was viewed alternatively through the prism of convergence and of barbaric yet vital soul. Still, the West could never make up its mind just what sort of beast confronted it, and the question constantly returned: was the Soviet zebra white with black stripes, or black with white stripes? and if the latter, was it not the zebra of Troy?

Although the four classic images of Russia were old, the historical context in which they recurred was new. For the "real twentieth century," in Akhmatova's expression, the century inaugurated by the First World War, would be the age par excellence of revolution and ideological politics. The Soviet impact on the West, consequently, was qualitatively different from that of old Russia. The latter, even at its strongest, was only a conservative, "follower" society in relation to Europe. But Soviet Russia, even at its weakest, cast itself in the role of a "leader" society and found many Westerners willing to accept this pretension. After 1917, therefore, Western-Soviet relations were of a different order of historical magnitude from Western-tsarist relations. Indeed, living with Soviet power constituted an essentially new problem, as the familiar fact of a Russian dynastic state was subsumed in the unprecedented fact of a Soviet Party-state with worldwide ideological reach.

And there was much the new Soviet state could reach into. In the two decades after October the outside world was in a constant flux of

294

social and national crises, as the Great Depression and the rise of fascism challenged the international system created at Versailles, not only within the West but far off in China and Japan. Since the new Russia was a constant catalyst of both hope and fear throughout these decades, it was correspondingly difficult for Westerners to bring her international role into any clear focus.

The difficulty of assessing Communist Russia was compounded by the fact that her internal order required the same span of time to find its own focus, in contrast with the imperial order at its beginnings. The internal structure of Peter the Great's Old Regime had appeared fully formed along with Russian international power. Petrine society was in no sense a creation de novo but a modernization of the Muscovite universal service state. When endowed with Western military organization and culture, therefore, it could pass for a variant of European absolutism and so had no disturbing effect on the existing European order: Peter's state appeared to Europe only as powerful but not as revolutionary. The state of Lenin and Stalin, however, was a different matter. Not only was its revolutionary impact on Europe manifest from the start, but for years outside observers were baffled by the Bolshevik revolution's meaning. Indeed, until the end of the 1930s, its leaders themselves were not sure what they were building, or where exactly they were headed; and the order they created emerged through a series of zigzagging improvisations.

The Soviet experiment has thus been called "the mistake of Columbus": the Party set sail for the spice-perfumed isles of Socialism but ended up, by the late 1930s, on the impassable continent of Stalinist totalitarianism and its offshore Gulag Archipelago—quite an achievement no doubt, but not precisely what the crew had in mind on enlistment.[3] Like Columbus, the Party never realized just where it had landed, but insisted to the end that its "soviet power" was indeed "real socialism." Since the Soviet leadership could never face up to its actual achievement, it is hardly surprising that ill-informed and ideologically confused Westerners grasped its nature much better. So the world spent the rest of the century contending with the new Russia, perceived (in Churchill's phrase) as a "riddle, wrapped in a mystery, inside an enigma."[4]

HEADS, THE EXPERIMENT: 1917–1945

I have been to the future, and it works.

—Lincoln Steffens (1919)

_____

The Russians have waged their Offensive [the First Five-Year Plan] for a new world along two vast all-embracing fronts—that of economics with the aim of creating a new economic order, and that of sociology with the aim of creating a new human personality. It is on the economic front that they have encountered their chief setbacks . . . difficulties, blunders, mishaps. But on the sociological front they have met slight opposition. . . . If by the word liberalism we mean tolerance of opposition, then there is not a vestige of it in Russia. But if we mean by it advanced ideas and practices in social accommodation then the Russian dictatorship has out-liberalized the most liberal statesmen in the world.

—Maurice Hindus, _The Great Offensive_ (1933)

The decisive part in the subjugation of the intelligentsia was played . . . by the word "Revolution," which none of them could bear to give up. It is a word to which whole nations have succumbed, and its force is such that one wonders why our rulers still need prisons and capital punishment.

—Nadezhda Mandelshtam,
Hope against Hope (1970, apropos of the 1930s)

_____

And they came over unto the other side of the sea into the country of the Gardarenes. And when he was come out of the ship, immediately there met him . . . a man with an unclean spirit, who had his dwelling among the tombs. . . . And [Jesus] said unto him "come out of the man, _thou_ unclean spirit." And he asked him "What is thy name?" And he answered saying, my name is Legion: for we are many. . . . Now there was there nigh unto the mountains a great herd of swine feeding. . . . And the unclean spirits went out, and entered into the swine: and the herd ran violently down a steep place into the sea . . . and were choked by the sea.

—Mark 5:1–13 (a source of Dostoevsky's
concept of demonic possession)

Within the fluid postwar world the four old images of Russia returned. Yet not everything had changed on the far side of 1917, so the West's perception of the new Russia was filtered through the aspirations of those familiar groups, the two heirs of the Enlightenment, the liberals and socialists on the one hand, and the foes of both liberalism and socialism, the neo-Romantic antirationalists, on the other. But it was the former group that was most profoundly concerned by the challenge of 1917.

And this for the good reason that Red October had for the first time in history brought a socialist government to power, for the first time

296

anywhere overthrowing capitalism and expropriating the bourgeoisie. Could it then be that Marx's prophecies had at last been fulfilled, and that the long anticipation which had been socialism's lot since 1848 had come to a happy end? Were the mere liberal democracy of 1789 and the Jacobin Republic thereby repealed and the logic of History sublated to its ultimate and highest level: the full democracy of Socialism? One thing at least was clear: 1917 had ritually negated and threatened with eventual destruction all the existing structures of the rest of Europe.

At first, therefore, in the 1920s and the early 1930s, most Westerners considered their new problem in the East to be not the resurgence of Asiatic barbarism, but the quite European issue of socialism. The two heirs of the Enlightenment judged Russia according to the universal categories of Right and Left: Bolshevism was a more extreme Jacobin dictatorship or a more enduring Paris Commune, either worse or better than its Western predecessors depending on one's politics, but still a familiar and commensurable phenomenon for all. It was red revolution against private property and laissez-faire capitalism, compounded with a Godless movement for the suppression of the family and traditional morality. Most Western opinion regarding the new Russia divided along the lines of its attitude toward socialism.

Thus the Western establishments of the day, wedded to liberal and individualistic ways, and grown more conservative in the troubled post-war world, found Bolshevism abhorrent, but as an expression of revolutionary socialism, not of Russia. Their practical policy toward it, expressed perhaps most forcefully by Winston Churchill, was to suppress it if they could, as when the Allies intervened on the side of the Russian Whites during the years 1918–1920, and when this failed, to seal it off from the rest of Europe with a *cordon sanitaire* of buffer states from the Baltic to Romania. Most Western governments, therefore, took years to recognize permanently the new regime in Moscow, the French until 1926, the English until 1929, and the Americans until 1933.[5]

More complex was the attitude of the minority among the Enlightenment's heirs that favored socialism. Here opinion divided over whether or not the Soviet regime represented true socialism and authentic Marxism. On the one hand, the Soviet regime declared itself Marxist and stood adamantly opposed to imperialist war; it indeed la-

beled the Social Democrats "renegades" for having voted for war credits in 1914. It had also ridden to power on a great wave of proletarian
and peasant anger, and it claimed to be the dictatorship of the former
exploited classes over their erstwhile exploiters. Finally, it had boldly
abolished private property and capitalism. Yet, on the other hand, it was
not democratic but a self-appointed dictatorship that had never won an
election; indeed, it had dispersed with bayonets the democratically chosen Constituent Assembly in 1918. The fact of a revolutionary dictatorship of the proletariat over the dispossessed bourgeoisie was not in itself
scandalous to pre-1917 socialists; this was a classical, if largely nominal,
part of their own program. But the Marxist proletarian dictatorship was
supposed to be that of an overwhelming majority over a small minority,
whereas in Russia matters were clearly the other way round. The Bolshevik dictatorship, moreover, dragged on interminably, instead of being the short-term affair Marxists had always envisaged.[6]

Western socialist opinion, therefore, divided between those who felt
that Bolshevism was a realization of their ideal because it had suppressed capitalism and those who felt it was a betrayal of that ideal
because it had also suppressed political democracy. And between these
two poles there were numerous waverers oscillating from one opinion
to the other. Broadly speaking, a majority of Western socialists, such as
the German SDs, firmly rejected Communism as a dangerous "Blanquist" or "putschist" deviation from Marxism; nor did they hesitate to
put down insurrectionary Communist movements at home with the
armed aid of the Right, as did Gustav Noske in Munich in 1919. A
minority of Western socialists, such as the leadership of the French
Socialist Party (SFIO) at the Congress of Tours in 1920, went over to
the Communist Third International because the Bolsheviks had dared
to make that revolution of the masses which Western socialists had
"betrayed" in 1914. An intermediate group, such as the German Independent Socialist Party judged Bolshevism, for all its dictatorial pro-
clivities, to be better on the whole than capitalism, eventually splitting
between the Socialist Party and the German Communist Party. This
intermediate position was approximated at times by such classical socialists as the British Labor Party in the 1920s, the French Socialists of
Léon Blum in 1936, and, farther on the Left, the Italian Socialists of

Pietro Nenni after the Second World War. Finally, numerous independent leftists, from Lincoln Steffens in the 1920s to Jean-Paul Sartre after the Second World War, were in and out of love with the Soviet experiment, depending both on its stage of evolution and on shifting political constellations in the West. Yet the extraordinary fact about most people who called themselves socialist is that, except for the orthodox Communists, they were never able to arrive at a clear opinion about the Soviet order and its relationship to their ideal.[7]

And no wonder. For the perennial confusion of the questing heirs of the Left Enlightenment arose for the good and sufficient reason that October had done nothing to resolve the riddle of socialism. On the contrary, the bewildering succession and bizarre character of the upheavals on the far side of the Western-Soviet divide only made the riddle appear more enigmatic still.

The Ride of the Troika

The world's first socialist revolution had broken out in the last place on earth one might have expected, in the laggard empire of the tsars. It was as if the West-East gradient of European history had been upended, delivering over seventy years of revolutionary anticipation and theoretical refinement to an improbable Petrograd Commune. Yet there the facts were. It was with the staggering Anglo-Franco-Germanic baggage of Marxism that Lenin had loaded up Gogol's troika (no screws, no metal) and headed off with all the Scythians to an Atlantis beyond the farthest Western isles.

He and Trotsky by no means wished to direct Russia East; rather they aimed ultra-West. Although their revolution had been made in Russia, it was intended as the first stage of a world upheaval, the beginning, at last, of the transition from socialism as theory to socialism as revolutionary practice. As Trotsky, quoting Goethe's Mephistopheles, repeated, "Gray, my good friend, is all theory, but everlasting green is the golden tree of Life."[8] Therewith the troika hurtled into a fourfold mistake of Columbus.[9]

Both Lenin and Trotsky held that backward Russia could not arrive at socialism by herself; final victory would come only when their gamble paid off in a Western revolution, above all in Germany—both the

European industrial powerhouse and the homeland of Marxism. Yet the Cunning of Reason was no kinder to Lenin and Trotsky than it had been to Marx. Just as socialist Paris had failed Marx in 1848, leaving Germany to her Old-Regime devices and ultimately to the iron chancellor, Bismarck, so Second International Germany failed the Bolsheviks in 1918–19, leaving the Soviet regime to its backward Russian devices and ultimately to a Leader of steel, Dzugashvili-Stalin. But this perverse result took time to emerge, and in the meanwhile the Bolsheviks groped their way unaided toward socialism through a succession of programs then known as the "experiment." This adventure unfolded in four dialectically related circles.

The first circle opened with the precipitate takeoff of Lenin's troika and led, during the Civil War of 1918–1920, to an attempted leap to immediate socialism known as War Communism. This label was adopted only after the policy's failure, however; and it was chosen to indicate that the episode had not been the Bolsheviks' considered program, but an emergency response to the crisis of war, a mere military Communism. In fact, it quite aptly characterizes the Bolsheviks' militant commitment to reaching full Communism at the time; for, while awaiting the Western revolution, in their war against the Whites they had indeed sought "to forge the institutions of the new world in the heat of the class struggle." This combined militant and military Communism thus escalated into full nationalization of industry and commerce (at least on paper), abolition of the market, eventually even of money, and a simulacrum of economic planning. This was precisely Marx's agenda for socialism as noncapitalism. Thus the Bolsheviks, though indeed prodded by the war emergency, wound up doing what they were ideologically programmed to do anyway.[10]

The first draft of their experiment failed dismally, in part owing to the decomposition of the economy begun by the World War and aggravated by the Civil War. But it was due at least as much to the coercive nature of War Communism itself. By 1921, the Bolsheviks' initial leap into utopia had produced the near-collapse of industry, while their policy of forced grain requisitions had alienated the peasantry and contributed to the famine of 1921–22.

War Communism had two enduring results nevertheless. It completed the liquidation of Russian civil society begun under the impact of foreign and civil war: by 1920 structured and autonomous social groups had disappeared in Russia, leaving only a fluid mass of workers and peasants. Furthermore, military mobilization for war against the Whites helped mold Lenin's recently underground party into a state apparatus. This promotion filled the void left by civil society's collapse with a bureaucracy that aspired to manage everything in the country, though it as yet lacked the real capacity to do so. Thus was created the framework of an unprecedented order—the Party-state—a system in which the official governmental structure, the workers' and peasants' "soviets," was in fact controlled by a parallel apparatus of Party "committees" staffed by co-optation from above. "Bureaucracy," however, is not really an appropriate term for such a structure, despite its usage from Trotsky onward to characterize the Soviet governmental apparatus. The Soviet regime was no state machine of the traditional Russian sort satirized by Gogol and Saltykov-Shchedrin. Rather, it was a partocracy that was omnicompetent in its purview and ideocratic in its purpose, a form of secular theocracy ruling in the name of the Socialist Idea. And given this ideological purpose, it became a superstate that in effect replaced the old social structure by a new political one.[11]

The second circle of the experiment opened in 1921 and, though called a "breathing spell," was in fact a retreat. By now it was clear that no Western revolution was imminent, and that for the foreseeable future the vanguard party would be a minority dictatorship in a backward country. On the theoretical plane, this anomaly was handled by declaring that "the stabilization of capitalism" was only temporary: by capitalism's very nature, a new economic crisis or another war would eventually bring world revolution. In the meantime, therefore, the Bolsheviks' task was to hold the socialist fort in Russia—a plausibly Marxist amendment to Lenin's theory of imperialism.

But how could they hold a proletarian fort in an overwhelmingly peasant country, especially once the economic disaster of War Communism had produced worker disaffection and peasant revolt? Lenin's answer was to improvise a New Economic Policy (NEP), which effected a partial return to the market. Peasant agriculture and petty commerce were largely freed from governmental control, while the "commanding heights" of heavy industry and credit remained in the hands of the Party-state. Although this policy quickly revived the economy, reliance on the capitalist principles of the market and private profit meant delaying indefinitely the transition to socialism. Trotsky and the Left, therefore, urged replacing the NEP with a plan for intensive industrial development; and even though they lost the struggle for power, their program was in effect adopted when the Party approved the draft of a first Five-Year Plan in 1927.[12]

Under the strain of this ambitious endeavor the NEP began to falter.[13] It did so, however, for political, not economic reasons: the Party violated its own semimarket policy by lowering agricultural prices administratively to funnel capital from consumption into the plan. Hence in 1928 the peasants drastically reduced their grain deliveries, and the regime was obliged to import food for its workers. The plan was threatened with collapse just as it was about to begin.

Thus, twelve years after October the revolution of the now dead Lenin and the exiled Trotsky had in effect failed—both in its international ambitions and its internal policy, and whether as full Communism or as a semimixed economy. With this second internal failure, the Party faced the alternative of abdicating to the peasants or finding a drastic way out.

As the crisis deepened the Party's leading theorist, Nikolai Bukharin, advocated raising grain prices, both to feed the cities and to fund the plan, a policy he called "growing into socialism through the market." In later years much would be made of this "Bukharin alternative" as the path to a more humane Soviet order than the one created by Stalin.[14] And indeed, Bukharin's program would have yielded satisfactory economic results. But this modest goal was not his own; and understandable enthusiasm for an alternative to Stalin should not lead us to think that by 1929 Bukharin had ceased being a Bolshevik and that "market socialism" or democratic Communism was now his program. Rather, he saw the market as a temporary expedient, merely a means to the goal he shared with all the other Bolsheviks; and this was the full noncapitalism of Marx, to be achieved under the full dictatorship of the Party of Lenin. In such a context, therefore, how realistic was it to continue temporary but prolonged cohabitation with the market?

Indeed, it soon became apparent that deepening the NEP would dilute the Party's dictatorship by conceding economic power to the independent peasant, and that this would in turn slow the looming socialist offensive to what Bukharin himself called "a snail's pace." But Lenin's Party was made of sterner stuff than such "conciliationism." Its raison d'être was the monopoly of power for struggle against all "class enemies," of whom the "petty-bourgeois" kulaks were the most retrograde specimens. By the end of the twenties, this Party was a million-member political army organized to follow a single "general line." Whoever commanded this apparatus, therefore, also commanded policy; and the commander of the *apparat* was now the "man of steel," General Secretary Stalin. As the crisis of the plan mounted, the "Gensek" did not hesitate to opt for the drastic way out of his Party's dilemma. The theorist Bukharin and his partisans were condemned as a "Right deviation"; Trotsky's program of giving priority to industry was appropriated without acknowledgment; and the fight was on to subdue the peasants and save the socialist plan, and with it the Party's hegemony.

So began the third and most crucial phase of the experiment. Stalin proclaimed himself the "Lenin of today" and launched a "second October" to complete the interrupted work of the first. He now sat alone atop the troika with all the reins in his own two hands; and he was headed for no misty Atlantis over the Western horizon, but for the concrete and steel of "socialism in one country." This time, moreover, Russia was really going to get there; and she would do it all on her own (no fancy foreign gaiters, no cosmopolitan intellectuals). Above all, there would be no further question of the vanguard Party of Ilich hitching its fortunes to "the peasant nag," or of the dictatorship of the proletariat capitulating to "capitalist" kulaks. So the experiment was swung full circle into the "great offensive" of forced collectivization and crash industrialization of 1929–1932. Called the First Five-Year Plan, this second leap into utopia produced the experiment's definitive form.

And, as it turned out, it amounted to an institutionalized version of its first draft, War Communism.[15]

This dire outcome has often been explained as a return to the Russian autocratic method of revolution from above to close the gap with the West, after the manner of Peter the Great or Ivan the Terrible. Stalin himself, in his later years, was fond of both comparisons, as have been numerous Western commentators ever since.[16] But the First Five-Year Plan was much more than a reversion to Muscovite practices. Not only was it revolution on a scale previously unknown in Russian history, but it was carried out with an ideological purpose unique in all history and quite peculiar to the Communist Party-state. For this incomparable instrument combined Marx's millenarian vision of progress through class warfare with Lenin's vanguard dictatorship of the toiling masses. Only such an ideology serviced by such an organization could produce the "liquidation of the kulaks as a class," for in this perspective their imputed petty-bourgeois essence replaced their human nature. Only by such logic did critics of the dictatorship, of whatever social origin, become "class-alien," "enemies of the people," and so sent the way of the kulaks. Only with such ideological alchemy could the world be divided between the "socialist camp" and everything else, which therefore became "objectively" the camp of reaction.

Stalin fully shared this ideological view of the world. Contrary to frequent assumption, he was no mere cynic, or madman, or "traitor" to the revolution. Cynics or madmen do not get as far as he did, nor do they find millions to follow them. Such a leader must have a purpose that is shared by others. And Stalin found that purpose in a life experience quite consonant with the ideology of his followers.

Born at the bottom of the old order, the son of a drunken village shoemaker turned factory worker and of a long-suffering, pious peasant mother, he was the most nearly proletarian of the Bolshevik chiefs, who were largely petty intelligentsia.[17] After failing to move up from the lower depths via an Orthodox seminary, where else but in "the revolution" could he have made a career? Once that revolution was in power, his background made him the closest among the Bolshevik chiefs to the plebeian Party cadres he soon came to command. His elevation to the rank of general secretary was no untoward accident or usurpation. On the contrary, it followed a quite Soviet *zakonomernost*, or logic: the Party's military and hierarchical structure cried out for personification in a leader, and the bulk of its functionaries could readily see this rude son of the people as their chief. Indeed, this new Leader, who had made it out of squalor and five years in Siberia to the Kremlin, had reason to see himself and his Party as "the wretched of the earth," the proletariat, in power, now justifiably lording it over their former lords. Yet at the same time, as a literal-minded believer in the science of Marxism-Leninism, he was convinced that he held such absolute power not for himself, but for the "cause" of Socialism.[18]

That same Marxist-Leninist science, moreover, told him that both he and his cause would be forever confronted with "enemies." And from Trotsky onward such enemies persistently arose to accuse him of usurping Lenin's mantle and creating a sham socialism. Yet once the deed was done, who could convincingly maintain that he had misread the science of Ilich? The magical mummy in its mausoleum on Red Square was now and forever silent, and not even Lenin's posthumously published "Testament," calling Stalin "too rude," could make the founder gainsay his chief heir. And so it was Stalin, as good a Leninist as any other, who at last proved to the world that in the decisive domain of practice the unicorn of Socialism was bloody real.

To accomplish this great but cruel task, the science of Ilich offered not only the negative sword of class warfare to wield against enemies. It also furnished the positive sword of technocratic progress through the machine; and it was with this weapon that the Party hacked its way through to socialism. For Marx, industrialism had been exploitative only in the hands of the bourgeoisie; but in the hands of the proletariat it became automatically liberating. Thus once Lenin made the Party the stand-in for the proletariat, as a practical matter "building socialism" came to mean laying out factories and firing up blast furnaces. Under Stalin, Marxism, which had originally been a doctrine of protest against working-class exploitation, became a doctrine of frenetic state-driven industrialization, entailing no small amount of working-class exploitation by its own dictatorship.

During the First Five-Year Plan, therefore, Marxism was inverted: the vehicle for proletarian revolt from below became the fulcrum for

Party revolution from above. The Cunning of Reason, this time, had proved most cruelly unkind; for as Marx had once done to Hegel, Dzhugashvili, the rude proletarian, now did to Marx, turning him quite on his philosophical head.

In another respect, however, Stalin took Marx pretty much as he stood. Marx had been an implacable foe of the "idiocy of rural life." He taught that bourgeois industrialization had required a "primitive accumulation of capital" achieved through the expropriation of the peasantry, as in the enclosures of eighteenth-century England. Should not socialist industrialization, too, Stalin asked, when undertaken in a backward country, require its own even more primitive accumulation through expropriation of the peasantry?[19] Thus the bloody process described in *Capital*—which had never occurred in England in the manner Marx described, and which had not furnished the basic accumulation he alleged—did in fact become the pivot of Russia's socialist plan, at the cost of six to eight million lives.

It was amidst such mass coercion and upside-down ideological intoxication that after 1929 the troika hurtled onward and eastward; and the result was indeed a second Bolshevik revolution, as its author maintained. By the mid-1930s the upheaval had virtually replaced the market with a state "plan" (though later observers more accurately called that instrument a "command economy"). At the same time, ideocratic bureaucracy became well-nigh universal and meaningful social autonomy was suppressed. To be sure, the Party-state's control was less total than it appeared to foreigners at the time or than Stalin wished it to be. Beneath the system's steel carapace, disorder was rife and even indirect resistance, ranging from simple theft of state property to covert entrepreneurship, was hardly unknown. And—yes—the peasants obliged Stalin to concede them their family plots and a minimarket for their kolkhoz products.[20] All the same, the basic fact of the new order was that it no longer recognized any sphere of social autonomy; all aspects of life were institutionally vulnerable to the power of the Party-state.

When Stalin's offensive was over, Russia lived under a far more awesome universal service order than had ever been dreamed of by the tsars. It was founded on state rather than seigneurial serfdom in agriculture and on the piecework exploitation of labor in industry, the whole buttressed by police terror and an institution not yet known to the outside world, the Gulag. Stalin then officially declared that Russia had arrived at Socialism and enshrined this achievement in a new constitution in 1936.

For once, the Cunning of Reason had been kind—to Marxism-Leninism, if not to the poor Scythians. Thus did the haunting Spectre of Communism at last receive a local habitation and a name, in Soviet Hyperborea, the land beyond the northern winds.

But the final circle of the experiment, and the fourth fold of the mistake, were yet to come. The new society was consolidated between 1936 and 1939 with a wave of purges designed to quell all doubts about the virtues of the system and the wisdom of its architect. This Great Terror is often explained as the rampage of a paranoid tyrant. Yet Stalin, though indeed given to morbid suspicion, found millions to help him in this new "class struggle," including many of its victims. His purges, therefore, are best understood as the logic of a militant utopia confronted in practice with its own moral failure. It was no accident that the mass terror began in 1936, just after the experiment's culmination and the proclamation of its alleged success. Until then socialism had lain in the future, and imperfections could be accepted as temporary. But with full nationalization and collectivization the instrumental means for achieving socialism had been put in place; yet the expected moral, and often material, result of their application had not followed. On the contrary, the outcome was a more sophisticated form of servitude coupled with chronic scarcity.[21]

This unanticipated contradiction could not be acknowledged if the system were to function. Socialism's obvious defects had to be blamed on a gigantic conspiracy of "traitors" and "wreckers," organized by Trotskyites and foreign "agents." Such "enemies" had either to be physically eliminated, exiled to the Gulag, or otherwise "repressed." And all were compelled to confess their "crimes." Fallen Bolshevik leaders did so at three show trials between 1936 and 1938. However, the overwhelming majority of the purged, also usually Party members, confessed behind prison doors, and their written admissions of guilt were seen only by their inquisitors. This charade, for all its surrealism, had a genuine function, which was to make its victims accomplices in their own undoing. Thereby the regime was absolved of all its crimes during the great offensive of the 1930s, while those skeptical of the "general line" were compelled to acknowledge that it had been inerrantly "correct." As word of their admission of guilt filtered back to society the population as a whole was compromised in the cause of Socialism triumphant—just as the masses were obliged to vote "yes" by 90-odd percent in otherwise meaningless elections.

Thus did Stalin complete a second revolution from above; and its result was to give him virtually a new Party. By 1939, some 80 percent of its members had joined after the midpoint of the decade, and hence were products of the new socialism, wedded both psychologically and ideologically to its achievements and personally beholden to its master builder. This Stalinist cohort would rule the Soviet Union until its most eminent product, Leonid Brezhnev, departed the scene in the mid-1980s. And they could enjoy this extended tenure because the purges had accumulated such a capital of fear as to underpin the system long after mass terror ceased on Stalin's death in 1953.

The human costs of the Stalin revolution were of course a state secret at the time, and it is not possible to determine them with precision even now. The figure most commonly advanced for the number of deaths during Stalin's twenty-five years of power—from collectivization, the Great Terror, and the routinized postwar terror taken together—is twenty million.[22] Yet whatever the final estimates may turn out to be, it is already clear that we are dealing with atrocity on a scale requiring seven zeroes to express. But few in the West guessed anything like the extent of the catastrophe at the time. And how many in the West recognize it even today? Surely, the average person's inability to believe the unbelievable was always a major cause of the West's highly uneven record in grappling with the Soviet enigma.

With the paroxysm of the purges, the voyage of the troika was over, the experiment had been completed, and the Scythians had arrived at their final destination. But just where did they find themselves once they got there? Stalin of course declared that they had reached station Terminus: Socialism. But where was this located exactly?

On the one hand, the Party had brought Russia to full noncapitalism: private property, profit, and the market were no more, and in their place a "planned," collective organization of labor and life had been created. To this degree, Marx's goal had been attained. Yet, on the other hand, the result was hardly his anticipated "leap from the kingdom of necessity to the kingdom of freedom." Instead a more stringent necessity had been imposed on everyone by the omnicompetent Party-state and its "command-administrative" plan.

This perverse outcome was no accident, however; it came as the lawlike result of Marxism itself. And it is necessary to insist on this fact, for many commentators have refused to recognize it, holding that Marx, unlike "utopian" socialists, offered no vision of the future but only "scientific" knowledge of history's laws. The reason for this strange blindness, of course, is that once Stalin implemented that very program by mass violence many Westerners backed away from it, preferring to believe that some other Bolshevik could have built a better socialism or choosing to read his doctrine only as a critique of capitalist society, as in the "Marxism without a proletariat" of the Frankfurt School.

In the master himself, however, it is quite clear that "human emancipation" requires the absolute "negation" of private property, profit, and the market. The concrete program for implementing this negation is spelled out unambiguously in part 2 of the *Manifesto*, "Proletarians and Communists." In it, the proletariat (here, read Party) is summoned to seize political power in order to "wrest, by degrees, all capital from the bourgeoisie," and then to "centralize all instruments of production in the hands of the State, i.e. of the proletariat organized as the ruling class." All production, moreover, would be "concentrated in the hands of the vast association of the whole nation" with "industrial armies, especially for agriculture," and a common plan. In short, "the theory of Communism may be summed up in the single sentence: Abolition of private property." Only under these conditions, for Marx, would the world at last function "rationally," like one immense factory, and human labor would produce not capital, but the flowering of the species' hitherto alienated creative potential.[23]

In fact, this instrumental program offers the perfect blueprint for all-encompassing state tyranny. The basic problem is simply this: when private property is abolished in favor of "public" or "collective" owner-ship, who in fact gets it? It cannot go directly to "society" as socialist supposition would have it, since society always needs an administrative instrument through which to act. All property, therefore, goes to that instrument, in other words, the state. Furthermore, when the market is suppressed, this does not mean that goods are now produced and dis-tributed according to "real human needs" instead of the "irrational" profit motive. It means rather that the state decides by administrative means what constitutes "rational" production and distribution. Accord-ing to what criteria, then, does the state make such decisions? The only possibility is by the moral or philosophical criteria of whoever controls the administrative apparatus. Ideology and politics rather than the mar-ket and private interest thus determine how the economy works, and consequently how society is shaped. And so a fully socialist state is also necessarily an ideocratic one.

In short, under a regime of noncapitalism, economic criteria, as ex-pressed in prices, are replaced by ideological criteria, as expressed through political directives. The suppression of private property and the market, therefore, is tantamount to the suppression of civil society and the absorption of all its former functions by the state. Such an omnicompetent state is no ordinary state, one *ruling over* society; it is a total state, one *replacing* society. Moreover, this total state must be controlled by the equivalent of Plato's guardians, a Party of ideocrats that incarnates rationality in an administrative apparatus. In practice, the ideocratic state must therefore be a partocratic one as well. Finally, since all this goes against the grain of mere mortal flesh, the partocracy must be a police state too. Thus the impossible Marxist utopia, if imple-mented in full, leads pitilessly to a totalitarian result. The result is all the more total in that it is not merely a coercive police operation, but is surrounded with an aura of humanism and arrayed with a mystique of science.

A second perverse outcome of Marxism's instrumental program is that its application necessarily betrays socialism's egalitarian inspira-tion. The socialist revolution was supposed to bring to power the prole-tariat as the only class whose self-interest coincides with the interests of humanity as a whole. Yet when workers under Bolshevism "overthrew the bourgeoisie" and established their dictatorship over society, they ceased to be workers and became instead full-time functionaries of the new partocracy. At least some of them did, because the majority remained where they had been in "class society," that is, at the bottom.

It turned out to be impossible for a *class* to accede to power as a whole; only upwardly mobile *individuals* promoted from the people (*vydvizhentsy*) could make such a transition.[24] They moved upward, moreover, not to greater affluence and independence in a pluralistic society, but to higher *rank* in the Party hierarchy, a status conferring privileges without independence. Consequently, social stratification, though no longer socioeconomic in nature, remained; and workers promoted to be managers and apparatchiki became a governing group, or a "new class," as Milovan Djilas called them in 1957, since they owed their position not to any relationship to the means of production, but to their political-administrative function.[25] Stalin called this group a stratum and bestowed on it the Old-Regime term "intelligentsia"—though its members were hardly intellectuals, and critical thought was definitely not among their functions. In practical terms, this social differentiation was no more scandalous than that existing in liberal societies, which offered only equality of opportunity, not of actual status. But since Soviet society pretended to offer real equality, or at least one higher than that of "bourgeois democracy," the system was confronted with a contradiction to which it could not admit lest it undermine its legitimizing ethos.

A final perverse outcome of Soviet Marxism was the new socialism's skewed relationship to its capitalist "predecessor." After the travail of the fabled Five-Year Plans of the 1930s, as an empirical matter they came down to something quite prosaic. Concretely, "building socialism" amounted to the appropriation of Western technology to give Russia the outward trappings of twentieth-century modernity: blast furnaces and factories, tractors and combines, trucks, tanks, and airplanes. Thus, in material terms, the result of Stalin's socialist revolution was not very different from Witte's capitalist achievements, at a slightly lower technological level, of a quarter of a century earlier. Both were imitative efforts to close the gap of modernity with the West—as Stalin's slogan had it, "to catch up with and overtake America." It might seem that such a "Soviet America" would be a disappointing result to revolutionaries committed to Marx's millenarian vision of human emancipation. But this was not the case; on the contrary, they viewed it as a world-historical triumph.

In fact, this outcome did represent an apt culmination of Marxism's historical career. The Marxist vision, after all, had been generated in order to overcome German backwardness vis-à-vis the Atlantic West; and it had had its grand Second International career in half-backward Central Europe. When it unexpectedly triumphed for the first time in still more backward Russia, its vocation for the modern world was appropriately consummated.

For it was the very incongruity of Marxism's victory in Russia that gave it a real, practical role, rather than the imaginary, visionary one to which it had hitherto aspired: its historical task became not to supersede capitalism, but to plagiarize it. This reversal of fortune arose from the paradox that since the Bolsheviks had seized power in a peasant country without a supporting Western revolution, they ended up in an unacceptable position for Marxists; they were a "superstructure" suspended in midair without the necessary proletarian and industrial "base."[26] Yet it was precisely this untoward fate that put revolutionary fire in their souls.

They resolved their dilemma by utilizing ideological Consciousness to determine social Being. Lenin had already shown the way when he invoked class struggle to subordinate the logic of history to Party will for the seizure of power. He was almost immediately left in the lurch, however, when the West failed to follow Russia's lead. To make up for the resulting deficit of modernity, Stalin then pushed the Leninist inversion of Marx to its culmination: he launched from above a second revolution that rebuilt Mother Russia as a Soviet pseudo-America and converted her superfluity of peasants into real proletarians. Thus the Party's supreme achievement was to transmogrify its status as "superstructure" into the demiurge for creating the industrial and worker "base" that was supposed to have created *it*.

So it came to pass that, ninety years after Marx had launched his theory, his heirs, Columbus-like, stumbled on its true meaning: Stalin demonstrated that Marxism's world-historical vocation was to spread eastward rather than westward, into ever more backward colonial and Third World countries. Marx's conviction that industrial Europe showed the rest of the world its future was perversely fulfilled by the Oriental despotism of Communism, in which the state is the proprietor of everything and everybody.

In still another way, Marxism played an unanticipated role in what may be called Communism's revolutionary mode of production. Of course, once socialism had been "built," Marxism's metaphysical and visionary aspects no longer had the direct relevance they possessed when Lenin and Stalin were firing up the Party for revolution, whether from below or from above. Even so, the doctrine remained indispensable to the revolution's end product; for it was the guarantee of the Party's legitimacy, and the Party's "leading role" was the linchpin of the institutionalized revolution. Thus, though now a "cold ideology,"[27] it deployed a veil of ideological categories to camouflage the nature of Soviet reality. To the regime's last days, it remained indispensable in a system that could never own up to what it was and yet survive.

The epic feat of building proletarian socialism in peasant Russia had produced a schizoid brave new world. On the one hand, the Revolution had culminated in the banal aping of the material appurtenances of the capitalism it had allegedly superseded; but this outcome at least provided imposing national power, and so could be counted a victory in the "international class struggle." On the other hand, the Revolution had generated a surreal Party-society, offering only the illusion of the masses in power; and this gap between pretension and performance made the system's material success dangerously vulnerable to empirical criticism. In the mature Soviet world, therefore, things could never be designated by their real names but were always cloaked in the now-stereotyped categories of Marxist metaphysics. The command economy was thus a "plan"; the purge of Party oppositions, and even of loyal Stalinists, was "class struggle"; and the exact copy of an American steel plant was beatified as "socialist" since the Party of Lenin had built it.[28]

Yet in the flush of Socialism's victory, these vulnerabilities were hardly apparent; and insofar as they were visible it was dangerous to say so. And so, as Stalin completed his work in 1939, it seemed that his two revolutions from above had salvaged the failed enterprise of Lenin and Trotsky for a long posterity.

Exegi Monumentum II

For decades the Soviet partocracy asserted that such posterity would be immortality; and this pretension focused on a talismanic eternal Lenin. The founder's apotheosis began on his death, when the Party transformed the city of Peter into the city of the Revolution by reannointing it Leningrad. The Bronze Horseman was thus dethroned as the symbol of national vitality and progress. For Ilich had aimed far higher than Russia's first Westernizer: He had cut a window through to Socialism. But the revolutionary Romanov was fully eclipsed only when the Party gave Lenin an undivided monument in the new capital, Moscow.

When Lenin's comrades found themselves orphaned, well before the revolution's work was done, they decided they must keep Him with them always. They did this in part out of reverence for the fabulous success he had brought them—and in part out of fear that without his prestige they might have difficulty controlling the country. The classic expression of their mood was given by the "drummer of the Revolution," Vladimir Maiakovskii:

> "Lenin" and "Death"—these words are enemies
> "Lenin" and "Life"—are comrades . . .
> Lenin—lived. Lenin—lives. Lenin—will live!

To ensure such eternal life, the Central Committee had the corpse embalmed for permanent preservation. Thus Lenin in afterlife could continue to legitimize Soviet power and mobilize the population behind it.

Some comrades were scandalized at this seeming play for the incense of peasant superstition by aping Orthodoxy's veneration of relics—an interpretation often shared by Western proponents of the thesis of "eternal Russia." In fact, the decision had nothing to do with this dark past. It was intended as a demonstration of Soviet superiority in science: what capitalist country could preserve a body indefinitely in a lifelike state, not like some wizened pharaoh? At the same time it bore witness to an underground Romantic current in Party culture: the belief of "God-builders" such as Minister of Enlightenment Anatolii Lunacharskii that socialism would one day raise men to a divine level thereby—perhaps—rendering them bodily immortal. Such a temptation indeed has venerable Enlightenment precedents. It may be considered an inverted version of Feuerbach's thesis that Heaven is an alienated reflection of Man's species-being; and it is in lineal descent from Condorcet's expectation that scientific progress would someday prolong human life "indefinitely."[29]

The Party, out of anxiety for its own life expectancy, in 1924 placed the embalmed Lenin in a porphyry mausoleum on Red Square, as the rock on which its infallibility was founded. Finished in 1930, just as Stalin's revolution was beginning, it would serve as the foundation of his grandeur for a quarter-century. Under his successors it remained Communism's high altar to the end.

In a way, physically immortalizing Lenin is a fitting symbol of Communism's ambition to transcend prehistory, thereby perfecting mankind's species-being; for Lenin had indeed led the world's first leap into the full fantasy of Marxism. Yet there is an obverse face to this symbol: the impossible leap out of real history would in fact lead to a dead-end world whose totem is, appropriately, a mummy in a mausoleum.

The Fascist Counterpoint

Thus, by 1939, Stalin had consolidated the only socialism the twentieth century would ever know. Its survival, however, was by no means assured. Russia was still only a second-rank power in a hostile world. Stalin's victory, moreover, was clearly flawed, even in the eyes of the experiment's Western sympathizers. If the full story of his terror was unknown, his public purge trials were scarcely convincing. Just as disturbing was his quasi-deification as Leader. But at this juncture, outside forces intervened to bring Soviet Russia's fortunes to new and more imposing heights.

These forces came from the near side of the mirror, where, in the crucial years of the experiment, events conspired to refurbish Soviet Russia's progressive credentials by contrast with Western crises and crimes. First came the Great Depression of 1929–1933, the gravest failure of capitalism in its history, and one that long appeared to signal its definitive bankruptcy. This collapse appeared all the worse through its coincidence with the victory of "rational" planning over "market anarchy" in the Soviet First Five-Year Plan.

The second dark force lending luster to Soviet Communism was the exploitation of the depression by fascism. This movement had appeared as no more than a small fist on the horizon with Mussolini's march on Rome in 1922, but it grew into a major menace after Hitler's advent to power in 1933, the Nazis' assassination of Chancellor Englebert Dolfuss in Vienna in 1934, and the abortive right-wing putsch of February 6 in Paris that same year. With the establishment of the Rome-Berlin Axis in 1936 and its simultaneous intervention in the Spanish Civil War, fascism seemed on the verge of engulfing Europe. Indeed, it appeared as a worldwide threat, for this alliance was almost immediately supplemented by the German-Japanese Anti-Comintern Pact; and the same year the Japanese began their attempt to conquer China. Since the Italians had already conquered Ethiopia, the world was confronted with a Rome-Berlin-Tokyo Axis actively on the march. At the same time, America's national hero, Charles Lindbergh, saw these bold new regimes as what his wife's best-selling book called the "wave of the future";[30] and the Nobel prize–winning novelist Sinclair Lewis, taking alarm, published It Can't Happen Here, the message of which was that it very well could, in fact precisely in Vermont. Despite what was beginning to be known by 1936 about the Soviet order under Stalin, Communist reality was significantly obscured by the more pressing needs of an antifascist coalition among all men of good will.

This reflex led to the formation of the French and Spanish popular fronts of 1934–1936, in a coalition of classical liberals, Social Democrats, and Communists against the Right. By 1936 this alliance permitted Léon Blum in France to attempt the first Western experiment, after that of Sweden, to build by democratic means, if not full socialism, then a welfare state that might be an initial step to something bolder. In the same year André Malraux, George Orwell, and Ernest Hemingway went to Spain to fight against the Axis alongside Stalin's agents (who, as it turned out, were rapidly taking over the beleaguered republic). To be sure, the popular front coalition was temporarily shattered in 1939 by

Stalin's pact with Hitler. But even this shocking act could be rationalized as a cruel necessity if Stalin were to avoid the trap of the Anglo-French imperialists to turn Hitler eastward against socialism.

Hitler's attack on Russia in 1941, however, restored the old syndrome of "no enemies to the left" so rapidly that the painful interlude of the pact was largely forgotten. This attitude persisted throughout what Churchill called the Grand Alliance of the Second World War, thereby making the conflict both a national war of the Allies against Germany and a civil war of the Left against the Right as resistance movements confronted collaborationists across the occupied continent. This international popular front continued in the coalition governments of resistance forces after the Liberation, in Paris, Rome, and Prague. Between 1934 and 1947, therefore, the West's perception of Russia was determined, and Russia's fortunes were furthered, less by the nature of the Communist regime itself than by the fact that, except for the glaring gap of 1939–1941, it projected the purest antifascist image in Europe.

Conversely, Communism was always a potent stimulus to fascism's development and to furthering its more ephemeral fortunes. These two extremes interacted constantly from the aftermath of the First World War until the ring was closed on Hitler in the Second. Indeed, long after Hitler and all other fascist regimes were gone, antifascism retained its power as a means for mobilizing world opinion on Communism's behalf.[31] An excursus into fascism's nature, therefore, is necessary here, since it is the negative and destructive counterthrust of fascism that finally made Communism into a planetary force.

But does fascism exist as a generic phenomenon?[32] The question is hardly an idle one, for "fascism" is used almost as indiscriminately, and is as charged emotionally, as is its Left antithesis, "socialism." In common usage "fascism" means Hitler, and thus has come to stand for absolute evil in the modern world.

Yet caution in speaking of a generic fascism ought to be in order a priori; for fascism, whatever else it might be, is an exacerbated form of nationalism, and nationalisms are by definition particularistic, if not given to outright mutual antagonism. Certainly, the first Fascist, Mussolini, though he learned much from Lenin, imitated Bolshevik techniques not to create a rival international movement, but to found a specifically Italian one. And Hitler, though he learned much from Mussolini, never considered his National Socialism to be a subspecies of some broader fascism. This remains true even though as the Second World War approached the various fascist regimes often coordinated their actions.

The concept of generic fascism was created not by those to whom it was applied, but by the Communists.[33] Although there was a loose sense of kinship among movements of the revolutionary Right in the 1920s and 1930s, the concept of fascism as an international movement was first enunciated in 1923 by the Third International. The occasion was Mussolini's triumph the previous year, an event all the more baffling to Marxists since it had been orchestrated by a former leader of the Italian Socialist Party; and the answer given to this conundrum was that Italian Fascism was simply a mask for "finance capital" in a state of terminal crisis. This explanation was later transferred to Nazism, thereby creating fascism as a social genus, and in this form it became the official doctrine of the Comintern in 1933. In this theory, fascism was the panicked reaction of "monopoly capitalism" to the threat of Communist revolution: the grand bourgeoisie, no longer able to dominate society through formal democracy, sought safety in populist dictators and street thugs, a desperate policy that could only end in a new imperialist war and Communism's world triumph. In short, fascism is the "highest" stage of imperialism, just as Lenin's imperialism had been the highest stage of classical capitalism.

Thus were the internal contradictions of capitalism constantly updated to keep the system pointed toward imminent revolution. Even though time had demonstrated that Marx's initial analysis of capitalism might be defective, his method, the dialectic of the class struggle, remained eternally valid. Indeed, the process of updating began with Marx himself: in the *Eighteenth Brumaire* he assuaged his bitterness that Louis Napoleon had buried the Revolution of 1848 by declaring that the "next time," once this Bonapartist adventurer had failed, the socialist revolution would surely triumph. So enduring is this faith in the Marxist method that fifty years after the end of the last fascist regimes, there are still theorists who tell us that we are living in "late capitalism."

In effect, the Communists' theory of fascism portrayed their new adversary as the mirror image of their alleged selves—that is, as an international class movement. By the same token, since for Communists there are only two ideological camps in the world—the "bourgeoisie" and their own "proletarian" Party—all non-Communist movements automatically tend toward "fascism." Liberals and Social Democrats are therefore especially suspect, for in the impending "final struggle" their timid policies obscure the fact that the only genuine alternative to fascism is Communism.

The notion that Communism is the only uncompromising and reliable antifascist force could work in two ways. It could serve, first, as a means of ideological intimidation to eliminate the center, thereby polarizing politics in favor of the hard Left. "Antifascism" thus offered a more radical version of the old principle of "no enemies to the left," since the new doctrine meant that the center was now allowed "no friends to the right" among traditional conservatives. In this mode, Communism's self-definition as quintessential antifascism was used after 1928, in the International's so-called third period, to brand Social Democrats as social fascists. Similarly, after the defeat of Hitler, his real international role was rhetorically transferred to the United States, and all American policies from the Marshall Plan to Ronald Reagan's Star Wars were stigmatized as a new fascist imperialism. A corollary to this use of antifascism was "the struggle for peace," which became a dominant theme in the early 1930s and then again after 1945, as another way to combat the "war-mongering" powers of the West.

However, as long as Hitler offered a real threat to the Soviet Union, "antifascism" was used in a second mode. It served to justify the popular front required to give protection to a vulnerable Soviet Union: the struggle for peace was now put in parentheses, and the Western powers were encouraged to rearm. This new position, adopted by the Comintern in 1936, nonetheless did not signify moral equality among the three components of the front: Communism, as the alleged polar opposite of fascism, retained its position as the one diamond-pure force of the Left, and its "bourgeois" allies always remained under suspicion of potential treason. So strong was the metaphysic of antifascism, that even Stalin's own (apparent) betrayal of its principles in 1939–1941 was rationalized as necessary to defend the land of the proletariat against Western machinations. Then, once the interlude of the pact had passed, Communist parties, without a hint of embarrassment, reclaimed leadership of the Left against fascism—and got away with it in the eyes of a fair part of European opinion. In truth, throughout the Soviet Union's existence, antifascism was as indispensable to its international strength as the manpower of its armies and the arsenal of its warheads.

The Communist theory of fascism, of course, has long since been refuted by events, yet a looser version of it lingers in modern political culture, clouding even today the discussion of the Soviet past. All postwar authoritarianisms that have overthrown constitutional government to repress Marxist forces—from General Augusto Pinochet in 1973 to the Greek colonels of 1975 to the Argentine generals of the early 1980s—were routinely denounced as fascist, even though these regimes were clearly national conservatisms which, however reprehensible their internal policies, threatened no one outside their borders. Even such a mystical patriot as General de Gaulle, on his return to power in 1958, was suspected of fascism by the Parisian mandarin Left. In this loose sense, fascism is seen as a constant component of modern politics, the permanent temptation of "bourgeois society."[34]

No matter how far the term "fascism" is stretched, it still carries a reference to the socioeconomic crisis of the interwar years. And so the argument recurs: even if the role of "monopoly capitalists" may have been exaggerated, is it not still true that general European fascism during the depression had a social base in "the lower middle class threatened with proletarianization"?

It is indeed true that Italian Fascism first, and German Nazism later, got their initial chance at power from the economic crises of 1918–1923, and even more from the Great Depression of the 1930s. It is also true that the fascist triad of people, party, and leader owed much of its power of seduction to the economic dislocations of the time. Nonetheless, all "bourgeois" societies experienced depression in the 1930s, yet not all such societies were vulnerable to subversion by Fascist or National Socialist minorities: many simply turned to a New Deal, to a welfare state on the Swedish Social Democratic model, or even to a popular front. The explanation for these differing reactions to the same economic crisis must therefore be sought in political rather than social circumstances.

The first of these circumstances is that in the Atlantic West constitutional democracy had long since struck deep roots, whereas in Italy and Germany it was a recent and fragile implant.[35] Even more important, democracy was handicapped in both countries by the legacy of the First World War. In Germany the republic bore the onus of its birth out of national defeat, and in Italy the still recent adaptation of constitutional government to universal suffrage (in 1912) was compromised by national humiliation at Versailles. These humiliations were all the more destructive of nascent political democracy since they had been preceded by a very different "democratic" experience—the military democracy of conscript armies fighting for four years in the trenches. The war of 1914–1918 was the first modern war (after the American Civil War) to be fought on both sides by citizen armies; and in the nations where this mass mobilization, with its enormous sacrifices, had ended in defeat the resulting frustration could easily generate a movement of revanche. It is this fact that constitutes the decisive condition for transforming nationalism into fascism. For Fascism and Nazism were much more than political authoritarianisms created in response to economic crisis: they were total movements for revolutionary regeneration in the wake of national failure in war. Their basic program was rejection of the restraints of constitutional democracy to achieve national mobilization for a return international engagement. Their revolutionary creed hence was summarized as the struggle of "the spirit of 1914 against the spirit of 1789."[36]

Fascism was created by war in order to wage further war; and its fate was to be destroyed by war. Far from being rampant throughout modernity, it was a phenomenon of the interwar period. And in that period it could aspire to power only among the dissatisfied powers of central and southern Europe. It is in this sense—precisely circumscribed in time and in place—that there is place for a feasible concept of generic fascism.

Yet even in central and southern Europe it is necessary to distinguish between militant and militaristic fascism on the one hand and national conservative authoritarianism on the other—even though the latter was often politically allied with fascism for circumstantial reasons. Schematically, the difference between these two types of regime is that the former is revolutionary, striving to create a new order and a new man, whereas the latter is traditional, seeking to thwart political and social democratization. In consequence, fascism is demotic or populist if not democratic, a mass mobilization regime that seeks to draw the entire nation into a single supraclass movement; conservative authoritarianism, by contrast, fears "the revolt of the masses" and seeks to contain them in unequal, pseudotraditional "corporatist" entities. Instrumentally, fascism militarizes society for foreign war in order to conquer an empire that would furnish raw materials for economic self-sufficiency and space for colonization *(Lebensraum)*—a quest for autarky that is in part an attempt by inland European powers to find a substitute for the overseas colonies acquired earlier by Atlantic nations. National conservatism, however, seeks to seal a population off from radical foreign contagion, and finds foreign military adventure internally destabilizing. Finally, fascism is hostile to religion as a matter of principle, because it proposes a competing secular religion, whereas national conservatism supports traditional religion as the bulwark of an inherited order.

In Europe there were only two states, Italy and Germany, where movements with such aspirations came to power on their own and created a *regime;* and the exercise of power is, after all, crucial to the fascist enterprise. (After the outbreak of war, Hitler's advance enabled lesser fascist regimes to emerge in Slovakia and Croatia, but they could not have achieved power by themselves.) There were, of course, numerous fascist *movements* in Europe that never attained power, notably Oswald Mosley's Fascist Union and arguably Charles Maurras's Action française. (As already noted, however, the Action française, with its elitist, royalist, and residually Catholic character, never became a mass mobilization movement, and so it had its chief practical impact through the national-authoritarian regime of Vichy.)[37]

Finally, there is another plausibly fascist state, Japan, which, though outside Europe, is quite relevant to Eurasian Russia. It is no accident that Japan was a cofounder of the Axis, for she pursued policies of national militarization, foreign conquest, and economic autarky similar to those of Germany and Italy. Still, Japan, though dominated by the military, attempted no internal social revolution; and her ideology of national regeneration drew on traditional resources of emperor worship and Shintoism quite different from the demotic myths of Mussolini and Hitler. Even so, despite the conservative form of the Japanese ideology, it too combined the creed of national uniqueness and superiority with modern populist mobilization, a mixture that has been called "Imperial fascism."[38]

In short, the three core "fascist" states were nations that in the interwar years stood a real chance of achieving the status of world powers, but that were thwarted in this ambition by historical circumstances. First, the three had emerged on the international scene as unified and modern nation-states only in the 1860s, when the world stage was already occupied by the maritime powers, Britain and France. The First World War was caused essentially by Germany's effort to break this monopoly, while Italy and Japan tagged along with the established powers in the hope (as it turned out a vain one) of co-optation by the Allies to higher things. It was the frustrations attendant on the settlement of 1918 that pushed the three new powers to launch a second general conflict. And, in fact, as of the 1930s, the correlation of forces in Eurasia was such that Germany and Japan could feasibly hope to dislodge Britain and France from their premier positions (though Italy would have had to ride Germany's coattails). It was largely the transoceanic, but at the time almost totally unarmed, American wild card that defeated the Axis's pretensions—and into the bargain gave Britain and France a short imperial afterlife following 1945. As for Russia in this period, though she had been a plausible aspirant to world-imperial status since Alexander I, after 1917 she was completely out of the running for any power beyond her borders. Her only weapon in the heyday of fascism was ideological—and this was the main point of the Soviet antifascist drumbeat.

The national authoritarian regimes of the interwar period are clearly different in nature and stature from the Axis three. They are, in order of appearance, Admiral Miklos Horthy's Hungary, Oliveira Salazar's Portugal, arguably Józef Pilsudski's Poland, and Francisco Franco's Spain. Of these, only Hungary was belatedly drawn into the fascist orbit by military occupation. Poland under Pilsudski's heirs, however, though partially a mobilization regime, was as hostile to Nazism as to Communism; and Portugal never approached fascism at all. To be sure, Franco, because of his dependence on Italian and German support during the Spanish Civil War, did for a time find a place for an ideologically fascist party, the Falange. But this body never governed, and Franco steered clear of Hitler's war because there was nothing in it for his tight peninsular realm. Thus Franco, though his record was distinctly more bloody than Mussolini's, should not be counted as a fascist: he was no populist demagogue in a stage uniform, but a real general fighting a national civil war against godless "reds." If Franco is nonetheless often equated with his civil war supporters, it is because that war crystallized fascism as a generic, worldwide movement.

There are, of course, elements of overlap in the forces that produced both national conservativism and fascism. Southern Europe was a zone of relative economic backwardness in which constitutional liberalism had never been successfully adapted to universal-suffrage democracy, while at the same time it was challenged on its left by a primitive and anarchistic syndicalism. Throughout this zone liberal democracy, caught between the postwar economic crisis and a surge of "red" strength, was relatively easy to overthrow in the name of national salvation. In such a fluid situation national conservatives could wind up paving the way for national revolutionaries, with the fortunes of each depending on overall circumstances. Thus, in the Iberian states, which lacked international ambitions, the postwar crisis stopped at national authoritarianism. In more ambitious Italy, slighted as it was by its allies at Versailles, it produced the original model of fascism in power.

But this model was far less draconian than its transalpine imitator. Although it was Mussolini who coined the term "totalitarian" (of course with a positive connotation) to designate the complete national mobilization he hoped to achieve, his practice fell far short of his ambition, as he was compelled to accommodate traditional forces. The monarchy remained in place, and the new regime had to accept a compromise with the church; the Fascist Party was subordinated to the state bureaucracy, rather than the other way around as in Germany; there was no serious state control of the economy, or leveling of the old social structure; there were no camps, and no Gestapo. And Il Duce did not dare challenge the existing international equilibrium until his Ethiopian War of 1935, when Hitler's rise to power made such secondary boldness feasible. Finally, although there was definitely a Fascist ideology of national vitality, expressed in a cult of youth, violence, and war, these regenerative values were founded on a culture of heroic virility, not on biological race. Anti-Semitism was not a principle of original Fascism (even though it is usually deemed essential to the concept of generic fascism). When anti-Semitism came to Italy, it was only in 1938, near the end of Mussolini's tenure, and under German hegemony.

Thus, as it turned out, the totalitarian ambition first formulated by Mussolini received its fullest implementation from Hitler; and this outcome can be understood only in the context of a Central European backwardness that is much more complex than the underdevelopment of southern Europe. The defining characteristic of the two defunct empires of Mitteleuropa is the already examined persistence of Old-Regime structures in societies that were otherwise in the forefront of modernity.[39] Already before 1914 progressives hoped, and conservatives feared, that it was only a question of time before this hybrid order gave way to Western-style democracy, even to socialism. Yet, when the Central European Old Regimes did give way, it was not to the domestic force of revolt against anachronistic privilege, but to the foreign force of military defeat, political collapse, and territorial amputation. The German democratic revolution, which had failed in the Springtime of the Peoples in 1848, succeeded out of season in 1918, and only as the fruit of national humiliation. And the same is even more true of cognate regimes in the former Dual Monarchy. Moreover, a German government at last founded on real universal suffrage, and into the bargain governed by socialists, was to the left of what a majority of the population wanted. Significant elements of society, in the bureaucracy, business, and the military, remained loyal to the Old Regime and hoped to recover Germany's prewar international prominence. To all these groups, and to the intellectual exponents of Germany's moral superiority as a mixed traditional-cum-modern society, Weimar and Versailles represented the conquest of native *Kultur* by Western *Zivilisation*. At the same time, since "Marxists" (that is, the SDs) were now in power, while still redder Communists were pressing in the wings and from the East, Germany seemed menaced by an even greater degradation than the Weimar Republic.

This situation was aggravated by the multinational and multicultural character of the two former empires of Mitteleuropa. For the Central Powers were summoned by the Allies to convert not only to democracy, but also to its logical counterpart, the self-determination of peoples. In the ethnic jumble of Central Europe, however, there was no way that political frontiers could be made to correspond to linguistically defined nationalities. Beginning with the jagged eastern ethnic borders of *Deutschtum* itself, everywhere independent national groups would in some measure be oppressed or oppressors or both, with one group, the Jews, scattered through all the other newly recognized nationalities— and so on to the equally jagged ethnic borders of the Soviet Union. Under the region's Old Regimes the pressures of national diversity, though never easy to manage, had been attenuated by the arbiter of the dynastic state. Under democracy, however, demagogic nationalism became a prime factor in the radicalization of politics; and it is no accident that modern racist theories had a special appeal in this area.

The instability of postwar Mitteleuropa, finally, was increased by a shared institutional heritage with Russia; and so the region became the only part of Europe, outside Russia herself, where Communism was a significant movement before the popular fronts of 1936. Despite much anti-Bolshevik panic throughout the Atlantic West and southern Europe in the wake of the First World War, Communist movements were small and ineffectual everywhere outside Mitteleuropa; indeed, until 1933, the largest Western Communist Party was that of Germany.

Communism in Central Europe after 1918, moreover, was an active revolutionary force, for the general situation there was revolutionary. As in Russia, military defeat had provoked the fall of the regime in Germany and both the fall of the regime and the disintegration of the state in Austria, leaving a void which even without the Russian example invited resort to extremism. But there *was* the Russian example, and it was all the more potent in that it came from a cognate, partially Old-

Regime society. As a result, Germany and the former Dual Monarchy saw Workers' and Soldiers' Soviets *(Räte)* almost everywhere, a Spartacist attempt at a German October in Berlin, and genuine if short-lived Soviet republics in Munich and Budapest. All these explosions fed on the hope, shared by Lenin, that if the *membra disjecta* of the three Eastern monarchies went red together, then the world would be theirs tomorrow. Nor did the red tide ebb in Central Europe until 1923. It was under these revolutionary Central European conditions that the Austro-German, Nazi radicalization of fascism was born. In a classic revolutionary dialectic, once the Bavarian soviets had been put down by the war veterans of the *Freikorps* (at the behest of the socialist government in Berlin), a more radical Right believed that its time had come to seize power; and this led to the abortive Beer Hall Putsch of the plebeian ideologue Hitler (and the wartime supreme commander, General von Ludendorff) in 1923.

The ideological thrust of Hitler's new National Socialism was to substitute for the proletarian millenarianism of Bolshevism a millenarianism of the *völkisch* nation—a concept of nationality, it will be recalled, in which the people was seen as a racial community rooted in a historic homeland. The party of the *völkisch* nation thus had to be both "national" and "socialist," since the entire community was summoned to form a supraclass unity to realize its world-historical destiny. As spelled out in the mid-1920s in *Mein Kampf,* this national version of socialism exploited a certain Central European combination of emotions: *Ressentiment* at the arrogant West and contempt, mingled with fear, of Slavo-Asiatic hordes pressing in from the East. This Nazi vision held that Germanic Mitteleuropa was beset on the one hand by the "capitalist" Western "plutocracies," and on the other by the "Jewish-Slavic" revolution of "Bolshevik slave-socialism." Both the Western and the Eastern menaces to Germany were aided and abetted by innumerable Jewish-capitalist-Bolshevik elements within Germany itself. Nazism thus had a vital need of Bolshevism as a foil to affirm its own identity as a revolutionary movement and to take the German masses away from the internationalist Left, whether Social Democratic or Communist. As a combination of all Nazism's enemies, Bolshevism was given a racial rather than a social meaning as Judeo-Slavism. More than anywhere else in postwar Europe, the socionational welter of the ill-defined East-ern marches of *Deutschtum*, as it descends the Danube, ascends the Elbe, or fords the Vistula, was propitious to producing such a heady hashish.

The central importance of racial doctrine in Nazism, however, should not obscure the similarities between the German and the Soviet re-gimes (and to a lesser degree the kinship of both with Italian Fascism). The first of these is that all three regimes offered what Lenin called "a party of a new type." Hitherto, dictatorship had meant the rule of an individual strongman *over* society. The three great dictatorships of the 1930s, however, were the first to develop after popular sovereignty had become the mandatory legitimating principle of society. These dicta-torships, therefore, had to be exercised *through* society, by means of the indispensable instrument of democratic politics, the political party. Lenin, as we have seen, adapted the structured and hierarchical organi-zation of the German Social Democratic Party to produce the Soviet Party-state.[40] And after the war, the Italian Fascists first, and the Ger-man Nazis later, adapted the Leninist model (and borrowed as well from the rival socialist parties at home) to produce their own versions of that great novelty of twentieth-century politics, the one-party state— which is in fact a nonparty, mass-mobilization state. In applying this formula, however, the Nazis were far more consequential than the Fas-cists. The former succeeded in completely subordinating the state to the party, thereby achieving a level of control quite comparable to that of the Soviet Communists.

Something similar can be said of Nazi and Soviet economic policies, though the form of state domination in the two cases was different. Private property, the market, and even profit continued to exist in Germany, whereas they were of course abolished in Russia. The reason for the difference was that Germany was already a highly industrialized society, and Hitler wished essentially to channel its power toward preparation for war. Soviet Russia, by contrast, had first to be reindus-trialized by the state before the country could contemplate an interna-tional military role. This difference does not mean, however, that Hitler left "capitalism" in place; rather, the German economy was subordinated to politics by a system of state regulation so thorough that it was called by its critics a *Befehlswirtschaft*, or command economy. Hence the fact that the German economy was not formally nationalized did not greatly affect the way it was run, and this was quite similar to the Soviet mode of subordinating economics to the politics of the state.

Underlying these organizational similarities between Communism and Nazism (and again, to a lesser degree Fascism) is the fact that both were ideocratic. That is, their policies, overall, were governed not by pragmatic considerations of state- or nation-building, but by overriding metahistorical goals—Socialism for the first and Aryan *Weltmacht* for the second. And these two ideological visions had real, though different, practical consequences for the policies of both the Communist and Nazi regimes.

The point bears emphasis because too often the role of ideology is dismissed in explaining the dictatorships of the 1930s, which, it is alleged, were moved essentially by considerations of power. In the case of fascism in particular, it is often claimed that it had no ideology but its rhetoric, or at best that its only ideology was its praxis. Fascist ideology is thus reduced to a diffuse and eclectic amalgam of slogans, symbols, and mock heroic theatricality—a *Duce* out of Verdi and a *Führer* out of Wagner—a crude politics of mass emotion, devoid of intellectual content. Certainly the primacy of will and the cult of action are the politically operative tenets of the two fascisms; and their "ideologies" are indeed unstructured mental nebulae. Still, this mythopoeic political culture did draw on a notable and potent intellectual genealogy.

The fascist mind-set derives from the progressive debasement of the European antirationalist tradition. This lineage begins with the early Romantics' proclamation of the superiority of feeling over thought, and with the correspondingly high value thereby placed on cultural uniqueness and national particularity as opposed to universal rationality. It acquires the cast of a cult with the substitution of art for religious transcendence and universal ethics at the hands of such spinners of neopagan myth as Nietzsche and Wagner (it is certainly pertinent to Hitler's politics that, although this one-time painter may not have been widely read, he knew Wagner by heart). The tradition becomes more harsh and virulent with the "conservative revolution" and "cultural despair" of the fin de siècle; and it sheds the last vestiges of a moral sense in the social Darwinism and scientism of the same period. This incremental radicalization of the anti-Enlightenment tradition was at its strongest in Germanic Europe. Pre-1914 Italy was more open to German influence than were either France or England. To be sure, neither Hitler nor Mussolini functioned as learned exegetes of this tradition in plotting their policies, in the way that Lenin and Trotsky utilized the Marxist canon. Yet the crucial fact is that by the period 1914–1918 a bastardized version of the antirationalist tradition had become the common discourse of large segments of the masses that the National Socialists wished to mobilize.

Communism, in contrast, is founded on the debasement of the European rationalistic tradition; and Marxism, whatever Romantic elements of eschatology and gnosis it carried, always appeared structured and universal in its import. Even in its simplified Leninist form, and indeed in its catechetical Stalinist guise, it remained an imposing intellectual construct offering a coherent answer to all human problems. Since legions of avant-garde Western intellectuals, from the Frankfurt School of the 1920s to Jean-Paul Sartre after the Second World War, were virtuosi of Marxist categories, they were automatically programmed to give the Soviet experiment the benefit of every doubt. Communism, therefore, no matter how bloodily it drove the class struggle, could always pass for a champion of progressive values. Fascism, however, never pretended to be virtuous; it boasted rather its commitment to national egoism, brute force, and selfish will.

Nonetheless, there were points of ideological, and not just organizational, convergence between Communism and Nazism. Both practiced a politics of ideologically illumined coercion in the name of the elect of history, the proletariat for the first and the master race for the second. Both in practice substituted the party and its leader for this alleged popular base, in a form of demotic autocracy. Above all, both understood politics as warfare by other means. Hence both concluded that all "enemies," whether "capitalistic" kulaks or "racially degenerate" Jews, are fair game for liquidation by whatever methods are at hand.

The reduction of politics to war leads, further, to the openly proclaimed scorn of both regimes for traditional morality, religion, and law. After all, the amoral principle of the survival of the fittest advanced by the social Darwinism underlying Nazism is not all that different from the amoral principle of Marxism that all history is the history of class struggle. Indeed, Marx had thought of dedicating *Capital* to Darwin, on the grounds that he was doing for the science of society what Darwin had done for biology; and he was relentless in denouncing formal democracy as "the universal brotherhood swindle."[41] Both Communism and Nazism, consequently, though enemies themselves, had an even more hateful common enemy in the moralistic, arrogant, yet "rotten" and doomed West. And so both movements held to the paradox that the parliamentary democracies were viciously imperialistic and at the same time indecisive and thus ineffectual internationally.

Yet this common cult of politics as war also produced crucial differences between *les frères ennemis* of Central and East Europe. The mystique of the world supremacy of a single, Aryan *Volk* is by definition exclusive. It can impose itself on others only by military conquest or at most with the aid of subsidiary *Völker*, such as Italians or Croats. The mystique of the proletariat, however, is universal and inclusive. It can feed on the crises of the liberal West at home and on guilt over colonialism abroad. Hence Soviet Moscow, unlike Nazi Berlin, rarely had need of military conquest to be an international force; and when it went the military route, as in Poland in 1920, in Finland in 1939, and in Korea in 1950, the enterprise backfired disastrously. The world reach of Soviet Moscow rested on manipulation of the moral conscience and the antifascist sentiments of the liberal world. Thus the West was ultimately able to answer Hitler in his own crude military terms, but to answer Communism proved to be a far more complex matter, as the decade-long American disaster in Vietnam demonstrated.

Dissimilar ideological orientations produced other practical differences as well. In the fascist regimes, the Leader came first and the Party second. Because the two regimes depended on the real charisma of a supreme chief, the tradition of each perished with its founder in the catastrophe of 1945. The contrast with Franco's noncharismatic dictatorship may serve to define the genuine totalitarian article. Spain's national authoritarianism was so far from totalitarian that it could even supply a Bourbon king to bring back La Passionaria from Moscow and to reinstate free elections. Spain thus made the transition to constitutional democracy without a revolutionary break, since beneath the carapace of Franco's purely political authoritarianism a classic civil society had always survived.

In Soviet Communism, unlike in fascism, there was no *Führerprinzip;* despite appearances during many years under Stalin, the Party of Lenin never depended on a given, single leader. Even though Stalin used the Russian equivalent of that term, *Vozhd*, it did not carry the magnetic connotations of its German and Italian equivalents; and the general secretary always preferred the simple title Comrade Stalin. This is not to say that the Soviet Party did not require a single apex of authority, indeed a single authoritative chief, for it clearly did. But this was a structural requirement of Communist dictatorship, not a mythic force for regime legitimation. Lenin, though he almost invariably got his way, dominated the Bolshevik apparatus by persuasion or threats of resignation, not as a personal dictator. Stalin, as an individual, had not an ounce of public charisma, and the "cult of personality" surrounding him was fabricated by the Party machine. Propelled by that machine, the Soviet regime survived four generations of leaders, while its erstwhile fraternal counterparts in China, Vietnam, and North Korea lived well into their second round of "chairmen."

In Communist totalitarianism, the Party, as the proletariat incarnate and the vehicle for the logic of history, is primordial and indispensable, while the individual leader is secondary and replaceable. When he concentrates absolute power in his hands, as did Stalin after 1937, he does this on the basis of the Party's antecedent legitimacy and as the "best pupil" of a totemic Lenin. Hence, with the routinization of the system after its great builders were gone, the Party's legitimacy was effectively assumed by a collective leadership of higher *apparatchiki* (with Brezhnev as a merely symbolic *vozhd*) presiding atop the life-giving pedestal of Lenin's tomb.

In sum, generic fascism, even if restricted to the interwar period, disintegrates as a concept when confronted with the awesome differences between Hitler and Mussolini; but generic Communism is quite real, and the genus maintained its unity from October to its ultimate routinization and decay. As a result, Leninist regimes have been remarkably uniform even when they are enemies internationally. They swear by the same canonical texts and speak in the same wooden language; they rest on the same Party and police structures; they engage in essentially similar command economic "planning." Indeed, their deceased charismatic founders have been mummified in mausoleums on the capital's main square—from Lenin to Ho to Mao.

Accordingly, the meaningful counterpoint to Communism is not fascism in general but Nazism specifically. Yet, even though structurally the two come the closest of the modern dictatorships to an ideal type of totalitarianism, historically they differ crucially in their practice of revolution. And this difference largely determined their contrasting fates.

The aim of Hitler's revolution was to forge a monolithic national community in order to resume the First World War, and to do so before he was fifty, while he was still young enough to win the second round. There was no time for his projected internal revolution, which would have been disruptive of society on the eve of battle; nor was the domestic transformation urgent since Germany's superior level of industrial development provided the wherewithal for the more pressing task of war. In internal affairs, Hitler stopped with an essentially political and cultural revolution, the *Gleichschaltung*—the "homogenization" or bringing into line—of all national institutions under the party's control. The projected social counterpart of this leveling was postponed until victory; and after 1936 the revolutionary impetus of Nazism was carried abroad in a succession of increasingly bold gambles. Nazism's life course thus turned out to be a permanent crisis—six years to prepare for war and six to wage it—with the result that Nazism never congealed into a stable system.

The aim of the Russian Bolsheviks, by contrast, once they were marooned by the West's failure to follow their example, was first of all to make an internal social and economic revolution, so that their backward base would someday be able to undertake the external fight against "imperialism." Their Marxist creed of class struggle was turned inward against the nation itself to produce the industrial society that the revolution's proletarian ideology presupposed. This meant a protracted process of forced development, while imperialism was kept at bay with the ideological resources of foreign Communist parties, antifascism, and popular fronts. Thus, in the two decades from 1917 to 1939 the Soviet regime had ample time to congeal into a stable system that would long outlast its builders.

Russia would pay for this stolid longevity, however, almost as dearly as Germany paid for Hitler's meteoric trajectory. For the Communists' primacy of domestic revolution meant that they in fact succeeded in "building socialism" internally, whereas Hitler's turn to imperial expansion precluded a comparably ambitious revolution on his domestic front. And socialism, as already indicated, if applied in its integral version, is the maximal formula for totalitarianism. It produces the economic and social, not just the political, *Gleichschaltung* of national life. The Soviet regime was thus far more "total" than its rival; and this has much to do with its survival for three-quarters of a century.

Hitler never had time to level Germany's existing social structure, because he did not push his political version of a command economy on to direct state management of the economy and full suppression of the market. When this lesser party-state was destroyed, the basic components of a civil society were still there; after 1947, therefore, Konrad Adenauer could resuscitate it with astonishing rapidity and on its foundation work a soon legendary "economic miracle." But after Stalin, the "universal emptiness of the Soviet night" was wholly filled by the Party-state. So when his remote successors in the 1980s tried to revitalize their heritage, they discovered that, once they had inadvertently provoked the system's collapse, the country was without any structured Russian civil society to take its place. There was only a gaping social void, out of which the orphans of Communism had to conjure up a market and a democracy. As it turned out, the Soviet "shadow economy" and its attendant mafia were the first to move into the void.

The contrasting revolutionary priorities of the Nazi and the Soviet regimes also explain the stark differences in their common recourse to mass terror. Nazi ideology as a national and racial doctrine meant that Hitler's terror was directed only secondarily inward, toward the homeland, to purge it of Jews, socialists, and other elements alien to the *Volk*. But it was directed massively outward, toward other peoples, whether

334

Jews, Poles, Ukrainians, gypsies, or Russians, whose "racial" otherness automatically made them enemies. Thus most Nazi camps were extermination camps, designed to clear *Lebensraum* in the East, and their victims were largely non-German. Communist ideology, by contrast, is a class ideology. Its terror thus was directed primarily inward against the "class-alien" among its own people and was designed to clear living space for the Party-state. Its camps, therefore, were primarily labor camps, with death coming "naturally" from toil, and the majority of its victims were Soviet citizens.

This difference between outer- and inner-directed terror is related to another difference between the political fortunes of the two regimes: from equal crime followed unequal punishments and rewards. Nazi terror mobilized the rest of Europe against Germany. Communist terror, however, touched few outside Soviet Russia, and in fact was long hidden away successfully in Siberia. It thus could not serve to mobilize Europe against the Soviet Union, while Hitler helped mobilize Europe at Soviet Russia's side.

Indeed, it was Hitler's racial policies that ultimately mobilized the Soviet people by Stalin's side. The jerry-built, terror-ridden socialism that Stalin had created by 1939 was by no means a sure bet to survive, nor did all Soviet people believe, as they had to intone in public, that theirs was the most advanced and happiest society in the world. Stalin had as yet to find out whether they would support him in a crisis, especially in the supreme crisis of modern total war—which had after all destroyed the tsar. When the gamble of his pact with Hitler broke down in June 1941, Stalin broke down with it, and national morale and military effectiveness almost broke down with him. In the first seven months of the war, some 3.9 million Soviet soldiers were taken prisoner, in part because Stalin's order never to retreat made it easy for the Germans to surround whole armies, and in part because the soldiers were not all that committed to the Soviet cause. Many Soviet citizens, moreover, felt that Russia could never hold off the technologically superior and traditionally more efficient Germans. In border areas, from the Baltic states to Ukraine, the population often greeted the Germans as liberators, and the collectivized peasantry everywhere hoped for dissolution of the kolkhozes and the reopening of their churches.[42]

It was Hitler's policy, not socialism's allure, that turned the tide. The Führer soon made it clear that the Slavic *Untermenschen* would be treated as the slaves they were born to be, and that he, too, needed the collective farms to exploit the region. As this news filtered back across the receding Soviet lines, the wavering elements of the population concluded "better our beast than theirs." The army's will stiffened and the Leader recovered his nerve just in time to save Moscow in December 1941—and along with it the fourfold fruits of the experiment. The following year the compounded blunders of Hitler gave Stalin the decisive victory in his namesake city on the Volga. As one Stalingrader later said, "Before the war our city gloried in the name of Stalin; after the war, Stalin gloried in the name of our city."[43]

Hitler thus gave Stalin something that had eluded every tsar since Alexander I: victory in a general European war, and over the major power of the day at that. For once, Stalin and his people had in fact "built" together. With this fund of national pride to draw on, the fruits of the experiment were secure for another half-century.

Where the Twain Meet

Yet when all the structural and ideological differences between Nazism and Communism have been recognized, the two remain, like Siamese twins, attached at the spine, and thus are equally unviable political formations. For both are perversions of the universal creed of modernity: democracy.

Previous chapters have followed the long gestation of the modern democratic idea from the Enlightenment onward; and its halting progress has been traced across the West-East cultural gradient. Periodic notice has been taken, moreover, of the stages by which this common creed bifurcated into socialism and nationalism. It is now necessary to bring these stages together in a single, dialectical genealogy.

When 1789 brought the democratic idea into the world on the ruins of Europe's most venerable Old Regime, it acted in the name of the "nation," an ancient Roman word for tribe or people. The Revolution's opening act was to transform the hierarchically divided Estates General into a monolithic National Assembly and to confer on it constituent, or founding, powers. In this context "nation" referred to the nonprivileged Third Estate, the overwhelming majority of the population. The term thus had as its first meaning the "people," composed of a mass of equal citizens; and the plenitude of authority, hitherto embodied in the majesty of monarchy, was now vested in the nation, henceforth endowed with the majesty of popular sovereignty.

Almost immediately, however, the infant republic of citizens came into conflict with still despotic, Old-Regime polities; and the term "nation" thus acquired a second meaning, one akin to the Roman original and identical to the current sense of a particular nation. It also became a militant concept; for in an egalitarian society, the logical counterpart of universal suffrage is the universal military service of the *levée en masse*. So rule of the people produced its first great offshoot, nationalism, in the sense of separate, unequal, and rival popular sovereignties. And these diverse sovereignties in practice found expression as the nation-state.

In the wake of the next revolutionary shock, that of 1830, modernity's common denominator, popular sovereignty, was given the more explicit Greek name—"democracy"—thereby erasing the taint of mob rule that government by the people had carried since Plato. Even more portentously, the egalitarian impetus of democracy produced its second great offshoot: socialism. Experience since 1789 had shown that replacing traditional estates with the equality of all citizens before the law did not make men equal as human beings; nor did the formal democracy of universal suffrage suffice to remedy this affront to the natural reason common to all men. Indeed, mere political emancipation masked the most invidious servitude of all: class exploitation resting on the unequal possession of wealth. The remedy was to abolish private property in favor of public ownership of the means of production and distribution—collective ownership that, as it turned out, would in practice be exercised by the same state that expressed the nation.

These diverse ramifications of generic democracy became fully clear in Europe's first anticipated revolution: that of 1848. By that date, in all European languages the term "people"—*peuple, Volk, narod*—meant both a nation and its laboring, lower classes, who were at the same time the most deprived and the most authentically national stratum of the population. The Springtime of the Peoples of 1848 was expected to be the universal Second Coming of 1789—democratic, social, and national all at once. Though the revolution failed on all three counts, the Western world has lived ever since in a shifting triangulation of democracy, socialism, and nationalism.

The three ideals were combined in quite unequal portions along the European cultural gradient: as modernity unevenly made its way eastward, citizen participation decreased and national obligations grew proportionately. Thus, as of 1914, the most democratic institutions from one end of Europe to the other were its national armies. It transpired, further, that both nationalism and socialism entail, as do modern armies, the mass mobilization of populations by the state. It is through this conflation of mobilizations that, in the politically or economically laggard portions of Europe, total democratic war produced the two demented faces of popular sovereignty. Communism pushed socialism to one totalitarian extreme, while Nazism drove nationalism to the other.

Yet the two remained united through their origins in the bicephalous modern "nation," whose nature is to be egalitarian and totalizing, social and national, at one and the same time. When this duality fuses with the modern religion of revolution—born in the wake of 1789 and magnified by 1914–1918—the dark face of modernity emerges in a single profile. National Socialism is thus hardly a contradiction in terms; it is one logical, if perverse, outcome of democracy; and internationalist socialism, when promoted by an omnicompetent party-state, yields a similarly perverse outcome. In this mixed formula, Soviet Russia emphasized the social component and Nazi Germany the national one; but each in its way aspired to the totality that the national-democratic ideal had always contained potentially.

It is just this diagnosis of our century's ills that the historian, Élie Halévy, as early as 1936, gave in his *Era of Tyrannies*. He saw the age as one long crisis, unleashed by the war of 1914–1918 and culminating at the time he wrote in the kindred "socialist" revolutions of the Axis and of Communism. He greatly feared that these unprecedented forms of tyranny would lead to another mass conflict—which of course they did. Yet he also foresaw that the runaway popular forces of our age could be tamed by the classical liberal tradition to which he was com-

mitted, and which he considered by no means closed to moderate socialist aspirations. This indeed was where the century would come
out.[44]

The two centuries since 1789 have demonstrated that the democratic ideal is saved from going overboard into demotic tyranny when it
is combined with constitutional government and the rule of law. It is
these practices, originally developed in oligarchic form by the Old Regime, and indeed possessing roots reaching far back into the feudal,
superstitious Middle Ages, that, for the most part, have enabled modern
democracy to become liberal and that have kept modern civilization
civilized. For the greater part of the twentieth century, however, this
outcome was in doubt, as rival totalitarianisms faced off across the entire European gradient from the Atlantic to the Urals.

To recapitulate the balance sheet as of 1945: Through the fascist-Com-
munist dialectic Hitler had saved Stalinist Russia's reputation as progressive by offering the contrast of fascism. Indeed, he helped implant
Communist strength west of the Rhine because this respectability made
possible the popular fronts of 1936. He then made the Soviet Union the
first power of Europe and a major force in the world by starting and
losing the Second World War, whereas Germany had won in the East
in 1918. The Hitlerian disaster, finally, obliterated Mitteleuropa: Stalin
gathered in almost all the old Habsburg empire and half of the Hohenzollern one as well. This partition of the continent along the Iron
Curtain brought the frontiers of what was now a Soviet Socialist empire
beyond Berlin to the Elbe. At the same time, in what remained of the
West, the legacy of the anti-Nazi resistance produced for the first time
mass Communist parties in France and Italy, where Marxism-Leninism
absorbed and disciplined the native syndicalist tradition. Simultaneously, on the other flank of the Stalinist empire, Japan's Imperial-fascist
adventure in the Far East made imminent the triumph of Mao Zedong
in China and the beginning of the career of Ho Chi Minh in Vietnam.

In these new circumstances, Communist Moscow had a leverage
undreamed of by the Old-Regime gendarme of the Winter Palace. The
black-brown shirts of fascism have been an indispensable source of
Communist strength wherever the Red Spectre has appeared, through-

out all of Eurasia. Indeed, the ultimate historical importance of fascism has been this negative one. For fascism brings with it war and social decomposition, and Communism, from the First World War through the Second, has been able to establish itself only in the vacuum left by the disintegration of a structured, civil society.

Thus, by Hitler's agency, the Cunning of Unreason at last wedded Stalinist socialism to Russian nationalism to create the winning national-socialism of the age. It was indeed all the more triumphant in that it never had to name its name, but could instead pass as internationalist and of panhuman validity. So Romulus slew Remus, and inherited the whole of the lupine empire of social-cum-national *Ressentiment* that lies on the dark side of modernity.

The Ride of Rozinante

It is with the steadily accumulating Marxist-Leninist-Stalinist baggage of two decades that, after October, the knights-errant of the Columbian West loaded up their poor steed Rozinante (no flesh, just notions and books) and journeyed East to find the Lady Dulcinea of their postwar, postcapitalist dreams. They quite understandably had to see the experiment for themselves; no secondhand accounts would do. Still, they traveled light indeed, for unlike Wallace or Leroy-Beaulieu of the previous century, almost none knew Russian or anything about Russia's past, and few took the trouble to learn. The result of their investigations was a veritable harvest of ideological *kliukvas*. In particular, the votaries of the experiment dismissed all émigré "Whites" as reactionaries, hostile to mankind's best hopes and fit companions only for sour Western conservative and interventionist liberals.

Yet there were more than a million of these émigrés in the West, and the majority were by no means tsarist officers as was commonly believed, but liberals, democrats, and socialists. Indeed, this emigration included a good half of the creative intelligentsia of the now defunct Russian civil society and the leaders of all Russian political parties but the Bolsheviks: the Mensheviks in Berlin; the Socialist Revolutionaries, the liberals, the monarchists, and the clergy in Paris; and a whole university of scholars in Prague. All these groups produced important and informed publications, which may be read with profit today. But it is striking that only spokesmen of the two extremes among the exiles—Trotsky and Berdiaev—obtained a real international hearing, whereas the mass of the immigration had minimal impact in shaping the West's new image of Russia.

(FACE LEFT)

The task of interpreting the new Russia, rather, fell primarily to the progressive intellectuals of the West, those philosophers, writers, and journalists who made up the modern republic of letters. They arrived at their evaluation of the experiment, moreover, in the same manner in which their predecessors had first built up the ideal of socialism itself—by negative extrapolation from the ills of the West itself. With the projections of these knights of the neo-Enlightenment, Russia and the West were back with the ghosts of Voltaire and Diderot.[45]

Just as the leaders of the first republic of letters, starting with Leibniz, had begun their idyll with the old new Russia by direct contact with its founder, so their latter-day successors began their romance with the new new Russia at the dawn of Red October. Thus was born the category of what Trotsky soon baptized "fellow travelers." The journalist John Reed, Harvard class of 1910, alienated from the American democracy of J. P. Morgan, after covering the revolt of Pancho Villa in Mexico in 1913, arrived in Petrograd in October 1917 just in time to witness its "ten days that shook the world," and to record them as seen through the eyes of Lenin and Trotsky.[46] Returning to the United States with this message, he was expelled from the Socialist Party in 1919 and so formed, with others, the Communist Labor Party. For this action he was indicted for sedition in the midst of the postwar Red Scare and fled back to Russia. There he died in 1920 of typhus; and his ashes now repose in a niche of the Kremlin wall just behind the mausoleum and beside the urn of Stalin.

In 1919 a muck-raking journalist and enemy of corporate corruption and machine politics, Lincoln Steffens, visited Russia to report on the results of October. On his return to the West he declared, in a remark soon heard round the world, "I have been to the future and it works." To develop this point, in 1920 he wrote *John Reed under the Kremlin*, published by the Walden Book Shop with an introduction by Clarence

Darrow.[47] Thus Bolshevism was wedded to the tradition of American radicalism and the heritage of Alexander I's old admirer, Thomas Jefferson.

Bolshevism was simultaneously wedded to other traditions as well, above all that of the Jacobins. In 1917 Captain Jacques Sadoul, an associate of the Socialist minister Albert Thomas, accompanied him to Russia on a French military mission. There he gained Lenin's confidence and, after vainly urging Paris to support the Bolsheviks against the Germans, went off to fight in the Red Army on his own and under the tricolor flag.[48] At the same time, the naval engineer André Marty led a mutiny against intervention in the French squadron at Odessa, but was later amnestied and returned to France.[49] Long a member of the Politburo of the French Communist Party and a heroic combatant in the Spanish Civil War, he always remained a staunch Communist internationalist; he hence wound up being expelled from the Party in 1952 for the "Left deviation" of protesting Stalin's policies in Eastern Europe.

But Bolshevism could fuse with other, quite antithetical traditions. In 1918 a minor member of the French mission, Pierre Pascal, a devout Catholic and a believer in Dostoevsky's vision of God-manhood, concluded, as had Aleksandr Blok, that October was the advent of the kingdom of Christ on earth. He too entered the Soviet service, in the Commissariat of Enlightenment (that is, Education) under the tender Bolshevik Anatolii Lunacharskii. Finally disabused of his faith by Stalin, he was pardoned by Paris in the 1930s and became a professor of Slavic literature at the Sorbonne and the leading scholar of the Russian Old Believers.[50] On yet another cultural front, in the late 1920s the ultra-modernist and antibourgeois movement of Surrealism disintegrated as an artistic avant-garde, and some of its members gravitated to politics. This schism brought the poet Paul Eluard and the poet-novelist Louis Aragon into the Party for life.[51] The former became the favorite bard of the Resistance during the war. The latter, married to the Russian writer and sister-in-law of Maiakovskii, Elsa Triolet, became a twentieth-century Melchior Grimm, Moscow's official man of letters in Paris. He supported Stalin unfailingly throughout his years in power, even though Elsa was basically aware of the real situation in Russia from

1936 onward; and he deplored Stalin's "errors" only once the Leader was gone and he and Elsa understood that this was now necessary for the cause.[52]

In Mitteleuropa, too, a similar pattern emerged. Although Rosa Luxemburg, the founder of German Communism, had criticized Lenin's putchist and antidemocratic actions, she was soon killed and the German Party Leninized. Indeed, guilty over its failure to make a revolution in Marxism's homeland, it soon became the most subservient of Western parties to its successful Russian brother. Symbolizing the new trend was Rosa's old friend Klara Zetkin, feminist and confidante of Lenin. It was she, in her *Reminiscences of Lenin*, who inaugurated the tradition of conversations with the current leader of the Kremlin designed to adapt his message for the Western public.[53]

At the same time, on the German cultural front Moscow beckoned to the artists, perhaps even more than in France. For the Revolution appeared there not only as a social avant-garde, but as an explosion of aesthetic modernism as well. Via Berlin, Europe became conscious of Gorky's proletarian realism, Maiakovskii's Futurism, Vsevolod Meyerhold's experimental theater, and above all Sergei Eisenstein's revolutionary cinematography. Under this spell Johannes R. Becher, the Expressionist poet, translated Maiakovskii and became such a faithful Leninist that, in 1949, he was made minister of culture in Communist East Germany.[54] Slightly later Bertolt Brecht inaugurated a more creative career as the leader of populist-modernist and ideologically committed theater. On the philosophical front, the Germanized Hungarian Gyorgy Lukács, under the impact of the postwar turmoil, challenged the positivistic Marxism of Engels with a dynamic, Hegelian interpretation of the doctrine; and he saw in Lenin the great practitioner of this Romantic, dialectical Marxism. This conversion set him on the road to becoming Europe's major Leninist-Stalinist philosopher and theorist of literature in a career that spanned four decades.[55]

Not all the pilgrims to the East remained convinced for so long, or even came away convinced at all. The neo-Enlightenment also had its doubting D'Alemberts and even its hostile Rousseaus. The American Left Communist Max Eastman, after visiting and studying in Russia in 1922, sided with Trotsky in 1925 against Stalin. From this position he moved to criticism of the whole of Soviet socialism in a series of increasingly vehement yet informed books—which after 1945 brought him into association with right-wing Republicanism.[56] Thus was created a special category of enemies, far worse than any conservatives: the renegades. More fortunate was Bertrand Russell, who became anti-Communist while remaining firmly on the Left. Just after the war he visited Russia with a Labor Party delegation and was accorded an interview with Lenin. Though most of the delegation was impressed, Russell himself was not; for his positivism immunized him to Marxist dialectics and his empiricism told him that the experiment was simply despotic without any redeeming enlightenment.[57] And he was one of the few major Western progressives never to succumb to Soviet temptation. Less gifted with grace, however, was the Reverend Hewlett Johnson, "red" dean of Canterbury, who in the 1920s inaugurated a career of low church Leninism that would take him beyond 1945.[58]

So Rozinante and all the fellow travelers rode on into the 1930s and those dark ranges of the Sierra Morena that mark the acme of the experiment. In 1931, amidst the bread lines of the depression, America's foremost cosmopolitan man of letters and purveyor of European modernism, Edmund Wilson, appealed to his fellow progressives:

> The truth is that we liberals and progressives have been betting on capitalism. . . . And now in the abyss of bankruptcy and starvation into which the country has fallen . . . liberalism seems to have little to offer beyond a recommendation of the public ownership of water-power . . . against . . . the beatings-up and murders of the working class by the owners.

Russia, however, seemed to represent the reality of the American dream:

> After all, the Communist project has almost all the qualities that Americans glorify—the extreme efficiency, combined with the ideal of a herculean feat to be accomplished by common action in an atmosphere of enthusiastic boosting—like a Liberty Loan drive—the idea of putting over something big in five years.[59]

344

A visit to the Soviet Union at the time of the purges, however, revealed to Wilson that the Communist project was perhaps not so near to the American dream after all. Still, he never really lost his illusions, and in 1940 he published *To the Finland Station*, an intellectual history of the socialist quest from the utopian Saint-Simon to Marx and on to Lenin. Just as his *Axel's Castle* of 1931 had introduced progressive Americans to the avant-garde of literature, so the *Finland Station* now brought them to the avant-garde of politics; and the *Partisan Review* pointed the moral that the two were organically linked.[60] Wilson therefore rejected the anti-Communist remonstrances of Vladimir Nabokov as émigré bitterness, yet cautiously turned his romance with Russia toward her literature, indeed eventually translating Pushkin's *Eugene Onegin*.[61]

Yet other fellow travelers were rather more devious. A notorious case is that of Walter Duranty, the *New York Times* correspondent in Moscow throughout Stalin's revolution from above. He knew fairly well how it was being conducted yet deliberately kept this knowledge out of his dispatches, in part not to lose his accreditation and in part because the home office did not want to hear the bad news.[62] His then colleague at the *Christian Science Monitor*, William Henry Chamberlin, though initially sympathetic to Stalin's revolution, eventually saw it basically for what it was, and so wrote *Russia's Iron Age;* in later years, like Eastman, he became a right-wing Republican.[63] Overall, however, in the 1930s the Western Left preferred to believe in the efficacy of Soviet planning as opposed to capitalist profiteering. Thus, beginning in 1928 Maurice Dobb of Cambridge University periodically updated, under one or another title, his *Soviet Economic Development since the 1917 Revolution*, to explain the success of the Five-Year Plans.[64] Until the 1960s, this donishly Stalinoid work remained the major textbook on the subject and was regularly assigned in all the best Western universities.

For those who rejected the Revolution's real outcome under Stalin yet refused to become renegades, there remained an alternative solution. In 1929 Trotsky was expelled from Russia and this "prophet outcast" and former commander of the Red Army abandoned the sword for the pen. Between 1929 and 1936 he published in rapid succession *Permanent Revolution, The History of the Russian Revolution*, and finally *The Revolution Betrayed*.[65] In the first two books he gave a polished

Bolshevik version of October and its world-historical significance; and this new vulgate was far more compelling dialectically and more satisfy- ❡ ing aesthetically than Stalin's *Short Course* history of 1938. In the third volume Trotsky produced a Marxist explanation of why the experiment had gone awry. His answer was that the Revolution had succumbed to Stalin because it had not spread beyond backward Russia. In the result- ing conditions of penury the Party "degenerated" into a "bureaucracy," appropriating society's scarce resources and ruling as a kind of class. Nevertheless, all hope was not lost for the experiment, since the bases of the system remained socialist: private property had been abolished and planning, however imperfect, had been instituted. Someday, there- fore, the workers would reclaim their state from Stalinism and bring about a glorious rebirth of October.

Through Trotskyism, Communism was in theory permanently ar- rested in its experimental stage, and true socialism was made out to be permanently imminent. This, for many of the perplexed, was an ideal solution, a veritable Grecian urn of October. One could thus both cherish the reality of a heroic 1917 and yet remain safely utopian. One could preserve eternally an ideal Leninism without having to accept its real historical consequences. This capacity to have the revolution both ways at once is the genius of Trotskyism, as it would be ever after of all sectarian Left Communist movements. Its attraction, however, was limited to intellectuals, for when Western workers adopted Commu- nism, they almost invariably preferred the Stalinist variety. Through- out the 1930s and beyond, therefore, those progressives who could not take their Communism as it really was had the alternative of taking it as it allegedly might have been.

More important than such sectarians were those progressives of the 1930s who remained in the mainstream Left, and whose literary spokesmen often associated the new socialism with Stalin's person. While the novelist Jules Romains stayed at home and described from afar the warmth of *cette grande lueur à l'est*,[66] his compatriot Romain Rolland was more forward. His once great international prestige rested on the fact that during the war of 1914 he had remained "au dessus de la mêlée" as a strict socialist and pacifist internationalist. By the 1930s he had become a disciple of Gandhi and of nonviolence, and in this mood, after writing about the war and the revolution in *The Death of a World* and the *Birth of Another*, in 1935 he visited Russia and found it to be in conformity with what he had already written.[67] Still more flattering for the new order and its builder was Henri Barbusse, who had been converted to revolution amidst the horrendous "fire" of the wartime trenches, which he had described in his first book. In 1935 he gave testimony to his faith with *Stalin: A New World Seen through a Man*, the first attempt at a portrait of the Leader.[68]

In these same years, across the Channel dramatist George Bernard Shaw went through a more complex evolution. He had been converted to socialism in 1883 by reading Marx's *Capital* in French translation (it had not yet been rendered into the language of Europe's premier capitalism), and soon thereafter became a founder of the Fabian Society. On the basis of these convictions, in the 1920s, he became a supporter of Mussolini—for was not his Fascism Europe's first attempt at socialism? On the basis of the same convictions, in the 1930s he switched his support to Lenin and Stalin, visited Russia, and found her socialism to be even better.[69] Soon thereafter, in 1935, another Fabian, H. G. Wells, renowned futurologist and president of the international PEN Club, was invited to a series of "talks" with Stalin in the Kremlin; though skeptical enough to question the Leader about literary freedom in Russia, he went away satisfied with the answer that it was provided for by Soviet "self-criticism." Wells concluded, "I have never met a man more candid, fair, and honest."[70] The next year the principal founders of British Fabianism, Sidney and Beatrice Webb, produced two apparently documented volumes, *Soviet Communism: A New Civilization?* whose discreet question mark suggested that the answer was in fact yes. The book was reprinted the following year without its question mark.[71]

German intellectuals of the Left went through a similar evolution, though in more convoluted form, since unlike the authors just mentioned they were now in exile. Some of them, such as Bertold Brecht, took refuge in the West, where they were safe not only from Hitler, but from Stalin as well. Others less prudently sought shelter in Moscow, where in various fashions they had to pay their way in ideological coin. Thus Lukács became in effect a cultural functionary of the Comintern; and the novelist Leon Furchtwänger, though substantially disabused by what he saw around him, nonetheless lavishly praised the Soviet system as the great bulwark against fascism and imperialism.[72] At the same time, at the opposite end of the Western political spectrum, Franklin Roosevelt's ambassador to Moscow, Joseph Davies, no socialist at all but a mere liberal, regularly reported to Washington that the West should be more "understanding" of Soviet Russia's problems, beset as she was by external enemies and internal deviationists. In particular, as he averred in his memoirs of 1938, the purge trials offered "proof . . . beyond reasonable doubt to justify the verdict of guilty of treason."[73]

Still, by 1936 the tide of neo-Enlightenment enthusiasm was beginning to turn; and by the end of that year, at the height of the popular front and the beginning of the purges the Soviet Union encountered its marquis de Custine. The foremost proletarian writer, Gorky, had just died (possibly poisoned by Stalin), and the Soviet Union of Writers invited the man then widely considered the foremost Western bourgeois writer, André Gide, to deliver the funeral oration on Red Square. Gide had long since moved away from his introspective involvement with "immoralistic" emancipation and Dostoevsky to a guilty concern with social injustice. He had recently returned from the Congo, after which he had written against the evils of colonialism; and by 1936 he was a prominent cultural patron of the popular front. But in addition to his concern for justice, Gide had a cult of sincerity. And so, as he was shown the Soviet Union from a private railway car while at the same time Bukharin was hustled from his hotel suite, he concluded that Soviet Russia had a disturbing number of points in common with the Congo. On his return home he felt obliged to reveal this fact himself, for he found that "too often the truth about the USSR is told with hatred and the lies with love."[74] But the tactic of loving truth did not work, for Romain Rolland and all the Left denounced his book as a stab in the back of the now faltering French Popular Front.

More telling intellectually than Gide's slight work was the *Stalin* of Boris Souvarine, a Franco-Russian member of the Party who had become disillusioned early on. This major study, published in 1935, was based on Russian sources and intimate acquaintance with the East; it is indeed the first work of serious scholarship, as opposed to journalism, about Soviet Russia to appear in the West outside émigré circles. Yet it

348

was greeted by most with disbelief or derision at the time and was not republished till 1977, for it came from the pen of a renegade.[75] More difficult to dismiss, however, was the work of an international commission headed by the liberal philosopher John Dewey, which in 1938 analyzed the evidence of the public purge trials and found it shot full of contradictions.[76] This blow, coming on the heels of Gide's defection, ended the idyll between Stalin and the Left liberals of the 1930s.

Stalin too had become disabused. After 1936 he concluded that the progressives of the West would be more blessed if they believed without having seen. Henceforth, no Western men of letters were invited to visit Russia; the number of newspaper correspondents was reduced to a handful, and these were kept within the strictest bounds. With the consolidation of the experiment through the purges, Soviet Russia retreated into an iron isolation from which she would not emerge for two decades. Her light now shone only from afar, as through a glass darkly. And this tactic in fact worked. Throughout the twenty years of isolation, and with Hitler's help, new generations would come forth and believe. Thus by 1945 Jean-Paul Sartre and Henry Wallace had replaced Gide and Ambassador Davies.

(FACE RIGHT)

But the reign of illusion regarding Soviet Russia was not only a phenomenon on the Left of Western culture, it was almost as powerful on the Right, among the heirs of the third of the pre-1917 perceptions of Russia, the neo-Romantic votaries of the Russian soul. This reaction was most marked in Germany, the most crisis-racked of Western societies and the one with the strongest antirationalist tradition. The neo-Romantics, moreover, at times did listen to the Russian émigrés, or at least to their radical Right fringe.

From the very beginning the Germans were both drawn and repelled by the new order in Russia, in part because it was so near to home and in part because it appeared so relevant to German conditions, whether as a hope or as a menace. Most of the pre-1917 admirers of Russian spirituality had their word to say about its relation to the explosion of Bolshevism. Thomas Mann, though moving toward the more sober and liberal Western attitudes of his brother Heinrich, still remained under the spell of the "mist and moonbeams that wrapped the Eastern havens" and so was half-fascinated and half-appalled by the vitality of the new order in the East. Such was the message in 1923 of a major essay on Goethe and Tolstoy, in which these two "aristocrats of nature" and "favorites of the gods" were presented as exemplars of an enriching tension between Western "humanism" and Eastern "genuineness"—between Goethe the Olympian spirit, and Tolstoy the pagan god who, like Antaeus, draws his power from Mother Earth. Somewhat later Mann declared Richard Wagner to be the Western pagan analogue to Tolstoy.[77]

Mann's major pronouncement on Russia came in 1924 in his allegorical novel *The Magic Mountain*, which sought to probe those maladies of modern civilization that had led to the cataclysm of 1914. The hero, Hans Castorp, represents a sickly Germany divided between Western order and humanistic culture on the one hand, and, on the other, Eastern freedom and authenticity. But it is the latter that is by far the more alluring, in the person of Clavdia Chauchat, a feline, "Kirghiz-eyed" Russian from Daghestan who exudes the Dostoevskyan vitality popularized by Dmitrii Merezhkovskii. She represents authentic prehumanist, prebourgeois selfhood, born of the nomad's craving for freedom and movement. Yet she is above all "passionate," "living for the sake of life alone," with that "passion which is self-forgetfulness," whereas Westerners live for mere "self-enrichment" and "revolting egotism."[78] In a still more exalted vein, Hermann Hesse in 1922 took a "look into chaos" in the East and applied the "prophetic" allegory of *The Brothers Karamazov* to its elucidation: "Already half of Europe, already at least the Eastern half of Europe is on its way to chaos, is heading drunken in a holy hallucination headlong into the Abyss, and it sings at the same time, sings out with a drunken hymn, as Dmitrii Karamazov sang. The bourgeois laughs insultingly over these songs, the saint and the seer hear them with tears." Nor was this evaluation confined to Germany, for T. S. Eliot picked up this very passage to help justify the cosmic pessimism about the modern world expressed that same year in his *Wasteland*.[79]

These aesthetic and religious sentiments easily fused with a more political view, which was equally ambivalent toward Russia. To popularizers of Nietzsche's cult of heroic barbarism and vital spirit the Bolshevik revolution appeared as a primitive, Asiatic version of that Dionysian national rebirth which the defeat of 1918 and the pusillanimity of the Weimar Republic had rendered imperative at home. Thus Möller van den Bruck resumed his old eulogies of young Russia with redoubled vigor. His new message was that since the fallen Second Reich of the kaiser had been replaced by the imported mediocrity of the republic, it was urgently necessary to establish a Third Reich, for which Bolshevik Russia provided a rough model. And there were other new prophets in this mode. The recently famous Oswald Spengler in his *Decline of the West* declared Russia to be "organically" different from the Occident, now in full decay; because of Russia's "young" yet "Byzantine" essence she possessed the inner strength to cast off the desiccating "civilization" imported from the Western "megalopolis" and return to true "culture." The vogue of Spengler was more than a German phenomenon, for his version of cultural pessimism soon became a great success throughout the war-disillusioned West.[80]

There were other new thinkers, however, who held that with the advent of Bolshevism the Russian soul had been transformed into Russian demonism, thereby giving what was in essence a deviant version of Dostoevsky's argument in *The Possessed*. René Fulop-Miller declared that Bolshevism's significance went "beyond that of a mere 'political experiment'; [Bolshevism] is the revolutionary eruption of an elemental spiritual destiny, for which the way had long been prepared in the thinking of the Russian intelligentsia." Probing still more deeply, he asserted: "the rationalism of the Bolsheviks . . . in fact has its roots in the peculiar soul-life of the Russian sects; the hopes of these men were always set on a paradise in this life, on achieving 'human Godhead.'" These ideas, too, were spread from Germany throughout the West, preparing the way for the later and more spectacular vogue of Nikolai Berdiaev.[81]

In the 1920s, likewise, the odd phenomenon of National Bolshevism made its appearance in German politics. In part this was the product of the international circumstances of the day: a defeated and isolated Germany needed the support of an equally isolated Russia against the victorious Western Allies; and this sentiment led to the revival of the "Eastern orientation" of German diplomacy going back to Bismarck, the Wars of Liberation, and even Frederick the Great. But National Bolshevism was also something new; for it combined these historical memories with cultural anti-Westernism, a concern for biological race, and nostalgia for the Russian soul. In the thought of its prime exponent, Ernst Niekisch, this ideology urged that the spirit of Potsdam should be wedded to that of Moscow to produce both a national Communist revolution in Germany and an alliance with Soviet Russia against the "Western plutocracies." This was deemed logical because the Prussian state had come into existence out of a mixture of German and Slavic blood, in contrast to the tainted parts of Germany west of the Elbe. A defeated Germany could be revived only by following the Soviet way of liberation. "The Bolshevik Revolution was a step of desperation. It was not a rape of the Russian essence, but rather the only creative way out for this essence, the only way to preserve itself." It followed that "insofar as Germany opts for Russia, she of course at the same time opts for *Asia;* she places her hope in Asia's need for vengeance against imperialist Europe."[82]

A still headier and more ambivalent attitude toward Russia emerged from the symbiosis between the extreme Right of the Russian emigration and nascent National Socialism. The Russian Revolution had brought to Germany, particularly to Munich, former members of the pogrom-prone Black-Hundreds, which had sprung up in opposition to the Revolution of 1905. With them came *The Protocols of the Elders of Zion*, a tsarist police forgery that purported to explain the events of 1905 as the result of an international Jewish conspiracy to subvert Holy Russia. The Revolution of 1917 also brought to Munich numerous Baltic Germans from the former Russian empire, notably Alfred Rosenberg, who were all the more stridently German in that, like Hitler himself, they came from a precarious Eastern march of *Deutschtum*. Rosenberg soon became a close collaborator of Hitler, the chief ideologist of Nazism, and the movement's "expert" on Russia, Jews, and the East. In Rosenberg's hands, the *Protocols* were reinterpreted to explain the Bolshevik revolution as a Jewish-Masonic plot victorious over a horde of Slavic slaves, which now threatened to engulf Germany herself. And in 1941 Rosenberg inspired, and to a degree directed, the application of Hitler's racial policies in the occupied Soviet territories.[83]

Thus an ambiguous blend of love and hate became the essence of what might be called the "vulgar Nietzschean" reaction to Russia among a variety of right-wing circles in postwar Germany. Reluctant love predominated in the 1920s and early 1930s while Germany herself was still "unregenerated." This was true even of the Nazis, who were the most ambivalent of these groups toward Russia and who accomplished the final debasement of the antirationalistic tradition. For although Hitler despised the German Communists, he admired the Russian Bolsheviks for their ruthless revolutionary methods. Once Hitler and his demotic Nietzscheans had at last "regenerated" their own fatherland, however, hatred of Russia displaced admiration, as the vitality they sought was no longer without but within. Russia again became a rival force, a menacing, Asiatic, and Jewish-Communist civilization, fit only to be conquered and destroyed. Thus the most unstable society of postwar Europe, for which Russian vigor was the most attractive and the most menacing, became, because of its own acute internal problems, the first to revive the half-forgotten sense of Russia's innate difference from the West. The Russian soul had now been transmuted into a mindless Asiatic beast—as it had once been for the young Marx and the Byzantinist Fallmerayer.

International Class Struggle

It was under the unfavorable conjunction of these various kinds of unreason, on both the Left and the Right, that Russia moved into her third century as a modern power. She did so, however, less as a European than as a Communist force. But there is no point in belaboring the international moral of the present chapter in the story of Western-Russian relations, for the balance sheet of the interwar years together with their military climax is quickly drawn.[84]

When Soviet Russia withdrew from the international market under War Communism in 1918–19, she simultaneously withdrew from the political concert of Europe by establishing the Third International. This act made Moscow the pivot of a centralized network of Communist parties that had as its mission world revolution and so promised, ultimately, the destruction of her neighbors. Diplomatic relations of the ordinary sort with other states were therefore ruled out, as were most classical or "rational" calculations of power and interest in the West's dealings with the Bolsheviks. By the end of the 1920s, Soviet Russia had established formal relations with most of the powers, and largely preserved them in peacetime thereafter. At the same time, she remained the seat of "the international proletarian movement" and this is what counted most. Thus after 1918 Moscow functioned in world affairs in a dual role: as head both of the Soviet State and of the World Communist movement. Western governments never quite knew which of these two "powers" they were dealing with, or which head of the new Russian eagle was the premier one.

The result was a type of foreign relations unique in modern history and reminiscent, *mutatis mutandis*, of those that once existed between the old concert of Europe and Ottoman Turkey. Moscow's foreign relations were conducted in an atmosphere of permanent ideological jihad, in which, despite tactical oscillations, she never really accepted more than temporary truces with her foes. The new pattern of Western-Russian relations thus was not an interaction between states, but a clash of civilizations. To this situation the Western powers, the Allies first and the Axis later, responded in kind. As a result of the Soviet impact, international politics were ideologized with a passion unknown in Europe since the sixteenth-century wars of religion.

In consequence, Soviet Russia never came to function rationally in European and world affairs. Whereas old Russia had been an integral part of numerous European coalitions from Peter the Great's Northern War to the Triple Entente of 1914, the Soviet Union never formed a genuine alliance with any power throughout its existence. It functioned rather in terms of a haphazard coincidence of interests with other states; and its brief ad hoc alliances were regularized diplomatically only after the fact of their emergence.

Concretely, during the interwar years Soviet Russia's most enduring association with a European power was with Germany. This link was first formed in 1922 at Rapallo, when an isolated Russia pressed on the equally isolated Weimar Republic a commercial and military agreement which aligned the two defeated nations of the continent against the victorious Allies. Russia thereby received needed industrial equipment, and Germany obtained both raw materials and a secret military training ground to evade the restrictions of the Versailles Treaty. This was hardly an authentic alliance, though, since Moscow was at the same time working through the German Communist Party to overthrow the Weimar Republic. On both sides it was only a temporary expedient. Abrogated by Hitler after 1933, this ad hoc alignment was in effect revived by the Nonaggression Pact of 1939—an expedient even more opportunistic than the first.

Soviet Russia's relations with the Western Allies were made of similarly opportunistic stuff. Moscow remained largely isolated from the maritime West until the rise of Hitler and the Comintern's adoption of the popular-front strategy in 1935. At the same time, she entered the League of Nations, hitherto castigated as a tool of Anglo-French imperialism, and signed a formal alliance with France in 1935. But this policy, too, proved transitory, and again for ideological reasons. Until 1938 the Entente powers could never make up their minds whether Nazi Germany or Soviet Russia was the main enemy. On the one hand, they half hoped that if Germany's ethnic-national grievances were satisfied Hitler might be turned into an anti-Bolshevik force; and on the other, they feared that outright support of Stalin against Hitler would lead to the westward spread of Communism. Thus, when the Entente made the Munich Agreement of 1938 with the Axis (without consulting Russia) the French alliance of 1935 and the policy of "collective security" through the league were in effect abrogated. When the Allies at last decided, in 1939, to seek Soviet support against Germany, it was too late. Stalin now preferred the more immediate and tangible benefits of his pact with Hitler, which offered the prospect of pitting him against the Allies while keeping Russia out of the impending war and thus, he believed, making him the arbiter of the conflict.

Nonetheless, a Soviet alliance with the West was finally achieved in 1941, but again only opportunistically. It was also essentially the work of the Axis. Hitler's attack on Russia made her the ally of Britain, and Japan's attack on Pearl Harbor, followed by Hitler's declaration of war against the United States, made America the ally of both England and

Russia. But this was quite unlike the coalitions of 1914–1917 or 1813–14, which were formed on both the Russian and Western sides deliberately and before, rather than after, the fact of war.

Nor did the Second World War unfold at all in the manner of Russia's two previous Grand Alliances with Western powers. The campaigns of 1813–14 against Napoleon were coordinated among the Allies. The war of 1914 was preceded by two decades of joint planning by the French and Russian general staffs. The campaigns of 1941–1945, by contrast, were conducted in two separate compartments; indeed, each half of the "alliance" went to considerable lengths *not* to tell the other much of what it was doing, from Russia's future plans for Poland to the Allied landing in Normandy—and of course the atom bomb.

To be sure, there was a period of Western enthusiasm for the improvised Grand Alliance of 1941. Indeed, the old interventionist, Churchill, who as late as 1939 had wanted to fight Stalin in defense of Finland, after 1941 took to courting "Uncle Joe" by regular visits to the Kremlin. And Franklin Roosevelt, in 1943, covered up Stalin's Katyn Forest massacres of several thousand Polish officers after the partition of 1939. At the same time, Ambassador Davies at last published his memoirs as *Mission to Moscow*; they became a best-seller in 1942, were serialized in the *Reader's Digest*, and made into a Hollywood movie.[85] For the duration of the war, to all the liberal West Stalin became respectable, and the Russian people admirable.

This enthusiasm, however, did not survive the victory of 1945. The Grand Alliance broke down, not only over the future boundaries and government of Poland, or the future fate of Germany; it broke down above all because it had never been a real alliance at all, since it had been built over a cultural and ideological abyss. Soviet Russia was no longer just another European power, as she had been in 1813–1815 or 1914. She was in truth a "new civilization," as the Webbs had thought, though not in the sense they believed, an ideocratic power for which "democracy," "peace-loving nation," and all the other common slogans of the war meant something radically different from what they meant in the West.

The contrast with old Russia was stark indeed. Under the imperial regime, Russian armies had been twice in Berlin and once in Paris, while Marshal Suvorov under Paul I had campaigned in Italy, Switzerland, and Holland. And none of this had occasioned panic, whether from Thomas Jefferson, the duke of Wellington, or Prince Metternich. But the arrival in 1945 of Soviet armies in Berlin, Prague, and Vienna produced the most profound fear throughout the West—not because those armies were Russian, but because they were Soviet and hence threatened to introduce a Communist order. Thus the war ended, not with a general peace treaty, but with a Polish settlement and a partition of Germany essentially imposed by Stalin. Alexander I, by contrast, had negotiated his acquisition of a Polish kingdom with the other members of the European Concert assembled at Vienna so as to ensure an even equilibrium of power from the Atlantic to the Urals.

It is indeed a striking fact that the Soviet Union to the end of its existence never signed a peace treaty with its chief adversary or its major allies in the Second World War, not unlike the custom of Suleiman the Magnificent in dealing with the West of his day. The nearest Europe ever came to a general settlement after the Second World War was the ambiguous Helsinki Accords of 1976—thirty years after the end of hostilities. The postwar structure of the European state system was not regularized until the reunification of Germany and the creation of the Conference on Security and Cooperation in Europe in 1990—and at that, with a post-Soviet Russian government.

TAILS, THE EMPIRE: 1945–1991

But for the Western student of the Soviet Union, at any rate, this [book] should have the same interest that a fish would have for an ichthyologist if it suddenly began to talk.

—Andrei Amalrik,
Will the Soviet Union Survive until 1984 (1970)

Rosy-fingered Eos, so often mentioned by Homer and called by the Romans Aurora, caressed with those fingers the first early morning of the Archipelago . . . the Archipelago was born under the fire of the cruiser *Aurora*.

The imagination and inner strength of Shakespeare's villains stopped short at ten or so cadavers. Because they had no ideology . . . It is thanks to ideology that it fell to the lot of the twentieth century to experience villainy on a scale of millions.

—Aleksandr Solzhenitsyn,
The Gulag Archipelago (1974)

It's incredible to me that after fifty years of Soviet power, paradise would have to be kept under lock and key.

We communists believe that capitalism is a hell in which laboring people are condemned to slavery. We are building Socialism. We have already been successful in many respects, and we will be even more successful in the future. Our life is undoubtedly the most progressive in the world at the present state of humanity's development. To use the language of the Bible again, our way of life is paradise for mankind.

—Nikita Khrushchev,
Khrushchev Remembers (1970)

What is Communism?
The radiant horizon of humanity.
What is the horizon?
An imaginary line that recedes the nearer one
    thinks he is getting to it.

—Classic Soviet joke

Over the entrance to the crematorium Jabberwocky read the words from the speech of the Sultanscrew pronounced on the occasion of the adoption of the Law of Death: Remember, No One, But No One Has Forced You To This! He did not know that over the exit of the oven were engraved the words from the last point of the Regulation on Death: When Leaving, Do Not Forget To Take Your Urn With You!

—Aleksandr Zinoviev, *The Yawning Heights* (1976)

With the victory of 1945 the Soviet experiment had ended in empire, and the voyage of the troika had indeed led to the opening of a new historical era. The prophecy of Tocqueville had at last come true regarding Russia and America: though "their starting point is different, and their courses are not the same, yet each seems marked out by the will of heaven to sway the destinies of half the globe." By the same

358

token, that "sixth part of the terrestrial orb," as Stalin designated the Soviet Union, had been given a new meaning; for (as Chaadaev had put it) Russia was now literally "leaning with one elbow on Germany and the other on China."

In other words, the political collapse of Europe, begun in 1914, was consummated with the partition of 1945. In 1914 the frontier of Europe had stood at the Urals, after 1917 it passed close by the Carpathians, and after 1945 it ran at the Elbe. There now existed only a rump Europe; and she was in truth what Paul Valéry had called her in prouder days, in awe at the contrast between her diminutive size and the miracle of her creativity: "that little cape on the continent of Asia."[86]

By 1945 the correlation of international forces that had existed in the world in 1939 had been completely overturned. The three late-starting powers of the class of 1870 in their joint drive for *Weltmacht* as the Axis had so fatally overreached themselves that they were eliminated from great-power competition. Henceforth they could function internationally only as allies, indeed, protectorates of the United States. Britain and France were able to play a while longer at grand-power politics, as at Suez in 1956, but increasingly they too had to align their policies on those of America. The United States, which had not been a significant international player before 1939, was suddenly elevated to the status of superpower.

The other great outsider of the prewar world, Soviet Russia, was simultaneously catapulted to the same rank, for the elimination of the Axis made her the preponderant force throughout Eurasia. In Europe her internal empire that was the "Union" was now augmented by an external empire of "People's Democracies" extending from the Baltic to the Adriatic. In Asia the collapse of Japan gave this empire the gift of a then "fraternal" Chinese Revolution, a Communist half-Korea, and a promising Communist insurrection in Indochina. All told, Stalin's gains in a decade were greater than those accumulated by Peter, Catherine, and Alexander I in over a century.

The Second World War thus brought the end of the multistate concert of Europe that had existed from the failure of the Habsburgs' attempt at world empire in the sixteenth century to the suicidal conflicts of the twentieth. In the place of the classic Eurocentric international system of five or six great powers, there now existed a bipolar world system in which the two foci lay outside the historic heartland of the West.

In this reordering of international affairs America hardly posed a problem for the West's identity, since she shared the same cultural and institutional heritage as her European allies. But the Soviet Union had come into being precisely to supersede that heritage, and the new division of the planet automatically entailed her exclusion from the West. Peter's window onto Europe was henceforth sealed up behind an Iron Curtain.

The new bipolar international system, therefore, was in no sense a "concert" of the world. Despite the attempt to create such an order with the founding of the United Nations, it soon became clear that the new global dispensation was a stark rivalry. The great question of the next forty-five years would be: was it a rivalry to the death, or could the interests of the two contestants be peacefully accommodated until they might someday cease to be conflicting? And so, by 1947, when the Truman Doctrine first enunciated the policy of containment to stop any further Soviet expansion, the fleeting peace of 1945 had given way to an unprecedented form of conflict, the Cold War. By the end of the decade, when the Soviets unexpectedly detonated an atomic bomb, it became apparent that this conflict had the potential of ending in Armageddon—a circumstance which meant that the conflict could never be permitted to become a "normal" war, since if it did both sides would lose.

The Cold War

The Cold War thus became the Third World War that never took place. But it was a real world war all the same, with stakes as high as in its two predecessors. Since this war could not be waged in actual battles, it was fought through endless logistical preparations for these nonbattles—the increasing refinement of nuclear and conventional weapons, the building of permanent alliances within each bloc, and rival programs of economic aid to Third World clients. Even more of a novelty, this contest was not about tangible national interests. Russia and America certainly had no conflicting territorial or economic interests; and

Russia and the states of Western Europe, once partition of the continent had given Moscow an ample security glacis, were in a similar relationship.

The source of the conflict, rather, was ideological or, in Moscow's terminology, "the international class struggle between the two social systems." Indeed, the Cold War is *the* great example in modern history of the power of "irrational," cultural forces in international affairs. In this context, what would otherwise have been a reasonable security alliance of East European states with the Soviet Union also meant adopting a Communist "social system." In this respect the Cold War continued the prewar anomaly of Soviet Russia's dual nature as both a sovereign state and the leader of an international revolutionary movement, an anomaly magnified many times over by the Soviet Union's new status as a superpower.

Before 1939, despite much inflammatory rhetoric from Moscow and echoing apprehension in the West, this international movement had never posed a serious threat to the existing world order; living with it had caused the powers minimal anxiety. After 1945, however, though the active revolution was over within Russia, its projection abroad at last became a political force which nobody could ignore. The internationalization of revolution was, of course, basically the product of the havoc wrought by the war. But the resulting radical surge was intensified since it was now sponsored by a superpower. And this superpower, in turn, was rendered all the more powerful because it had such an international radical movement at its disposal. Under this combination of circumstances—geopolitical, military-technological, ideological—the Cold War, widening the social and cultural abyss created in 1917, transformed the old debate about Russia and the West into a radically new kind of problem.

Concretely, the initial issues in the Cold War were the future of Germany in the West and that of China and its neighbors in the East. The conflict between the two blocs went through three phases and, broadly speaking, produced a Western victory in Germany and a Communist victory in the East.[87]

Stalin's last years marked the first and most acute phase of conflict. In Europe, tension mounted dangerously up to the Soviet blockade of

Berlin and the answering Allied airlift in 1948–49; it was resolved only with the partition of Germany through the creation of two separate German states and the foundation of the North Atlantic Treaty Organization (NATO) in 1950. In Asia, though Stalin had expected that his Chinese allies would conquer no more than half the country, the Revolution of 1949 gave them the whole thing, thereby creating a contiguous Communist empire from the Elbe to the Yellow Sea. The following year, as this bloc attempted to round out its frontiers in Korea, the Communist and Western worlds at last came to an open clash.

The second phase was marked by Khrushchev's retreat from such stark confrontation to "peaceful coexistence," which meant not peace *tout court* but pursuit of Communism's victory by nonviolent means. Tension remained high, and nuclear and ballistic competition now began in earnest. At the same time the Soviet Union, although it at last accepted Western predominance in Germany as definitive, for the first time penetrated the Third World to pick up what it could of the debris of abandoned European empires. These overseas adventures eventually produced the most dangerous confrontation of the entire Cold War, the Cuban missile crisis of 1962.

The resulting fright inaugurated a third phase of East-West relations called détente. Begun under Leonid Brezhnev, for some in the West it meant a serious attempt at accommodation, even convergence, between the two blocs, while for others it signified simply controlled conflict. This effort lasted until 1980, when it too collapsed over Soviet intervention in Afghanistan and the repression of Solidarity in Poland.

Kaleidoscopic Vision

It was in the context of these three phases of conflict that after 1945 the four old Western images of Russia returned for the second time since 1917, in a renewed effort to find an answer to what was now a planetary enigma. The first step in this process was for the West to adjust to its own altered internal configuration.

After 1945 the West's center of gravity had crossed the Atlantic to the United States; and this Yankee parvenu, gorged with wealth and reeking of success, suddenly became the economic, military, and even

362

cultural sheet anchor of the "free world." As Stalin sought to expand his East European glacis into Germany, the United States answered with a vast program of economic reconstruction under the Marshall Plan of 1948–1952, and ultimately with the military alliance of NATO in 1950, to which the German Federal Republic was admitted in 1953. The European populations on the whole were relieved that the Americans were there and the Russians were not. Even so, old Europe, hitherto the only part of the world that really counted, was understandably uneasy about the fact itself of dependence.

The rump West of partitioned Europe reacted to this unprecedented situation in two ways. The first was to seek a new form of independence vis-à-vis the United States, as well as of security in the face of the Soviet empire, precisely by building "Europe" through some kind of supra-national organization. This began in the economic sphere in 1951 with the "pooling" of the French and German coal and steel industries; by 1959 it had become a Common Market of the six core continental countries; in 1973 it incorporated Britain, and eventually it become the European Union. Overall it turned out to be one of the great economic success stories of the century, though it cannot be claimed that it fundamentally altered Western Europe's need of a close American alliance.

The second reaction to Europe's changed world status was the emergence in many quarters of an ardent anti-Americanism. This current held that it was capitalist America, not Communist Russia, that presented the real threat to European independence, social progress, and international peace. These attitudes clearly existed on the Left, especially among intellectuals, who after 1945 transferred from Germany to the United States the dishonor of being the world center of imperialism and racism, and who saw in Senator Joseph McCarthy the herald of the coming American fascism. But anti-Americanism also existed on the Right, as in Gaullism after 1958, which saw in American leadership a threat to European independence and in the Soviet Union simply a new mutation of traditional Russian nationalism. It was therefore just another state with which one could engage in the classical play of power politics, balancing its weight against that of the United States to recreate a *Europe des patries*, extending "from the Atlantic to the Urals." On many occasions Right and Left, nationalism and progressivism, could unite in a common hostility to the encroachments of the "American empire," with its tentacular multinationals, its stealthy Central Intelligence Agency, its hegemonic NATO "leadership," and its barbaric popular culture.

If the defects of America were visible for all to see, it was far more difficult to assess the nature of its Eastern rival, to which, if only by default, those suspicious of America were obliged to turn. After the war, Stalin's Russia had become a land whose bourn no traveler now visited and from which no traveler returned. The West thus was soon in a state of fractious division about the meaning of the Eastern superpower. In Europe, a large minority, nurtured in the antifascist Resistance, continued the prewar Sovietophilia of the republic of letters. In America, a clear majority repudiated the naïveté of Ambassador Davies and Vice President Henry Wallace in favor of mobilization against the looming spectre behind the Iron Curtain. As the Communists were expelled from the postwar resistance governments in Paris and Rome in 1947, and as they took over the whole government in Prague in 1948, the Western Left and Center of the wartime popular front divided in a domestic cold war.

This intra-Western conflict, however, developed quite differently in the United States and in Europe. In America, beginning with the fiasco of Henry Wallace's presidential campaign in 1948 and the Alger Hiss affair, the far Left was largely suppressed under the pressure of such figures as J. Edgar Hoover and Senator Joseph McCarthy. Known leftists did not get jobs in American universities or in Hollywood, and labor unions were purged of their reds by such former Communist sympathizers as Walter Reuther of the United Automobile Workers and onetime New Deal Democrat Ronald Reagan.

American "exceptionalism" (a term created by baffled Communist leaders) had always refused political legitimacy to the European idea of socialism; and the same was true a fortiori of Communism. The reason for this anomaly, as we have seen, was that America had never known an Old Regime. Thus in America the habitual rallying cry of radicals has not been equality, but liberty; and all political movements have had to invoke its name to secure a hearing. Amid the twentieth-century surge of social concern this heritage produced a notable deformation of the

American political vocabulary: reforming New Deal intellectuals, who in Europe would have been Social Democrats, called themselves liberals; hard-left socialists and Communists therefore became mere radicals; and in reaction to this leftward shift of traditional national terms, the New Deal's opponents, who in Europe would have been called liberals, were now labeled conservatives. Moreover, since no one could be an avowed Communist and survive politically, radicals of that extreme persuasion had to work clandestinely within other "progressive" organizations. Thus Communism in America invariably connoted subversion; and once it had been rooted out of the labor movement, it was largely confined to intellectual circles oriented toward European cultural modernism.

In Europe, by contrast, not only did socialism have long-standing legitimacy, but Communism, though hardly regarded as just another political force, was quite up front politically; indeed in many progressive quarters allegiance to it was worn as a badge of honor. Hence the postwar ideological battle in Europe was much closer and more protracted than in America. This battle, moreover, took place in a West that was for the first time open to the Hegelian-Marxist tradition. Although Marx was indeed one of the seminal thinkers of the nineteenth century, outside Central and Eastern Europe most people were not aware of this fact until the next century. Only after 1917, indeed only in the 1930s, did Marx and with him Hegel really become assimilated by the intelligentsia west of the Rhine. Such figures as the American socialist philosopher and pragmatist Sidney Hook, and Alexandre Kojève, a Russian émigré who had become a French banker, explained to the heirs of mere positivist *lumières* the mysteries of the dialectical path from Hegel to Marx.[88] At the same time, the works of Trotsky and Stalin familiarized Westerners with the political world of the Russian Revolution. It was in this Germano-Russianized ideological culture, which purported to establish an organic link between reason and revolution, that the Western Left and Right squared off for battle.

Yet the central postwar issue was by no means abstruse: it was concretely the question of terror and concentration camps. The last year of the war had for the first time revealed its supreme barbarism, the Nazi extermination camps. At the same time, rumors began to filter through from the East that terror certainly, and camps probably, existed also in the Russia of Stalingrad. At first these doubts were expressed only in imaginative literature. In 1945 George Orwell, disillusioned by his experiences with Communists in Spain, published the antiutopian novel *Animal Farm*.[89] In the same year, the still more sensational *Darkness at Noon* (which had languished in relative obscurity since 1940), by the Hungarian-German and former Communist Arthur Koestler became an international best-seller; it probed the mystery of the purge trials by presenting a fictional Bukharin interpreted in a Dostoevskyan mode that exactly suited the anxious mood of the moment.[90] And this book, together with Orwell's devastating *1984*, published in 1949, began to turn the tide of Left-Center opinion against the Soviet Union.[91]

But this was still merely fiction, not hard evidence. The latter came in 1946 with Victor Kravchenko's *I Chose Freedom*, the first major work by a Soviet defector.[92] His motives were immediately impugned when it was suggested that this cosmopolitan diplomat, stationed in Washington, merely wished to get rich by furnishing propaganda for the Cold War. Indeed, *Les Lettres françaises* (the cultural review of the French Communist Party edited by Louis Aragon) published an alleged admission by an alleged American that the Office of Strategic Services had forged Kravchenko's book. Kravchenko then sued the periodical for libel, and in 1949 a grand judicial spectacle opened in Paris. The Communist defense flew in Kravchenko's ex-wife and various high Soviet officials from Moscow (and into the bargain brought the "red dean" from Canterbury) to testify to the villainy of the renegade and the admirable freedom prevailing in Russia. In rebuttal Kravchenko's lawyer, a Resistance hero and socialist, produced witnesses who had been in Soviet camps, most notably Mme. Margarete Buber-Neumann, a German Communist leader sent to Siberia by Stalin in 1937, then turned over by him to Hitler after 1939 to spend the war in Ravensbruck. Kravchenko won his case hands down, and the non-Communist press agreed with the verdict.[93] All the same, he largely lost his reputation for he had dared besmirch the land of Stalingrad, and the resulting harassment was such that he eventually took his life.

But the case against Stalin soon rested on much more than the testi-

366   mony of one man. After Stalin released his Polish prisoners in 1941–42, many of them made their way abroad; among them, Jerzy Gliksman was the first to publish, in 1948, his experiences under the title *Tell the West*.[94] On the basis of these and similar materials, in 1947 the old Mensheviks David Dallin and Boris Nicolaevsky produced an extended analysis of the Soviet camp system.[95] In 1949, the British Labor Member of Parliament Richard Crossman published a collection of autobiographical accounts by European intellectual celebrities such as Gide and Ignazio Silone who now saw Communism as *The God that Failed*.[96] These efforts to counter Communism's allure in the West culminated in 1950 with the formation of the Congress for Cultural Freedom, under the leadership of such liberal-to-Left intellectuals as Koestler, Raymond Aron, and David Rousset, an organization which published the periodicals *Encounter*, *Preuves*, and *Der Monat*. This organization was later discovered, in 1967, to have received financing from the U.S. Central Intelligence Agency, a circumstance which led other liberal-to-Left intellectuals to view the whole enterprise as "tainted."[97] Such, however, was the occupational hazard of opposing Communism from a "progressive" position; for what often counts in such a contest is less the substance of what one says than the associates one acquires in saying it.

Thus, the mounting evidence that the Soviet Union had some dark secrets to hide by no means brought unanimity in the West or closed the debate. Rather, Western opinion divided three ways. A majority, overwhelming in the United States and somewhat smaller in Europe, believed the new facts and turned resolutely against Soviet Russia. A minority of perhaps a quarter of the population in France and Italy and a smaller, though highly influential, group in England denied the facts were facts and continued to hold that Soviet Russia was more prosperous and democratic than the West. This mass hallucination fed on the conviction that the facts were simply calumnies fabricated by the "lubricous vipers" of warmongering imperialism. A third group admitted that the facts might be true, or at least partially so, but maintained it was reprehensible to say this publicly, claiming undue candor only played into the hands of American imperialism. And that great moral conscience of the postwar era, Jean-Paul Sartre, even advocated lying about the matter, in order not to throw the workers of the Billancourt into despair—"pour ne pas désespérer Billancourt."[98] When his existentialist colleague Albert Camus replied that the truth was the truth and that perhaps the despair of the poor Scythians should also be taken into account, he was excommunicated from the company of progressive men. The philosopher and sociologist Raymond Aron entered the lists against this upside-down view of the world in 1955 with *The Opium of the Intellectuals.*[99] For this heartless appeal to reason, his old classmate and colleague on *Les Temps modernes*, Sartre, refused to speak to him for twenty-five years. Of course, in the interval Sartre came to acknowledge some of the facts about Russia and regularly signed petitions in favor of Soviet dissidents. He could make this about-face with an unperturbed conscience, since during that same interval he discovered that true socialism had moved on, first to Cuba and then to China.[100]

Yet after 1945 Soviet Russia's image was no longer formed predominantly by philosophers and writers of the republic of letters. This task was gradually taken over by humbler commentators laboring in the cloisters of academe. These researchers knew the Russian language, in addition to one or another scholarly discipline. They were, moreover, largely trained by émigré Russian scholars who could tell a *kliukva* when they saw one, men such as the economists Wassily Leontief and Alexander Gerschenkron, the historians George Vernadsky and Michael Karpovich, and the linguist-critic Roman Jakobson and the literary historian Gleb Struve. Though most of the younger researchers had never been to Russia, they could regularly consult with such figures as Boris Nicolaevsky in New York, Isaiah Berlin at Oxford, or Boris Souvarine in Paris. At long last the old diaspora of Russian civil society in exile was able to make a capital contribution to the stammering West's understanding of the new Russia. The result, by the mid-1960s, was that for the first time since October the West possessed a corpus of reasonably informed literature on Soviet Russia, which could plausibly be compared to the pre-1917 achievements of Mackenzie Wallace and Anatole Leroy-Beaulieu. Soon the fruits of this effort began to filter through to the broader press and the media.

Still, this empirical enterprise required some overarching mode of explanation. And it so happened that the Soviet superpower's emergence on the world scene coincided with the breakthrough of systematic social science in Western academic culture. The results of the seminal social thinkers of the nineteenth and early twentieth centuries, fairly isolated figures in their time, were now drawn together in various combinations to produce what was intended to be a comprehensive science of society comparable in rigor to the natural sciences. In America, Talcott Parsons had already synthesized Émile Durkheim with Max Weber, and others soon brought Marx, Freud, and Tocqueville into the mix. Within a decade, these new approaches were exported back to the countries of the great founders. Thus, in the postwar years the social sciences staked out their claim to be the third great area of human inquiry, alongside the humanities and the exact or natural sciences. In this new social-science culture the nascent investigation of Soviet Russia had to find its niche.

It did so first with the concept of totalitarianism.[101] The term "totalitarian," it will be recalled, was created by Mussolini in the 1920s and was used in a positive sense to designate the restructuring of society as an organic, corporate, or "total" whole. The term was given a negative meaning in Germany in the early 1930s by opponents of Nazism, and in the second half of the decade was carried abroad, especially to the United States, by refugees from Hitler, such as the philosophers of the Hegelo-Marxo-Freudian Frankfurt School. This migration produced the noun "totalitarianism" as a generic concept to designate the revolutionary tyrannies of the twentieth century, so much more ruthless and thorough than all those of the past.

At the same time, in Russia the consolidation of Stalin's order made it difficult to fit the Soviet Union into the traditional categories of Left and Right; so Trotsky took to calling his rival's regime "totalitarian." Still, throughout the late 1930s the more pressing danger of Nazism prevented the unqualified extension of Mussolini's term to Russia by men of good will. The Nazi-Soviet Nonaggression Pact of 1939, however, at last broke the spell, and in 1940 a symposium of the American Philosophical Society for the first time put all three "dictatorships" into the same "totalitarian" basket.[102] The Grand Alliance of the war years temporarily put such comparisons out of bounds, at least in public discourse, but the cold peace of 1945 quickly restored them to prominence in all liberal and many socialist quarters of the West.

With Hitler gone, Stalin's Russia became the archtotalitarian society for most of the Atlantic world. Even in this new situation, however, the social-science notion of totalitarianism as an historically unique form of politics continued to be based on the perceived equivalence of the Nazi and Communist regimes. The process of elaborating a concept common to the two began with Hannah Arendt's philosophical and humanistic investigation of the problem in her *Origins of Totalitarianism* of 1951.[103] The new concept became a formal "model" at the hands of Carl J. Friedrich and Zbigniew Brzezinski in 1953, who defined totalitarianism's essence in six points: (1) an elaborate ideology, (2) a single mass party, (3) terror, (4) a technologically conditioned monopoly of communication, (5) a monopoly of weapons, and (6) a centrally controlled economy.[104] Soviet Russia consequently came to be analyzed essentially in terms of a "permanent purge" in the service of the "Leviathan-state's" drive to "maximize power."[105]

The defining characteristic of the totalitarian model thus is to view its subject in political and ideological terms. It has often been pointed out that this approach oversimplifies matters, since social and economic forces are eclipsed behind the monolith of state power. It is less often noted that in the abstract totalitarian model, ideologies, though recognized as a governing factor, are not distinguished one from another but are given a common functional role in the system: thus Communism and Nazism serve equally to justify terror and purges. Indeed, both the strengths and the limitations of the totalitarian model represent a classical liberal view of the primacy of politics in explaining how the world works. For to the liberal the distinguishing characteristic of any society is whether it is "free" or "despotic," while only secondary attention is devoted to the social setting and ideological thrust of the politics in question. And what appeared most alien to the liberal West after 1945 was precisely the "total" organization of political power in the regimes of both its late enemy and its recent ally.

The totalitarian model is thus the intellectual reaction of a threatened liberal world to the resurgence of autocratic power in an age when, according to all liberal notions of progress, such power ought to have been a thing of the barbaric past. To the partisans of liberal individualism, the inner workings of such a power have always appeared alien; but they come to appear demonic when liberal society is too weak to afford the luxury of probing the historical forces behind the political forms in its adversaries' camp. In circumstances of imminent danger, the endeavor to understand all leads dangerously near to excusing too much, and Olympian detachment ill fitted the mood prevailing in the remnants of the liberal world during the period of its greatest insecurity, from the rise of Hitler in 1933 to the death of Stalin in 1953. Under these circumstances all liberalism's adversaries were conflated into a single antithesis: totalitarian dictatorship. What began as an effort to account for the wartime danger of Mussolini and Hitler was also used to account for the postwar danger of Stalin.

By 1950, therefore, the truncated West of NATO had in effect revived, in highly magnified form, the early nineteenth-century image of Russia as an Oriental despotism. Belief in Russia as an enlightened despotism, so frequent in the 1930s and during the war, did not entirely disappear; but it was increasingly confined to the intellectual hard Left. The insecure Atlantic fringe of the "free world" displayed a combination of fear and bafflement in the face of Stalin's empire, now installed in the heart of the continent, similar to that of the "maritime powers" before the Cossacks of Nicholas I in Poland and Hungary. Soon, however, not even the totalitarian model sufficed to account for the Stalinist phenomenon, for in his last years the rule of the surviving major dictator became increasingly incomprehensible and Oriental.

After the devastations of the war, Stalin had to consolidate and tighten the Soviet internal order for a second time. All contacts with the West were severed and independent thought was stifled as Stalin's cultural commissar, Andrei Zhdanov, attacked the poet Anna Akhmatova and the satirist Mikhail Zoshchenko. To the nationalism bred of the war the regime added anti-Semitism through a campaign against "rootless cosmopolitans" and Zionists "in the service of American imperialism." Moscow alleged further that one or another homespun Popov had pioneered everything from the radio to atomic fission. After Tito's defection in 1948, the new "People's Democracies" were subordinated to the Kremlin in public purges reminiscent of the Moscow trials of the 1930s. Sergei Eisenstein was commissioned to make a film on Ivan the Terrible, which was in fact a glorification of Stalin's terror. To complete this picture, the Leader, as "universal genius" and "coryphaeus of all the arts and sciences," acted as the arbiter of linguistic theory in a controversy over the work of Nikolai Marr, just as he had earlier decided against Mendelian biology in the Lysenko affair. And Western Communist intellectuals had to defend these condemnations to their amazed colleagues. Contemplating this weird spectacle, foreigners were at least as baffled as they were alarmed; the prevailing opinion was now best expressed by the resurrection of Churchill's verdict, at the time of the 1939 pact, that Soviet Russia was "a riddle, wrapped in a mystery, inside an enigma."

Even the powers of the new social science would not suffice to penetrate this mystery, and so some commentators turned to more intuitive modes of explanation. Weapons were drawn from history to explain Stalinism as a resurgence, with a twentieth-century technological apparatus, of eternal Russia's character as an Asiatic despotism. To illustrate this thesis, the first choice of a precursor was, of course, Nicholas I. By 1951, the old best-seller of Custine was back in print, doing almost as well as the first time around. As Ambassador George Kennan later observed, so great were the marquis's powers of imagination that, "although it is a bad book about the Russia of Nicholas I, it is an excellent one about the Russia of Stalin."[106] In a similar vein, by 1952 the authority of Marx and Engels was invoked with ironic emphasis by reprinting their Russophobic articles under the title *The Russian Menace to Europe*.[107] Although Lord Palmerston's name had long been rehabilitated, equally highly placed personages, now on the banks of the Potomac rather than the Thames, came under similar suspicion in the more panicky circles of the West.

Yet even the heritage of Nicholas would not suffice to explain the new Russian menace. The tradition of Ivan the Terrible and of Tartary were therefore invoked as in the days of the young Marx and Fallmerayer; and of course Philotheus of Pskov and the theory of the Third Rome were rediscovered as the source of Russia's imperial messianism.

But from the Third Rome it was only a step to the Second and the Sacred Palace of Byzantium, the *fons et origo* of Eastern despotism, in which the Caesaro-papism of Orthodoxy devolved from Constantine to the Communist autocracy of Stalin.[108]

As if this appeal to history were not enough, metahistory was called upon to supplement it. Although Oswald Spengler was now in eclipse because of his semiassociation with Nazism, the more respectable Arnold Toynbee could be quoted to defend the thesis that Russian civilization was a distinct historical species, quite unrelated to the West.[109] And Russian literature was mined to argue the same organic difference: a favorite illustration was Gogol's troika hurtling with primitive force over the limitless steppes and "bidding all the nations and peoples to step aside and make way for its path." The roots of Bolshevism were found in Russia's warped national psychology as portrayed by Dostoevsky's Ivan Karamazov and his Grand Inquisitor, and the key to the purge trials was discovered in his novel *The Possessed*.

These explanations seemed all the more compelling since they could be found in analyses of Communism made by Russian thinkers themselves. Thus the old émigré Berdiaev gained a new popularity by expounding, in a mixture of Dostoevsky and Merezhkovskii, the sublime satanism of Bolshevism in *The Origin of Russian Communism* and *The Russian Idea*.[110] Berdiaev, a former Marxist who had converted to philosophical intuitionism combined with religious nationalism, held that the soul of Holy Russia was innately religious, but that once this spiritual essence had been perverted by Western rationalism, it became demonic. Yet in either its positive or its negative guises Russian soulfulness was superior to the shallowness of the West. Russia, at least, did nothing half-way, whether good or evil. The fall of Russia in 1917 was thus the paradigm of the fall of modern man; and the demonism of Bolshevism, paradoxically, was therefore the proof of Russia's higher spirituality. Berdiaev's message took hold in Western circles where the war had induced a pessimism about the human condition similar to that expressed after the previous war in T. S. Eliot's *Wasteland*. So it was that the perception of Stalinism as the return of Oriental despotism shaded off into a metaphysical vision of Communism as upside-down Russian soul, the realm of cosmic demonism.

As in the years after 1830, these reactions had mixed causes with varying degrees of rationality. The Soviet Union's military power on the continent after 1945 and her increasingly clear determination to transform the states of Eastern Europe into satellites furnished real reasons for alarm. This alarm was enormously increased when a Communist revolution triumphed in China in 1949. For that event, though not directly promoted by Russia, seemed to create a monolithic red bloc extending from the Elbe to the Yellow Sea, thereby forming the world's largest land empire since Genghis Khan had ruled over the same Eurasian mass. The West's anxiety about Communist expansion was brought to a climax when in 1950 Stalin sought to round out his gains through the Korean War. Even if one makes allowance for the fact that Soviet policy in these years was less premeditated and coherent than it appeared at the time, the ceaseless expansion of Communist power between 1945 and 1950 could only have provoked the deepest fear in the West.[111]

Fear would not have been half so great, however, had not the liberal West itself been in grave internal crisis during the same period. In the years of postwar reconstruction, when the continent's economy was in shambles and social discontent was rife, Communism appeared to stand a real chance of seizing power in what survived of liberal Europe. In 1947 and 1948 France and Italy were convulsed by quasi-insurrectional strikes, and a Communist revolt broke out in Greece. To many observers, it seemed that a Stalinist solution was possible in the very heartland of the liberal world, and that the historic West might well be submerged by "Asia."

Khrushchev's Thaw

In 1953, however, "The Great Khan died," in Churchill's phrase, and the situation in both Soviet Russia and the West began to change. Indeed, by middecade it seemed to resemble, *mutatis mutandis*, what it had been just a century before, when in Russia the iron regime of Nicholas I gave way to the reforming rule of Alexander II, while in the West industrial society was beginning its great era of Victorian prosperity and stability. Commentators immediately drew this parallel.

The prolonged crisis of liberal society that had begun with the Great

Depression and the rise of Hitler in the 1930s came to an end sometime after 1950. The Marshall Plan and Keynesian economics soon gave Europe a constantly expanding economy, and on this basis generous national systems of social security were instituted everywhere west of the Elbe. This neoliberal order, in contrast to the economic and political turbulence of the interwar years, proved to be remarkably stable. Indeed, the "Atlantic world," as the West was now called, embarked on the most prodigious economic expansion in history, a boom which continued without major slowdown until the "oil shock" of 1973. This great prosperity, and the consequent rise in living standards for all categories of the population, finally restored the self-confidence of the postwar West, which now organized itself into the North Atlantic Treaty Organization. As had been the case after 1856, therefore, growing confidence in its own destiny diminished the West's fear of Russia and her Warsaw Pact of conscript "fraternal" socialisms.

In a quite different way, the transformation of the 1950s was equally dramatic on the Soviet side. After Stalin's death, Russia appeared to have discovered a Soviet Alexander II in his successor, Nikita Khrushchev. The new government immediately mitigated the terrors of the regime by diminishing the power of the political police and liquidating its chief, Lavrentii Beria. Most of the Siberian labor camps were closed and their surviving inmates "rehabilitated" and returned home. In taking these bold steps, Khrushchev and his colleagues wished, first of all, to ensure that no new Stalin would emerge to direct terror inward against the Party, for this was clearly the aspect of the late Leader's rule that scandalized them most. But they also believed that terror was economically inefficient and socially wasteful; by abating it, they hoped to spur growth so as to shift the global "correlation of forces" against the capitalist West.[112]

For a time it seemed to the West that they might well succeed. By the end of the 1950s there was a "Khrushchev boom": industrial growth rates shot up, the standard of living of the population began to improve for the first time since the NEP, and even the perennial sick man of socialism, Soviet agriculture, seemed to develop through such crash programs as the opening of the "virgin lands" of Central Asia and the introduction of corn fodder from Iowa. In response, the most serious

Western newspapers, such as the *New York Times*, and even more *Le Monde*, opined that Khrushchev's goal of advancing Russia, already the world's second industrial power (or so they believed), to the rank of the first by 1981 was a feasible enterprise.

This impression of socialist success was dramatized even to the simplest Western citizens by Soviet prowess in weaponry and space. As early as 1949 Moscow unexpectedly ended the American monopoly on nuclear arms by exploding its first atom bomb; and in 1953 it closed the gap with the United States a second time by moving up to the hydrogen category. That all this was linked to major ballistic missile capacity was demonstrated in spectacular fashion in 1957, when Russia launched, ahead of the Americans, the world's first satellite, or "sputnik." This succession of feats was capped by the voyage into outer space of the planet's first cosmonaut, Yurii Gagarin, in 1961. By that date, the Atlantic world no longer needed convincing that a highly competitive economic system and technological capacity existed behind the facade of the totalitarian state. The West took the deepest alarm: America upgraded its schools' mathematical curriculum to meet this new and subtler type of Soviet menace; and President John Kennedy mobilized the nation's resources to be first to put a man on the moon, for fear that if the Soviets conquered the empire of the air, they might also win the empire of Earth.

The impression of a new Russia was reinforced after 1955 by sharp changes in her international posture. Stalin had nominally abolished the Comintern in 1943 to mollify his wartime allies, but he reinstated it under the name of Cominform in 1946 in order to wage the Cold War. Khrushchev abolished this new body in 1954, in part to win back such dissidents as Yugoslavia's Tito but also to improve Russia's overall international position. Soon the various Communist parties acquired a new type of independence from Moscow that the Italian leader Palmiro Togliatti baptized "polycentrism." Finally, with the Chinese schism of 1961, the monolithic world Communism of Stalin's day came to an end—although most Western observers did not grasp this fact until American intervention in Vietnam was well under way.

What is more, Khrushchev moderated the militant stance that had produced the Berlin blockade of 1948–49 and the Korean War of 1950–

1953, and indeed proclaimed a policy of "peaceful coexistence." This of course did not mean renouncing the goal of ultimate socialist victory over capitalism, since Khrushchev firmly believed that history was inevitably working to that end. His conviction was manifested in the boast "We'll bury you," which sounded so sinister to his American hosts in 1959. For as a true-believing Marxist-Leninist, Khrushchev was confident that socialism was inherently more efficient than capitalism, and hence that Russia could afford to abandon Stalin's truculence for a policy of waiting out the West. The concrete meaning of peaceful coexistence thus was that henceforth Communism's victory would be pursued not by military means but through economic and ideological competition, or at the most through "wars of national liberation" and guerilla insurgency, as in the case of Vietnam. So the Cold War melted down a bit, at the same time as an internal thaw came to Russia. Confrontation was mitigated by summitry between the heads of state, beginning at Geneva in 1955.

Other major changes followed rapidly. After the Geneva summit, the Iron Curtain was partially raised. Correspondents returned to Moscow in large numbers, as did even a few men of letters like the American Communist Howard Fast and the sempiternal Louis Aragon. In their wake came junior statesmen, such as Vice President Nixon (who famously debated Khrushchev in the kitchen of an American exchange exhibit), and statesmen in their prime, such as Chancellor Konrad Adenauer, Prime Minister Harold Wilson, and President de Gaulle, and then, at the end of the decade, President Nixon. In addition, student and scientific exchanges were established with Western universities, while tourism became a regular business. Simultaneously, there was movement in the opposite direction. Soviet delegations traveled abroad, and Russian culture was exported via the tours of the Bolshoi Ballet and the successful poetry readings of such mildly "oppositional" figures as Evgenii Evtushenko and Andrei Voznesenskii.

So dramatic was the contrast between this movement and the stagnation of Stalin's time that by the early 1960s much of the Western public had concluded, like MacKenzie Wallace in the 1870s, that the Russians, even under Communism, "are human beings like ourselves." Nor did the all-too-human Khrushchev himself, disquieting as his rocket rattling often was, seem the nightmarish figure his predecessor had been. For he traveled widely abroad, "living it up" (as he once said to his retinue of journalists) all over the Western world, thumping with his shoe on the desk of the United Nations and crashing the gates of President Eisenhower's White House—though the line was drawn at letting him into Disneyland.

But Khrushchev did one more supremely important thing, for Soviet Russia and all the world: he destroyed the mystique of Stalin, and with this act there began the erosion of the mystique of Communism itself. Khrushchev, as a good Leninist and enthusiastic participant in Stalin's First Five-Year Plan, was convinced that if Stalin's later errors were corrected the Soviet system would indeed be the most progressive, productive, and admirable in the world. After all, had not Soviet power put such a humble coal miner as himself at the head of the people's Party and state? At the Twentieth Party Congress, in 1956, he delivered what was intended as a "secret speech" denouncing certain of Stalin's crimes against the Party (though not against the population at large); and through Polish sources the speech was leaked to the world. The importance of the speech was not that it told the West anything basic that it did not already know, and still less that it told the full story about Stalin, for it did neither of these things. Its importance lay rather in the fact that the Kremlin itself now certified part of the truth about Stalin; and only such an imprimatur made it possible for that truth to pierce the ideological armor that had hitherto protected the Father of the Peoples. The hypnotic spell that Stalinism had exercised over both adherents and opponents in the West was suddenly broken.[113]

For its votaries, Stalinism's fascination had lain in the seeming infallibility of Communist policy; and for its foes, fear had been magnified by the Soviet myth's apparent invulnerability to empirical refutation. Khrushchev's frankness stripped away the aura of invincibility surrounding the late Leader; and by the same token, the Soviet system itself lost something of its frightening mystery. Russian society was partially "demystified," as Marxists would say, and so assumed a more prosaic character in Western eyes. With Khrushchev's bold stroke, the greatest mass hallucination in modern history was ended.

But this very fact meant that Khrushchev's own problems were only beginning. For he was under the illusion that de-Stalinization could be carried out as a limited operation: one swift, surgical incision and the Soviet patient would be cured. He clearly had not read Tocqueville about what happens to bad governments when they start to reform themselves; nor had he even pondered the record of Alexander II. By October of 1956 Poland was in near revolt, and Hungary was in open insurrection. Some threat of force and more diplomacy brought Poland back into line, but a bloody military invasion alone could recover Hungary. Under the impact of these events, legions of Western believers lost their faith in the country of the Soviets. Even in Russia herself the apparent conformity of the intelligentsia began to dissolve into criticism and dissent. As early as 1954 Ilia Erenburg had whispered the need for a "thaw," and in 1956, the year of Budapest, Boris Pasternak, in *Doctor Zhivago*, went so far as to suggest that the Revolution had been a death-bearing illusion from the beginning.[114]

Pasternak had therefore to be silenced as surely as Budapest had been suppressed.[115] Nonetheless, a fissure had opened in the system, both at home and abroad. Indeed, the question was now posed: could Soviet socialism survive with the truth and without the combined mystique and terror of Stalin? Or, put more positively, could Communism eventually reform and liberalize itself? As for the reign of Khrushchev himself, despite the repression in Budapest, the answer to both questions seemed to be "yes." For, once socialist order had been restored in Eastern Europe after 1956, the reform of Soviet society continued, though at a more gradual pace.

Thus, after 1956, the Soviet situation offered grounds for the creation of the next Western image of Russia: that of "modernization," allegedly leading to "convergence." At the same time, cultural conditions in the West, where the new social sciences had by now hit full stride, furnished the conceptual categories for such a perception. Beginning in the late 1940s with the work of Colin Clark and Simon Kuznets, reflection on the long stagnation of the depression, in conjunction with the engineered economic development of the Soviet Five-Year Plans, had led to the beginning of the economics of "growth," a notion left undeveloped by the classical theorists of the previous century.[116] Soon, too, economists developed the techniques to calculate gross national product, while Wassily Leontief explored the mechanisms of "input-output" valid in any type of industrial economy, whether capitalist or socialist.[117] After the Second World War the problems of economic recovery in Western Europe, as well as Soviet-Western competition for the allegiance of the "new nations" of the Third World, made development the focus of social-science attention. When this economic perspective was synthesized with borrowings from sociology's concern with the transition from traditional to modern society, modernization emerged as the driving dynamic of history.

And so, by around 1955, modernization theory offered a materialistic version of the ceaseless changeability of contemporary society whose aesthetic facet Baudelaire had called modernity. The new theory held that the entire world, in the wake of Western Europe and America, was destined to move from "backwardness" through "underdevelopment" to the culmination of history in an industrial, urban, literate, and functional-rational order. The theory asserted, further, that everywhere the imperatives of this process were approximately the same, as was the outcome—all of which is a unilinear version of what Marx had said a century earlier about the dialectical dynamics of capitalism. Political and cultural forms, finally, were held to be secondary in this process to the logic of socioeconomic change.

The emergence of this new model coincided with Khrushchev's mitigation of what was most blatantly alien to the West in the Soviet system. The old concept of totalitarianism, and even more the notion of Communism as the perversion of the Russian soul, ceased to be so compelling in explaining the Soviet enigma, at least for the Left and Center of public opinion. Concurrently, these same groups perceived what they took to be a core of likeness with the reformed Soviet system, namely, the rational organization of life to meet the needs of an advanced technological order. All societies trying to meet such needs, it was widely believed, must therefore develop basic similarities of structure, as well as of attitudes and values, no matter what their political regimes.

Hence the Soviet Union under Khrushchev, though still regarded as an unpleasant neighbor, came to be viewed as endowed with sufficient cognate features to be comprehensible to the West. Churchill's phrase about riddles and enigmas was quoted less frequently, and prevailing sentiment was better rendered by the aphorism of the American diplomat Charles Bohlen: "Soviet Russia is not a mystery, it is only a secret."[118] Western liberals increasingly felt that if only they had enough information about the Soviet Union they could understand the workings of its society and the policies of its government by applying, with modifications to be sure, the concepts that they used to explain modern society everywhere.

By around 1960, the West's overriding preoccupation with the Soviet Union's methods of maximizing political power began to give way to a view which emphasized instead economic growth and social transformation.[119] The brutal course of the Soviet Union's development was increasingly interpreted as the form of modernization peculiar to a society handicapped by an exceptional burden of backwardness, in other words, as a local form of a worldwide process of industrial transformation. Accordingly, the causes of Russia's rate of economic growth and the reasons for her appeal to underdeveloped countries now received considerably more attention in Western scholarship and journalism than did her system of political controls or the techniques of purge and brainwashing.

The new emphasis was common to virtually the whole range of Western social science; and politically it could be used to support either trust or distrust of Soviet Russia. Its most effective popularizers were such cautious liberals as Walt Rostow, in his *Stages of Economic Growth*, and Raymond Aron, in his *Dix-huit leçons sur la société industrielle*,[120] both of whom were firmly anti-Soviet. Their recognition of the success of Soviet development, therefore, was tinged with alarm, as well as qualified by the conviction that over the long haul a market economy was a better means of modernization than a planned one—at the time, by no means a self-evident proposition.

In other liberal quarters, however, belief in the global logic of industrial development led to a less cautious view soon known as "convergence." This theory was first enunciated in 1941 by a Trotskyite turned conservative, James Burnham, in *The Managerial Revolution*.[121] His thesis was that the true masters in all industrial societies, whether nominally capitalist or socialist, were the "managers" of the complex modern "technostructure." To Burnham, this perspective was intended as an argument for the withering away of socialism and its ideological utopianism. But it could just as easily be used to predict the withering away of proprietary capitalism, and the two predictions together added up to the convergence of East and West, a step taken by such works as John Kenneth Galbraith's *The New Industrial State* in 1967.[122] The burden of this left-leaning convergence theory was that, since the Soviet Union was already a "mature" industrial society like the West, the two systems were destined to go the further mile by converging in their social and political forms as well. The managers of the technostructure would be obliged to introduce economic planning in the West and individual liberty in the East, since such were the imperatives of *any* developed industrial-technological order. And with the fusion of the two socioeconomic systems, the political differences between their respective governments could also be expected to disappear.[123]

Thus the social-science model of universal modernization, although it began as a fairly neutral enterprise, was adopted with particular enthusiasm in circles hoping to achieve a "democratic socialism." Just as the primacy of politics in the totalitarian model reflected a classical liberal sensibility, so the primacy of socioeconomic forces in the modernization model appealed above all to a socialist sensibility. As this became apparent, the more cautious Western social scientists, such as Aron, backed away from it. The model thus never had more than a marginal role in shaping Western policy toward Russia. In the socialist countries themselves, however, the same overlap between social science and socialism gave convergence theory a real role, for "modernization" there came to mean the liberalization of Stalinist structures. Convergence theory hence became an important intellectual stimulus to the Prague Spring of 1968, and indeed to Gorbachev's *perestroika* of the 1980s. The reason for this cross-fertilization is that "convergence" is no more than another term for the famous "third way" between Leninist Communism and "capitalism" that has haunted, and eluded, progressive spirits both West and East through much of the twentieth century.

The shift in models from totalitarianism to modernization coincided with another phenomenon of the 1960s: the fulgurous career of the

New Left. As its name indicates, this largely juvenile movement was opposed to the old Left of Communism, which in its eyes had become ossified and bureaucratic, both in the Soviet Union and in still Stalinist Western Communist parties. The New Left, therefore, sought its models and heroes in such Third World rebels as Cuba's Che and Vietnam's Ho. Hostility to the old-style Left therefore did not mean taking the side of the West in the Cold War. On the contrary, "imperialism" continued to be reviled, indeed much more than Stalinism, since it was the West's own wickedness. The New Left thus remained partial to the communist ideal, and in fact continued to hope that it might yet emerge from established Communism, if the latter were purged by some Guevarist "revolution within the revolution."[124]

These ideological vicissitudes yielded a new variant of that classic law of political thermodynamics known as "no enemies to the left." Thus, in America, once McCarythism attacked Communism in order to tar liberals as subversive, anti-Communism became disreputable; in consequence anti-anti-Communism became honorable for some, and so Communism itself wound up appearing half-way acceptable too. This reflex was reinforced by the long-standing international context; for ever since Hitler's challenge to Communism, generic antifascism had conferred pseudodemocratic legitimacy on his adversary. This was all the more true in that Communism was clearly a revolutionary force in the Third World; hence its eventual regeneration in the Soviet Union was not to be ruled out. The problem then was to explain why the original Soviet experiment had gone (somewhat) awry. And the answer, of course, was a variant of the standard Trotskyite explanation: the culprit was Russian backwardness. As Isaac Deutscher paraphrased the master: it was Mother Russia that had spoiled the Revolution; and it was reactionary mockery to suggest that revolutionary Marxism might have ruined Mother Russia. Thus was anti-anti-Communism made sociologically respectable, as political-ideological emotion lent passion to the social-science debate about modernization and convergence.

Of course, the majority of Western opinion did not succumb to the roseate mirage of convergence. All the same, almost everyone was compelled to recognize that Russia after Stalin was a significantly different place. So long as Soviet Russia had been ruled by a single dictator, she seemed to be still in the same totalitarian category as the regimes of Mussolini and Hitler. With Stalin gone, however, she appeared to be changing into something else—not a democracy to be sure, but clearly something less total than before. Her political structure was increasingly perceived as having evolved from totalitarianism to "authoritarianism." And this change, in conjunction with her (seemingly) clear-cut success at economic development, led many observers to conclude that the ostensibly ideological dictatorship of the proletariat had all along been no more than an ordinary "modernizing dictatorship"—such as existed in much of the still "developing" Third World.

In sum, at the end of Khrushchev's tenure, Soviet Russia was deemed sufficiently different from the West to require permanent caution, and yet sufficiently similar to permit indefinite coexistence. As early as 1951, Raymond Aron had summed up the dynamic of the Cold War with the aphorism, "paix impossible, guerre improbable"—peace is impossible, war improbable.[125] Although this rule remained valid under Stalin's successors, there were nonetheless important changes in Western-Soviet relations, both in tone and in substance.

The Road to Détente

In the years immediately after 1945 the Soviet Union was still painfully recovering from the devastations of a war she had long thought she might well not win, and was certainly in no condition to embark on far-flung foreign adventures. Stalin was ready to gather in all the fruits of his victory over Hitler in the west and to press on if possible into Greece and Persia in the south. But beyond this, he lacked the means, and no doubt also the intention, to go. At the same time the United States possessed an overwhelming preponderance of wealth and power, as well as the only nuclear armaments in the world. Nevertheless, Western, especially American, anxiety about the menace of Russian imperialism was at its height, and discussion of the Soviet system was shrill and passionate. The principal cause of this disparity between the real magnitude of the Russian threat and the virulence of the West's reaction lay in the conjunction of the final, macabre period of Stalin's rule with the social disarray of continental Europe.

By the end of the 1950s, however, Russia had not only rebuilt her shattered economy but was expanding it at what seemed to be an ever more dynamic rate. She had developed nuclear and ballistic power which was increasingly comparable to that of the United States, and she was politically active throughout the Third World, from the Near East, to Southeast Asia, and on into the heart of Africa—as well as "only ninety miles from Miami," in Cuba. For the first time she posed a real and immediate threat to major Western interests.

Nevertheless, though highly alarmed by the new global reach of Soviet power, the West did not feel terrorized, as it had during the Berlin blockade of 1948 or at the outbreak of the Korean War in 1950. Public discussion of the Soviet presence in Egypt, the Congo, or Indonesia—where neither the tsars nor Stalin had ever dreamed of carrying Russian power—now eschewed reference to the messianism of Philotheus of Pskov. Instead, Western debate about Khrushchev's aims, while marked by a worried tone and concern over a possible "missile gap" in Russia's favor, was conducted in fairly "rational" terms, focusing on the objective relationships of power and interests on each side. This remained true even when in 1961 Khrushchev revived the threat to Berlin and thus to Allied positions throughout Western Europe, underlining his determination with a virtual ultimatum and pushing matters to the construction of the Wall of Shame. Western nerves continued to hold up amid the gravest crisis of all, the Cuban missile confrontation of 1962, when the world for the first time seemed close to a Western-Russian nuclear war.

The source of the West's relative *sang-froid* throughout these crises did not lie in the international sphere alone, since the real Soviet threat increased rather than diminished between Stalin's time and Khrushchev's. The source lay, rather, in the self-confidence produced by European reconstruction and the consequent diminished possibility of internal Communist subversion. Western fortitude was reinforced by Russia's partial openness, which in turn was due to her economic reconstruction and the consequent diminution of the insecurity bred by her internal postwar difficulties. The old mystery surrounding Russia dimmed as the Kremlin attenuated the controls employed by Stalin to cloak his country's weakness. In fact, Western fear of Soviet Russia had always been due as much to the ideological zealotry and terroristic practices of Stalin's system as to the reality of his nation's international power.

At the same time, once the Sino-Soviet breach became final in the early 1960s, these Stalinist qualities seemed to pass from Moscow to Beijing, and the focus of Western fears followed this eastward movement. Once the bombastic Khrushchev had fallen from power, in 1964, he was replaced by a committee of humdrum apparatchiki; and these gray masters of the once eerie Kremlin began to speak about the mysteries of the erstwhile fraternal regime of Mao Zedong in the same tones with which Westerners spoke of China or in which Churchill had spoken of the Soviet enigma. Thus Soviet Russia, though hardly just another European nation, looked distinctly less Asiatic than in the days of the Great Khan. Instead, she appeared increasingly in her role as a superpower, susceptible of responding in a "rational" manner to calculations of national self-interest. The way opened for a more positive West-East relationship than mere peaceful coexistence.

The alarms and excursions of the Khrushchev years had frightened and chastened both sides, and so gradually the two groped their way toward a kind of deal. Eventually called détente, this new modus vivendi was sketched in following the Cuban missile crisis by President Kennedy with the Nuclear Test Ban Treaty of 1963 and the first sale of American wheat to Russia that same year. The process even continued throughout the "escalation" of the Vietnam War by President Lyndon Johnson, since his policy was, after all, one of relative restraint designed to avoid direct conflict with China and, if possible, to entice the Soviets to moderate North Vietnam. Yet the high noon of détente was the Nixon-Kissinger years following the American failure in Vietnam.

Mature détente meant three things.[126] First of all it signified a continuing process of arms control negotiations, an effort which produced ceilings on the numbers of warheads and missiles, as well as the limitation of antiballistic missile systems, through the Strategic Arms Limitation Talks (SALT) I treaty of 1972. Second, it meant what the Germans called *Ostpolitik*, a variant of which was practiced by the principal Western powers on both sides of the Atlantic and under the leadership of such different political leaders as Chancellor Willy Brandt, Charles de Gaulle, and Richard Nixon. Its program was increased trade and investment in the Soviet Union and the People's Democracies to forge bonds of mutual self-interest that would reduce the risk of war and at the same time soften the Eastern dictatorships. Finally, détente was supposed to mean mutual restraint in all areas of potential conflict between the two superpowers, in Europe categorically and in the Third World relatively, since proxy wars were implicitly tolerable if they remained local and limited. Vietnam was tacitly written off by the United States as a lost cause, and Castro's Cuba was tacitly accepted as permanent for the same reason. But, in the West at least, détente meant that no further alterations in the world balance of power were to be expected.

By the mid-1970s this combination of explicit and tacit deals was widely regarded in the West as marking the end of the Cold War. However, not everyone was satisfied with the terms of the armistice, or even agreed that the conflict was over. On the Right, the Committee on the Present Danger felt that Nixon and Kissinger had foolishly conceded too much, and that the Soviet Union had by no means abandoned its goal of world supremacy.[127] On the Left, the opinion was widespread that existing arms control agreements were too modest, and that America's role in the Third World was overall more retrograde than that of the Soviet Union. And these sentiments were usually supported by the social-science theorem that "modernization" was gradually moving a now merely "authoritarian" Russia in the direction of "pluralism," and thus that the deepening of détente would accelerate this liberalization.

From the beginning of détente, however, there were strong signals that this might not be so. For a start, the Prague Spring of 1968, the first effort since Khrushchev to reform Communism, ended like its predecessor in repression. In the Third World, moreover, the Soviet Union proved unable to pass up any chance at revolution, as was demonstrated when Brezhnev airlifted Cuban troops to Angola and Ethiopia in the second half of the 1970s. And much more ominously, not even the status quo in Europe was secure, for in 1978 Russia began to deploy SS-20 intermediate-range missiles against Western Europe.[128] The aim of this maneuver was to separate American from European security interests, in effect neutralizing NATO by making it possible to intimidate the Western European nations without automatically producing American intervention. The final blow to détente came during Brezhnev's last two years and involved both the Third World and Europe. In December 1979 the Soviets invaded Afghanistan to save a sinking Communist regime; and in 1981, they put an end to the sixteen months of defiance by the Solidarity labor movement in Poland through the proxy intervention of the Polish Communist regime.

In the midst of these convulsions, SALT II was not even submitted to the American Senate for ratification. After Ronald Reagan's election in 1980 Western rearmament gathered full momentum. In 1982, NATO, urged on by the socialists François Mitterrand and Helmut Schmidt, proceeded to deploy Pershing missiles in Europe to counter the SS-20s. And in 1983 Reagan launched the Strategic Defense Initiative, commonly referred to as Star Wars. These measures have often been called the "second Cold War," as if the original conflict had once been resolved to the satisfaction of both parties, but it is hard to find a date or an event that marks the suspension of the postwar contest between East and West. All that one can find in the record is the fleeting hope, between SALT I in 1972 and the Helsinki Accords in 1975, that postwar international stability had at last been achieved. But the cascade of confrontations between 1975 and 1981 indicates that this belief had been in fact an illusion.

In reality, East-West confrontation was a constant as long as the Soviet regime existed, changing only in the style of the contest—from Stalin's overt hostility to Khrushchev's peaceful coexistence to Brezhnev's détente. And the goal the Soviets proclaimed was always the same: to someday shift the global "correlation of forces" irrevocably in favor of the "socialist camp." By 1980, therefore, détente turned out to have been no more than the pursuit of the Cold War by other means.

For that conflict was like no other in modern history, not simply because it took place in a hitherto unprecedented bipolar system of international power, nor because it was conducted under the shadow of the even more unprecedented novelty of nuclear weaponry. It was unique above all because it was driven by an ideology of the insurmountable incompatibility of "socialism" and "capitalism," an ideology in which international relations were no more than "international class struggle." Believing this, in fact made it so, on both sides in the contest, even when at the start the "capitalist camp" held no such metaphysical view of the world. For there was no conflict of *national* interests between America and Russia, or even between the Western European nations and Russia. But there was a deep conflict of "social systems," as the Soviet vocabulary had it, between East and West. The Cold War was thus not the result of a failure of communications, or of Western ill-will in accommodating legitimate Soviet security needs. This conflict-unlike-all-others was rather a given of the Soviet Union's nature as a system-unlike-all-others, and of its real incompatibility with the social and political order existing on the rest of the planet. The two systems could not converge, nor could they be meshed; one could only displace or supersede the other, just as Soviet doctrine held.

But it was difficult for most Westerners to see this clearly while the Cold War lasted. Its end, however, immediately made the conflict's nature transparent. The Cold War did not end because the contestants reached an agreement; it ended because the Soviet Union disappeared. And this left the West facing only Russia. To be sure, she was still one of the world's two major nuclear powers and not without a prickly national sensitivity. All the same, mere Russia the nation was hardly enough to polarize the planet ideologically or to generate the tensions for a new cold conflict; for her internal order was now simply a crude version of a system-like-all-others.

The Waltz of the Models

By the early 1980s, on the eve of Gorbachev's accession to power, the four classical images of Russia had been applied twice to the Soviet Union, once in the prewar, experimental period of Communist development, and again in the postwar period of imperial Communism. None of the four images, clearly, had been useful in understanding the prewar period. Neither the conservative Winston Churchill, nor the enlightened Webbs, nor the soulful Thomas Mann, nor even the dialectical Lukács had ever grasped the extraordinary combination of dynamism and horror that characterized the Soviet experiment. So are the four old images in their postwar guises any more helpful in explaining the Soviet empire?

The perception of Soviet socialism as converging with the West in some common, modern destiny has been challenged in an earlier chapter, and more will be said about its deficiencies shortly. As for the inverted Russian soul of Berdiaev, so tempting in the intense polarization of Stalin's last years, it may be dismissed as the recurring neo-Romantic fantasy that it clearly is. Similarly unhelpful is that more prosaic form of the argument from "eternal Russia": permanent Byzantine-Muscovite autocracy. Postwar Communism has been a force in too many places outside Russia, from East Berlin, Prague, and the "red belt" of Paris to Cuba and Vietnam, to be accounted a specifically Russian phenomenon, whatever surface plausibility such a view may have had when the movement was confined to the Soviet Union. Far more plausible, by contrast, is the modern successor to the image of Oriental despotism, the concept of totalitarianism. Just as worthy of attention is the contemporary mutant of the image of enlightened despotism, modernization through developmental dictatorship.

Assessing the merits of these models is nonetheless a delicate matter, for the totalitarian Lion and the modernizing Unicorn contended not only as social-science explanations of the Soviet phenomenon, but also as policy positions for dealing with it.[129] The totalitarian model was regnant in Western Sovietology from the end of the Second World War until the mid-1960s, that is, during the most acute phases of the Cold War under Stalin and Khrushchev. In this context it signified, first, that Soviet Communism was totally "other" and, second, that by its very nature the system could not reform itself in any significant way: cold hostilities with such a neighbor would therefore be a permanent state of affairs. The modernization model was dominant among "revisionist" Sovietologists in the Brezhnev and Gorbachev years when the Cold War had been mitigated, or more exactly routinized, by détente. Here it meant, first, that Soviet Russia could reform itself significantly and, second, that the Cold War should be wound down through arms control and trade; at the end of détente, therefore, was the possibility of Soviet democratization, and for some even of convergence.

Hence, in the heat of methodological battle over Soviet Russia's nature, "totalitarianism" came to be seen as the sociology of the hawks and "modernization" that of the doves; and the two camps were equated further with "conservatives" and "liberals" in domestic Western affairs.

In fact, of course, the political alignments on the issues in these debates were hardly so neat as a simple Right-Left dichotomy would suggest: good socialists could be ardent cold warriors and good conservatives could champion détente. Still, it remains overall true that late-twentieth-century Westerners, in arguing about Soviet Russia, were also arguing about the pace of reform in the West, just as early-nineteenth-century Westerners, in arguing about tsarist Russia, had also been arguing about support of or resistance to their own contemporary revolutions. As it turned out, in the twentieth century the Left was a poor vantage point for understanding Sovietism since it led to undue optimism regarding reform—just as, in the early nineteenth century, the same position had been a handicap for understanding tsarism since it produced excessive pessimism about its capacity for change.

It is because of the Cold War interaction between social science and politics that the obvious resolution of the warm war of the models never prevailed. As a strictly conceptual matter, both possess a measure of validity: Soviet Russia was in fact an all-encompassing dictatorship; and at the same time this dictatorship's central goal was economic development (whether for "building socialism" or simply for catching up with the West). Thus the real question is whether the dictatorship was merely instrumental to the economic end, or whether it was the essence of the system, an end in itself, in which economic growth was only a means to international power. Given the Soviet Union's dismal economic record overall, and the inordinate cost of command-administrative methods in achieving it, the answer to this question can only be that the Soviet Party-state throughout its existence subordinated economics to politics; and this of course is the essence of the totalitarian model, considered as an ideal type rather than a precise description. There are such better ways than a Communist dictatorship to accelerate economic development that it is untenable to make modernization per se the essence of the Soviet system, or to present the unique Soviet experiment as merely a local variant of a worldwide process of "becoming modern."[130]

And so, none of the four old images of Russia, even those promoted to the rank of social-science models, proved more satisfactory in resolving the Soviet riddle than had any of them been in the wake of 1917.

Despite Khrushchev's partial demystification of Russia, the Communist enigma was still largely opaque. Although the Soviet Union had become much less of a secret, at the deepest level it still remained a mystery.

Voices Off

At this point, around 1970, once the dynamism of the Khrushchev decade had given way to the stagnation of the Brezhnev era, there appeared a new and fifth image, emerging like a wan presence over the Eastern horizon. And this image came from the poor Scythians themselves.

It was indeed the first time that they had had anything to say about how outsiders perceived their world. Until the late 1960s the Western image of postrevolutionary Russia had been the product above all of Westerners, of the Soviet government, and, at the beginning at least, of such of its partisans as "the drummer of the Revolution," Vladimir Maiakovskii, the symbolist Scythian Aleksandr Blok, the icon maker Sergei Eisenstein, or Leon Trotsky. Émigré Russians formed under the Old Regime, largely ignored before 1939, after 1945 belatedly came to influence the West's perception of Russia; but their knowledge of her postrevolutionary state was vicarious, derived from study rather than experience. Only in the late 1960s did born-and-bred products of the Soviet system begin to have an impact on Western opinion. Much as occurred under the Old Regime—when, after Turgenev's emergence in the wake of the Crimean War, Russians first took the lead in explaining their ways to the world—so now a group known as the dissidents became a fresh source of insight into the Soviet enigma. To the world's astonishment, as Andrei Amalrik claimed, the hitherto silent Soviet "fish began to talk."[131]

This came about because of Khrushchev's parting gift to his countrymen, his second de-Stalinization campaign of 1961–62. Not only had he still not read Tocqueville or pondered the lesson of Alexander II, he had not even pondered his own record of 1956. The result, this time, was an explosion whose effects would be felt until the end of Soviet power.

Frustrated at the flattening out of his economic "boom" in 1961,

Khrushchev sought to shake up a sclerotic Party at the Twenty-Second Congress of that year by launching a public attack on Stalin. The late Leader's body was removed from the mausoleum and buried beside the Kremlin wall, while Stalingrad was rebaptized Volgograd. In 1962, frustrated by the failure of his foreign policy in Cuba, he went further and authorized the publication of a short novel about the camps, *One Day in the Life of Ivan Denisovich*, written by an inmate of eleven years, Aleksandr Solzhenitsyn.[132] All Russia trembled, whether with joy or with fear, for it seemed that the very foundations of the system might be challenged. This Moscow Spring, however, was soon stifled by the Party, and in 1964 Khrushchev himself was deposed, to be succeeded by the far more cautious Brezhnev. In 1966 the new leader publicly tried and exiled to Siberia two writers, Andrei Siniavskii and Iurii Daniel, for slandering the Soviet Union by publishing books in the West.[133] Nonetheless, the irreparable had occurred: the genie of dissidence was out of the bottle and it would never be put back in again.

This circumstance interacted with another, almost contemporaneous event. In 1968 Czechoslovakia entered into the process of de-Stalinization that the rest of Eastern Europe had undergone a decade earlier. And, once again, the process got out of hand. The Czechoslovak Communist Party under Alexander Dubček radicalized so quickly that it seemed that, for the first time, a Leninist regime might transform itself into a quasi–social democracy. The enlightened of the West and the reformist intelligentsia of the East hoped that the promises of Marx would at last be made good, and that the world would see its first example of "socialism with a human face," as the Czechs famously phrased their goal. Unfortunately, however, liberal Communism appeared to Brezhnev and his colleagues to be a contradiction in terms. The Prague Spring was (bloodlessly) crushed with a parade of Soviet tanks and Czechoslovakia was "normalized." This blow to expectations previously so high signaled to many in the West, as well as to many Eastern dissidents, that a Leninist regime, by its very nature, could not reform itself and that anticipation of convergence with the liberal world was a delusion. To be sure, not all Western observers abandoned hope that "the next time" Communism's liberalization would succeed. Still, for most of them, the idea that economic modernization would necessarily soften authoritarian politics was compromised; and achieving meaningful cooperation with the Soviet Union appeared correspondingly more complex.

The hardening of Soviet policy between 1962 and 1968 only emboldened Soviet dissenters. In the latter year some of them began publishing a *Chronicle of Current Events* devoted to factual reporting, without commentary, of the Soviet government's violations of its own laws defining individual rights; and in 1970 the "father of the Soviet hydrogen bomb," Academician Andrei Sakharov, and other elite figures took the risk of launching a "democratic movement for human rights" and of appealing to Western opinion for support.[134] At the same time long-forbidden authors, whose very names symbolized moral resistance to the regime, came once again to the fore. Anna Akhmatova, disdaining that "little invention of Gutenberg," as she put it, reappeared after almost thirty years of silence with the clandestine reproduction of some of her work at home in *samizdat* and its fuller publication abroad in *tamizdat;* and Osip Mandelshtam, who had been swept away in 1937 during the purges, was posthumously resurrected by the partial publication of his poetry in Russia and the appearance abroad of the memoirs of his widow, Nadezhda.[135]

But most of this literature was new, and the first theme it developed was that broached by *Ivan Denisovich:* the camps. Perhaps the most notable example of this genre was Evgeniia Ginzburg's *Into the Whirlwind* of 1967, which explored their worst specimen, the Kolyma valley.[136] Other authors, meanwhile, sought less to unmask the system's criminality than to satirize its absurdity. The master of this genre was Aleksandr Zinoviev, who portrayed "free" Soviet society as enmeshed in a web of ideological lies that had been foisted on it by the regime but that much of the population had internalized. Thus, in the title of his main work of socialist surrealism, *The Yawning Heights*, he changed the first letter of the regime's slogan regarding the "radiant heights" of Communism in order to assert that those heights were in fact a "gaping" abyss.[137] He explained, furthermore, that no one would dare say such a thing publicly, not just out of fear of the KGB (the Committee for State Security), but because in Soviet logocratic culture people "spoke Sovietese" spontaneously. Indeed, a good case in point is Brezhnev's straight-faced reply to the Czechs' demand for a "human-faced" socialism: but you already have "really-existing socialism!"—which thereupon became the regime's new defining slogan.

Among the classics of dissidence there was one name that led all the rest, Aleksandr Solzhenitsyn. As a result of the furor occasioned by *Ivan Denisovich*, after 1963 his works could no longer appear in Russia, so he continued his mission of unmasking the Soviet camp system by publishing two major novels abroad, *The First Circle* and *Cancer Ward*. With this corpus of writings he resurrected the great nineteenth-century Russian tradition of literature as moral and social protest; and by 1971 he had received the Nobel prize.[138] For the first time under the new regime, Russia had produced a rough analogue to Tolstoy or Dostoevsky under the old, a figure of prophetic stature, but one who like most such personages had his inflexible, indeed arrogant, side.

The dissident movement not only produced literary writers; it brought forth social analysts as well. Among the first to emerge was the Marxist Roy Medvedev. In *Let History Judge*, published abroad in 1971, he delivered a detailed indictment of Stalin's thirty-year "usurpation" of power, an aberration he explained in part by Stalin's warped personality and in even greater part by the penetration of the Party bureaucracy by "petty bourgeois" elements.[139] The explanation was an obvious one for a Communist loyalist. From Marx's commentary in the *Eighteenth Brumaire* on the failure of 1848 to the Third International's analysis of the rise of fascism, the "petty bourgeoisie's" corrupting role had been used to explain revolutionary disappointments; so it was only natural to account for Stalin's subversion of Lenin's revolution in the same manner. The inconvenience of this tack, however, was that its influence was restricted to those who believed the Soviet system could be corrected by returning to "true" Leninism, and these were increasingly rare among the Russian intelligentsia of the 1970s. Indeed, the book's argument was essentially a restatement, with different data, of Trotsky's thesis that the revolution had been betrayed by Stalinist bureaucracy. Although Medvedev's sanitized Party history helped Western "revisionists" formulate their answer to the totalitarian model, his book in fact offered a less impressive social analysis of Communism than had Milovan Djilas's *The New Class* some twenty years earlier.

The genuine dissidents abandoned Marxism entirely, and with far more probing results. The opening shot came in 1970, when Andrei Amalrik posed the startling but central question, *Will the Soviet Union Survive until 1984?*[140] His answer was that the West took the Soviet Union much too seriously both as a rival "social system" and as a super-power. For, in fact, its "planned" economy was a haphazard and graft-ridden affair; its "scientific" Marxism was a spent force that only stifled society's creativity; and the regime's sole ambition now was to hold on to power. Despite appearances, the Soviet system was already a derelict, with no way to keep going but through foreign adventure. Although Amalrik mistakenly believed that this desperation would lead to conflict with the regime's ideological rival, Red China, events would bear out the essentials of his diagnosis of Communism's domestic state. Even his terminal date was approximately accurate.

In a less categorical vein Sakharov had already issued, in 1968, a manifesto called *Progress, Coexistence, and Intellectual Freedom.*[141] In part this was a critique of the dead weight of Communist ideology and of the Leninist Party-state, coupled with a warning that they were eroding the country's vital forces; and in part it was a plea for "convergence" be-tween Western freedom and what remained of valid socialism in Soviet structures. (He had obviously been reading Western social scientists.) By 1975, however, in *My Country and The World*, he had changed his position to agree, in effect, with Amalrik, that the morally bankrupt Soviet system offered nothing worth converging with, and indeed that her decomposing order was a "danger" to the world.[142] In 1974 an even starker evaluation of the Soviet failure was given in a volume of essays by Solzhenitsyn and others, published under a title which was in itself a whole program, *From under the Rubble*. Its message was brutally simple: the experiment, the empire, and indeed socialism itself had been a disaster that had brought only ruin to Russia and the threat of ruin to the world.[143]

Similarly bold sentiments were displayed in the "fraternal" nations of Central Europe. In Hungary György Konrád and Ivan Szelényi gave another quasi-Marxist analysis of Communism's failure, which they explained as the usurpation of power by the Party intelligentsia—a variant of Trotsky's "bureaucratic degeneration" and Djilas's "new class."[144] In Czechoslovakia Vaclav Havel gave an ethical explanation of the grand failure; the presumption of Communism to exercise total power, resting as it did on an impossible "universal theory of everything," would one day be answered by the moral "power of the powerless."[145] In Poland dissent was more open and active than anywhere else. Adam Michnik, while helping workers to organize, appealed for an alliance of the non-Communist Left with religion in *The Church and the Left*.[146] And Leszek Kolakowski, who had been obliged to emigrate because of his "humanistic" revisions of Marxism, soon renounced it altogether. In 1978 he published abroad *Main Currents of Marxism*, a monumental analysis of the roots of what he considered to be the grand illusion of our century.[147] Building on Lukács's return to the Hegelian foundation of Marx, he explained Communism's perverse outcome as the result of its metaphysical origins: Marxist socialism transposed Hegel's philosophical religion into socioeconomic terms to yield a "fantasy" of human self-deification, which in practice could only produce human bondage. And so, between the Prague Spring of 1968 and the birth of Poland's Solidarity in 1980, Eastern European dissidence found a more philosophic voice than was possible under the harsher conditions of Russia.

Still, dissidence could effectively challenge Brezhnev's "really-existing" socialism only from within the Soviet heartland. The great blow came in 1974: in the wake of the KGB's discovery of his most important manuscript on the camps, *The Gulag Archipelago*, Solzhenitsyn was expelled into Western exile. He had nonetheless taken his precautions, and his three-volume work was immediately published in all Western languages. Here at last was a literary monument bearing irrefutable witness to the bankruptcy of the Soviet order.[148] It recounted with epic sweep and in minute detail the rise of the Soviet camp system from the first shot of the cruiser *Aurora* in October 1917 to the days of Khrushchev. It traced in clinical precision and with moral passion the development of the human "sewage system" of the camps and the "metastasis" of the "cancer" of terror, not only throughout the Siberian archipelago, but in nominally free Soviet society. With this work the West indeed discovered that, despite the research of Nikolaevsky and Dallin, and later of Robert Conquest, it had not known all that much about Soviet terror and repression. It had not known anywhere near the full facts; above all, it had never been exposed to the existential "feel" of the Soviet world under Stalin, in which even the "free" population lived in the shadow of his camps.

But Solzhenitsyn did not simply describe that world; he also offered an explanation of the dementia that for sixty years had engulfed Russia: "The greatest villains of Shakespeare never went beyond ten or so cadavers, because they had no *ideology*. . . . It is thanks to *ideology* that the twentieth century has experienced villainy on a scale of millions."[149] By "ideology" he meant blind faith that an impossible utopia was a scientific social project, an illusion that permits its bearers to impose their project on life through institutionalized terror. Only the supreme delusion of ideology could produce the criminal will that had driven Communism ever since the "rosy-fingered dawn" of October.[150]

Clearly, this veritable crime against human nature could not endure indefinitely. Whence, however, might liberation come? Solzhenitsyn's answer was the injunction: "Refuse to live according to the Lie."[151] Although this admonition might seem excessively abstruse, it had a practical, political purpose. For the power to name things, or to define the terms of discourse, is to a degree the power to control the terms of real life. This is partially true in any society; but in a world where there is only one permitted discourse, it is magnified into a total power. The West usually dismissed Soviet jargon as crass propaganda or an absurdity not to be taken seriously. In fact, this jargon was the real keeper of the gates of the Soviet police state: Communist Russia was just as surely governed logocratically, by the Party's monopoly of the Word, as by the KGB or the *nomenklatura*.

Yet, every syllable in the regime's discourse was a falsehood, an inversion of reality: "democratic centralism" for dictatorship, "Union" for empire, "fraternal republics" for satellites, "popular" or "soviet power" for Party autocracy, and "radiant heights" for quotidian squalor; and nothing under the sun was left unnamed by the Central

Committee and the editors of *Pravda*. Speaking "Sovietese," therefore, automatically signified obeisance to the regime's values and submission to its power. In such a world, calling things by their real names was the first step toward reclaiming life from the logocratic Lie. It was the beginning of individual self-emancipation and at the same time a politically seditious act, which, if repeated often enough, would liberate society as a whole.

Powerful though Solzhenitsyn's message was, the demonic Soviet world he depicted was a bit much for reasonable men in the West to believe. Although his *Gulag* became an international best-seller, and its title a new word in all languages, there was also a campaign of doubt, even denigration against him. In Britain *The Observer* and *The Guardian* attacked him for being "one-sided" and taking insufficient account of the Soviets' positive "achievements."[152] In France *Le Monde* even suggested that his account of the desperation of Soviet defectors who formed the Vlasov movement during the war implied sympathy for collaboration with Nazism.[153] At the same time, conservative President Gerald Ford, on the advice of *Realpolitiker* Henry Kissinger, refused to receive Solzhenitsyn at the White House since it might ruffle the allegedly smooth waters of détente—even though Soviet tanks had recently made possible the conquest of South Vietnam by the North, and though Brezhnev was then preparing to airlift Fidel Castro to Africa. Kissinger, of course, knew fairly well how ruffled the waters of his policy really were, but, faced with the inveterate difficulty of mobilizing a democracy for foreign policy, he saw no other way than détente to buy peace with the Soviet Union, which as an autocracy was permanently mobilized for power politics.

And so mainstream Western opinion, while admiring the dissidents' courage, was by and large distrustful of their political judgment. Many indeed felt that they at times could be dangerous to international equilibrium, as when Solzhenitsyn imperiously told the West in his Harvard speech of 1976 that the enlightened West was in fact spiritually myopic and into the bargain obtuse about the danger of Communism.[154]

Yet even if one was put off by the alleged "Slavophile" and reactionary Solzhenitsyn, preferring instead the more low-keyed "Westernizer" and liberal Sakharov, there remained a remarkable consensus among all the dissidents (except those few Leninist loyalists, such as Medvedev, who are better described as oppositionists).

For the dissidents by the end of the 1970s were not talking about "abuses," "aberrations," or even "criminal distortions" in the Soviet system—human rights violations, economic incompetence, or pervasive censorship—matters that could conceivably be corrected without changing the nature of the system itself. Rather, they were declaring that Communism from its inception had been a failure and a fraud; it was "criminal" in its very essence, an enterprise that merited—yes—the theological epithet "evil." It was thus deserving of the supreme infamy in twentieth-century political discourse: moral equivalence with Hitler and fascism, as Vasilii Grossman made so bold as to assert in his *Life and Fate*, written in the 1960s but published abroad only in 1984.[155] It was this globally negative judgment that mainstream Western opinion found difficult to believe; for it seemed improbable that such a great and mighty nation had nothing positive to offer.

True, by the time the dissidents appeared on the scene most of Western opinion had shed its cruder illusions about the Soviet system: by and large people knew that it was a despotism and that living standards under it were well below Western norms. Hence the dissidents' message was generally read to mean that the system's "abuses" were worse than the outside world had previously suspected—but that, nevertheless, there fortunately existed Soviet reformers prepared to remedy matters. And many observers would add that "cold warriors," therefore, should abstain from pressuring Moscow so as not to undermine those reformers' efforts to liberalize the system.[156] Yet—once again—this was not the burden of the dissidents' message; indeed, Eastern intellectuals regularly told the Western Left to step up pressure on the Communist regimes, Sakharov even endorsing Reagan's rearmament so that in arms negotiations the United States "would have something to give up."[157] Nonetheless, Westerners of good will persisted in missing the point, since the "socialism" the dissidents described was too fantastic for sober suburbanite citizens to imagine as really existing anywhere short of the moon.

Yet the dissidents had been unmistakably explicit: Communism by nature was a fraudulent and unviable enterprise destined, someday, to end on the ash heap of history—though they had no idea how that might come about. They were agreed, further, that the root cause of the disaster lay in the Marxist design for utopia and the Leninist Party used to build it. The product of an impossible ambition realized by lawless means could only be a monstrosity. Marxism-Leninism was therefore something much more all-encompassing than Oriental despotism as defined by Herodotus, Montesquieu, or Marx, and far more crushing than what that concept denoted when applied to Russia's Old Regime. Communism was a phenomenon *sui generis* in history; and its end result was a burnt-out fantasy, a moral black hole, an anti-world. The fifth, dissident image of Soviet Russia thus proclaimed that the Spectre of Communism was indeed just that: for a spectre, after all, is a dead soul.

The realm of the Soviet Spectre hence was a "looking-glass world" (*zazerkol'noe obshchestvo*, the dissidents said), a surreal world on the far side of human possibility. And in truth, Communism had pushed to the point of inversion the propensity of the Russian *Sonderweg* to telescope the phases of European development. Recall that Lenin had been able to put Marx's theory into practice only by turning it upside down, subordinating the proletariat to the Party and the logic of history to the voluntarism of class struggle. Stalin had then completed Marxism's inversion by employing the Party "superstructure" to create from above the industrial and worker "base" that was supposed to have created Soviet power from below. "Really-existing" Socialism therefore remained a permanently inverted world—an imitative and lumbering developmental dictatorship attempting to pass itself off as capitalism's higher negation and its world-historical successor.

But the Communists had inverted not only old Russia; they had inverted modernity itself, and with it the entire historical experience of that Europe to which Russia had belonged until 1917. For what they imposed on Russia was the ultimate Western utopia, the culminating product of that Anglo-Franco-Germanic ideological quest for human emancipation which had been on the march since the Enlightenment and its Romantic antithesis. The Soviet Party-state therefore was hardly an alien entity, some eternally Russian "Other"; it was our Western selves turned upside down and backside front. And its world-historical lot was to play Socialist surreality to mundane bourgeois reality—to figure as the dark doppelgänger of our luminous modernity, perversely created by attempting to overreach that reality in a superhumanity.

It is precisely for these reasons that, while it lasted, the inverted modernity of Communism enjoyed a truly fabulous career. For the Bolsheviks, by daring to incarnate the ultimate in Western utopia, conferred on Russia a power beyond anything her poor Scythian steppes could ever have afforded. So the laggard Eastern train of Europe came to haunt world politics for seven decades, polarizing the planet before the riddle of the Soviet Sphinx. Never before in Western history has such a monumental failure been such an irresistible success.

Yet, although the dissident image of Soviet reality turned out to be eminently prescient, at the time it seemed somewhat too surreal for sane Westerners to believe—indeed, almost as improbable as Dostoevsky's *The Possessed* and Conrad's *Under Western Eyes* taken together. So on the near side of détente and SALT II, most Westerners preferred to trust in accommodation with the "really-existing" Soviet regime. They therefore held to the hope that, despite the Soviet Union's still primitive autocracy and her persistent inflexibility on many questions of foreign affairs, a sufficient correspondence of interests—if only for mutual survival and the preservation of the hard-won fruits of development—would eventually emerge to permit a durable coexistence. To the average citizen, the continuing success of the Soviet economy—according to the CIA, 60 percent of the American gross national product—and the resulting parity of nuclear weaponry seemed to preclude any other course. To more optimistic observers, this limited convergence of interest continued to presage, as under Khrushchev, a lessening of the political differences between the Soviet and the Western worlds, and Russia's ultimate assimilation into some postindustrial, "service" or "information" society.

Over and Out: Gorbachev

But soon, as we have seen, the West found itself on the far side of détente. With the invasion of Afghanistan, SALT II went by the board;

and with Sakharov's exile to Gorkii for protesting it, the last of the dissidents was silenced. By the turn of the 1980s Soviet Russia offered the world a bleaker visage than at any time since Stalin's death. In the first half of the decade, Western public opinion on the Right anxiously echoed Reagan's castigation of the Evil Empire, and on the Left it agonized over the dangers of a new Cold War.

As it turned out, these bleak years were the prelude to a Western romance with Russia the like of which the world had not seen since the days of Voltaire and his Cateau. This began when Mikhail Gorbachev was elected general secretary in 1985, the first change at the top in Russia in twenty years. His election soon led to a campaign of domestic reforms known as *perestroika*, or "restructuring," and to the announcement of bold "new thinking" in international relations. Between these two initiatives, the frustrated expectations that generations of Western progressives had placed in the Soviet experiment seemed on the point of realization.[158]

The change that touched the widest circle in the West was the one that concerned everyone directly: the attenuation and then the end of the Cold War. It soon became apparent that "new thinking" meant that the Soviet Union was withdrawing from the arms race, and doing so essentially on Western terms. Most crucially, she gave up the SS-20s, an abdication sealed by the Intermediate-Range Nuclear Forces agreement of December 1987. Then, at the beginning of 1989 the Soviet government withdrew from Afghanistan, liquidating the last vestiges of the so-called second Cold War.

The great question, of course, was why the Soviet Union, after decades of denouncing the West for "dealing from positions of strength," suddenly became so accommodating. One answer, perhaps predominant at the time, was that the Soviet regime had undergone a genuine change of heart, abandoning class struggle for "universal human values," as Gorbachev asserted. So, one might conclude, Communism had not been entirely bad, after all. Another explanation, discretely subscribed to by Western governments, was that the Soviet economy was flagging so badly that Gorbachev had no alternative to accommodation with the far stronger West; and if the Soviet leaders accepted their capitulation so graciously, it was because they themselves had lost faith in Communism's superiority. Both explanations are undoubtedly true, though the decline was the more basic and indeed the cause of the change of heart.[159]

In any event, with the Cold War as good as over, Western attention shifted to the internal drama of *perestroika*. It proceeded to unfold in a dizzying succession of reforms: a (modest) economic liberalization; a policy of *glasnost*, or limited freedom of expression; and then "democratization," or an effort to transfer some power from the Party to elected soviets. This process culminated in May and June of 1989, with the meeting of the First Congress of People's Deputies. Among these deputies were Medvedev, working to save the system through reform, and the recently liberated Sakharov, working to undo the system by abolishing "the leading role of the Party."

Here were changes, surely, that put paid to the Cold War notion that the Soviet Union was a "totalitarian" system incapable of reforming itself. It seemed clear that Soviet modernization, despite the inordinate costs of the Stalinist "aberration," had produced a developed, "pluralistic" society with which Western democracies could "do business," in conservative Prime Minister Margaret Thatcher's words. Indeed, for many observers Gorbachev's *perestroika* meant more than Soviet Russia's drawing abreast of Western democracy; it meant that, after rectifying Stalin's departures from Leninism, she was at last on the verge of "socialism with a human face." The principal proponents of the Soviet system's capacity for reform, Professors Stephen Cohen and Jerry Hough, propounded this view (though with less direct terminology) on television and in the op-ed columns of the major national newspapers.[160]

Indeed, "Gorbi," as he was now called worldwide, was a hero to all ideological camps, from Ronald Reagan to the students on Tiananmen Square to Berliners ready to assault their infamous Wall; he was the "man of the decade" for *Time* magazine, the welcome guest of the pope, and the laureate of the Nobel peace prize. No Communist leader had ever evoked such international enthusiasm, neither "Uncle Joe" in the darkest days of the Second World War, nor Comrade Lenin among the first generation of Cominternists. Among pre-Communist Russian leaders, not even the Agamemnon of the European coalition against

Bonaparte, Alexander I, approached the veneration accorded Gorbi. Indeed, the only comparison for the adulation he evoked is that of the *philosophes* for the Semiramis of the North.

This "Gorbomania," however, presents us with something of an enigma—though, this time, a Western rather than a Russian one. Although relief at the Cold War's ending accounts for part of this enthusiasm, it is hardly enough to explain the extravagant lengths to which it was carried. Gorbachev was hailed as if he and *perestroika* had brought the answer to some great questions of human destiny, as if there was meaning in his reforms far beyond their significance for Russia herself. It was as if *perestroika* meant that Communism had at last redeemed itself in some non-Marxist way by healing the schism within modern civilization through the convergence, not of institutions and economies, but of existential values. Of course, in reality, nothing of the sort had occurred; the Soviet system had simply given up being Soviet. But this was indeed enough to produce a great international catharsis. This is perhaps what was involved in the West's lyrical Gorbachev moment, as the Spectre turned out to be something of a kitten after all.

Then, at the height of the euphoria, everything fell apart. The general secretary, like his predecessor in reforming Communism, Khrushchev, had clearly not read Tocqueville on the dangers for bad governments that attempt to transform themselves; nor had he even adequately pondered his predecessor's fate. In the same month as the Congress of People's Deputies, Poland's Communist reformers held elections—which were won by a re-legalized Solidarity. When the Poles and the other East Europeans saw that Moscow was too weak to react, the fraternal dominoes started falling one by one. By November the Berlin Wall was down, and by December the regime of Nicolae Ceauşescu in Romania had perished violently. The hard-won external empire and the hitherto vital security glacis vanished into thin air without Moscow offering the slightest resistance.

At the end of this *annus mirabilis* it was only a question of time before the Soviet Union itself would implode. The boomerang of *perestroika* crossed back over the frontier in January 1990, as Lithuanians took to the streets to demand "sovereignty"; by June Boris Yeltsin had prevailed on the Russian Federation's parliament to declare "sovereignty," too; soon all the other Soviet republics followed suit, thereby in effect dismantling the internal empire.

The next prop of the system to collapse was the command economy. The limited experiments of *perestroika* with cooperatives, partial autonomy from the plan for state enterprises, and joint ventures with foreign concerns quickly escalated into demands for a genuine market economy. By the fall of 1990, Gorbachev and Yeltsin together had agreed to a Five-Hundred-Day Plan for conversion to the market. And this step triggered, the following year, the collapse of the system's core institution: the Party.

The terminal crisis of 1991 began with the inevitable reaction against the escalating changes since 1989. Party diehards attempted to repress the Lithuanians with military force. They then tried to depose Yeltsin as chairman of the Russian Supreme Soviet, or parliament. So Yeltsin and the parliament replied by instituting democratic elections for a new office: president of the Russian Federation. In June Yeltsin won the election on the first round.

This outcome could only provoke the final confrontation. In August the Soviet government (quaintly referred to at the time in the West as "coup plotters") declared a state of emergency. When Gorbachev failed to endorse it, as they seem to have expected, they declared him deposed. The government failed utterly, however, to put down the resistance of Yeltsin and the democrats to what had now become an illegal coup. In consequence, though Gorbachev was nominally restored, the victorious democrats proceeded to disestablish the Soviet system. In September, the Party was dissolved and then banned. In December, the "Union" was abolished out from under Gorbachev.

In the euphoric years 1989–1991, therefore, everywhere behind the now shattered iron looking-glass the peoples undertook to invert "really-existing" socialism. One after another they set about restoring private property, profit, and the market as the basis for replacing partocracy with democracy, thereby negating that "negation of the negation" which for Marx had defined Socialism. From the Elbe to the Urals and beyond they proclaimed their determination to transform themselves back into "normal societies" and so "return to Europe."

Thus, amid the ruins of the empire the fruits of the experiment were liquidated too. The reputedly world-historical turning of October was annulled and all its results were repealed. The Party, the Plan, the Police, and the new civilization purportedly fostered by those institutions—all wound up on the notorious "ash heap of history" to which Trotsky had consigned Bolshevism's adversaries in October. It was as if 1917 had never occurred.

History's "logic" was hence set back to the level of 1789–1793. For despite the shadow of the Terror, the universal citizenship posited by the Jacobin Republic has turned out to be the irreversible political norm of modernity—a formula implicitly containing whatever distributive justice the sovereign citizenry might legislate. And so, by 1991 it had been proved beyond a reasonable doubt that there exists no such thing as a Socialist society at the exit from capitalism; there waits only a Soviet-type regime, and such a regimen *is* reversible. All Europe was thus set right side up again, and the continental gradient returned to its normal, West-East declivity.

What had happened to produce so precipitous a fall from the heights of superpower status and of vanguard social model? And why did a regime that had made a career of armed coups and coercive revolutions from above give up without a fight?

A favorite explanation is that the return of the repressed nationalities was the primary cause of the collapse.[161] And indeed, in the last year of *perestroika* their "parade of sovereignties" was a visible component of the system's decomposition. Nationalist disaffection, however, was less a cause than an effect of the decay: after all, for seven decades the Party had easily repressed its minority nationalities. Similarly, it was less the strength of Russia's democrats than the Party's weakness that made it possible to overthrow the regime in August 1991; for every Communist chief from Lenin to Brezhnev had made short shrift of critics and oppositionists. So what had changed to make the structure suddenly so vulnerable?

The answer really is quite simple, and the dissidents had spelled it out well before the actual day of reckoning. The cause of the Soviet collapse was the intrinsic unviability of the upside-down Leninist Party-state as a "social" system; this, in turn, derived from the intrinsic impossibility of the Marxist fantasy of human emancipation through socialism-as-noncapitalism. In consequence, after the initial success of Stalin's red-hot drive to build socialism, the system congealed into a systemic Lie concealed only by the "wooden language" of the One True Teaching. Soviet socialism had in fact been an illusion throughout its career; ideology alone had made it appear to be as real as its obverse on the capitalist side of the looking glass.

Concretely, the chain reaction of the collapse unfolded as follows: The chief legitimizing postulate of the regime had been that socialism is more productive as an economic system than capitalism. Under Stalin, and indeed as late as Khrushchev, it seemed that this might well turn out to be true. As the Cold War wore on, however, it became increasingly clear that the Soviet economy, except for its military arm, was declining relative to the West. Yet Gorbachev—to the end committed to the "socialist choice made in October"—believed he could revive the system and hence preserve its superpower status. He therefore undertook to reanimate the system with a whiff of *glasnost* by permitting the comrade fish to speak out critically and, as he hoped, constructively.

Instead, the Soviet intelligentsia transformed itself into a veritable Third Estate of dissidents. A few months of speaking the truth and—behold!—the logocratic spell that held the decrepit structure together was broken. Just as Marx had "found Hegel standing on his head and stood him on his feet again," so the dissidents did the same to the world's premier Marxist regime. Radiantly inverted Soviet pretensions were set on their real clay feet and "demystified"; and soon all Sovietdom saw that the Party-emperor had no clothes.

Forthwith the country ceased to live according to the Lie. And without the protection of the Lie, the regime lost confidence in its legitimacy, thereby depriving the once ruthless instrument of Lenin and Stalin of the will to coerce. Hitherto impotent democrats and nationalists could therefore challenge a superpower with impunity. And so, that power perished like an insubstantial phantasmagoria when its guiding ideology was confounded by "really-existing" modernity.

CONCLUSION

The West and Russia are like a tree with a double trunk which has the same roots and whose branches are increasingly intertwined; however, that part of the tree which looks towards the steppes, and against which the winds of Asia have long blown, has sprouted fewer leaves, many of its branches are dead, and the trunk itself almost broke on several occasions.

—Wladimir Weidlé, *La Russie absente et présente* (1949)

Let us assume for the sake of argument that recent research had disproved once and for all every one of Marx's individual theses. Even if this were to be proved, every serious Marxist would still be able to accept all such modern findings without reservation and hence dismiss all of Marx's theses *in toto*—without having to renounce his orthodoxy for a single moment. Orthodox Marxism, therefore, does not imply the uncritical acceptance of the results of Marx's investigations. It is not a "belief" in this or that thesis, nor in the exegesis of a "sacred" book. On the contrary, orthodoxy refers exclusively to *method*.

—Gyorgy Lukács, *History and Class Consciousness* (1920)

After the rising of June 17 [1953]
[the East German regime declared that]
The people had forfeited the confidence of the
  government
And could only win it back by doing twice as
  much work.
Would it not be easier to
Dissolve the people and
Elect another?

—Bertolt Brecht, "The Solution" (1953)

If, beginning with the eleventh century, you look at what was happening in France from one fifty-year period to another, at the end of each fifty years you will notice that a double revolution has taken place in the state and society. The noble has moved down on the social scale and the commoner has moved up. . . . Each half-century brings them closer, and soon they will touch.

. . .

The whole book that you are about to read was written under the impression of a sort of religious terror produced in the soul of the author by the sight of that irresistible [egalitarian] revolution which has been marching for so many centuries through so many obstacles, and that one sees still today marching on amidst the ruins that it has created.

—Alexis de Tocqueville, *Democracy in America*, Introduction (1835)

n the cold light of the post-Soviet dawn no Red Spectre remained to haunt Europe and the world. All that could be found in the East was Russia, much the worse for wear after three-quarters of a century of Communism, but still quite recognizably Russia.

Nevertheless, after contending for so long with the Soviet phantasmagoria, the West had difficulty in focusing on its real new neighbor. As Westerners awoke from their looking-glass dream, they anxiously asked whether the land behind the spectre had in truth become "just another country," a candidate "market democracy," and a prospective member of the "new world order." In short, would Russia *rediviva* resume her "convergence" with the West—as inaugurated by the Bronze Horseman, accelerated by the Tsar Liberator, and fractured by Lenin's October? Or would reborn Russia turn out to be a mutant of that "eternal Russia" of the West's perennial nightmares from Nicholas I to Stalin? The Lenin Mausoleum, after all, still stands on Red Square.

Whither the Troika Now?

Only eight years after Communism's demise it is clearly too early to assert that, this time, Russia will complete her real convergence with the West. But it is not too early to assert that, in the normal course, she hardly has anywhere else to go. Communism, the great utopian adventure of our age, is over for good: the Soviet experiment at least demonstrated that. Fascism is not a likely destination, either; for it was never an alternative "social system" to anything, only a temporary and local response to interwar conditions, as well as an ideological foil to Communism. So with the Red Spectre and its black-brown doppelgänger both safely on Trotsky's "ash heap of history," our familiar twentieth century—the ideological century par excellence—is closed.

Nor is Russia likely to revert to some nativist *Sonderweg* of development. To be sure, if conditions in Russia deteriorate enough, an attempt might be made to establish a national, "Slavophile" regime, but it would hardly last. In the long run, the pressures of a now global economic and technological society are too great for any one nation, no matter how proud of its distinctive tradition, to go it alone and to survive as a power; and Russia is too big a country, and too used to being a power, to accept any lesser destiny. As has ever been the case since Peter, if Russia wants to be strong, she will have to Westernize. With her Communist identity gone, and with no other ideological identity possible, she has little choice but to become, as before 1917, just another "normal" European power, with an equally normal internal order.

IMPERIUM PERENNUM?

But might not even this normal Russia be a menace to the West, as she was so often perceived to be when her "normal" Old Regime was converging with Europe? As she now approaches her tricentennial as a European power, a glance backward over her whole career in that role may provide an answer.

During those three centuries she was usually an expansionist, even "imperialist," power, annexing vast territories in almost every reign. Indeed, she began this imperial career well before Peter, with Ivan the Terrible's conquest of Kazan in 1552; and by 1639, she had reached the Pacific Ocean. Frightening calculations have been made to demonstrate that Russia then absorbed the "territorial equivalent of modern Holland for 150 years running," thereby displaying a unique capacity for imperialism.[1] The crudest form of the essentialist argument, of course, is the familiar reference to the sixteenth-century prophecies of Philotheus of Pskov making Moscow the Third and final Rome, a messianic pretension also considered unique among European nations.

No matter that Philotheus was speaking only of the church, not the state, and that pre-Petrine Muscovite foreign policy was never governed by this precept—Russian messianism nonetheless became a staple of international polemics. It first entered the historiography when the Poles, after the Revolution of 1830, used it (for quite understandable reasons) to explain their oppression by Russia.[2] It was then taken up by Western Europeans in general to explain Nicholas I's designs on Constantinople and the Straits. And so it was repeated through the various Turkish and Balkan crises down to 1914, and then recycled to account for Stalin's Central European empire.

However, we should not forget that beginning with a rough contemporary of Philotheus—Christopher Columbus—*all* Europe was expansionist, a behavior that continued until the great partitions of Africa and Asia on the eve of the First World War. Russia's imperial career during these four centuries was in many ways the Eastern front of what may be called the European conquest of the planet. When the maritime powers first went colonizing among overseas heathens during the sixteenth and seventeenth centuries, Russia expanded southward and eastward against the nomads of the steppes and the politically weak peoples of Siberia, who were often also infidel Muslims. We have seen how, with Peter, Russia first pushed westward to the Baltic in order to break out of landlocked isolation, and how Catherine combined this orientation with a new southward thrust to close the steppe frontier and drive the Turks across the Black Sea—a process of expansion in Europe that was completed when Alexander I profited rather too handsomely from the collapse of the Napoleonic empire. Finally, on the Eastern front again, Alexander II absorbed Turkestan, or Central Asia. Thus, the Russian empire, in the form in which it would endure until 1917, was constituted.

It was indeed an enormous affair—one-sixth of the globe's land surface, as the Soviets boasted about their dominion over the same rough area. But it was hardly more extensive than the territories put together by little Britain from the seventeenth to the early twentieth centuries— one-quarter of the world's land surface by 1918, as the British also proudly pointed out, and which as late as 1945 they had no intention of giving up. The British holdings, moreover, were far larger and richer proportionately to the "mother" country than were Russia's Siberian steppes, forests, and tundra relative to old Muscovy. Nor were the

Russian domains different in nature from the second modern global empire, that of France, or from the more concentrated colonial territories of the Netherlands, Belgium, and Portugal, all larger and more populous than their owners.

Granted, Russia's expansion was viewed as disastrous by her close neighbors, Sweden, Turkey, and especially Poland; but it was hardly different in kind from Louis XIV's advance on the Rhine or in the Low Countries; or the Austrian Habsburgs' drive down the Danube; or England's resolve to keep any major power from the mouth of the Scheldt, "pointed like a pistol at the heart" of Britain; or, later, America's determination with the Monroe Doctrine to keep all foreign states out of a whole hemisphere.

Empire building is simply what great powers do. As Thucydides, in analyzing the expansion of the Athenian empire, concluded twenty-five hundred years ago: "Of the gods we believe, and of men we know, that by a necessary law of their nature they rule wherever they can."[3] Power abhors a vacuum, and if one lupine state does not fill it another will. The principal difference between Russian imperialism and that of the Columbian West is that the latter operated overseas while Russia operated over land. But this is in reality a sign of poverty and backwardness rather than of unique aggressiveness. Siberia could be occupied by a handful of fur trappers; ships and soldiers were required to expand into the Americas or the Indies. The limitations of Russia's imperial reach were perhaps most dramatically demonstrated by the pitiful performance of her navy, the firstborn of Peter's conquering innovations, against upstart Japan at Tsushima in 1905.

Moreover, there was quite probably more messianic ideology in Western overseas expansion than in its Russian counterpart over land: Spanish and Portuguese colonization was conducted in part as a religious crusade, continuing the impetus of the Iberian *reconquista*; the New England Puritans migrated to build a godly "city on a hill" as a beacon to mankind (their heirs are still at it in secularized form with the superiority of the "American way of life"); the British have considered it their "white man's burden" to elevate "lesser breeds without the law"; and the French have had their *mission civilisatrice* and the "universal principles of 1789." It is difficult to see how all this is intrinsically different from the Russians' (rather archaic) pan-Slav concern for Orthodox Christians under the Turks in the Balkans during the nineteenth century.

Nonetheless, though these similarities are—or ought to be—beyond serious empirical dispute, we have also seen that Western Europeans as often as not failed to see Russia in such "rational" fashion—because of the persisting belief, traced in these pages, that Russian despotism (despite some "enlightened" interludes) was an intrinsically alien, threatening civilization. In fact, however, during Russia's three hundred years in Europe, only twice was she in a position to threaten anyone beyond her immediate neighbors; and she had these two opportunities because of a temporary, and somewhat fortuitous, inflation of her power.

Russia has been an international force of the first magnitude in only two periods of her history: from Peter the Great to 1815 and from her victory at Stalingrad in 1943 to the 1980s. In both periods she was successful because her meager resources were mobilized to a maximum by the coercive authority of the state.[4] In both cases, moreover, she sought to counterbalance her poverty by appropriating Western techniques and modes of organization, while at the same time avoiding political dependence on Western powers.

Under the Old Regime, an army with state-of-the-art technology and strategy but resting on peasant serfs conscripted for life defeated the declining powers of Sweden, Poland, and Turkey, and so created the Russian empire in Europe. This empire became for a brief time, after 1815, the major power of the continent not because of its inherent strength, but because Napoleon's megalomania led him to throw away the most modern military force of the age by invading Russia's vast expanse, thereby temporarily creating a power vacuum as far west as Paris. However, Russia chose to fill the void only long enough to dispose of Napoleon, and then withdrew to leave the rest of Europe to the restored Old Regime. And this was her first and only chance at *Weltmacht* under her own Old Regime.

But when this enserfed empire took on the industrialized powers of

Britain and France in the Crimean War of 1854–1856, it lost pitifully. Thereafter, because of persistent backwardness, it was thwarted uninterruptedly, in another Turkish war in 1876–1879 and in the Russo-Japanese conflict of 1905, before disintegrating completely in the test of 1914–1917. Nonetheless, throughout most of this period, the world champion imperialists of modern history, the British, were in a permanent state of hysteria about the chimera of Russia advancing over the Himalayas to India.[5]

Under the Soviet regime, once the First World War and Lenin's revolution had set the Russian economy back twenty-five years, Stalin's "building of socialism" from above, in order to compete in the "international class struggle," achieved a mode of national mobilization unprecedented in Russia's or any other country's history. Russia won the first round of this struggle—against Hitler—less because of the efficiency of her new socialism than because the Fürher's hubris led him to repeat Napoleon's mistake and plunge into Russia without adequately weighing the risks. The Nazi defeat created another unprecedented power vacuum in Europe, this time up to the Elbe. It did not remain a vacuum for long, however, for the Soviet Union, unlike the Russia of Alexander I, moved in to fill it indefinitely.

Yet here the parallel with tsarist power stops; for the allure of socialism and of antifascism gave the Soviet Union an imperial reach far beyond the range of the tsars, or even of its own armies. The socialist mystique projected Russia's influence into the West in the form of Communist parties, fellow-traveling intellectuals, and "peace movements" and throughout the Third World with "wars of national liberation."

However, Russia's second, ideologically driven mobilization in its turn proved incapable of sustaining great-power status. The strains of the next round of "international class struggle"—the Cold War—proved to be more than the Soviet command economy could bear, as its performance increasingly failed to match capitalism's level of productivity and technological innovation. In an attempt to reverse this decline, the regime launched *perestroika*'s foredoomed effort to liberalize the Soviet system without de-Communizing it, and so inadvertently precipitated systemic collapse and with it Russia's superpower pretensions.

Russia, therefore, is now back at geopolitical square one: a poor power trying to modernize in the real world after the failure of its caricature modernization in the surreal world of Soviet socialism. It is quite unlikely that in the foreseeable future she will have caught up economically with the West—or even with China—sufficiently to move into any vacuum in Central Europe. Nor would neo-Russian nationalism act as a magnetic mystique abroad any more than tsarism had. Finally, even if by some extraordinary exertions Russia recovered the still poorer republics of the late "Union," this would not make her a significant threat.

For at the end of the twentieth century international power rests not on the extent of territory a state controls but on its level of economic and technological development. Politically, economically, and morally the age of territorial empires is over: crossing frontiers with armies is no longer a permissible road to national aggrandizement. The United States manages to be quite globally imperial without controlling any significant foreign territory, not even its "own" Panama Canal. Thus Russia, no matter how organized politically, must first become rich if she wishes again to be powerful; and getting rich, with the handicap of a Soviet legacy, will take no small length of time.

Still, wealth, rather than power, is for the first time a serious alternative for Russia. Until the twentieth century the constraints of a severe northern climate made it difficult to exploit the country's boundless oil, mineral, and other natural resources. The steppes, forests, and tundra of Siberia, for all their vastness, were therefore less valuable than the tropical "sugar islands" or rubber plantations of Western powers; and within the twentieth century the Soviet Gulag was hardly the best way to maximize that region's potential. With modern science and technology, however, in conjunction with participation in the world market, Russia now has the capacity to turn the wealth of Siberia into a major source of national development overall.[6] And if Russia takes the route of riches she will surely become a different nation internally from the

418

poor, self-exploited power she has been throughout her history. Hence, it may be hoped, she will also become a more self-confident and relaxed member of the international concert of nations.

A FIFTY-YEAR RULE?

So what are the chances of her effecting a successful "transition to the market and democracy," as the West defines its hopes for present-day Russia as Europe once again regained? A glance backward over her irregular "curve of convergence" since Peter may provide an answer.

To recall: as we move along the West-East cultural gradient, we find that Russia ushered herself into the European concert at Poltava on the last surge of the military revolution that had been advancing eastward since the early sixteenth century. And she did so approximately fifty years after her nearest parvenu neighbor, Brandenburg-Prussia under the Great Elector. From then until the end of the Old Regime she could continue to march in Prussia's footsteps, and only slightly behind the third "court of the North," Austria, at a close interval. Thus under Catherine she became a state-of-the-art "enlightened police state" only some twenty-five years after Frederick II had perfected the model. After 1789 she would continue to imitate the Central European example of reacting to the shock of the French Revolution through monarchical revolution from above. Thus under Alexander II, the Great Reforms of the 1860s almost exactly replicated Prussia's Stein-Hardenberg reforms of 1807–1812. And, again some fifty years after Prussia, Russia in 1905 accepted the further reform of a "granted" constitution establishing a legislative Duma.

But do these correspondences—and they are more than coincidences—permit us to conclude that there exists some "fifty-year rule" governing Russia's convergence with Europe, or at least with Mitteleuropa, analogous to the pattern Tocqueville found in Western Old-Regime history? Perhaps, but only if we introduce an enormous zigzag in the middle of the process; for the First World War threw all of Europe east of the Rhine far off Western course. The movement toward liberalism and democracy inaugurated by the Enlightenment seemed, after 1914, about to be reversed. First, the East veered to totalitarianism of the Left, while the Center veered to the totalitarian

Right. Then, after a quarter-century of catastrophe, the fortunes of war again redirected history, as a second world conflict destroyed the totalitarianisms of the Right—though with an inconclusive outcome. Germany and Italy at last became stable, constitutional democracies; in Central Europe east of the Iron Curtain, totalitarianism of the Left took over. The full liquidation of the consequences of 1914 did not come until 1989–1991, with the collapse of the Soviet Union and its satellites. The great antidemocratic hiatus of 1918–1945 was at last closed across the entire continent—with Russia returning to the constitutionalist movement halted in 1917 just fifty years after the other interwar totalitarianisms had done so. Indeed, as regards imperial reach, Russia cut back well beyond her position in 1914, for Yeltsin abandoned all the conquests of Peter, Catherine, Alexander I, and Alexander II combined; and he did so around fifty years after the Atlantic imperial powers had given up their overseas colonies.

Of course, such a pattern—and it is a genuine pattern—does not constitute a *Gesetzmässigkeit*, a lawlike movement of history. At any time the treacherous Cunning of Reason could again upset the world's equilibrium. Even so, it is at present possible, unlike in 1914, to say that the potential for such an upset is nowhere perceptible. To this it may be added that, if the existing situation continues, the predominance of private property and the market (that is, a "normal" modern society) will in the long run produce the same effects in Russia that they have everywhere in the contemporary world: the formation of a civil society and a pluralistic culture. In this perspective, then, the real question is: how long will the long run take?

Given Russia's heavy heritage of poverty and despotism, it could be quite long indeed. But given also the fact that in the twentieth century history moves much faster than in earlier ages—and at the end of the century faster even than at its beginning—Russia's current long run may turn out to be not so long after all. Nor should we forget that what we call "democracy" (that is, constitutional government combined with universal suffrage) is barely a hundred and twenty years old in westernmost Europe, and hardly older in the United States. So at the end of our accelerating century Russia's chances for convergence would seem to be still further enhanced.

And Whither the Spectre?

Now that Russia no longer offers Marx's Communism a local habitation and a name, does his Spectre have any other prospects for the future? Although most people, both East and West, would doubtless prefer to believe that the "old mole" (another of Marx's metaphors) is now extinct, so simple an end to such a grand career is hardly likely. Remember that Marx's utopia, despite its lurid record in practice, was born as a species of idealistic socialism and thus as a reaction against the scandal of human inequality. So long as inequality exists therefore—and there is no likelihood of it disappearing in any foreseeable future—the drive for the full democratization of society will be with us. The only question is the form it will take. A glance backward over the combined career of generic socialism-cum-Marxism may provide an answer as to what those forms might be.

At the time of Communism's collapse the socialist idea had existed for about one hundred and sixty years, and Marxism for some one hundred and forty. This sesquicentennial of radical egalitarianism surely gives us enough perspective to discover, if not a *Gesetzmässigkeit* of its development, then a pattern of recurrences from which to divine its possible future. Even at a casual glance, however, one fact is obvious: from 1848 to 1917 socialism-as-noncapitalism was a movement in opposition, and its career was one of anticipation; from 1917 to 1991 it was an idea in power, and its story was one of failed application. Can the socialist idea now be reborn as a movement of anticipation?

THE OLD MOLE

Let us recall that anticipation has been of the essence of socialism ever since the maximalist egalitarian ideal emerged in the *entre-deux-révolutions* of 1830–1848. Revolutionary socialism's theories of anticipation, moreover, display a pattern. They have all been primarily the work of intellectuals. They necessarily invest their hopes in one or another variant of the "people" as the most dehumanized social stratum and thus the quintessential human class. Just as regularly, they impute to the masses an inborn commitment to the theory which these masses are one day supposed to realize. However, ever since 1848 the people have consistently disappointed the professional revolutionaries by developing a "consciousness" inadequately informed by theory. When this becomes clear, a crisis ensues in which the intellectuals must either abandon their vision and become small-deeds reformers or pursue their "noble dream" in the people's place through a dictatorship representing the "true" popular consciousness.

The first such crisis occurred in the seed time of socialism itself. The socialist sects of the July Monarchy were politically weak, as their insurrectionary failures of 1832 and 1834 clearly demonstrated. And if they got a fleeting chance at power in February 1848, it was not because of the strength of the street but because the propertied classes abandoned Louis Philippe when he refused to extend the suffrage: so in June they were crushed by the new democratic republic. Reacting to this accumulation of failures, the die-hard theorist Auguste Blanqui, building on the heritage of Babeuf,[7] concluded that a Communist revolution could triumph only as an elite conspiracy. After the culminating failure of 1848, his movement went underground to emerge in the fortuitous "revolution" of the Commune of 1871, which, insofar as it had a theory, indeed followed Blanqui's precepts or Proudhon's anarchism (but not Marx's competing canon).

The second time the crisis of anticipatory theory occurred was with the Russian Populists of the 1870s; as already indicated, they are best understood not as a movement apart, but as the Eastern expression of a common European current of leveling democracy.[8] And indeed, their commitment to revolution as the motive force of history owed an indispensable debt to the recent French examples of 1848 and 1871. It was in the hope of marching in this Western tradition that, in 1874, the student intellectuals took the first step of "going to the people" with a call for revolution. However, when the peasants failed to respond with the requisite insurrectionary "consciousness," some Populists created the conspiratorial People's Will to make the revolution in their place. And when this, too, failed, Plekhanov's wing of Populism decided, not to abandon socialist theory, but to exchange it for a better, Marxist one.

As for Marx and Engels themselves, they never had to face the crisis of deficient proletarian consciousness, because on each occasion in their lifetimes that "the revolution" failed them—in 1848–49 and in 1871—this could be explained away as the result of superior state force employed against the people. So in two brilliant pamphlets, the *Eighteenth Brumaire* and the *Civil War in France*, Marx annexed the clientele of Blanqui and Proudhon to the myth of his own, future proletarian revolution. As for the moment of its coming, he and Engels fell back on a permanent "next time"; and in 1885, Engels was still writing that the impending European upheaval was "now soon due (the European revolutions, 1815, 1830, 1848–52, 1870 have occurred at intervals of fifteen to eighteen years)." In this way, the Second International became the institutional embodiment of the "next time."

But as the wait lengthened unduly, disappointment grew apace; and the International began to fissure on all sides. In France, Georges Sorel created the syndicalist myth of the general strike to accelerate the *grand soir* of revolution. In Italy, Benito Mussolini, the editor of the Socialist Party's newspaper, *Avanti*, opted for aggrieved nationalism to produce the revolutionary regeneration of which the proletariat had proved incapable. It was in this rough generational company that Bernstein and Lenin, in their opposite ways, came to terms with the deficit of the proletariat's revolutionary consciousness under mature capitalism—the former by turning parliamentary reformer, the latter by making an intelligentsia vanguard the keeper of the revolutionary flame.

In opting for Party over people, Lenin indeed echoed the People's Will. But the parallel stops with this broad option, for Lenin made a more realistic choice of popular "base" than his predecessors: an urban force concentrated in key political centers. Lenin's strategy in fact recalls most of all those other elitist revolutionaries with whom he has often been compared by his socialist rivals: the Jacobins and Blanqui, both of whom sought to promote minority revolution from a radical urban base. And if these Western predecessors failed where he succeeded, one of the reasons was because the French peasantry, revolutionary in 1789, had largely cooled off by 1793 and was downright conservative in 1848, whereas the Russian peasantry in 1917 was at its peak of radicalism. The Russian jacquerie, therefore, was able to neutralize the entire country while Lenin's Jacobins put their urban Party-

Commune in power (though without making the Bolsheviks in any way beholden to their rural cohorts).

An analogous process of rectifying the revolutionary process emerged from the disappointed expectations attendant on socialism's exercise of power. Once the Social Democratic vote for war credits in August 1914 brought to naught that long anticipation which was Second International "orthodoxy," as a practical matter Marx's goal of Communism as noncapitalism could be achieved only through Lenin's intelligentsia vanguard. With this revolution made, however, still greater disappointments arose: to the perennial inadequacy of the masses were now added the caprices of the logic of history. The anticipation inspiring October had been that war-bred world revolution would come to socialist Russia's rescue; but this expectation was quickly refuted by events. So the Party substituted itself for the logic of history by improvising a policy of crash War Communism to replace the missing European revolution; yet this course, too, was thwarted by events. In desperation, the Party temporarily abandoned Marx's goal for a partial return to "capitalism" with the NEP.

Thus Marxist-Leninist socialism after four years in power found itself caught in internal contradictions even worse than those of prewar Social Democracy. At this humiliating juncture Trotsky advocated a modified version of War Communism: comprehensive "planning" in a "temporary" market context. Bukharin, however, went so far as to mimic Kautsky, though within Leninist coordinates, by producing a Soviet version of evolutionary revolution: just as Kautsky had hoped to reach socialism through democracy, Bukharin advocated "growing into socialism through the market."

Yet the basic dilemma of maximalist socialism in power remained: for Lenin's Party could hardly have achieved Marx's goal either through Trotsky's reliance on "rational" planning, which would have killed the market, or through Bukharin's recourse to the market, which would have destroyed the Party's monopoly of power. The only solution that would be true to both Marx and Lenin was Stalin's military use of that monopoly to force society into noncapitalism. With this squaring of the Marxist circle, socialism as anticipation was declared ended: it was at last "really existing." However, since what now existed was the inevitably vitiated product of an impossible theory, Stalin's achievement also offered the impetus for a new birth of anticipation. And so, alternative Marxisms unfolded—from the Czechs' "socialism with a human face," to Mao's, to Che Guevara's.

The course of Socialism from Marx to Lenin to Stalin thus was a progression toward realizing the theory's instrumental program paralleled by a degeneration of its initial moral-egalitarian ideal. And this paradox is indeed the *Gesetzmässigkeit*, the logic, of the movement. For at each turning point in this combined ascent-descent, the alternative was not some evolutionary "third way," whether that of Kautsky, or Bukharin, or "convergence." Rather, at each of Socialism's moments of truth, the alternative was to abandon the impossible Marxist enterprise and to settle, roughly, for what liberal Europe was well on its way to achieving by 1914.

For Russia this would have meant, economically, Witte's state-guided industrialization and use of the international market to attract foreign investment, a policy that yielded rates of industrial growth quite comparable to Stalin's in the 1930s, and with nothing like the human cost. Such methods, however, were precluded after 1917, because Soviet Russia withdrew from the world market, not for economic reasons, but for the ideological purpose of preserving the world's sole bastion of Socialism. And, socially, the alternative to Communism for Russia and Europe together would have been Bernstein's liberal democratic welfare state, which requires capitalism and the market to finance it. Indeed, this is just where the story came out worldwide after the seven-decade hiatus of Communism.

This outcome, moreover, contradicts the widespread assumption that Communism, for all its faults, was at least a champion at modernizing a backward country. In fact, it will be recalled, Marxism's covert vocation from the beginning was not to revolutionize advanced countries but to shake up the status quo in laggard ones. Yet, by 1991, when this substitute vocation had run its course, it became apparent that Marxism was not even all that good at crash modernization. The Soviet Union at the end of its career turned out to be an industrial museum-piece unable to compete in the international market (except for the limited domain of armaments), and thus was forced to earn the Yankee dollar like some Third World country by exporting raw materials.

By contrast, Witte's methods before 1914 were not only as effective as Stalin's economically, they were also compatible with the political modernization called constitutional government that Russia had inaugurated in 1905. Moreover, after Stalin's death, his command-administrative mode of economic development had only a truncated career. The heyday of the Soviet model in the world extended approximately from 1950 to 1970, when it was adopted integrally in China, Vietnam, and Cuba and partially in India, Egypt, Algeria, much of sub-Saharan Africa, and finally Ethiopia. In the early 1970s, however, the tide turned: authoritarian regimes, from Korea and Taiwan to Brazil and Chile, combined run-of-the-mill military dictatorship with the market and private property to far outpace the now declining Soviet Union and its imitators. Into the bargain, by the late 1980s these countries had embarked upon the political modernization of constitutional democracy as well. Simultaneously, China adopted the economic half of this model with perhaps more spectacular results than East Asia's "little tigers." In the twentieth century overall, then, the winning formula for crash modernization has proved to be market dictatorship, not Marxism. And this difference is due, of course, to the fact that Marxism dogmatically precludes the market and private property, making its dictatorship total, while such total power ultimately stifles economic innovation.

Thus, both economically and politically Communism has been the great blind alley of our century, a hiatus in Russian and world history. And this is why, once the Soviet regime collapsed, it left no usable heritage to posterity. No matter how bloody and destructive Western "bourgeois" revolutions often were, they all created institutions that have endured to this day, together with ideals whose moral appeal is still intact—a combination we now crudely summarize as "market democracy." The Russian Revolution, by contrast, when at last it gave up the ghost in 1991, left behind nothing but rubble, wormwood, and squalor. Indeed, in retrospect, its most prominent accomplishment was to keep Marxist ideology alive for seven decades after 1914 as "the inescapable philosophy of our age," in Sartre's phrase.

To see why, let us review the post-1914 alternatives to Communist maximalism. For a start, the scrupulously orthodox Western Social Democrats had in reality liquidated Marxism as a revolutionary force with their patriotic vote for war credits in 1914. It therefore took Lenin's voluntaristic, Jacobin Marxism to save the doctrine from the debacle—yes, debacle—of the democratic Second International. Similarly, Bukharin, with his policy of slouching toward socialism through the market, would never have made good Lenin's October gamble. Once again, his policy would have slowly suffocated Marxism as a world revolutionary force by attempting to do through Party capitalism what real capitalism did far better without the Party. It was Stalin's Promethean brutality alone that reversed the incipient debacle—yes, debacle—of the NEP, and so maintained the Spectre in its haunting orbit to the end of the century.

WHAT THEN REMAINS

But does this Spectre now have a future? After all, Marx's central thesis that capitalism would be transcended through proletarian revolution has been "disproved once and for all." What Lukács envisaged as a mere hypothesis is now an accomplished fact. The refutation was provided, basically, by postwar capitalism's extraordinary success, first in its Western homeland and then in the more dynamic countries of the Third World. The capstone of the process, however, was the collapse of the counterworld of Communism. It is simply no longer credible that industrial workers will someday overthrow capitalism for a nationalized and planned "socialism." Marxism (and indeed generic socialism) as a specifically proletarian movement is thus a spent force; and in this basic and literal sense its career is over.

Yet in a broader sense a diffuse Marxism—a generic distillation of Marxism—will be with us as long as social differentiation exists. True, for Marx the proletariat was the indispensable savior class, and *Capital* was devoted entirely to deriving its revolutionary role from the specific conditions of (early) industrial society. Yet at bottom his proletariat was the universal class for much less circumscribed reasons: it was the social Messiah above all because it was the victim class, the most dehumanized class, and thus the only class whose cause was the cause of humanity itself. But it is obvious that victimization and dehumanization can be produced by circumstances other than industrial wage-labor. And such dehumanization can also generate the sublime wrath, the revolutionary consciousness, that for Marx was the motive force propelling history to "human emancipation." Hence, even though the proletariat failed its own cause, and even though the Leninist Party eventually proved incapable of replacing it, the Spectre will surely continue on its haunting rounds as the vehicle of the Marxist "method."

Lukács's self-evidently absurd proposition that even if all of Marx's theses were disproved *in toto* the dialectical *method* nonetheless remained valid thus holds up in a looking-glass sort of way. For it is true to the social psychology of anticipation; and it is accurate as a description of the way Marxism has in fact operated in history. The essence of this method is the parareligious theorem that alienation, suffering, and death are the eternal wellsprings of rebirth and transfiguration, a destructive-creative dialectic that Hegel temporalized in history and that Marx then secularized into a class struggle. Viewing the totality of society from the standpoint of its most oppressed class yields the universal consciousness that will "emancipate" the entire species. It is this alluring redemptive method that underlay "every one of Marx's individual theses." When Lukács advanced his unabashedly metaphysical view of Marxist orthodoxy in 1920, his purpose was to argue that Lenin's voluntarism, rather than Kautsky's scholasticism, embodied the one true Marxist Method. Yet Lenin's dictatorship of the proletariat, too, has become just another "individual thesis" of Marxism.

All the theses of both Marx and Lenin have been "disproved" by history. Even the fallback vocation of Marxism as developmental dictatorship has been discredited. So what remains?[9] The Method does. For, if interpreted more broadly than Lukács himself ever envisioned, this translates as the proposition that the negation of existing society by the oppressed, of whatever social category, is the only way to make humanity human. Whether this now constitutes orthodox Marxism or not is a pointless question; but it *is* a logical extension of Marxism's primal

428

impulse. Socialism is in the first instance a negation, a morally motivated refusal of the "really-existing" world; and it develops its anticipated programs by extrapolation from its accumulated negations. The heartbeat of the Method is thus a benign version of the Mephistophelian "spirit that eternally denies," thereby eternally accomplishing a higher good.

THE RIDE OF THE METHOD

Not only does the Marxist Method remain, however; it has its old familiar quarry to bite into. The proletariat may have deserted, but the bourgeoisie is still at its post; and though socialism failed, capitalism is very much with us. As the Soviet lodestar progressively lost its luster, Marxism therefore took on ever new faces of negation and anticipation. There were, first, those revisionisms that remained within the Marxist-Leninist fold, from Trotskyism to Titoism to Maoism and Castroism— the revolution within the revolution, in the phrase of one of its latter-day theorists.[10] Their common premise was that, since Communism had realized the basic formula of communism by abolishing private property and the market, it must someday produce the "human face" necessarily inherent in the formula. Thus, the Western votaries of these offshoots of October—of whom Sartre is only the most illustrious exemplar—directed their fire less against the venial vices of Soviet socialism than against the mortal sins of American imperialism. And this remained the pattern until the dissidents, above all Solzhenitsyn, succeeded in equating the Soviet system with totalitarianism, thereby fundamentally compromising Communism for the fellow-traveling Left. Sartre ended his career without a utopia, indeed marching in protest in 1977 alongside his old comrade and foe, Aron, against the fate of the Vietnamese boat people just like any bourgeois liberal.

More interesting than this long afterglow of October is the post-Party, postproletarian Left, which transformed socialist negation and anticipation into what may be called generic critical theory. The founders of this tendency were, of course, the Frankfurt School of the inter-war years. These philosophic sociologists were disillusioned with both Kautsky and Lenin, with the now "petty bourgeois" Western workers and the "state-capitalist" Soviet Union. What they offered the Left was not some new path to socialism, but the relentless cultural criticism of bourgeois society: its obscurantist enlightenment, its technological hubris, its formalistic democratic politics, its liberal pseudofreedoms, its stultifying consumerism, its vulgar popular culture, its repressive sexual morality—in sum, its debased mass society.[11] To make this case they mingled their basic Marx with Freud's liberation of the repressed drives of the subconscious and Nietzsche's advocacy of aesthetic elitism, and of course with Hegel's method of progress through negation. Critical theory thus developed a syncretistic Marxism: without a proletariat-redeemer, it was turned into the negation of bourgeois culture as itself the supreme creative act and the means of "human emancipation"—a posthistorical state defined only by the denials necessary to reach it. As if to confirm this diagnostic of the self-destruction of bourgeois civilization, Nazism triumphed as the critical method was being elaborated. The Frankfurt School was thus driven to America and a new career in the 1960s.

By then, postwar Europe was producing kindred transmutations of the Marxist paradigm. The pathbreaker was Michel Foucault. Contrary to the previously reigning Parisian mandarin, Sartre, he did not accept Marxism as an inescapable philosophy; and unlike the Frankfurt School he did not purport to build on Marx. His aim rather was to transcend Marxism with a new philosophy drawing on Heidegger and Nietzsche together with structural linguistics. Nevertheless, in this new philosophy, too, the negation of modern "enlightenment" and bourgeois "humanism" (including its existential Sartrean variety) proved an end in itself, without any positive hero. For Foucault, dehumanization was the result less of institutional tyrannies than of the categories and language of modern rationalism, the modes of "discourse" that "humanist" civilization had generated purportedly to liberate man, but which in fact constituted so many forms of mandarin "power" subordinating the weak to the strong and the many to the few. The insane asylum, the prison, the hospital, the school, traditional sexual ethics, and above all the rationalistic social sciences that generate the discourses of domination producing this "great confinement"—all these are facets of that one carceral modernity from which man still vainly awaits his liberation.[12]

This message coincided with the return to prominence of the Frankfurt School in the persons of such old representatives as Herbert Marcuse in America and such new ones as Jürgen Habermas in Germany.[13] These two currents of generic critical theory, in conjunction with dim perceptions of Mao's cultural revolution and the heroics of Castro and Che, furnished the ideological background of the New Left that emerged on both sides of the Atlantic with the student revolts of the 1960s. This Left was "new" first because it repudiated the old Left of Communism as state-capitalist repression and domination. It was new also because it expected emancipation to come less from the proletariat (brainwashed into moderation as it was by Western Communist and SD parties) than from any element whatsoever in "consumer" (that is, bourgeois) society that was intellectually "critical" or socially oppressed.

Thus unfolded the first post-October visitation of the Spectre. And a strange visitation it was—all superstructure and no base, critical theory riding on a magic carpet of thin air and gesticulating with theatrical revolutionism. Its class warriors were the apprentice intellectuals mass-produced by the "knowledge factory" of the postwar mega-university; their aim was to turn their institutions into "critical universities" to overthrow consumer capitalism at home and American imperialism in Vietnam and Latin America. The New Left's creed turned out to be an amalgam of traditional Marxist negations with post-Communist, even anti-Communist, critical theory—the two elements held together by the belief that "the desire to destroy is a creative desire," to borrow Bakunin's famous formulation, in 1842, of the anarchist impulse. A surreal West had thus come to answer a surreal East.

And this neo-antinomianism added up to the grandest negation ever in Western history. A generic critical theory had stood the Enlightenment of the *philosophes* on its head as thoroughly as Marx had ever done to Hegel. Whereas the *philosophes* had sought to liberate man from the "superstition" of religion through reason, the Frankfurt School and Foucault sought to liberate him from the mind-formed manacles of

Reason triumphant. The practical task of the New Left was to carry this philosophical negation into politics, and into the street. Whereas classical socialism sought to liberate man from the "swindle" of liberal democracy, the neo-anarchists now aimed at liberating him both from the yoke of the bourgeoisie and the fraud of "really-existing" socialism. In the dark enlightenment of the 1960s the whole Western progressive tradition from the original Enlightenment onward was proclaimed a snare and a delusion, a veritable regression into "civilized barbarism." And what did these new equerries of Rozinante anticipate might emerge from such global negation? Their goal never received a name, nor did they have a program other than some grand social *charivari* that would turn the existing world upside down.

The vaulting ideological negation of the New Left failed utterly. When the movement burned out in the early 1970s, capitalism had suffered nary a dent, and American imperialism had been thwarted in Vietnam not by new-Left mimicry of revolution, but by the military power of old-Left and nationalistic North Vietnam. All that remained of the psychodrama of the 1960s was the style of its counterculture, now mass-produced for consumer society, and its antitraditional sexual mores—changes relevant above all to the bourgeoisie. The "people" were never at ease with what they saw as a nihilistic assault on traditional values.

Still, the burnout gave off some disturbingly spectral flames. The sixties movement had begun as an ultrademocratic and unstructured protest against social inequality, with a style that mingled flower power with sham barricades and that was as much playful as threatening in its provocations. Yet, as time passed and it failed to arouse the masses, it turned—like the Russian student Populists of the 1870s—to elitist terror and a protototalitarian political style. Hence, in the early 1970s it went down fighting, quite literally—from the Red Brigades in Italy to the Baader-Meinhof gang in Germany, to the "Maos" (initially blessed by Sartre and Foucault) in France, to the Weathermen in America. To be sure, this mock guerilla warfare never menaced existing society in the least. Nonetheless, morally and psychologically, the New Left, in its fantasy reenactment of the grand tradition of popular insurrection inaugurated by the Bastille, replicated the degeneration of democratic impulse into elitist coercion endemic on the ultra-Left from Babeuf to Lenin.[14]

So, after this most recent failure of para-Marxist, parasocialist anticipation, we must again ask: what remains? The first survivor, it transpires, is old-fashioned, anticapitalist Marxism as updated to the conditions of the late twentieth century. Just as Marx had not been disheartened by the failure of his original expectations in 1848 but deferred them to the "next time," so former partisans of the Soviet experiment were not crushed by its collapse but continued to look for new "internal contradictions" of capitalism. And since there are always crises and injustices of some kind in this unhappy world, such contradictions are never hard to find. Consequently, just as earlier in the century the "highest stage" of capitalism was declared to be "imperialism" and then later "fascism," so at the century's end the system's terminal stage is held to be "globalization." Indeed, it has been argued that Marx, with wizard-like clairvoyance, had foreseen this one hundred fifty years ago in the *Manifesto*'s description of the emerging world market.[15]

But this persistence of the old belief is not the most promising expression of the underlying paradigm. Its future, rather, belongs to new permutations of the quest for human equality. Since that objective is still an unachieved one, we can only expect that the old mole of the Method will burrow its way into ever new egalitarian movements. Indeed, in the tumult of the 1960s the waning cause of the proletariat was supplemented by incorporating other groups of the excluded into the Method's basic paradigm, to wit, that the most dehumanized group in society constitutes society's quintessentially human element. In Europe this new group was the peoples of the Third World then struggling for liberation from colonialism. In the United States the newly recognized cause was that of blacks struggling for their civil rights.

Yet, overall, it was America that pioneered the postproletarian liberation movement. This meant expanding on the civil rights movement to create a new feminism going beyond the long since realized goal of full universal suffrage to the social, even existential equality of the "genders"; finally, the expansion extended to the rights of sexual minorities.

And this escalation of causes was soon taken up in old Europe, whose Third World dependents were now on its own territories as well as overseas. In consequence, the basic paradigm of emancipation came to read that the oppressive "power structure" of society extended outward in a continuum from class, to race, to gender, while society perpetrated oppression through a discursive continuum from capitalism, to racism, to sexism.[16]

Of course, most of the new egalitarian movements were neither Marxist nor Marxist-influenced. Rather, the new movements sprang from very real social grievances; and each modeled its activism on that of its predecessor—as in American feminism's debt to the black civil rights movement—rather than on the now remote Marxist principle of proletarian class struggle formulated in 1848. Nevertheless, all these causes vibrated, whether consciously or only mimetically, to the old dialectic of the Method, for twentieth-century culture is saturated with it (on this point Sartre was right, at least as a matter of description). Thus, each of these causes carried intimations of a struggle for the cause of humanity itself; and each struggle has implied that, in its person, the time has arrived for the last to be made first, since only in this way could humanity become whole.

Nevertheless, there are important differences between the current multiplicity of egalitarianisms and the unitary, ecumenical ideal embodied by Marx's proletariat. Whereas equality once meant social fraternity, it now requires group diversity. The relentless, leveling logic of modernity has fragmented humanity's species-being, its oneness, into politically recognized cultural and ethnic subspecies. In the eyes of classical liberals, this outcome flatly contradicts democracy's universalistic values. If so, however, it does not do this any more than classical socialism did in its day.

In fact, the quest for diversity represents the transposition onto hitherto deprived groups of the basic socialist intuition, namely, that mere political equality is a mask for social hierarchy. Both socialism and diversity are at one and the same time a consequence and a contradiction of liberal democracy. In the eyes of the most modern Left, therefore, the civic uniformity promoted by formal democracy becomes a mask for ethnic hierarchy; and the formal recognition of group cultural identity becomes the means for equalizing real social status. Yet here the parallel with the old logic of socialism stops; for none of the multicultural egalitarianisms can offer a plausible universal class.

The workers were supposed to be the single world-historical class not only because of their deprivation and dehumanization, but because they were the overwhelming majority of society. All the new insurgent groups, however, are "minorities," and proudly so; even the numerically majoritarian women are a minority in a sociological sense in what remains "a man's world" (and a white-European one to boot). Nor do any of these minorities stand in the same crucial relationship to society's basic "mode of production" as the proletariat once did. The liberation of these groups, even when added together in a continuum, can hardly pretend to anything so grand as closing out prehistory and achieving the fullness of humanity's species-being.

It would thus seem that there is no manna here for the Spectre to batten on. Indeed, in a society whose ethos is egalitarian, one can only welcome the prospect that justice might at last be rendered to all. There is no gainsaying the need to persevere in that quest, both on grounds of democratic principle and as a practical matter of preserving social peace—all quite true. Yet is it not also true that enlightened aspirations, if pursued as absolutes founded on science, can bring the quest for justice to a dark and sinister end?

If we have learned anything from our century's experience, it must surely be that enlightened intentions hardly guarantee emancipatory results. Indeed, it would seem that the nobler the cause, the greater the damage when it spins out of control. And the noblest cause that the modern world has produced is the central promise of the Method: that the last shall be made first, the slave shall become master, and mankind shall finally be made One. We have seen the results of this illusion in the grand tragedy of 1917 in Russia, and after 1949 in the Third World of East Asia. We have seen it also as Western farce in the 1960s.

It would therefore be a piece of market-democracy hubris to conclude that we have come to the "end of ideology,"[17] as de-Stalinization led some to believe in the 1950s, or to the "end of history,"[18] as others opined in the wake of the Communist collapse. Ever since the Enlightenment was answered by its Romantic negation we have known that modern history moves, not in a straight line, but in paradoxical zigzags. And ever since social prophets of the generation of 1848 took to melding Enlightenment and Romanticism, we have known how capricious those zigzags can be. It would thus be wise to anticipate that, amid some as yet unforeseen crisis of modernity, the Cunning of Reason may visit us with a new mystic rationalism distilled from some good cause by an overdose of the Method.

So out of rational respect for the irrational in human affairs, the prudent moral to draw from the tricentennial of Russia-in-the-West—and the sesquicentennial of the Spectre, in modernity everywhere—is to leave the moralizing, this time, to the readers themselves.

INTRODUCTION

1. From Trotsky and his biographer, Isaac Deutscher, onward, referring to the backwardness of "Mother Russia" has been the standard way of explaining why the Revolution ended up in Stalinism. See especially Isaac Deutscher, *The Prophet Unarmed: Trotsky, 1921–1929* (New York: Oxford University Press, 1959).

2. For this planetary shock as it appeared at the time, see James Burnham, *The Struggle for the World* (New York: John Day Company, 1947); Raymond Aron, *Le grand schisme* (Paris: Gallimard, 1948); John Foster Dulles, *War and Peace* (New York: Macmillan, 1950); Waldemar Gurian, *Bolshevism: An Introduction to Soviet Communism* (Notre Dame: University of Notre Dame Press, 1952); Anthony T. Bouscaren, *Imperial Communism* (Washington, D.C.: Public Affairs Press, 1953). For the beginning of the descent from this high peak of estrangement, see Wladyslaw W. Kulski, *Peaceful Coexistence: An Analysis of Soviet Foreign Policy* (Chicago: Henry Regnery, 1959); John Lukacs, *A History of the Cold War* (New York: Doubleday, 1961).

3. Hajo Holborn, *The Political Collapse of Europe*, 6th ed. (New York: Knopf, 1959).

4. See, for example, Robert Lee Wolff, "The Three Romes: The Migration of an Ideology and the Making of an Autocrat," *Daedalus* 88, no. 2 (Spring 1959).

5. The paradigmatic example of equating internal despotism with external aggression is the marquis de Custine; Karl Marx held exactly the same position. See the section "Europe as the Two and the Three" in Chapter 2.

6. The Western literature treating Russia as, in some sense, a non-European society is extensive. The most wide-ranging exemplar of the genre is Jan Kucharzewski, *Ot belego do czernego orla* [From the White to the Red Eagle], 9 vols. (Warsaw, 1922). There exists a one-volume English abridgement of this work, *The Origins of Modern Russia* (New York: Polish Institute of the Arts and Sciences in America, 1948). Donald W. Treadgold, *The West in Russia and China: Religious and Secular Thought in Modern Times*, vol. 1, *Russia, 1472–1917* (Cambridge: Cambridge University Press, 1973) gives a straightforward account of Russia's cultural dealings with the rest of Europe, but by casting this

in a diptych with China he also asserts that Russia is fundamentally non-European. A more [...] statement of Russia's non-European character is Karl August Wittfo[gel, Orienta]l Despotism: A Comparative Study of Total Power (New Haven, Conn.: [...] ersity Press, 1957). An extreme statement of cultural, in particular re[...] terminism in Russian history is Alexander Yanov, The Origins of Auto[cracy: Ivan] the Terrible in Russian History (Berkeley: University of California Pre[ss, 1981]. For the bitter Russophobia of a Central European ex-Communis[t, see Tibo]r Szamuely, The Russian Tradition, ed. Robert Conquest (New Y[ork: McGr]aw-Hill, 1974); chap. 6 of this book gives a capsule history of the [...] Oriental despotism from Herodotus and Aristotle to the twentieth [...] r a contemporary journalistic assessment of Russia's uniqueness, se[...] Steele, Eternal Russia: Yeltsin, Gorbachev, and the Mirage of Democracy (Cambridge, Mass.: Harvard University Press, 1994). The roots of Stalinism in the heritage of Ivan the Terrible and Peter the Great is an important theme in Robert Tucker's Stalin in Power: The Revolution from Above, 1928–1941 (New York and London: Norton, 1990). For a more spiritual, and favorable, view of Russia's distinctiveness, see James H. Billington, The Icon and the Axe: An Interpretive History of Russian Culture (New York: Knopf, 1966). Currently the most prominent exponent of the idea of Russia's essential otherness, characterized as permanent "patrimonial" autocracy, is Richard Pipes, in his Russia under the Old Regime (New York: Charles Scribner's Sons, 1974), The Russian Revolution (New York: Knopf, 1990), and Russia under the Bolshevik Regime (New York: Knopf, 1994).

7. Russia's essential difference from Europe is an equally common theme in Russian historical literature, although the difference is more often than not perceived as a sign of Russia's superiority. For an overview of such opinion until the late nineteenth century, see Alexander von Schelting, Russland und Europa im russischen Geschichtsdenken (Bern: A. Francken, 1948). For an analysis of such opinion down to the present, see Iver B. Neumann, Russia and the Idea of Europe (New York: Routledge, 1996). The most serious and influential statement of the peculiarities of Russia's development is given by the liberal historian and Westernizer Pavel Miliukov, Ocherki po istorii russkoi kul'tury, first published beginning in 1896, and recently republished (Moscow: Progress-Kul'tura, 1995). See especially vol. 1 on the relationship of Russia's autocratic state to geography and climate, and vol. 3, Natsionalizm i evropeizm, on her cultural development. Miliukov's views were partially taken up by Georgii Plekhanov, Istoriia russkoi obshchestvennoi mysli (Moscow: Mir, 1914–15); and they influenced Lenin's castigation of Russia's "Asiatic" lack of "culture" once he was in power. Another school of Russian historiography held that Russia is neither European nor Asiatic but "Eurasian." See, most notably, Nikolai Sergeevich Trubetzkoy, The Legacy of Genghis Khan and Other Essays on Russia's

[handwritten marginal note: R's essential / otherness - but my / view]

Identity, ed. Anatoly Liberman (Ann Arbor: Michigan Slavic Publications, 1991), and George V. Vernadskii, *Opyt istorii Evrazii: s poloviny VI veka do nastoiashego vremeni* (Berlin: Izdanie evraziitsev, 1934). See also Nicholas Riasanovksy, "The Emergence of Eurasianism," in *California Slavic Studies*, vol. 5 (Berkeley and Los Angeles: University of California Press, 1967). For a positive evaluation of Russia's apartness from Europe, though without reference to Oriental despotism, there is Nicholas Berdiaev, *The Origin of Russian Communism* (Ann Arbor: University of Michigan Press, 1960), and *The Russian Idea* (Westport, Conn.: Greenwood Press, 1979).

The theme of Russia's radical otherness returned in force as the Soviet system was collapsing. The first such statement, emphasizing the permanence of backwardness and despotism in Russian history, and hence the continuity from Ivan to Peter to Stalin, is Vasilii Seliunin, "Istoki" [Origins], *Novyi mir*, no. 11 (1988). This is also an important theme of Igor Kliamkin, "Kakaia ulitca vedet k khramu?" [What Street Leads to the Temple?], *Novyi mir*, no. 11 (1987). This idea has been given a scholarly development by Evgenii Anisimov, *The Reforms of Peter the Great: Progress through Coercion in Russia* (Armonk, N.Y.: M. E. Sharpe, 1993). Russia's Eurasian uniqueness has been celebrated with great learning and no small amount of intellectual fantasy by the Orientalist Lev Nikolaevich Gumilev, *Drevniaia Rus i velikaia step'* [Ancient Russia and the Great Steppe] (Moscow: Mysl', 1989), and *Iz istorii Evrazii* [From the History of Eurasia] (Moscow: Iskusstvo, 1993).

8. The most comprehensive survey of this body of opinion, covering the period from Peter the Great to the mid-nineteenth century, is Dieter Groh, *Russland und das Selbstverständnis Europas* (Neuwied: Hermann Luchterhand Verlag, 1961). The author's position is that Russia is not part of Europe, and that her impact since Peter thus has represented a challenge to Europe's own identity.

9. For the original "convergence theory," see, for example, John Kenneth Galbraith, *The Affluent Society* (Boston: Houghton Mifflin, 1958). A similar position is implied in the views of such a major economist as Wassily Leontief, "The Decline and Rise of Soviet Economic Science," *Foreign Affairs* 38 (January 1960): 261–272. Even Raymond Aron, usually highly skeptical of Soviet accomplishments, for a time considered that some measure of economic convergence might be possible, *Dix-huit leçons sur la société industrielle* (Paris: Gallimard, 1962). For a critique of the idea of convergence at the time of its vogue, see Bertram D. Wolfe, "The Convergence Theory in a Historical Perspective," in *An Ideology in Power: Reflections on the Russian Revolution* (New York: Stein and Day, 1969).

10. Viewing modern Europe in terms of such a gradient is hardly confined to Germany; it comes quite naturally to citizens of any of the nations between the Rhine and the Urals, from the Czechs and Hungarians to the Poles to the

440

Russians. For the view from Central Europe, see Jéno Szúcs, *Les trois Europes* (Paris: L'Harmattan, 1985). In Russia the concept of gradient (though the term itself was not used) was at the heart of the debate between Bolsheviks and Mensheviks about whether Russia's forthcoming revolution would be "bourgeois" or "bourgeois-cum-proletarian"; and Trotsky's once famous "law of combined and uneven development" as the key to modern Russian history is a by-product of that debate. See the section "Leninist Practice" in Chapter 4. The concept of a European gradient is the essence of the highly influential model of industrial development used by Alexander Gerschenkron. See his *Economic Backwardness in Historical Perspective* (Cambridge, Mass.: Belknap Press of Harvard University Press, 1962). Gerschenkron's thesis is that the farther east one goes in Europe the greater becomes the role of banks and of the state in fostering industrialization, a pattern complemented by the prevalence in backward areas of socialist or nationalist ideologies.

11. Such a perspective was employed by Alexander Gerschenkron to test Max Weber's thesis on the Protestant ethic and capitalism by investigating the "this-worldly asceticism" of the Russian Old Believers. See *Europe in the Russian Mirror: Four Lectures in Economic History* (London: Cambridge University Press, 1970).

1. RUSSIA AS ENLIGHTENED DESPOTISM

1. Dennis Hay, *Europe: The Emergence of an Idea*, rev. ed. (Edinburgh: Edinburgh University Press, 1968); Frederico Chabod, *Storia dell'idea d'Europa* (Bari: Editori Laterza, 1962); Jacques Le Goff, *La veille Europe et la nôtre* (Paris: Editions du seuil, 1994); J. B. Duroselle, *L'idée d'Europe dans l'histoire* (Paris: Denoel, 1965); Rémi Brague, *Europe, la voie romaine* (Paris: Criterion, 1993).

2. Dimitri Obolensky, *The Byzantine Commonwealth: Eastern Europe, 500–1453* (New York: Praeger Publishers, 1971).

3. See Pavel Miliukov, *Ocherki po istorii russkoi kultury*, vol. 3, *Natsionalizm i evropeizm*, and Donald W. Treadgold, *The West in Russia and China: Religious Thought in Modern Times*. vol. 1, *Russia, 1472–1917* (Cambridge: Cambridge University Press, 1973).

4. See Treadgold, *Russia and China*, vol 1., chaps. 1 and 2, and Paul Pierling, S.J., *La Russie et le Saint-Siège* (Paris: Plon-Nourrit, 1896).

5. Although Russia's propensity for imperialism has long been a commonplace, serious study of her empire building is fairly recent. This interest, moreover, seems directed in part to filling the void in Russian Studies left by the collapse of what had previously furnished the central concern, Communism. See John LeDonne, *The Russian Empire and the World, 1700–1917* (New York: Oxford University Press, 1997); Geoffrey Hosking, *Russia: People and Empire, 1552–*

1917 (Cambridge, Mass: Harvard University Press, 1997); Michel Heller, *Histoire de Russie et de son empire*, trans. Anne Coldefy-Faucard (Paris: Plon, 1997). See also William Fuller, *Strategy and Power in Russia, 1600–1914* (New York: Free Press, 1992).

6. The most pertinent works on eighteenth-century diplomacy are Matthew S. Anderson, *The Rise of Modern Diplomacy* (New York: Longman, 1993); Derek McKay and H. M. Scott, *The Rise of the Great Powers, 1648–1815* (London: Longman, 1983); and especially Paul W. Schroeder, *The Transformation of European Politics, 1763–1848* (Oxford: Clarendon Press, 1994). For the early nineteenth-century ideology of the European concert, see Carsten Holbrand, *The Concert of Europe* (London: Longman, 1970). Still indispensable is Albert Sorel, *L'Europe et la Révolution française*, 8 vols. (Paris: Plon, Nourrit et cie, 1885–1904); see especially vol. 1, *Europe and the French Revolution: The Political Traditions of the Old Regime*, trans. Alfred Cobban (London: Collins, 1969).

7. The fact that the modern European state system was created by the simultaneous emergence of England and Russia as great powers is highlighted by J. S. Bromley, ed., *The Rise of Great Britain and Russia, 1688–1725*, in *The New Cambridge Modern History*, vol. 6 (Cambridge: Cambridge University Press, 1970). See especially chap. 21, M. S. Anderson, "Russia under Peter the Great and the Changed Relations of East and West," pp. 716–740.

8. The most pertinent works on Russian foreign policy are Hugh Ragsdale, ed., *Imperial Russian Foreign Policy* (Cambridge: Cambridge University Press, 1993), especially the "Introduction" by Albert Rieber, which gives a long-term view of Russian foreign policy close to that of this study; Ivo Lederer, ed., *Russian Foreign Policy: Essays in Historical Perspective* (New Haven, Conn.: Yale University Press, 1962), especially the article of Hajo Holborn, "Russia and the European Political System"; Wolfgang Windelband, *Die auswärtige Politik der Grossmächte in der Neuzeit von 1494 zur Gegenwart*, 3d ed. (Essen: Essener Verlagsanstalt, 1936); Sir Charles Alexander Petrie, *Diplomatic History* (London: Hollis and Cartar, 1946). For the Soviet perspective, see V. P. Potemkin, ed., *Geschichte der Diplomatie*, 3 vols. (Moscow: Verlag für fremdsprachige Litteratur, n.d.).

9. Schroeder, *Transformation of European Politics*, pp. vii and viii.

10. Ragsdale, *Russian Foreign Policy*, pp. 75–82, and Orest Subtelny, "'Peter I's Testament': A Reassessment," *Slavic Review* 33 (1974): 663–678.

11. Matthew S. Anderson, *Britain's Discovery of Russia, 1553–1815* (New York: St. Martin's Press, 1958). Dietrich Gerhard, *England und der Aufstieg Russlands* (Munich: R. Oldenbourg, 1933).

12. Schroeder, *Transformation of European Politics*, pp. 43–45.

13. Lucien Febvre, "Civilisation: évolution d'un mot et d'un groupe d'idées," in Centre International de Synthèse, ed., *Première semaine internationale de syn-*

442

thèse, Civilisation, le mot et l'idée (Paris: Renaissance du livre, 1919–1930), pp. 1–56.

14. Febvre, "Civilisation."

15. For the genesis and structure of Old-Regime Europe in the *longue durée*, see Dietrich Gerhard, *Old Europe: A Study of Continuity, 1000–1800* (New York: Academic Press, 1981). For Russia's organic assimilation into this Europe in the early modern period, see Marc Raeff, *The Well-Ordered Police State: Social and Institutional Change through Law in the Germanies and Russia, 1600–1800* (New Haven, Conn.: Yale University Press, 1993).

16. Manfred Riedel, "Gesellschaft, bürgerliche," in Otto Brunner, Werner Conze, and Reinhart Koselleck, eds., *Geschichtliche Grundbegriffe. Historisches Lexikon zur politisch-sozialen Sprache in Deutschland*, vol. 2 (Stuttgart: Ernst Klett, 1975); Quentin Skinner, *The Foundations of Modern Political Thought*, 2 vols. (Cambridge: Cambridge University Press, 1978).

17. For the historic importance of Christian Europe's exposed eastern flank, see William McNeill, *Europe's Steppe Frontier, 1500–1800* (Chicago: University of Chicago Press, 1964).

18. The relevant studies are Michael Roberts, "The Military Revolution, 1560–1660," in Roberts, *Essays in Swedish History* (London: Weidenfeld and Nicolson, 1966); Geoffrey Parker, *The Military Revolution: Military Innovation and the Rise of the West, 1500–1800* (New York: Cambridge University Press, 1988); William H. McNeill, *The Pursuit of Power: Technology, Armed Force, and Society since A.D. 1000* (Chicago: University of Chicago Press, 1982). Bruce Porter, *War and the Rise of the State: The Military Foundation of Modern Politics* (New York: Free Press, 1993); Richard M. Hellie, *Enserfment and Military Change in Muscovy* (Chicago: University of Chicago Press, 1971).

19. The term "feudal" is now generally used to designate any agrarian economy or preindustrial, "traditional" society. This is essentially Marx's meaning, and it is fundamentally misleading for analyzing the Old-Regime world. "Feudal" here applies exclusively to the political-military institutions of medieval Europe, roughly between 900 and 1400, such as they are described, for example, by Marc Bloch.

20. Alexis de Tocqueville, *Democracy in America*, ed. J. P. Mayer and Max Lerner, trans. George Lawrence (New York: Harper and Row, 1966). Or, in his own words, America "is reaping the results of the democratic revolution taking place among us [Europeans] without experiencing the revolution itself," p. 11. Louis Hartz, *The Liberal Tradition in America* (New York: Harcourt, Brace, 1955), develops the thesis that America did not produce a socialist movement because it never had an Old Regime.

21. For Europe as a constantly expanding force from its medieval beginnings, see

Robert Bartlet, *The Making of Europe: Conquest, Colonization, and Cultural Change, 950–1350* (Princeton, N.J.: Princeton University Press, 1993).

22. For Russia's eighteenth-century institutional convergence with Europe and her maturity as an Old Regime, see Raeff, *Well-Ordered Police State*, and his *Origins of the Russian Intelligentsia: The Eighteenth Century Nobility* (New York: Harcourt Brace, 1966). For the reign of Semiramis in particular see Isabel de Madariaga, *Russia in the Age of Catherine the Great* (New Haven, Conn.: Yale University Press, 1981). R. R. Palmer, *The Age of the Democratic Revolution: A Political History of Europe and America, 1760–1800*, 2 vols. (Princeton, N.J.: Princeton University Press, 1959), concurs in this assessment of Russia's Europeanization; see vol. 1, pp. 402–404.

23. Frederick the Great, *Oeuvres* (Berlin: Imprimerie royale, 1846–1857), vol. 2, pp. 23–24.

24. See Norbert Elias, *The Civilizing Process*, trans. Edmund Jephcott, 2 vols. (Cambridge, Mass.: Blackwell, 1994).

25. It is a commonplace that the exceptionally polished nature of correct French is due to the action of the state since the founding of the Académie Française by Richelieu in 1636. That the King's French was molded especially by the cult of elegant conversation among the aristocracy of the court has been emphasized recently by Marc Fumaroli, for example, in *Le genre des genres littéraires français: la conversation* (Oxford: Clarendon Press, 1992).

26. See Emile Haumant, *La culture française en Russie (1700–1900)*, 2d ed. (Paris: Hachette, 1913).

27. See Bernard Lewis, *Cultures in Conflict: Christians, Muslims, and Jews in the Age of Discovery* (New York: Oxford University Press, 1995); Lewis, *Islam in History: Ideas, People, and Events in the Middle East* (1993); Lewis, *Islam and the West* (New York: Oxford University Press, 1993).

28. Voltaire, *Histoire de Charles XII, roi de Suède* (Paris: Larousse, 1925). See also Albert Lortholary, *Le mirage russe en France au XVIIIe siècle* (Paris: Boivin, 1951), pt. 1, chap. 2; Dimitri S. von Mohrenschildt, *Russia in the Intellectual Life of Eighteenth-Century France* (New York: Columbia University Press, 1936).

29. Montesquieu, *L'esprit des lois* (Paris: Bibliothèque de la Pléiade, 1951); see vol. 2., book 19, chap. 15, for Russia's European nature, and book 13, chap. 6, for her despotic constitution.

30. Voltaire, *Histoire de l'empire de Russie sous Pierre le Grand*, 2 vols., published respectively in 1759 and 1763.

31. Voltaire, *La Russie sous Pierre le Grand*, vol. 1, pp. 1–2.

32. Ibid., vol. 2, p. 276.

33. One of the most pertinent works on enlightened despotism is H. M. Scott, ed., *Enlightened Absolutism: Reform and Reformers in Later Eighteenth-Century Europe*

(Ann Arbor: University of Michigan Press, 1990); see especially Scott, "Introduction: The Problem of Enlightened Absolutism," and Derek Beales "Social Forces and Enlightened Policies." See also Leonard Krieger, *Kings and Philosophers, 1689–1789* (New York: Norton, 1970), and *An Essay on the Theory of Enlightened Despotism* (Chicago: University of Chicago Press, 1975); François Bluche, *Le despotisme éclairé* (Paris: A. Fayard, 1968); John G. Gagliardo, *Enlightened Despotism* (Arlington Heights, Ill.: Harlan Davidson, 1967). C. B. A. Behrens, *Society, Government, and the Enlightenment: The Experiences of Eighteenth-Century France and Prussia* (London: Thames and Hudson, 1985), and *The Ancien Regime* (New York: Norton, 1989); Pierre Chaunu, *La civilisation de l'Europe des lumières* (Paris: Arthaud, 1971). For the relativization of the concept of absolutism, see Nicholas Henshall, *The Myth of Absolutism: Change and Continuity in Early Modern European Monarchy* (London: Longman, 1992).

Of particular value in relating ideology to politics throughout the century are Palmer, *Democratic Revolution*, and Franco Venturi, *Settecento Riformatore*, 5 vols. (Turin: Einaudi, 1969–1987). Both works are comparative in nature—ranging indeed from the Appalachians to the Urals—and both consider enlightened despotism integral to the Enlightenment overall.

34. Liselotte Richter, *Leibniz und sein Russlandbild* (Berlin: Akademie der Wissenschaften zu Berlin, 1946); W. Guerrier, *Leibniz in seine Beziehungen zu Russland und Peter dem Grossen* (Berlin: Akademie der Wissenschaften, 1873).

35. William Fiddian Reddaway, ed., *Documents of Catherine the Great: The Correspondence with Voltaire and the Instruction of 1767* (Cambridge: Cambridge University Press, 1931). For Catherine's relations with the ensemble of the *philosophes*, see Lortholary, *Le mirage russe*, pt. 2, esp. chap. 5. For her courtship of the Encyclopedists, see Maurice Tourneux, *Diderot et Catherine II* (Paris: Calmann Lévy, 1899); Dmitrii Fomich Kobeko, "Ekaterina i D'Alembert," *Istoricheskii vestnik*, April–May 1884, pp. 107–142, 294–299; Iakov Karlovich Grot, "Pis'ma Imperatritsy Ekateriny II k Grimmu, 1774–1796," in *Sbornik imperatorskogo russkogo istoricheskogo obshchestva*, 148 vols. (St. Petersburg, 1867–1916), vol. 23 (1878).

36. Charles W. Everett, *Jeremy Bentham* (London: Dell, 1966); Mary Peter Mack, *Jeremy Bentham: An Odyssey of Ideas* (New York: Columbia University Press, 1963). For British contacts with Russia generally, see Peter Putnam, ed., *Seven Britons in Imperial Russia* (Princeton, N.J.: Princeton University Press, 1952).

37. Reddaway, *Documents of Catherine*, p. 216.

38. Richard Wortman, *Scenarios of Power: Myth and Ceremony in Russian Monarchy* (Princeton, N.J.: Princeton University Press, 1995), pp. 135–138.

39. Waclaw Lednicki, *Pushkin's Bronze Horseman: The Story of a Masterpiece* (Berkeley: University of California Press, 1955).

40. For Western Europeans' exploration of Central Europe and Russia in the

eighteenth century, see Larry Wolff, *Inventing Eastern Europe: The Map of Civilization on the Mind of the Enlightenment* (Stanford, Calif.: Stanford University Press, 1994).

41. L'abbé Chappe d'Auteroche, *Voyage en Siberie, fait par ordre du Roi en 1761* (Amsterdam: n.p., 1769–1770).

42. Jean-Jacques Rousseau, "Considérations sur le gouvernement de Pologne (1771)," in C. E. Vaughan, *The Political Writings of Jean-Jacques Rousseau*, vol. 2 (Cambridge: Cambridge University Press, 1915).

43. The juxtaposition of Voltaire's Russia with Rousseau's Poland is employed in chaps. 5 and 6 of Wolff's *Inventing*.

44. Jean-Jacques Rousseau, "The Social Contract," in *The Essential Rousseau*, trans. Lowell Bair (New York: New American Library, 1974), p. 40.

45. Reddaway, *Documents of Catherine*, pp. 194–200.

46. De Madariaga, *Catherine the Great*; J. P. LeDonne, *Ruling Russia: Politics and Administration in the Age of Absolutism* (Princeton, N.J.: Princeton University Press, 1984).

47. Venturi, *Settecento*, and Palmer, *Democratic Revolution*, argue, with different emphases, both that the French Revolution brought the culmination of the eighteenth-century reform movement inspired by "philosophy" and that enlightened despotism was an integral part of this movement.

48. Jeremy Bentham, *Works*, 1st ed., 11 vols. (Edinburgh, 1843–1859), vol. 4.

49. Thomas Jefferson to Joseph Priestly, November 1802, in Paul Leicester Ford, ed., *The Works of Thomas Jefferson*, 12 vols. (New York and London: G. P. Putnam's Sons, 1904–1905), vol. 8, p. 179. See also N. Hans, "Tsar Alexander I and Jefferson: Unpublished Correspondence," *Slavonic and East European Review* 32, no. 78 (December 1953): 215–225.

50. Jefferson to Alexander I, April 1806, *Works*, vol. 8, p. 430.

51. Jefferson to John Adams, March 1814, *Works*, vol. 9, p. 461.

52. The most pertinent works on the Enlightenment as an intellectual movement are Ernst Cassirer, *The Philosophy of the Enlightenment* (Princeton, N.J.: Princeton University Press, 1951), and *Kant's Life and Thought*, trans. James Haden, intro. Stephan Korner (New Haven, Conn.: Yale University Press, 1981); Paul Hazard, *La crise de la conscience européene, 1680–1715* (Paris: Gallimard, 1968), translated as *European Thought in the Eighteenth Century, from Montesquieu to Lessing* (Gloucester, Mass.: Peter Smith, 1973); Norman Hampson, *The Enlightenment* (New York: Penguin Books, 1990); Peter Gay, *The Enlightenment: An Interpretation*, 2 vols. (New York: Knopf, 1966–1969). For the pivotal case of France, see Daniel Mornet, *Les origines intellectuelles de la Révolution francaise, 1715–1789* (Paris: A. Colin, 1933), esp. pt. 3; Alphonse Dupront, *Qu'est-ce que les lumières* (Paris: Gallimard, 1996, though this course of lectures had been given thirty years earlier).

446

53. The antiecclesiastical meaning of "civil society" is omitted in Riedel, "Gesell-schaft, bürgerliche." The genealogy of this aspect of the concept is given in Georges de Lagarde, *La naissance de l'esprit laïque au déclin du moyen age*, 6 vols. (Paris: Presses universitaires de France, 1948); Marsilio is treated in vol 2.

54. For background information, see Alfred North Whitehead, *Science and the Modern World* (New York: Macmillan, 1953); Herbert Butterfield, *The Origins of Modern Science, 1300–1800*, rev. ed. (New York: Free Press, 1965); Alexandre Koyré, *From the Closed World to the Infinite Universe* (New York: Harper, 1958); Marie Boas Hall, *The Scientific Renaissance, 1450–1630* (London: Collins, 1962); Rupert A. Hall, *The Revolution in Science, 1500–1750*, 3d ed. (London and New York: Longman, 1983).

55. Jean Le Rond D'Alembert, *Preliminary Discourse to the Encyclopedia of Diderot*, trans. Richard Schwab (New York: Bobbs-Merrill, 1963), p. 12.

56. Marquis de Condorcet, "Sketch for a Historical Picture of the Progress of the Human Mind," in Keith M. Baker, ed., *Condorcet: Selected Writings* (Indianapolis: Bobbs-Merrill, 1976), pp. 233, 279–280. For the full story of this scientistic utopianism, see Keith M. Baker, *Condorcet: From Natural Philosophy to Social Mathematics* (Chicago: University of Chicago Press, 1975).

57. Hegel, *Philosophy of History*, trans. J. Sibree (New York: Dover Publications, 1956), section 3, chap. 3. The translation has been slightly modified here. The same image of inversion occurs in his *Phenomenology of the Spirit*, trans. A. V. Miller (Oxford and New York: Oxford University Press, 1977), p. 355. This image is the source of Marx's own references to standing Hegelian idealism on *its* head.

58. Karl Marx, "Theses on Feuerbach," in Robert Tucker, ed., *Marx-Engels Reader*, 2d ed. (New York: Norton, 1978), p. 143.

59. Written in 1736, for years *Le mondain* circulated only in manuscript.

60. John Bury, *The Idea of Progress: An Inquiry into Its Origins and Growth* (New York: Dover Publications, 1955). The precise terminology—"ancient," "medieval," "modern"—was a mid-eighteenth-century coinage of the German historian Johann Matthias Gesner, and it did not become commonplace until the nineteenth century. But the substance of this triad, with its characterization of the middle period as the Dark Ages, was clearly present from the 1740s onward.

61. See especially Albert Soboul and Philippe Goujard, *L'Encyclopédie ou Dictionnaire raisonné des Sciences, des Arts et des Métiers: textes choisis* (Paris: Editions sociales, 1984), and Albert Soboul, "Les philosophes et la révolution," in Jacques Le Goff and Bela Köpeczi, *Intellectuels français, intellectuels hongrois, XIII–XX siècles* (Paris: Editions du CNRS, 1985).

62. For Old-Regime society in France, see Roland Mousnier, *The Institutions of France under the Absolute Monarchy, 1598–1789*, trans. Brian Pearce (Chicago:

University of Chicago Press, 1979–1984); Pierre Goubert, *L'ancien régime*, vol. 1. *La société;* vol. 2, *Les pouvoirs* (Paris: A. Colin, 1969–1973); Pierre Chaunu, *La civilisation de l'Europe des lumières* (Paris: Arthaud, 1971); François Furet, "La Révolution, 1774–1880," in *L'histoire de France*, 4 vols. (Hachette: Paris, 1989); Keith Baker, *Inventing the French Revolution: Essays on French Political Culture in the Eighteenth Century* (Cambridge: Cambridge University Press, 1990).

63. For the institutional and social "base" of the Enlightenment, see Daniel Roche, *Les républicains des lettres: gens de culture et de lumières aux XVIIIe siècle* (Paris: Fayard, 1988), and *Le siècle des lumières en province: académies et académiciens provinciaux, 1680–1789* (Paris: Mouton, 1978); Robert Darnton, *The Business of Enlightenement* (Cambridge, Mass.: Harvard University Press, 1979); Jean Proust, *Diderot et l'Encyclopédie* (Paris: A. Michel, 1995); John Lough, *Essays on the Encyclopédie of Diderot and D'Alembert* (London: Oxford University Press, 1968), esp. Appendix C, "A List of Subscribers to the Quarto Edition"; Jürgen Habermas, *The Structural Transformation of the Public Sphere: An Inquiry into a Category of Bourgeois Society*, trans. Thomas Burger (Cambridge, Mass.: MIT Press, 1991).

64. Robert Darnton, *The Literary Underground of the Old Regime* (Cambridge, Mass.: Harvard University Press, 1982).

65. The famous thesis of Alexis de Tocqueville, in *The Old Regime and the French Revolution*, trans. Stuart Gilbert (Garden City, N.Y.: Doubleday, 1955).

66. Peter Gay, *The Party of Humanity: Essays in the French Enlightenment* (New York: Knopf, 1964).

67. Kingsley Martin, *The Rise of French Liberal Thought: A Study of Political Ideas from Bayle to Condorcet* (Westport, Conn.: Greenwood Press, 1980).

68. Peter Gay, *Voltaire's Politics: The Poet as Realist* (Princeton, N.J.: Princeton University Press, 1959), chap. 2.

69. Gay, *Voltaire's Politics.* Gay, however, dismisses Catherine's commitment to the Enlightenment much too lightly. Venturi presents her more accurately.

70. Venturi, *Settecento*, vols. 3, 4.

71. In the Marxist view this means that the base of enlightened despotism was second serfdom. See Soboul's comments in Bela Köpeczi, Albert Soboul, Eva Balázs, and Domokos Kosáry, eds., *L'absolutisme éclairé* (Paris: Editions du CNRS, 1985).

72. See Gagliardo, *Enlightened Despotism*, and Scott, "Problem," in *Enlightened Absolutism*, p. 19.

73. Karl Vorlander, *Immanuel Kants Leben* (Leipzig: F. Meiner, 1911), pp. 55–57, and Ernst Sandvoss, *Immanuel Kant: Leben, Werk, Wirkung* (Stuttgart: Kohlhammer, 1983), pp. 11–12.

74. To this practical concern the French minister for foreign relations, the comte

448

de Vergennes, added a "philosophic" note by denouncing the first partition of Poland as immoral. See Scott, "Problem," in *Enlightened Absolutism*, p. 29.

75. For the general situation in Europe at the time, see Schroeder, *Transformation of European Politics*, pt. 1, chap. 1.

76. Herbert Kaplan, *The First Partition of Poland* (New York: Columbia University Press, 1962).

77. De Madariaga, *Catherine the Great*, pt. 4, chap. 13.

78. Isabel de Madariaga, *Britain, Russia, and the Armed Neutrality of 1780* (New Haven, Conn.: Yale University Press, 1962).

79. Hugh Ragsdale, "Russian Projects of Conquest in the Eighteenth Century," in his *Russian Foreign Policy*, pp. 82–102.

80. The key work remains Robert Lord, *The Second Partition of Poland* (Cambridge, Mass.: Harvard University Press, 1915).

81. For the Polish Enlightenment that Catherine snuffed out, see Jean Fabre, *Stanislas-Auguste Poniatowski et l'Europe des lumières* (Paris: Institut d'etudes slaves, 1952).

82. For the partitions as viewed from Russia, see de Madariaga, *Catherine the Great*, pt. 8, chaps. 27–28. For the partitions as viewed from Poland, see Norman Davies, *God's Playground: A History of Poland*, 2 vols. (New York: Columbia University Press, 1982), vol. 1, chap. 18.

83. This thesis is suggested by Schroeder, *Transformation of European Politics*, pt. 1, chaps. 1–3.

84. Quoted by Lord, *Second Partition*, p. 503.

85. The comparison is that of de Madariagra, *Catherine the Great*, p. 451.

2. RUSSIA AS ORIENTAL DESPOTISM

1. Hay, *Europe: The Emergence of an Idea*, pp. 125–126; Mark Bassin, "Russia between Europe and Asia: The Ideological Construction of Geography," *Slavic Review* 50, no. 1. (Spring 1991); W. H. Parker, "Europe: How Far?" *Geographical Journal* 126 (1960): 278–297.

2. The most convenient introduction to imperial Russian foreign policy for this period is Barbara Jelavich, *A Century of Russian Foreign Policy, 1814–1914* (New York: Lippincott, 1964). For the Congress of Vienna, see C. K. Webster, *The Congress of Vienna* (London: Oxford University Press, 1919), and his *The European Alliance, 1815–1825* (Calcutta: University of Calcutta, 1929); Harold Nicolson, *The Congress of Vienna: A Study in Allied Unity, 1812–1822* (New York: Harcourt, Brace, 1946). For the diplomacy of the age as a whole, see Norman Rich, *Great Power Diplomacy, 1814–1914* (New York: McGraw-Hill, 1992); Schroeder, *Transformation of European Politics*.

3. Jefferson to Dr. Logan, July 23, 1816, in Albert Ellery Bergh, ed., *The Writings*

of Thomas Jefferson, 20 vols. (Washington D.C.: Thomas Jefferson Memorial Association, 1905–1907), vol. 15, pp. 47–49.

4. John H. Gleason, *The Genesis of Russophobia in Great Britain: A Study of the Interaction of Policy and Opinion* (Cambridge, Mass.: Harvard University Press, 1950); Raymond T. McNally, "Das Russlandbild in der Publizistik Frankreichs zwischen 1814 und 1843," in Horst Jablonowski, ed., *Forschungen zur Osteuropäischen Geschichte* (Berlin: Historische Veröffentlichungen des Osteuropa-Instituts an der Freien Universität Berlin, 1958), vol. 6; Oscar J. Hammen, "Free Europe versus Russia, 1830–1854," *American Slavic and East European Review* 11, no. 1 (February 1952): pp. 27–41.

5. For the beginnings of Socialism, see G. H. Cole, *Socialist Thought*, vol. 1, *The Forerunners, 1789–1850* (London: Macmillan, 1953); Élie Halévy, *Histoire du socialisme européen* (Paris: Librairie Gallimard, 1948); George Lichtheim, *The Origins of Socialism* (New York: Praeger, 1969), and *A Short History of Socialism* (New York: Praeger, 1970); Alexander Gray, *The Socialist Tradition: Moses to Lenin* (London and New York: Longmans, Green, 1947); David O. Evans, *Social Romanticism in France, 1830–1848* (Oxford: Clarendon Press, 1951); Jacques Droz, ed., *Histoire générale du socialisme*, vol. 1, *Des origines à 1875* (Paris: Presses universitaires de France, 1972); Eric Hobsbawm, *The Age of Revolution, 1789–1848* (New York: New American Library [Mentor Book], 1962).

6. Tocqueville, *Democracy in America*, "Author's Introduction," pp. 5–6. The translation has been revised here.

7. Marquis de Custine, *The Empire of the Czar: A Journey through Eternal Russia*, no trans. (New York: Doubleday, 1989), and *Lettre de Russie: La Russie en 1839* (Paris: Gallimard, 1975). See also George F. Kennan, *The Marquis Custine and His "Russia in 1839"* (Princeton, N.J.: Princeton University Press, 1971).

8. Michel Cadot, *La Russie dans la vie intellectuelle française, 1839–1856* (Paris: Fayard, 1967), and Charles Corbet, *L'opinion française face à l'inconnue russe, 1799–1894* (Paris: Didier, 1967).

9. This phrase is Aleksandr Herzen's pithy summation of Custine's long condemnatory peroration. See Herzen, *Polnoe sobranie sochinii* (Moscow: Akademiia nauk, 1954–1965), vol. 2, p. 311.

10. Custine, *Empire of the Czar*, pp. 613–614.

11. This diatribe has not been published in any of the standard editions of Marx's works. It may be found in *Karl Marx: La Russie et l'Europe*, trans. B. P. Hepner (Paris, 1954). A full inventory of the opinions of Marx and Engels on Russia is given by H. Krause, "Marx und Engels und das zeitgenössische Russland," in *Marburger Abhandlungen zur Geschichte und Kultur Osteuropas* (Giessen: W. Schmitz, 1958).

12. See Gleason, *Genesis*, chap. 7; Karl Marx, "Revelations of the Diplomatic History of the Eighteenth Century," in *Free Press* (London, 1856–57).

450

13. Francois P. G. Guizot, *Histoire de la civilisation en Europe depuis la chute de l'Empire Romain jusqu'à la Révolution française* (Paris: Didier, 1875), first published 1828. Now remembered chiefly for the slogan "get rich," Guizot was one of the most influential historians of the nineteenth century; his general European history was particularly widely read. See, for example, *The History of Civilization, from the Fall of the Roman Empire to the French Revolution*, trans. William Hazlitt, 3 vols. (London: G. Bell and Sons, 1875–1880); Pierre Rosanvallon, *Le moment Guizot* (Paris: Gallimard, 1985); Stanley Mellon, *The Political Uses of History: A Study of Historians in the French Restoration* (Stanford, Calif.: Stanford University Press, 1958).

14. Jules Michelet, *Histoire de France* (Paris: Les amis de l'ambassade du livre, 1965), first published in 17 vols. between 1833 and 1869; *Le peuple*, intro. Paul Viallaneix (Paris: Flammarion, 1974).

15. Michel Cadot, ed., *Publications de Jules Michelet: légendes démocratique du Nord* (Paris: Presses universitaires de France, 1968).

16. Charles Quenet, *Tchaadaev et les Lettres philosophiques: contribution à l'étude du mouvement des idées en Russie* (Paris: H. Champion, 1931); Raymond T. McNally, trans., *The Major Works of Peter Chaadaev* (Notre Dame, Ind.: University of Notre Dame Press, 1969), and *Chaadayev and His Friends: An Intellectual History of Peter Chaadayev and His Russian Contemporaries* (Tallahassee, Fla.: Diplomatic Press, 1971).

17. Nicholas Riasanovsky, *Russia and the West in the Teaching of the Slavophiles: A Study of Romantic Ideology* (Gloucester, Mass.: P. Smith, 1965), first published in 1952; P. K. Christoff, *An Introduction to Nineteenth Century Russian Slavophilism: A Study in Ideas*, vol. 1, *A. S. Xomjakov* (The Hague: Mouton, 1961).

18. This point of view is best exemplified by Hans-Ulrich Wehler, *The German Empire, 1871–1918*, trans. Kim Traynor (Dover, N.H.: Berg Publishers, 1985), and Ralph Dahrendorf, *Society and Democracy in Germany* (London: Weidenfeld and Nicolson, 1967). For a Marxist critique of the *Sonderweg* thesis, see David Blackbourn and Geoffrey Eley, *The Peculiarities of German History: Bourgeois Society and Politics in Nineteenth-Century Germany* (Oxford and New York: Oxford University Press, 1984).

19. For the origin of the term "culture" as an antithesis to "civilization," see Elias, *The Civilizing Process*, chap. 1. For the full history of the two terms, see Jörg Fisch, "Zivilisation, Kultur," in Otto Brunner, Werner Conze, and Reinhart Koselleck, eds., *Geschichtliche Grundbegriffe: Historisches Lexikon zur politisch-sozialen Sprache in Deutschland*, vol. 7 (Stuttgart: Klett-Cotta, 1992).

20. The most pertinent works on the German revival are James Sheehan, *German History, 1770–1866* (New York: Oxford University Press, 1989); Hajo Holborn, *A History of Modern Germany*, vol. 2, *1648–1840* (Princeton, N.J.: Prince-

ton University Press, 1982); Jacques Droz, *L'Allemagne et la Révolution française* (Paris: Press universitaires de France, 1949); Thomas Nipperdey, *Deutsche Geschichte, 1800–1866: Burgerwelt und starker Staat* (Munich: C. H. Beck, 1983); Henri Brunschwig, *Société et romantisme en Prusse au XVIIIe siècle* (Paris: Flammarion, 1973); Walter Bruford, *Germany in the Eighteenth Century: The Social Background of the Literary Revival* (Cambridge: Cambridge University Press, 1935); Klaus Epstein, *The Genesis of German Conservatism* (Princeton, N.J.: Princeton University Press, 1966).

21. Otto Müller, *Intelligentcija: Untersuchung zur Geschichte eines politischen Schlachwortes* (Frankfort: Athenaum Verlag, 1971); John Zammito, *The Genesis of Kant's Critique of Judgment* (Chicago: University of Chicago Press, 1992), esp. chap. 1.

22. Leonard Krieger, *The German Idea of Freedom: History of a Political Tradition* (Boston: Beacon Press, 1957).

23. Immanuel Kant, "What Is Enlightenment?" in *Kant* (New York: Modern Library, 1949).

24. The best guide to Kant remains Cassirer, *Kant's Life and Thought.*

25. Elias, *The Civilizing Process*, chap. 1.

26. Ibid.

27. Friedrich Schiller, *Ausgewählte Werke* (Stuttgart: Kohlhammer, 1954), pp. 350–355.

28. Nigel Reeves, *Heinrich Heine: Poetry and Politics* (London: Oxford University Press, 1974).

29. Friedrich Meinecke, *Cosmopolitanism and the National State*, trans. Robert Kiber (Princeton, N.J.: Princeton University Press, 1970); Hans Kohn, *Nationalism: Its Meaning and History* (Princeton: Van Nostrand, 1955); Jean-Rene Suratteau, *L'idée nationale de la Révolution à nos jours* (Paris: Presses universitaires de France, 1972).

30. See "Nation" and "Souveraineté," in François Furet and Mona Ozouf, eds., *Dictionnaire critique de la Révolution française* (Paris: Flammarion, 1988); Reinhart Koselleck, "Volk, Nation, Nationalismus, Masse" in Otto Brunner, Werner Conze, and Reinhart Koselleck, eds., *Geschichtliche Grundbegriffe: Historiches Lexikon zur politisch-sozialen Sprache in Deutschland*, vol. 7 (Stuttgart: Ernst Klett, 1992).

31. Walter M. Simon, *The Failure of the Prussian Reform Movement: 1807–1819* (Ithaca, N.Y.: Cornell University Press, 1950); Reinhart Kosseleck, *Preussen Zwischen Reform und Revolution: Allgemeine Landrecht, Verwaltung, und Sozialbewegung von 1791–1848* (Stuttgart: Klett, 1967); Johann G. Fichte, *Addresses to the German Nation* (London: Open Court Publishing Company, 1922); Hans Rosenberg, *Bureaucracy, Aristocracy, and Autocracy: The Prussian Experience, 1660–1815* (Cambridge, Mass.: Harvard University Press, 1958).

452

32. Arthur Lovejoy, "On the Discrimination of Romanticisms," in *Essays in the History of Ideas* (Baltimore: Johns Hopkins University Press, 1948).

33. Some key works on Romanticism in general are H. G. Schenk, *The Mind of the European Romantics: An Essay in Cultural History* (New York: Anchor Books, 1969); René Welleck, "The Concept of Romanticism in Literary History," and "Romanticism Re-examined" in his *Concepts of Criticism*, ed. Stephen G. Nichols, Jr. (New Haven, Conn.: Yale University Press, 1963); Paul van Tieghem, *Le romantisme dans la littérature européene* (Paris: A. Michel, 1969); Meyer Abrams, *Natural Supernaturalism: Tradition and Revolution in Romantic Literature* (New York: Norton, 1971); Abrams, *The Mirror and the Lamp: Romantic Theory and the Critical Tradition* (New York: Oxford University Press, 1953); Nicholas Riasanovsky, *The Emergence of Romanticism* (New York: Oxford University Press, 1992); Rudolf Binion, *After Christianity: Christian Survivals in Post-Christian Culture* (Durango, Colo.: Logbridge-Rhodes, 1986); Jacques Barzun, *Classic, Romantic, and Modern*, 2d ed. (Boston: Little, Brown, 1961), and *Darwin, Marx, Wagner: Critique of a Heritage* (Boston: Little, Brown, 1941), and *Romanticism and the Modern Ego* (Boston: Little, Brown, 1943); Andrzej Walicki, *Philosophy and Romantic Nationalism: The Case of Poland* (Oxford: Clarendon Press, 1982).

    The principal works that consider Romanticism as a phenomenon enduring throughout the nineteenth century are those of Paul Bénichou: *Le sacre de l'écrivain, 1750–1830: essai sur l'avènement d'un pouvoir spirituel laïque dans la France moderne* (Paris: J. Corti, 1973); *Le temps des prophètes: doctrines de l'âge romantique* (Paris: Gallimard, 1977); *Selon Mallarmé* (Paris: Gallimard, 1995). See also Mario Praz, *The Romantic Agony*, trans. Angus Davidson (New York: Oxford University Press, 1954), first published in 1933.

34. Robert T. Clark, *Herder: His Life and Thought* (Berkeley: University of California Press, 1955); Frederick M. Bernard, *Herder's Social and Political Thought: From Enlightenment to Nationalism* (Oxford: Clarendon Press, 1965); Isaiah Berlin, *Vico and Herder: Two Studies in the History of Ideas* (New York: Viking Press, 1976).

35. August Wilhelm von Schlegel, "Lectures on Dramatic Literature," in John B. Halsted, ed., *Romanticism* (New York: Harper Torchbooks, 1969), pp. 43–55; Arthur Lovejoy, "The Meaning of 'Romantic' in Early German Romanticism," in *Essays in the History of Ideas* (Baltimore: Johns Hopkins University Press, 1948).

36. Novalis, "Christendom or Europe," in Halstead, *Romanticism*, pp. 122–138.

37. Victor Hugo, "Prefaces to Cromwell and Hernani," in Eugen Weber, ed., *Paths to the Present: Aspects of European Thought from Romanticism to Existentialism* (New York: Dodd, Mead, 1969).

38. Heinrich Heine, "De l'Allemagne depuis Luther," *Revue des deux mondes*, March 1, November 15, December 15, 1834, trans. Charles Godfrey Leland as *Germany*, vol. 1 of *The Works of Heinrich Heine* (New York: Dutton, 1906); Hajo Holborn, "Der deutsche Idealismus in sozialgeschichtlicher Beleuchtung," *Historische Zeitschrift* 174, no. 2 (October 1952): 359–384.

39. Ernst Cassirer, *Rousseau, Kant, Goethe: Two Essays*, trans. James Gutman and Paul Oskar (New York: Harper and Row, 1963).

40. Richard Kroner, *Von Kant bis Hegel*, 2 vols. (Tubingen: Mohr, 1921–1924).

41. Some of the more important modern commentaries on Hegel are Jean Hyppolite, *Genèse et structure de la phénomenologie de l'Esprit* (Paris: Aubier, 1946), English translation 1974, and *Introduction to Hegel's Philosophy of History*, trans. Bond Harris and Jacqueline Bouchard (Gainesville: University Press of Florida, 1996); Charles Taylor, *Hegel* (New York: Cambridge University Press, 1975); Shlomo Avineri, *Hegel's Theory of the Modern State* (London: Cambridge University Press, 1972); Walter Kaufmann, *Hegel: Reinterpretation, Texts and Commentary* (New York: Doubleday, 1965).

The religious and neo-Platonic components of Hegel's thought have been noted by Holborn, "Idealismus"; Karl Löwith, *From Hegel to Nietzsche* (New York: Garland, 1984), and *Meaning in History* (Chicago: University of Chicago Press, 1949); Enrico de Negri, *Interpretazione de Hegel* (Florence: G. C. Sonsoni, 1943); Wilhelm Dilthey, "Die Jugendgeschichte Hegels," in *Die Jugendgeschichte Hegels und andere Abhandlungen zur Geschichte des deutschen Idealismus* (Leipzig and Berlin: B. G. Teubner, 1921). The case is given its most extensive historical grounding by Laurence Dicky, *Hegel: Religion, Economics, and the Politics of the Spirit, 1770–1807* (New York: Cambridge University Press, 1987).

42. Abrams, *Natural Supernaturalism*.

43. For the genealogy of the idea of historicism, see Friedrich Meinecke, *Historicism: The Rise of a New Historical Outlook*, trans. J. E. Anderson (London: Routledge and Kegan Paul, 1972); Ernst Troeltsch, *Der Historismus und sein Überwindung* (Berlin: R. Heise, 1924); George Iggers, *The German Conception of History: The National Tradition of Historical thought from Herder to the Present* (Middletown, Conn.: Wesleyan University Press, 1968).

44. Theodore von Laue, *Leopold Ranke: The Formative Years* (Princeton, N.J.: Princeton University Press, 1950); Leonard Krieger, *Ranke: The Meaning of History* (Chicago: University of Chicago Press, 1977).

45. James Westfall Thompson, *A History of Historical Writing* (New York: Macmillan, 1942), vol. 2., pp. 171–172.

46. See notes 13 and 14 above for France and note 44 for Germany. For Romano-Germanic Europe as a whole see Hegel, *The Philosophy of History*.

454

47. This perspective on European history is developed more fully in Martin Malia, "A New Europe for the Old?" *Daedalus* 126, no. 3 (Summer 1997): 1–22.

48. Custine gives just such a checklist; see his *Empire of the Czar*, chap. 37.

49. Dieter Groh, *Russland und das Selbstverständnis Europas* (Neuwied: Hermann Luchterhand, 1961), pp. 65–80.

50. See note 34 above for Herder's general worldview.

51. Johann Gottfried Herder, *Ideen zur Philsophie der Geschichte der Menschheit* (Frankfurt: Deutsche Klassiker Verlag, 1989), pp. 698–699. The work was first published in Riga and Leipzig over the years 1785–1792.

52. Anne L. G. de Staël, *Dix années d'exil*, ed. Paul Guatier (Paris: Plon, 1904).

53. Hegel, *Philosophy of History*, p. 350.

54. Benoît Hepner, *Bakounine et le panslavisme révolutionnaire* (Paris: Rivière, 1950).

55. Hans Kohn, *Panslavism* (New York: Random House, 1960); Michael Petrovich, *The Emergence of Russian Panslavism, 1856–1870* (New York: New York University Press, 1956).

56. Jenó Szúcs, *Les trois Europes* (Paris: L'Harmattan, 1985).

57. See Malia, "A New Europe for the Old?"

58. Andrzej Walicki, *The Slavophile Controversy: History of a Conservative Utopia in Nineteenth-Century Russian Thought*, trans. Hilda Andrews-Rusiecka (Oxford: Clarendon Press, 1975), pp. 161–165. For Baader, see Groh, *Russland*, pp. 117–124; Heinrich Stammler, "Wandlungen des deutschen Bildes vom russischen Menschen," *Jarbücher für die Geschichte Osteuropas* 5, no. 3 (1957): 280–282. For Chaadaev's Western connections, see McNally, *Chaadayev and His Friends*, pp. 180–181, and his "Chaadaev's Evaluation of Western Christian Churches," *Slavonic and East European Review* 42, no. 99 (June 1964): 370–387.

59. Walicki, *The Slavophile Controversy*, pp. 161–165.

60. Robert Triomphe, *Joseph de Maistre: etude sur la vie et sur la doctrine d'un matérialiste mystique* (Geneva: Droz, 1968); Joseph de Maistre, "Cinq lettres sur l'éducation publique en Russie à M. le Comte Rasoumowsky, ministre de l'instruction publique," in *Oeuvres choisies de Joseph de Maistre* (Paris: R. Roger et F. Chernoviz, 1910), p. 187.

61. A. F. L. M. Freiherr von Haxthausen, *Studien über die inneren Züstande, das Volksleben und insbesondere die ländlichen Einrichtungen Russlands*, 3 vols. (Hannover and Hahn, 1847–1852). There is an abridged English version, *Studies on the Interior of Russia, August von Haxthausen*, ed. S. Frederick Starr (Chicago and London: University of Chicago Press, 1972); see especially the editor's introduction.

62. Andrzej Walicki, "Adam Mickiewicz's Paris Lectures and Russian Slavophilism," and (for Lelewel), "Alexander Herzen's 'Russian Socialism' as a Response to Polish Revolutionary Slavophilism," in his *Russia, Poland, and Univer-*

sal Regeneration (Notre Dame, Ind.: University of Notre Dame Press, 1991). See also his *Philosophy and Romantic Nationalism*, pt. 1, chap. 3.

63. Martin Malia, *Alexander Herzen and the Birth of Russian Socialism, 1812–1855* (Cambridge, Mass.: Harvard University Press, 1961).

64. Nicholas V. Riasanovsky, *A Parting of Ways: Government and the Educated Public in Russia, 1801–1855* (Oxford: Clarendon Press, 1976).

65. Paul Debreczeny and Jesse Zeldin, trans. and eds., *Literature and National Identity, Ninteenth-Century Russian Critical Essays* (Nebraska: University of Nebraska Press, 1970).

66. "Ia pamiatnik sebe vozdvig nerukotvornyi" (I have raised to myself a monument not created by human hands). Most Russians know this poem by heart; it is inscribed on the Pushkin monument inaugurated in Moscow in 1881 with speeches by Turgenev and Dostoevsky.

67. The most successful effort to treat imperial Russia's internal development in European context is Raeff, *The Well-Ordered Police State*. See also his *Origins of the Russian Intelligentsia* (New York: Harcourt and Brace, 1966). Perry Anderson, *Lineages of the Absolutist State* (London: New Left Books, 1974), offers a Marxist perspective on Russia's place in Europe. Some works relevant to assessing Russia's *Sonderweg* are Natan Eidelman, *Revoliutsiia sverkhu v Rossii* (Moscow: Izdatel'stvo "Kniga," 1989); John P. LeDonne, *Absolutism and Ruling Class: The Formation of the Russian Political Order, 1700–1825* (New York: Oxford University Press, 1991); Eric Amburger, *Geschichte der Behördenorganisation Russlands von Peter dem Grossen bis 1917* (Leiden: Mouton, 1966).

68. Vladimir Nahirny, *The Russian Intelligentsia: From Torment to Silence* (New Brunswick, N.J.: Transaction Books, 1983).

69. Alan Pollard, "The Russian Intelligentsia: The Mind of Russia," *California Slavic Studies* 3 (1964): 1–32.

70. Riasanovsky, *Slavophiles*.

71. P. R. Roosevelt, *Apostle of Russian Liberalism: Timofei Granovsky* (Newtonville, Mass.: Oriental Research Partners, 1986).

72. Malia, *Herzen*; E. H. Carr, *Michael Bakunin* (London: Macmillan, 1937). Eugene Lampert, *Studies in Rebellion* (London: Routledge and Kegan Paul, 1957).

73. Nicholas Riasanovsky, *Nicholas I and Official Nationality in Russia, 1825–1855* (Berkeley: University of California Press, 1967, 1959).

74. The scene is described in Alexis de Tocqueville, *Recollections*, ed. J. P. Mayer and A. P. Kerr, trans. George Lawrence (Garden City, N.Y.: Doubleday, 1970), pt. 2, chap. 7; the slogan is repeated in Karl Marx, *The Eighteenth Brumaire of Louis Bonaparte* (New York: International Publishers, 1963), p. 119.

75. Edmund Schramm, *Donoso Cortes: Leben und Werk eines spanischen Antiliberalen* (Hamburg: Ibero-amerikanisches Institut, 1935).

76. Quoted in Michael Florinsky, *Russia: A History and an Interpretation* (New York: Macmillan, 1961–1963), vol. 2, pp. 867–868.

77. Harold W. G. Temperley, *England and the Near East: The Crimea* (London and New York: Longmans, Green, 1936), p. 374.

78. Jacob Phillip Fallmerayer, *Fragmente aus dem Orient* (Stuttgart: J. G. Cotta, 1877, first published in 1845). See also Groh, *Russland*, pp. 213–218.

79. The view of Nicholas I's foreign policy depicted here is roughly that expressed by V. Puryear, *England, Russia, and the Straits Question, 1844–1856* (Berkeley: University of California Press, 1931), and by Riasanovsky, *Nicholas I and Official Nationality*, chap. 5. See also Norman Rich, *Why the Crimean War? A Cautionary Tale* (Hanover, N.H.: University Press of New England, for Brown University, 1985), and Gooch, "A Century of Historiography on the Origins of the Crimean War," *American Historical Review* 62 (October 1956); David Goldfrank, *The Origins of the Crimean War* (New York: Longman, 1994); David Wetzel, *The Crimean War: A Diplomatic History* (Boulder, Colo.: Eastern European Monographs, 1985).

80. Contrary to the opinion expressed here, Gleason's *Genesis of Russophobia in Great Britain* interprets the phenomenon he is discussing as, on the whole, the "rational" reaction to a fundamental conflict of interests between England and Russia over the Straits, although the evidence of virulent hatred he adduces would not seem to support his own thesis. See also R. McNally, "The Origins of Russophobia in France, 1812–1830," *American Slavic and East European Review* 17, no. 2 (April 1958): 173–189.

3. RUSSIA AS EUROPE REGAINED

1. At one time the historiography insisted on the promising nature of the Great Reforms. See A. A. Kornilov, *Krestianskaia reforma* (St. Petersburg: Vaisberg and Gershunin, 1905); a summary of his views is given in *Modern Russian History*, no trans. (New York: Knopf, 1916–17); Jacob Walkin, *The Rise of Democracy in Pre-Revolutionary Russia: Political and Social Institutions under the Last Three Tsars* (New York: Praeger, 1962). Terence Emmons, *The Russian Landed Gentry and the Peasant Emancipation of 1861* (London: Cambridge University Press, 1968). Terence Emmons and Wayne Vucinich, eds., *The Zemstvo in Russia: An Experiment in Local Self-Government* (Cambridge: Cambridge University Press, 1982). Later attention shifted to the alleged reformist potential of the Soviet regime as represented, for example, by the "Bukharin alternative" (see the section "The Ride of the Troika" in Chapter 5). Since the Soviet collapse, however, reformist efforts under the imperial regime are again receiv-

ing more attention, a tendency that began even before 1991. See Bruce Lincoln, *In the Vanguard of Reform: Russia's Enlightened Bureaucrats* (De Kalb: University of Illinois Press, 1982), and his *The Great Reforms* (De Kalb: University of Illinois Press, 1990).

2. For the beginnings of Populism, see Chapter 2, notes 68, 69, and 72; for the movement's further development, see Franco Venturi, *Roots of Revolution: A History of the Populist and Socialist Movements in Nineteenth Century Russia*, trans. Francis Haskell (London: Weidenfeld and Nicolson, 1960); Eugene Lampert, *Sons against Fathers* (Oxford: Clarendon Press, 1965); Aileen Kelly, *Mikhail Bakunin: A Study in the Psychology and Politics of Utopianism* (Oxford: Clarendon Press; New York: Oxford University Press, 1982).

3. William Wochrlin, *Chernyshevskii: The Man and the Journalist* (Cambridge, Mass.: Harvard University Press, 1971); Irina Paperno, *Chernyshevsky and the Age of Realism: A Study in the Semiotics of Behavior* (Stanford, Calif.: Stanford University Press, 1988); Norman Pereira, *N. G. Chernyshevsky: An Intellectual Biography* (Berkeley: University of California Press, 1970).

4. Still of value is the classic of A. A. Kornilov, *Obshchestvennoe dvizhenie pri Aleksandre II, 1855–1881* (Moscow: Russkaia mysl, 1909).

5. Henry Adams, *The Education of Henry Adams* (New York: Modern Library, 1946), p. 439.

6. For the past twenty-five years or so 1905 and the crisis leading up to it have usually been treated in the West as a "workers' revolution," and thus "the general rehearsal for 1917" in Trotsky's expression. For the 1890s, see for example Allan Wildman, *The Making of a Workers' Revolution: Russian Social Democracy: 1891–1903* (Chicago: University of Chicago Press, 1967). A corrective in the direction of politics is offered by John Keep, *The Rise of Social Democracy in Russia* (Oxford: Clarendon Press, 1967). The Revolution of 1905 itself is now coming into its own as a revolution of the whole of society with the aim of achieving constitutional democracy. See Abraham Ascher, *The Revolution of 1905*, 2 vols. (Stanford, Calif.: Stanford University Press, 1988–1992), and Terrence Emmons, *The Formation of Political Parties and the First National Elections in Russia* (Cambridge, Mass.: Harvard University Press, 1983).

7. For awareness of the profound gulf in Western society, see Louis Chevalier, *Laboring Classes and Dangerous Classes in Paris during the First Half of the Nineteenth Century*, trans. Frank Jellinek (Princeton, N.J.: Princeton University Press, 1973), and Benjamin Disraeli, *Sybil, or, The Two Nations*, ed. Sheila M. Smith (Oxford and New York: Oxford University Press, 1981).

8. The basic works are Erich Eyck, *Bismark*, 3 vols. (Erlenbach and Zurich: Eugen Rentsch Verlag, 1941–1944), and Otto Pflanze, *Bismark and the Development of Germany*, 2d ed., 3 vols. (Princeton, N.J.: Princeton University Press, 1990).

9. For the "internal contradictions" of imperial German society, see Arthur

458

Rosenberg, *The Birth of the German Republic, 1871–1918*, trans. Ian F. D. Morrow (New York: Russell and Russell, 1962); Thorstein Veblen, *Imperial Germany and the Industrial Revolution* (New York: Macmillan, 1915); Ralf Dahrendorf, *Society and Democracy in Germany* (Garden City: Doubleday, 1967); Hans-Ulrich Wehler, *The German Empire, 1871–1918*, trans. Kim Traynor (Dover, N.H.: Berg Publishers, 1985), *Bismarck und der Imperialismus* (Koln and Berlin: Kiepenheuer und Witsch, 1969), and *Deutsche Gesellschaftsgeschichte* (Munich: C. H. Beck, 1987); Blackbourn and Eley, *The Peculiarities of German History.*

10. Alexandre Dumas, *Adventures in Czarist Russia* (London: P. Owen, 1960); S. Duriline, *Alexandre Dumas père en Russie* (Paris: O. Zeluck, 1947).

11. Carl Ackerman, "'Alice' Goes to Russia," unpublished paper (University of California at Berkeley, 1992); Lewis Carroll, *The Russian Journal and Other Selections from the Works of Lewis Carroll* (New York: E. P. Dutton, 1935).

12. Alfred Rambaud, *History of Russia from the Earliest Times to 1882*, trans. L. B. Lang, 3 vols. (Boston: Estes and Lauriat, 1886); Alexander Brückner, *Geschichte Russlands bis zum Ende des 18. Jahrhunderts*, 2 vols. (Gotha: Perthes, 1896–1913).

13. Sir Donald Mackenzie Wallace, *Russia*, 2d ed. (London and New York: Cassell and Co., 1912), pp. 98, 129, 131.

14. Anatole Leroy-Beaulieu, *The Empire of the Tsars and the Russians*, trans. Zénaïde A. Ragozin (from 3d French ed.), 3 vols. (New York and London, 1893–1896), vol. 1, pp. 303, 498.

15. Jules Verne, *Michael Strogoff*, first published 1876 and *Aventures de trois Russes et de trois Anglais*, 14th ed. (Paris: J. Hetzel, 1877).

16. George Kennan, *Siberia and the Exile System*, 2 vols. (New York: Century Co., 1891).

17. Richard Pipes, "Max Weber and Russia," *World Politics* 7 (1955): 371–401; Max Weber, *The Russian Revolutions*, trans. and ed. Gordon C. Wells and Peter Baehr (Cambridge: Polity Press, 1995).

18. Paul N. Miliukov, *Russia and Its Crisis* (Chicago: University of Chicago Press, 1905).

19. For Marx's relation to Russia, see Maximilien Rubel, "Karl Marx et le socialisme populiste russe," *La revue socialiste* 11 (May 1947): 547–559; Rubel, "La Russie dans l'ouevre de Marx et d'Engels: leur correspondance avec Danielson," *La revue socialiste* 36 (April 1950): 327–349. See also Kostas Papaioannou, "L'Occident et la Russie, I: introduction à la russophobie de Marx," *Contrat social* 12, no. 1 (January–March 1968), and "L'Occident et la Russie, II: Marx russophobe," *Contrat social* 12, nos. 2–3 (April–September 1968). For a full collection of Marx and Engels's pronouncements on Russia see Karl Marx and Friedrich Engels, *Die russische Kommune; Kritik eines Mythos*, ed. Maximilian Rubel (Munchen: C. Hanser, 1972).

20. Karl Marx and Friedrich Engels, *Perepiska K. Marksa i F. Engel'sa s russkimi politicheskimi deiteliami*, 2d ed. (Moscow: Gosudartsvennoe izdatel'stvo politicheskoi literatury, 1951).

21. Carl Schorske, *German Social Democracy, 1905–1917: The Development of the Great Schism* (Cambridge, Mass.: Harvard University Press, 1955); J. Peter Nettl, *Rosa Luxemburg* (London and New York: Oxford University Press, 1966).

22. Élie Halévy, *The World Crisis of 1914–1918*, trans R. K. Webb (Oxford: Clarendon Press, 1930), p. 19.

23. Lewis Namier, *The Revolution of the Intellectuals* (London: Oxford University Press, 1962).

24. Carlton Hayes, *The Historical Evolution of Modern Nationalism* (New York: R. R. Smith, 1931).

25. Ernst Gellner, *Nations and Nationalism* (Ithaca, N.Y.: Cornell University Press, 1983).

26. Benedict Anderson, *Imagined Communities: Reflections on the Origin and Spread of Nationalism*, rev. ed. (London and New York: Verso, 1991).

27. Prosper Mérimée, *Études de littérature russe*, 2 vols. (Paris: H. Champion, 1931–32, vols. 10–11 of *Oeuvres complètes*).

28. Charles Miller, "Nietzsche's Discovery of Doestoevsky" *Nietzsche-Studien* 2 (1973).

29. Hugh McClean, "The Development of Modern Russian Literature," *Slavic Review* 21, no. 3 (September 1962): 389–410, 428–432.

30. David Magarshak, *Stanislavsky: A Life* (New York: Chanticleer Press, 1951); Nikita S. Sibiriakov, *Stanislavskii i zarubezhnyi teatr* (Moscow: Iskusstvo, 1967).

31. Richard Leonhard, *A History of Russian Music* (New York: Funk and Wagnalls, 1970).

32. Sergei Lifar', *Istoriia russkogo baleta* (Paris: n.p., 1945).

33. See, e.g., Lionello Venturi, *Chagall: Biographical and Critical Study* (New York: Skira, 1956); Marc Chagall, *My Life* (London: Owens, 1965); Jacques Lassaigne, *Kandinsky: Biographical and Critical Study* (Cleveland: World, 1964); Will Grohmann, *Wassily Kandinsky: Life and Work* (New York: Abrams, 1958).

34. For an illuminating discussion of the ideology underlying modern Russian painting, see Alain Besançon, *L'image interdite, une histoire intellectuelle de l'iconoclasme* (Paris: Fayard, 1994), chap. 8. An excerpt from Kandinsky's text is given in Eugen Weber, ed., *Paths to the Present* (New York: Dodd, Mead, 1960).

35. Baudelaire, "Qu'est-ce que le romantisme?" in *Oeuvres*, Bibliothèque de la Pléiade (Paris: Gallimard, 1951), p. 602.

36. Baudelaire, "Correspondances" and other poems in *Les fleurs du Mal*, in *Oeuvres*, Bibliothèque de la Pléiade (Paris: Gallimard, 1951).

460

37. The best introduction to Wagner is Ernest Newman, *Wagner as Man and Artist* (New York: Vintage, 1952).

38. Baudelaire, "Richard Wagner et Tannhäuser à Paris," in *Ouevres*, Bibliothèque de la Pléiade (Paris: Gallimard, 1951), p. 602.

39. Bernard Denvir, *Impressionism: The Painters and the Paintings* (New York: Mallard Press, 1991), p. 347.

40. For different aspects of Romanticism's transformation into other things, see Praz, *The Romantic Agony*; Renato Paggioli, *The Theory of the Avant-garde*, trans. Gerald Fitzgerald (Cambridge, Mass.: Harvard University Press, 1969); Edmund Wilson, *Axel's Castle: A Study in the Imaginative Literature of 1870–1930* (New York: Charles Scribner's Sons, 1939).

41. Currently the baseline of Nietzsche studies is Walter Kaufmann, *Nietzsche: Philosopher, Psychologist, Antichrist* (New York: Vintage Books, 1968). See also Tracy B. Strong, *Friedrich Nietzsche and the Politics of Transfiguration* (Berkeley: University of California Press, 1975). For a compendium of opinion, see Bernard Magnus and Kathleen Higgins, eds., *The Cambridge Companion to Nietzsche* (Cambridge: Cambridge University Press, 1996).

42. Friedrich Nietzsche, *The Birth of Tragedy*, trans. Francis Golffing (New York: Doubleday, 1956), p. 9. Where possible references to Nietzsche are to readily accessible English translations. Most other references to Nietzsche are in *Werke in Drei Bänden*, ed. Karl Shchlechta, 3 vols. (Munich: Carl Hanser Verlag, 1966).

43. Friedrich Nietzsche, *The Gay Science*, ed. Walter Kaufmann (New York: Vintage, 1974), bk. 5, and *Werke*, vol. 2., pp. 205–206.

44. Friedrich Nietzsche, *Twilight of the Idols* in *The Portable Nietzsche*, ed. Walter Kaufmann (New York: Viking Press, 1954), and *Aus Dem Nachlass Der Achtzigerjahre*, in *Werke*, vol. 3, p. 444.

45. Friedrich Nietzsche, *Nachlass*, in *Werke*, vol. 3, p. 422.

46. It has long been known that Nietzsche's projected book, "The Will to Power," was never completed but that its intended message survived in numerous fragments. The first part of this work was to have been a "History of European Nihilism." This has been reconstructed by Elisabeth Kuhn, *Friedrich Nietzsches Philosophie des europäischen Nihilismus* (Berlin and New York: Walter de Gruyter, 1992). Its outline parallels closely *Beyond Good and Evil*, in which he made his most striking comments about Russia.

47. For the atmosphere of this period, see Roger Shattuck, *The Banquet Years: The Arts in France, 1885–1918* (New York: Harcourt, Brace, 1958), and Poggioli, *Theory*.

48. K. Mochul'skii, *Dostoevskii: zhizn' i tvorchestvo* (Paris: YMCA Press, 1947).

49. Boris Eikenbaum, *Lev Tolstoi*, 2 vols. (Leningrad and Moscow: Priboi, 1928). For the role of Tocqueville's *Ancien régime* in sensitizing Tolstoy to the fact

that he was living the end of Russia's Old Regime, see Kathyrn B. Feuer, *Tolstoy and the Genesis of War and Peace*, ed. Robin Feuer Miller and Dona Tussing Orwin (Ithaca, N.Y.: Cornell University Press, 1996).

50. Fedor M. Dostoevsky, *The Possessed*, pt. 2, chap. 1, section 7.

51. E. M. de Vogüé, *The Russian Novelists*, trans. J. L. Edmonds (Boston, 1887), pp. 211–212, 224, 269.

52. Ibid., pp. 224, 269.

53. André Gide, *Dostoevsky*, intro. Arnold Bennett (London and Toronto: J. M. Dent and Sons, 1925), p. 9. The essay was first written in 1908.

54. Bennett's introduction to Gide, *Dostoevsky*; Mischa Harry Fayer, *Gide, Freedom, and Dostoevsky* (Burlington: Lane Press, 1946).

55. Oscar Wilde, "Vera, or the Nihilists," in *The Plays of Oscar Wilde*, 4 vols. (Boston and London: J. W. Luce, 1905–1920), vol. 3.

56. Oscar Wilde, *De Profundis* (New York: Philospohical Library, 1960), esp. p. 112.

57. André Gide, *The Immoralist*, trans. Dorothy Bussey (New York: Knopf, 1954).

58. T. S. Eliot, *Selected Essays* (New York: Harcourt, Brace, 1950), p. 344.

59. Berdiaev, *The Origin of Russian Communism*; Berdiaev, *The Russian Idea*, trans. R. M. French (London: G. Bles, Centenary Press, 1947).

60. Heinrich Stammler, "Wandlungen des deutschen Bildes vom russischen Menschen," *Jahrbücher für Geschichte Osteuropas* 5, no. 3 (1957): 274.

61. Rudolph Binion, *Frau Lou: Nietzsche's Wayward Disciple* (Princeton, N.J., Princeton University Press, 1968).

62. Quoted in Stammler, "Wandlungen des deutschen Bildes," p. 290. English translation of verses by John Zammito.

63. Stammler, "Wandlungen des deutschen Bildes," pp. 290, 296. See also André von Gronika, "Thomas Mann and Russia," *Germanic Review* 20, no. 2 (April 1945); Leon Löwenthal, "Die Aufassung Dostojewskis in Vorkriegsdeutchland," *Zeitschrift für Sozialforschung*, 3 (1934): 343–382.

64. Bernice Glatzer-Rosenthal, ed., *Nietzsche in Russia* (Princeton, N.J.: Princeton University Press, 1986). See also Dmytro Čiževsky, *Dostojevskii und Nietzsche* (Bonn: n.p., 1947).

65. Nietzsche, *Werke*, vol. 3., pp. 619, 726, 1254.

66. Nietzsche, *Beyond Good and Evil*, trans. Walter Kaufmann (New York: Vintage Books, 1966).

67. Nietzsche, *Nachlass*, in *Werke*, vol. 3., p. 690.

68. Nietzsche, *Ecce Homo*, trans. Walter Kaufmann (New York: Vintage Books, 1969), p. 327 and *Werke*, vol. 2, p. 1153.

69. Friedrich Nietzsche, *Sämtliche Werke in Zwölf Bänden*, 12 vols. (Stuttgart: Kröner Verlag, 1964), vol. 11, p. 365.

70. Nietzsche, *Beyond Good and Evil*, p. 131.

71. Nietzsche, *Twilight*, p. 543.

72. Stammler, "Wandlungen des deutschen Bildes," p. 292.

73. Fritz Stern, *The Politics of Cultural Despair: A Study in the Rise of the Germanic Ideology* (Berkeley: University of California Press, 1961).

74. Ibid., p. 209.

75. Ibid., p. 211.

76. Sigmund Freud, "Dostoevsky and Parricide," in *Sigmund Freud: Collected Papers*, vol. 5 (New York: Basic Books, 1959), pp. 222–242.

77. Stammler, "Wandlungen des deutschen Bildes," p. 304.

78. J. S. Mill, *Autobiography* (Indianopolis: Bobbs Merrill, [Library of the Liberal Arts], 1957), pp. 152–153.

79. George Dangerfield, *The Strange Death of Liberal England* (New York: H. Smith and R. Haas, 1935); Carlton Hayes, *France: A Nation of Patriots* (New York: Columbia University Press, 1930).

80. The standard account of the Action Française is Eugen Weber, *Action Française; Royalism and Reaction in Twentieth-Century France* (Stanford, Calif.: Stanford University Press, 1962). Other works often fail to make the necessary distinction between fascism as a movement and fascism as a regime. Nolte, *Three Faces*, puts Charles Maurras on the same level as Mussolini and Hitler; Zeev Sternhell, *La droite révolutionnaire: les origines françaises du fascisme, 1885–1914* (Paris: Editions du Seuil, 1978), makes the Third Republic the epicenter of European fascism. See also Mario Sznajder and Maia Asheri, *Naissance de l'idéologie fasciste* (Paris: Fayard, 1989), note on "fascism" in chap. 4.

81. For the "internal contradictions" of imperial German society, see note 9 above. See also Robert Wohl, *The Generation of 1914* (Cambridge, Mass.: Harvard University Press, 1979).

82. Wolfgang Sauer, "Das Problem des deutschen Nationalstaates," in Hans-Ulrich Wehler, ed., *Moderne deutsche Sozialgeschichte* (Cologne and Berlin: Kiepenhauer und Witsch, 1966), pp. 407–436; Karl Dietrich Bracher, *The German Dictatorship: The Origin, Structure, and Effects of National Socialism* (New York: Praeger, 1970).

83. For the ideology of Mitteleuropa, see Henry Cord Meyer, *Mitteleuropa in German Thought and Action, 1815–1945* (The Hague: H. Nijhoff, 1955), chap. 9, pp. 194–217.

84. Fritz Ringer, *The Decline of the German Mandarins: The German Academic Community, 1890–1933* (Cambridge, Mass.: Harvard University Press, 1969).

85. Stern sums up the average view on these issues: "America was all civilization, Russia all culture; in ideal societies, as in the Germany of the future, the two would be perfectly balanced." Stern, *The Politics of Cultural Despair*, p. 197.

86. Klemens von Klemperer, *Germany's New Conservatism: Its History and Dilemma in the Twentieth Century* (Princeton, N.J.: Princeton University Press, 1957);

Stern, *The Politics of Cultural Despair*. For the pre-1870 background, see Leonard Krieger, *The German Idea of Freedom* (Boston: Beacon Press, 1957); Fritz Stern, "The Political Consequences of the Unpolitical German," *History*, August 1960.

87. Heinrich Mann, *Essays* (Berlin: Aufbau-Verlag, 1954).
88. George L. Mosse, *The Crisis of German Ideology: Intellectual Origins of the Third Reich* (New York: Grosset and Dunlap, 1964).
89. Nietzsche, *Beyond Good and Evil*, p. 131.

4. WAR AND REVOLUTION

1. Raymond Aron, *Les guerres en chaine* (Paris: Gallimard, 1951).
2. The best single guide to the international relations of this period is A. J. P. Taylor, *The Struggle for the Mastery of Europe, 1848–1918* (Oxford: Clarendon Press, 1954).
3. Some of the standard works on the buildup to the First World War are Sidney Fay, *The Origins of the World War*, 2 vols. (New York: Macmillan, 1928); William Langer, *The Franco-Russian Alliance, 1890–1894* (Cambridge, Mass.: Harvard University Press, 1929); Boris Nolde, *L'alliance franco-russe: les origines du système diplomatique d'avant-guerre* (Paris: Droz, 1936); Raymond J. Sontag, *Germany and England: Background of Conflict, 1848–1894* (New York and London: Appelton-Century, 1939); William Langer, *European Alliances and Alignments, 1871–1890*, 2d ed. (New York: Knopf, 1950); Langer, *The Diplomacy of Imperialism, 1890–1902*, 2d ed. (New York: Knopf, 1951); Fritz Fischer, *Germany's Aims in the First World War* (New York: Norton, 1967).
4. Taylor, *Struggle*, p. xxiv.
5. See the section "Culture and the German *Sonderweg*" in Chapter 2.
6. This point is forcefully made by François Furet, *Le passé d'une illusion: essai sur l'idée communiste au XXe siècle* (Paris: R. Laffont, Calmann-Lévy, 1994).
7. Norman Stone, *The Eastern Front, 1914–1917* (London: Hodder and Stoughton, 1975); Alan Clark, *Suicide of the Empires: The Battles of the Eastern Front, 1914–1918* (New York: American Heritage Press, 1971).
8. The crucial role of the army in producing the Russian Revolution is analyzed by Allan Wildman, *The End of the Russian Imperial Army: The Old Army and the Soldiers' Revolt (March–April 1917)* (Princeton, N.J.: Princeton University Press, 1980), and *The Soldiers' Plebiscite: Soviet Power and the Committee Revolution at the Front, October–November 1917* (Washington, D.C.: Wilson Center, Kennan Institute for Advanced Russian Studies, 1982).
9. For some of the literature on socialism, see Chapter 2, note 5. The most comprehensive histories of socialism are G. D. H. Cole, *A History of Socialist Thought*, 5 vols. (London: Macmillan; New York: St. Martin's Press, 1953–

1960); Carl Landauer, *European Socialism: A History of Ideas and Movements from the Industrial Revolution to Hitler's Seizure of Power*, 2 vols. (Berkeley: University of California Press, 1959).

10. See the section "The 'Two' and the 'Three'" in Chapter 2.

11. The best discussion of these crucial years is Lichtheim, *The Origins of Socialism.*

12. Robert Tucker, ed., *Marx-Engels Reader*, 2d ed. (New York: Norton, 1978), p. 475, note 8, appended to the English translation of 1888.

13. Martin Malia, *The Soviet Tragedy: A History of Socialism in Russia, 1917–1991* (New York: Free Press, 1994), chap. 1.

14. This is the title of the classic study in historical demography of Peter Laslett, *The World We Have Lost*, 2d ed. (New York: Scribner, 1973, 1971). *The Communist Manifesto* gives an almost lyrical evocation of this past: "The bourgeoisie . . . has put an end to all feudal, partriarchal, idyllic relations. It has pitilessly torn asunder the motley feudal ties that bound man to his 'natural superiors'. . . . It has drowned the most heavenly ecstasies of religious fervour, of chivalrous enthusiasm, of philistine sentimentalism, in the icy water of egotistical calculation." Tucker, *Marx-Engels Reader*, p. 475.

15. See Klaus Epstein, *The Genesis of German Conservatism* (Princeton, N.J.: Princeton University Press, 1966), and Johnathan Knudsen, *Justus Möser and the German Enlightenment* (New York: Cambridge University Press, 1986).

16. Ferdinand Tönnies, *Community and Society*, trans. and ed. Charles P. Loomis (East Lansing: Michigan State University Press, 1957).

17. Mona Ozouf, "Fraternité" in François Furet and Mona Ozouf, eds., *Dictionnaire critique de la Révolution française* (Paris: Flammarion, 1989). Marcel David, *Fraternité et Révolution française, 1789–1799* (Paris: Aubier, 1987), takes this elusive concept back to Rousseau, with whom the modern idea of socialism may also be plausibly linked.

18. "Theses on Feuerbach," in Tucker, *Marx-Engels Reader*, p. 145.

19. Traditionally, commentators on Marx have treated him as a social scientist who derived his theories directly from the observation of society. See, for example, Cole, *Socialist Thought*, and Landauer, *European Socialism.* This approach, however, appeared increasingly inadequate after the publication in the 1930s of his more Hegelian writings—the manuscripts of the 1840s and the *Grundrisse* of 1857–58—a corpus which in fact was not assimilated by scholarship until the 1950s. Assessments of the metaphysical substratum in Marx, however, have varied notably.

Marxology has been further complicated by the fact that since 1917 most of it was produced by Westerners writing in one or another degree of tension with Soviet Communism yet with no direct experience of it. Briefly, there are first the Western Marxists for whom, after the manner of György Lukács, the metaphysical Marx offers a "critical philosophy" for contending with the ills of bourgeois society. For this group the Soviet performance came increasingly to be embarrassing or simply irrelevant; and consequently, they have had little of value to say about the relationship of Marxism to Soviet Communism. See, for example, Herbert Marcuse, *Reason and Revolution*, 2d ed. (New York: Humanities Press, 1954), and his *Soviet Marxism: A Critical Analysis* (New York: Columbia University Press, 1958). See also Perry Anderson, *Considerations on Western Marxism* (London: Verso, 1979). For a critical evaluation of this movement, see J. G. Merquior, *Western Marxism* (London: Paladin, 1986).

Second, there are Western Social Democrats for whom Soviet Communism represents a deviation from, indeed a betrayal of, genuine Marxism. This group has nontheless made important contributions to the historical understanding of Marxism. In particular, George Lichtheim, in *Marxism: A Historical and Critical Study* (New York: Praeger, 1961), has given what amounts to a Marxist analysis of Marxism by situating it in comparative political and cultural context. At the same time, however, while fully recognizing Marx's Hegelian background, Lichtheim tends to minimize its significance, along with the fire-eating Marx of 1848. Early Marxism thus becomes an immature version of the real thing, and by the same token it appears as an adumbration of Leninism. Obversely, Lichtheim tends to view Social Democracy as the genuine culmination of the Marxist tradition. An even more categorical Social Democratic version of Marxism is Shlomo Avineri, *The Social and Political Thought of Karl Marx* (Cambridge: Cambridge University Press, 1968).

Finally, there are writers from the former socialist countries. Some of these, notably in Hungary, have attempted to give a Marxist analysis of Marxism's failure in power; and the result has usually been to identify a "new class" that has "betrayed" the revolution. See for example George Konrád and Ivan Szelényi, *The Intellectuals on the Road to Class Power* (New York: Harcourt, Brace, Jovanovich, 1979). Other East Europeans, however, have found Communism's fatal flaw to lie not in any social group but in the metaphysical nature of Marx's ideas themselves.

Here the decisive break was made by Leszek Kolakowski, in his *Main Currents of Marxism*, trans. P. S. Falla, 3 vols. (Oxford: Clarendon Press, 1978). This monumental work opens with the phrase "Karl Marx was a German philosopher," by which the author means that Hegelian metaphysics is not simply one aspect of Marxism, but its defining characteristic. Kolakowski's conclusion was that Marx's Promethean "fantasy" of total human emancipation through class warfare, if followed literally as in Leninism, yielded not liberation, but total social bondage. This perspective has been adopted here. A kindred approach is employed by Andrzej Walicki, *Marxism and the Leap to the Kingdom of Freedom: The Rise and Fall of the Communist Utopia* (Stanford, Calif.: Stanford University Press, 1995), who takes the analysis from Marx himself

466

down to Communism's collapse in 1991. At the same time, however, the author does consider that part of Marx is "scientific," by which he seems to mean empirically grounded. This second aspect of Marx is also known as "modernization theory." For a fuller discussion of this "Warsaw School of the history of ideas," see Martin Malia, "The End of the Noble Dream" *Times Literary Supplement*, November 7, 1997.

Other pertinent works on Marxism are Auguste Cornu, *Karl Marx et Friedrich Engels: leur vie et leur oeuvre*, 3 vols. (Paris: Presses universitaires de France, 1955–1962); David McLellan, *Karl Marx, His Life and Thought* (London: Macmillian, 1973); Frank Manuel, *A Requiem for Karl Marx* (Cambridge, Mass.: Harvard University Press, 1995); and especially Maximillien Rubel, *Karl Marx, essai de biographie intellectuelle* (Paris: M. Rivière, 1957). See also Robert Tucker, *Philosophy and Myth in Karl Marx* (Cambridge: Cambridge University Press, 1964); Eugene Kamenka, *The Ethical Foundations of Marxism* (London: Routledge and Kegan Paul, 1962); Louis Dupré, *The Philosophical Foundations of Marxism* (New York: Harcourt, Brace and World, 1966); Jerrold Seigel, *Marx's Fate: The Shape of a Life* (Princeton, N.J.: Princeton University Press, 1978); Roman Szporluk, *Communism and Nationalism: Karl Marx Versus Friedrich List* (New York: Oxford University Press, 1988); and Trygve R. Tholfsen, *Ideology and Revolution in Modern Europe: An Essay on the Role of Ideas in History* (New York: Columbia University Press, 1984).

For the related subject of utopianism, see Frank Manuel, *Utopias and Utopian Thought* (Boston: Beacon Press, 1965), and his *The Changing of the Gods* (Hanover, N.H.: University Press of New England, 1983); James Billington, *Fire in the Minds of Men: Origins of the Revolutionary Faith* (New York: Basic Books, 1980); Melvin Laski, *Utopia and Revolution: On the Origins of a Metaphor, or, Some Illustrations of the Problem of Political Temperament and Intellectual Climate and How Ideas, Ideals, and Ideologies Have Been Historically Related* (Chicago: University of Chicago Press, 1976).

20. "Afterword," to the German edition of 1873, in Tucker, *Marx-Engels Reader*, p. 302. Also see the section "Enlightenment and the Police State" in Chapter 1.

21. On Left Hegelianism in general, see Sidney Hook, *From Hegel to Marx* (Ann Arbor: University of Michigan Press, 1962); William Brazill, *The Young Hegelians* (New Haven, Conn.: Yale University Press, 1962); David McLellan, *Marx before Marxism*, 2d ed. (London: Macmillan, 1980); Jean Hyppolite, *Etudes sur Marx et Hegel* (Paris: M. Rivière, 1965), English trans. 1969; Karl Löwith *Von Hegel zu Nietzsche* (Zurich and Wien: Europa Verlag, 1941, 1949), English trans. 1984.

22. "The German Ideology: Part I," in Tucker, *Marx-Engels Reader*, pp. 146–200.

23. "Contribution to a Critique of Hegel's *Philosophy of Right*: Introduction," in

Tucker, *Marx-Engels Reader*, p. 64; David Lovell, *Marx's Proletariat: The Making of a Myth* (New York: Routledge, 1988).

24. "Philosophy of Right and Law, Preface" in C. J. Friedrich, ed., *Hegel* (New York: Modern Library, 1953), p. 227.

25. For this metaphysical notion of prehistory, see "Preface to *A Contribution to the Critique of Political Economy*," in Tucker, *Marx-Engels Reader*, p. 5.

26. *Capital*, vol. 1., chap. 32, quoted from Tucker, *Marx-Engels Reader*, p. 438.

27. Tocqueville, *Recollections*, p. 65.

28. See the section "Culture and the German *Sonderweg*" in Chapter 2.

29. "Critique of Hegel's *Philosophy of Right*," in Tucker, *Marx-Engels Reader*, p. 65.

30. Richard Pipes, *Struve, Liberal on the Left* (Cambridge, Mass.: Harvard University Press, 1970).

31. Editor's introduction to "Address of the Central Committee of the Communist League," in Tucker, *Marx-Engels Reader*, p. 501.

32. For the pre-Marxist Russian revolutionary movement, see Chapter 2, notes 63, 68, and 72, and Chapter 3, notes 2–4. See also Arthur Mandel, *Dilemmas of Progress in Tsarist Russia: Legal Marxism and Legal Populism* (Cambridge, Mass.: Harvard University Press, 1961). Samuel Baron, *Plekhanov: The Father of Russian Marxism* (Stanford, Calif.: Stanford University Press, 1963). Albert L. Weeks, *The First Bolshevik: A Political Biography of Peter Tkachev* (New York: New York University Press, 1968). E. L. Rudnitskaia, *Russkii blankizm: Petr Tkachev* (Moscow: Nauka, 1992).

33. In 1882, the year before his death, Marx wrote in the introduction to a Russian translation of the Manifesto: "If the Russian Revolution becomes the signal for the proletarian revolution in the West, so that both complement each other, the present Russian common ownership of land may serve as the starting-point of a Communist development." Tucker, *Marx-Engels Reader*, p. 472. For Marx's relation to Populism, see Andrzej Walicki, *The Controversy over Capitalism* (Oxford: Clarendon Press, 1969).

34. The most convenient collection of Lenin's principal writings is Robert C. Tucker, *The Lenin Anthology* (New York: Norton, 1973). The most thorough and judicious biography of Lenin is Robert Service, *Lenin: A Political Life*, 3 vols. (London: Macmillan, 1991, 1995). For Lenin's talents as a politician, see Adam Ulam, *The Bolsheviks: The Intellectual and Political History of the Triumph of Communism in Russia* (New York: Collier Books, 1976, 1965). For Lenin's ideological development, see Alain Besançon, *The Intellectual Origins of Leninism*, trans. Sarah Matthews (Oxford: Basil Blackwell, 1981). New, and generally negative, archival material can be found in Dmitrii Volkogonov, *Lenin: A New Biography* (New York: Free Press, 1994). See also Neil Harding, *Lenin's Political Thought* (London: Macmillan, 1977); A. J. Polan, *Lenin and the End of Politics* (Berkeley: University of California Press, 1984).

468

35. Robert Michels, *Political Parties: A Sociological Study of the Oligarchical Tendencies of Modern Democracy* (New York: Free Press, 1962).

36. Pipes, *Struve, Liberal on the Left*, p. 195.

37. Cole, *Socialist Thought*, vol. 3. pt. 1., *The Second International*, esp. chap. 5; James Joll, *The Second International* (London: Weidenfield and Nicolson, 1955); Peter Gay, *The Dilemma of Democratic Socialism: Eduard Bernstein's Challenge to Marx* (New York: Columbia University Press, 1952); Manfred B. Steger, *The Quest for Evolutionary Socialism: Eduard Bernstein and Social Democracy* (Cambridge: Cambridge University Press, 1977).

38. David Lovell, *From Marx to Lenin: An Evaluation of Marx's Responsibility for Soviet Authoritarianism* (Cambridge and New York: Cambridge University Press, 1984).

39. Quoted from Kolakowski, *Main Currents of Marxism*, vol. 2, p. 387.

40. *Communist Manifesto*, in Tucker, *Marx-Engels Reader*, p. 484; emphasis added.

41. For the development of Marxism in Russia, see above notes 32 and 34 and Theodore Dan, *The Origins of Bolshevism*, trans. and ed. Joel Carmichael (London: Secker and Warburg, 1964), first published in Russian in 1946 in New York; Leopold Haimson, *The Russian Marxists and the Origins of Bolshevism* (Cambridge, Mass.: Harvard University Press, 1955); John Keep, *The Rise of Social Democracy in Russia* (Oxford: Clarendon Press, 1963); Allan Wildman, *The Making of a Workers' Revolution: Russian Social Democracy, 1891–1903* (Chicago: University of Chicago Press, 1967); Israel Getzler, *Martov: A Political Biography of a Russian Social Democrat* (London and New York: Cambridge University Press, 1967); Abraham Ascher, *Pavel Axelrod and the Development of Menshevism* (Cambridge, Mass.: Harvard University Press, 1972). For criticism of the impact of Marxist political intellectuals on the Russian workers' movement, see the émigré Menshevik Selig Perlman, *A Theory of the Labor Movement* (New York: Augustus M. Kelley, 1928, 1949, 1970).

42. Service, *Lenin*, vol. 1. pp. 6–8.

43. The prime example of this in English-speaking countries is Eric Hobsbawm's trilogy on nineteenth- and twentieth-century Europe. See especially *The Age of Revolution, 1789–1848* (Cleveland, Ohio: World Publishing, 1962).

44. This is pointed out forcefully by Alfred Cobban, *The Social Interpretation of the French Revolution* (Cambridge: Cambridge University Press, 1964).

45. Walicki, *Controversy over Capitalism*.

46. A basic theme of Tocqueville, *The Old Regime and the French Revolution*.

5. THROUGH THE SOVIET-RUSSIAN LOOKING-GLASS

1. George Lichtheim, *Marxism*, 2d ed. (New York: Praeger, 1965), p. 382.

2. As cited in the Introduction, note 6, this is the title of Jan Kucharzewski's work.

3. Wiktor Sukiennicki, *Kolumbowy Blad, Szkice z historii, teorii i praktyki sowieckiego "kommunizmu"* (Paris: Kultura, 1959). I owe this reference to Professor Andrzej Walicki.

4. Winston Churchill, *His Complete Speeches, 1897—1963*, vol. 6 (New York: Chelsea House, 1974), pp. 62.

5. For Soviet Russia's role in international affairs between the wars, see Louis Fischer, *The Soviets in World Affairs, 1917–1929*, 2 vols. (Princeton, N.J.: Princeton University Press, 1951); Jonathan Haslam, *Soviet Foreign Policy, 1930–33: The Impact of the Depression* (London: Macmillan, 1983); and his *The Soviet Union and the Struggle for Collective Security in Europe, 1933–39* (New York: St. Martin's Press, 1984). Still valuable is Franz Borkenau, *World Communism: A History of the Communist International* (Ann Arbor: University of Michigan Press, 1962), first published in 1939.

6. For a listing of the body of published material relevant to the West's reaction to Soviet Russia, see Thomas Hammond, ed., *Soviet Foreign Relations and World Communism: A Selected, Annotated Bibliography of 7000 Books in 30 Languages* (Princeton, N.J.: Princeton University Press, 1965). Some the more important items of this literature are Stephen Graubard, *British Labor and the Russian Revolution, 1917–1924* (Cambridge, Mass.: Harvard University Press, 1956); Royal Institute of Internationl Affairs, *The Impact of the Russian Revolution* (London: Oxford University Press, 1967); Christopher Lasch, *American Liberals and the Russian Revolution* (New York: Columbia University Press, 1962); Peter G. Filene, ed., *American Views of Soviet Russia, 1917–1965* (Homewood, Ill.: Dorsey Press, 1968); David Caute, *Communism and French Intellectuals, 1914–1960* (New York: Macmillan, 1964); Annie Kriegal, *Les communistes francais, essai d'ethnographie politique* (Paris: Editions du Seuil, 1968).

7. For an early attempt to define the new regime in Russia, see Walter Batsell, *Soviet Rule in Russia* (New York: Macmillan, 1929).

8. Leon Trotsky, *My Life: An Attempt at an Autobiography* (New York: Pathfinder Press, 1970), p. 356.

9. The sketch of Soviet history offered here is not the currently predominant view. The prevailing "master narrative" treats the Revolution as the result of a more or less "normal" social process, of which the Bolshevik regime is thus an authentic, if somewhat skewed, expression. Perhaps the most succinct epitome of this view is Sheila Fitzpatrick, *The Russian Revolution* (New York: Oxford University Press, 1982, 2d rev. ed. 1995). The perspective presented here privileges instead ideology in explaining Soviet development. It builds on the author's *The Soviet Tragedy: A History of Socialism in Russia, 1917–1991* (New York: Free Press, 1994). The fullest treatment of the role of Marxism in Soviet policy is Walicki, *Marxism and the Leap to the Kingdom*. The most balanced general history of Soviet Russia, treating ideology, politics, and society to-

470

gether, is Geoffrey Hosking, *The First Socialist Society* (Cambridge, Mass.: Harvard University Press, 1985, 1990, 1993).

10. Sylvana Malle, *The Economic Organization of War Communism, 1918–1921* (Cambridge: Cambridge University Press, 1985). See also Walicki, *Marxism and the Leap*, where he analyzes War Communism.

11. Abdurakhman Avtorkhanov, *Proiskhozhdenie partokratii,* 2d ed. (Frankfurt am Main: Posev, 1981–1983).

12. Issac Deutscher, *The Prophet Unarmed: Trotsky, 1921–1929* (New York: Oxford University Press, 1959).

13. Alan M. Ball, *Russia's Last Capitalists: The NEPmen, 1921–1929* (Berkeley: University of California Press, 1987).

14. Stephen Cohen, *Bukharin and the Bolshevik Revolution: A Political Biography, 1888–1938* (New York: Knopf, 1973), and Moshe Lewin, *Political Undercurrents in Soviet Economic Debates: From Bukharin to the Modern Reformers* (Princeton, N.J.: Princeton University Press, 1974).

15. Adam Ulam, *Stalin: The Man and His Era* (New York: Viking Press, 1973), chap. 8; Robert Conquest, *Harvest of Sorrow: Soviet Collectivization and the Terror Famine* (New York: Oxford, 1986); Andrea Graziosi, *The Great Soviet Peasant War, Bolsheviks and Peasants, 1917–1933* (Cambridge, Mass.: Harvard Papers in Ukrainian Studies, 1996).

16. Robert Tucker, *Stalin in Power: The Revolution from Above, 1928–1941* (New York: Norton, 1990); Robert McNeal, *Stalin, Man and Ruler* (New York: New York University Press, 1988).

17. The largely peasant background of the Bolshevik Party membership has been appropriately emphasized by Orlando Figes, *A People's Tragedy: A History of the Russian Revolution* (New York: Viking, 1997).

18. See the author's introduction in Lars Lih, *Stalin's Letters to Molotov, 1925–1936* (New Haven, Conn.: Yale University Press, 1995).

19. Alexander Erlich, *The Soviet Industrialization Debate, 1924–1928* (Cambridge, Mass.: Harvard University Press, 1960); Moshe Lewin, *Russian Peasants and Soviet Power: A Study of Collectivization*, trans. Irene Nove (Evanston, Ill.: Northwestern University Press, 1968).

20. Sheila Fitzpatrick, *Stalin's Peasants* (New York: Oxford University Press, 1995).

21. Igor Birman, *Ekonomika nedostach* (New York: Chalidze Publications, 1983), and his *Personal Consumption in the USSR and the USA* (Basingstoke: Macmillan, 1989).

22. Robert Conquest, *The Great Terror: A Reassessment* (New York: Oxford University Press, 1990), epilogue. See Alec Nove, "The Scale of the Purges," in Nove, ed., *The Stalin Phenomenon* (New York: St. Martin's Press, 1993), pp. 29–33; Nove, "Victims of Stalinisim: How Many?" in J. Arch Getty and Roberta Manning, eds., *Stalinist Terror: New Perspectives* (New York: Cambridge Uni-

versity Press). For a salutary corrective to Western downplaying of this matter see Stéphane Courtois et al., *Le livre noir du communisme: crimes, terreur, répression* (Paris: Laffont, 1997).

23. Tucker, ed., *The Marx-Engels Reader*, pp. 483–491.

24. Sheila Fitzpatrick, ed., *Cultural Revolution in Russia, 1928–1931* (Bloomington: Indiana University Press, 1978), editor's introduction.

25. Milovan Djilas, *The New Class: An Analysis of the Communist System* (New York: Holt, Rinehart and Winston, 1957). For a later version of the new-class thesis, see Konrád and Szelényi, *The Intellectuals on the Road to Class Power*.

26. Moshe Lewin, *The Making of the Soviet System: Essays in the Social History of Interwar Russia* (New York: Pantheon, 1985), chap. 11. For a corrective to such reductionist social history, see Stephen Kotkin, *Magnetic Mountain: Stalinism as a Civilization* (Berkeley: University of California Press, 1995), which appropriately construes the culture of society as a response to the ideological purposes of the regime.

27. Kostas Papaioannou, *L'idéologie froide, essai sur le déperissement du marxisme* (Paris: J. J. Pauvert, 1967).

28. For the logocratic nature of the Soviet system, see Françoise Thom, *La langue de bois* (Paris: Julliard, 1987).

29. See the section "Enlightenment and the Police State" in Chapter 1.

30. Anne Morrow Lindbergh, *The Wave of the Future* (New York: Harcourt, Brace, Jovanovich, 1940).

31. This is a major thesis of Furet, *Passé d'une illusion*.

32. The most important general treatment of fascism is Stanley G. Payne, *A History of Fascism: 1914–1945* (Madison: University of Wisconsin Press, 1995), an outgrowth of his *Fascism: Comparison and Definition* (Madison: University of Wisconsin Press, 1980). Other important works relevant to the subject are Ernst Nolte, *Der Faschismus in seiner Epoche* (Munich: R. Piper, 1963), trans. *Three Faces of Fascism*, by Leila Vennewitz (New York: Holt, Rinehart and Winston, 1966); Eugen Weber, *Varieties of Fascism* (New York: Van Nostrand, 1964); George L. Mosse and Walter Laqueur, eds., *International Fascism, 1920–1945* (London: Harper and Row, 1966); F. L. Carsten, *The Rise of Fascism* (Berkeley: University of California Press, 1967; New York: New Viewpoints, 1975); Walter Laqueur, ed., *Fascism: A Reader's Guide* (Berkeley: University of California Press, 1976); Hans Rogger and Eugen Weber, eds., *The European Right: A Historical Profile* (Berkeley: University of California Press, 1965); Wolfgang Sauer, "National Socialism: Totalitarianism or Fascism?" *American Historical Review* 63 (1967): 404–422; A. James Gregor, *Interpretation of Fascism* (Morristown, N.J.: General Learning Press, 1974); Renzo de Felice, *Fascism: An Informal Introduction to Its Theory and Practice* (New Brunswick, N.J.: Transaction Books, 1976), and his *Interpretations of Fascism* (Cambridge, Mass.: Har-

vard University Press, 1977); Karl Dietrich Bracher, *The German Dictatorship* (New York: Praeger, 1970); Karl Dietrich Bracher, W. Sauer, and G. Schulz, *Die Nationalsozialistische Machtergreifung* (Koln: Westdeutscher Verlag, 1960). An interesting attempt at a marxian theory of right-wing revolutionism is Arno J. Mayer, *Dynamics of Counterrevolution in Europe, 1870–1956: An Analytic Framework* (New York: Harper and Row, 1971).

33. Leonid Luks, *Entstehung der Kommunistischen Faschismustheorie* (Munich: Deutsche Verlags-Anstalt, 1985).

34. In this broad perspective fascism comes to be something like a secular equivalent of original sin. Evil is redefined in essentially political terms, while at the same time fascism loses all historical specificity. For a typical statement, see Umberto Eco, "Eternal Fascism," *New York Review of Books*, June 22, 1995. "Nevertheless, even though political regimes can be overthrown . . . behind a regime and its ideology there is always a way of thinking and feeling, a group of cultural habits, of obscure instincts and unfathomable drives. . . . Ur-Fascism grows up and seeks for consensus by exploiting and exacerbating the natural *fear of difference.* . . . Thus Ur-Fascism is racist by definition . . . one of the most typical features of historical fascism was the *appeal to a frustrated middle class*, a class suffering from an economic crisis . . . and frightened by the pressure of lower social groups. . . . For Ur-Fascism there is no struggle for life but, rather, life is lived for struggle. . . . *Life is a permanent warfare.* . . . Ur-Fascism can come back under the most innocent of disguises. Our duty is to uncover it and to point our finger at any of its new instances—every day, in every part of the world" (pp. 12–15). As Furet comments on this eternal mindset: "Jamais régime déshonoré n'aura eu tant d'imitations posthumes dans l'imagination de ses vainqueurs" (Never has an abominated regime been credited with so many posthumous imitations in the imagination of its conquerors). Furet, *Passé d'une illusion*, p. 190. "Life as permanent warfare" was also the perspective of Marx and Nietzsche.

35. Stern, *The Politics of Cultural Despair*, pp. 247–248.

36. For the interaction of Communist and Nazi ideologies, see Walter Laqueur, *Russia and Germany: A Century of Conflict* (Boston: Little, Brown, 1965). For German Communism, see Ruth Fischer, *Stalin and German Communism: A Study in the Origins of the State Party* (Cambridge, Mass.: Harvard University Press, 1948); Werner Angress, *Stillborn Revolution: The Communist Bid for Power in Germany, 1921–1923* (Princeton, N.J.: Princeton University Press, 1963); Franz Borkenau, *The Communist International* (London: Faber, 1938); Hermann Weber, *Die Wandlung des deutschen Kommunismus: Die Stalinisierung der KPD in der Weimarer Republik*, 2 vols. (Frankfurt am Main: Europäische Verlagsanstalt, 1969).

37. See Chapter 3, note 80.

38. For the debate over Japanese fascism, see Andrew Gordon, *Labor and Imperial Democracy in Prewar Japan* (Berkeley: University of California Press, 1991); Masao Maruyama, *Thought and Behavior in Modern Japanese Politics* (New York: Oxford University Press, 1969); Peter Duus and Dan Okimoto, "Fascism and the History of Prewar Japan: The Failure of a Concept," *Journal of Asian Studies* 39, no. 1 (November 1979): 65–76. For the deterioration of the Japanese military ethos, see Robert B. Edgerton, *Warriors of the Rising Sun: A History of the Japanese Military* (New York: Norton, 1997), and Iris Chang, *The Rape of Nanking* (New York: Basic Books, 1997).

39. See the section "The Roots of Aesthetic Nihilism" in Chapter 3.

40. See the section "Leninist Practice" in Chapter 4.

41. For example, Marx, *Eighteenth Brumaire*, p. 34.

42. Alexander Dallin, *German Rule in Russia, 1941–1945: A Study of Occupation Policies* (New York: Octagon Books, 1980).

43. This remark was made to the author in conversation.

44. Élie Halévy, *The Era of Tyrannies*, trans. R. K. Webb (New York: Anchor Books, 1965). For his classification of Nazism and Communism as "socialist"—a not uncommon opinion at the time—see *Histoire du socialisme* (Paris: Gallimard, 1948).

45. For American opinion on Communism, see Peter G. Filene, *Americans and the Soviet Experiment: 1917–1933* (Cambridge, Mass.: Harvard University Press, 1967). For a sampling of this opinion, see Filene, ed., *American Views of Soviet Russia: 1917–1965*. For the literary community in particular, see Daniel Aaron, *Writers on the Left: Episodes in American Literary Communism* (New York: Columbia University Press, 1992), first published 1961. For French reactions to Communism, see Furet, *Passé d'une illusion*, chap. 3. For a critical appraisal of the reaction of Western intellectuals generally to Communism, see Paul Hollander, *Political Pilgrims: Travels of Western Intellectuals to the Soviet Union, China, and Cuba, 1928–1978* (New York: Oxford University Press, 1981).

46. John Reed, *Ten Days That Shook the World* (New York: International Publishers, 1919). Republished in 1935 by the Modern Library with a foreword by V. I. Lenin and an introduction by Granville Hicks.

47. Lincoln Steffens, *John Reed under the Kremlin* (Chicago: Ransom, 1922).

48. Jacques Sadoul, *Notes sur la révolution bolchevique (Octobre 1917–Janvier 1919)*, with a preface by Henri Barbusse (Paris: Editions de la Sirène, 1919).

49. André Marty, *The Epic of the Black Sea Revolt* (New York: Workers Library, 1941), based on his "La révolte de la Mer Noire" (Paris, 1932).

50. Pierre Pascal, ed., *Selections from Lenin*, trans. J. Fineburg (New York: International Publishers, 1929), and *Avvakum et les débuts du raskol: la crise religieuse au XVIIe siècle en Russie* (Paris: Librairie ancienne H. Champion, 1938).

474

51. Pierre Daix, *Aragon, une vie à changer* (Paris: Seuil, 1975), and *Ce que je sais du XXe siècle* (Paris: Calmann-Levy, 1985).

52. Dominique Desanti, *Elsa-Aragon: le couple ambigu* (Paris: Belfond, 1994).

53. Klara Zetkin, *Reminiscences of Lenin: Dealing with Lenin's Views on the Position of Women and Other Questions* (London: Modern Books, 1929).

54. Simone Barck, *Johannes R. Bechers Publizistik in der Sowjetunion, 1935–1945* (Berlin: Akademie-Verlag, 1976).

55. Gyorgy Lukács, *History and Class Consciousness*, trans. Rodney Livingstone (London: Merlin Press, 1971); Mary Gluck, *Georg Lukács and His Generation, 1900–1918* (Cambridge, Mass.: Harvard University Press, 1985).

56. Max Eastman, *Artists in Uniform* (New York: Knopf, 1934), and his *The End of Socialism in Russia* (Boston: Little, Brown, 1937).

57. Alan Ryan, *Bertrand Russell: A Political Life* (New York: Hill and Wang, 1988). Bertrand Russell, *The Autobiography of Bertrand Russell* (Boston: Little, Brown 1967–1969).

58. A. T. D'Eye, *Russia Revisited: With the Dean of Canterbury through the U.S.S.R.* (London: Russia Today Society, 1945).

59. Edmund Wilson, "An Appeal to Progressives," *New Republic* 65 (January 14, 1931), quoted from Peter G. Filene, ed., *American Views of Soviet Russia, 1917–1965*, pp. 74–77.

60. Edmund Wilson, *Axel's Castle: A Study in the Imaginative Literature of 1870–1930* (New York: Charles Scribner's and Sons, 1931), and *To the Finland Station: A Study in the Writing and Acting of History* (London: Macmillan, 1972), first published in 1940.

61. Simon Karlinksy, ed., *The Nabokov-Wilson Letters: Correspondence between Vladimir Nabokov and Edmund Wilson, 1940–1971* (New York: Harper and Row, 1979).

62. S. J. Taylor, *Stalin's Apologist: Walter Duranty, the New York Times Man in Moscow* (Oxford: Oxford University Press, 1990).

63. William Henry Chamberlin, *Russia's Iron Age* (Boston: Little Brown, 1934), *America's Second Crusade* (Chicago: Regnery, 1950), and *The Evolution of a Conservative* (Chicago: Regnery, 1959).

64. Maurice Dobb, *Soviet Russia and the World* (London: Sedgwick and Jackson, 1932), and *Soviet Economic Development since the 1917 Revolution* (New York: International Publishers, 1928, 1948, 1967).

65. For Trotsky's career in exile, see Isaac Deutscher, *The Prophet Outcast: Trotsky, 1929–1940* (New York: Oxford University Press, 1963).

66. Jules Romains, *Cette grande lueur à l'est*, vol. 19 of *Les hommes de bonne volonté* (Paris: E. Flammarion, 1932–1946).

67. Romain Rolland, *Quinze ans de combat, 1919–1934* (Paris: Riedler, 1935), trans. as *I Will Not Rest*, by K. S. Shelvanker (London: Selwyn and Blount, 1935).

68. Henri Barbusse, *Staline: un monde nouveau vu à travers un homme* (Paris: E. Flammarion, 1935).

69. Paul Hummert, *George Bernard Shaw's Marxian Romance* (Lincoln: University of Nebraska Press, 1973).

70. Herbert George Wells, *Stalin-Wells Talks* (London: New Statesman and Nation, 1934); Anthony West, *H. G. Wells: Aspects of a Life* (New York: Random House, 1984).

71. Sidney and Beatrice Webb, *Soviet Communism: A New Civilization?* 2 vols. (New York: Charles Scribner's Sons, 1936).

72. David Pike, *German Writers in Soviet Exile, 1933–1945* (Chapel Hill: University of North Carolina Press, 1982).

73. Joseph Davies, *Mission to Moscow* (New York: Simon and Schuster, 1941).

74. André Gide, *Retour de l'URSS* (Paris: Gallimard, 1936).

75. Boris Souvarine, *Staline: aperçu historique du Bolchevisme* (Paris: Plon, 1935).

76. "Preliminary Commission of Inquiry into the Charges Made against Leon Trotsky in the Moscow Trials" (commonly called the Dewey Commission, after its convener, John Dewey), eds., *The Case of Leon Trotsky: Report of Hearings on the Charges Made against Him in the Moscow Trials* (New York: Harper, 1937).

77. Thomas Mann, "Goethe and Tolstoi" (1922), in *Essays of Three Decades*, trans. H. T. Lowe-Porter (New York: Knopf, 1948).

78. Thomas Mann, *The Magic Mountain*, trans. H. T. Lowe-Porter (New York: Knopf, 1934) pp. 205, 260–280 *passim*, 422–434 *passim*.

79. Hesse, as quoted by T. S. Eliot, "The Wasteland" (1922), in *Collected Poems, 1909–1935* (London: Faber and Faber, 1936).

80. Oswald Spengler, *The Decline of The West* (New York: Knopf, 1926). First published in German in 1920; Arnold Toynbee, *A Study of History*, abbr. ed., 2 vols. (New York: Oxford University Press, 1947–1957), esp. vol. 2, pp. 152–153.

81. Berdiaev, *The Origin of Russian Communism*.

82. Uwe Sauermann, *Ernst Niekisch und der revolutionäre Nationalismus* (Munich: Bibliotheksdienst Angerer, 1985).

83. Laqueur, *Russia and Germany*, chaps. 5 and 12.

84. For the relevant literature on the Soviet Union's international posture between the wars, see note 5 above. The generalizations offered here, however, are the author's.

85. See Filene, ed., *American Views of Soviet Russia, 1917–1965*, p. 142.

86. Paul Valéry, "La crise de l'esprit," in *Variété* (Paris: Gallimard, 1924), p. 25.

87. The main outlines of the Cold War period are now fairly clear. See especially Vojtech Mastny, *The Cold War and Soviet Insecurity* (New York: Oxford University Press, 1996); John Gaddis, *We Now Know* (New York: Oxford Univer-

476   sity Press, 1997); Vladislav Zubok and Constantine Pleshakov, *Inside the Kremlin's Cold War: From Stalin to Khrushchev* (Cambridge, Mass.: Harvard University Press, 1996); David Holloway, *Stalin and the Bomb* (New Haven, Conn.: Yale University Press, 1995). Adam Ulam, *Expansion and Coexistence*, 2d ed. (New York: Praeger Publishers, 1974), and his *The Rivals: America and Russia since World War II* (New York: Viking Press, 1971), hold up very well even with the archives largely open.

88. Sidney Hook, *From Hegel to Marx: Studies in the Intellectual Development of Karl Marx* (New York: Reynal and Hitchcock, 1936); Alexandre Kojève, *Introduction à la lecture de Hegel: leçons sur La phénoménologie de l'esprit, professées de 1933 à 1939* (Paris: Gallimard, 1947).

89. George Orwell, *Animal Farm* (London: Secker and Warburg, 1945).

90. Arthur Koestler, *Darkness at Noon*, trans. Daphne Hardy (New York: Macmillan, 1941).

91. George Orwell, *Nineteen Eighty-Four* (New York: Harcourt, Brace, 1949).

92. Victor Kravchenko, *I Chose Freedom: The Personal and Political Life of a Soviet Official* (New York: Scribner and Sons, 1946).

93. Guillaume Malaurie, ed., *L'affaire Kravchenko*, with Emmanuel Terrée (Paris: R. Laffont, 1982).

94. Jerzy G. Gliksman, *Tell the West: An Account of His Experiences as a Slave Laborer in the Union of Soviet Socialist Republics* (New York: Gresham Press, 1948). The classics of this body of literature are Jozef Czapski, *The Inhuman Land*, foreword by Daniel Halévy, intro. by Edward Crankshaw, trans. from the French by Gerard Hopkins (London: Chatto and Windus, 1951), and Gustaw Herling-Grudzinski, *A World Apart*, trans. Joseph Marek (New York: Roy Publishers, 1951), reprinted 1986 and 1996 by Penguin, New York; see also Gustav Herling, *Welt ohne Erbarmen*, trans. Hansjurgen Wille (Berlin: Verlag fur Politik und Wirtschaft, 1953).

95. David J. Dallin and Boris I. Nicolaevsky, *Forced Labor in Soviet Russia* (New Haven, Conn.: Yale University Press, 1947).

96. Richard Crossman, ed., *The God That Failed* (New York: Harper, 1949).

97. Peter Coleman, *The Liberal Conspiracy: The Congress for Cultural Freedom and the Struggle for the Mind of Postwar Europe* (New York: Free Press, 1989).

98. For the intellectuals and Soviet Russia in general, see Hollander, *Political Pilgrims*. For the special case of France, see Tony Judt, *Past Imperfect: French Intellectuals, 1944–1956* (Berkeley: University of California Press, 1992). For the special case of Sartre, see Annie Cohen-Solal, *Sartre: A Life*, trans. Anna Cancogni, ed. Norman Macafee (New York: Pantheon Books, 1987).

99. Raymond Aron, *The Opium of the Intellectuals*, trans. Terence Kilmartin (Garden City, N.Y.: Doubleday, 1957). Aron's first work appeared in French in

1955; Albert Camus, *The Rebel*, no trans. (New York: Knopf, 1956); Germaine Bree, *Camus and Sartre: Crisis and Commitment* (New York: Delacorte Press, 1972). Jean-François Sirinelli, *Sartre et Aron, deux intellectuels dans le siècle* (Paris: Fayard, 1995).

100. For the intellectual history of the period overall, see Raymond Aron, *Mémoires* (Paris: Julliard, 1983).

101. For a history of the concept, see Abbott Gleason, *Totalitarianism: The Inner History of the Cold War* (New York: Oxford University Press, 1995).

102. "Symposium on the Totalitarian State," *Proceedings of the American Philosophical Society* 82, no. 1 (February 23, 1940): 1–102. See also Kes K. Adler and Thomas G. Patterson, "Red Fascism: The Merger of Nazi Germany and Soviet Russia in the American Image of Totalitarianism, 1930's–1950's," *American Historical Review* 75, no. 4 (April 1970): 1046–1064.

103. Hannah Arendt, *The Origins of Totalitarianism* (New York: Harcourt, Brace, 1951).

104. American Academy of Arts and Sciences, *Totalitarianism: Proceedings of a Conference Held at the American Academy of Arts and Sciences, March 1953*, ed. Carl J. Friedrich (New York: Grosset and Dunlap, 1954); Carl J. Friedrich and Zbigniew K. Brzezinski, *Totalitarian Dictatorship and Autocracy* (Cambridge, Mass.: Harvard University Press, 1956).

105. Zbigniew K. Brzezinski, *The Permanent Purge: Politics in Soviet Totalitarianism* (Cambridge, Mass.: Harvard University Press, 1956).

106. Marquis de Custine, *A Journey for Our Time: The Journals of the Marquis de Custine*, ed. and trans. Phyllis Penn Kohler (New York: Pellegrini and Cudahy, 1951); Kennan, *Marquis de Custine*, p. 124.

107. Paul W. Blackstock and Bert F. Hoselitz, eds., *The Russian Menace to Europe: A Collection of Articles, Speeches, Letters, and News Dispatches*, by Karl Marx and Friedrich Engels (Glencoe, Ill.: Free Press, 1952).

108. This view of Eastern Orthodoxy is common to Spengler and Toynbee, among others. Also see the Introduction note 4.

109. Toynbee, *A Study of History*, esp. vol. 2, pp. 152–153.

110. Berdiaev, *The Origin of Russian Communism* and *The Russian Idea*.

111. Adam Ulam, *The Communists* (New York: Scribner's, 1992).

112. For the Khrushchev era in general, see Carl A. Linden, *Khrushchev and the Soviet Leadership* (Baltimore: Johns Hopkins University Press, 1966); James G. Richter, *Khrushchev's Double Bind: International Pressures and Domestic Coalition Politics* (Baltimore: Johns Hopkins University Press, 1994).

113. Nikita Khrushchev, *The Crimes of the Stalin Era: Special Report to the 20th Congress of the Communist Party of the Soviet Union*, annotated ed. (New York: New Leader, 1962).

478

114. Ilia Erenburg, *The Thaw* (Chicago: H. Regnery Co., 1955); Joshua Rubenstein, *Tangled Loyalties: The Life and Times of Ilya Ehrenburg* (New York: Basic Books, 1996).

115. Robert Conquest, ed., *The Pasternak Affair: Courage of Genius, a Documentary Report* (Philadelphia: Lippincott, 1961).

116. Colin Clark, *The Conditions of Economic Progress* (London: Macmillan, 1940), and his *A Critique of Russian Statistics* (London: Macmillan, 1939); Simon Smith Kuznets, *Toward a Theory of Economic Growth, with Reflections on the Economic Growth of Modern Nations* (New York: Norton, 1968).

117. Wassily Leontief, *Input-Output Economics* (New York: Oxford University Press, 1966). For his optimistic assessment of the Soviet economy, see "The Decline and Rise of Soviet Economic Science," *Foreign Affairs* 38 (January 1960): 261–272.

118. This remark is generally attributed to Ambassador Bohlen. See his *Witness to History* (New York: Norton, 1973).

119. Cyril E. Black, *The Transformation of Russian Society: Aspects of Social Change since 1861* (Cambridge, Mass.: Harvard University Press, 1960).

120. Walter W. Rostow, *The Stages of Economic Growth* (Cambridge: Cambridge University Press, 1960); Raymond Aron, *Dix-huit leçons sur la société industrielle* (Paris: Gallimard, 1962).

121. James Burnham, *The Managerial Revolution: What Is Happening in the World* (New York: John Day Company, 1941).

122. John K. Galbraith, *The New Industrial State* (Boston: Houghton Mifflin, 1967).

123. Alfred Meyer, "Theories of Convergence," in Chalmers Johnson, ed., *Change in Communist Systems* (Stanford, Calif.: Stanford University Press, 1970); Clark Kerr, John Dunlop, Frederick Horbison, and Charles Meyers, *Industrialism and Industrial Man* (Cambridge, Mass.: Harvard University Press, 1960); Gur Ofer, *The Service Sector in Soviet Economic Growth, a Comparative Study* (Cambridge, Mass.: Harvard University Press, 1973), and his *Soviet Economic Growth, 1928–1985* (Santa Monica, Calif.: Rand/UCLA Center for the Study of Soviet International Behavior, 1988). For a critique of convergence theory see Wolfe, "The Convergence Theory in a Historical Perspective," (in *An Ideology in Power*).

124. Regis Debray, *Révolution dans la révolution? lutte armée et lutte politique en Amerique latine* (Paris: F. Maspero, 1967).

125. This is the title of the first chapter of Raymond Aron, *Le grand schisme*.

126. John L. Gaddis, *Russia, the Soviet Union, and the United States* (New York: McGraw, 1979), chap. 9. See also his *The Long Peace: Inquiries into the History of the Cold War* (New York: Norton, 1983)

127. See, for example, Kenneth W. Thompson and Steven L. Rearden, eds., *Paul*

H. Nitze on Foreign Policy (Lanham, Md.: University Press of America and Charlottesville, Va.: White Burkett Miller Center of Public Affairs, University of Virginia, 1989).

128. David Holloway, *The Soviet Union and the Arms Race* (New Haven, Conn.: Yale University Press, 1983).

129. For the debate over "totalitarianism," see Gleason, *Totalitarianism*; Guy Hermet, Pierre Hassner, and Jacques Rupnik, eds., *Totalitarismes* (Paris: Economica, 1984); Pierre Hassner, "Une notion insaisissable mais irremplaçable," in his *La violence et la paix* (Paris: Editions Esprit, 1995); Malia, "The End of the Noble Dream," and "L'histoire soviétique," in *Axes et méthodes de l'histoire politique* (Paris: Presses universitaires de France, 1998).

130. Alex Inkeles and David H. Smith, *Becoming Modern: Individual Change in Six Developing Countries* (Cambridge, Mass.: Harvard University Press, 1974).

131. Andrei Amalrik, *Will the Soviet Union Survive until 1984?* (New York: Harper and Row, 1970).

132. In *Novyi mir*, no. 11 (1962); Aleksandr Solzhenitsyn, *The Oak and the Calf: Sketches of Literary Life in the Soviet Union* (New York: Harper and Row, 1980).

133. Andrei Siniavskii, *Siniavskii i Daniel na skame podsudimykh* (New York: Mezhdunarodnoe Literaturnoe Sodruzhestvo, 1966).

134. Andrei Sakharov, *On Sakharov*, ed. Alexander Babyonyshev (New York: Vintage Books, 1982); Valerii Chalidze, *The Soviet Human Rights Movement: A Memoir* (New York: Jacob Blaustein Institute for the Advancement of Human Rights, American Jewish Committee, 1984); Ludmilla Alekseeva, *Soviet Dissent: Contemporary Movements for National, Religious, and Human Rights* (Middletown, Conn.: Wesleyan University Press, 1985).

135. Nadezhda Mandelshtam, *Hope against Hope: A Memoir*, trans. Max Hayward (New York: Atheneum, 1970).

136. Evgeniia Ginzburg, *Into The Whirlwind*, trans. Paul Stevenson and Manya Harari (London: Collins Harvill, 1967).

137. Aleksandr Zinoviev, *The Yawning Heights*, trans. Gordon Clough (New York: Random House, 1979).

138. Edward Ericson, *Solzhenitsyn and the Modern World* (Washington, D.C.: Regnery Gateway, 1993).

139. Roy Medvedev, *Let History Judge: The Origins and Consequences of Stalinism*, trans. Colleen Taylor (New York: Knopf, 1971). A fuller version was published by Spokesman Books for the Bertrand Russell Peace Foundation, European Socialist Thought 7 (Nottingham, Eng., 1976); Roy Medvedev, *An End to Silence: Uncensored Opinion in the Soviet Union from Roy Medvedev's Underground Magazine "Political Diary,"* ed. Stephen Cohen (New York: Norton, 1982).

480

140. Amalrik, *Will the Soviet Union Survive?*

141. Andrei Sakharov, *Progress, Coexistence, and Intellectual Freedom*, trans. *New York Times* (New York: W. W. Norton, 1970).

142. Andrei Sakharov, *My Country and the World*, trans. Guy V. Daniels (New York: Knopf, 1975).

143. Aleksandr Solzhenitsyn, *From under the Rubble*, trans. A. M. Brock (Boston: Little, Brown, 1975).

144. Konrád and Szelényi, *The Intellectuals on the Road to Class Power.*

145. Vaclav Havel, *The Power of the Powerless: Citizens against the State in Central-Eastern Europe* (Armonk, N.Y.: M. E. Sharpe, 1985).

146. Adam Michnik, *The Church and the Left*, ed. and trans. David Ost (Chicago: University of Chicago Press, 1993); first published in Polish in 1978.

147. Leszek Kolakowski, *Main Currents of Marxism*, 3 vols., trans. P. S. Falla (Oxford: Clarendon Press, 1978).

148. Aleksandr Solzhenitsyn, *The Gulag Archipelago, 1918–1956: An Experiment in Literary Investigation*, 3 vols. (New York: Harper and Row, 1974–1978).

149. Solzhenitsyn, *Gulag Archipeglago*, vol 1., p. 181.

150. Ibid., p. 1.

151. Solzhenitsyn, *Zhit' ne po lzhi* (Paris: YMCA-Press, 1975).

152. Ericson, *Solzhenitsyn*, pp. 92–93. For a nuanced intellectual portrait of Solzhenitsyn, see David Remnick, *Resurrection* (New York: Random House, 1997), chap. 4.

153. *Le Monde*, April 15, 1974.

154. Aleksandr Solzhenitsyn, *A World Split Apart: Commencement Address Delivered at Harvard University, June 8, 1978* (New York: Harper and Row, 1978).

155. Vasilii Grossman, *Life and Fate: A Novel*, trans. Robert Chandler (London: Collins Harvill, 1985).

156. Stephen Cohen, Alexander Rabinowitch, and Robert Sharlet, eds., *The Soviet Union since Stalin* (Bloomington: Indiana University Press, 1980); Stephen Cohen, *Rethinking the Soviet Experience: Politics and History since 1917* (New York: Oxford University Press, 1985), and *Sovieticus: American Perceptions and Soviet Realities* (New York: Norton, 1985).

157. Andrei Sakharov, "The Danger of Thermonuclear War: An Open Letter to Dr. Sidney Drell," *Foreign Affairs* 61, no. 5 (Summer 1983): 1001–1016.

158. See for example Moshe Lewin, *The Gorbachev Phenomenon: A Historical Interpretation* (Berkeley: University of California Press, 1988, updated 1991). This work is an application to Gorbachev's *perestroika* of the author's defense of the "Bukharin alternative" in his *Political Undercurrents in Soviet Economic Debates: From Bukharin to the Modern Reforms* (Princeton, N.J.: Princeton University Press, 1974), republished during *perestroika* as *Stalinism and the Seeds of Soviet Reform: The Debates of the 1960s* (Concord, Mass.: Pluto Press, 1991).

159. Important works published during the Gorbachev period or immediately after are Geoffrey Hosking, *The Awakening of the Soviet Union* (London: Heinemann, 1990); Hedrick Smith, *The New Russians* (New York: Random House, 1991); Robert Kaiser, *Why Gorbachev Happened: His Triumphs, His Failure, His Fall* (New York: Touchstone, 1991, rev. ed., 1992). The first and most vivid postmortem is David Remnick, *Lenin's Tomb* (New York: Random House, 1993). Important works that appeared after the fall are John B. Dunlop, *The Rise of Russia and the Fall of the Soviet Empire* (Princeton, N.J.: Princeton University Press, 1993); John Keep, *Last of the Empires: A History of the Soviet Union, 1945–1991* (New York: Oxford University Press, 1995); Jack Matlock, *Autopsy on an Empire: The American Ambassador's Account of the Collapse of the Soviet Union* (New York: Random House, 1995).

160. Stephen Cohen's principal forum was the "MacNeil-Lehrer News Hour" on PBS. For Jerry Hough, see his *Russia and the West: Gorbachev and the Politics of Reform* (New York: Simon and Schuster, 1988, 2d ed. New York, N.Y.: Touchstone, 1990).

161. Ronald Suny, *The Revenge of the Past* (Stanford, Calif.: Stanford University Press, 1993).

CONCLUSION

1. Richard Pipes, *Survival Is Not Enough* (New York: Simon and Schuster, 1984), p. 37.

2. N. Ulianov, "Kompoleks filfeia," *Novyi zhurnal* 45 (June 1956). For the origins of the ideology, see Dimitri Strémooukhoff, "Moscow the Third Rome: Sources of the Doctrine," *Speculum* 28 (January 1953): 91–101. For the oldest Western stereotypes regarding Russia, there is Marshall Poe, "Russian Despotism: The Origins and Dissemination of an Early Modern Commonplace," (Ph.D. diss., University of California, Berkeley, 1993).

3. Thucydides, "The Melian Dialogue," in *The Peloponnesian War*, trans. Crawley (New York: Modern Library, 1982), p. 334.

4. Georges Sokoloff, *La puissance pauvre: une histoire de la Russie de 1815 à nos jours* (Paris: Fayard, 1993). The view that post-Soviet Russia is necessarily postimperial Russia has been vigorously propounded on the basis of recent data by Anatol Lievin, *Chechnya: Tombstone of Russian Power* (New Haven, Conn.: Yale University Press, 1998).

5. Peter Hopkirk, *The Great Game: On Secret Service in High Asia* (London: Murray, 1990).

6. Daniel Yergin and Thane Gustavson, *Russia 2010* (New York: Vintage Books, 1995).

7. See the section "Marxist Theory" in Chapter 4.

482

   8. See the section "Leninist Practice" in Chapter 4.

   9. See Christa Wolf, *What Remains and Other Stories*, trans. Heike Schwarzbauer and Rick Takvorian (New York: Farrar, Straus, and Giroux, 1993).

  10. Régis Debray, *Revolution dans la revolution? lutte armée et lutte politique en Amerique latine* (Paris: F. Maspero, 1967).

  11. Max Horkheimer, *Eclipse of Reason* (New York: Seabury Press, 1974).

  12. Martin Jay, *The Dialectical Imagination: A History of the Frankfurt School and the Institute of Social Research, 1923–1950* (Boston: Little, Brown, 1973); Luc Ferry and Alain Renaut, *French Philosophy of the Sixties: An Essay on Antihumanism*, trans. Mary H. S. Cattani (Amherst: University of Massachusetts Press, 1990); J. G. Merquior, *From Prague to Paris: A Critique of Structuralist and Post-Structuralist Thought* (London: Verso, 1986), his *Foucault* (London: Fontana, 1985), and his *L'esthétique de Lévi-Strauss* (Paris: Presses universitaires de France, 1977).

  13. Herbert Marcuse, *One-Dimensional Man: Studies in the Ideology of Advanced Industrial Society* (Boston: Beacon Press, 1964); Jürgen Habermas, *The Philosophical Discourse of Modernity*, trans. Frederick G. Lawrence (Cambridge, Mass.: MIT Press, 1987).

  14. Todd Gitlin, *The Whole World Is Watching: Mass Media in the Making and Unmaking of the New Left* (Berkeley: University of California Press, 1980); Paul Berman, *A Tale of Two Utopias: The Political Journey of the Generation of 1968* (New York: Norton, 1996).

  15. See the "Introduction" by Eric Hobsbawm to *The Communist Manifesto: A Modern Edition* (London and New York: Verso, 1998). For a spate of similar pronouncements, see "Marx's Stock Resurges on a 150-Year Tip," *New York Times*, June 27, 1998.

  16. Joan Scott, *Gender and the Politics of History* (New York: Columbia University Press, 1988).

  17. Daniel Bell, *The End of Ideology: On the Exhaustion of Political Ideas in the Fifties* (Glencoe, Ill.: Free Press, 1960).

  18. Francis Fukuyama, *The End of History and the Last Man* (New York: Free Press, 1992).

ACKNOWLEDGMENTS

A stammering *Urschrift* of this book was sketched in 1962. It outlined matters only down to 1855, yet already expressed the central themes developed here, namely, European civilization's unity in diversity and the fluctuation of the Western image of Russia in terms of the West's internal cultural climate. This first draft was helpfully criticized that year by the writer and critic Kornei Chukovskii during a trip to Russia and by the philosopher and intellectual historian Isaiah Berlin on my return to the West. I had much to learn from both.

A subsequent draft in the late 1960s, bringing matters into the twentieth century, benefited from extensive comments by the wide-ranging intellectual historian Andrzej Walicki of the Institute of Philosophy of the Polish Academy of Sciences. Around the same time, Eugene Rice of Columbia University gave me the helpful impressions of a historian outside the Russian field. Again in the 1960s I benefited greatly from conversations about European intellectual history with my then colleague at Berkeley Carl Schorske, who also looked at the *Urschrift*. I have a similar debt over a longer term to another colleague, Nicholas Riasanovsky, who read still another, longer version of the manuscript.

The book was basically completed around 1977 with the addition of sections on the Soviet experience treated, in the spirit of the dissidents, as a surreal phantasmagoria. I was led to hesitate about this approach, however, by the feeling that I might have overgeneralized from their judgments—against the increasingly positive assessment of the Soviet experience by Western scholarship. So when Communism began to disintegrate, beginning with the Solidarity movement in Poland, I put aside the present work to follow, and comment on, the unfolding collapse, writing the whole process up after its culmination in 1991 as *The Soviet Tragedy*. These changes led me to rework the present book again,

484   putting increased emphasis on culture and ideology as the sources of the failed Communist fantasy.

I am grateful to Aida Donald of Harvard University Press for her patience, throughout these long vicissitudes, in not calling in her bets. Finally, I am grateful to Terence Emmons of Stanford University, who had helped with the first draft of the manuscript when he was my graduate assistant and who became the only person on whom I imposed a full reading of the manuscript's penultimate version in 1997. It goes without saying that none of these persons is an accomplice of any of the views expressed in the finished product.

A work so long in the making obviously required the help of numerous students and other assistants at Berkeley. I wish in particular to thank Laurence Dickey, Stephen Vincent, Dallas Clouatre, and especially John Zammito, members of a graduate generation for whom intellectual history was still central. More recently, I have had the aid of David Schneer, Ron Bialkowski, Jason Ostergren, and Michael Katten, mostly graduate students in Russian history, in assorted tasks of typing, advice, editing, and the verification of references. In this work I also received the assistance of current or recent undergraduates at Berkeley: Stephen Jungels, John Grandy, Hun Kim, José Pamintuan, Daniel Silver, and especially Tom Anderson. To all, heartfelt thanks.

Absolutism, 5–6, 29, 30, 60, 63, 65; in Russia, 50, 71, 97, 168; enlightened, 59, 70, 71, 123, 283; revolution against, 63, 279; in Europe, 84, 106, 139, 140, 163, 294

Academy of Sciences (France), 38, 65, 70

Academy of Sciences (Prussia), 46

Academy of Sciences (Russia), 41, 46, 206

Action Française, 222, 321

Adams, Henry, 173, 221

Adams, John Quincy, 173

Adenauer, Konrad, 333, 376

Adler, Victor, 267

Aestheticism, 59, 120, 124, 165, 195, 201, 203, 204, 207, 221, 222, 342, 429

Afghanistan, 361, 387, 401, 402

Africa, 34, 280, 398, 413, 425

Aggression and imperialism dyad, 6, 7, 99, 151

Akhmatova, Anna (pseud. of Anna Andreyevna Gorenko), 235, 236, 293, 370, 393

Alexander I, 39, 94, 168, 173, 206, 341; expansionist policies of, 26, 87, 88, 89, 356, 358, 413, 419; liberalism and reforming policies of, 56–59, 73, 89–90, 91–92, 92, 141, 170; Europeanization under, 163; Congress of Vienna and, 243

Alexander II, 171, 173, 175, 176–177, 180, 378, 391, 413; reforming policies of/Great Reforms, 10, 176, 181, 205, 373, 418; revolution from above and, 163, 174; expansionist policies of, 419

Alexander III, 181–182, 191

Alexis, czarevich of Russia (son of Peter the Great), 44

Algeria, 151, 425

Alienation concept, 255, 258, 260, 261, 299, 308. See also Marxist theory

Alliance system during First World War, 239–244. See also specific countries

Amalrik, Andrei, 391, 395

American Philosophical Society, 368

American Revolution. See United States: Revolutionary War

Anarchy, 172, 221, 246, 278, 421

Ancient world, 65, 101

Andreas-Salomé, Lou, 211–212

Anecdotes of Peter the Great (Voltaire), 43

Anglo-Russian Convention (1907), 167

Animal Farm (Orwell), 365

Anna, Empress of Russia, 39

Anna Karenina (Tolstoy), 205

Anti-anti-Communism, 382

Anti-Comintern Pact (Germany and Japan), 315

Anti-Dühring (Engels), 259

Antifascism, 318–319, 322, 330, 333, 363, 416; Communism and, 315, 316, 318–319, 382. See also Fascism; Popular front

Antirationalism, 165, 215, 216, 328, 329, 348, 352

Anti-Semitism, 219, 351; in Russia, 175, 370; in France, 222; generic fascism and, 324; in Italy, 324; of Nazi ideology, 329, 333

Arabs, 31

Aragon, Louis, 341–342, 365, 376

Arendt, Hannah, 369

Argentina, 319

Aristocracy, 64, 133; in Europe, 36, 59; in France, 38; international, 38–40; in Russia, 38–40, 168; hereditary privilege of, 68, 96, 109; reforming policies of, 69, 72; Tory ("Ultra"), 175–176; in Germany, 226; revolution against, 279

Aristotle, 60

Armed Neutrality concept, 157

Armies. See Universal military service

Arms control, 385, 386, 389, 399, 402

Aron, Raymond, 235, 366, 367, 380, 381, 383, 428

Art, 113, 115–117, 122; folk, 114, 120, 122; as culture, 114–115; as religion, 123–124, 328; civic, 169, 193; in Russia, 193, 205, 207–217; painting, 197–198, 200–201; Romanticism in, 198; ab-

Art (continued)
stract, 201; decadent, 201, 204, 209, 219, 222; avant-garde, 205, 341; Surrealism, 341
Aryan state, 328, 330. See also Anti-Semitism; Hitler, Adolf: racist policies of
Asia, 20, 27, 128, 129, 150, 280, 361, 413
Atheism, 136, 169, 202, 215, 296
Atlantic West, 34, 56, 70, 97, 165, 189, 311, 320, 325, 419
Atlantic world, 369, 370, 374
Atlee, Clement, 247
Atom bomb, 355, 359, 375. See also Weapons
Aurora cruiser, 396
Austria, 21, 22, 96, 97, 135, 243, 418; War of Succession, 23; relations with Russia, 24–26, 77–80, 148, 237, 243; monarchy in, 33, 35, 97; Russia viewed as menace by, 75, 84, 91, 149, 150, 156; territorial compensation to, 78, 237; in Triple Alliance, 90, 150, 239, 240, 241; Compromise of 1867 and, 164; expelled from Germany by Prussia, 177, 178; revolutionary movements in, 185, 325; relations with Germany, 237; in League of the Three Emperors, 237–238; during Crimean War, 238; relations with England, 238; national revolution in, 244; Soviet occupation of, 356
Austria-Hungary, 174, 267. See also Dual Monarchy
Autarky, 321–322
Auteroche, Chappe d', 51, 52, 54
Authoritarianism, 320–323, 330
Autocracy, 6; Eastern, 5, 71; military, in Muscovy/Muscovite Russia, 31; in Imperial Russia, 40, 43, 50, 55, 84, 92, 93, 96, 137, 139, 140–146, 150, 168, 171, 184, 273, 278, 279, 293, 303; resurgence of, after Second World War, 329, 369–370; in Soviet Union, 398, 401
Avant-garde, 205, 278; philosophic, 71; intellectual, 329; artistic, 341; social, 342; literary, 344; political, 344
Avanti newspaper, 422
Axel's Castle (Wilson), 344
Axis powers, 315, 321, 322, 337, 353, 354, 358

Baader, Franz von, 136
Baader-Meinhof gang (Germany), 431
Babeuf, Gracchus/Babouvists, 250, 255, 421, 432
Backwardness, ideological, 440n10. See also Germany: viewed as backward soci-
ety by Marx; Russia, culture and character: viewed as backward society
Bakunin, Mikhail, 100, 134, 170, 188–189, 255, 258, 269, 270, 278; champions peasant revolt in Russia, 144–145; anarchist politics of, 190, 430
Balance of power, 9, 30, 155, 238; as basis for concert of Europe, 4, 23, 88, 153, 155, 238; initiated by Congress of Vienna, 21–22, 88; achieved through territorial compensation, 23, 83; influences on, 25–27, 76, 190; in favor of Russia, 82–83, 90; European state system and, 83, 88; partitions of Poland and, 157; international, in First World War, 240; alliance system and, during First World War, 242; détente and, 386
Balkans/Straits/Balkan Wars, 21, 24, 77, 152, 155, 158, 188–189; Christianity in, 40, 79; Ottoman Turks' occupation of, 76; Russia viewed as menace by, 153–154, 156; Russian occupation of, 157, 166; Russia's interests in, 180, 237, 238, 240, 243, 413
Ballanche, Pierre, 255
Ballets Russes, 197, 198, 206, 209
Baltic Sea/Baltic provinces, 20, 23, 80, 128, 131, 296; trade relations, 25; European expansion into, 34; German occupation of, 39, 334; under Peter the Great, 74, 413; Russian military strength in, 148
Balzac, Honoré de, 98
Barbarism/barbarous society, 27, 125, 350, 431; heroic cult of, 350. See also Ottoman Empire; Russia, culture and character
Barbès, Armand, 147, 250, 264
Barbusse, Henri, 346
Barrès, Maurice, 221
Baudelaire, Charles, 197, 198, 200, 201, 203, 204, 205, 206, 210, 212, 223, 378
Bebel, August, 250
Becher, Johannes R., 342
Becoming concept, 121, 125, 126, 199
Beer Hall Putsch, 326
Beethoven, Ludwig van, 116, 200
Being concept, 261, 264, 277
Belgium, 110, 414
Benkendorff, Alexander, 39
Bennett, Arnold, 209
Benois, Aleksandr, 197
Bentham, Jeremy, 49, 57, 71, 164–165
Berdiaev, Nikolai, 211, 218, 350, 372, 389
Beria, Lavrentii, 374
Berlin, 34, 38, 74, 389

Berlin, Isaiah, 367–368
Berlin Academy, 46
Berlin blockade, 360–361, 375, 384
Berlin Wall, 384, 403, 404
Bernanos, George, 210
Bernstein, Eduard, 248, 275, 276, 284, 422, 424
Bessarabia, 88, 89, 153
Beyond Good and Evil (Nietzsche), 213, 230
Biron, Ernst-Johann, 39
Birth of Another (Rolland), 346
Bismarck, Otto von, 24, 127, 149, 164, 166, 174, 188, 203, 244, 299; relations with Russia, 167, 176; legitimist Bonapartism of, 176–177, 266; creates German empire (1871), 177–178; conservative radicalism, 178; defeat of liberalism, 223; League of the Three Emperors, 237–238, 239; use of universal military service, 242; German diplomacy, 351
Black Hundreds, 351
Black Sea, 20, 26, 155, 157, 413
Blackstone, William, 47, 49, 50
Blanqui, Auguste, 147, 171, 184, 250, 255, 264, 271, 297, 421, 422
Blok, Aleksandr, 246, 341, 391
Blum, Léon, 297, 315
Boehme, Jacob, 120
Bohemia, 133, 135
Bohlen, Charles, 380
Boileau, Nicolas, 59
Bolshevism, 184, 211, 216n, 271, 280, 296, 331; in First World War, 236; after Russian Revolution, 244, 246, 297, 332–333; Marxism and, 266; voluntarism of, 269; socialist experiment of, 273, 299–307; perception of, by West, 293, 294, 296; Communism as goal of, 299; dictatorship of, 310; as model for Mussolini, 316–317; in Germany, 326, 350–351; after Second World War, 339; Jacobinism and, 341; radical politics in United States and, 341; Russian spirituality and, 348–349, 350–352. *See also* Communist Party: Soviet Russia; Leninism; Mensheviks; Russian Revolution
Bolshoi Ballet, 376
Bonaparte. *See* Napoleon Bonaparte
Boris Godunov (Mussorgsky), 196, 209
Borodin, Aleksandr, 197
Bosnia, 237
Bourbon, House of, 22, 24, 28–29, 30, 33, 58; in Spain, 70, 330
Bourgeoisie, 64, 65–66, 95, 96, 101, 102, 106, 220, 428, 431; German critique of, 229–230; economic, 249, 268; intelligentsia, 250; society, 259, 429; as ally of the proletariat, 272; as agents of revolution, 273, 279, 282, 283; in Russia, 280; abolition/suppression of, 297, 310; Communism and, 308, 318; fascism and, 317, 319; revolution, 425. *See also* Petty bourgeoisie; Third Estate
Boyars, 31, 37
Brainwashing, 380
Brandenburg, Mark, 135
Brandenburg-Prussia, 178, 418
Brandt, Willy, 385
Brazil, 425
Brecht, Bertolt, 342, 346
Brezhnev, Leonid, 307, 331, 361, 386, 387, 389, 390, 398, 406; dissident Soviet writers and, 392; Prague Spring and, 392; relations with Czechoslovakia, 393–394; "really-existing" socialism, 394, 396
Briand, Aristide, 221
Britain, 33, 79, 87, 157; military revolution in, 32; imperialism/colonialism of, 34, 239, 413–414, 416; constitutional government, 69, 101, 170; relations with India, 151; industrialization of, 157; trade with Ottoman Empire, 157; Russia viewed as menace by, 157–158, 166, 416; as maritime power, 158, 322; perception of Russia, 237; alliance with Japan against Russia, 239; relations with France, 239; use of universal military service, 242; relations with Russia, 243; political economy, 257; as international power, 358; perception of Soviet Union, 398. *See also* Crimean War; England
Bronze Horseman, The (Pushkin), 7, 51, 236
Bronze Horseman monument, 50–51, 313–314
Brotherhood of peoples, 188, 190, 191, 330
Brothers Karamazov (Dostoevsky), 215, 216, 217, 349, 372
Bruck, Möller van den, 350
Brückner, Alexander, 180
Brzezinski, Zbigniew, 369
Buber-Neumann, Margarete, 365
Buchez, Philippe-Joseph, 255
Buddha, 215
Buddhist soul concept, 208
Buffer states, 81, 296
Bukharin alternative, 301, 302, 423, 424, 426, 456n1

Bulgaria, 189
Bundist (Jewish) movement, 186
Bunin, Ivan, 194
Buonarroti, Philippe-Michel, 250
Bureaucracy, 32, 70; separation of powers
    and, 50; in Germany, 109; in Russia,
    142, 300; rational, 182; in Italy, 323; in
    Soviet Union, 394
Burke, Edmund, 81, 101, 116, 125, 126,
    136, 137, 156, 158
Burnham, James, 380–381
Byron, Lord, 116
Byzantium, 5, 18, 19, 41, 100, 103, 129,
    146, 372, 389

Calas family, 49
Calvinism, 83
Camps/camp system of detention. *See*
    Concentration camps; Gulag Archipel-
    ago; Siberian exile system
Camus, Albert, 367
Cancer Ward (Solzhenitsyn), 394
Capetian realms, 30, 135
Capital. *See* Wealth
Capital (Marx), 183, 259, 263, 284, 305,
    330, 346, 426
Capitalism, 229, 251, 261, 267, 274, 297,
    381, 407, 416, 432, 433; international
    market economy of, 173, 424; in Rus-
    sia, 173, 182, 267, 284; peasant com-
    munes and, 183, 268; nationalism and,
    189; in England, 225; in France, 225; in
    United States, 225, 247, 273, 362; as en-
    emy of Communism, 252, 329, 426;
    Marxism and, 259, 266, 267, 273, 274,
    426; socialism and, 268, 270, 279, 285,
    400; welfare state and, 276; contradic-
    tions of, 280, 432; finance, 280; laissez-
    faire, 296; revolution and, 300; industri-
    alization and, 305; monopoly, 315, 317,
    319; in Germany, 327–328; in Third
    World, 426. *See also* Materialism
Capital punishment, 47
Carbonari, 170, 187, 272
Carlowitz, treaty of, 40
Carmen (Mérimée), 193
Carroll, Lewis, 179–180
Castro, Fidel, 386, 398, 428, 430
Categorical Imperative. *See* Kant, Im-
    manuel
Catherine II (Catherine the Great), 9, 23,
    57, 58, 140; expansionist policies of, 7,
    25, 26, 48–49, 54, 75–79, 82–83, 87, 89,
    237, 358, 413, 419; enlightened despot-
    ism of, 9, 49–50, 60, 72, 141; reforming
    policies of, 35, 47, 48, 49–50, 51, 52,
    57, 80; Europeanization under, 39, 163;

lumières of, 47, 51, 54, 56, 76, 78; as
    Semiramis of the North, 47, 48, 51, 56,
    76, 404; and Poland-Lithuania, 49, 52,
    57, 76–77, 79, 80, 82, 83, 89–90, 93,
    154, 237; religion and, 49, 77, 78, 83;
    support of *Encyclopédie*/Encyclopedists,
    49, 55; *Nakaz* document, 50, 51, 89;
    commissions The Bronze Horseman
    monument, 50–51; advancement of civi-
    lization in Russia and, 53, 54, 55, 58;
    police/police state of, 55–56, 418; as
    Messalina of the North, 56; French En-
    lightenment and, 73; war with Ottoman
    Turks, 76, 78, 79, 130, 157, 237, 413;
    Greek project, 79–80, 83, 100, 157; rela-
    tions with Austria, 80
Catholicism, 18, 19, 64, 122, 136, 321; re-
    lationship to Orthodox Muscovy, 19–
    20; separation of church and state, 41;
    in Poland, 92; Romantic, 138; in
    France, 222. *See also* Papacy
Cavour, Camillio, 188
Ceauçescu, Nicolae, 404
Censorship, 54, 99, 169, 170, 399
Central Asia, 151, 166, 374, 413
Central Committee (Soviet Union),
    398
Central Europe, 395, 417, 419; universal
    service system, 33; nationalism in, 147,
    188, 189; relations with Russia, 151–
    152, 155, 176; revolution from above,
    164; Romanticism in, 165; ethnic na-
    tionalities in, 325; under Stalin, 413.
    See also Revolutions of 1848
Central Intelligence Agency (CIA), 363,
    366, 401
Century of Louis XIV (Voltaire), 45
Chaadaev, Petr, 102–103, 136, 358
Chagall, Marc, 197
Chamberlin, William Henry, 344
Charles II, 22
Charles XII, king of Sweden, 42, 240
Charter of the Nobility, 35
Chartism, 96, 176, 221, 250
Chateaubriand, René de, 116, 124, 125,
    202
Chekhov, Anton, 194
Chernyshevskii, Nikolai, 169, 170, 183,
    197, 269, 270
Chesmé, battle of, 78
Chile, 425
China, 4, 5, 45, 46, 190, 247, 294, 361,
    385, 403, 417, 425; Communist, 285,
    331, 338; war with Japan, 315; as issue
    in the Cold War, 360; Communist revo-
    lution (1949), 361, 373; de-Staliniza-
    tion programs, 375; relations with So-

viet Union, 385; relations with United States, 385; cultural revolution, 430
Chinese Revolution (1911), 185, 358
Chopin, Frederic, 93
Christendom, 46, 63, 64; Christian West, 18, 20; Latin, 102, 127; papal, 115, 128; cultural revolution and, 115–116, 124; during Restoration, 136
Christianity, 30, 46, 60, 65, 101, 107, 253; separation of church and state, 41; in China, 46; superstition and, 118; generic, 127; Romanticism and, 127; medieval, 128; during Restoration, 136–137; democracy as, 202; socialism as, 202
Christian Science Monitor, 344
Chronicle of Current Events, 393
Church: universal service system and, 31, 33; autonomy of, 68; constitutional reforms and, 69. *See also* Clergy; Dissent: religious; Religion; Separation of church and state
Church and the Left (Michnik), 396
Churchill, John, duke of Marlborough, 22
Churchill, Winston, 295, 296, 316, 355, 371, 373, 380, 385, 387
Church Slavonic, 140
Citizenship/citizens, 107–110; universal, 406
City-states, 31, 129, 138, 178, 214
Civility. See *Moeurs douces*
Civilization, 42, 53, 125, 219, 227; in Russia, 26, 55, 140, 143–144, 150, 163, 180–181; concept of, 27–28, 37, 100–102, 103, 107, 130–131; police/police state as designation of, 28; geographical directions of, 35–36; social class and, 37; in Europe, 65, 84, 128, 133, 157, 236; culture and, 103–104; Enlightened/Romantic redefinition of, 128; as plurality of cultures, 130–132; crisis of modernity, 165, 219, 220; in Germany, 225, 229, 325
Civil liberties/rights, 49, 275, 393, 432–433
Civil society, 28, 30, 32, 34, 42, 60, 103–105, 123; in Russia, 35, 71, 140, 141–144, 170, 171, 174, 339, 367, 419; in France, 65, 70; changing structures of, 65–67; in Europe, 70, 108; intelligentsia/intellectuals as substitute for, 143; suppression of, 258, 300, 309, 339; universal-suffrage democracy and, 275–276; freedoms of, 285; in Spain, 331; in Germany, 333; modernization of, 379. *See also* Social class; Society
Civil War (Russia), 299, 300

Civil War (Spain), 315, 323, 341
Civil War (United States), 173, 320
Civil War in France (Marx), 422
Clark, Colin, 378
Class-alien concept, 334
Class struggle, 101–102, 126, 258, 261–262, 267, 274, 285, 400; Marxist dialectic of, 65, 102, 228, 257, 259, 260–262, 303, 317, 332, 427, 433; as basis for Bolshevism/Communism, 245, 246, 281; as historical force, 261; voluntarism and, 264; under Bolsheviks, 299, 302, 306–307, 318; international, 312, 352–356, 360, 387–388, 416; abandonment of, in Soviet Union, 402. *See also* Proletariat; Social class
Claudel, Paul, 210, 222
Clemenceau, Georges, 221
Clergy: privilege of, 29–30, 66, 68; opposition to religious reforms of Peter the Great, 44; radical politics and, 44; supernatural claims of, 44, 49, 67, 68, 69, 78; in France, 101; in Germany, 105, 107. *See also* Church; Religion; Separation of church and state
Cobbet, William, 252
Code Napoleon, 50, 87, 113
Cohen, Stephen, 403
Cold War, 4–5, 7, 8–9, 12, 24, 359–361, 389, 402, 403, 407, 416; as outcome of First World War, 235; propaganda, 365; Soviet-Western relations during, 383–388; détente and, 386, 387, 388
Coleridge, Samuel Taylor, 116, 217
Collective security policy, 354
Collège de France, 93, 102
Colonialism, 330, 347, 413, 432
Columbus, Christopher, 34, 413
Cominform, 375
Comintern, 317, 346, 354, 375, 403
Command economy. *See* Economy: command
Committee on the Present Danger (United States), 386
Common Market, 362
Communards, 201
Commune, the, 200–201, 221, 421
Communes. *See* Peasantry: commune system
Communism, 96, 312, 387, 400; collapse of, 6, 391–403, 405–407, 412, 420, 434, 465n19, 466n19; in Soviet Russia/Soviet Union, 12, 271, 298, 333, 432; utopian, 250, 411; defined as non-capitalism, 251, 252; as social system, 252, 360; revolutionary, 258, 333; humanist,

Communism (continued)
285; during Russian Civil War, 299;
democratic, 301; as despotism, 312,
343; as antifascism, 315, 316, 318–319;
fascism and, 317, 318, 328, 329, 338,
382; proletariat and, 318, 329, 400; in
Central Europe, 325; Nazism and, 327–
328, 329–330, 332, 335–339, 369; socialist goals of, 328, 337, 345; antirationalist tradition and, 329;
antireligious principles of, 329; ideology, 329, 334, 345, 382, 395, 397, 424;
progressivism and, 329, 366; subordination of party to state, 329; amoral principles of, 329–330; generic, 331; similarities with Nazism, 335–339;
totalitarianism and, 331, 337; world
revolution as goal of, 353; during Cold
War, 360, 361; liberalization of, 392; social analysis of, 394, 395–396; inverted
modernity of, 400–401; Marxist, 420,
423; maximalist, 426; in West, 430. See
also Class struggle; First International;
Party-state apparatus; Second International; Soviet Russia/Soviet Union;
Spectre of Communism; Third International; War Communism
Communist Labor Party (United States),
340
Communist League (Germany), 272
Communist Manifesto (Marx), 246, 249,
259, 264, 272, 274, 308, 432
Communist Party, 318, 333, 375, 416; in
Soviet Russia/Soviet Union, 247, 327,
331, 333, 397–398, 405, 406–407; in
Germany, 297, 325, 342, 352, 354; in
France, 338, 341; Italy, 338; in United
States, 342–343, 343; Western, 382,
431; in Czechoslovakia, 392
Communist politics/regimes: in Germany,
325; in China, 331, 385, 395; in North
Korea, 331; in Vietnam, 331; in Soviet
Russia/Soviet Union, 352, 382, 387; in
Asia, 358; in Korea, 361; in Czechoslo-
vakia, 363; in United States, 363–364,
376, 382; in Europe, 364; in Spain, 365;
Western, 371; in Italy, 375; in North
Vietnam, 385, 398; in Poland, 387
Communist Russia. See Soviet Russia
Compensation, territorial and diplomatic,
23, 74, 78, 82, 83, 88–89, 237
Compromise of 1867 (Ausgleich), 164, 178
Comte, Auguste, 165, 169, 229, 269
Concentration camps, 324, 364, 365–366,
393, 394. See also Stalin, Joseph: Soviet
camp system (Gulag) under
Concert of Europe, 4, 21–27, 39, 70, 88,

142; Russia as member of, 10, 13, 14,
21, 24, 42, 73–76, 88–89, 139–140, 238,
246, 356, 418; French Revolution and,
79; territorial compensation policy, 88–
89; Ottoman Turks and, 154, 353; collapse of, 189–190, 358–359; Soviet Russia's withdrawal from, 352
Condorcet, Marie Jean, 61, 70, 113, 314
Conference on Security and Cooperation
in Europe, 356
Congo, 384
Congress for Cultural Freedom, 366
Congress of Berlin, 88, 160, 237
Congress of Tours, 297
Congress of Vienna, 9, 21, 87, 94, 149,
239; territorial compensation and creation of status quo in Europe, 88–89, 91,
96, 147; Russia and, 156, 157
Conquest, Robert, 397
Conrad, Joseph, 216fn, 401
Consciousness: revolutionary, 264, 275,
276, 421, 422, 427; scientific, 278; ideo-
logical, 311; popular, 421
Conscript armies. See Universal military
service
Conservatism, 165; revolution and, 215,
217, 249; in Germany, 226, 227–228,
230; radical, 226; in Europe, during
First World War, 241; national, 319,
321, 323; in United States, 343; model
of, 389–390; détente and, 390
Conspiracy of the Equals, 250
Constantine, grandson of Catherine II
(Catherine the Great), 79
Constantine the Great, 5
Constantinople. See Ottoman Empire/
Ottoman Turks
Constantinople, See of, 19
Constituent Assembly (Russia), 297
Constitutional government, 56–58, 419;
reforming policies of, 69, 73; liberal,
145; ideal of, 251; in Germany, 265; in
Spain, 331; in Soviet Russia, 425
Constitutionalism, 29, 91–92, 185; liberal,
164, 279; in Russia, 168, 170, 245, 246,
419; democratic ideal and, 338
Consumer society, 431. See also Bourgeoi-
sie
Containment, policy of, 359
Contract, theories of, 29
Convention of 1792, 94
Convergence/convergence theory, 411,
412, 418, 419, 424; of practical inter-
ests, 7, 25; cultural, 12–13, 75–76; illu-
sion of, during Cold War, 12–13; West-
East cultural gradient, 12–13;
Muscovy/Muscovite Russia with Old

Regime Europe, 32; of political and social structures, 75, 167, 192, 237, 381,
382–383, 395, 401; Russia with universal civilization, 165; of conflicting perceptions of Russia, 293; modernization
policies and, 378, 380; détente and,
389; socialism with liberalism, 392; of
values/value systems, 404. *See also* West-
East cultural gradient
"Copernican revolution," 118
Corn Laws (England), 176
Corporate privilege, 29, 30
Corporatism, 229, 321
Correspondences (Baudelaire), 199, 200
Cortés, Donoso, marquis de Valdegamas,
148
Cosmopolitanism, 114–115, 117, 119–
120, 122, 130–132, 187, 190
Cossacks, 31, 55, 97, 147, 149, 176–177,
191, 370
Council of Florence, 19
Counterculture, 431
Courbet, Gustave, 200
Crimea, 79, 157
Crimean War (1853–1856), 10, 154–155,
156, 157, 158, 160, 166, 175, 178, 179,
192, 193, 237, 238, 391, 416
Critical thought, 54, 64, 71, 117, 118,
169, 310, 428, 430
Croatia, 321, 330
Cromwell, Oliver, 33, 83
Crossman, Richard, 366
Crusades, 18–19, 128, 157, 414
"Crystal Palace" as metaphor for future,
169, 285
Cuba, 285, 382, 384, 386, 389, 392, 425
Cuban missile crisis, 361, 384, 385
Cubism, 201
Culture: in Germany *(Sonderweg)*, 103–
111; as national identity, 130–131; con-
cept of, 135–136; in East Central
Europe, 189–190; in Russia, 206, 207,
214, 220, 229, 231; in Germany *(Kul-
tur)*, 215, 222–223, 224, 225–227, 229,
264–265, 325, 342; in Europe, 217;
mass, 219; harmony with society, 223;
politics and, 223, 227
Cunning of Reason. *See* Hegel: Cunning
of Reason principle
Custine, marquis de, 98–99, 137–138,
139, 140, 145, 179, 193, 347, 371
Cyprus, 237
Czartoryski, Adam, Prince, 57, 94
Czechoslovakia, 188, 339, 392, 396, 424;
Soviet occupation of, 356; relations
with Soviet Union, 393–394. *See also*
Prague Spring

D'Alembert, Jean, 48, 61, 66, 70, 119
Dallin, David, 366, 397
Damiens (would-be assassin of Louis XV),
47
Daniel, Iurii, 392
Dante, 210–211
Dark Ages, 62
Darkness at Noon (Koestler), 365
Darrow, Clarence, 340–341
Darwin, Charles/Darwinism, 222–223,
264, 329, 330
David, Jacques-Louis, 200
Davies, Joseph, 347, 348, 355, 363
Death of a World (Rolland), 346
Debussy, Claude, 196
Decadence, 226. *See also* Art: decadent
Decembrist conspiracy, 92, 138, 139, 141,
143, 144, 188
Declaration of Independence, 282
Decline of the West (Spengler), 350
Defectors, Soviet, 365, 398
Defensor Pacis, 60
De Gaulle, Charles, 319, 376, 385
Dehumanization, 260, 261–262, 427, 429,
432, 434
Delacroix, Eugène, 200
De Maistre, Joseph, 15, 51, 137, 139
Democracy/democratic government, 6,
52, 53, 72, 95, 96, 125, 126, 130, 147,
148, 335, 419, 420; nationalism and,
108–109, 189, 335; pan-Slavism and,
134; constitutional, 165, 273, 320, 425;
in Poland, 170; in England, 175–176; in
France, 175–176; peasant communes
as, 180, 267; in Russia, 182, 405, 419;
liberal, 219, 323, 337–338, 430; in
West, 220; in Germany, 224, 419; egalitarian, 229, 282, 284, 336; political,
236, 253; universal-suffrage, 250, 257,
323; bourgeois, 267, 268, 310; classical,
267; formal/legitimate, 278, 281, 433;
defined, 282, 419; socialism and, 284,
335, 336, 337–338; military, 320; National Socialism and, 337; in United
States, 340, 419; market, 411, 434; in
Italy, 419; universal, 433
Democratic Legends of the North (Michelet),
102
Democratic revolution. *See* Revolutions of
1848
Democratic society, 252
Denmark, 148
De Profundis (Wilde), 210
Descartes, René, 49, 61, 62, 107
Despotism, 29–30; enlightened, 9, 41, 45,
70, 71, 72, 100, 110, 293, 370, 372, 389;
Oriental/Asiatic, 6–7, 43, 138, 139, 146,

Despotism (continued)
172, 184, 293, 312, 370, 371, 372, 400,
437n6; humane, 180. See also specific
countries
De Staël, Mme., 217
De-Stalinization 375, 377, 382–383, 391–
392, 401, 434
Détente, 361, 383–388, 389, 390, 398,
401
Deutscher, Isaac, 382
Deutschtum, 114, 325, 327
Development economics, 207
De Vogüé, Melchior, 208, 210
Dewey, John, 348
Diaghilev, Sergei, 197, 198
Dialectical materialism. See Marxist theory
Di Borgo, Pozzo, 39
Dictatorships, 327, 328, 397; populist,
317; totalitarian, 368, 370; modern-
izing, 383, 389
Diderot, Denis, 48, 49, 50–51, 52, 56, 66,
73, 119, 340
Discourse on the Origins of Inequality (Rous-
seau), 53
Dissent: religious, 40, 44, 64, 65, 77, 78,
104–105, 353; philosophic, 70; Soviet,
367, 390–401, 402, 406, 407, 428
Divine authority/Providence, 29, 60–61,
62, 73, 97, 122, 257
Division of labor, 249, 261
Dix-huit leçons sur la societé industrielle
(Aron), 380
Djilas, Milovan, 310, 395, 396
Dobb, Maurice, 344
Doctor Zhivago (Pasternak), 378
Dodgson, Charles (Lewis Carroll), 179–
180
Dogger Bank incident, 166
Dolfuss, Englebert, 315
Domesday Book and Beyond (Maitland), 207
Don Carlos (Schiller), 131
Dostoevsky, Feodor Mikhailovich, 11,
194, 195, 198, 204, 209, 218, 347, 350,
372, 394, 401; God-manhood and relig-
ious conversion of, 205–206, 210, 211,
341; cultural influence of, 212–213,
228; success in Germany, 215–217; re-
jection of modernity, 229–230
Doux commerce, 64
Dreyfus Affair/Dreyfusards, 220, 221,
222, 224
Dual Monarchy, 241, 324, 325
Dubček, Alexander, 392
Dumas, Alexander, 179
Duranty, Walter, 344
Durkheim, Émile, 368
Dvorianstro. See Non-noble service gentry

Dynastic state/polity, 29, 32, 35, 36, 38,
42, 70, 133, 187, 189; in England and
France, 28–29; in Russia, 30, 35, 37–38,
59, 150, 294, 325; in Austria, 29; in
Prussia, 29, 35, 122–123

East Asia, 425
East Central Europe, 133–134, 135, 188–
189
Eastern Europe, 45, 135, 225, 360, 373,
396
East Germany, 342
Eastman, Max, 343, 344
East Prussia, 24, 35, 74
East Rome, 30, 40, 153
Ecclesiastical immunities. See Clergy:
privilege of
Economic theory, 61, 257, 258, 259, 260,
374, 378–379
Economy, 32, 373; in Europe, 64, 374;
centralized, 254, 275; nationalization
of, 254, 275; planned, 255, 256, 299,
308, 315, 332, 345, 381, 395, 423, 426;
bourgeois, 267; Great Depression, 294,
314–315, 319–320; in Russia, 300–301,
309, 312; command, 305, 312, 328,
332, 333, 390, 405, 416; crises in, 319,
323; state management of, 327–328,
333; in Soviet Russia/Soviet Union,
333, 375, 401, 402, 416; industrial,
378–380; socialist, 379; market, 380,
405; global, 412. See also Autarky; Capitalism
Education, 54, 55, 73, 109, 168, 220. See
also Universities
Egalitarianism/egalitarian society, 53, 67,
68, 108, 145, 207, 248, 250, 253–254,
261, 283, 420; of Communism-Marx-
ism, 261, 432–433; socialist, 309–310.
See also Civil society
Egypt, 384, 425
Eighteenth Brumaire of Louis Bonaparte, The
(Marx), 259, 272, 283, 317, 394, 422
Eisenhower, Dwight D., 377
Eisenstein, Sergei, 205, 342, 371, 391
Eliot, T. S., 210, 349, 372
Elitism, 10–11, 27, 30, 42, 53, 62, 132,
272, 429, 431–432; in Russia, 37, 38,
55, 139–146; in England, 222; in
France, 222, 421
Elizabeth, Empress of Russia, 38, 39, 43,
47
Éluard, Paul, 341
Emancipation Edict of 1861 (abolition of
serfdom), 168, 169, 170, 181, 182
Emancipation of Labor Group (Russia),
270

Émigrés: Russian, 100, 348, 351, 364, 367–368, 372, 391; French, 347; Polish, 396
Émigré "Whites," 339–352
Empire des tsars et les Russes, L' (Leroy-Beaulieu), 181
Empiricism, 60–61, 60–62, 113, 114, 118, 164, 203, 276
Encounter periodical, 366
Encyclopédie/Encyclopedists, 46, 48, 49, 52, 54, 55, 66, 114, 117, 119; empiricism of, 61–62, 164
Engels, Friedrich, 183, 184, 251, 261, 268, 421–422; Russophobia of, 191, 371; Marx and, 249, 258, 343; Lenin and, 343
England: perception of Russia, 8; European status of, 21, 22, 26, 96; relations with Russia, 25, 167; trade with Russia, 25, 79, 172–173; colonialism of, 26, 38, 71, 78, 79, 88; as flank power, 26, 88, 96; military revolution, 33, 64; as civil society, 58–59, 104, 107, 108; empiricism in, 61, 114; as maritime power, 69, 88, 96, 108; military strength, 69; constitutionalism in, 69, 71, 176, 185, 220; relations with Ottoman Empire, 77; relations with Poland-Lithuania, 77; Russian expansionist policies and, 77, 78, 79, 80, 100, 156, 237, 414; in Triple Alliance (1815), 90, 150; nation-state formula in, 127, 189; relations with France, 156, 238; industrialization in, 158, 250, 252; reforming policies of, 158, 163, 176, 250; Germany viewed as menace by, 166; support of South, in Civil War, 173; territorial compensation to, 237; relations with Austria, 238; foreign policy of autonomy, 239; in First World War, 240–241; Glorious Revolution (1688), 248; economic development, 249, 283; perception of Soviet Russia, 296, 366; Communism and, 329; alliances during Second World War, 354. *See also* Britain
Enlightenment, 11, 34, 64–65, 117, 118, 136, 137, 224, 254, 329, 400, 418; in Russia, 84, 144; failure of, 113, 204, 218–219; in England, 117, 118; in France, 117, 118; social and political institutions, 136–137; concept of progress, 204, 281; culture and, 217; egalitarian perspective on, 253, 254; in Germany, 257; Romanticism and, 434–435. *See also* Despotism: enlightened; *specific countries*
Entente Cordiale, 239, 354
Epistemology, 117, 118–119

Era of Tyrannies (Halévy), 337
Erenburg, Ilia, 378
Erfurt Congress, 223–224, 274
Essai sur les moeurs (Voltaire), 68
Estates General, 71, 72, 168
État de droit, 29–30
"Eternal Russia" concept, 3, 6, 313–314, 389, 411
Ethics, 61, 62, 107, 114, 118, 119, 204, 221, 227, 328
Ethiopia, 315, 324, 386, 425
Ethnic identities, 433–434
Eugène, Prince of Savoy, 22
Eugene Onegin (Pushkin), 344
Eurasia, 6, 321, 322, 339
Europe, 10, 27, 33–34, 133, 147, 220; relations with Russia, 8, 21, 206, 207; perception of Russia, 10–11, 23, 75, 82–83, 139, 153–154, 165, 167, 179, 236–237; as civilization, 18, 35–36, 133; expansion of, 33–34, 128, 129, 413; relations with Ottomans, 39–42; "of the Two and of the Three" (divided in 1870), 96–97, 150–151, 164, 190, 192, 238–239; cultural identity of, 128; radical politics in, 147, 249; as maritime power, 151, 164, 165, 221, 235; international relations in, 238–239; Marxist influence in, 267; industrialization, 298; partition of, after Second World War, 358–359, 362; during Cold War, 360, 386, 387. *See also* Balance of power
European cultural gradient, 110. *See also* West East cultural gradient
European state system, 17, 22–23, 25–26, 26, 88, 127, 128, 236, 237, 356; England and Russia as flank powers of, 26, 77, 88, 96; balance of power and, 83; collapse of, 189–190; division of, 239–240
European Union, 362
Evtushenko, Evgenii, 376
Existentialism, 367
Expressionism, 342
Extermination camps, 334, 365. *See also* Concentration camps

Fabian Society/Fabianism, 248, 267, 346
Falange party (Spain), 323
Falconet, Etienne-Maurice, 51
Fallmerayer, Jakob, 152–153, 352, 371
False Dimitri, The (Schiller), 131
Famine in Russia (1921–1922), 299
Far East, 166, 185, 239, 338
Fascism, 6, 11, 222, 235, 294, 315–317, 338–339, 399, 432; as revolutionary movement, 235, 320–321, 462n80; co-

494

Fascism *(continued)*
    alitions against, 315; nationalism and,
    316, 320, 324, 329; generic, 316–317,
    320–321, 323, 331; as nationalism, 316–
    317; Communism and, 317, 318, 328,
    329, 338, 382, 411–412; Imperial (Ja-
    pan), 317, 322, 338; social, 318; triad of
    people, party, and leader, 319, 323, 327,
    330; authoritarianism and, 320–321;
    religion and, 321, 323; Nazi radicaliza-
    tion of, 326, 338; ideology of, 328,
    329
Fascist regimes/Fascist Party, 317, 321,
    323, 462n80; in Germany, 316, 317,
    321, 322; in Italy, 316–317, 319, 321,
    322–323, 327; in Croatia, 321; in
    Slovakia, 321; in Japan, 321–322; in
    Russia, 322; in Hungary, 322–323; in
    Central Europe, 326; in United States,
    362
Fascist Union (Britain), 321
Fast, Howard, 376
Fathers and Sons (Turgenev), 204
Faust (Goethe), 115, 120
Feminism, 432, 433, 434
Feudalism, 29–31, 67, 101–102, 251, 252,
    259, 261, 274, 279, 283, 338, 442n19;
    chivalry, concept of, 115, 128. *See also*
    Middle Ages; Serfs
Feuerbach, Ludwig, 169, 202, 257–258,
    260, 269, 314
Fichte, Johann-Gottlieb, 109, 120, 132
Film/motion pictures, 205, 342
Finland, 26, 45, 88, 89, 168, 330, 355
Firebird, The (Stravinsky), 196
First Circle, The (Solzhenitsyn), 394
First Congress of People's Deputies, 403,
    404
First International, 183, 186, 278
First World War, 84, 135, 189, 190, 204,
    224, 236–244, 293, 418; war credits,
    190, 191, 246, 296, 423, 426; political
    effects of, 235, 242, 320, 325; universal
    military service in, 236, 320; alliance
    system during, 239–244
Five-Hundred-Day Plan, 405
Five-Year Plans in Russia, 301, 344, 378;
    First (1929–1932), 302–303, 304, 310,
    315, 377
Flaubert, Gustave, 193, 194, 208
Fletcher, Giles, 20
Fleurs de mal, Les (Baudelaire), 210
Fokine, Mikhail, 197
Ford, Gerald, 398
Foucault, Michel, 429, 430, 431
Fourier, Charles, 250
Fourteenth Amendment, 282

France, 267; perception of Russia, 8, 237;
    European status of, 21, 96; revanchist,
    26, 237, 320; military polity, 33; as mili-
    tary monarchy, 35; level of civilization,
    36, 58; under Louis XV, 55, 56; empiri-
    cism in, 61, 114; radical politics of, 65–
    66, 171; reforming policies of, 65–66,
    79; expansionist policies of, 87–88, 157,
    414; as constitutional monarchy, 94–95;
    revolt of the bourgeoisie (12th century),
    101, 102; class struggle in, 101–102; ab-
    solute monarchy in, 102; as civil soci-
    ety, 104, 106, 107, 108; classicism, 115;
    nation-state formula in, 127, 189; trade
    relations, 156, 173; Russian occupation
    of, 158; Third Republic, 81, 95, 164,
    176; Russian expansionist policies and,
    237; political development, 249; percep-
    tion of Soviet Russia, 296, 366; popular
    front coalition, 315–316; as maritime
    power, 322; Estates General, 335; Na-
    tional Assembly, 335; universal suffrage
    in, 421. *See also* French Enlightenment;
    French Revolution
France, international politics: relations
    with Russia, 17, 24, 58, 87–88, 154–
    155, 173, 191, 239; relations with Po-
    land-Lithuania, 24, 76, 77; relations
    with Sweden, 24; alliance of Russia and
    England against, 25, 26; in War of
    American Independence, 26; relations
    with Spain, 28–29, 31; relations with
    Ottoman Turks, 40; relations with Ot-
    toman Empire, 77; relations with Amer-
    ica, 79; relations with Britain, 87–88,
    156, 238, 239; in Triple Alliance, 90,
    150; occupation of Prussia, 109–110; re-
    lations with Algeria, 151; relations with
    Germany, 166–167; relations with Aus-
    tria, 238; relations with Prussia, 239;
    European coalition against Bonaparte,
    240, 403–404; in First World War, 241,
    242; territorial compensation to Russia,
    243; resistance movement in Second
    World War, 341, 363; relations with
    Soviet Russia, 354; as international
    power, 358
Franco, Francisco, 322, 323, 330
Franco-Prussian War, 166, 167, 176, 177,
    189, 358, 421, 422
Frankfurt School, 308, 329, 368, 428, 429,
    430
Franz-Joseph, emperor of Austria, 148,
    149
Frederick II (Frederick the Great), king of
    Prussia, 23–26, 46–49, 73, 75, 105, 120,
    130, 351; view of Russia, 36, 37, 74; en-

lightened despotism, 72, 418; partition of Poland-Lithuania and, 74, 77; cultural ambitions, 106; coalition against, 240
Frederick William I, king of Prussia, 22, 35, 38
Frederick William II, king of Prussia, 237
Frederick William IV, king of Prussia, 148
Freedom, 28, 67, 68, 96, 100–101, 128, 129, 168, 181, 182, 222, 275; repression of, 97; constitutional, 102; individual, 263, 282, 381, 400, 432–433; national, 282; political, 285, 286. *See also* Civil liberties; Serfs: emancipation of, in Russia
Free Press (England), 99
Free Youth Movement (Germany), 229
Freiligrath, Ferdinand, 117
Freitag, Gustav, 193
French Enlightenment, 61, 65–66, 73, 144
French language, 38
French Revolution, 29, 58, 63, 72, 73, 79, 87, 88, 93, 94, 102, 116, 414–415, 432; effects of, 97, 101, 107, 108, 110, 124, 126, 137, 141, 248–249, 283, 337, 338, 422; philosophical opposition to, 111–112; failure of, 113, 282; Romanticism and, 115, 124; perception of, by foreign intellectuals, 123; universal military service during, 241; ideals of, 248, 253, 335–336; socialism and, 250, 253; Germany and, 265; as model, 266; democratic ideal of, 335–336
Freud, Sigmund, 211, 216–217, 219, 368, 429
Friedrich, Carl J., 369
From under the Rubble (Sakharov, ed.), 395
Fronde, the, 64
Fuggers, the, 104
Furchtwänger, Leon, 346–347

Gagarin, Yurii, 375
Galbraith, John Kenneth, 381
Galicia, 243
Galileo, 60, 61
Gandhi, Mohandas, 345
Garnett, Constance, 209, 216, 220
Geneva summit (1955), 376
Genius, cult of, 203, 222, 258, 371
Genius of Christianity, The (Chateaubriand), 124
"Genius rebel" cult, 114, 125
Gentry: emancipation from universal service, 35, 38, 40, 55; in Russia, 142, 169, 170
George, Lloyd, 220, 221

George, Stephan, 228
Georgia, 151
German Federal Republic, 362
German Ideology (Marx), 258–259
German language, 38, 110
Germany, 127, 134, 167, 177–178, 332, 364–365, perception of Russia, 8, 225–226, 228, 342; Russian occupation of, 23–24, 46, 87, 149; national revolution in, 32, 244; unification of, 88, 148, 150, 164, 177–178, 238, 239; as civil society, 105, 106; French occupation of, 107; national identity, 107, 108, 114–115, 223–225; cultural identity and achievements, 112, 114–124, 127, 140, 218, 223–226, 228, 230; religion during Romantic era, 117–118, 119; corporate institutions, 138; democratic aspiration of, 148; military strength of, 166, 167, 239; viewed as menace by England, 166; economy, 167, 223, 224, 225, 239; radical politics in, 171, 265, 267; trade with Russia, 173; Reich formed 1870, 177, 182; Russian literature and, 211, 215–216, 217; anti-Romantic era in, 222–223; men of property and culture, 223, 224–225, 265; as nation-state, 223; antimodernity in, 224–225, 226; social policies, 225; aesthetic revolution in, 226, 227; perception of West, 226; division of, as basis for balance of power in Europe, 238; patriotism in, 242; viewed as backward society by Marx, 265, 267, 311; Marxist influence and revolution in, 265–266, 267, 268; industrialization policies of, 267, 274, 327, 332; partition and reunification of, 356, 361; Soviet occupation of, 356. *See also* Weimar (culture); Weimar Republic
Germany, international politics: Russian/French alliance against, 17; Slavic nationalism and, 134; military supremacy in Europe (1870), 166–167; relations with France, 167; relations with Russia, 167, 239, 243; in First World War, 224, 229, 240–241, 242; political gap with the West, before First World War, 224–225; relations with the East, 225; relations with Austria, 237; in League of the Three Emperors, 237–238; in Triple Alliance, 239, 240; victory in East Europe, 338; as issue in Cold War, 360
Gershenkron, Alexander, 367–368, 440n10
Gestapo, 324
Gibbon, Edward, 101, 117, 127

Gide, André, 209, 210, 215, 218, 347, 348, 366
Giercke, Otto von, 229
Ginzburg, Evgeniia, 393
Glasnost, 403, 407
Gliksman, Jerzy, 366
Glorious Revolution (Britain), 101
"God-manhood" concept, 205–206, 211, 341
God that Failed, The (Crossman, ed.), 366
Goethe, Johann Wolfgang von, 105, 107, 114, 115, 119, 120, 130–131, 132, 203, 298, 349
Gogol, Nikolai, 140, 193, 194, 205, 215, 298, 300, 372
Golden Horde, 5, 146
Gold standard, 173, 174
Goncharov, Aleksandr, 194
Gorbachev, Mikhail, 12, 381, 387, 389, 402–407
Gordon, Peter, 39
Gorky, Maxim, 342, 347
Götterdämmerung, 241
Grand Alliance. *See* Second World War: Allied powers
Great Depression, 294, 314–315, 319–320, 343, 373–374, 378
Great Elector of Brandenburg, 35, 168, 418
Great Northern War. *See* Peter I: victory over Sweden at Poltava
Greece, 6, 65, 319, 383; class revolt in, 40; ancient, 60, 101, 111, 115, 223; Catherine the Great and (Greek project), 79, 80, 83, 100; revolt against Ottoman Turks, 91; independence of, 153–154, 158, 187; city-states, 214; Communist revolt in, 373
Greek Orthodoxy, 18–19, 79, 127
Grey, Edward, 241
Grimm, brothers, 117
Grimm, Frédéric-Melchior, 48–49, 341
Grossman, Vasilii, 399
Grotius, Hugo, 49
Guardian, The, 398
Guardini, Romano, 211
Guevara, Che, 382, 424, 430
Guild system production, 253, 263, 282
Guizot, François, 101, 102, 125–129
Gulag Archipelago, 294, 306, 417
Gulag Archipelago, The (Solzhenitsyn), 396, 398
Gunpowder weaponry, 31–32
Gustavus Adolfus of Sweden, 83
Gutenberg, Johann, 41, 393
Gypsies, 334

Habsburg/House of Habsburg, 4, 24, 40, 135, 149, 156; in Austria, 22, 135, 185, 338, 414; in Spain, 22, 31; war with Bourbons, 22, 24; relations with Russia, 148; Compromise of 1867, 178; Dual Monarchy of, 185; expansionist policies of, 358
Halévy, Élie, 337
Hamlet (Shakespeare), 216
Hamman, Johann, 114, 122
Hanover, House of, 29
Hanska, Mme. de, of Ukraine, 98
Hardenberg, Friedrich (Novalis), 116, 120, 123, 136
Harvard speech of Solzhenitsyn, 398
Havel, Vaclav, 396
Haxthausen, Freiherr von, 137–138, 139
Hegel, Georg Wilhelm Friedrich/Hegelianism, 6, 11, 63, 108, 122, 124, 126, 201, 202, 247, 269, 364; Marx and, 63, 112, 122, 257–258, 262, 305, 343, 364, 430; Absolute Idea concept (pantheism), 120–122, 136, 144, 202, 260, 262; Cunning of Reason principle, 122, 262, 264, 286, 299, 305, 306, 419, 435; historicism of, 128, 429; view of civilization, 132; dialectic of reason, 133, 264; radical interpretation of, 145, 257–258; radical politics of, 171, 265; idealistic dialectic, 257–258; spiritual dialectic/theological philosophy, 260, 262, 265; philosophical religion of, 396; neo-Platonic elements of, 453n41
Heidegger, Martin, 429
Heine, Heinrich, 96, 116, 117
Helphand-Parvus, Aleksandr, 186, 267
Helsinki Accords, 356, 387
Hemingway, Ernest, 315
Henriad, The (Voltaire), 45
Henry IV, 29, 45, 69, 71, 72
Herberstein, Sigismund von, 20
Herder, Johann-Gottlieb, 114–115, 120, 122, 130–133, 187
Hernani (Hugo), 116
Herodotus, ix–x, 6, 400
Heroism, cult of, 200, 202, 211, 218, 220, 223, 324, 350; in Russia, 216n, 345; during First World War, 224; in Germany, 229; mock, of fascism, 328
Herwegh, George, 117
Herzen, Aleksandr, 117, 138, 144–145, 169, 170, 269
Hesse, Hermann, 212, 230, 349
High Church Movement (England), 137
Hilferding, Rudolf, 267, 280
Hiss, Alger, 363

Historical consciousness, 100–101
Historicism/historicity, 111, 127, 128, 129, 130, 132, 257, 276, 283; national particularity of, 100–101, 115, 133, 316, 328; Romanticism and, 111, 123, 124–129; cultural particularity of, 113, 133; cosmopolitan view of, 114–115, 117; religion and, 120, 124; reason and, 121–122; vs. concept of progress, 126; revolution and, 248–249
Historiography, 13, 36, 45, 100–103, 107, 413, 438n7
History: philosophy of, 43–44, 132; triad of antiquity, Middle Ages, and modernity, 65; economic, 207; social, 207; as logical progression toward socialism, 247, 251, 252, 257, 259, 260–261, 261, 263–264, 274, 276, 282, 376; Marxist view of, 249, 259, 260, 263–264, 270–271, 279; logic of, 264, 270–271, 274, 275, 279, 280, 281, 285, 311, 331, 400, 406, 423; as logical progression toward noncapitalism, 281; laws of, 308; as logical progression toward modern society, 379, 435
History of Charles XII (Voltaire), 42, 43
History of Civilization in Europe (Guizot), 101
History of France (Michelet), 102
History of the Russian Empire under Peter the Great (Voltaire), 43–44
History of the Russian Revolution, The (Trotsky), 344–345
Hitler, Adolf, 103, 322, 323, 351, 368, 369, 383, 399; rise to power, 315, 354, 370, 374; Nonaggression Pact with Stalin, 316, 334, 354, 368; viewed as menace by Soviet Union, 318, 354; Beer Hall Putsch, 326; racist policies of, 326, 328, 333, 334, 352, 415; social structure of Germany and, 326, 333–334; preparation for war, 327; Wagner and, 328; Mussolini and, 331; revolutionary aims of, 332; expansionist policies of, 333; defeat in Russia, 335; Stalin and, 338, 339, 354, 382–383; national idealism, 352, 354; attack on Soviet Russia, 354; declares war on United States, 354–355. See also Nazism
Ho Chi Minh, 338, 382
Hoffman, E. T. A., 205
Hofmansthal, Hugo von, 228
Hohenzollern empire, 24, 74, 109, 135, 149, 338
Holland, 21, 22, 283, 356
Holy Alliance (Alexander I), 9, 91, 97, 117, 136, 146, 147, 149, 150, 187, 237
Holy Family, The (Marx), 258
Holy League, 22
Holy Roman Empire, 127, 134
Holy Spirit, age of, 256
Holy Synod, 41, 44, 172
Hook, Sidney, 364
Hoover, J. Edgar, 363
Horace, 141
Horthy, Miklos, 322
Hough, Jerry, 403
Hugo, Victor, 116
Huguenots, 38
Humanism, 60, 96, 115, 128, 202–203, 227, 309–310, 420–421, 429; in Germany, 131, 202; in Russia, 140, 193; socialism and, 224
Humanity, concept of, 67, 114, 131, 181, 261
Hume, David, 67, 107, 117, 118
Hungary, 133, 135, 370, 395; foreign occupation of, 22, 31, 158, 322–323, 326, 378; cultural-linguistic nationalism in, 110–111; Russian intervention in, 147–149, 151, 152; Compromise of 1867 and, 164, 178; refusal of democratic suffrage, 185; anti-Communist revolution (1956), 378
Huns, 74
Hurons, 45
Huysmans, Joris, 221
Hydrogen bomb, 375, 393

I Chose Freedom (Kravchenko), 365
Iconoclasts, 18, 66
Idealism, 119, 120, 144, 265; philosophical, 103, 104, 111; absolute, 121; post-Kantian, 123; creative, 215
Imperial Ballet, 196
Imperialism, 280, 281, 333, 382, 417, 432; classical capitalism as, 317; fascism as, 317, 322, 338. See also specific countries
Impressionism, 200–201, 203
Independent Socialist Party (Germany), 185, 297
India, 151, 158, 416, 425
Individualism, 136, 138, 211, 220, 222, 370
Individual liberties. See Freedom
Indochina, 358
Indonesia, 384
Industrialism/industrial society, 13, 146–147, 215, 219, 252, 266, 283, 284, 373; socialism and, 249, 305; under First Five-Year Plan, 302; capitalism and,

Industrialism/industrial society *(continued)* 305; in Soviet Union, 374–375; logic of, 380–381
Industrial Revolution, 249
Industrial Workers of the World, 185
Information society, 401
Inherited order and structures, of civilization, 65, 67, 126, 321. *See also* Nobility
Input-output mechanism of economy, 379
Intelligentsia/intellectuals, 66, 67, 72, 362; as class of professionals, 67, 68, 276; in Germany, 103–111, 119, 120, 223, 226–227, 228, 229–230, 265, 324–325; in Russia 139–146, 163, 169, 170–171, 173, 207, 269, 270, 284, 412; radical politics of, 169, 170–171, 173; socialism and, 171, 269, 284; nihilism of, 181; bourgeois, 250–251; Communist/Marxist politics of, 269, 276, 278, 396; as agents of revolution, 276, 277, 278, 279, 420–421, 422, 423; Leninist politics of, 277–278; workers as, in Russia, 310; emigration of, from Soviet Russia, 339–340; in Soviet Russia/Soviet Union, 350, 378, 394, 400, 407, 416; in United States, 364; reformist, 392. *See also* Dissent
Interdynasticism, 38–40
Intermediate-Range Nuclear Force agreement, 402
International Workingmen's Organization (First International), 190
Into the Whirlwind (Ginzburg), 393
Ireland, 79, 185, 220, 263
Iron Chancellor. *See* Bismarck, Otto von
Iron Curtain, 33, 338, 363, 370, 376, 419
Irrationalism, 44, 45, 68, 219, 222, 223, 228, 435; political, 8–9, 63; in international politics, 244, 360; of profit motive, 309
Islam, 18, 40
Italian War of 1859, 189
Italy, 31, 33, 35, 87, 96, 115, 126, 157, 330, 356; Renaissance, 36, 101; enlightened despotism in, 70; constitutionalism and democracy in, 71, 91, 320; unification of, 88, 238; cultural-linguistic nationalism in, 110–111; Russia and, 149; independence of, 157, 158, 187; in Triple Alliance, 239, 240; Marxist influence in, 267; tradition of revolution in, 272; conquest of Ethiopia, 315; status as world power, 322; relations with Spain, 323; German influence on, 329; resistance movement in, 363; perception of Soviet Russia, 366

It Can't Happen Here (Lewis), 315
Ivan the Terrible, 5, 303, 371, 412

Jacobin Republic/Jacobinism, 56, 81, 120, 220, 250, 271, 282, 296, 406, 422–423; Bolshevism and, 341; Marxism and, 426
Jakobson, Roman, 367–368
James, Henry, 193, 194
James I, king of England, 105
Japan, 294, 338, 354, 358; war with Russia, 160, 166, 167, 185, 239, 241, 414, 416; in First World War, 240; war with China, 315; status as world power, 322
Jaurès, Jean, 267
Jefferson, Thomas, 57, 58, 59, 71, 73, 90, 341, 356
Jesuits, 20, 46
Jews, 186, 214, 325, 326, 351–352, 352; culture of *Ressentiment*, 203; Nazi Germany's policy toward, 333–334
Jihad, 41, 353
Joachim of Floris, 120
Joan of Arc, 102
John Reed under the Kremlin (Steffens), 340–341
Johnson, Hewlett, 343
Johnson, Lyndon, 385
Joint ventures, 405
Joseph II, 47, 79, 80
Joy (Bernanos), 210
July Monarchy, 144, 164, 272, 283, 421
July Revolution, 94, 95, 97, 116, 146, 151, 239, 249, 250, 336
June Days insurrection. *See* Revolutions of 1848
Junkers, 74, 149–150, 178, 223

Kaiserreich, 223, 224, 226, 229, 272
Kandinsky, Wassily, 197
Kankrin, Egor, 39
Kant, Immanuel, 59, 62–63, 66, 74–75, 106, 107, 112, 119–120, 130, 144, 202, 204, 254, 257; doctrine of the moral will, 118, 201; pure/universal reason theory, 118, 121; Categorical Imperative, 119, 124; critical Idealism, 121
Karpovich, Michael, 367–368
Katyn Forest massacres, 355
Kautsky, Karl, 250, 267, 275, 276, 278, 280, 423, 424, 428
Kennan, George, 181–182, 182, 371
Kennedy, John, 375, 385
Kepler, Johannes, 61
Keynes, John Maynard, 374
KGB (Committee for State Security), 393, 397

Khomiakov, Alexei, 136, 137
Khrushchev, Nikita, 361, 374–380, 383,
384, 385, 387, 389, 390, 396, 404; de-
Stalinization policies, 377, 391–392,
401; Communist reforms of, 386; for-
eign policies of, 392
Kiev, 30, 129
Kireevskii, Ivan, 136
Kissinger, Henry, 385, 386, 398
Kleber, Johann, 109
Kliuchevskii, Vassilii, 206–207
Koestler, Arthur, 365, 366
Kojève, Alexandre, 364
Kolakowski, Leszek, 396
Kolkhoz, 5, 334
Kondriatiev, Nikolai, 207
Konrád, György, 395–396
Korea, 330, 425
Korean War, 373, 375–376, 384
Kościuszko, Thaddeus, 81, 93
Kossuth, Louis, 148–149
Kravchenko, Victor, 365
Kropotkin, Petr, 190, 210
Kuchuk-Kainardji, Treaty of, 79
Kulaks. See Petty bourgeoisie: in Russia
Kuznets, Simon, 207, 378

Labor: agitation, 221; Marxist concept of,
255, 259, 260, 261; surplus value of,
259
Labor camps, 334. See Concentration
camps; Siberian exile system
Labor movements, 274, 276; in Britain,
250; in Europe, 250; socialist, 275; in
United States, 364
Labor Party (Britain), 221, 247, 275, 297,
343
Labriola, Antonio, 267
LaHarpe, Frédéric-César de, 49, 73
Laissez-faire doctrine, 66, 263,
296
Lamennais, Félicité de, 126
Land and Freedom organization, 169–170
Language: as culture, 114; differences in,
133; of propaganda, 397–398; structural
linguistics, 429. See also Vernacular
revolution; specific languages
Lasalle, Ferdinand, 258
Latin America, 430
Latin Christianity, 156–157
Latin language, 64
Latin West, 18–19, 19, 41
Lavrov, Petr, 183, 284
Law, 50, 58, 61, 68, 261, 330; recodifica-
tion of/reform, 47, 49–50, 56–57; inter-

national, 89; due process of, 168; rule
of, 220, 338
Leadership styles/"cult of personality,"
331, 342, 343, 346–348. See also Stalin,
Joseph: cult of personality
League of Armed Neutrality, 79
League of Nations, 354
League of the Three Emperors, 237–238
Lebensraum as policy of colonization, 321,
334
Le Bon, Gustave, 219
Lefort, Francis, 39
Leibniz, Gottfried Wilhelm, 46, 47, 130,
136, 206, 340
Lelewel, Joachim, 138
Lenin, V. I., 122, 186, 243, 276, 312–313,
340, 345–346, 403, 406, 427, 428, 432;
Bolshevik Revolution (Red October) of,
3, 4, 244, 246, 266, 270, 271, 279, 281,
340, 411, 416, 426; revolutionary the-
ory/permanent revolution, 184, 248,
272; bourgeois intelligentsia concept of,
250, 277, 278; Marxist politics of, 267,
272, 276, 277, 329, 400, 426, 427;
worker-peasant alliance, 272; theory of
capitalism, 280, 381; Communist utopia of, 285; perception of, by West,
294; in troika of Soviet Russia, 298–
314; theory of imperialism, 300; New
Economic Policy (NEP), 300–301, 302,
374, 423, 426; dictatorship of, 301, 303–
304; critics of ("enemies of the people"), 303, 306–307, 329; class struggle,
304, 311; Party-state apparatus of, 304,
327, 395; socialist goals of, 313–314,
344, 422; expansionist policies of, 317,
326; style of leadership, 331; Engels
and, 343
Leningrad, 313–314
Leninism, 271–286, 331–332; role of proletariat in revolution (vanguard party),
250, 272, 276, 277, 278, 280, 281, 300,
302, 423; Marxism and, 271, 273, 278,
280, 281, 311; orthodox, 273; ideal,
345; reformist, 392
Leninism-Stalinism, 343
Leontief, Wassily, 207, 367–368, 379
Leopardi, Giacomo, 116–117
Leroux, Pierre, 125
Leroy-Beaulieu, Anatole, 181, 339, 367
Leskov, Nicolai, 194, 215
Lessing, Gotthold, 107
Let History Judge (Medvedev), 394–395
Lettres françaises, Les (review), 365
Lewis, Sinclair, 315
Liberal International, 186, 187

500

Liberalism/liberal politics, 11, 103, 125, 130, 225, 251, 318, 370; classical, 94, 146, 186, 190, 220, 253, 337–338, 381, 433; in Britain, 94, 175, 176, 187, 220, 221, 224, 225, 250; in France, 94, 175, 176, 187, 220, 225; Western, 94, 151, 160, 182, 191, 380; in Russia, 132, 141–142, 143–144, 148, 168, 170, 175, 181–182; constitutional, 145, 323; in Poland, 93–94, 152; in Europe, 164, 174, 175, 176; in Prussia, 178; bourgeois, 186, 428; conservative, 186–187; symbolism and, 217; heroic age of, 218; collapse of, in Europe, 220; working class and, 220–221; in Germany, 223, 224, 226; in United States, 225; capitalism and, 252; totalitarianism and, 370; crisis of, 373–374; in Soviet Union, 386; model of, 389–390
Liberty. *See* Freedom
Liberty, Equality, Fraternity (slogan), 253
Lichtheim, George, 465n19
Liebknecht, Karl, 185
Life and Fate (Grossman), 399
Lincoln, Abraham, 173
Lindbergh, Charles, 315
Literacy, 37, 219
Literature, 190, 213, 218, 344; about Russia, 51, 98, 137, 179, 180–182; anti-Russian, 51–52, 54, 98–103, 137–138; imaginative, 59, 371; lyric, 59, 116; in Germany, 114–115, 348–352; fiction/novels, 115, 193–195, 215, 230, 341, 346–347; in England, 201; about Soviet Russia, 339–352, 367–368, 371; anti-Soviet, 342–343, 371; about camp system, 365–366, 392, 393, 396
Literature in Russia, 140–141, 207, 215, 230, 344, 372; golden age of, 193–195; spiritualism in, 208–211, 213, 216n, 217, 372; pessimism in, 210; "primitive," 215; antibourgeois, 228; about Russian Revolution, 364; dissident, 390–401; surreal, 393
Lithuania, 404, 405
Living standard, 64, 274, 374, 399
Lobachevskii, Nikolai, 206
Locke, John, 29, 61, 114, 117
Logic, 60, 61, 97. *See also* History: logic of; Reason
London Exposition (1851), 169
Louis Napoleon Bonaparte, 238, 266, 317. *See also* Napoleon III
Louis Philippe, 421
Louis XIV, 4, 22, 26, 28, 29, 38, 43, 64, 65, 72, 83, 84, 91, 105, 142, 240, 414
Louis XV, 45, 47, 55, 56, 68, 72

Louis XVI, 70, 81, 169
Low Countries, 31, 87, 189, 414
Ludendorff, Erich von, 243, 326
Lukács, György, 343, 346, 387, 396, 426, 427, 464n19
Lumières, 58, 101, 124, 156; in Russia, 47, 51, 54, 56, 76, 78; in Germany, 123; legacy of, 364. *See also Philosophes*
Lunacharskii, Anatolii, 314, 341
Lutheranism, 77, 83, 104, 120, 122; in Germany, 105, 107, 119
Luxemburg, Rosa, 184, 185, 186, 267, 268, 280, 342
Lyricism, 116, 124, 194, 208, 222, 228
Lysenko affair, 371

Mably, Gabriel, 54
Mafia, 333
Magic Mountain, The (Mann), 349
Magyars, 30, 188
Mahler, Gustav, 211
Maiakovskii, Vladimir, 205, 313, 341, 342, 391
Maid of Orleans, The (Schiller), 131
Main Currents of Marxism (Kolakowski), 396
Maitland, Frederick, 207
Malevich, Kazimir, 205
Mallarmé, Stéphane, 201
Malraux, André, 315
Managerial Revolution, The (Burnham), 380–381
Mandelshtam, Nadezhda, 393
Mandelshtam, Osip, 291, 393
Manet, Édouard, 200
Mann, Heinrich, 226, 348
Mann, Thomas, 212, 225, 230, 348–349, 387
Mao Zedong, 190, 247, 338, 385, 424, 428, 430, 431
Marcuse, Herbert, 430
Maréchal Maurice de Saxe, 38
Margaret, Jacques, 20
Maria Stuart (Schiller), 131
Maria Theresa of Austria, 77
Market(s), 252, 285, 327, 405; anarchy of, 254–255, 315; abolition/suppression of, 299, 305, 308, 309, 327, 333, 428; capitalist principles of, 301; socialism, 301–302, 419, 423, 426; democracy, 411, 425, 434; international/global, 424, 425, 432. *See also* Capitalism; Economy
Marlborough, duke of, 38
Marr, Nikolai, 371
Marshall Plan, 318, 362, 374
Marsilio of Padua, 60
Martel, Charles, 18

Marty, André, 341
Marx, Karl, 11, 96, 112, 122, 139, 144,
179, 198, 251, 364, 421–422; Hegel
and, 63, 126, 199, 257, 407, 430; attitude toward Russia, 99–100, 158, 171,
182–184, 352, 371; rejects utopian socialism, 255, 256, 407; Feuerbach and,
257; German revolution and, 262, 264,
265–267, 273, 311; Darwin and, 330;
writings on, 464n19. *See also* Class
struggle; Communism; Spectre of Communism
Marxism-Leninism, 12, 304, 306, 311,
338, 400, 423, 428
Marxism/Marxist politics, 11, 368; revolutionary tradition and, 144, 249, 250,
256, 264; in France, 186; in Germany,
186, 223–224, 325; in Poland, 186; in
Russia, 186, 272, 273, 311; "orthodox,"
259, 270, 271, 273, 275, 276, 279, 281,
282, 285, 427–428; historical determinism of, 267, 427; party Consciousness,
277; ideological divisions of, 284–285;
welfare state and, 284–285; in troika of
Soviet regime, 298–314; social effects
of, 310; Bolshevism and, 311, 312;
Communism as goal of, 420, 423; modernization and, 424; generic, 426; Marxist Method, 427–428, 432–434, 435
Marxist-Populist symbiosis, 284
Marxist theory, 144, 256–271, 277–279,
281–282, 312, 329, 426; of socialism,
144, 252, 256, 305, 308, 344, 405, 420;
of proletariat, 145, 190, 262, 297, 426–
427; of science, 222–223, 270, 395; of
revolution, 223–224, 268, 270, 275,
279, 282, 283, 382, 426–427, 427; humanistic goals of, 257–258, 260, 285,
311, 407; of materialism, 259, 260, 262;
utopia and, 260, 420; class categories,
272; noncapitalism as goal of, 274, 275,
277, 281, 311, 317, 432; economics and
Five-Year Plans, 304–305, 425; of industrialization, 305, 312, 332–333; abo-
lition/suppression of private property,
428. *See also* Alienation; Class struggle;
Communism; Production; Socialism;
Society
Materialism, 222, 225, 262, 269; Marxist
dialectic of, 259, 260, 262. *See also* Capitalism
Mauriac, François, 210
Maurras, Charles, 321
Mazzini, Giuseppe, 96, 126, 139, 187
McCarthy, Joseph, 362, 363, 382
Medvedev, Roy, 394–395, 399, 403
Mehemet Ali, 153, 154, 156

Mein Kampf (Hitler), 326
Mendel, Gregor, 371
Mendeleev, Dmitrii, 206
Men of parts *(hommes à talents)*, 66–69,
105–106, 226
Mensheviks, 184, 271, 280, 339
Menshikov, Aleksandr, 156
Merezhkovskii, Dmitrii, 214, 215, 218,
349, 372
Mérimée, Prosper, 193, 208
Messianism. *See* Russia, international poli-
tics: world domination as goal of
Metaphysics, 100, 118, 202, 276, 396, 427,
464n19
Metternich, Prince of Austria, 91, 237,
244, 356
Mexico, 173, 340
Meyerhold, Vsevolod, 342
Michelet, Jules, 102, 117, 125, 127, 128,
129, 139, 267
Michels, Robert, 272
Michel Strogoff, Courier of the Tsar (Verne),
181
Michnik, Adam, 396
Mickiewicz, Adam, 93, 102, 117, 126, 138,
187
Middle Ages, 30, 60, 65, 101, 102, 115,
129, 143, 223, 338. *See also* Feudalism;
Serfs
Miliukov, Paul, 182, 184
Miliutin, Dimitrii, 167
Mill, John Stuart, 11, 218, 220, 269
Missile gap, 384
Missile systems. *See* Weapons: nuclear
Mission to Moscow (Davies), 355
Mitteleuropa, 134, 164, 165, 175–179,
188, 192, 220, 225, 338, 342; Marxist
influence in, 267; Old Regime struc-
tures in, 324, 418; Communism in, 325
Mitterrand, François, 275, 387
Modern art, 198–205
Modernism, 65, 112, 204–206, 342; in
Russian literature, 217; in Europe, 343,
364
Modernity, 10–11, 11, 13, 14, 56, 71,
136, 219, 379, 406, 407, 435; in Russia,
140, 228, 310–311, 312, 400; rejection
of, 215, 221–223, 227–229, 253; in
Germany, 227–228; in Europe, 241,
244; egalitarian democracy and, 282;
Second World War and, 337
Modernization, 381, 386, 424; as step toward convergence, 378, 380; the-
ory/model, 379–380, 381–383, 389,
390; political, 425
Moeurs douces, 36–38, 42, 58, 68; as civilized conduct, 36–38

Molière, 64, 105
Möller van den Bruck, Artur, 214–215, 217, 220, 226, 228, 230
Monarchy, 69; relation to subjects, 30, 36, 73; sovereign, 30; centralized, 33; enlightened, 43, 45, 47, 58, 73, 92; in Russia, 45, 47, 54, 56, 58, 92, 97, 183, 184; civilized society and, 68–69, 70, 71–73; reforming policies of, 68–69, 69, 71–72; in Central Europe, 83; autocratic, 97; absolute, 102; national, 128; in Austria, 178, 183; in Prussia, 183, 184; in France, 222; Russian Revolution and, 245; bourgeois, 249; in Italy, 323
Monat, Der, periodical, 366
Monde, Le, 375, 398
Monet, Claude, 200
Mongol-Byzantine tsarism, 183
Mongols, 5, 17, 30–31, 31, 146
Monroe Doctrine, 414
Montesquieu, Charles de, 6, 29, 43, 50, 400
Moral ideals and laws, 114, 118, 119, 255, 256, 329
Morgan, J. P., 340
Morris, William, 221, 253
Moscow, 313, 342, 352–353, 392, 412
Moscow Art Theater, 195
Möser, Justus, 125, 252
Mosley, Oswald, 321
Mountain, Jacobin, 191
Müller, Adam, 252
Munich Agreement, 354
Münnich, Count Burkhard, 39
Muscovy/Muscovite Russia, 19, 20, 23, 31, 77; expansionist policies of, 6, 178, 412–413; European status of, 17, 42; religion in, 18–20, 19, 20, 41; isolation of, 20, 30–31; as military autocracy, 31; universal military service in, 32, 163, 294; as patriarchal society, 143, 389; opposition to, in West, 151
Music, 116, 195–196, 199–200, 201, 206
Muslims, 44, 128, 413
Mussolini, Benito, 315, 317, 322, 323, 324, 331, 346, 368, 370, 383, 422
Mussorgsky, Modest, 196, 204, 209
My Country and the World (Sakharov), 395

Nabokov, Vladimir, 344
Nakaz document of Russian laws, 50, 51, 89
Napoleon Bonaparte, 4, 58, 84, 87, 89–91, 94, 96, 109, 113, 132, 147, 203, 413; coalition against, 240, 403–404; use of universal military service, 241; invasion of Russia, 415

Napoleon III, 175–176, 176–177, 188
Napoleonic Wars, 24, 39, 82, 87, 88, 93, 140
National Bolshevism (Germany), 350–351
Nationalism, 6, 11, 114–115, 130, 177, 189, 222; particularity of, 100–101, 115, 133, 316; in France, 108, 109; cultural, 110, 120, 227, 328; cultural-linguistic, 110–111; Romantic, 110–111; in Germany, 115, 120, 148, 188, 242; messianic, 126; pan-Slav, 134, 188; in Europe, 187, 189, 362; in Italy, 188; capitalism and, 189; mass, 224, 337; fascism and, 316, 320, 324, 329; democracy and, 335–336; in Russia, 362; religious, 372; in Soviet Union, 417
National Socialism. *See* Nazism
Nation building, 69, 110, 328
"Nation" concept, 335–336
Nation-states, 188, 189, 214, 219, 223, 322, 336
NATO. *See* North Atlantic Treaty Organization
Natural reason, 42, 62, 67, 253
Natural supernaturalism, 123, 126, 198–199, 202, 204
Nature, 229; laws of, 60–61; external world of, in philosophy, 117, 118, 121
Naumann, Friedrich, 225
Nazism (National Socialism), 230, 317, 319, 326, 327, 329, 332, 333, 337, 364–365, 368, 429; as revolutionary movement, 235, 320, 326, 332, 333; Hitler's rise to power and, 315; economic policies, 319, 327; Bolshevism and, 326; racial doctrine of, 327, 333–334; Communism and, 327–328, 329–330, 332, 335–339, 369; antireligious principles of, 329; master race concept, 329; subordination of party to state, 329; amoral principles of, 329–330; social Darwinism and, 330; ideology, 333–334; extinction of Soviet citizens, 334; nationalism and, 337; Soviet Russia and, 352; defeat of, 416
Near East, 99, 128, 154, 157
Nekrasov, Nikolai, 169, 197
Nenni, Pietro, 297
Neo-Enlightenment, 340, 343, 347
Neo-Jacobinism, 268
Neo-Platonism, 121, 453n41
Neo-Romanticism, 348, 389
Nesselrode, Count Karl, 39
Netherlands, 29, 414
New Christianity, (St. Simon), 255
New Class, The (Djilas), 395

New Deal, 319, 363, 364
New Economic Policy (NEP). *See* Lenin,
   V. I.: New Economic Policy
New Industrial State (Galbraith), 381
New Left, 382, 430, 431–432
Newman, John Henry (later Cardinal),
   137
New Model Army (Britain), 33
Newton, Isaac, 60, 61, 64, 119, 120
New York Times, 344, 375
Nicholas I, 7, 9, 39, 102, 136, 140, 145,
   172, 187, 244, 370, 371; police/police
   state, 5; autocracy of, 9–10, 92, 150,
   167, 373; relations with Poland, 94,
   152, 153, 155; repression under, 97–98,
   99, 146, 150; cultural revolution under,
   139–140; West's perception of Russia
   under, 147, 155–156, 175, 371; armed
   interventions in Hungary and Romania,
   147–149, 152, 154–155; expansionist
   policies of, 152, 176, 237, 413; Eastern
   Question, 152–153, 155; and Ottoman
   Empire, 153–155; occupation of Romania, 154–155; relations with Central
   Europe, 155, 176; foreign policy, 158;
   Europeanization under, 163, 167–168;
   doctrine of Official Nationality, 174.
   See also Crimean War
Nicholas II, 166, 245
Nicolaevsky, Boris, 366, 367–368, 397
Niekisch, Ernst, 351
Nietzsche, Friedrich Wilhelm, 11, 194,
   197, 201, 202, 210, 211, 328, 352, 429;
   aesthetic nihilism of, 202, 203, 204; theory of slave morality *(Ressentiment)*,
   202–203, 227; cultural influence of,
   212, 213, 227, 228; politics of, 213–214,
   227; rejection of modernity, 223, 227;
   critique of bourgeois civilization, 230;
   concept of the will, 230–231; cult of heroic barbarism, 350
Nihilism, 172, 226, 228, 269; aesthetic,
   169, 193, 202, 204, 205, 208, 209, 213,
   217–219, 231; ethical, 217
Nijinsky, Vaslav, 197
Nikon, patriarch of Moscow, 137
1984 (Orwell), 365
Nixon, Richard, 376, 385, 386
Nobility, 36–38, 44; hereditary, 29, 31,
   42; in Russia, 35; in East Europe, 37,
   135; privilege of, 37, 66, 67; social reform and, 44, 72; in France, 106. *See
   also* Gentry; Inherited order and structures
Noble Savage, 215
"No enemies to the left" principle, 316,
   318, 382

Nonaggression Pact (1939), 316, 334,
   354, 368
Noncapitalism, 281; as goal of Marxism,
   274, 275, 277, 281, 302, 423; class strug-
   gle for, 281; as goal in Russian Revolu-
   tion, 284, 285; as socialism, 285, 299,
   420; in Russia, 308, 309
Non-noble service gentry, 31, 33, 35, 36,
   66; elite, 36, 66, 105, 107
Normandy, Allied landing at, 355
North Atlantic Treaty Organization
   (NATO), 361, 362, 363, 370, 374
Northern War. *See* Peter I: victory over
   Sweden at Poltava
North Korea, 331, 358, 361
North Vietnam, 398, 431
Noske, Gustav, 297
Notes from the Underground (Dostoevsky),
   194
Novalis. *See* Hardenberg, Friedrich (No-
   valis)
November Revolution (Germany), 278
Novgorod (city-state and republic), 30,
   31, 129, 138, 178
Novikov, Nikolai, 56, 141
Nuclear Test Ban Treaty, 385
Nuclear war, 384

Observer, The, 398
October general strike, 191
October Manifesto, 174
October Revolution. *See* Russian Revolution (1917)
"Ode to Joy" (Schiller), 116
Odoevski, Vladimir, 136
Official Nationality policy of Nicholas I,
   174
Oil shock (1973), 374
Old Regime, 29, 30, 62, 68, 125, 187, 241,
   242, 251; in Europe, 13–14, 21, 32–36,
   59, 70, 76, 83, 87, 96, 108, 126, 147,
   150, 237, 238–239; in Russia, 27–39,
   55, 70–71, 73–84, 75–76, 91, 98, 137,
   140, 141–142, 156, 160, 164, 168, 170,
   172, 174, 207, 270, 278–279, 294, 325–
   326, 391, 400, 412, 415, 418; in Germany, 35, 105, 106, 109, 110, 164, 203,
   229, 265, 267, 270, 299, 324; polity, 40;
   attacks on, by *philosophes*, 45, 68, 70; political and social structures, 62, 66, 68,
   70, 267; Christendom as, 63; in France,
   65, 72–73, 94, 113, 157, 335, 336; in
   Europe, 96, 235, 236, 244, 245, 249,
   252, 282, 415; Romanticism and, 115–
   116; in Austria, 150; in Prussia, 150,
   177; in Central Europe, 178, 190, 324;
   in Austria-Hungary, 267

"Old Russia" (Andreas-Salomé), 211–212
One Day in the Life of Ivan Denisovich
  (Solzhenitsyn), 392, 393, 394
On the Government of Poland (Rousseau), 52
On the Spiritual in Art (Kandinsky), 197
Opium of the Intellectuals, The (Aron),
  367
Oriental despotism. *See* Despotism: Orien-
  tal/Asiatic
Origin of Russian Communism (Berdiaev),
  372
Origins of Totalitarianism (Arendt), 369
Orthodox Christianity, 18–20, 41, 92,
  103, 136–137, 415
Orthodox Russia, 46, 60, 136, 143
Orthodoxy, 64, 77, 83, 106, 188, 372
Orwell, George, 315, 365
Ostermann, Andrew, 39
Ostpolitik, 385–386
Ottoman Empire/Ottoman Turks, 17, 18,
  77, 79, 135; conquest of the Balkans,
  19, 88; war against Muscovy/Muscovite
  Russia, 20, 24; occupation of Hungary,
  22, 31; Russian expansionist policies
  and, 25, 48, 99, 238, 414, 415; warfare
  technology, 31, 39, 41; relations with
  Europe, 39–42; concert of Europe and,
  40, 41–42, 88, 353; janissaries/slave system, 40; relations with France, 40, 77;
  religious wars, 40; as barbarous society,
  41, 76, 78; relations with England, 77;
  war with Russia, 79–80, 81, 82, 130,
  237, 268; war with Greece, 91; Slavic
  nationalism and, 134; anticipated dissolution of (Eastern Question), 152, 153;
  Russian protectorate in, 153–155, 155,
  157; constitutionalist revolt in, 185. *See
  also* Crimean War
Owen, Robert, 250

Palestine, Holy Places of, 154, 156, 157
Palmer, Rev. William, 137, 139
Palmerston, Lord, 96, 100, 180, 371
Panama Canal, 417
Pan-Germanism, 167, 188, 190, 225
Pan-Slavism, 134–135, 188, 190, 225, 415
Pantheism, 144, 198, 199, 202. *See also*
  Hegel, Georg Wilhelm Friedrich: Abso-
  lute Idea concept
Papacy, 20, 22, 60, 127, 128, 136. *See also*
  Catholicism
Paris Commune, 171–172, 176, 184, 268,
  284, 296
Parliamentary government, 58, 72, 94,
  174, 214, 219, 220, 235, 274, 330
Parsons, Talcott, 368
Partisan Review, 344

Partocracy, 300, 309, 405
Party-state apparatus (Germany), 334
Party-state apparatus (Soviet Union), 294,
  300, 301, 302, 303, 304, 308, 309, 310,
  311, 312, 314, 327, 333, 337, 390, 400,
  406, 422–423; under Stalin, 302, 304,
  312; under Lenin, 304, 327, 395; ideoc-
  racy of, 309, 312; organization of the
  economy, 309, 312; industrial and
  worker base for, 311, 400; as institutionalized revolution, 312; Central Committee, 313. *See also* Communist Party
Pascal, Pierre, 113, 341
Paskevich, Ivan, Prince of Poland, 148,
  149
Pasternak, Boris, 378
Patriotism, 221, 242, 268
Paul I, 56, 73, 356
Pavlov, Ivan, 206
Pavlova, Anna, 197
Peaceful coexistence policy, 361, 376, 383,
  385, 387, 401. *See also* Cold War
Pearl Harbor, 354
Peasantry, 35, 37, 173, 180, 181, 184, 186,
  189, 300, 305; commune system, 5,
  129, 138, 143, 180, 183, 268, 270, 283;
  religion and superstition of, 55, 205–
  206, 313; socialism of, 138–139, 144–
  145, 169, 248, 269, 283; as agent of
  revolution, 144–145, 149, 283–284,
  297, 300, 421, 422–423; emancipation
  of, 163; capitalism and economic power
  of, 183, 268, 302; in First World War,
  242, 245; in Russian Revolution, 246,
  281, 422; democratic, 267, 280; Marxist
  influence on, 270; proletariat and, 272,
  281, 283–284, 311; collectivization of,
  275, 302, 306, 307, 308, 334, 335; under Stalin, 305–306; Hitler and, 334,
  335. *See also* Feudalism; Serfs
Péguy, Charles, 222
PEN Club, 346
People's Budget (England), 220, 221
People's Democracies, 358, 371, 386
People's Will, 171, 216n, 270, 271, 420–
  421, 422
Perestroika, 12, 402, 403–406, 416–417
"Permanent purge" concept of, 369
Permanent Revolution (Trotsky), 344–345
Permanent revolution theory, 186, 246,
  248, 266, 272, 344–345, 394, 472n34.
  See also Revolution: tradition of
Persia, 6, 7, 45, 151, 185, 239, 383
Peter I (Peter the Great), 5, 20, 35, 56, 58,
  84, 130, 136, 141, 237, 294, 415;
  Europeanization/modernization poli-
  cies of, 7, 27, 32, 36, 39, 42, 43, 53, 143,

146, 168, 179, 303, 412; enlightened
despotism, 9, 60; victory over Sweden
at Poltava (Northern War), 9, 17, 21–
25, 42, 43, 44, 75, 353, 415, 418; expansionist policies of, 17, 23, 24, 26, 46, 87,
89, 100, 152, 358, 359, 412, 419; concert of Europe and, 21, 23, 238; po-
lice/police state under, 28, 30, 44, 45,
53, 58; reforming policies of, 31, 32, 35,
43–46, 98, 136; nobility and, 36; promotion of science, 41, 206; subordination
of church to state, 41, 44, 49; founds St.
Petersburg, 50; autocracy of, 92, 150;
civil society under, 143–144
Peter III, 130
Petipa, Marius, 196
Petöfi, Eötvös, 117, 149
Petrograd Commune, 298
Petrushka (Stravinsky), 196
Petty bourgeoisie, 272, 277, 394, 428–
429; in Russia, 302, 303, 329
Philip II, 22, 83
Philosophes, 42, 43, 47, 54, 56, 59, 72, 94–
96, 124, 130, 179, 187, 430; opposition
to Old Regime, 45, 70; Russia and, 47,
54, 217; egalitarian goals of, 49, 68;
radical politics of, 63, 70, 71–72, 125;
reforming policies of, 67–68, 125, 140;
religion and, 102, 202, 257; Romanti-
cism and, 115, 122, 124, 125; reason
and, 118, 125; French Revolution and,
137; in Russia, 140, 141; liberal politics
of, 141. See also *Lumières*
Philosophical Letters (Voltaire), 69
Philotheus of Pskov, 5, 7, 19, 371, 384,
412, 413
Physiocrats, 66
Pilsudski, Józef, 322, 323
Pinochet, Augusto, 319
Plato, 60, 309, 336
Plekhanov, Georgii, 184, 270, 284, 421
Pluralism, 29, 386, 403, 419
Pobedonostsev, Konstantin, 172
Poetry, 59, 114, 123, 193, 201, 341, 342;
in Germany, 106, 107–108; "universal
poetic" concept of, 115; in Russia, 169,
195, 210, 393; in England, 201, 349; in
France, 201, 206; in Soviet Union, 376
Poland, 334, 370, 404; cultural-linguistic
nationalism in, 110–111; insurrection
of 1863 in, 216n, 413; Marxist influence
in, 267; national revolt, 268; authoritarian regime, interwar period, 322–323;
relations with Soviet Russia, 330; during Second World War, 355, 356; political unrest in, 378; dissent in, 396. *See
also* Solidarity movement

Poland/Congress Poland, 89–90, 126,
133, 135, 138, 157, 243; Russian occupation of, 88, 89, 102, 147, 149, 151,
158, 216n; insurrection of 1830, 92–93,
98, 138, 143, 145, 151, 176–177, 183;
Slavic nationalism and, 134; nationalism, 138; Romantic Catholicism in,
138; independence of, 148, 170, 187;
Hungarian uprising and, 149, 152; government by constitution, 168; pan-Slavism and, 187
Poland-Lithuania *(Rzeczpospolita)*, 8, 18,
20, 21, 24, 30, 31, 35; relations with
France, 24, 77, 93; relations with Russia, 24, 57; relations with Sweden, 24;
expansionist policies of Russia toward,
26, 48, 356, 414, 415; expunged from
map of Europe, 33, 81–82, 157; government (Diet), 52–53, 58, 80; Republic of,
71, 77; partitions of, 74, 76–79, 81–84,
134, 154, 156; reform movement/revo-
lution, 77, 80–82, 92–93; relations with
England, 77; wars with Russia, 77, 93;
nobility, 78; Patriot Party, 80–81, 92;
relations with Prussia, 81; reunification
of, 87; government (Constitution), 93;
Russian occupation of, 93
Police/police state, 5, 10, 28–30, 68, 71,
84, 309; in Russia, 5, 44, 55, 56,
72, 90, 140; in France, 27; in Germany,
27, 105, 106; as enlightened governance, 27–28; in dynastic polities, 32;
statecraft and, 32; ideal of, 55–56; en-
lightenment and, 59–73; of Old Re-
gime, 66; in Prussia, 72
Polish Democratic Society, 138
"Politics of cultural despair," 215, 226, 329
Poltava, Battle of. *See* Peter I: victory over
Sweden at Poltava
Polycentrism, 375
Poniatowski, Józef, Prince of Poland, 93
Poniatowski, Stanislas Augustus, King of
Poland, 76
Pope, Alexander, 59, 61
Popular front, 315–316, 319, 325, 333,
338, 347, 354, 363
Popular sovereignty, 242, 327
Populism/Populist movement *(narodniki)*,
180, 212, 272, 273, 279, 317; in Russia,
169–171, 183, 186, 258, 267, 269–270,
284, 421, 431; national, in Germany,
206, 227. *See also* Socialist Revolution-
aries
Porte. *See* Sublime Porte
Portugal, 91, 189, 322, 323, 414
Positivism, 11, 112, 165, 208, 217, 222
Posnania, 243

Possessed, The (Dostoevsky), 206, 215, 216n, 350, 372, 401
Postproletarian liberation movement, 432–433
Potemkin, Grigorii, 79
"Potemkin villages," 79
Prague Spring, 285, 386, 392, 396. *See also* Czechoslovakia
Pravda, 398
Prevues periodical, 366
Priestly, Joseph, 57
Principia Mathematica (Newton), 64
Printing press, 41, 393
Private property, 260, 261, 327, 405, 419, 425; rights, 94, 95; abolition/suppression of, 248, 254–255, 256, 263, 274, 285, 297, 308–309, 327, 336, 345, 428
Production/mode of production, 7, 259, 260, 261, 274, 309; private ownership of, 254; centralization of, 263; bourgeois, 273; collective ownership of, 308–309; public ownership of, 336
Profit/profit motive, 254–255, 259, 285, 301, 308–309, 327, 405
Progress: concept of, 28, 65, 70, 114, 115, 121, 122, 125, 126, 128, 199, 259, 281; unilinear, 229
Progress, Coexistence, and Intellectual Freedom (Sakharov), 395
Progressivism, 190, 343–344, 362, 366, 367, 381, 431
Proletariat, 95, 173, 186, 330, 422; as agents of revolution, 126, 261–262, 270, 275, 276, 277, 279–280, 282, 283, 297, 304–305, 309–310, 312, 353, 422, 426, 432, 433; Marxist politics of, 145, 262, 270; class consciousness of, 249; economics of, 257; dehumanization of, 260, 261–262; under capitalism, 261; as universal class, 266, 270, 277, 278; as ally of the petty bourgeois peasantry, 272, 311; in Russia, 273, 281, 282, 297; Communism and, 308, 318. *See also* Class struggle
Property. *See* Private property
Protestantism, 18, 19–20, 41, 49, 64, 136, 137; in England, 29, 64; in Holland, 64; in Germany, 136
Protocols of the Elders of Zion, The, 351–352
Proudhon, Pierre-Joseph, 250, 255, 258, 284, 421, 422
Providence, concept of, 114, 263
Prussia, 23–24, 36, 96, 127, 135, 152, 418; European status of, 21, 97; military rule of, 22, 33, 35, 167; monarchy in, 33, 35, 72, 80, 97, 176; Napoleonic invasion of, 39; military revolution in, 77; relations with Poland-Lithuania, 81; relations with Russia, 84, 130, 149; territorial compensation to, 88–89; relations with France, 109–110, 149, 239; state system in, 127; military strength of, 135; emancipation of serfs, 149; German unification and, 150, 176, 237; aristocracy in, 164; as civil society, 168, 169, 174; revolution from above, 176, 177; formation of German empire and, 176–178; in Seven Weeks' War, 189, 237; universal military service in, 242; antiliberal policies of, 239, 265; industrialization of, 283
Psychoanalysis, 219
Public opinion, 10, 70; balance of power and, 9, 76; partitions of Poland-Lithuania and, 81–82; Soviet Union and, 376, 379–380, 391, 398, 399, 402
Pugachev, Emelian/*Pugachevshchina*, 55, 137, 146, 170, 173
Purge techniques, 369, 380. *See also* Stalin, Joseph: purges/Great Terror
Puritans, 69
Pushkin, Aleksandr, 7, 51, 117, 138, 140–141, 193, 236, 344

Racism, 325, 326, 327, 351, 433; in United States, 362, 432. *See also* Anti-Semitism
Radek, Karl, 186
Radetsky, Joseph, 148
Radical Republicans (France), 220
Radishchev, Aleksandr, 56, 141
Rambaud, Alfred, 180
Ranke, Leopold von, 127–128, 129
Rationalism, 49, 62–63, 66, 103, 229, 372, 429; social, 46, 66–67; in philosophy, 59–60; Romanticism and, 112; of the Enlightenment, 116, 128; Russia and, 132, 182, 206, 207, 217; mystic, 216n, 435; criticism of, 217, 218, 226; Germany and, 226; technology and, 379
Ravensbruk concentration camp, 365
Raynal, Guillaume, 54
Reagan, Ronald, 318, 363, 387, 399, 402, 403
Realism, 195, 208
Realpolitik, 8, 188, 237, 398
Reason, 50, 58–60, 62, 107, 113, 257, 262; deductive, 60; abstract, 63; pure logic of, 75, 121; equality and, 96, 254; Romanticism and, 117, 118, 119; practical, 118, 201; religion and, 119; subjective/objective, 121; historical, 121–122; in the Enlightenment, 199,

430–431; universal, 224, 228; revolution and, 364
Red Army, 341, 344
Red Brigades (Italy), 431
Reed, John, 340
Reflections on the Revolution in France (Burke), 116
Reform (general discussion), 67, 68, 71–72, 169
Reformation, 18, 64, 65, 126–128, 248
Reform Bill (England): of 1832, 94; of 1867, 163; of 1882, 250
Reichstag, 164, 177–178
Reinsurance Treaty, 237
Religion, 19, 119, 122, 254, 414; culture and, 60, 61, 113; revealed, 60, 61, 101, 115, 146; superstition and, 118, 257, 430; ethics and, 119; art and, 209–210, 328; philosophical, 257; fascism and, 321, 323; secular, 321. *See also* Clergy; Dissent: religious; Separation of church and state; *specific religions*
Reminiscences of Lenin (Zetkin), 342
Renaissance, 36, 60, 65, 101, 126, 127, 128, 248
Renan, Ernest, 222
Representative government, 68, 69
Republicanism/Republican party: in France, 221; in United States, 343, 344
Republic of letters, 42, 45, 46, 48, 54, 59, 106; in Europe, 47–48, 363, 367–368; empiricism and, 62; reforming policies of, 67; after Russian Revolution, 340–352. See also *Philosophes*
Respublica Christiana. See Christendom
Ressentiment, culture of, 203, 227, 326, 339
Restoration, 94, 101, 136, 149, 265
Resurrection (Tolstoy), 194, 205
Reuther, Walter, 363
Revelations of the Diplomatic History of the Eighteenth Century (Marx), 99–100
Revisionism, Marxist, 126, 247–248, 275, 278, 281, 285, 396, 428
Revisionism, in Soviet writings, 394–395
Revolution, 364; from above, 46, 70, 71, 91, 163, 164, 174, 176, 177, 303, 307, 311–313, 344, 416, 418; from below, 70, 91, 174, 312; anarchistic, 172; popular insurrections, 176, 332; as motive force of history, 248–249, 421; models and theories of, 248–250, 266, 270, 279, 280; anticipatory, 249, 268–269, 278, 279, 282, 298, 336–337, 420–423, 427; tradition of, 268–269, 272, 420–421, 431–432; the "people" as agents of, 270, 332; preventive, 271; worker/peasant alliance in, 272, 283–

284; evolutionary, 276; social, 276, 279, 332, 333; bourgeois, 279; institutionalized, 312; national, 323; conservative, 328–329; economic, 332, 333; within the revolution, 382, 428
Revolution Betrayed, The (Trotsky), 344–345
Revolutions of 1848 ("Springtime of the Peoples"), 99, 103, 110, 113, 129, 134, 144, 147, 149, 151, 152, 154–155, 270, 421; failure of, 164, 171, 182, 188, 199, 221, 222, 263, 274, 299, 317, 324, 336–337, 421, 422; compared to Russian revolution, 174; effects of, 199, 256; June Days insurrection, 221; defeat of liberalism, 223; democratic, social, and national goals of, 336–337; proletariat in, 433
Rhineland, 88
Ricardo, David, 258
Richelieu, Cardinal, 29, 36, 38–39, 69
Richter, Jean-Paul, 108
"Rights of Man," 95, 282
Rilke, Rainer Maria, 211, 218
Rimbaud, Arthur, 201
Rimsky-Korsakov, Nikolai, 196
Roerich, Nicholas, 197
Rolland, Romain, 345–346, 347
Romains, Jules, 345
Roman Empire, 101
Romania, 147–149, 152, 154–155, 188, 296
Romano-Germanic world, 128, 129, 133, 134
Romanov, House of, 34, 35, 74, 93, 135, 179, 243, 244
Romantic Enlightenment, 126, 147, 434–435
Romanticism, 11, 103, 104, 107, 125, 136, 193, 400; literary, 111, 120; as reaction to the Enlightenment, 111–124; in Germany, 112, 114–124, 127, 132, 218; defined, 112–113, 123; reason and, 119, 133; religion and, 123, 124; in Russia, 130; Western, 143, 164, 165, 217; French Revolution and, 203; aesthetic revolution and, 205; cultural ideal of, 328
Rome, 65, 136, 137; ancient, 111, 214
Rome-Berlin-Tokyo Axis, 315
Roosevelt, Franklin, 347, 355
Rosenberg, Alfred, 214, 351–352
Rostovtseff, Michael, 207
Rostow, Walt, 380
Rousseau, Jean-Jacques, 56, 94, 117, 125, 204; Russia and, 52, 53, 54, 73, 130; critique of empiricism, 114, 119; egalitarianism of, 254

"Rousseaus of the gutter," 66
Rousset, David, 366
Royal academies, 105
Royal Academy of Sciences, 70
Rubinstein, Anton, 195
Ruskin, John, 221, 223
Rus, Kievan, 30
Russell, Bertrand, 343
Russia (Wallace), 180–181
Russia: isolation of, 20, 98, 413; military
    strength of, 88–90, 91, 97, 150, 157,
    166, 167, 175, 178; Western investment
    in, 173; reforming policies of, 182; eth-
    nic minorities in, 243; industrial econ-
    omy, 245, 246; after collapse of Soviet
    Union, 387, 417–418. *See also* Soviet
    Russia/Soviet Union
Russia, culture and character: otherness
    of, 3, 5, 7, 84, 135–136, 293, 389, 400–
    401; viewed as backward society, 6, 13,
    20, 382, 414, 416, 424; as barbarous so-
    ciety, 20, 30, 36, 37, 46, 55, 74, 98, 128,
    129, 147, 184, 191, 197, 214; cultural as-
    similation into Old Regime Europe, 35,
    38, 42, 75–76, 207; level of civilization,
    36, 58–59; as civil society, 75–76, 163,
    169; cultural identity, 112, 131, 132,
    136, 138, 163, 192–213, 218; "Russian
    soul" and, 138, 165, 207–217, 218, 222,
    230, 348–352, 379, 389; aesthetic revo-
    lution, 193–207; commonality with
    Germany, 228, 230; classical images of,
    387–391
Russia, domestic politics: modernization,
    7, 13, 146; Europeanization, 34, 103,
    172, 180, 181, 415; Great Reforms
    (1860–1874), 141–143, 163, 165, 167–
    175, 183, 184; underground political or-
    ganizations, 169–170; revolutionary
    movement, 169–171, 173, 325; industri-
    alization policies, 172, 267, 269, 270,
    301, 415–416, 417–418; revolution
    from below, 174; postreform, 181, 182,
    207; revolution from above, 303
Russia, government: absolute monarchy,
    50, 53, 99, 102–103, 138, 139, 151, 158,
    270, 371, 419; as enlightened despot-
    ism, 58, 73, 370, 415; democratic poten-
    tial in, 138–139; as Oriental despotism,
    99–100, 146, 172, 184, 279, 370, 389,
    400; Duma parliament, 174–175, 191,
    245, 418; Provisional Government,
    182, 245–246
Russia, international politics: world domi-
    nation as goal of (messianism), 5, 46,
    53–54, 99–100, 151–154, 156–157, 330,
    412–414; as international power, 21,

26, 111, 167, 237, 415, 417–418; trade
    relations, 25, 79, 172–173, 173, 301;
    European status, 25–27, 39, 42, 50, 88–
    89, 97, 100–101, 102, 137, 139–140,
    146, 163, 175, 181, 184, 236; as flank
    power, 26, 77, 88; assimilation into
    Europe, 38, 39, 73; expansionist poli-
    cies, 46, 53–54, 75, 93, 99, 151, 153,
    239, 240, 355–356, 412–414; relations
    with Poland-Lithuania, 57, 76–77, 80;
    relations with West, 59, 246, 294; rela-
    tions with Austria, 77, 79, 237, 243; as
    maritime power, 78, 153, 414; territo-
    rial compensation to, 78, 89; as Euro-
    pean power, 82, 88–90, 150, 151, 152,
    153, 163, 188, 236–237, 415; viewed as
    menace, by West, 84, 89, 91, 99, 146–
    159, 151, 152, 167, 231; as "gendarme
    of Europe," 92, 99, 140, 158–159, 338;
    non-European status, 128, 129, 135,
    147, 150; pan-Slavism and, 134, 188,
    415; relations with Poland, 149, 152;
    Eastern Question (anticipated dissolu-
    tion of Ottoman Empire), 152–153,
    155; relations with Britain, 167, 243; re-
    integration into Europe, 186, 190, 191;
    relations with France, 25, 26, 191, 239;
    in League of the Three Emperors, 237–
    238; relations with Germany, 239, 243;
    in coalitions, 353
Russia, wars and revolutions: in Second
    World War, 21, 32, 76, 415; military
    revolution in, 33, 34, 77, 418; partitions
    of Poland-Lithuania, 74, 77–82; war
    with Ottoman Turks, 77, 78, 79–80, 81,
    82, 151, 160, 189, 237, 268, 413, 416;
    war with Sweden, 81; coalition of Great
    Powers against, 90; war with France,
    132, 154–155; intervention in the Bal-
    kans, 153–154, 157, 240, 241; war with
    Japan, 160, 166, 167, 185, 239, 241,
    414, 416; in First World War, 182, 240,
    242–243, 416, 434; use of universal mili-
    tary service, 242; occupation of Paris,
    355; occupation of Berlin, 355
Russian Federation, 404–405
Russian Idea, The (Berdiaev), 372
Russian language, 140, 195, 257
Russian Menace to Europe, The (Marx and
    Engels), 371
Russian Revolution (1905), 182, 183, 184–
    186, 231, 351
Russian Revolution (1917), 112, 235, 244,
    279, 285, 296, 326, 396–397, 423; fall
    of imperial regime, 3, 10; Marxism and,
    266, 345; noncapitalism as goal of, 284,
    285; socialism and, 298; political effects

of, 301; religious interpretation of, 341; Western criticism of, 344; historical significance of, 345, 406, 425–426, 428; as spiritual nationalism, 372; collapse of Soviet Union and, 406, 425
"Russian soul." *See* Russia, culture and character
Russian Whites, 296, 299, 300
Russia's Iron Age (Chamberlin), 344
Russie en 1839, La (Custine), 98
Russophobia, 8, 99–100, 147, 183, 190, 191, 193, 228, 456n80. *See also* Russia, international politics: viewed as menace by West; Spectre of Communism
Rzeczpospolita. See Poland-Lithuania

Sacre du printemps, Le (Stravinsky), 196
Sadoul, Jacques, 341
Sage of Ferney, 48
Saint-Simon, Henri de, 125, 249–250, 255, 258, 260, 344
Sakharaov, Andrei, 393, 395, 399, 402, 403
Saladin the Turk, 37
Salazar, Oliviera, 322
Salon de refusés, 200
Salon of 1846 (Baudelaire), 198
SALT. *See* Strategic Arms Limitation Talks
Saltykov-Shchedrin, Mikhail, 300
Samizdat, 393
Saracens, 18
Sartre, Jean-Paul, 297, 329, 348, 366–367, 426, 428, 429, 431, 433
Savigny, Karl Friedrich von, 125
Schelling, Friedrich, 120, 136, 144
Schiller, Johann, 107, 108, 114, 115, 116, 131
Schlegel, August, 115, 116, 120, 131–132, 218
Schlegel, Friedrich, 115, 116, 120, 131–132, 136, 218
Schmidt, Helmut, 387
Schopenhauer, Arthur, 199–200, 201–202
Schwarzenberg, Felix, Chancellor of Austria, 149
Science, 41, 60, 70, 101, 128, 277, 308, 309, 329, 434; concept of immortality and, 61, 313–314; scientific method, 61–62, 204; pre-Enlightenment, 113; during Enlightenment, 118, 119; in Russia, 193, 206; religion and, 202–203; socialist concept of utopia and, 263; natural, 368. *See also* social science
Scientific revolution and progress, 60–61, 64–65, 105, 126, 276, 314
Scientific socialism. *See* Marxist theory
Scott, Walter, 117, 187

Second International, 184, 186, 190, 259, 267, 273, 274–276, 280, 281, 299, 311, 422, 423, 426
Second Reich, 350
Second Rome, 372
Second World War, 4, 189, 190, 204, 297, 337, 419; Allied powers, 316, 322, 325, 351, 354–355, 368–369; Western-Soviet relations during, 353, 354; postwar reconfiguration, 356, 357–360, 361–363, 373
Self-determinism/self-government, 106, 109, 242, 325; in Russia, 52, 168, 175. *See also* Constitutionalism; Democracy
Separation of church and state, 41, 44, 49, 62, 220, 222
Separation of powers, 50
Serbia, 40, 241
Serfs/serfdom, 33–35; in Russia, 31, 32, 35, 37, 55, 137, 141–145, 149, 415; in Germany, 35, 109; in Prussia, 149; emancipation of, in Russia, 168, 169, 170, 181, 182; state, 305–306; in Austria, 415. *See also* Feudalism; Peasantry
Seven Weeks' War, 189, 237
Seven Years' War, 23, 24, 25, 74, 77, 130, 240
Shakespeare, William, 105, 107, 115, 208, 216, 397
Shaw, George Bernard, 346
Shelley, Percy, 116
Shintoism, 322
Short Course (Stalin), 345
Siberia, 413, 414, 417
Siberian exile system, 56, 92, 93, 170, 181–182, 205, 213, 216n, 304, 334, 365, 374, 392, 397
Sieyès, Emmanuel Joseph, 66
Silone, Ignatio, 366
Siniavskii, Andrei, 392
Slavery, 252, 259, 261; in Africa, 34; in United States, 173; of the family, 260, 296; wage, 261; class, 261–262
Slavophiles, 103, 136, 138, 143, 145, 156, 398, 412
Slavs/Slavdom, 128, 131, 132–135, 138, 148, 188–189, 225
Slovakia, 321
Smith, Adam, 123, 260
Sobieski, Jan, King of Poland, 18
Social class, 37, 102, 221, 318; hierarchy, 28, 68, 122–123, 433; unequal division and tensions, 29, 95, 219, 253–254, 255, 261; status and privilege, 37, 66; in Germany, 107, 224, 226, 227, 228; in England, 175–176; in France, 175–176, 222; in Prussia, 178; educated, 227,

Social class *(continued)*
228; exploitation of, 255, 257, 258, 297,
336, 427; universal, 262, 266, 270, 284,
427, 434; identity, 276–277; ideology,
334. *See also* Bourgeoisie; Class struggle; Clergy; Nobility; Proletariat; Society; Third Estate; Working class
Social contract, 73
Social Contract (Rousseau), 52, 53
Social Darwinism, 330
Social democracy, 271; in Germany, 177–
178, 264; in Russia, 186, 247, 273, 278–
280, 296, 423; Communism and, 223–
224, 226, 318; in Sweden, 247, 275,
319; in France, 275; Marxism and, 285;
antifascist coalition of, 315; Western,
465n19
Social Democratic (SD) Parties (Western), 426, 430
Social Democratic (SD) Party (Germany),
185, 186, 191, 223, 272, 274–275, 297,
325, 327
Social Democratic (SD) Party (Russia),
423
Social engineering, 62
Socialism, 11, 147, 187, 252, 253–254,
256, 309, 337, 416, 423; theory of, 71,
314; in France, 96, 112, 185, 257; in
Russia, 100, 138; generic, 112, 254,
264, 267, 420, 426; science and technology and, 125, 264; utopian, 169, 249–
250, 251, 263; revolutionary, 172, 184,
248, 255, 259, 296, 298–299, 309–310,
420–421; humanism and, 224, 285, 309–
310; rejection of, in Germany, 226; during Russian Revolution, 245–246;
defined, 247–249, 251–252, 254; industrialization as source of, 249, 304, 305,
308, 312; origins of, 250–251; ideal of,
250, 251–256, 252, 253, 255, 256, 345,
400; maximal, 254, 423; as combination
of Enlightenment and Romanticism,
257, 259, 260, 268; noncapitalism and,
285, 299, 308, 407, 420; egalitarian,
286, 309–310, 424; liberal, 286; "building," 310, 312, 333, 390; proletariat,
312; national, 326, 339; totalitarianism
and, 333; democracy and, 335, 336,
381; internationalist, 190, 337; social
science and, 381; "really existing," 394,
396, 400, 401, 405, 424, 431. *See also*
History: as logical progression toward
socialism; Marxism
Socialism: Utopian and Scientific (Engels),
259
Socialist Party: in France (SFIO), 221,

297; in Italy, 297–298, 317; in United
States, 340. *See also* Social democracy
Socialist politics/regimes, 252, 406–407;
in Soviet Union, 12, 378, 387–388, 417;
in Russia, 138, 144, 145, 169, 170, 183,
245, 246, 251; in Europe, 144, 145,
182, 184, 245, 296, 364; in France, 169,
220, 269; in Germany, 224, 229, 241,
324, 326; in Russia, after Russian Revolution, 243, 246, 272, 305–306, 312–
313; in Britain, 250; in Soviet Russia,
296, 337, 343, 428; under Stalin, 334,
345; in China, 367; in Cuba, 367; in
Eastern Europe, 378
Socialist Revolutionaries (SRs), 186, 216n,
272, 339
Social science, 13, 258, 368, 369, 378–
382, 386, 429; social-science model,
389, 390
Society, classless and stateless, 255, 259,
262, 274. *See also* Civil society;
Society of orders/estates, 29, 30, 33, 42,
63, 66, 95, 108, 109, 253
Socioeconomic processes, 257, 267, 274,
310, 379–380, 381, 396
Sociology of community, 252–253
Socrates, 202, 203
Solidarity movement (Poland), 361, 387,
396, 404
Solzhenitsyn, Aleksandr, 392, 394, 395,
396, 397–398, 428
Sombart, Werner, 229
Sonderweg, 103–111; in Russia, 139–146,
412; in Germany, 223, 226; in Soviet
Union, 400
Sophie, Princess of Anhalt-Zerbst (Cath-
erine II), 23
Sophocles, 216
Sorel, George, 422
South Vietnam, 398
Souvarine, Boris, 347, 367–368
Sovereignty, 336, 337, 404, 406
"Soviet" (council), 184, 245, 246
Soviet Communism: A New Civilization?
(Webb and Webb), 346
*Soviet Economic Development since the 1917
Revolution* (Dobb), 344
Soviet Russia/Soviet Union, 3, 4, 74, 112,
190, 235, 244, 285, 307, 325, 356, 358,
360, 370–371, 375, 376, 402; collapse
of, 6, 247, 387, 404–407, 417, 419, 424–
425, 425; perception of, by West, 292–
293, 295–296, 297–298, 339–354, 366–
368; as international power, 293–294,
295, 330, 338, 352–356, 355, 358, 371,
373, 377, 390, 412; troika of Lenin and

Trotsky in, 298–314; purges, 306–307, 371; America as model for, 311, 312; Hitler and, 318, 352, 354; industrialization of, 327, 328, 354, 381, 400, 424–425; relations with Finland, 330; relations with Korea, 330; relations with Poland, 330, 355; emigration of intelligentsia from, 339–352; relations with Weimar Republic, 353–354; relations with France, 354; in Second World War, 354–355, 416; contrast with old Russia, 355–356; occupation of Austria, 356; occupation of Czechoslovakia, 356; occupation of Germany, 356; expansionist policies of, 359, 362, 373, 383, 398, 416; in Cold War, 359–360; superpower status of, 360, 363, 367–368, 384, 385, 395, 398, 406, 407, 416–417; relations with Eastern Europe, 373; as police state, 374, 397, 406; military strength of, 375, 386–387; space program, 375; Khrushchev's reforms, 375–378, 380, 383–384, 390, 392–393; de-Stalinization in, 382–383; peaceful coexistence, 383; relations with China, 385; trade with West, 385–386, 389; relations with Cuba, 392; social analysis of, 394, 395–396; Gorbachev's reforms, 403–404. *See also* Russia

Spain, 18, 31, 79, 91, 128, 198, 323; European status of, 21, 22; enlightened despotism in, 70; popular front in 315–316; national authoritarianism in, 322, 330, 331

Spartacus League, 185

Species-being concept, 258, 260, 261, 314, 434

Spectre of Communism, 3, 6, 8, 9, 96, 147, 235, 245, 306, 338, 340, 354, 356, 363, 398, 400, 404, 411, 412, 420, 426, 427, 430, 434, 435

Spencer, Herbert, 229

Spengler, Oswald, 350, 372

Speranskii, Mikhail, 73, 141

Spirit of the Laws (Montesquieu), 43

Sportsman's Sketches, A (Turgenev), 193

"Springtime of the Peoples." *See* Revolutions of 1848

Sputnik, 375

Staël, Mme. de, 132

Stages of Economic Growth (Rostow), 380

Stalin (Souvarine), 347

Stalin: A New World Seen through a Man (Barbusse), 346

Stalin, Joseph, 5, 24, 122, 299, 303–304, 305, 312, 314, 318–319, 341, 377, 382, 387, 394; in Second World War, 76, 335, 383; perception of, by West, 152, 294, 315, 346–348; totalitarianism under, 294, 369; purges/Great Terror, 301, 306–307, 308, 314, 344, 348, 355, 371, 374, 378, 380, 384–385, 393, 397, 426; class warfare, 304; industrialization policies of, 304, 305, 424, 425; Marxism and, 305, 329; revolution from above, 311, 312, 313, 344, 416; Hitler and, 316, 334, 338, 339, 354, 371, 383; cult of personality, 331, 345–348, 371, 377, 378, 394, 403; partition of Germany, 356; expansionist policies of, 358, 360–362, 373, 375, 383, 389; writings of, 364; Soviet camp system (Gulag) under, 365–366, 393; Iron Curtain and, 370

Stanislavsky, Constantin, 195

Steffens, Lincoln, 297, 340

Stein, Heinrich vom, 39

Stein-Hardenberg Reform Movement (Prussian Reform Movement), 109, 110, 123, 265, 418

Steppenwolf (Hesse), 212

Straits. *See* Balkans

Strategic Arms Limitation Talks (SALT) treaty: I, 385, 387; II, 387, 401

Strategic Defense Initiative (Star Wars), 387

Stravinsky, Igor, 196, 197

Strikes, 268, 422; in Russia, 174, 184, 185, 191, 245; in Europe, 185, 221, 373

Struve, Gleb, 367–368

Struve, Petr, 273

Sturm und Drang movement, 114, 115, 120, 187, 218

Sublime Porte, 40–41, 77, 79, 153, 154, 157

Suez war (1956), 358

Suffrage: property, 94; universal, 94–95, 108–109, 164, 177, 185, 219, 220, 235, 250, 253, 257, 275, 282, 323, 336, 419, 432; in Europe, 147, 177, 274, 320, 324; in Russia, 174, 235

Sukhomlinov, Vladimir, 167

Suleiman the Magnificent, 356

Supernaturalism, 67, 218. *See also* Natural supernaturalism

Superstition, 49, 55, 62, 101, 118, 125, 313, 338, 430

Supreme Soviet, 405

Surrealism, 341, 430

Suvorov, Aleksandr, 356

Sweden, 22, 32, 83, 315; war with Russia, 20, 24, 80, 81, 414; rule over Baltic provinces, 25, 74; social democratic government, 275, 285. *See also* Peter I: victory at Poltava
Swinburne, Algernon, 201
Swiss Confederation, 29, 71, 356
Symbolism, 11, 112, 197, 200, 202, 214, 217; in art and literature, 197, 198, 201, 212; religious, 198–199; aesthetic revolution and, 204
Syndicalism, 220, 284, 323, 338
Szelényi, Ivan, 395–396

Table of Ranks, 36
Taine, Hippolyte, 194
Taiwan, 425
Tamizdat, 393
Tatars, 17, 20, 54, 139, 206, 246, 371
Taxes, 31, 32, 254, 282
Tchaikovsky, Petr Ilich, 195, 196
Technology, 70, 258, 304, 379, 412, 416; military, 32, 35, 41; socialism and, 125, 310–311; Russian, 375, 415
Technostructure, 381
Telescoping, historical, 144, 266, 271, 280, 400
Tell the West (Gliksman), 366
Temps modernes, Les, 367
Terror/terrorism, 113, 333, 334, 364–365, 369, 397, 431. *See also* Stalin, Joseph: purges/Great Terror
"Testament" of Frederick II (Frederick the Great), 74
"Testament" of Lenin, 304
"Testament of Peter I," 24, 80, 100
Thatcher, Margaret, 403
Theater/drama, 195, 342
Thermidor, 250
Third Estate, 37, 67, 69, 71–72, 108; in France, 66, 72, 102, 282, 336; of dissidents, 407
Third International, 6, 190, 297, 317, 318, 352, 394
Third Reich, 226, 350
Third Rome, Moscow as, 5, 371–372, 412
Third Section, 5, 100, 149
Third World countries, 312, 359, 383, 416, 434; Soviet-Western competition for, 379, 384, 432, 433; Communism in, 382; détente and, 386, 387; United States and, 386
Thirty Years' War, 22, 32, 104–105
Thomas, Albert, 341
Through the Looking Glass (Carroll), 180

Thucydides, 414
Tiananmen Square protest, 403
Tito, Marshal, 190, 370–371, 375, 428
Tkachev, Petr, 271
Tocqueville, Alexis de, 66, 95–96, 169, 214, 263, 264, 286, 357, 368, 378, 391, 404
Togliatti, Palmiro, 375
Tolstoy, Leo, 193–195, 204, 205, 208, 211, 394; anti-modernism of, 205, 229–230; German literature about, 349
Tonio Kröger (Mann), 212
Tönnies, Ferdinand, 229, 252–253
Tory ("Ultra") aristocracy in France and England, 175–176, 221
Totalitarianism, 3, 5–6, 309, 338, 383, 418–419; in Russia, 217, 295, 403, 428; in Italy, 323; socialism and, 333; generic, 368–369; model, 369–370, 379, 381–382, 389; liberalism and, 370
Total war concept, 334, 335, 337
To the Finland Station (Wilson), 344
Toynbee, Arnold, 372
Tractarian Movement (England), 137
Trade unions, 221, 224, 252, 274, 275, 276
Transcaucasia, 151
Transcendentalism, 118, 120
Trans-Siberian Railroad, 172
Treaty of Brest-Litovsk, 244
Treaty of Nystadt, 23
Treaty of Unkiar Skelessi, 154
Treaty of Utrecht, 18, 22
Treaty of Versailles, 294, 320, 323, 354
Treaty of Westphalia, 22, 238
Triolet, Elsa, 341–342
Triple Alliance (1814), 90, 150, 239, 240
Triple Entente (1914), 239, 240–241, 243, 353
Troika: of Gogol, xi; Soviet, 298–314, 357
Trotsky, Leon, 306, 313, 340, 345, 382, 391, 396, 406, 412, 428; theory of permanent revolution, 186, 248, 344–345, 394; Russian Revolution and, 266; 267, 329; in troika of Soviet Russia, 298–314; industrialization policies of, 301, 302, 423; opposition to Stalin, 343; writings of, 344–345, 364
Troubadours, medieval, 115
Truman, Harry/Truman Doctrine, 24, 359
Tsarism, 3, 5, 172, 175, 191, 225; in Russia, 138–140, 142, 145, 147, 148, 160, 167, 174, 179, 294, 390, 411; repression under, 181–182; Mongol-Byzantine, 183; indifference of West to, 187
Tugan-Baranovskii, Mikhail, 207

Turgenev, Ivan, 169, 193–194, 204, 206, 208
Turgot, Anne Robert Jacques, 70, 169
Turkey. *See* Ottoman Empire/Ottoman Turks

Ukraine, 31, 78–79, 130, 178, 243, 334
Under Western Eyes (Conrad), 216n, 401
Union of Brest, 20
Union of Florence, 20
Union of Writers (Soviet Russia), 347
Unions. *See* Labor movements; Strikes; Trade unions
United Automobile Workers, 363
United Nations, 359, 377
United States, 59, 164, 214, 318, 359, 376; Revolutionary War, 26, 79, 81, 93, 157, 248, 282; under British, 34, 57, 71, 81; industrialization policies of, 173; in First World War, 182, 240; labor unions and strikes, 185; Triple Entente and, 240; universal military service in, 242; Marxist influence in, 267; perception of Soviet Russia, 296, 343–344, 414; in Second World War, 322, 354–355; Vietnam War, 330, 375, 376, 385, 430, 431; superpower status of, 358, 361–362, 383, 384; Cold War/détente politics of, 359–360, 376, 398; expansionist policies of, 362, 363, 366, 370, 414, 417, 430, 431, 432; tension with Europe, 362–363; political movements in, 363–364; modernization of, 379; anti-Communism in, 382; relations with China, 385
Universal military service, 108, 109, 168, 236, 336; during First World War, 241–242; under Stalin, 305–306
Universal service system in Russia, 31, 32, 33, 35, 38, 40, 163, 294
Universal suffrage. *See* Suffrage: universal
Universities, 92, 93, 368, 430; in Germany, 105, 107, 109; in Russia, 168, 206; Western, 376. *See also* Education
University of Berlin, 109
Urquhart, David, 99, 100, 139, 158, 180, 183
Utilitarianism, 112, 164–165, 169, 203
Utopia/utopianism, 71, 219, 345, 365, 381, 466n19; socialist, 169, 283, 299, 302–303, 308; revolutionary, 216n, 306; rationalist, 217, 218; Romantic, 218; Russia as, 231; Marxist, 249–250, 251, 260, 276, 308, 309, 400, 420; anarchy as, 255; social science concept of, 263; Communist, 281, 285, 411

Valéry, Paul, 358
Value systems, 73–74, 84, 93, 103–104, 140, 258, 431
Vanguard party. *See* Leninism: role of proletariat in revolution (vanguard party)
Varangians, 133
Verlaine, Paul, 210
Vernacular revolution, 64–65, 107, 108, 140. *See also* Language
Vernadsky, George, 367–368
Verne, Jules, 181
Verochka (Wilde), 209
Vichy regime, 321
Vietnam War, 330, 331, 338, 375, 376, 382, 385, 389, 425, 428, 430, 431
Villa, Pancho, 340
Vinogradoff, Paul, 207
Vlasov movement, 398
Volk, völkisch ideology, 227–228
Voltaire, François, 7, 11, 52, 59, 61, 64, 66, 68, 69, 101, 105, 106, 117, 127, 140, 340; idealization of Russia, 42, 43–44, 45, 47, 48, 52, 54, 58, 69, 73, 78, 130, 402; philosophy of history, 43–44, 132; as court *philosophe* in Prussia and Russia, 47–48, 69, 132
Voluntarism, 264, 269, 400, 426, 427
Voznesenkii, Andrei, 376

Wagner, Richard, 196, 197, 199–200, 202, 203, 205, 206, 210, 223, 349
Wallace, Henry, 348, 363
Wallace, Mackenzie, 180–181, 339, 367, 376
War, total, 334, 335
War and Peace (Tolstoy), 194, 205, 208
War Communism, 299–300, 303, 352, 423
War of American Independence. *See* United States: Revolutionary War
War of Austrian Succession, 23
War of Liberation (Germany, 1814), 265
War of Polish Succession, 22–23
War of Spanish Succession, 22
Warsaw Pact, 374
Wasteland, The (Eliot), 210, 349, 372
Wealth, 64, 70, 252; public control of, 254; capital, 254–255; accumulation, 259, 305; unequal distribution of, 336
Weapons: conventional, 359; nuclear, 359, 361, 375, 383, 384, 385, 401; ballistic missile, 361, 375, 384, 386, 387
Weathermen radical movement (United States), 431
Webb, Beatrice, 346, 355, 387
Webb, Sidney, 346, 355, 387
Weber, Max, 182, 183, 224, 229, 253, 368

Weimar, duke of, 105
Weimar (culture), 103–111, 130, 131, 132, 202
Weimar Republic, 324–325, 350, 354; constitutional democracy in, 320; Russian émigrés to, 351; perception of Soviet Russia, 348–352; relations with Soviet Russia, 353–354. *See also* Germany; Germany, international politics
Weitling, Wilhelm, 250
Welfare state, 177, 254, 275, 276, 284–285, 315, 319, 374, 424
Wellington, duke of, 156, 158, 356
Wells, H. G., 346
West-East cultural gradient, 6–9, 10, 12, 13, 35, 74, 168, 206, 418; during Cold War, 4–5; divergence, 12; before Peter I, 18; in Europe, 47; concept of *Sonderweg* and, 103, 104; in Russia (1789–1848), 139–146; 1870 division of Europe and, 164; European status of Russia and, 217; Bolshevism/Bolsheviks and, 269; democracy and, 335; during Second World War, 337, 338
What Is to Be Done? (Chernyshevskii), 169
Whitehead, Alfred North, 217
Wilde, Oscar, 201, 209–210, 218
Wilhelm Meister (Goethe), 115
Will, concept of, 214, 407; rational moral, 118, 201; heroic, 201–202, 203; as expressed by Nietzsche, 230–231; Party political, 267, 281, 311; fascism and, 328–329
William II, 239
Will the Soviet Union Survive until 1984? (Amalrik), 395
Wilson, Edmund, 343–344
Wilson, Harold, 376
Wilson, Woodrow, 182
Windischgrätz, Alfred, 148
Witte, Sergei, 172, 173, 174, 269, 270, 310, 424, 425
Wordsworth, William, 113, 202
Working class/workers, 185, 191, 221, 259, 269, 276, 300, 434; /peasant alliance, 272; exploitation of, 280–281, 304, 305–306; industrial, 283, 427; as agents of revolution, 283–284, 310, 457n6; political/administrative function, 310; in Soviet Russia, 326, 345; preference for Stalinist Communism, 345. *See also* Proletariat
World as Will and Representation, The (Schopenhauer), 118, 201
Worldling, The (Le Mondain) (Voltaire), 64
World of Art, The review, 197
World Spirit concept, 121, 122, 123

Yawning Heights, The (Zinoviev), 393
Yeltsin, Boris, 404, 405, 419
Young Europe, 186
Young (Left) Hegelians, 257
Young Turks, 185
Youth, violence and war cult, 324
Yugoslavia, 190, 370–371, 375

Zarathustra (Nietzsche), 203, 211, 231
Zetkin, Klara, 342
Zhdanov, Andrei, 370
Zinoviev, Aleksandr, 393
Zionism, 370
Zola, Émile, 208
Zoshchenko, Mikhail, 370